A System of Health Accounts 2011

REVISED EDITION

Please cite this publication as:
OECD, Eurostat and World Health Organization (2017), *A System of Health Accounts 2011: Revised edition*, OECD Publishing, Paris.
http://dx.doi.org/10.1787/9789264270985-en

ISBN 978-92-64-27097-8 (print)
ISBN 978-92-64-27098-5 (PDF)

European Union
ISBN 978-92-79-64619-5 (print)
ISBN 978-92-79-64620-1 (PDF)

Catalogue number
No.: KS-05-19-103-EN-C (print)
No.: KS-05-19-103-EN-N (PDF)

Photo credits: Cover illustration: © Adam Gault/OJO Images/Getty Images.

Corrigenda to OECD publications may be found on line at: *www.oecd.org/publishing/corrigenda*.

Foreword

Health care systems in all countries continue to evolve in response to changing demographics and disease patterns, rapid technological advances and more and more complex financing and delivery mechanisms, to name but a few factors. In striving towards some of the common health care system goals of equity, efficiency and effectiveness of care, one of the key questions for policy makers is "How much do we spend on health and is it measured in a comparable way?"

To meet the increasing demands of analysts and policy makers for such health expenditure information, A System of Health Accounts (SHA) *proposes a framework for the systematic description of the financial flows related to health care. The aim of SHA is to describe the health care system from an expenditure perspective both for international and national purposes.*

Since the publication of the original A System of Health Accounts by OECD in 2000 and the subsequent WHO/WB/USAID Producers Guide for producing national health accounts with specific applications in low and middle income countries in 2003, almost ten years of country experience in health accounting has been gathered together. This prompted the need for an update to rectify some of the shortcomings apparent in the original manual but also provided an opportunity to take into account some of the new developments in health care systems. With the goal of producing a global standard in health accounting, a formal collaborative effort between OECD, Eurostat and WHO was agreed in 2006 to oversee the revision of the SHA Manual.

A System of Health Accounts 2011 *is the result of a four-year extensive and wide-reaching consultation process gathering inputs and comments from a multitude of national experts and other international organisations around the world. All their contributions are gratefully acknowledged. The Manual strives to reach a consensus while also reflecting different perspectives and priorities within the expanding domain of health accounts.*

The publication was prepared by the International Health Accounts Team (IHAT), comprising the following health accounts experts from the three organisations: Roberto Astolfi, Rebecca Bennetts, Hartmut Buchow, William Cave, Didier Dupré, Patricia Hernández, Sandra Hopkins, Dorota Kawiorska, Luca Lorenzoni, Nathalie Van de Maele, David Morgan, Cornelis van Mosseveld, Eva Orosz, Markus Schneider, Tessa Tan Torres and Jens Wilkens as well as comments on the various drafts from other colleagues. Appreciation also goes to the senior management of the three co-ordinating organisations including Anne Clemenceau, Marleen De Smedt, David Evans, Mark Pearson, and Peter Scherer for their assistance in steering the SHA revision process. The Manual is a co-edition of the OECD, the European Union and the World Health Organization.

Table of Contents

Tables

Figures

Acknowledgments

This publication has benefitted from the many comments and inputs to the manual throughout the consultation process from a large number of experts and organisations including: Sawsan AbdulKarim, Aw Abou, Hedi Achouri, Nicoleta Adamescu, Baktygul Akkazieva, Faisal Al Gohaly, Fatina Al Halwani, Eyob Asbu, Maria Angelica Borges dos Santos, Daniel Arán, Luis Armando Ruiz Morales, Leticia Avila, Osmat Azzam, Vinod B. Annigeri, Ernesto Báscolo, D. Bayarsaikhan, John Beard, Tahmina Begum, Pedro Bivona, Marc Bura, Alexandra Carvalho, Leonor Cedillo, Kwok Cho Tang, Andrea Collado, Cathy Cowan, Jonathan Cylus, the Subdirección General de Análisis Económico y Fondo de Cohesión, Ministerio de Sanidad y Consumo (Spain), Finka Denkova, Tesfaye Dereje, Michel Duée, Varatharajan Durairaj, Zine Eddine Elidrissi, Irina Falkovich, the Centers for Medicare and Medicaid Services (United States), Ministry for Health and Prevention (Denmark), Milena Gajic, Gauden Galea, Charu Garg, Ketevan Goginashvili, Rozita Halina Tun Hussein, Hilda Harb, John Henderson, Jakub Hrkal, Jacques Huguenin, Mie Inoue, the Canadian Institute for Health Information, Georgeta Istrate, Natalja Jedomskihh-Eigo, Hyoung-Sun Jeong, Ben Jesse, Solomon Kagulula, Moussa Keita, Maryam Khoshakhlagh, Geoffrey Kimani, Felicia Knaul, Michal Kozinski, Joe Kutzin, Jennifer Ligoton, Christina Liwendahl, Joses M. Kirigia, Redencion M. Ignacio, Ricardo M. de Moraes, Sigita Maciuikiene, Richard Madden, Ajay Mahal, Vittorio Mapelli, Nora Markova, Awad Mataria, Colin D. Mathers, Thomas Mbeeli, Diana Miguez, Gloria Miriam Rubio, Dirk Moens, Alejandro Moliné, Michael Müller, Laurent Musango, Stephen N. Muchiri, Juliet Nabyonga, the National Board of Health and Welfare (Sweden), Manuela Nöthen, the Ministry of Health and Social Affairs (Sweden), Wadji Ndack, Alana Officer, Marie-Jeanne Offossé, Alireza Olyaee Manesh, Alain Palacios, Lassina Pare, Rámon Perez Minaya, Margarita Petrera, Vincent van Polanen Petel, Augusto Portocarrero Grados, Jean-Pierre Poullier, Isabel Quintela, Rachel H. Racelis, Azizur Rahman, Ravindra Rannan-Eliya, Magdalena Rathe, Saadiya Razzaq, Cynthia Regalado, Jorge Relano, José Luis Reséndiz Jacinto, Carmen Reyes, Mary Reyes, Cruz Rivero Carlos, Molly Robinson, Rosa Maria Rodríguez Skewes, Raymond Rossel, Tomas Roubal, Sarit Rout, Racquel Dolores Sabeñano, Belgacem Sabri, Rocío Sáenz, Auguste Sagbohan, Hossein Salehi, Farba Sall, Luis Salvador-Corulla, Shekhar Saxena, Arthur Sensenig, Aparnaa Somanathan, Alice Soumaré, Sidikou Soumaré, Romaric Somé, Samrit Srithamrongsawat, Kristina Stig, Bernd Struck, Ruben Suarez, Statistics Sweden, the Swedish Association of Local Authorities and Regions, Páll Szilárd, Viroj Tangcharoensathien, Jeffrey Tshabalala, Alexander Turdziladze, Ricardo Valladares, Jan van Tongeren, Chitpranee Vasavid, Piet Verbiest, John Verrinder, Ana Vicente, Nilhda Villacres, Raymond Wagener, Quan Wan, Xiaoping Xie, Catherine Zaidman, Jameela Zainuddin, Tiemin Zhai, Xiaorui Zhang, Yuhui Zhang, Yuxin Zhao and André Zida.

The various drafts of the chapters also benefitted from comments made by delegates at the annual meetings of OECD Health Accounts Experts, Eurostat Technical Group on Care and the WHO Regional Consultation meetings organised in Ouagadougou, Shanghai, Cairo, Mexico City, Geneva, Seoul, Cuernavaca, Nairobi, Punta Cana, Manila and Beijing.

The revision process has also received welcome financial support from the Bill and Melinda Gates Foundation and the European Commission.

Acronyms

ADL	Activities of Daily Living
ART	Antiretroviral Therapy, Assisted Reproductive Technologies
ATC	Anatomic Therapeutic Chemical Classification
BPM6	IMF Balance of Payments Manual 6th Edition
CHE	Current Health Expenditure
COFOG	Classification of Functions of Government
COI	Cost of Illness
CFC	Consumption of Fixed Capital
CPA	Classification of Products by Activity
CPC	Central Product Classification
DNA	Deoxyribonucleic Acid
DRG	Diagnosis-related Groups
ESA	European System of Accounts
ESSPROS	European System of Integrated Social Protection Statistics
FS	Classification of Revenues of Health Care Financing Schemes
GBD	Global Burden of Disease
GCF	Gross Capital Formation
GFCF	Gross Fixed Capital Formation
GFSM	Government Financial Statistics Manual
HC	Classification of Health Care Functions
HETUS	Harmonised European Time Use Survey
HF	Classification of Health Care Financing Schemes
HIV/AIDS	Human Immunodeficiency Virus/Acquired Immune Deficiency Syndrome
HLE	Healthy Life Expectancy
HMO	Health Maintenance Organisation
HPV	Human Papillomavirus
HP	Classification of Health Care Providers
HRH	Human Resources for Health
HS	Harmonised Commodity Description and Coding System
IADL	Instrumental Activities of Daily Living Restrictions
ICD	International Classification of Diseases
ICHA	International Classification for Health Accounts
IEC	Health-related Information, Education and Communication
IHAT	International Health Accounts Team
IMF	International Monetary Fund
ISCO	International Standard Classification of Occupations
ISHMT	International Shortlist for Hospital Morbidity Tabulation

ISIC	International Standard Industry Classification of All Economic Activities
JHAQ	Joint Health Accounts Questionnaire (OECD-Eurostat-WHO)
LMIC	Lower- and Middle-Income Countries
MDG	Millennium Development Goals
MGEN	Mutuelle générale de l'Éducation nationale (French mutual health insurance company)
MoH	Ministry of Health
MoP	Mode of Production or Mode of Provision
MRI	Magnetic Resonance Imaging
MSA	Medical Savings Accounts
NACE	Nomenclature des activités économiques dans la Communauté européenne
NAICS	North American Industry Classification System
NGO	Non-governmental Organisation
NHA	National Health Accounts
NHI	National Health Insurance
NPISH	Non-Profit Institutions Serving Households
NRCMS	New Rural Co-operative Medical Scheme (China)
OECD	Organisation for Economic Co-operation and Development
OTC	Over-the-Counter Medicines
PAHO	Pan American Health Organisation
PBR	Psychological and behavioural rehabilitation
PFI	Private Finance Initiative
PG	WHO NHA Producers Guide (Guide to Producing National Health Accounts)
POM	Prescription only medicines
PPP	Purchasing Power Parities *(n.b. PPP can also be used to mean public-private partnership)*
RNA	Ribonucleic acid
RoW	Rest of the World
SHA	System of Health Accounts
SHI	Social Health Insurance
SNA	System of National Accounts
TCAM	Traditional Complementary and Alternative Medicine
THE	Total Health Expenditure
TPE	Total Pharmaceutical Expenditure
UN	United Nations
UNGASS	United Nations General Assembly Special Session
USAID	United States Agency for International Development
VPHI	Voluntary Private Health Insurance
WB	World Bank
WHO	World Health Organization

PART I

Foundations of the *System of Health Accounts*

PART I

Chapter 1

Introduction

Background

Health systems across the globe are continuing to evolve in response to a multitude of factors, including improvements in medical technology and knowledge, increased information about health and health services and greater access to it, changes in health policy priorities to meet shifting disease and demographic patterns, new organisational methods and more complex financing mechanisms. Health accounts also need to adapt to deal with these developments and to anticipate foreseeable future trends.

Health accounts provide a systematic description of the financial flows related to the consumption of health care goods and services. Their intent is to describe a health system from an expenditure perspective. But as more countries implement and institutionalise health accounts, there are increased expectations from analysts, policy makers and the general public alike for the more sophisticated information that can be gained through the greater volume of health expenditure data now available. Health accounts are increasingly expected to provide inputs (along with other statistical information) into improved analytical tools to monitor and assess health system performance. One high priority is to develop reliable, timely data that is comparable both across countries and over time. This is indispensable for tracking trends in health spending and the factors driving it, which can in turn be used to compare it across countries and to project how it will grow in the future. Health accounts are thus used in two main ways: internationally, where the emphasis is on a selection of internationally comparable expenditure data, and nationally, with more detailed analyses of health care spending and a greater emphasis on comparisons over time. Health accounts are crucial for both of these uses.

The Manual itself draws inspiration from and builds on a number of international manuals and guidelines on health expenditure accounts, most notably: *A System of Health Accounts* ("SHA 1.0") (OECD, 2000); the *Guide to Producing National Health Accounts* ("The Producers Guide") (WHO, World Bank, USAID, 2003); and the *SHA Guidelines* (Eurostat/UK ONS, 2003). The wealth of experience gained in implementing these various guidelines around the world, the results of specific health accounting research projects and efforts in international data collections[1] have been significant inputs into the Manual's development.

The formal process of producing SHA 2011 started in 2007 as a co-operative activity of health accounts experts from the OECD, WHO and Eurostat, known collectively as the International Health Accounts Team (IHAT). The resulting manual has been the subject of an extensive and wide-reaching consultation process aimed at gathering inputs from national experts and other international organisations around the world. It strives to reach a consensus, while also reflecting different perspectives and priorities within the expanding domain of health accounts. In developing the material, great importance has been given to policy relevance, feasibility and sustainability. The Manual is based on the conceptual framework of the System of Health Accounts, but must also address practical possibilities and analytical needs.

Differences and improvements between SHA 1.0 and SHA 2011

SHA 2011 introduces a number of changes and improvements compared with SHA 1.0. First and foremost, though, it reinforces the *tri-axial* relationship that is at the root of the System of Health Accounts and its description of health care and long-term care expenditure – that is, what is consumed has been provided and financed. This triangulation maintains the guiding principles of SHA 1.0 and the *Producers Guide*. SHA 2011 offers more complete coverage within the functional classification in areas such as prevention and long-term care; a more concise picture of the universe of health care providers, with closer links to standard industry classifications; and a precise approach for tracking financing in the health care sector using the new classification of financing schemes.

Based on this tri-axial approach to health care expenditure, SHA 2011 also develops three analytical interfaces – the health care consumer, provision and financing interfaces – which allow countries to focus on specific areas of national health policy interest and, by expanding health accounts in this direction, also facilitates a more comprehensive analysis. Building on the methodological work of the *Producers Guide*, SHA 2011 further develops the health care financing interface to allow for a systematic assessment of how finances are mobilised, managed and used, including the financing arrangements (Financing schemes), the institutional units (Financing agents) and the revenue-raising mechanisms (Revenues of financing schemes). The production interface delves into the cost structures of health care provision (Factors of provision) and provides a separate treatment of capital formation so as to avoid some of the past ambiguity regarding the links between current health spending and capital expenditure in health care systems. The consumer health interface is of particular interest to the study and further analysis of the functional dimension, as it helps in exploring the breakdown of health care expenditure according to beneficiary characteristics, such as disease, age, gender, region and socio-economic status. In addition, the Manual updates the discussion in a number of other areas where methodologies are still being tried and tested, such as developing price and volume measures in the health sector or measuring international trade in health care.

Overall, however, great emphasis has been given to the need to preserve the investment and efforts of countries to date in institutionalising health accounts. Subject to successful data piloting and methodology verification, any proposed changes to classifications and accounting methods should be introduced in a gradual and stepwise approach so as to ensure a smooth transition from SHA 1.0 to SHA 2011.

The role of the Manual and its organisation

The global reference proposed by this Manual should assist in the development of consistent methodologies for the compilation of health expenditure accounts. At the same time, the content of the Manual must have relevance and applicability for users – governments, health institutions, health analysts and policy makers – with a wide range of health system priorities, as well as different organisational, economic and statistical structures.

SHA 2011 represents a significant step in the development of health accounts, and it reflects the professional technical view of the three co-ordinating international organisations and country experts at the time of writing. It should be seen as a staging post, an effort to provide guidance in health accounts that will be relevant for an extended period of time. At the same time, health accounting is an evolving discipline and as such this Manual can also be considered as work in progress. Particular sections and chapters are highlighted in the Manual to indicate the need for further development, pilot testing and validation. Like any statistical manual, it will be useful to the extent that countries use and implement various aspects of it, and countries will undoubtedly concentrate on those parts that are most relevant to their own circumstances. In this respect, the Manual does not and cannot make an automatic connection with data collection. Countries, health statistics agencies and international organisations may accord very different priorities to different sections of the Manual, and will decide to what extent they implement or adapt SHA 2011 with regards to dimensions and levels of detail based on their own health expenditure priorities, policy information needs and statistical resources. For instance, many analysts, not exclusively in lower and middle income countries, may view the tracking of the revenues of health care financing schemes as an inherent part of the development of their health accounts, while some EU countries may give more importance to estimations of trade in health care or to developing price and volume measures. In summary, SHA 2011 is intended as a flexible toolkit for health accountants.

This first part of the Manual continues with an overview of the System of Health Accounts: its foundations, purposes and principles are set out in Chapter 2, the main accounting concepts and aggregates in Chapter 3 and a discussion of the boundaries of health care in Chapter 4. The next three chapters provide a detailed description of the dimensions of the consumption framework: health care functions (HC), health care providers (HP) and financing schemes (HF). The second part of the Manual then considers the financing, provision and uses of health care goods and services in turn, looking specifically at the revenues of financing schemes (Chapter 8), factors of provision (Chapter 9) and the possible distribution of health spending by beneficiary groups (Chapter 10). The second part also provides new material on a number of concepts of health accounts that countries may find useful; these include the area of capital spending (Chapter 11), the development of trade in health care between countries (Chapter 12) and the measurement of price and volume in health (Chapter 13). The Manual concludes with some summary guidance on accounting and compilation processes (Chapter 14) and a presentation of results (Chapter 15). A number of annexes provide further relevant information, including links to other classifications, the relationship between SHA and the System of National Accounts, a classification of products and some supplementary accounting tools.

It should be emphasised that the order of the chapters does not necessarily reflect their relative importance. Based on the user's perspective and needs, the Manual could equally be used in other ways, such as bringing together the financing interface into one module, the consumer health interface into another module, and the provision interface into a third module.

Note

1. The Joint OECD, Eurostat and WHO Health Accounts Questionnaire (JHAQ), used since 2005.

PART I

Chapter 2

Purposes and Principles of Health Accounts

Introduction

A System of Health Accounts 2011 reflects a desire to make health accounts more adaptable to rapidly evolving health systems around the world by further enhancing the cross-country comparability of health expenditure and financing data and thereby increasing the information base for its analytical use. Moreover, it is hoped that the new version of the SHA will make it more useful as a tool in the assessment and monitoring of health systems and in the analysis of the importance of health expenditures from a consumption perspective in the economy as a whole.

This chapter therefore provides an overview of the purposes of the System of Health Accounts, and then describes the principles from which it has been derived. The chapter concludes with a discussion of how information on health expenditures has been used in the past and of some of the anticipated analytical uses of information generated from SHA 2011.

Background

Efforts to describe financial flows associated with the consumption of health care can be traced as far back as the 1920s (Fetter, 2006). In the early 1960s, Abel-Smith and others carried out a number of studies measuring health expenditures in developing countries (Abel-Smith, 1963; Abel-Smith, 1967). In the 1970s (and in some country cases such as France and the Netherlands, the 1950s), OECD countries regularly began to estimate health expenditures, with relatively aggregated information on private and public expenditures.[1] Of these initial efforts, perhaps the most comprehensive exercise was undertaken by the United States, which provided detailed information on the sources of health financing, along with associated expenditure data (Waldo, 1996). The above efforts reflect, in part, the systematic development of national economic accounts as a means to measure aggregate economic activity.[2] Over the years, studies have also been undertaken to describe financial flows for a subset of health consumption expenditure categories such as HIV/AIDS, regions and socioeconomic groups.

In more recent years, there have been two major efforts to systematise the collection of information on financial flows related to health care. These include the publication of *A System of Health Accounts* (SHA 1.0) by the OECD in 2000, including an associated set of classifications of financial flows known as the International Classification of Health Accounts (ICHA); and the combined efforts of the WHO, World Bank and USAID that led to the development in 2003 of the "Guide to Producing National Health Accounts", otherwise referred to as the *NHA Producers Guide* (PG). These were the first standards to receive wider acceptance and use in producing health expenditure data globally. These have led to the compilation of internationally comparable data sets within the framework of joint data collection by the OECD, Eurostat and WHO, and each manual has contributed to a considerable number of studies in higher-income countries (SHA 1.0) (Orosz and Morgan, 2004) and in low- and middle-income countries (*NHA Producers Guide*). Since their publication, the international organisations have sought to support the efforts of countries to implement these standards through various means, including, *inter alia*, grants directed to individual countries, methodological workshops for country experts, or various cross-country projects to enhance data analysis and the development of indicators based on the SHA methodology. Other guidelines have been produced targeting a regional coverage and using varying approaches (Eurostat/UK ONS, 2003; PAHO, 2005), and many adjustments have been made to guide national policy (see, for example, van Mosseveld and Smit, 2005) as well as sub-national estimations (see, for example, Kamp-Nielsen, 2002; Schneider *et al.*, 2002; and Brændvang, 2008).

Purposes and objectives of the *System of Health Accounts 2011*

SHA 2011 provides a standard for classifying health expenditures according to the three axes of consumption, provision and financing. It gives guidance and methodological support in compiling health accounts. More specifically, the purposes of the System of Health Accounts 2011 are:

- to provide a framework of the main aggregates relevant to international comparisons of health expenditures and health systems analysis;
- to provide a tool, expandable by individual countries, which can produce useful data in the monitoring and analysis of the health system;
- to define internationally harmonised boundaries of health care for tracking expenditure on consumption.

In order to pursue these purposes, SHA 2011 provides the basis for collecting, cataloguing and estimating all the monetary flows related to health care expenditure.

Principles of the *System of Health Accounts 2011*

The guiding principles in defining the dimensions and classifications of SHA 2011 have been the relevance and usefulness for health analytical purposes, continuity with existing standards and improved links to the System of National Accounts (SNA). The starting point for SHA 2011 is the consumption of services and goods by the resident population of a country or region. This influences the structure of the classifications in that, in describing the system, it is the final consumption by residents which is given priority, over production.

This Manual has been developed by applying a functional approach to what is provided and consumed in health care. This means that health expenditures are included regardless of how or by whom the service or good is funded, or how and by whom it has been provided. For example, health services provided and consumed outside the SNA-defined health branch (such as occupational health services or medical services in residential long-term care) are part of the final consumption of health services of the resident population, and thus included in SHA. The way health care is financed, for example, whether or not the final consumed health service is paid for or reimbursed by a public entity, is not decisive for inclusion or exclusion in the health accounts.

Health systems and the System of Health Accounts

Health systems have complex, nationally determined frameworks that are strongly influenced by culture, politics and economics, with links across economic sectors, public administration and various activities related to social participation. Due to the multi-factorial nature of health and the multi-sectoral contribution to health status, a health systems framework is much wider than the SHA approach, notably with respect to the boundaries of health expenditure. While health systems can vary significantly among countries, SHA aims to enhance international health care expenditure data by delineating the boundary of health care according to a functional classification.

The health system framework described by the World Health Organisation is defined as consisting of all the organisations, institutions, resources and people whose primary purpose is to improve health (WHO, 2000). Four components or *functions* in this framework are essential to reaching the final objectives, which also serve as the standards by which its performance is ultimately measured:

- *Governance*: oversight of the system including policy-making and appropriate regulation and monitoring;
- *Resource generation:* investment in personnel as well as in key inputs and technologies (human, physicaland knowledge);
- *Human resources:* investments in, and provision of, a well-performing health workforce;
- *Medical products and technology:* production and provision of cost-effective medical goods, pharmaceuticals and knowledge;
- *Capital goods:* investments in fixed and other types of capital to be used in future health provision;
- *Financing:* raising revenue for health, pooling resources and purchasing services;
- *Service delivery* (provision): "combination of inputs into a service production process that delivers health interventions to individuals or to the community (...); aims at producing the best and most effective mix of personal and non-personal services, and making them accessible" (WHO, 2005a).

This health system framework also defines a set of objectives. These objectives can vary in importance over time and between countries, but their attainment is dependent on how the health system performs. All these objectives are, in various forms and by various names, subject to measurement for the analysis and monitoring of health systems performance. Figure 2.1 shows how the various dimensions of the SHA nestle between the different health system functions and the objectives of the health system framework, reflecting the policy relevance of these dimensions. The subsequent text explains and defines these dimensions.

All four functions of the health system (governance, resource generation, financing and service delivery) can be linked to the three axes of health accounts: consumption, provision and financing. Each axis is associated with specific classifications, but there is no unique classification matching each axis. For example, the financing axis can be measured equally by financing schemes and financing agents. Consumption is the starting point, and the goods and services consumed with a health purpose (functions) set the boundary of the health accounts (see Chapter 4). What has been consumed has been produced and provided, thus another axis is provision. Finally, what has been consumed and provided has been financed. This means that the third axis, financing, as well as the second axis on provision are measured according to the consumption.

The associated key health accounting dimensions include:

- Classification of health care functions (HC);

Figure 2.1. **Linkage between the frameworks of health systems and health accounts**

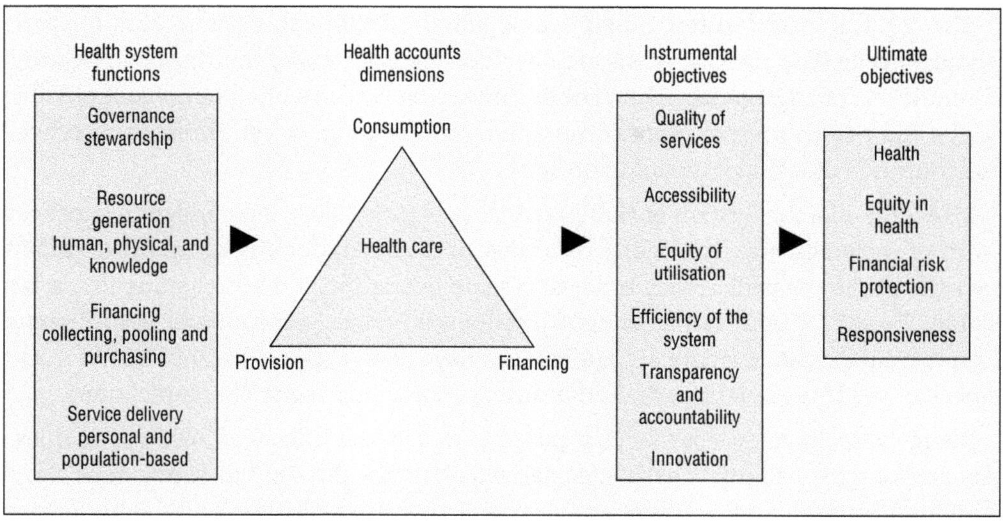

Source: Adapted from WHO (2000).

- Classification of health care providers (HP);
- Classification of financing schemes (HF).

SHA 2011 defines additional dimensions compared to SHA 1.0 that allow the compilation of complementary indicators of the health system:

- Classification of types of revenues of health financing schemes (FS) (Chapter 8);
- Classification of factors for health care provision (FP) (Chapter 9);
- Classification of beneficiaries: age, gender, disease, socioeconomic characteristic or region (Chapter 10);
- Classification of human resources in health care using ISCO 2008 (Annex C);
- Classification of health care goods and services (Annex E).

For financial flows under SHA to be policy relevant, they should help monitor and assess the attainment of objectives relevant to any given health care system. The health systems framework guides us to produce data that are useful for the analysis of health care. Indicators for some of the objectives can be developed using expenditure data only. Data arranged in health accounts tables show where the money comes from, who manages it and what it is used for, which enhances the *transparency and accountability* of the health system. For countries that receive significant amounts of external resources, tracking these financial flows over time can capture trends associated or consistent with aid volatility, additionality and fungibility as well as the potential implications for sustainability. Indicators for *financial risk protection* can be developed with data on the amounts of out-of-pocket spending and the levels of various forms of pre-paid resources. Indicators for *equity in financing* can be developed with data on the sources of funds, on expenditure (in combination with utilisation and income), and on types of revenue and beneficiaries.

Other objectives, however, need a combination of expenditure and non-expenditure data. For example, data on expenditure in combination with utilisation can be used to develop indicators of *accessibility* and *equity*. Expenditures on the different functions in health care can, under certain assumptions, be used as indicators of *efficiency* in combination with data on outcomes.

SHA 2011 is intended to be a statistical standard that can provide data for various analytical needs. The classifications are developed in such a way that they can be used on different levels of aggregation. The various dimensions are intended to make it possible to describe the health system more comprehensively from an expenditure perspective for those countries that find it useful to do so.

SHA 2011, like the System of National Accounts (SNA 2008), is intended to constitute a system of *comprehensive*, internally *consistent* and internationally *comparable* accounts, which should be *compatible* with other aggregate economic and social statistics as far as possible. Overall, SHA 2011 has sought to adopt, wherever appropriate, definitions and concepts from existing statistical systems that have been approved and defined under the auspices of the United Nations and other international and regional organisations.

Being *internally consistent* makes it possible to use identities and accounting rules for cross-checking the validity of estimates derived along the different dimensions of the SHA and to identify gaps and deficiencies in current reporting systems and health accounts, thereby indicating priorities for the continued improvement of the data quality. During the implementation of SHA 1.0 and the *Producers Guide*, considerable progress was made in terms of *comprehensiveness*. The accounts and the data produced have increasingly provided a more comprehensive picture of countries' health systems, as can be seen in the OECD-Eurostat-WHO joint questionnaire data collection from 2005 onwards. In developing SHA 2011, it has been particularly important to respect alignment with the first edition and with the *Producers Guide* in order to help countries to migrate from the old system towards a new standard, and to build time series that are consistent according to the revised classifications. These demands were at the same time constraints in the development of SHA 2011, *e.g.* the quality criteria of the SHA are competing with the goals of *timeliness* and *precision* in reporting.

Analytical uses

The allocation of resources involves a continual decision-making process in the health system, and better-informed decision-making selectively uses the available knowledge in order to make sustained choices. Health accounts have been developed to help decisions linked to the allocation of resources to better meet the objectives of the health system. They are expected to be used by people analysing resource use in the health system for the purposes of both accountability and planning.

The focus and importance of different policy aspects and research interests have evolved since the first version of the SHA, and they will continue to change. The analytical use of SHA will depend on how well it meets these changing needs, and how well it can capture developments in health systems. The financing of health care has become even more complex, with innovative mixtures of funding arrangements. Private and public mixes in financial contributions and organisational arrangements are increasing, as are the forms of prepaid arrangements. Medical and information technologies are developing with increasing speed which has a strong impact on how services are delivered. For example, the Internet and the increased availability of information is promoting health literacy. Individuals are increasingly engaged in self care, including preventive and even curative care. Individuals can now check their medical records, monitor themselves, relay information to their practitioners and order drugs on the Internet. There are strong trends towards the consumption of alternative medicine and engagement in health-promoting activities. Similarly, we live in an increasingly globalised world, resulting in an increasing movement of goods, services and patients across national borders. One clear manifestation is the phenomenon of medical travel. These emerging health trends not only make it more difficult to capture the flow of funds at country level, but also make it more important to define, assess and monitor them. They also enlarge the range of interested users of the expenditure estimates.

Uses of national health accounts and SHA data

Information from national health accounts and associated efforts has been used in a variety of ways by policy makers and researchers. For example, information on NHA-derived health expenditure flows has been used to study the growth of health expenditures and its potential determinants in the United States and other OECD and EU countries, and also, more recently, in China and India (Newhouse, 1992; Yip and Mahal, 2008). Newhouse, for instance (1992), used health expenditure for the United States to argue that technological change was the single most important factor driving health care costs in the United States. Other studies have sought to measure the relationship between GDP growth and health spending to assess the "income elasticity of demand" for health care, and to project health care spending (Chawla *et al.*, 1997).

Another popular use of data on national health expenditure has been to assess the impact of ageing on health expenditures (Gerdtham *et al.*, 1992), in particular through the use of the panel structure of health expenditure data (cross-sectional time series). While the literature suggests that the effects of ageing on medical care spending are likely to be small *per se*, projections of age-related expenditure in the EU 2009 Ageing Report indicate that the combined effects of health status and age will place strong upward pressure on long-term care spending in the future (European Commission, 2009). Some of the work in this area has focused on how the concentration of health spending in the time shortly before death, and not so much ageing *per se*, is a major driver of health expenditures (Zweifel, 2004; Polder *et al.*, 2007). Most of these analyses rely heavily on individual-level information from insurers and household surveys.

Cross-country and cross-provincial health expenditure data, in conjunction with information on indicators of health outcomes, such as life expectancy at birth, have been used to assess the "overall efficiency" of health spending, often using sophisticated stochastic frontier techniques (Swedish Association of Local Authorities and Regions *et al.*, 2007). Moreover, some studies have used specific components of health spending information available from health accounts data, for instance, public spending on health, to consider that particular component's impact on health (Anand and Ravallion, 1993). Some analyses have also compared health system characteristics across countries so as to identify their relative impact on health expenditures (OECD, 1990).

In a survey of the literature, Berman (1997) argued that careful national health accounts analyses can contribute towards a better understanding of the health system. He noted, for instance, how national health accounts data shed light on the fact that the public sector played only a small role in the provision of primary care in India, despite years of public investment in such provision (D'Çruz and Barat, 2001). In Mexico, the use of the NHA methodology led to significant upward revisions in estimates of both private and overall national health spending (Frenk *et al.*, 2003). National health accounts data could offer a useful aggregate picture of the impact of health reform efforts, including to make expenditure projections and to assess sustainability (Berman *et al.,* 2003). Information on patterns of financing, such as a high share of private out-of-pocket spending by households, has been used in various policy documents to highlight the lack of risk-pooling mechanisms (Kutzin, 2008). The large share of foreign funding in health has also been used to point out potential problems with the predictability and sustainability of funding (Peeples, 2009).

More recent instances of how data from national health accounts analyses have been used at a country level include the case of Turkey, which highlighted differences in health spending by age and socio-economic groups (Government of Turkey, 2003). Moreover, recent studies and analyses have seen SHA-based data broken down by beneficiary characteristics, such as disease, age and gender (see Chapter 10). Country-level analyses have also focused on disease-specific sub-accounts, specifically HIV/AIDS, highlighting both overall allocations, the distribution of spending between preventive and curative care, and patterns of international financing (see *e.g.* Avila-Figueroa *et al.*, 2002). The reporting of expenditure on HIV/AIDS is now a global effort and is part of the annual UNGASS report.[3] Some of the Millennium Development Goals (MDG)[4] reported by countries also include expenditures.

At a European level, SHA data is currently used to develop common EU indicators on health and long-term care expenditure, as well as to monitor various EU policy objectives, such as the goals of social inclusion and social protection, which encompass health care.[5] Both national and EU level reports have made use of SHA data to help evaluate health care system performance as well as to assess the impact of both health care reforms or unexpected events (such as the global financial crisis that started in 2008) on the living conditions of EU citizens.[6]

A study of how NHA data has been used in 21 low- and middle-income countries gives several examples of how new data has informed decision-making (De *et al.*, 2003). The study showed that the main users in these 21 countries are the ministries of health and the donors and gave the following examples:

- Off-budget and fragmented donor support to the health sector revealed in the NHA work supported the development of a Sector-Wide Approach in Tanzania;
- NHA and non-expenditure health data were instrumental when Egypt increased spending on primary health care, after data showed a lack of alignment between actual spending and public policy, and a heavy reliance on households' payments;
- NHA studies in South Africa have shown how inequitably health was funded, across regions and across income groups.

Analyses of the impact of reform efforts – such as the introduction of user fees in India, or medical savings schemes in China – typically rely on individual level information that is not accessible from NHA data. For example, analyses of the introduction of a school health insurance scheme in Egypt (Yip and Berman, 2001) and price controls on hospital services in China (Eggleston and Yip, 2004) all required information either at the household level or at the level of individual hospitals. In Burkina Faso, national health accounts data encouraged the government to reallocate the ministerial budget, giving priority to improving access to health care in poorer regions.[7]

There is no doubt from the preceding section that the information on financial flows from existing health accounts work has been used for different types of policy and research activities, and particularly for cross-country and cross-provincial comparative analyses. These achievements notwithstanding, it is clear that, when viewed in the context of the broader research and policy agenda on health financing and health systems, health accounts data need to be complemented with other types of health expenditure data.

Notes

1. Since the late 1970s, Jean-Pierre Poullier was the driving force in creating comparable national expenditure series on health for OECD member states, resulting in a database of health spending and background information. See OECD (1977), OECD (1985) and OECD (1990). See also Scheiber and Poullier (1989); Poullier *et al.* (2002); Murray and Evans (2003); van Mosseveld (2003); Schneider (1995).
2. A comprehensive manual for assembling internationally comparable national accounts data was first developed under the auspices of the United Nations in 1953. SNA 2008 is the fifth revision of the SNA. It is jointly published by the EC, IMF, OECD, UN and WB.
3. Available at *www.unaids.org.*
4. See *www.undp.org/mdg.*
5. Country reports and EU Joint Reports on Social Protection and Social Inclusion are available at *http://ec.europa.eu/social/main.jsp?catId=757&langId=en.*
6. See Joint report on health care systems, European Union, Economic and Financial Affairs, available at *http://ec.europa.eu/economy_finance/publications/occasional_paper/2010/pdf/ocp74_en.pdf.*
7. For example, the study highlighted that Amnesty International used data from Burkina Faso's 2008 reproductive health subaccount to support its argument that government expenditure on reproductive health remained insufficient (Zida *et al.*, 2010).

A System of Health Accounts 2011: Revised edition

PART I

Chapter 3

Accounting Concepts and SHA Aggregates

Introduction

This chapter presents an overview of the main accounting concepts and aggregates used throughout the Manual. While each aggregate is considered in further detail in the following chapters, here the focus is on the relationship between the consumption of health care goods and services and all the other possible uses of health care goods and services in the economy. The range of possible uses includes intermediate consumption (or factors of provision), analysed in Chapter 9, capital formation, presented in Chapter 11, and exports, examined in Chapter 12 together with imports. This chapter examines the central concept of consumption, considering the distinction between final consumption expenditure and actual final consumption and discusses the role of capital transfers. Various issues concerning the valuation of market and non-market transactions are also explored.

The chapter both starts and concludes with a discussion of the main similarities and differences between the System of Health Accounts and the System of National Accounts (SNA); it relates information on the health sector to the national economy accounting rules and considers differences in the production boundaries of the two systems.[1]

Accounting and national accounting as a base for the *System of Health Accounts*

Accounting is, in the words of the American Institute of Certified Public Accountants (AICPA), "*the art of recording, classifying and summarising in a significant manner and in terms of money, transactions and events which are, in part at least, of financial character, and interpreting the results thereof*". When this refers to the accounting of the individual actors or "institutional units" in the economy, such as households, enterprises and public bodies or government agencies, this is sometimes referred to as micro-economic accounting. When this refers to the measurement of a nation's economic activity (as compared to business activities, which are recorded in business accounts), we may talk about national accounts or macro-economic accounts. Health accounts, in turn, refer to summary accounts for expenditure with a health purpose in a particular economic territory or a nation, which aggregates the expenditure of different actors for this purpose. This sits in between micro and macro-accounting, and is sometimes referred to as meso-economic accounting.

The System of Health Accounts draws upon and relies on health care-related accounts of both individual units and organisations, as well as certain aggregates compiled as part of the national accounts. The more closely SHA can link to business accounting and public accounting standards, to international and national health recording guidelines, and to national accounting definitions, the more feasible it will be to produce health accounts and the more useful they will be for analyses. Accounts that can be linked to national accounts are known as satellite accounts to the national accounts framework. Although SHA uses methodologies that are closely linked to the main national accounts methodology, the system is not bound to employ exactly the same concepts and can focus more on health specific issues. As SHA focuses on current health spending for consumption purposes and is tri-axial – linking consumption to provision and to financing – it does not qualify as a full SNA satellite account. In order for the SHA to become an SNA satellite account, it would need additional information on the production of the health care industries.[2] Annexes A and B discuss in more detail the links and mappings between health accounts and national accounts statistics that are required to support the development of health accounts using national accounts information.

National accounts typically present the whole range of the production, distribution and consumption activities of an economy's *institutional units* (corporations, government, households and non-profit institutions). They measure the stocks (accumulation to a point in time) and the flows (over time) in an economy. The main aggregate measures in national accounts are gross domestic product (GDP), gross value added, disposable income, saving and external trade. The typical national accounts tools include input-output tables (showing how industries interact with each other in the production process), and the national balance sheet (showing assets on one side and liabilities and wealth on the other). The accounts are derived from data sources, including surveys, administrative and census data and official records. They are structured in a sequence of accounts components that include current accounts (production, income and expenditure accounts), capital accounts, financial accounts and balance sheets. Each account has a balancing item, which is obtained by subtracting the total value of the entries on one side of an account (uses or assets) from the total value on the other side (resources or liabilities). This ensures that the accounts balance, and provides information such as value added, operating surplus, disposable income, saving, net lending/net borrowing and net worth.

The final section of this chapter examines in more detail the relationship between expenditure on health, as defined in the System of Health Accounts, and the components of consumption, as defined in the national accounts.

The consumption, availability and use of health care goods and services

This section examines the central SHA concept of the *consumption* of health care goods and services in relation to the SNA perspective of the *use* of health care goods and services. The boundary of what constitutes health care under the SHA is delimited in Chapter 4, and the health care goods and services within that boundary are classified in the functional classification in Chapter 5.

All health care goods and services that are available in a country are either supplied by domestic providers or have been imported from the rest of the world. They can then be put to different uses, either to satisfy the health needs of the population, or as inputs to produce other health care goods and services. For example, a radiologist might provide a consultation to patients resident in the country, to foreign tourists, or to another health provider (a colleague or a hospital, for example). Those health care goods or services produced and imported in the economic territory and used by a resident to satisfy an individual or collective need are classified as final consumption and included in the health accounting framework. However, the following cases are considered to lie outside the boundaries of the SHA accounts, which encompass functions, providers and financing schemes:

- If the user is non-resident, the products are considered as exports;
- If the health care goods and services are used by other health care providers, they are considered as factors of provision (intermediate consumption); and

- If the health care goods are stored for future use they are accounted for as a change in inventories or stocks of goods.

Figure 3.1 presents, in schematic form, all the possible uses of health care goods and services. The two main uses are: as inputs into the production of other health care goods and services (as factors of provision), and as final uses. Final uses itself can be broken down into final consumption expenditure; investment (or gross capital formation); and exports. The shaded area represents the total *final consumption expenditure* on health care goods and services, which corresponds to current health expenditure and the triangular identity between consumption, provision and financing, introduced in Chapter 2 as the basis of the System of Health Accounts.[3]

Intermediate uses consist of those health care goods and services that are consumed (used-up or transformed) in the production process. Examples include a radiology consultation provided to another health care provider and medical materials used in operating theatres. The provision of a service from, say, one hospital to another is counted as an input into the overall service to the patient by the second hospital, and only at this point counted as final consumption. In this example, the additional compilation of the consultation of the first hospital would lead to double-counting from a consumption point of view and is therefore not shown separately. Such products, which could be either produced by domestic firms or imported from the rest of the world, are used together with other "intermediate consumption" goods and services produced by the rest of the economy (*e.g.* electricity, water, fuel and protective wear) and capital goods. Capital goods, which include MRI machines and hospital buildings, are characterised by the fact that they are used repeatedly and for more than one year in the delivery of health care services by providers.

Figure 3.1. **The uses of health care goods and services**

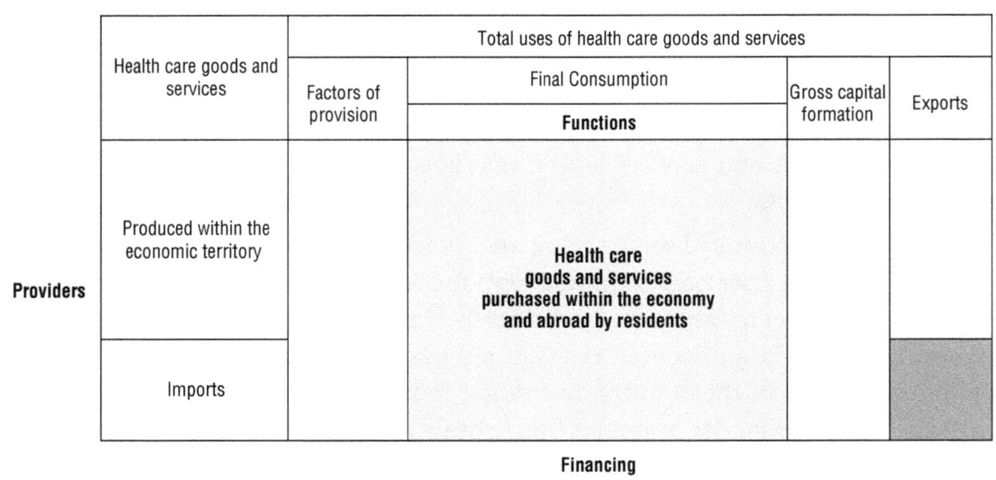

Source: IHAT for SHA 2011.

Within the category of final consumption, household final consumption expenditure consists of the expenditure incurred by resident households for the individual consumption of goods and services, including the consumption of goods and services acquired abroad.

Final consumption expenditure by general government consists of expenditure incurred by government units, which itself can be divided into two types: those expenditures incurred for the benefit of individual households (individual) and those incurred for the benefit of the community as a whole, or of large sections of the community (collective).

Individual goods and services are thus distinguished from collective or public goods and services and have the following characteristics:

- It must be possible to observe and record the acquisition of the good or service by an individual household or member thereof and also the time at which the acquisition took place;
- The household must have agreed to accept the provision of the good or service and to take whatever action is necessary to make it possible, for example, by attending a school or clinic; and
- The good or service must be such that its acquisition by one household or person, or possibly by a small, restricted group of persons, precludes its acquisition by other households or persons.

By contrast, collective services have the following characteristics:

- Collective services are delivered or made available simultaneously to every member of the community or to particular sections of the community, such as those in a particular region of a locality;
- The use of such services is usually passive and does not require the explicit agreement or active participation of all the individuals concerned; and
- The provision of a collective service to one individual does not reduce the amount available to others in the same community or section of the community. There is no rivalry over acquisition.

With relation to health services, collective health services refer notably to some preventive and health promotion services, but also by convention cover the governance and administration services of the health system.

The treatment of consumption expenditures incurred by non-profit institutions serving households (NPISH)[4] is very similar to that for general government. However, whereas government expenditures are financed in large part out of taxation, NPISH expenditures are financed principally out of subscriptions, contributions or donations, or property income. NPISH final consumption expenditure consists of the expenditure incurred by resident NPISH on individual consumption goods and services and on collective consumption services.

Final consumption expenditure, as detailed above, refers to "who incurs". But the total of final consumption may also be viewed from another angle, that is, "who consumes". In this way *actual final consumption of households* is measured by the value of all the individual consumption goods and services acquired by resident households, irrespective of who incurs the expenditure. Therefore, we can identify three sets of goods and services entering into household actual final consumption: those acquired through the final consumption expenditure of households themselves and those acquired as social transfers in kind both from government and from NPISH, that is, goods and services purchased on behalf of individuals. The goods and services can be the output of these institutions as non-market producers, or they may have been purchased by these institutions from market producers for onward transmission to households for free or at prices that are not economically significant.

Main aggregates of health expenditure

Total expenditure on health (SHA 1.0)

The approach taken in SHA 1.0 was to sum up the two aggregates of "current expenditure on health" and "gross capital formation" to arrive at "total health expenditure". However, the use of the aggregate "total health expenditure" tended to be misunderstood. In effect, while current health expenditure refers to final consumption, which is the demand for health care goods and services by households, government and non-profit institutions, gross capital formation refers to the demand for capital goods by health providers. Thus, it could be argued that the two aggregates cannot be directly summed up as they refer to different timings of consumption, since capital formation enables future provision. For this reason, it is recommended to keep the two aggregates "current expenditure on health care" and "gross capital formation in health care" separate under SHA 2011, and to discourage the use of the aggregate "total health expenditure", at least with respect to how it was used in SHA 1.0.

Current expenditure on health care

In measuring expenditure on health care goods and services, current expenditure on health can be defined as follows.

> ***Current expenditure on health care*** = final consumption expenditure of resident units on health care goods and services, including the health care goods and services provided directly to individual persons as well as collective health care services.

In other words, current expenditure on health quantifies the economic resources spent on the health care functions as identified by the consumption boundaries set in Chapter 4. Furthermore, SHA concerns itself primarily with the health care goods and services consumed by resident units *only*, irrespective of where that consumption takes place (*i.e.* in the economic territory or in the rest of the world), or indeed who is paying. Therefore, exports of health care goods and services (provided to non-resident units) are *excluded*, whereas imports of health care goods and services for final use, for example, those goods and services consumed by residents while abroad, are *included*.

Expenditure on gross capital formation in the health care system

The distinction between current expenditure on health care goods and services and capital expenditure in health care industries is an important one. Capital goods are an essential component of the demand of health care providers and play a crucial role in the provision of health care goods and services by maintaining or expanding their production.

Gross capital formation in health care is defined as the acquisition of produced assets; that is, assets intended for use in the production of other goods and services over a period of one year or more. It is the sum of the values of the following three components:

- Gross fixed capital formation;

- Changes in inventories; and
- Acquisitions less disposals of valuables.

Therefore, gross fixed capital formation is one of the three elements included in the wider aggregate called gross capital formation.

In calculating the acquisition of produced assets in capital formation, the disposal of existing assets should be deducted from the value of the acquired capital goods. Such capital may be tangible assets, for example, hospital buildings, ambulances or MRI machines, or intangible assets, such as investment in software and databases.[5] Gross capital formation can be further broken down according to the health care provider industry. It should be noted that, for the most part, capital goods are produced by branches or industries outside the realm of health care providers.

The guiding criterion for the recording of gross capital formation is the ownership of the assets by the health providers. The only category of health providers for which capital formation would not be recorded is the rest of the world, as the acquisitions of capital by non-resident providers will be recorded in the country of residence of the provider.

The inclusion of all providers (except the rest of the world) is a departure from SHA 1.0, which excluded the net acquisition of capital assets by retailers of medical goods (as the retail sale of medical goods is regarded as a supporting activity). The recommendation to also record the value of gross capital formation acquired by retail sellers is motivated by the fact that retail sales are part of the health system. Retail sellers are part of the distribution of medical goods – they are a different type of provider, but arguably as relevant as medical offices. In summary, the definition of "capital formation" is the following:

> ***Gross capital formation*** in the health care system is measured by the total value of the *assets* that providers of health services have *acquired* during the accounting period (less the value of the disposals of assets of the same type) and that are used repeatedly or for more than one year in the provision of health services.[6]

Capital transfers to health care providers

Capital transfers[7] from financing agents to health providers for the purpose of capital formation may deserve particular attention.

The extent to which the remuneration of the health services covers operating together with capital costs can vary widely across and indeed within countries (Box 3.1). In a few countries, the payments that providers receive for the delivery of health services include operating costs only, while capital expenses are covered by separate grants that health providers receive from different levels of government or by philanthropic organisations. For example, the financing system used in Germany for the remuneration of hospital services, based on diagnosis-related groups (DRG), excluded from the payment for health services the capital costs of reconstruction and medical equipment, which are subsidised by capital transfers by the German States ("*Länder*") based on their investment programmes, in co-ordination with their strategic hospitals plans.

More common, at least in OECD countries, is the case of partial coverage of capital expenses through the payment received for the delivery of the health services, with the remaining part funded by specific investment grants. For example, in Luxembourg, hospital charges paid by the *Sécurité Sociale* covered 20% of capital costs, while the remaining 80% is paid with government investment grants funded out of taxes. Similar situations have occurred in France, where charges for hospital services covered only part of the capital costs.

By contrast, there are also payment schemes that cover both the operating costs and capital expenses. For example, Medicare fees for hospital services in the United States include the full coverage for capital expenses. Similarly, in Canada the costs for major medical equipment may be reimbursed through operating expenses. In Germany, investment surcharges are included in fees for some long-term care services.

Typically, for private providers in OECD countries, charges for service delivery very often fully cover capital expenses, although even here in a few cases governments may also make capital transfers for the purchase of medical equipment.

Looking at some further examples, in December 2007, the Federal Parliament in Switzerland passed a reform of the hospital financing system that introduced a DRG payment system. Under the new arrangement, payments to hospitals remunerate both the operating costs and capital costs. In the Netherlands, a case-mix system based on "diagnosis treatment combinations (DBC)" was introduced for the reimbursement of hospitals and medical specialist care in 2005. Prices negotiated between health insurers and hospitals include capital costs, while prices based on fixed tariffs do not. However, hospitals that get paid on a fixed price basis may be compensated in the following year by the Ministry of Health for the capital costs incurred.

The presence of such wide-ranging payment mechanisms, and the different extent to which capital costs are included in prices, can potentially affect the comparability of health expenditure across countries, between parts of the same health system, or over time. A possible solution to the potential loss of comparability is to adjust current health expenditure by adding the capital transfers that financing agents transfer to the health providers to fund the part of capital expenses not covered by charges for operating costs.

This Manual proposes the sum of "current health expenditure" plus "capital transfers", which could be called "overall health expenditure", as an additional aggregate, and encourages further research to gather empirical evidence on the potential of this concept to improve international comparability compared to the use of "current health expenditure" alone.

Research and development

In the 2008 SNA, research and development is considered as an intellectual property product and as such included as part of capital formation. The results of research and development (R&D) "consists of the value of expenditures on creative work undertaken on a systematic basis in order to increase the stock of knowledge, including knowledge of man, culture and society, and use of this stock of knowledge to devise new applications. This does not extend to including human capital as assets within the SNA. The value of research and development (R&D) should be determined in terms of the economic benefits it is expected to provide in the future. This includes the provision of public services in the case of R&D acquired by government. In principle, R&D that does not provide an economic benefit to its owner does not constitute a fixed asset and should be treated as intermediate consumption. Unless the market value of the R&D is observed directly, it may, by

Box 3.1. **Layers of the core accounts and health financing**

Pricing policies of health providers can vary widely between countries and providers and over time. Sometimes financing schemes, rather than paying for the outputs, pay for the inputs, that is, the factors of provision, such as compensation of employees and capital services. All the diverse types of transactions that reimburse providers for the provision of health care in the current period should be considered in the measurement of health expenditure. As outlined in Chapter 9, the valuation of the cost of services includes the consumption of both interest and fixed capital. The valuation of the transactions covering consumption (HC) should comprise their full cost and all the current payments made by financing schemes (HF) or financing agents (FA) to providers (HP). Accounts capture the sales and other revenues of providers that equal the purchases of financing schemes:

Total consumption and provision of *health care* for residents *equals* total revenues of domestic health care providers for health care *less* provision for non-residents *plus* residents' purchases of health care abroad:

$$\sum_{i=1}^{9} HC_i^{residents} = \sum_{j=1}^{8}\left(HP_j^{total} - HP_j^{non-residents}\right) + HP_9^{residents} = \sum_{k=1}^{6}\sum_{l=1}^{n} FA_{kl}^{residents} \quad [1]$$

The kind of economic transactions *(l=1,....,n)* for the purchase of services vary in the income statements of provider accounts and financing agents. The main categories are direct payments, global budgets, lump-sums, fee-for-service payments, cost-sharing, in-kind reimbursement, subsidies and possibly also transfers for capital cost/expense. Suppose that in equation [1] the index l=n stands for capital transfers, then the following equations hold for current health care expenditure and capital transfers for health care:

$$\text{Current health care expenditure} = \sum_{i=1}^{9} HC_i^{residents} - \sum_{k=1}^{6} FA_{kn}^{residents} \quad [2]$$

$$\text{Capital transfers for health care} = \sum_{k=1}^{6} FA_{kn}^{residents} \quad [3]$$

It is recommended to give special attention to the revenues of providers coming from government and other financing agents in the form of expenses for capital formation, investment grants and other transfers, because these transfers might include transfers for capital formation of future periods that do not affect the consumption of health care in the current period (see Chapter 11). Capital transfers might also be difficult to assign to specific functions, and therefore should be reported for providers. The compilation of the demand of capital goods by health care providers is further outlined in Chapter 11.

For the consumption and provision of *health-related activities*, the following equation holds:

$$HC_R = \sum_{j=1}^{9} HP_{R,j}^{total} - \sum_{j=1}^{9} HP_{R,j}^{non-residents} = \sum_{k=1}^{6}\sum_{l=1}^{n} FA_{R,kl}^{residents} \quad [4]$$

The subscript R denotes the health-related activities of consumption, provision and financing. Health-related activities consumed abroad are not included.

convention, be valued as the sum of costs, including the cost of unsuccessful R&D..." (SNA 2008, 10.103).

Although according to the SNA, R&D of health care providers should be recognised as part of capital formation, for practical reasons the SHA regards R&D in health as a capital-related expenditure and therefore to be recorded as a memorandum item to the capital account.

Examples of R&D include those linked to the generation of specific products such as vaccines and pharmaceuticals that result from basic research and biomedical, clinical research and research on risk factors.

The *Frascati Manual*, which provides detailed guidelines for the estimation of expenditure on research and development in health (OECD, 2002a, Annex 4), may be a source of useful examples. Further information on international comparisons and examples of national initiatives can be found in "Measuring expenditure on health-related R&D" (OECD, 2001). The separate recording of expenditure on R&D as a component of capital formation is suggested and is expected to be an area for further development.[8]

Expenditure on "education and training" is treated in a similar way to Research and Development in that it is conceptually close to capital when it refers to investment in human capital. In the SHA, it is treated as capital-related expenditure and therefore recorded as a memorandum item to the capital account. As is stated in the SNA, when training is part of programmes to ensure an improvement of ongoing activities, it is considered as intermediate consumption.[9] This means that all resources involved in training in those circumstances should be accounted for as intermediate consumption: the salaries paid during the training (to trainers and to trainees) as well as the specific additional resources to undertake the activities, which is part of the resources used in the various health programmes, and thus recorded above the line within the programmes in the functions.

Rest of the world

A measure of final consumption expenditure of *residents* needs to consider interactions with the rest of the world. Imports and exports of goods and services are defined by the existence of a transaction (sale, barter, gift, grant, etc.) in goods and services between residents and non-residents. Given the increasing importance of trade in health care goods and services, a consistent and comparable aggregate of health care expenditure that takes account of this trade is necessary.

In this respect it is important to clarify the concepts of residence and what is to be included under imports and exports. Residents include any individual, enterprise or other organisation ordinarily domiciled domestically. To ensure compatibility with other macroeconomic statistics, SHA takes its lead from the definitions contained in the Balance of Payments Manual (BPM6) (IMF, 2009): "The residence of each institutional unit is the economic territory with which it has the strongest connection, expressed as its centre of predominant economic interest. Each institutional unit is a resident of one and only one economic territory determined by its centre of predominant economic interest."

Health care goods and services acquired by non-residents from resident providers are *exports*. For example, health care provided to non-resident tourists represents an export. Exports can, however, take other forms which do not necessarily imply the movement of the user across the border. Consider, for example, the increasing importance of e-health, tele-diagnosis, or the purchase of medical goods through the Internet. Another example relates to health professionals providing services abroad on a temporary basis. Health services provided to foreign enclaves such as embassies are also part of exports.

In the System of Health Accounts, the category *rest of the world*, relating to non-resident units, is referred to in the provider and financing schemes classifications. However, with respect to imports and exports of health care goods and services, it is important to clarify that it is the provision rather than the financing by non-resident units that is of interest here. For example, if a foreign government or non-resident non-governmental organisation (NGO) pays for health services for residents, but these services are actually provided by a domestic provider, then these services are indeed financed by the rest of the world, but are not classed as an import. If, however, the services are *provided* by a foreign government to a resident, then this is indeed accounted for as an import.

In SHA tables, therefore, imports of goods and services from non-resident units are recorded under the provider category *rest of the world* (HP.9) and can be cross-classified against the functional and financing classifications. Within the current health expenditure account, exports are not included since they refer to consumption by non-residents. During compilation, the direct purchase of health care goods and services by non-residents will therefore often need to be explicitly excluded from domestic provider revenues. However, for transparency and reconciliation, it is recommended that *exports* should also be reported in a supplementary trade table (Chapter 12).

Transactions in the health care sector

SHA recommends the standard SNA/ESA[10] approach when referring to transactions in the health care sector. Hence, the definition of a transaction can be interpreted as an economic flow or a kind of formalised relationship between various units acting in the health care sector, that is, between consumers and providers, providers and financing units, or consumers and financing units. It usually takes the form of an agreement or contract under which the quantity, price (or payment) and quality characteristics of the transaction is articulated. As in SNA, transactions in SHA can be divided into four main groups, as follows:

- Transactions in products, which refers to final consumption of health care goods and services;
- Distributive transactions, which encompasses transfers granted to households for the specific purpose of providing health care services to family members;
- Financial transactions, which comprises either acquisitions or disposals in financial assets and liabilities such as loans to health care providers from financing agents;
- Other flows, which refers to the consumption of fixed capital and acquisitions less disposals.

Time of recording

The timing of recording of final consumption expenditures within SHA has two elements:

- Calendar year versus fiscal year;
- Accrual versus cash accounting.

First, a particular period must be chosen within which the activities took place. Most often this is a fiscal year or a calendar year. This choice may seem trivial, but in practice it can pose problems. For example, government entities may report spending on the basis of a fiscal year while private entities report on the basis of a calendar year. For the purposes of international comparability, the calendar year is preferred. In such a case, the health accountant must adjust the figures reported so that only one time period is used (the *Producers Guide* provides practical guidelines).

The second element of the time boundary is the distinction between when the activity took place and when the transaction that paid for the activity took place. In practice, this involves a choice between accrual accounting and cash accounting. Health accounts should use the accrual method, in which expenditures are attributed to the time period during which the economic value was created, rather than the cash method, in which expenditures are registered when the actual cash disbursements took place.

The same treatment should be made when considering exports and imports; these are recorded at the time when a service is delivered or, in the case of goods, when the change in ownership of real assets occurs.

The measurement of consumption and output: market and non-market production

By convention, final uses are valued at the prices agreed to by the parties to the transaction. These prices are described as market prices or purchasers' prices. In the case of full direct payment by households, they correspond to the price paid to the health provider, *e.g.* hospital, physician or pharmacy. The prices of final uses include non-deductible VAT, other taxes on products (such as sales taxes and specific duties) and transport and marketing costs.

However, there are a large range of activities for which the notion of sales is non-existent, particularly in the health care sector. These constitute the non-market sector, and cover mainly services provided by general government and non-profit institutions. The organisations concerned do not sell their services, or if they do, the prices do not cover the full cost, and it is therefore necessary to find a different measure of valuation of their output. Non-market providers are those that provide services, and in some cases goods, either free of charge or at prices that are not economically significant, typically meaning, in practice, prices that cover less than half the full cost of production (*i.e.* including any subsidies or other transfers).[11] In such cases, the value of the good or service is, by convention, measured as equal to the sum of its production costs, including:

- Intermediate consumption, *e.g.* electricity, water, as well as other medical goods and services used up in the production process;
- Compensation of employees (gross salaries in cash and in kind, actual and imputed social contributions and taxes);
- Consumption of fixed capital, which is the utilisation cost of the equipment used by non-market producers; and
- Other taxes paid on production (taxes on ownership or use of land, buildings or other assets used in production).

General government bodies constitute the bulk of the non-market producers, but there are others, like the non-profit institutions. Most of the services provided by general government are provided to the general public without charge. These services may be financed through taxation and social contributions, but there is no direct link between the payment of the tax and the level of services received. A tax is a compulsory transfer to general government and is not the price of a public service. Certain services provided by general government, like education and health care, are provided to households on an individualised basis, meaning that it is possible to know who consumes them. Other services are provided only on a collective basis (*e.g.* mass health information and education campaigns), meaning it is impossible to know who consumes what.

In the case of individual services, if prices are fully paid by patients or third-party payers (on the patients' behalf), the provision is valued at market prices. If patients do not pay the full price, for example if government charges only part of the price to the consumer, and this price is well below the production costs of the services consumed, the value of the good or service is conventionally measured as equal to the sum of its production costs, as above.

In some cases, even when government corporations are engaged in market-oriented production, they may still offer health care services to their workers and their relatives free of charge. In such cases, the valuation should also be made through an input cost approach.

The treatment of subsidies and other transfers to provider industries

According to SNA, "subsidies" are current unrequited payments that government units make to enterprises on the basis of the levels of their production activities or the quantities or values of the goods or services that they produce, sell or import (SNA 2008, 7.98). Subsidies on products (payable per unit of good or service) should be distinguished from other subsidies on production (not calculated per unit of good or service) that often take the form of regular transfers paid to cover persistent losses. It is important to recall that, "Subsidies ... do not include grants that governments may make to enterprises in order to finance their capital formation ... such grants being treated as capital transfers" (SNA 2008, 7.99).

Subsidies to public corporations and quasi-corporations[12] consist of regular transfers that are intended to compensate for persistent losses (that is, negative operating surpluses) incurred on their productive activities as a result of charging prices that are lower than their average costs of production as a matter of deliberate government economic and social policy. In order to calculate the basic prices[13] of the outputs of such enterprises, it will usually be necessary to assume a uniform *ad valorem* implicit rate of subsidy on those outputs determined by the size of the subsidy as a percentage of the value of sales plus subsidy (SNA 2008, 7.105).

In health care provision and finance, current government transfers and subsidies are frequently used to reduce the prices paid by final consumers or insurance funds for certain goods or services (especially for institutionalised care). These government transfers have two different forms, according to whether they are paid to market or non-market providers of health care. Transfers to market producers are identical to the category of "subsidies" in national accounts in so much as subsidies can only occur in market production. In many countries, however, subsidies for market production in health care are of relatively minor importance compared with transfers that go to non-market producers. In the latter case, these are recorded as "current transfers".

Chapter 29 of SNA 2008 gives two options for reporting on subsidies:

"... either consumption is valued differently from the core framework in order to include the value of consumption subsidies, or consumption is valued as it is in the central framework and specific current transfers must include consumption subsidies" (SNA 2008, 29.69).

SHA abides by the first option. Final consumption values of, for instance, hospital services should be recalculated (whenever possible) by adding subsidies to the recorded costs. This solution provides for a uniform treatment of national totals and for functional and institutional breakdowns, when shares in total expenditure on health are compared across countries. The exclusion of subsidies could lead to distortions in cross-country comparisons. In practice, subsidies for health care are almost exclusively related to inpatient care.

Also relevant to the issue of subsidies and current transfers is the provision of in-kind goods and services to health providers. It may be the case in the health care sector that the cost of certain intermediate goods and services may be met by central government directly, with these services being made available to health care providers at no or a very low nominal charge. An example of this would be the provision of electricity or water services to public health care providers, with the government covering all or part of the cost directly. A similar example may be the provision of blood products from publicly run blood banks and blood transfusion centres to hospitals free of charge. In both cases, the valuation of non-market services should attempt to take into account these costs.[14]

The production boundary of health care services

SHA recommends following the standard SNA rules for drawing the production boundary of health care services, albeit with two notable exceptions:

- Occupational health care is included in the national totals of health care spending. In SNA, this item is recorded as ancillary services and part of intermediate production of enterprises;[15] and
- Part of the cash transfers to private households for care givers of home care for the sick and disabled are treated as the paid household production of health care.

Occupational health care

Occupational health care expenditure is the sum of expenditures incurred by corporations, general government and non-profit organisations on the provision of occupational health care. Occupational health care can be provided in-house or contracted out.[16] Occupational health care includes the surveillance of employee health (routine medical check-ups) and therapeutic care (including emergency health care services) on or off business premises.

Household provision of health care

The provision of health care services not only takes place in health care facilities, but also in private households, where care for the sick, disabled or elderly is provided by family members. The own-account provision of these personal care services by members of the household for their own final consumption is excluded from measured production in conventional national accounting practice. However, the boundary line drawn in SHA includes personal health services provided within households by family members in the case where they correspond to social transfer payments granted for this purpose.

This valuation is based on the assumption that the value of the unpaid care work performed in the household is worth what social programmes are willing to grant. This is of course not a totally satisfactory treatment, since the actual amount of time spent on health care work is not taken into consideration. Nevertheless, it is preferable to no valuation at all, and therefore to no consideration of the hours spent on care, which is the case when no formal care or monetary support is granted to households.

Health care as part of the informal sector

The concealed production of health services (to avoid the payment of income or other taxes or to achieve hidden additional income besides that under contract with health insurance and/or government programmes) may amount to a sizeable share of the real medical benefits accruing to private households. It may also be the case that such non-declared payments may be made to health care providers on top of their "official" revenues for reported health services. In both cases, an estimate of the amounts should be part of total current expenditure on health as defined by SHA, as differences in the treatment of the informal health care sector can distort international comparisons.

Illegal actions should in principle be recorded in the accounts in the same way as legal actions, if they fall within the health care boundary – see also Chapter 4.

The relationship between current expenditure on health and the SNA components of consumption

SHA and national accounts differ in their primary perspective of the economic activity of a society. While SHA concerns itself with the consumption, provision and financing of health care goods and services only, national accounts refer to the supply of all goods and services, the use of those goods and services, and the generation and distribution of income in the whole economy.

Although, as stated, the primary interest of SHA is the consumption of health care goods and services, the health provision boundary linked to the basic health consumption boundary is important, as it involves some differences from SNA production boundaries. The expenditure of production units on providing occupational health services for their employees is recorded as intermediate consumption of the respective units under SNA, while it is recorded as output of the respective units in SHA. In another departure from SNA, the production of households that take care of their dependents is not considered as an economic activity under SNA and is therefore not recorded. Under SHA, however, it is recorded as health expenditure, although restricted to the case where there are social transfers made to carers.

In SNA, the output of products is recorded at basic prices. The basic price is defined as the amount receivable by the producer from the purchaser for a unit of a good or service produced as output minus any tax payable and plus any subsidy receivable on the product as a consequence of its production or sale. It excludes any transport charges invoiced separately by the producer.

The use of products is recorded at purchasers' prices. The purchaser's price is defined as the amount payable by the purchaser, excluding any deductible VAT or similar deductible tax, in order to take delivery of a unit of a good or service at the time and place required by the purchaser. The purchaser's price of a good includes any transport charges paid separately by the purchaser to take delivery at the required time and place. The difference in value recorded for a product between when it is produced and the moment it is used for, say, final consumption expenditure can be considerable. In the health sector, the main component of this difference is "taxes less subsidies on products payable by the producer".

Table 3.1 shows the link between current expenditure on health as defined in SHA and the main components of consumption as defined in SNA 2008. Although the concept of current expenditure on health mainly overlaps with the SNA aggregate "final consumption expenditure" (which is much wider as it covers all goods and services consumed in the economy), as described above it also includes some components that are not considered as consumption in SNA.

Table 3.1. **Relationship between SHA current expenditure on health and SNA terminology**

SNA 2008 code	*Description*
P.31	Individual consumption expenditure on health
P.32	Collective consumption expenditure on health
P.3	Final consumption expenditure on health (= P.31 + P.32)
D.31-D.21	Government subsidies to health care providers (net) in order to lower price of output
P.31*	Occupational health care (intermediate consumption within establishments) minus an estimated share of occupational health in health providers' and other medical industries net administration
P.31*	"Remunerated" unpaid household production in the form of transfer payments (social benefits in cash) for home care of sick, disabled and elderly persons provided by family members
P.3*	Adjusted total final consumption expenditure on health (= P.3 + D.31 – D.21 + P.31*)
	CURRENT EXPENDITURE ON HEALTH (≈ P.3*)

* The production boundaries used in SHA for the estimation of this item differ from SNA rules. Please see Annex A for a more detailed discussion of the differences.

Source: Source: IHAT for SHA 2011.

Notes

1. A more detailed examination of the relationship between SHA and SNA is presented in Annexes A and B.
2. To become an SNA satellite account, SHA would need extra information and accounts such as a production account; intermediate inputs to the health care industries; as well as gross capital stock and an input-output table of health care industries. See SNA 2008, 29.139 to 29.141.
3. There are differences in the SNA and the SHA boundaries relating to the treatment of occupational health care and household provision of health care which are discussed later in the chapter.
4. In most countries non-profit health care providers have market oriented practices. As in the SNA (4.83) health non-profit institutions are legal or social entities, created for the purpose of producing goods and services, whose status does not permit them to be a source of income, profit or other financial gain for the units that establish, control or finance them. In practice, their productive activities are bound to generate either surpluses or deficits but any surpluses they happen to make cannot be appropriated by other institutional units according to the articles of association by which they are established.
5. A full classification by type of asset is detailed in Chapter 11.
6. Please note the use of "provider of health services" instead of "health care services" so to include those economic units providing health administration services.
7. Capital transfers are defined as "unrequited transfers where either the party making the transfer realises the funds involved by disposing of an asset (other than cash or inventories), relinquishing

a financial claim (other than accounts receivable) or the party receiving the transfer is obliged to acquire an asset (other than cash) or both conditions are met" See SNA 2008, 10.19.

8. An OECD "Handbook on deriving capital measures of intellectual property" is under preparation at the time of writing. Its purpose is to provide guidance on deriving capital measures (gross fixed capital formation, consumption of fixed capital, capital services, and the stock of capital) of R&D and other intellectual property products.
9. "[W]hen training is given by an employer to enhance the effectiveness of staff, the cost is treated as intermediate consumption" (SNA 2008, 1.54).
10. The European System of Accounts (ESA) is the system of national accounts and regional accounts used by members of the European Union.
11. Although SNA itself does not set such a level of costs to distinguish between market and non-market production, European System of Accounts (ESA) does set a 50% borderline as a criterion for this distinction. It is therefore recommended for the purposes of SHA to follow this practice so that when the price covers less than 50% of the cost, the provider is treated as a non-market producer.
12. "Some unincorporated enterprises function in all (or almost all) respects as if they were incorporated. These are termed quasi-corporations" (SNA 2008, 4.42). In the health system, these are typically public health service providers exercising a degree of market activity and a certain autonomy from government control.
13. Basic prices are prices before taxes on products are added and subsidies on products are subtracted (SNA 2008, 2.63).
14. See Box 9.1 in Chapter 9 for a further discussion of intermediate consumption in the health system.
15. This excludes remuneration in kind in health care goods and services that do not constitute intermediate consumption, but household actual final consumption.
16. The item corresponds to *Item 05.2: Health* in the Classification of the Outlays of Producers by Purpose (COPP).

A System of Health Accounts 2011: Revised edition

PART I

Chapter 4

Global Boundaries of Health Care

Introduction

Achieving consensus on a common boundary of health care activities is crucial for the complex task of international comparisons. In pursuing this objective, SHA refers to a functional approach based on selected health care activities that can be captured by transactions. Transactions are valued activities that take place between different actors or organisations. The transactions recorded in the SHA accounting framework relate to health care goods and services provided and consumed to improve the health status of individuals and of the population as a whole.

It has to be emphasised that health itself is a condition, and is therefore not exchangeable, in contrast to health care. Health has value in use and not in exchange. Therefore, in health accounts, it is the demand, supply and distribution of health care goods and services, rather than health *per se*, that define the transactions measured. Consequently, the focus of this chapter is on the boundaries of health care, and not of health.[1]

In particular, this chapter focuses on the boundaries of health care activities that underlie the core accounting framework of SHA 2011. In addition, it introduces interfaces to the core accounting framework, which allow the compilation of a broader set of tables and indicators for useful analytical purposes and for exploring their relationships with other statistical systems.

Defining current health care expenditures

Health care boundary: Focus on functions

The functional classification of health care (ICHA-HC) delineates the boundaries of health care activities from an international perspective.[2] Following the concept underlying the design of the ICHA-HC classification, the boundary contains **all activities with the primary purpose of improving, maintaining and preventing the deterioration of the health status of persons and mitigating the consequences of ill-health through the application of qualified health knowledge** *[medical, paramedical and nursing knowledge, including technology, and traditional, complementary and alternative medicine (TCAM)]*. This primary purpose is pursued by the following groups of health care activities:

- Health promotion and prevention;
- Diagnosis, treatment, cure and rehabilitation of illness;
- Caring for persons affected by chronic illness;
- Caring for persons with health-related impairment and disability;
- Palliative care;
- Providing community health programmes;
- Governance and administration of the health system.

In carrying out the above activities, the prerequisite of a basic level of medical, paramedical and nursing knowledge is one of the main delineation criteria. In most cases, but not exclusively, this refers to national standards of accreditation, licensing and other regulation or practices related to health care personnel and care givers. These procedures qualify them to practice their medical and nursing knowledge as well as to provide more complex services within an institutional framework.

Administration is an embedded activity in the provision of health care goods and services, for example, the administrative activities carried out in a hospital or a physician's practice, and as such it is included as an inherent part of the functions specified above. The functional classification does, however, distinguish separate categories of the health system governance and administration performed, for example, by ministries of health or health insurance enterprises, as follows:

- *Governance and health system administration* (HC.7.1): necessary for the design, operation, management and control of health care policy;
- *Administration of health care financing* (HC.7.2): necessary for managing the process of health care financing.

The basic dividing lines for structuring the health care functions are individual versus collective health care goods and services, the basic purposes of care (*e.g.* curative, rehabilitative, long-term care), and the modes of provision (*e.g.* inpatient, outpatient). SHA 2011 distinguishes (as did SHA 1.0) the health care functions (HC) and certain health care-related functions (HCR). The latter can be closely linked to health care in terms of operations, institutions and personnel, but should, as far as possible, be excluded when measuring activities belonging to the health care functions themselves. For example, many activities that may accompany or follow the provision of health care services such as long-term social care or activities related to enhancing the social integration and participation of disabled persons are not counted as health care functions. Similarly, activities such as the control of food hygiene and drinking water, environmental protection and the multi-sector promotion of healthy life styles, which are well known as health determinants, should in general be recorded as health care-related functions and not health care functions, except in certain cases where there is a strict relation to preventive health care programmes.

The core and extended accounts of SHA

It is necessary to delineate a common boundary of the health care system that will permit international comparisons concerning both the amount and the structure of expenditures for health care goods and services. Central to the framework are three classifications related to health care functions, provision and financing, which will be subsequently referred to as the core classifications or the core framework. Other classifications complement these. In total, SHA 2011 distinguishes three main groups of classifications:

- The core framework, encompassing the three classifications that measure current health care expenditure by functions, providers and financing schemes;
- Capital formation, with its related classification of assets;
- And other classifications that allow for the compilation of additional indicators in the extension of the core accounting framework.

The core accounting framework is organised around a tri-axial system for the recording of health care expenditure, namely classifications of the functions of health care

(ICHA-HC), health care provision (ICHA-HP), and financing schemes (ICHA-HF),[3] as presented in Figure 4.1. These three core classifications address the three basic questions:

- What kinds of health care goods and services are consumed? (Chapter 5)
- Which health care providers deliver these goods and services? (Chapter 6)
- Which financing scheme pays for these goods and services? (Chapter 7)

The ultimate goal of data compilation of the core accounts is to answer these three questions with respect to each transaction that incurs health care expenditures – in other words, to use the three axes of the International Classifications for Health Accounts (ICHA), namely, function, provider and financing, to describe each financial flow in the health care sector.

Around the core accounting framework of the SHA, a number of complementary classifications might be added that are closely linked to one of the three axes. Some of these additional classifications, related to human resources, beneficiaries, revenues of financing schemes and factors for provision of health care, were introduced to varying extents in SHA 1.0 and/or in the *Producers Guide*, albeit in some cases with different names. SHA 2011 revisits some of these classifications with the aim of, *inter alia*: proposing a more comprehensive structure of classifications, as in the case of the beneficiary and factors of provision classifications; recommending a new breakdown to existing classifications, as in the classification of revenues of financing schemes; and offering better guidelines to particular aspects of health accounts, for instance, in the area of external trade in health care or capital formation, which are subjects of growing interest for both national and international policy. From an economic perspective, these classifications encompass activities that help to understand the health system in a wider context.

The health care functions of ICHA-HC refer to the health purpose of activities and determine the boundaries of health care consumption in the strict sense. The transactions related to the consumption of health care goods and services on the one hand and the transactions related to capital formation, education and training, as well as to research and development for future health care provision, on the other hand, serve different purposes. The first group of transactions relate to the current health expenditure account directly and serve the purpose of promoting, developing and maintaining the health status of individuals and the population as a whole. Here it should be noted that collective health care service provision is considered to be for the direct final use of health care by the community as a whole. The second group of activities are those relating to resource generation that have the purpose of supporting health care provision by developing technology, human resources and capital formation. In SHA 2011, these different purposes are clearly separated, while maintaining the tri-axial account of current health expenditures of SHA 1.0. As a consequence, the boundaries of the second type of transactions are included in extended expenditure accounts, whose boundaries relate to those of the first type (health care consumption) of transaction, but do not equate to them.

Figure 4.1 shows the core health expenditure accounts of SHA 2011 and their extensions. The three core classifications in the middle of this figure represent the consumption of health care goods and services, which equals their provision and financing. Each of the three dimensions provides interfaces to further breakdowns or dimensions. Details of the links between core and extended accounts are described in more detail in Part 2 and in the annexes.

Figure 4.1. **The core and extended accounting framework of SHA 2011**

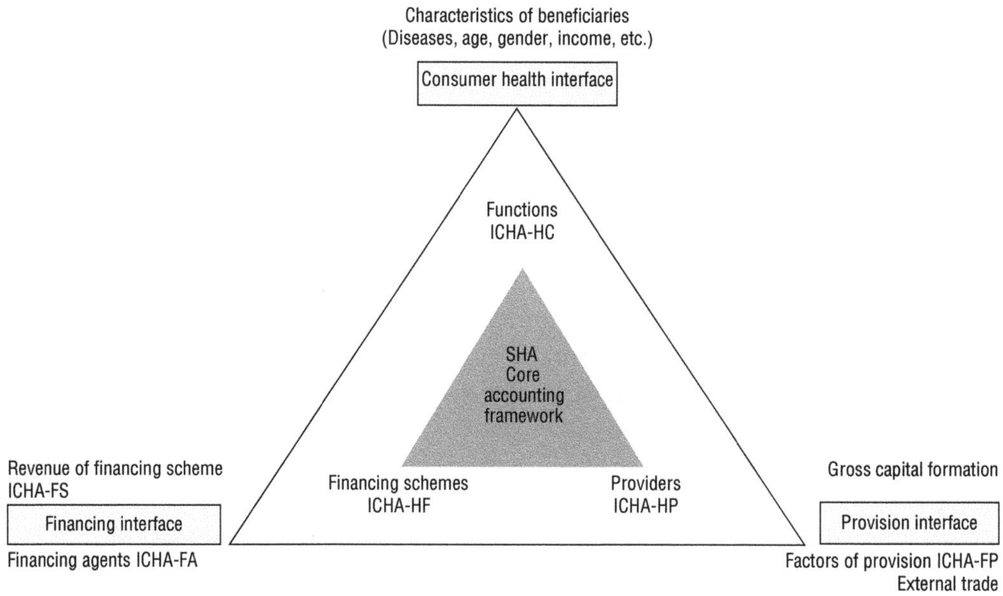

Source: IHAT for SHA 2011.

The consumer health interface related to the core accounts is of a different nature to the other two interfaces. The aim of developing the consumer health interface to ICHA-HC under the SHA is to provide more detailed information on health care expenditure in relation to the uses and beneficiaries of the health care system. The distribution of health care expenditure by patient characteristics (*e.g.* age, gender, socioeconomic status or diseases/condition of beneficiaries), population morbidity (incidence or prevalence of diseases), and its burden both in monetary and non-monetary terms can give health care policy makers important information for re-designing health care priorities and re-allocating available resources. While information derived from the consumer health interface can be used as an input to priority setting, the information from either the financing or the provision interfaces gives insights into the type and level of resources available. Accordingly, information on the revenues of the financing schemes, on health care exports and imports (external trade), on the cost of inputs used in health care provision or, importantly, information on capital formation, education, training, and research in the health sector, can provide further support to decisions on changes in the allocation of health care sector resources.

Criteria in boundary setting

Countries differ in financing and organisation of their health care system and in the range of goods and services consumed. From an international perspective, developing a common boundary of functionally defined health care systems means setting the limits on the scope of health care activities to be included in order to improve the comparability of cross-country data. Four main criteria are set out to determine whether an activity should be included within the core expenditure account of the SHA; these are presented below, in order of importance:

- The primary intent of the activity is to improve, maintain or prevent the deterioration of the health status of individuals, groups of the population or the population as a whole as well as to mitigate the consequences of ill health;

- Qualified medical or health care knowledge and skills are needed in carrying out this function, or it can be executed under the supervision of those with such knowledge, or the function is governance and health system administration and its financing;
- The consumption is for the final use of health care goods and services of residents;
- And there is a transaction of health care services or goods.

The main criterion to include or exclude certain activities relates to their role in enhancing health status, diminishing ill-health, or preventing the deterioration of the health of individuals and/or the population as a whole. Here, by convention, the administration and governance of the health care system is also included. Although direct contact with the patient is not explicitly introduced as a criterion, it is obvious that for cure and treatment as well as in personal prevention direct contact is a necessary prerequisite. In the case of collective prevention activities, both direct and indirect contacts with the target group of population are possible. Another criterion is the amount of medical, nursing or health knowledge needed to perform the activities, or the degree to which medical, paramedical or nursing professionals are involved in the provision process. The last two criteria imply that it is also important to distinguish whether the health care goods and services subject to the transactions are consumed by patients, or utilised by the target population groups, or further transformed and used up within the production process as intermediate consumption,[4] or increase the stocks of goods as capital formation. All four criteria are further discussed in the next section.

Consequently, neither the reimbursement of the cost of health care goods and services nor information and data historically collected by a country's statistical system are a key criterion for inclusion or exclusion. In reality, this means that certain goods and services recorded by a particular country under health care might not be included for the purpose of international data collection, and that some goods and services not recorded might be included. Furthermore, the specific health care transactions requested under the SHA may not always be in agreement with the available data or the way that the statistical system is designed at a national level. Both over- and under-estimation of the aggregates may occur, as well as a certain level of ambiguity concerning the transactions, due to a lack of detailed data, which might be difficult to prevent. From a data comparability point of view, any departures from SHA should be minimised as far as possible, and well documented.

The boundary of the current health care expenditure account

The consumption frame of health care goods and services

The boundaries of the current health expenditure account are established by the purposes of the consumption of the health care goods and services included. These purposes are discussed in detail in Chapter 5 "Classification of health care functions" (ICHA-HC). Here, however it is essential to clarify certain aspects of the general structure, which can provide a bridge across accounting concepts and definitions, as described in Chapter 3, and the health care boundary criteria set up in operational terms, including specific rules on how to handle borderline issues.

Boundary criteria in operational terms

In accordance with the *purposes*, health care comprises health care goods and services provided directly to individual persons as well as collective health care services. The latter covers health care prevention programmes as well as administration of both the health care system itself and its financing. The prevention tasks and collective health care services commonly include epidemiological surveillance and other measures of health promotion and disease prevention, including the establishment and enforcement of good practices or standards in public health, as well as the provision of health care prevention programmes and their administration. Governance and administration of the health care system comprises activities related to planning, management and regulation of the health care sector as a whole in order to ensure its effectiveness, including tasks related to collecting, pooling and distributing funds by government units and/or health insurance, as well as other financing agents (see Chapter 5).

Health care goods and services provided to and consumed by individuals comprise the majority of transactions recorded in the core accounting framework and grouped under the specific functions, such as curative and rehabilitative services, long-term care (health), preventive immunisation or screening, or pharmaceuticals and other medical goods. The ICHA-HC functional classification also distinguishes on the second-digit level between different types of settings, so-called *modes of provision*, by which the services are provided: inpatient care, day-care, outpatient care and home care. One should note that health care services offered at the workplace or school, although provided in specific settings, are also included here, as the purpose is health improvement, regardless of the provider settings or facilities and their regulatory status. Among health care goods and services consumed by individuals, *occupational health services* require particular attention, because these services are often provided by specialists of occupational medicine within an industry setting.[5] When occupational medical services for employees are outsourced (contracted out to offices of medical specialists), caution in data compilation is recommended to avoid the potential for double-counting.

Regarding the *level of medical knowledge and skills* that are needed to carry out health care activities, SHA 2011 refers to the International Standard Classification of Occupations (ISCO). This classification recognises medical occupations by classifying them under health professionals and associate professionals, including medical and paramedical, nursing and other health professionals based on both the tasks and duties undertaken as well as educational and skill type criteria. Therefore it is recommended that the ISCO be used as background information on the set of medical occupations characterised by the application of *qualified medical knowledge and skills*. In operational terms, the reference is to ISCO categories 2200 and 3200, excluding veterinary occupations – see Annex C. Activities related to Traditional, Complementary and Alternative Medicine (TCAM) goods and services are in general included – although to be dealt with individually on a country by country basis – on the scope of tasks provided by both TCAM professionals and associate professionals as classified in ISCO (groups 2230 and 3230).[6]

Regarding the notion of activities to be carried out under the *supervision of those with qualified medical or health care knowledge and skills*, application of this criterion will generally be left to the discretion of the countries, as national arrangements of health care delivery can differ significantly. Nevertheless, the common understanding is that a minimum level of such supervision should consist of basic introductory training and occasional visits or consultations by the qualified medical professional (a supervisor) in order to ensure the services are performed by the care givers satisfactorily.

The current health care expenditure account of SHA focuses on *final consumption* and not on intermediate consumption of services and goods. In other words, SHA does not aim to account for health care goods and services provided as intermediate output to other providers. This is the case, for example, when one hospital provides or carries out a laboratory test for another hospital. In the case of inpatient and day-care services, health expenditure should comprise all medical services and goods received during the episode of care, regardless of the provider or the payer. The provision of a laboratory test by Hospital A to Hospital B leads to expenses for B and revenues for A. However, the laboratory tests are part of the treatment processes offered by Hospital B. Therefore, the provision of laboratory tests by Hospital A is counted, but as a part of the output and billing of Hospital B, and as such is considered in SHA as final consumption of health care goods and services. In this example, the additional compilation of the laboratory test of Hospital A would lead to double-counting from a consumption point of view and is therefore not shown separately. In fact, it is essential that total expenditures for hospital care or any other providers are reconciled for interflows among providers. Intermediate consumption is not limited to goods and services that are delivered by health care providers to other providers, but also includes goods and services that might be delivered by units of the rest of the economy, such as electricity and water.

SHA focuses on the consumption of health care goods and services by the resident population irrespective of where this takes place. This implies the *inclusion of imports* (from non-resident providers) and the *exclusion of exports* (health care goods and services provided to non-residents). In practice, when business or establishment surveys of resident providers are the starting point for the construction of the SHA, this may result in the inclusion of exports of health care (delivered to non-residents but provided by resident units) and the neglect of imports of health care from non-resident providers. As the extent of cross-border trade becomes more important, other sources of information, such as travel surveys or insurance claims for reimbursement of services bought abroad, may be considered as an estimating factor (see Chapter 12 for further boundary considerations related to cross-border trade).

Another aspect to be considered in the consumption of health care is the *non-observed economy*, *i.e.* unrecorded, illegal or informal activities that are not always captured or reported in regular statistical sources. The reason for this may be that the activity is informal, and thus escapes the attention of official surveys; it may be that the producer is anxious to conceal a legal activity, or it may be that the activity itself is illegal. In some countries the consumption of health care goods and services is often related to informal payments, so-called "envelope payments" or "under-the-table payments". Whether these payments relate to normal or additional services provided to patients or represent a patient's additional gratitude to the physician, these extra unrecorded payments increase the incomes of health care providers on one side and add to the financial burdens of the consumer on the other side. The non-observed health economy may account for a significant part of the health care system for some countries. It is therefore particularly important to try to make estimates of the total consumption of health care, even if it cannot always be separately identified as such.[7]

SHA refers to *valued transactions*, *i.e.* transactions under which payments are made to providers in exchange for health care goods and services received by consumers. In other words, the flow of health care goods and services is accompanied by a flow of financial or other means. Usually, these payments go to health care providers and are made directly by patients or indirectly by other actors in the health care system (for example, government or health insurance) on behalf of individuals or groups of the population. However the recipient of these payments may not necessarily be a typical health care provider like a hospital or physician but a household which, under certain circumstances, may provide some health care services to other members of the family. These circumstances refer to the *provision of health care services at home* (home health care) that are usually made under supervision of medical or paramedical professionals or on the condition that the family member who provides them possesses certain medical knowledge that could be used for this purpose.

This requires that SHA considers households not only as a financing agent that pays for health care goods and services purchased or consumed, but also as a specific health care provider that can deliver services under certain circumstances.[8] The scope of health or health care-related services provided at home by family members often is *a mixture of health and social care services*. This leads to the problem of how to split the health care component from the social one when classifying these activities under SHA. For the health care component, SHA recommends taking into account nursing care activities, which are often provided in combination with personal care services, notably assistance with activities of daily living (ADL).[9] If these activities are paid, for instance, via "nursing allowances" or other transfers granted for the care of household members due to their health problems, then they are to be included in the current health care expenditure account. The interpretation here is that benefits granted for care to members of households are included if they are paid. It is also assumed that behind the decision to grant benefits, there is usually a preceding medical examination and periodic supplementary examinations to evaluate whether or not the person is still eligible for the benefits. Other benefits in cash, such as benefits for sickness leave or maternity leave or pensions for disabilities or work accidents, are granted for the purpose of income maintenance and are therefore excluded from the core accounting framework.

Consumption is valued at purchasers' prices including any (non-deductible) value added tax (VAT). This means that the value of medical goods and services is based on what purchasers pay.[10] Even if medical services and pharmaceuticals are provided free of charge, it is necessary to estimate the *values that are equivalent to market prices*. Often, health care services and medical goods are provided free of charge or at user charges which are below prices "that are economically significant".[11] When reliable market prices cannot be obtained, a second best procedure is to value the output to be equal to the sum of its cost of provision: that is, as the sum of selected inputs, including transport charges and trade margins. More detailed information about the type of factors of provision is provided in Chapter 9.

Many prices of health care goods and services are the result of complex institutional pricing arrangements in which the prices contracted, for example, by health insurance, may not include the cost of capital services, which can be paid separately by government or other financing agents. One of the costs of providers' services is the consumption of fixed capital (CFC), or what is called *depreciation* in business accounting,[12] for example for hospital buildings, medical equipment or expired pharmaceuticals that can no longer be prescribed. This is the value loss of the capital assets used up in the process of delivering health care goods and services during the current period, resulting from physical deterioration, normal obsolescence or damage. It measures the decline in the usefulness of a fixed asset for purposes of health care provision. Within the core accounting framework, CFC should always be included in the price of health care goods and services. As discussed in Chapter 3, in some cases purchases of health care goods and services by financing schemes (or agents) do not cover the cost of capital, so the respective amount has to be estimated.

Borderline cases

SHA consumption frame draws the borderline irrespective of where and by whom (although with reference to the second criteria) the activities are provided and how they are financed. The functional classification of health care sets the borderline according to purpose. In some cases, such as with cosmetic surgery, the transportation of patients, home help services, sunglasses or condoms, it might not be clear whether or not to classify these services and goods under the current health expenditure account. In general, borderline cases refer to specific goods and services that are situated on the boundaries of health care and health care-related or non-health-care products.[13] As it is not always easy to make a distinction between these, as a rule of thumb the four criteria for health care boundary setting should be verified at the outset, followed by specific rules on how to handle borderline cases. In many cases, a reference to medical recommendations can serve as additional guidance (see Table 4.1 for further details). Here, three particular areas of borderline cases are briefly discussed:

- Multi-sectoral issues;
- Wellbeing;
- Social care.

A large group of borderline cases relate to *multi-sectoral issues* such as road safety, intentional injuries or improving health equity by reducing poverty. The main criterion for the decision to include or exclude these activities in SHA is whether the primary purpose of these activities is health and whether an application of medical knowledge and technology is involved. For example, road safety measures are quite important to reducing road injuries; however, the primary purpose is public safety and movement from one place to another, rather than health. Therefore, it would be misleading to include the cost of road construction, road signs and crash barriers in the accounts in addition to the cost of medical treatment of injured persons. Similarly, safety tests for cars, seat belts or policy activities geared towards road safety are considered outside the boundary of health care goods and services. However, preventive measures related to the above activities can be recorded as an additional layer to the consumption frame, in particular as health care-related activities proposed in SHA 2011.

Another group of borderline cases concerns *well-being* services, such as those provided in spas and wellness centres. The perception of health services is evolutionary, inter-cultural and social (Petrera and Vicente, 2008). The understanding of the relationship between welfare, well-being, lifestyle and health status as well as the scrutiny of the effectiveness of health care goods and services might vary between countries. The current health care expenditure accounts aim to measure neither the impact on welfare nor the effectiveness of health care services. Goods and services directed primarily to well-being, such as fitness training or specific diets, might well have a health impact but are excluded from the consumption frame unless they are part of activities recommended medically and thus conform to the four health care boundary criteria (for details, see Chapter 5).[14] In the case of cosmetic surgery or dental work for aesthetic purposes (*e.g.* teeth whitening), this should be excluded (when it can be separately identified); despite the medical knowledge, technology and personnel involved in its provision, it does not meet the first criterion.[15]

The aim of *social care* is to provide services and support, by formal and informal caregivers, to individuals who, for reasons of disability, illness or other dependency, need help to live as normal a life as possible, either within a residential care setting or in their own home. Social care covers a wide range of services, including professional advice and support, accommodation, various types of assistance in carrying out daily tasks, home visits, home help services, provision of meals, special equipment, house adaptation for disabled persons as well as assessment and care management services. Often local authorities are responsible for assessing the care needs of their populations as well as the planning and provision of services. In reality, there may be a mixed economy of social care provision (by public, non-profit and for-profit providers), various mechanisms for its financing (direct payments, reimbursements, benefits in cash, etc.) and different arrangements for its delivery (pure social components or a mixture with various levels of medical care). The latter mix of services often makes it difficult to separate between health components and social components with services related to help with activities of daily living (ADL) and instrumental activities of daily living (IADL).[16] An assessment of care needs frequently involves input from medical professionals and often is in response to an underlying medical condition or disability. Therefore, long-term care (health) in SHA 2011 includes personal "body help" type services (*e.g.* help with ADL) under health expenditure, while "assistance or home help" type services (*e.g.* help with IADL) should be separately counted as long-term care (social) outside the core health care boundary and recorded under the *health care-related* category (HCR.1). If, however, long-term care (social) services are also delivered as part of a service package in which a medical or nursing care component dominates, then the expenditure for these should also be included under health care, and *vice versa*.[17] This aside, the health accounting framework leaves open the possibility to identify total long-term care spending, that is, the aggregate of the health and social components, which may be of greater policy relevance.

Layers of the consumption frame

The layers of the consumption frame can serve different purposes. In SHA 1.0, the "*health care-related functions*" were introduced as additional layers to the functional classification, encompassing areas that overlap with the health domain on the one hand but go beyond the health care boundary on the other hand. Seven health-related functions were proposed: 1) capital formation of health care provider institutions; 2) education and training of health personnel; 3) research and development in health; 4) food, hygiene and drinking water control; 5) environmental health; 6) administration and provision of social services in kind to assist living with disease and impairment; 7) administration and provision of health-related cash-benefits. In the joint OECD, ESTAT and WHO SHA data collection, the "*memorandum items*" were introduced with reference to aggregates on specific expenditure categories such as totals of pharmaceuticals and of ancillary services (in both cases including inpatient and other modes of provision) that cannot be directly obtained from the functional classification categories. All these functions and items are of interest, as they constitute relevant parameters for health policy.

As far as the different layers are concerned, SHA 2011 recognises the importance of the purposes behind both the "health care-related functions" and the "reporting items" layers. However, it recommends that they refer to the consumption of health care goods and services following one of the main criteria under this frame. Accordingly, certain modifications and additions to SHA 1.0 concept are made in the functional classification in Chapter 5. In general:

- *Capital formation* is considered *separately* due to the complexity of this subject, the experiences hitherto of international data collection as well as the different nature of spending on capital formation compared to consumption spending on health care. Chapter 11 of SHA 2011 proposes a set of guidelines for estimating capital formation with a more comprehensive approach than in SHA 1.0. In addition, it addresses both the education and training of human resources as well as research and development as memorandum items.
- From a wide range of multi-sectoral *health care-related activities*, SHA 2011 recommends distinguishing two groups of activities, *i.e. i)* the *social part of long-term care*, and *ii)* activities of *prevention linked with multi-sectoral health care* that may involve a public safety interest in a wide sense.
- As *reporting items* for the totals of specific expenditure categories, it is proposed that three groups be captured under the functional classification: *i) pharmaceuticals* (including that of inpatient care), *ii) TCAM* and *iii) prevention*. The latter classifies expenditure according to SHA 1.0 subcategories of prevention and public health services.

The boundaries of the additional expenditure accounts of SHA

Dimensions of extension

Depending on the additional activities considered, the boundaries of the extended health accounts can differ from current health expenditure captured under the core accounting framework. There are three main interfaces, offering additional classifications and further breakdowns of expenditure, which link the core health expenditure account to a broader set of statistical areas (see Figure 4.1):

- The consumer health interface;
- The provision interface;
- The financing interface.

The derived additional expenditure accounts of SHA give the opportunity to develop all these areas in more detail. In the following, only a general overview of the interfaces and their relation to the boundary of the core accounting framework is presented. Some of them are discussed further in Part 2 and in the annexes.

Consumer health interface

The consumer health interface is of particular interest to the study of the relationship between the consumption of health care goods and services and the associated health enhancement of the population. Although health is only partly determined by the consumption of health care, the breakdown of health care expenditures by *various characteristics of beneficiaries* (see Chapter 10) helps to improve the understanding of the observed distribution in overall health spending. Health differences among individuals and population groups are apparent along many dimensions, including age, gender, socio-economic status (SES) and geographic area. Age and gender are demographic characteristics of beneficiaries that form an intrinsic epidemiological part of identifying and measuring the utilisation of health care goods and services by type of disease.

Some components of the consumer health interface are closely connected to the social area. Organising equal access to health must take into account the diversity of people's social, cultural and ethnic backgrounds.[18] Identifying and measuring the burden of health care financing in different social groups of the population adds to the understanding of both consumption and financing patterns. It also helps to improve the consistency of health accounts. Health expenditures are quite unevenly distributed among population groups. Socio-economic variables may determine not only health, but also, in public financing schemes, any exemptions from co-payments. "Catastrophic" health expenditures and out-of-pocket expenditures that low-income households face are therefore of particular interest for health accounts and add valuable information to the knowledge about both the demand for health care and its accessibility (O'Donnell *et al.*, 2008).

Employing consistent methodology and data sources can ensure that expenditures for various diseases can be compared and that the sum of expenditures for all diseases equals the estimate of current health expenditure. SHA offers the possibility to develop consistent *expenditure by disease accounts*. In practice, this means mainly a top-down approach to the allocation of health expenditures by specific health status classifications based on the International Classification of Diseases (ICD), keeping the boundary of the current health care expenditure account.[19] The cost of disease is different from the total cost faced by the patient. One reason is the inclusion of indirect costs. Indirect costs in the estimation of the so-called Cost Of Illness (COI[20]), or productivity loss, measures the loss in earnings as a result of death, illness or time spent undergoing treatment for the population as a whole. The loss of earnings comprises both those of the patient and those of family members caring for the patient. Usually indirect costs are larger than health-related cash benefits, because these benefits do not fully replace the loss of income. The cost framework might also include intangible costs, *e.g.* costs of pain, suffering, anxiety, grief and loss of leisure time, for which a monetary value is assigned.

Current health expenditures can be considered as the product of the annual prevalence of patients receiving health care goods and services and the average value of these health care goods and services. The ability to *link monetary with non-monetary data* gives opportunities to gain information about utilisation, incidence and prevalence that is essential for measuring unit costs of health care services. Unit costs may be important for developing health price indices (see Chapter 13). In addition, information about unit costs could be used for checking the consistency of the accounts.

Provision interface

The provision interface offers links to additional dimensions and accounts, such as the classification of factors for health care provision (see Chapter 9) or the capital formation account (see Chapter 11). The focus switches here from consumption to the provision approach. In the current health expenditure account, the total of provision equals the total of consumption and the total of health care financing. It is important to distinguish between "provision" as the output of health care products and the "production" of providers as a process that relate inputs to outputs. Health care provision for final consumption differs from the production of health care providers by the external trade in health care goods and services, the production of non-health products, and the production of health care goods and services used as intermediate consumption. From an economic perspective, the total value of the production of the health care system and the related value added are of interest. Such a broader economic perspective is taken in full health care satellite accounts that compile both the supply and the use of health care goods and services.[21]

The *factors of provision* (FP) are the factor inputs used by providers to produce the goods and services consumed or the activities conducted in the system. The boundary for measuring factors of health care provision is derived from the outputs of health care providers. Usually this differs from the boundary of health care consumption of the core health expenditure account. One particular issue concerning the factor of provision account is that the factor costs of health care providers also include items related to non-health products and exports. Chapter 9 recommends taking account of these in order to preserve the current health expenditure boundary. The extension of the core account of SHA to FP might be of interest for various reasons, *e.g.* the cost of the various components driving the expenditure increase varies according to the organisation of purchase and provision and the strength of health professionals in the health care market. In many high-income countries, human health resource costs are the most important group of variables among the factors of the health care provision account, including wages and salaries as well as social dues to be paid on earnings. By contrast, in lower-income countries, the cost of medicines can play a significant role. Furthermore, the compilation of intermediate consumption in the factors of provision account of SHA 2011 allows the measurement of the intermediate use of health care goods and services by health care providers and allows for checking interflows among providers.[22]

The *generation of resources* by investment in key inputs and technologies (capital, human and knowledge) determine the capacities of the health care system. Information and communication technologies as well as medical equipment are nowadays integrated in almost all health care provision processes and give opportunities for further improvements. Capital formation is a crucial factor in the provision of health care goods and services by health care providers and in the enhancement of their quality. Capital formation deals with changes in the equipment, buildings and instruments used by providers, including amongst other things the acquisition and application of new medical technology. Gross capital formation is measured in the capital account by the sum of three components: gross fixed capital formation plus changes in inventories plus acquisitions less disposals of valuables. A human capital account would record expenditures for the formation of human capital in health care as well as the human resources in health care. Human capital and health knowledge are, like physical capital, crucial factors in the provision of health care goods and services by health care providers and in the enhancement of their quality. Human capital within the health care system consists of the stock of knowledge, skills and experience embodied in the labour force, including all types of skills, ranging from medical to IT, cleaning and management, which is taken as a proxy for human capital. SHA 1.0 recognised the importance of the labour force and proposed the measurement of human resources in health care in a stock-flow approach and expenditures for activities involving education and training (SHA1.0: HC.R.2). Furthermore, the amount of resources devoted to innovation, science and inventions is measured in the form of expenditures for research and development in health (SHA1.0: HC.R.3). Both types of expenditures are not for current final consumption, but influence final consumption in the future. Like capital formation, they are invested by health care providers as inputs into the future capacities of the health care system (see Chapter 11, memorandum items).

Financing interface[23]

The financing interface offers the possibility to expand the accounting of health care financing to a detailed analysis of the revenue side of financing schemes (see Chapter 8) and their linkages with the institutional sectors of the SNA. Information about health care financing is limited in the core expenditure account to answering the questions: "*where does the money go to?*" and "*which types of different services are financed?*" (HFxHPxHC). The financing interface aims to provide a more comprehensive picture about financing flows in health care, by providing answers to the questions: "*where does the money come from?*" and "*what instruments are used for fund raising?*". Two types of information can be gained from the revenues of schemes account. On the one hand, it may focus on tracing back the funds that are at the disposal of financing schemes, *i.e.* the flows from the institutional units of the economy (general government, non-financial corporations, financial corporations, households and NPISH) and from the rest of the world to the financing schemes. On the other hand, of particular interest might be information on contribution mechanisms, *i.e.* the way the health care funds were collected (government contributions, health insurance premiums, grants, transfers, etc.) in relation to issues of the fiscal stability, sustainability and equity of health care financing.

Identifying financing agents, which are the institutional units, and the types of revenues for each financing scheme, allows for a better interpretation of public and private funding in the health care sector. For example, "households", as an institutional sector, belongs to the private sector, so household out-of pocket direct payments for purchasing health care goods and services are considered as private funding. However, social health insurance contributions paid by households via health insurance premiums are considered as elements of public funding, in contrast to the voluntary health insurance premiums paid by households, which are considered as elements of private funding. In addition, the revenues of financing schemes account can provide information about discrepancies between the receipts and the expenses of financing schemes. Revenues and expenditures of financing agents/schemes may not be balanced. The total expenditure in HCxHF and the HPxHF tables does not necessarily equal the total revenue in the HFxFS table.[24] The differences show the surplus or deficit of the particular health care financing schemes. A related issue concerns intergenerational imbalances in the financing system. Contributions (private and public) and premiums paid by one generation are by definition not always equal to the payments necessary for service delivery for that generation (Auerbach *et al.*, 1994).

To sum up, the extension to the revenues of financing schemes does not change the consumption boundary considered in the core health care expenditure account, but adds distributive transactions to the health accounts at the financing interface. Imbalances between the revenues and expenditures of schemes might be accumulated over several years. These deficits or surpluses change the financial position of the financing schemes, *i.e.* their financial assets and liabilities. SHA 2011 does not provide guidelines for the recording of financial assets and liabilities. If accountants are interested in expanding the financial accounts further, they should follow the rules laid down by the Government Finance Statistics Manual (GFSM, IMF, 2001) and SNA.

Table 4.1. **Selected borderline cases of the SHA core accounting framework**

Borderline activity	*Criteria in boundary settings*				Main arguments and recommendations to include/exclude from health care function
	Primary purpose – health	*Qualified medical and health knowledge and skills*	*Consumption for final use*	*Transaction of health care goods and services*	
Cosmetic surgery for reconstruction of traumatic damage	yes	yes	yes	yes	Included.
Other cosmetic or plastic surgery	?	yes	yes	yes	Often no health purpose; performed by medical (surgeons) professionals; using medical technology; presence of transitions. Pure aesthetic services should be excluded.
In-vitro or artificial fertilisation	yes	yes	yes	yes	Included.
Autopsies	?	yes	?	?	Might be no health purpose (*e.g.* criminal evidence), as well as not for final consumption. Included under condition of collective health purpose and final consumption.
Forensic medicine	yes	yes	yes	?	Forensics makes large use of health knowledge and technology (incl. psychology); autopsies and forensics are linked services linked. Included for personal and collective health purpose and final consumption; excluded as intermediate consumption.
Telemedicine	yes	yes	yes	?	Performed using medical and paramedical knowledge and technologies. Included for personal and collective health purpose and final consumption; excluded as intermediate consumption.
Psychological therapy/psychotherapy related to mental or physical abuse	yes	yes	yes	yes	Included.
Chiropractors' services	yes	yes	yes	yes	Included if medically prescribed and provided by health professionals (see ISCO 08).
Alternative healers/ alternative medicine	yes	?	yes	yes	Included if follows the rules for TCAM ISCO 08 (2230 Traditional and complementary medicine professionals, and 3230 Traditional and complementary medicine associate professionals).
Acupuncture	yes	yes	yes	yes	Included if medically prescribed and provided by health professionals (ISCO 08: see above).
Services provided by balneology institute	yes/no	yes/no	yes	yes	The very large spectrum of such services often provided by non-health professionals; seldom prescribed as part of a medical treatment. Included, if curative, rehabilitative, or prevention function, and if provided by health professionals. Excluded as sports, wellness or leisure purposes.
Long-term care	yes	yes	yes	yes	Included: nursing long-term care and personal care with a health purpose, contrary to social care.
Summer camp for disabled people and/or for whole family with disabled children providers	?	?	yes	yes	Pros: the main purpose of such services may be support to activities of daily living (ADL); could have a rehabilitative component. Cons: included in health-related functions; activities go beyond daily living. Excluded if the social component is main purpose (only medical/health components are included).
Orphanages (orphans and disable children) home for children	?	?	yes	yes	Generally considered as institutions of social care. Excluded if social component is main purpose (only medical/health components are included).
Crèches for 0-3	?	no	yes	yes	Generally considered as institutions of social care related to the purpose of supporting women's participation in labour market. Excluded.
Housing adaptation such as automatic staircase lifts	?	no	no	no	There is a large spectrum of such technical devices, which are generally not bound to health services or provided by health professionals. It is investment rather than care. It doesn't improve health but standard of living. Excluded.
Recreational services (in mental health or residential care settings)	?	no	yes	yes	Excluded. Only medical/health components are included.
Massages	?	?	yes	yes	Included, if provided by health professionals and medically prescribed (see ISCO 08: 2264 Physiotherapist and 3255 Massage therapist). Excluded are Beauticians and related workers (ISCO08: 5142).
Fitness activities	?	?	yes	yes	Excluded unless these activities are under medical recommendation.
Nutritional products	?	?	yes	yes	Pros: contribute to improvement of health, products sold in pharmacies and/or prescribed by doctors. Cons: also sold in supermarkets; Included in case of health purpose and under the supervision of health professionals.
Vitamins and minerals	yes	?	yes	yes	Included in HC.5.1.2 Over-the-counter drugs (OTC) even if provided by supermarkets.

Table 4.1. **Selected borderline cases of the SHA core accounting framework** *(cont.)*

Borderline activity	*Criteria in boundary settings* *Primary purpose – health*	*Qualified medical and health knowledge and skills*	*Consumption for final use*	*Transaction of health care goods and services*	Main arguments and recommendations to include/exclude from health care function
Maternal and child health	yes	yes	yes	yes	Both prevention and cure elements with a wide range of health care services (*e.g.* genetic counselling and prevention of specific congenital abnormalities, etc.) Included.
Occupational health care	yes	yes	yes	yes	Included as final consumption in SHA (in SNA intermediate consumption).
Blood pressure instruments	yes	yes	yes	yes	Included under HC.5.2.9 for Households. If intermediate output for professionals then to be excluded.
Sunglasses	?	?	yes	yes	Included but on a restrictive basis, only when medically prescribed or advised with a clear health purpose distributed by health professions (ISCO 08). Exclude fashion articles for pure aesthetic purposes.
Sun cream	?	?	yes	yes	Included but on a restrictive basis, only medically prescribed.
Condoms and other mechanical contraceptive devices	?	?	yes	yes	Included in HC.5.1.3 Other medical non-durable goods.
Patient transport to and from facilities for the purpose of receiving medical care, by taxi or other conventional vehicles use	yes	no	yes	yes	Pros: the transportation service is needed because of the health status or to get a health provision. Cons: the service is generally not provided by health professionals; when provided in a health institution, this expenditure is already included in the main product (intermediate consumption, not final use). Included if provided under medical recommendation
Ambulance services which do not result in the transport of patients	yes	yes	no	yes	Intermediate consumption. Excluded.
Services of patient-supporting organisations in relation with diseases	yes	?	yes	?	Included if services (consultation) directly related to heath purpose (except legal services).
Orthopaedic shoes	yes	?	yes	yes	Included if prescribed by a licensed medical practitioner and provided by orthopaedic technicians.
Other medical goods industry	?	?	?	?	Usually intermediate products. Excluded if these goods are not directly provided to the patient.
Health policy formulation outside central government/consultancy	yes	?	no	yes	In health programmes and donor programmes consultancy can be offered as part of the package. Usually excluded because kept as intermediate products.
Activities of organ banks	yes	yes	?	yes	Not included as it is intermediate consumption of other health providers.
Export of health services	yes	yes	yes	?	Transactions not related to resident population. Excluded.
Health care production for own final use	yes	?	yes	?	In SHA (contrary to SNA) is treated as replacement of professional health care under certain conditions (*e.g.* nursing allowance granted to households for care of one family member, usually case of home LTC). Included if payment involved.
Medical association, nurses unions and the like (umbrella organisations for professionals)	?	?	?	?	Not a health activity toward patient. Excluded (intermediate services).
Refresher training (courses to be followed by professionals on an obligatory or voluntary basis)	no	yes	no	?	Excluded (intermediate consumption/input factor).
Biochemical engineering	?	?	?	?	Pros: performed for public health institutions or the pharmaceutical industry. Cons: these products are integrated as intermediate consumption in health care goods and services. Excluded.

Source: IHAT for SHA 2011.

Notes

1. Measuring health and its improvement or deterioration is an important aspect of health economics and statistics, as is reflected, for example, in such measures as life expectancy, healthy life years (HLY) and quality/disability-adjusted life years (QALY, DALY). SHA 2011, like SHA 1.0, does not aim at such measures, but at measurements of health care expenditure. This means that the SHA accounting framework is part of a larger model, in which several determinants of health, one of them being the provision of health care, play a crucial role.
2. SHA describes the international concept and boundaries of health accounts. However, countries have their own responsibility to define what is in or out of the national health care services boundary. As a result, national boundaries may deviate from the international boundaries.
3. A set of tables to present the interaction of these three axes is included in Chapter 15.
4. Intermediate consumption consists of the value of the goods and services consumed as inputs by the process of provision, excluding the cost of fixed assets whose consumption is recorded as consumption of fixed capital.
5. Occupational health care is treated by SNA as intermediate consumption and therefore not included in the consumption of health care services by households. In contrast, SHA includes occupational health care as health expenditure because of the health benefits for employees. It is governed in most countries by detailed regulations. Occupational health care includes surveillance of employee health (routine medical check-ups) and therapeutic care (including emergency health care services) on or off business premises. The expenditure incurred in occupational health care can be approximately estimated as the cost of the personnel involved.
6. Occupations in traditional and complementary medicine whose practice requires an extensive understanding of the benefits and applications of traditional and complementary therapies, developed as the result of extended formal study of these techniques as well as human anatomy and elements of modern medicine, are classified in unit group 2230, Traditional and complementary medicine professionals. Those whose practice requires a less extensive understanding, which is based on relatively short periods of formal or informal education and training or that is developed informally through the traditions and practices of the communities where they originated, are included in Unit group 3230, Traditional and complementary medicine associate professionals.
7. For details about the accounting of non-observed health activities see OECD (2002b) and United Nations (2008a).
8. Here, two problems appear. The first concerns data availability. Despite the progress in the measurement of health care provision by households, few data about health care provided at home by relatives or neighbours are available. Furthermore, household provision consists of a large variety of different activities that are presently not standardised (see Eurostat, 2003).
9. The basic activities of daily living (ADL) consist of certain self-care tasks that could be supported or provided by a family member if the person is not able to do them by him/herself: personal hygiene, dressing and undressing, eating, transferring from bed to chair and back, voluntarily controlling urinary and faecal discharge, or moving around (as opposed to being bedridden).
10. SNA aims to measure all inputs (productive activities) related to the production of goods and services and to balance this with all outputs either used by industries, consumed, invested or exported. The view of consumption in SHA requires a different approach than the view of production in SNA. Therefore, the value of the consumption of medical goods is measured at purchasers' prices including total VAT within the core accounting framework. In contrast, in SNA, "The output of retailers is measured by the total value of the trade margins realised on the goods they purchase for re-sale (valued at actual prices)." The reason is that in SNA the production of pharmaceuticals is measured as output of the pharmaceutical industry. In general, the productive activity of pharmacies is restricted to distribution. The cumulative values of the production of pharmaceuticals by industries, transportation, and wholesalers of pharmaceuticals would have to be incorporated to measure the total production value of pharmaceuticals.
11. Prices of health care services are dealt with in more detail in Chapter 13.
12. The difference between depreciation and consumption of fixed capital can be important, due to the historic cost versus opportunity cost principle. To avoid confusion, the term "consumption of fixed capital" is used in SNA to distinguish it from "depreciation" as typically measured in business accounts (SNA 2008, 1.66).

13. Products that are excluded from the SHA boundaries might be considered by some countries for their inclusion in the complementary expenditure framework for analytical use.
14. Chapter 5 proposes a memorandum item for health promotion in multi-sectoral settings, notably to capture joint intervention of the health system and other branches, *e.g.* alcohol level detection in drivers.
15. If it is not possible to separate the aesthetic purpose from the medical purpose, this should be documented under metadata.
16. Instrumental Activities of Daily Living (IADL) comprises activities such as shopping, cooking, doing laundry, managing household finances and housekeeping. To perform these activities, medical, paramedical or nursing knowledge is not required.
17. In case a separation is not possible between the health care components and the social care components, a clear description in the metadata is required.
18. For example, the Primary Health Care model as articulated at Alma-Ata explicitly stated the need for a comprehensive health strategy that not only provided health services but also addressed the underlying social, economic and political causes of poor health. Call for global action on the social determinants of health with the aim of achieving health equity see WHO (2008a).
19. Estimating current health expenditure according to disease is comparable with direct health cost in Cost-of-Illness accounts (COI). One should note that direct non-health cost, such as transportation and lodging for family members if the health provider is far from home or childcare for dependent children during hospital stay, is not included. COI may consider different time frames for cost estimation: the annual time frame (prevalence-based) or the lifetime frame (incidence-based). Because prevalence-based models have a simpler data requirement, they have been more widely used than incidence-based ones (see Chapter 9).
20. COI studies are not standard in their content, so that the indirect costs are not always included and the coverage of the indirect costs is not unified. See Polder (2001).
21. SNA 2008, Chapter 29, describes such an approach that balances supply and use of health care goods and services in the outline of an input-output model. This is further discussed in Annex E.
22. SHA 2011 aims to measure only the activities of the providers of health care. The intermediate use of health care products and services by other industries are not considered, because it would require the compilation of a complete input-output table.
23. The financing interface is developed in detail in Chapters 7 and 8.
24. In Chapter 8, Table 8.3 shows a possible presentation of the operating balance of health care financing schemes and discusses the possible accounting of loans that may be taken to cover the expenditure of the financing schemes not balanced by their revenues.

A System of Health Accounts 2011: Revised edition

PART I

Chapter 5

Classification of Health Care Functions (ICHA-HC)

Introduction

Within the health accounting framework, the underlying principle may be formulated as "what is consumed has been provided and financed". Clearly, there is no one-to-one relationship between health care functions and the provision and financing categories. The same type of health care goods and services can be consumed from different types of providers and at the same time purchased using various types of financing schemes. But to achieve the tri-axial perspective (consumption-provision-financing), the starting point is to measure consumption (see Chapter 4), which in a health functional approach describes the direct consumption by the population according to the type of health purpose. The boundaries of health care are set based on this consumption purpose. It is therefore important to have a clear understanding of what consumption with a health purpose is, and which are the relevant categories to be identified.

The functional classification in the health accounting framework focuses on the estimation of current spending and involves the contact of the population with the health system for the purpose of satisfying health needs. Therefore, investment is not included here but treated separately in Chapter 11 "Capital formation in health systems".

The conceptual and taxonomic exercise to generate the functional classification, as with other classifications, must take account of feasibility constraints. Experience has shown that the compilation can be limited by the nature of national health statistical systems, which seldom correspond to a classification based on health purpose. Hence, what is to be classified can differ according to both the data available and the ability to implement an accounting framework.

This chapter continues with a discussion of the concept of "function" and the uses of a function-based classification within the SHA framework. A summary of the main changes from SHA 1.0 is also provided. The full classification of health care functions is then presented, together with definitions and examples, and those areas requiring further development to strengthen accountability are identified.

Health care consumption by purpose

In an accounting sense, a "function" relates **"to the type of need a transaction or group of transactions aims to satisfy or the kind of objective pursued"**. Transactions on the expenditure side deal with the question "for what purpose?" (SNA 2008, 2.42).

The accounting process involves the identification of the transactions and the resources involved in the process of satisfying health needs.[1] In summary, the classification of functions refers to groups of health care goods and services consumed by final users (i.e. households[2]) with a specific health purpose (see Chapter 4).

Health care is generally consumed as an integrated service package. In fact, a contact with the health system normally includes a personalised mix of services, for example, of preventive, curative or rehabilitative care. Those services may or may not be delivered on an organised programme basis. Thus, it may not be possible to separate each of the components of the package distinctly into prevention, cure or rehabilitation consumption when they are not part of a programme with specific expenditure records.[3]

Health care can be consumed in two ways: by collectives or individuals.[4] As health status is an attribute of individuals, most consumption of health services is undertaken by specific individuals; and thus is related to private consumption and individual needs. This is important because, although expenditure on health is frequently estimated as an aggregate, the link between the distribution of services among those in need and the distribution of the resources involved is a key issue in policy formulation.

By contrast, collective services are aimed at the whole population (or sections of the population) and aim to improve overall health standards or the effectiveness and efficiency of the health system with benefits to all users simultaneously. These services are diverse and not directly related to individual users but linked to interventions on the whole health system or sub-components, such as the monitoring and evaluation of specific disease control programmes, in addition to governance and administrative services.

Uses of the functional approach

The main uses of a functional classification are:

- A grouping of health care goods and services by purpose;[5]
- A cross-classification of these groups with other relevant health accounting classifications;
- The generation of indicators, such as relative shares of preventive/curative expenditure, the ratio of inpatient to outpatient spending, and other indicators from cross-classifying with financial or provision information, such as: private spending on groups of health care goods and services (*e.g.* medical goods paid as out-of-pocket spending) or services by mode of provision (*e.g.* inpatient/outpatient). Note that indicators needed for national monitoring may differ, and may be linked to more detailed reporting levels.

Features of SHA 2011 functional classification

The following refinements have been introduced into the functional classification in SHA 2011.

- *Functional nomenclature.* An effort has been made to enhance the functional approach both in the labels and definitions of the first-level purpose categories. In that regard, individual consumption categories previously linked to mode of provision categories have been renamed on a more functional basis, although the content remains unchanged [*e.g.* medical goods (HC.5) and ancillary services (HC.4)].
- *Current spending.* Capital formation is acquired as a means of production, and is an investment. In order to refocus the measurement to that of final consumption, the expenditure associated with capital formation has been moved to a specific capital account. The re-structuring also includes human resource formation and research and

development services, which do not fit the final consumption purpose and are thus excluded from this classification. The focus on final consumption improves the operation of the tri-axial approach.[6]

- *Prevention.* The functional category has been better aligned to the purpose of consumption, *i.e.* one of the objectives of contacting the health system is to receive preventive care. The boundary criteria (as described in Chapter 4) have been applied to better differentiate health prevention from the health care-related categories (HC.R) of SHA 1.0. Refined definitions should ensure comprehensive, exhaustive and mutually exclusive categories and increase the comparability of HC classes across countries. The "prevention and public health" class of SHA 1.0 has been unclear in its content, because the categories were based on a mix of criteria: "public" referred at the same time to government-financed services, place of delivery (public-owned services) and the beneficiaries involved (population priority groups). Thus, "preventive and public health" has been restructured into a preventive class, which is better distinguished by purpose from the curative components (see Tables 5.1 and 5.2 and the definitions developed in the section below).
- *Memorandum items* have been created to allow further analysis of policy and resource allocation. Two groups are presented, based on their content:
  - *Reporting Items* identify policy relevant categories that are not identified through a specific HC class even though their content falls within the health care boundary: for example, the total expenditure on pharmaceuticals (including that of inpatient care), or an alternative grouping of health care goods and services that are not separately identifiable in the main HC classification, such as TCAM (see Table 5.3 and definitions developed in the section below).
  - *Health care-related classes* also identify policy relevant areas that are related to health but go beyond the health care boundary. This is the case, for example, for programmes that come under the social part of long-term care (LTC) or areas involving cross-sectoral health promotion (see Table 5.1 and definitions developed in the section below).
- *Research and development* is not part of the population's health final consumption. It has been excluded from the health care-related classes[7] and is now a memorandum item of the capital account in SHA 2011.
- *Education and training of human resources for health* (HRH) is not part of health final consumption by the population. It has been excluded from the health care-related classes and is now a memorandum item of the capital account in SHA 2011.[8]

The revised functional health care classification is displayed in Box 5.1. The first-digit categories identify the purpose of health care, or the various potential needs of a consumer of health care. The list reflects the aggregates used by most countries to develop a comparative spending profile. Memorandum items are included, to be measured when relevant at national level, such as where countries have an interest in tracking continued prevention and public health categories according to SHA 1.0.

Box 5.1. **The classification of health care functions at the first-digit level**

HC.1	Curative care
HC.2	Rehabilitative care
HC.3	Long-term care (health)
HC.4	Ancillary services (non-specified by function)
HC.5	Medical goods (non-specified by function)
HC.6	Preventive care
HC.7	Governance and health system and financing administration
HC.9	Other health care services not elsewhere classified (*n.e.c.*)
Memorandum items: reporting items	
HC.RI.1	Total pharmaceutical expenditure
HC.RI.2	Traditional complementary alternative medicines
HC.RI.3	Prevention and public health services (according to SHA 1.0)
Memorandum items: health care related	
HCR.1	Long-term care (social)
HCR.2	Health promotion with a multi-sectoral approach

Rationale of the functional classification

Categories of health care consumption by purpose

The first-level categories of the functional classification aim to distribute health consumption according to the type of need of the consumer (*e.g.* cure, care, prevention, etc.).

The contact[9] with the system of an individual in search of health care includes a standard set of components that can be disaggregated into a sequence designed to:

- Establish a diagnosis;
- Formulate a prescription and therapeutic plan;
- Complement the process with imaging, laboratory and functional tests for diagnosis and assessment of the clinical evolution;
- Complement the therapeutic plan to include pharmaceuticals and other medical goods as well as procedures such as surgery;
- Monitor and assess the clinical evolution.

This sequence is adjusted to the appropriate type of care based on individual needs; for example, in the case of prevention this can entail monitoring a healthy condition, prescribing a healthy life style, establishing early case detection through imaging, laboratory and functional tests, and in some cases, through the prescription of medical goods, *e.g.* bed nets as part of a malaria programme or anti-malaria medicines to reduce the risks of acquiring the disease.

A *contact* with the health system is an event covering one or more of the components described above according to the specific needs for which the sequence is initiated. The approach in this framework is that the basis of measurement is each contact with the health system, and not the entire duration of the disease or health condition. For example, during a pregnancy, each visit to the medical officer, laboratory service or antenatal class or each associated provision of medicines is independently accounted for as a contact. A contact is distinct from the complete treatment, which comprises all the contacts to treat a health condition.

The *natural history of disease* qualifies the various components of the health system contact and allows a breakdown by specific type of service. It displays a rationale for the progression of a disease or other health condition (disorder, injury, ageing), from the moment of exposure, incident or onset, to the factors that cause health conditions (causal agents) until recovery, functional decline or death, and it determines the purpose of each contact with the health system (see Figure 5.1).[10] Interventions by the health system are intended to handle each of the stages in such a way that the development of the health condition is stopped, and when this is not feasible, it is delayed, or its effects reduced.

The starting point of this process is a healthy condition. At this stage, interventions aim to enhance health status and to maintain a condition of low risk of diseases, disorders or injuries – in other words, to *prevent* their occurrence (HC.6), through vaccinations or an injury prevention programme, for example. Preventive interventions also cover individuals at specific risk and those who have either no symptoms of the disease or early signs and symptoms, where early case detection will assist in reducing the potential damage by enabling a more successful intervention. Take the examples of breast and prostate cancer, where age and sex affect the risk; certain lifestyle choices increase the risks, as smoking does for lung cancer.

From the onset, a disease, injury or disorder is identified by the emergence of symptoms or signs that lead to a search for an appropriate treatment for or by the patient. When the symptoms correspond to an acute condition, a remission or *cure* (HC.1) is sought and expected. Many conditions cannot, however, be completely cured and lead to chronic conditions with some degree of functional decline. Treatment then involves recurring contacts for control as well as the patient's personal involvement in monitoring and controlling symptoms and treatment.[11] Curative care is the most frequent reason why people initially contact the health system. However, based on the specific needs of each consumer the services received typically include a basket of components that mixes preventive and rehabilitative as well as curative care.

Co-morbidity may also occur. When an additional morbid process emerges while the first one is still active, this usually entails additional treatment for the new acute condition. It is also possible that the treatment given during a contact may carry iatrogenic risks, that is, a disease, injury or side effects may be generated by the treatment received, which also require treatment. Complications frequently imply a more complex treatment. A relapse or recurrence is another potential outcome, in which case the treatment has to be re-established or modified. Sequelae, the negative consequences of a condition, can persist.

Impairments, limitations in functioning capacity and consequences of treatment may be *rehabilitated* (HC.2). Both an acute and a chronic condition may deteriorate, causing disability of some degree of severity, from mild to complete. A decline across several domains of functioning could leave the individual unable to handle their own care, and when rehabilitation is not feasible, a *long-term care* (HC.3) option is pursued. This aims to maintain the best quality of life and to reduce suffering and limit deterioration. Palliative care is a component of this final stage.

Figure 5.1. **The natural history of disease and the purpose of health care goods and services**

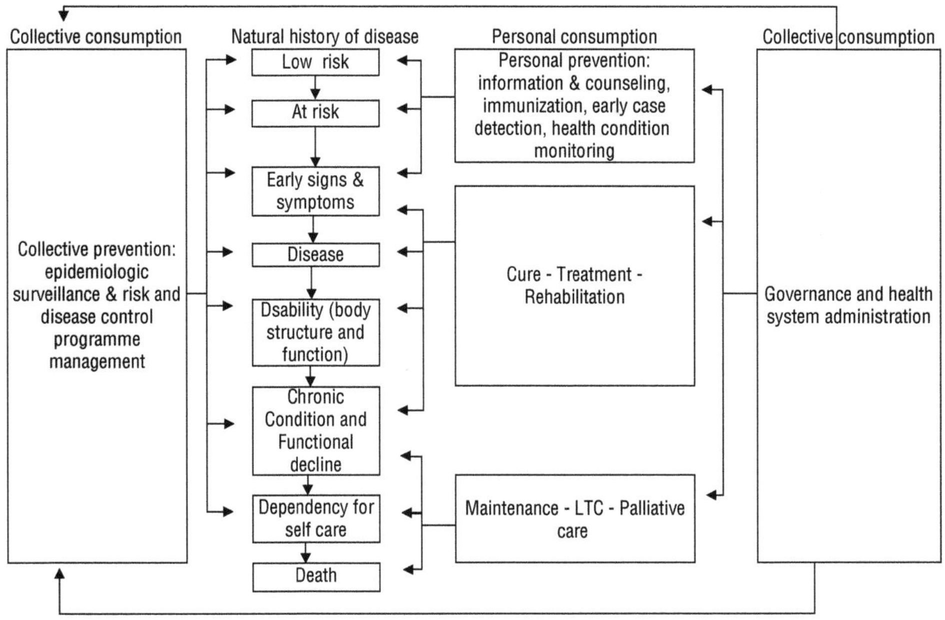

Source: Adapted from Norman (2003).

Collective services are aimed at the whole population (or sections of the population) and aim to improve overall health standards or the effectiveness and efficiency of the health system, which benefits all users simultaneously. This refers in particular to some *preventive services* (part of HC.6) and to *governance and health system and financing administration* (HC.7).

An illustration of the application of the structure of the natural history of disease is presented in Figure 5.2, which uses a decision tree to classify transactions based on the purpose of health care. Note that the codes sequence of the HC classification does not follow the pathway of the history of the disease. The codes follow those developed in SHA 1.0 to facilitate continuity in time series.

Mode-of-provision categories

The categories relating to cure, rehabilitation and long-term care (HC.1-HC.3)[12] are broken down at the second level of classification by a mode-of-provision (MoP) approach, which is based on the specific organisational and technological arrangements of the services consumed. There is no unique block of goods and services to be consumed under each MoP. Each can correspond to a single product or a group of health care goods and services used to cope with an individual's health condition. The services consumed by type of MoP also vary according to the characteristics of the health care system and to the preferences of both the consumer and those prescribing treatment.[13]

The MoP approach responds to particular policy interests but also recognises the structure of national data sources. It is also meant to differentiate between products that are similar but frequently display a different quality, most notably in terms of the technology utilised and the intensity, length and continuity of the health care interaction.

Figure 5.2. **Decision tree for the functional classification**

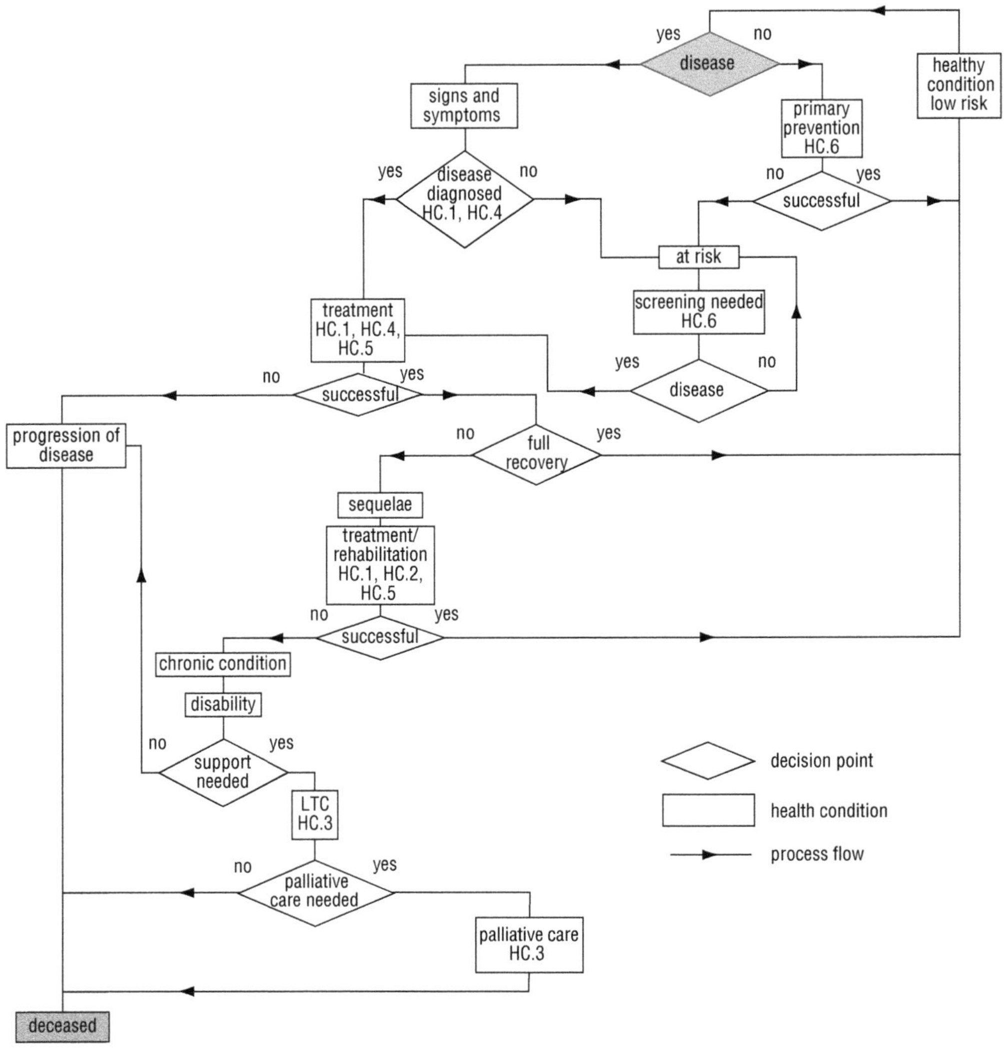

Source: IHAT for SHA 2011.

For example, surgical and some medical non-surgical procedures in inpatient and outpatient settings may be identical in all but one respect: inpatient settings include accommodation and additional nursing care. The role of ancillary services and medical goods are the same regardless of whether they are provided to an inpatient or an outpatient. In all cases, consumption includes the total value of the resources involved in the provision of the service, including management and administrative costs.

The identified MoP categories are: *inpatient, day care, outpatient and home-based care*. The main criteria to differentiate the categories are:

- Inpatient care and day care involve formal admission to a health care facility, whereas outpatient and home-based care do not;
- Inpatient care involves an overnight stay after admission, whereas day care requires the patient to be discharged on the same day;
- Outpatient and home-based care can be differentiated based on the location from where the services are provided; home-based care is provided at the patient's place of residence, whereas outpatient services are delivered from the health care providers' premises.

Inpatient care

An inpatient contact comprises a formal admission into a health care facility for treatment and/or care that is expected to constitute an overnight stay. The classification as inpatient care is irrespective of the type of provider; this may be a hospital, nursing care facility, or facilities classified as ambulatory care providers but which perform occasional procedures requiring inpatient care and are thus able to provide overnight accommodation. It can also include health facilities within any type of establishment that accommodates patients justifying an overnight stay. Tuberculosis hospitals and sanatoriums are often organised to include accommodation along with medical treatment, which is the predominant purpose during a stay in such facilities.

The inclusion of accommodation with medical and ancillary care constitutes the main distinction between outpatient and inpatient care. Accommodation is mostly required because inpatient contacts are typically more complex medical cases that require longer diagnostic procedures and pre- or post-operative intensive surveillance; care with accommodation typically translates into relatively more severe medical cases.

- Contacts lasting less than 24 hours but including an overnight stay, such that the individual leaves the health care facility the day following the day of admission, are normally counted as inpatient care irrespective of the original intention. Emergency cases and urgent admissions should be included only when they result in an overnight stay and formal admission to an inpatient facility, but otherwise are considered as outpatient cases.
- Contacts on a recurrent basis lasting less than 24 hours are classified as day cases, though in some cases these may be *night cases,* for example, mental health patients who need surveillance during the night (in addition to care provided in day-care centres or at home).

All health care goods and services received during an inpatient contact for care should be included regardless of the provider or the payer, such as when pharmaceuticals are provided directly by health professionals or by relatives who had to acquire them in a pharmacy, either hospital-based or elsewhere.

In the case of developing countries, where services provided by patients' relatives in hospitals are more common, any direct expenditure or reimbursement – including expenditure on food, nursing care and medical goods (if not provided by the health facility) – should be recorded under inpatient care. These are often reported in the reimbursement records of the financing schemes or captured in household surveys.

Day care

Inpatient and outpatient services are practically universal. However, the day-care approach is still incipient in many countries and is often linked to specific objectives such as cost containment and waiting list reduction. In contrast to inpatient and outpatient care, **day care comprises planned medical and paramedical services delivered to patients who have been formally admitted for diagnosis, treatment or other types of health care** *but* **with the intention to discharge the patient on the same day**. Day care can relate to preventive, curative, rehabilitative and long-term care services. Day-care services can be delivered in hospitals, ambulatory premises or free-standing day-care centres. Day-care elective surgery is often performed in institutions or wards that specialise in planned services. This can include any elective invasive therapies provided, usually under general or local anaesthesia, to day-care patients whose post-surveillance and convalescence care requires no overnight stay as an inpatient (for example, laser surgery, dialysis and so on). It may also include non-invasive recurrent and planned therapy (such as rehabilitation in individual or group sessions).

In some countries day-care services are, for reporting purposes, often aggregated with outpatient or inpatient services. A contact for a patient who is admitted as a day-care patient, but then due to a complication is retained, should be re-classified as an inpatient case, where feasible. A day patient (or "same-day patient") is usually admitted and then discharged after staying between 3 and 8 hours on the same day. Services for non-admitted patients that are extended to formal admission for day-care are considered as day care. Chapter 14 offers some suggestions on how to deal with aggregated records.

Outpatient care

Outpatient care comprises medical and ancillary services delivered to a patient who is not formally admitted to a facility and does not stay overnight. An outpatient is thus a person who goes to a health care facility for a consultation or treatment, and who leaves the facility within hours of the start of the consultation without being "admitted" to the facility as a patient. "Outpatient" under the SHA framework has a wider meaning than in many national reporting systems, because it refers to any care offered to a non-admitted patient regardless of where it occurs: the outpatient service may be delivered in the outpatient ward of a hospital (including accident and emergency departments), a dedicated hospital outpatient centre, an ambulatory care centre, a physician's private office, or a health care practice within a work place, school or prison, or even on the street (*e.g.* vaccinations, injections, blood pressure or temperature measurement), but not at the patient's place of residence.

Health services have evolved to include a set of miscellaneous non-admission services that can be classified as outpatient care, such as consultation and group support services. These are not to be classified as collective, but as individual outpatient care, since such services are delivered simultaneously but to selected individuals without an overnight stay. As an MoP, *outpatient care* involves a service demand by the patient in a medical setting, regardless of the complexity, location and the type of outpatient facility. As the key criterion concerns the location of the provider rather than the patient, non-face-to-face contacts, such as via e-mail or telephone, generated from the health professional's location are considered as outpatient care, and not home-based care.

- *Includes:* all clinic visits referred visits, observation services and emergency department visits.
- *Excludes*: direct purchase of pharmaceuticals, medical goods and ancillary services; and services consumed at home or in a day-care facility.
- *Clarifying cases*: any outpatient contact that subsequently turns into an admission to a hospital should be modified and recorded as inpatient care. This includes visits to the emergency department, which are recorded as outpatient visits, but when the person is subsequently admitted to the inpatient areas of the hospital are to be recorded as inpatient.[14] Services provided in the street are also considered as outpatient; however, if a person is stabilised in the street by a paramedical officer and then transported to hospital by ambulance, this whole expenditure would be counted as "patient transport

and emergency rescue" (HC.4.3). Non-face-to-face encounters, such as telephone, radio or Internet consultations, could be considered as home-based care; however, the criterion is the place from where the service is provided, *i.e.* the health facility, and therefore should be classed as outpatient care.[15]

Home-based care

Home-based care comprises medical, ancillary and nursing services that are consumed by patients at their home and involve the provider's physical presence. Included are obstetric services at home, home dialysis and all health care services consumed in a home-setting, regardless of the provider, which may be a relative, a health professional or a community trained worker. This is recorded as home-based care, regardless of the duration of the service. It includes health services consumed at the family home and in other individual or collective residences where the individual is located on a permanent basis (*e.g.* prisons, convents, boarding schools). Health care received by persons residing in a health care facility (*e.g.* a residential long-term care facility) is to be considered as inpatient care.

Note that the consumption of health services in any health facility (regardless of its size) located within a residence, such as a medical centre in a residence for the elderly or disabled, or in a school or prison, should be classified as inpatient or outpatient according to the aforementioned criteria: that is, if it involves an admission with an overnight stay then it would be referred to as an inpatient service, and if not, then as an outpatient visit.

Further detailed functional groupings

Each country can opt for a level of aggregation in the reporting as required for its policy analysis and depending on the feasibility related to data and resource constraints. Greater detail within a class does not necessarily imply more detailed reporting, but rather greater clarity about the content of the aggregates. As with other classifications, the greater the detail presented, the less uncertainty there is while classifying, and the more comparable the results. Additional benefits can be found when breakdowns of the HC classes are compatible with those in other available classifications. The division into general and specialised health services for inpatient and outpatient care should be compatible as far as possible with the COFOG (UN, 1999). Within these settings, general and specialised services relate to the technological characteristics of the provider. Specialised services may involve providers that focus on a specific type of patient or need, such as a mental facility service, either for inpatients or outpatients, or a hospital for gynaecology and obstetrics, which may involve more complex technology than a simple maternity unit.

Curative care categories include a breakdown into *general* and *specialised* services. A further separation by basic and more complex types of treatment may be a useful input in assessing effectiveness and efficiency, by cross-classifying providers and functions. For countries where this is relevant, some comments are provided in Chapter 15. In the case of *outpatient care*, an additional category of *dental care* is added, due to its specific importance. Dental services that are provided in a hospital or through the day-care MoP usually do not represent a large component, and thus are included under specialised services. No third-digit breakdown is proposed for rehabilitative services or long-term care (health) services.

Health care goods and services non-specified by function

Health care can be complemented by other goods and services, such as diagnostic laboratory and imaging services, or pharmaceuticals. Such services can be related to preventive care, curative care, rehabilitation or long-term care, thus the purpose of the service itself is unknown. In inpatient care (and day care) such goods and services are normally an integral part of the service package. However, they can be directly consumed as a result of a prescription or individual initiative or self care.[16] In this latter case, there is often no record linking the treatment to other parts of the health care system, only a transaction linked to a retail sale.

Two categories group this direct consumption: ancillary services[17] (HC.4) and medical goods (HC.5). For "ancillary services", there is a second-level breakdown into laboratory services, imaging services, and patient transportation and emergency rescue. "Medical goods" are split into pharmaceuticals and other medical non-durable goods, and therapeutic appliances and other medical durables. Pharmaceuticals are then sub-divided into prescribed and over-the-counter (OTC), with a separate subclass for other non-durable goods, while therapeutic appliances are separated into four main goods categories.

Memorandum items

Different approaches can be taken in accounting for goods and services with a health purpose. The HC classification is based on the natural history of disease and on mode of provision (MoP) approaches. But other approaches (*e.g.* the type of care: modern or traditional; or the type of component: physical examination, procedures performed, laboratory analysis) may also be relevant for decision-making. In addition, important components of the programme and intervention may go beyond the health care boundary and involve non-health activities (*e.g.* rehabilitation and long-term care involve health and social services). Therefore, components of health expenditure identified using different approaches and the reporting of components that lie beyond the health care boundary are targeted through two different memorandum categories. These are termed *reporting items* and *health care-related classes*, respectively.

Reporting items

The categories of the functional classification reflect what is considered the most important from a health policy point of view, and in compliance with the rules of any classification construction process, the classes are designed to be both exhaustive and mutually exclusive. However, some components contained within the health care boundary but not fully disaggregated as separate categories on their own may also have strong analytical relevance. This is the case for pharmaceutical consumption, a key component of health care, for which only the direct purchase by the consumer is reported as a separate class: HC.5.1. A total expenditure figure on pharmaceutical consumption is also considered useful to inform decision makers, thus a separate reporting item comprising all pharmaceutical consumption is proposed. Another selected component is Traditional, Complementary and Alternative Medicines (TCAM). TCAM is part of the health system and difficult to isolate, but it is also recognised to be an expanding component. Decisions about health regulations for expanded coverage programmes, as well as a monitoring process by type of delivery, require TCAM information.

Table 5.1. **Classification of health care functions**

Code	Description	SHA 1.0 codes
HC.1	**Curative care**	**HC.1**
HC.1.1	Inpatient curative care	HC.1.1
HC.1.1.1	General inpatient curative care	
HC.1.1.2	Specialised inpatient curative care	
HC.1.2	Day curative care	HC.1.2
HC.1.2.1	General day curative care	
HC.1.2.2	Specialised day curative care	
HC.1.3	Outpatient curative care	HC.1.3
HC.1.3.1	General outpatient curative care	HC.1.3.1
HC.1.3.2	Dental outpatient curative care	HC.1.3.2
HC.1.3.3	Specialised outpatient curative care	HC 1.3.3
HC.1.4	Home-based curative care	HC.1.4
HC.2	**Rehabilitative care**	**HC.2**
HC.2.1	Inpatient rehabilitative care	HC2.1
HC.2.2	Day rehabilitative care	HC2.2
HC.2.3	Outpatient rehabilitative care	HC2.3
HC.2.4	Home-based rehabilitative care	HC2.4
HC.3	**Long-term care (health)**	**HC.3**
HC.3.1	Inpatient long-term care (health)	HC.3.1
HC.3.2	Day long-term care (health)	HC.3.2
HC.3.3	Outpatient long-term care (health)	part of HC.3
HC.3.4	Home-based long-term care (health)	HC.3.3
HC.4	**Ancillary services (non-specified by function)**	**HC.4**
HC.4.1	Laboratory services	HC.4.1
HC.4.2	Imaging services	HC.4.2
HC.4.3	Patient transportation	HC.4.3
HC.5	**Medical goods (non-specified by function)**	**HC.5**
HC.5.1	Pharmaceuticals and other medical non-durable goods	HC.5.1
HC 5.1.1	Prescribed medicines	HC.5.1.1
HC 5.1.2	Over-the-counter medicines	HC.5.1.2
HC 5.1.3	Other medical non-durable goods	HC.5.1.3
HC.5.2	Therapeutic appliances and other medical goods	HC.5.2
HC.5.2.1	Glasses and other vision products	HC.5.2.1
HC.5.2.2	Hearing aids	HC.5.2.3
HC.5.2.3	Other orthopaedic appliances and prosthetics (excluding glasses and hearing aids)	HC.5.2.2
HC.5.2.9	All other medical durables, including medical technical devices	HC.5.2.4- HC.5.2.9
HC.6	**Preventive care**	**HC.6, part of HC.R.4, HC.R.5**
HC.6.1	Information, education and counseling programmes	Part of HC.6.9, part of HCR 4, HC.R.5
HC.6.2	Immunisation programmes	Part of HC.6.3
HC.6.3	Early disease detection programmes	Part of HC.6.3, HC.6.4
HC.6.4	Healthy condition monitoring programmes	Part of HC.6.1, HC.6.2, HC.6.5
HC.6.5	Epidemiological surveillance and risk and disease control programmes	HC.6, part of HC. 4, HC. 5
HC.6.6	Preparing for disaster and emergency response programmes	Part of HC.6
HC.7	**Governance, and health system and financing administration**	**HC.7**
HC.7.1	Governance and Health system administration	HC.7.1
HC.7.2	Administration of health financing	HC.7.2
HC.9	**Other health care services not elsewhere classified (*n.e.c.*)**	
Memorandum items		
Reporting items		
HC.RI.1	Total pharmaceutical expenditure (TPE)	
	of which Inpatient pharmaceutical consumption	

Table 5.1. **Classification of health care functions** *(cont.)*

Code	Description	SHA 1.0 codes
HC.RI.2	Traditional, Complementary and Alternative Medicines (TCAM)	HC.1-HC.6.1
HC.RI.2.1	Inpatient TCAM	HC.1.1
HC.RI.2.2	Outpatient and home-based TCAM	
HC.RI.2.3	TCAM goods	
HC.RI.3	Prevention and public health services (according to SHA 1.0)	HC.6
HC.RI.3.1	Maternal and child health; family planning and counseling	HC.6.1
HC.RI.3.2	School health services	HC.6.2
HC.RI.3.3	Prevention of communicable diseases	HC.6.3
HC.RI.3.4	Prevention of non-communicable diseases	HC.6.4
HC.RI.3.5	Occupational health care	HC.6.5
HC.RI.3.9	All other miscellaneous preventive care services	HC.6.9
Health care related		
HCR.1	Long-term care (social)	
HCR.1.1	In-kind long-term social care	Part of HCR.6
HCR.1.2	Long-term social care cash-benefits	Part of HC.R.7
HCR.2	Health promotion with multi-sectoral approach	HC.6, HC.R.4, HC.R.5

Source: IHAT for SHA 2011.

Health care-related classes

The functional classification focuses on the grouping of health care goods and services consumed with a defined health purpose. A similar set of services and goods can be consumed with a non-health purpose. This is the case where health care is inter-linked with well-being or with social care, such as medical services with a cosmetic non-health purpose or social support as part of long-term care. Some of this related spending may also be of major relevance for policy purposes. This is the case for the expenditure on social services and cash benefits that are offered as part of long-term care expenditure and HIV/AIDS control and support programmes, for which a total value, including both the health care component as well as the social care component, is vital for the purpose of resource allocation. The classification therefore proposes some additional health care-related classes that allow the construction of relevant indicators to sum up the health and non-health components.

Additional classes could be included for country-specific policy requirements. One case could be the registration of purely cosmetic health activities, as these are provided by qualified health professionals in a professional environment using specific health knowledge and techniques, but do not meet the criterion of a primary health intent. However, in some countries the provision and consumption of cosmetic health services is big business.

Detailed descriptions and definitions of both the reporting items and health care-related classes are included in the explanatory notes at the end of this chapter.

Explanatory notes to the ICHA-HC classification of health care functions

HC.1 Curative care[18]

Curative care comprises **health care contacts during which the principal intent is to relieve symptoms of illness or injury, to reduce the severity of an illness or injury, or to protect against exacerbation and/or complication of an illness and/or injury that could threaten life or normal function.**

A contact for curative care comprises an individual contact with the health system and can be made up of a sequence of components, such as to establish a diagnosis, to formulate a prescription and therapeutic plan, to monitor and assess the clinical evolution or to complement the process by imaging, laboratory and functional tests for diagnosis and evolution assessment. The contact can also include various therapeutic means such as pharmaceuticals and other medical goods (*e.g.* ortheses, such as glasses, and prosthetic appliances, such as artificial teeth or limbs), as well as therapeutic procedures, such as surgical procedures, which require additional follow-up. Routine administrative procedures such as completing and updating patient records are also an integral part of the service.

- *Includes*: all components of the curative care of illness or the treatment of injury; the surgery performed; diagnostic and therapeutic procedures; and obstetric services.
- *Clarifying cases*: treatment and disease management contacts for chronic diseases for which a cure is not feasible should be recorded as curative care when a partial recovery is expected, regardless of the initial clinical condition of the patient (including dependent patients). When a decline in health condition is expected in dependent cases, coupled with increasing dependency needs, this should be classified as long-term care (health): HC.3.

Curative care by mode of provision

The second level refers to the categories of inpatient, day care, outpatient and home-based curative care (see description of modes of provision above). In all cases the main purpose of curative care remains the same, but the technology and place of provision change: in the case of an overnight stay in a health care facility the mode of provision is *inpatient*, or *home-based* if services are consumed at the patient's place of residence. When a patient is admitted for planned care or treatment involving specific organisational arrangements but does not involve an overnight stay then this is *day care*,[19] otherwise it is an *outpatient* contact.

- HC.1.1 Inpatient curative care;
- HC.1.2 Day curative care;
- HC.1.3 Outpatient curative care;
- HC.1.4 Home-based curative care.

General and specialised care

Since curative care categories can cover more than a third of health expenditure, a further breakdown may be appropriate. Curative care can be broken down at a third-digit level into general and specialised care under each mode of provision. The underlying principles are:

a) More common health care needs can be solved through less complex services (basic or general care) while a narrower set of needs require an increasing level of technological complexity (specialised care);

b) The health system usually operates based on the selectivity of needs, with wider availability of basic or general services, generally at lower cost and with diverse means of use (in dense or scattered population areas). A progressive reduction in service availability is expected for more complex health care needs, with treatment requiring higher technology. They are also likely to be of higher cost and often accessed through a referrals system;

c) There can be a gap between health needs and the availability of services and resources required, *e.g.* some countries lack high technology equipment to deal with cancer or renal failure cases, thus only basic care is consumed regardless of care needs;

d) The disaggregation is relative to the technology and resources available in the whole country. Levels of technology can differ in various countries, but specialised care should always refer to a higher level of complexity than services classified as basic or general.

General care. General care is often the entry point to the health care system, before referral is made to a specialist when a more complex health condition is found. General care involves the components of the contact for care, such as routine examinations, medical assessments, prescription of pharmaceuticals, routine counselling of patients, dietary regime, injections and vaccination (unless covered under preventive programmes) of all patients. It includes, for instance, basic maternity and routine diagnosis and follow-up of reproductive health for non-complicated cases and can be part of an initial medical consultation or check-up, or part of a follow-up inpatient or outpatient contact.

In reality, an initial contact can be made with a specialised health provider as the entry point. These initial contact services, including basic diagnosis and assessment, are of a general type. Ideally, records should be appropriate to classify these basic services as such, regardless of the specialised level of the provider. General care excludes curative care services with a higher level of specialisation.

Specialised services. These services relate to curative care involving a higher level of technology, which are expected to be consumed by selected cases of less frequent and more complex health care needs. These services are linked to a deep but narrower set of conditions that require a high technology service, involving more complex diagnostic and treatment procedures. They are frequently performed by providers devoted to a particular condition, disease or class of patients. There are four basic medical fields, which are internal medicine, gynaecology and obstetrics, surgery and paediatrics. Specialised services often involve a breakdown of these fields, such as neurosurgery (surgery), allergology (internal medicine), paediatric allergology (paediatrics) or reproductive medicine or genetics (gynaecology and obstetrics), etc.

General inpatient care (HC.1.1.1) covers four types of services: general surgery, general internal medicine, general paediatrics and general gynaecology and obstetrics. Admissions focus on routine treatment, such as maternity cases without complications, appendicitis, hernias, diarrhoea and dehydration in children, non-complicated diabetes and so on.

General outpatient services (HC.1.3.1) also are expected to cover the more frequent and uncomplicated cases of all medical fields, such as monitoring and non-complicated cases of communicable and non-communicable common paediatric diseases and non-complicated cases of acute and chronic disease follow-up in adults.

With respect to dental care, curative care services focus on oral health, including teeth, gum and other related disorders. It includes the whole range of services usually performed in an outpatient setting, such as tooth extraction, the fitting of dental prostheses, and dental implants and orthodontics. The vast majority of dental care is performed as outpatient care, and therefore a separate third-digit category for dental care is included under the outpatient mode of provision (HC.1.3.2). Dental surgery provided as an inpatient service is classified as an inpatient specialised service (HC.1.1.2).

A further breakdown at the fourth-digit level by type of speciality or by component, such as for performance of procedures, pharmaceuticals and consumption of ancillary services included in a curative inpatient service, could also be used.

HC.2 Rehabilitative care

Rehabilitation is an integrative strategy that aims at empowering persons with health conditions who are experiencing or are likely to experience disability so that they can achieve and maintain optimal functioning, a decent quality of life and inclusion in the community and society.

Whereas curative services focus primarily on the health condition, rehabilitation services focus on the functioning associated with the health condition. Rehabilitation services stabilise, **improve or restore impaired body functions and structures, compensate for the absence or loss of body functions and structures, improve activities and participation, and prevent impairments, medical complications and risks.** Functioning and disability are conceived as a continuum that embraces everyone at some time during the life course.[20] Functioning involves a dynamic interaction between health conditions, environmental factors and personal factors. Rehabilitation is relevant over the course of the health condition, along a continuum of care from the hospital to rehabilitation facilities and to the community and across sectors from health, education and labour to social affairs. As stated in Chapter 4, the criteria boundary is also applicable to rehabilitative care; thus, only rehabilitative components with a primary purpose related to health functioning should be included. For comparative purposes, labour and social purposes have to be identified and excluded from health care.

Rehabilitation services are consumed by individuals experiencing functional difficulties associated with a broad range of health conditions (disease, disorder and injury), which may be acute or chronic, congenital or acquired, and affect people with disabilities[21] of all ages, independent of, or in conjunction with, specialist health care services (*e.g.* hip replacement, heart transplant, specialist eye treatment or treatment for acute depression). Rehabilitation services are based (where possible) on a functional assessment and diagnosis to determine the goals and plan for rehabilitation. These are followed by agreed interventions (including biomedical and technological approaches as well as peer support) to optimise a person's capacity. Rehabilitation plans are monitored and adapted in accordance with an individual's needs and resources. The careful monitoring of outcomes related to specific interventions may help determine improvements to the intervention so as to optimise functioning and minimise disability.

The scope of rehabilitation is wide and includes psychological, assistive technological, environmental, cardiopulmonary, geriatric, neurological, orthopaedic and paediatric rehabilitation, among others. As rehabilitation involves all areas of an individual's functioning, it may happen that for some of them the health care boundary criteria are not matched, notably in areas that are job-related, social-related or leisure-related, when the primary focus goes beyond the health purpose (see Box 5.2). For comparative purposes, a selection of those primary health purpose components should be made.

- *Includes*: consumption of services aimed at reaching, restoring and/or maintaining optimal physical (*e.g.* complementing body structure through a prosthesis), sensory (*e.g.* complementing hearing recovery with a prosthesis), intellectual (*e.g.* recovering memory capability after a stroke), psychological (*e.g.* reducing depression and stress through supported learning to use a prosthesis) and social functional levels (*e.g.* by re-establishing control of basic functions such as swallowing and speaking after a stroke), all of which are health consequences of disease, disorders or injury.

- *Excludes*: rehabilitative services with a primary social, leisure or labour purpose. Some examples of the social focus are those linked to a primary purpose of creative, cultural and educational interactive routines, as well as vocational training and re-training and education and job placement.
- *Clarifying cases*: there can be an overlap of curative treatment, *e.g.* in the case of stroke, when complemented with early rehabilitation treatment, such as speech therapy and physiotherapy. Both functions can be run in parallel. This may also be a possible overlap between rehabilitation services and long-term care services: rehabilitation is consumed on a continued or recurrent basis with a recovery purpose, whereas long-term care has a maintenance purpose.

Rehabilitation by mode of provision

Rehabilitation services can be divided into the same four modes of provision: inpatient, day care, outpatient and home-based. The four modes of provision could be further broken down into the various specialised rehabilitation types identified as appropriate to the health care boundary:

- HC.2.1 Inpatient rehabilitative care;
- HC.2.2 Day rehabilitative care;
- HC.2.3 Outpatient rehabilitative care;
- HC.2.4 Home-based rehabilitative care.

It should be noted that while preventive, curative and rehabilitative care services are very different in their purposes and characteristics, in terms of health statistical systems (*e.g.* hospital records) it may be difficult to separate into the three components. In such cases, a single aggregate of curative-rehabilitative care has been used for data collection and reporting purposes. Alternative record development or prorata procedures can also be used, which should be clearly indicated in the methodological information.

HC.3 Long-term care (health)

Long-term care (health) consists of **a range of medical and personal care services that are consumed with the primary goal of alleviating pain and suffering and reducing or managing the deterioration in health status in patients with a degree of long-term dependency.**[22]

To date, estimates of spending on services for long-term health care have been mostly limited to higher-income countries, due to the fact that in most low- and middle-income countries (LMIC) long-term health care is provided as informal care, *i.e.* usually consumed at home, provided by relatives and without any transaction or record involved.[23] However, it is evident that needs are emerging and expanding in all countries,[24] along with the rise in life expectancy, an epidemiological transition and the increasing involvement of health systems with long-term care in the wake of social and economic changes.

Box 5.2. **Examples of rehabilitation services**

Occupational therapy services enhance an individual's skills, capacity and performance in interaction with their personal and environmental contexts. Services may be directed at the individual or the environment to improve activities (*e.g.* activities of daily living) and participation (*e.g.* speaking recovery capabilities). Occupational therapy is centred on the individual, but may also involve the family, carers and the broader community. Occupational therapy services include, among others:

- Therapeutic use of meaningful and purposeful occupations (occupation understood as any activity on which time is spent by a person),
- Adaptation of environments and processes to enhance functioning and participation,
- Programmes involving graded tasks and activities as prerequisites to engagement in functional training for activities of daily living (including self care),
- Prescription or design, fabrication, application, adaptation and training in the use of assistive technology or orthotic or prosthetic devices.

Physical therapy involves services to "develop and maintain maximum movement potential and functional ability throughout the lifespan" (WCPT, 2007). This includes services to restore the integrity of body systems essential to movement, maximise functional ability and recuperation, minimise incapacity, and enhance the quality of life in individuals and groups of individuals, by dealing with functional limitations and disabilities in relation to the physical, psychological and emotional spheres and in terms of social well-being. Circumstances where movement and function are threatened include congenital, age, injury, disease or determined environmental factors. Services are adapted on an ad-hoc basis and may include, among others:

- Manual therapy techniques, electrotherapeutic, physical agents and mechanical modalities (WCPT, 2007);
- Prescription, application and, as appropriate, fabrication of devices and equipment;
- Skin repair and protection techniques, airway clearance techniques (*e.g.* in obstructive respiratory diseases) and therapeutic exercise.

Physical and rehabilitation medicine (PRM) involves services to diagnose health conditions, assess functioning and prescribe biomedical and technological interventions that treat health conditions and optimise functional capacity. The services include, among others:

- Prescription of an integrated range of biomedical, psychological and social interventions, *e.g.* drug treatment, physiotherapy, occupational therapy, speech and language therapy, dysphagia management, rehabilitation nursing, neuropsychological interventions, psychological interventions, nutritional therapy, provision of assistive technology, prosthetics and orthotics and the education of patients and families.

Psychological and behavioural rehabilitation (PBR) is a collection of services to diagnose impairments in cognitive functions and other psychosocial functional limitations that affect the life and well-being of individuals and the manner and effectiveness of dealing with their health conditions and disability. Among PBR services are:

- Individual psychotherapy, including cognitive behavioural therapy and neurocognitive therapy to improve the self-recognition of health conditions related to psychological and behavioural problems and empowerment with skills to manage them to enhance the quality of life;

Box 5.2. **Examples of rehabilitation services** *(cont.)*

- Psycho-education and adaptive strategies, reduction of expressed emotion, behavioural management, and for primary care-givers, including the family, services to improve supportive social networks.

Prosthetics and orthotics rehabilitation aims to enhance the quality of life for people with physical disabilities who require improvements in mobility or independence, through practices associated with the provision of prosthetic and orthotic care, rehabilitation engineering and related areas such as wheeled mobility (ISPO, 2005). The technological devices to complement the function (orthoses) or substitute the structure (prostheses) of the human body are a key component of these services, which include, among others:

- The formulation of treatment through examination, prescription of devices and related rehabilitation;
- The fabrication and fitting of the device, including instructing the user in the use and care of the device;
- Evaluation and follow-up, including maintenance, repair and replacement of the device.

Speech and language therapy aims at restoring people's capacity to communicate effectively and to swallow safely and efficiently. It aims at identifying types of communication problems and the best way to treat them. As such, the services include, among others:

- Clinical and/or instrumental screening, assessment, identification, diagnosis, treatment and management of disorders related to speech, voice, language, fluency, and swallowing that impact on the individual's ability to communicate.

Selection and development of augmentative and alternative communication systems and devices for individuals who are limited in their ability to communicate verbally, and provision of education and training in their use.

To plan services and develop policy, there is a need for separate reporting of the health and social care components as well as for measures of total long-term care (LTC).[25] Due to the strong link between long-term care and the ageing process, policy interest in many countries is understandably centred on elderly age groups. Therefore, a differentiation of long-term care by dependency level, with a cross-classification by age, is likely to be of significant policy relevance; for instance, if health promotion for the aged is successful, the need for long-term health care services should be delayed until more advanced ages. It may also be important to break down age-related payment strategies so as to link the various layers to public and private payments as well as to the public-private mix in provision (Huber and Rodrigues, 2008).

From a final use point of view, LTC typically comprises an integrated package of services and assistance to patients with an increased level of dependency (also understood as impairment, activity limitation and/or participation restriction) on a continued or recurrent basis, and over an extended period of time. The greater the dependency level, the more comprehensive the set of services included in the package. A continuum of care can be tracked, from more intensive medical or nursing services, through personal care services, to lower-level social assistance-type services and other social care. This care is aimed at the dependent population with chronic or recurrent psychiatric conditions, such as physically disabled people and mental health and substance abuse patients.

The continuum of care may not necessarily require the whole range of services offered or the same delivery path. For example, care may consist of regular, short-term health interventions over a long period, or recurrent and chronic consumption over extended periods. In some cases, long-term care implies supportive care offered to people at any stage of their condition, or palliative care, in the case of life-threatening illness. It also includes terminal care, understood as the management of patients during the last months of life. Even with incurable diseases, many people may live with a functional impairment for many years, and in some cases lead an otherwise largely normal life. Terminal cancer patients receiving palliative care may have radiotherapy or chemotherapy treatment courses from time to time to keep their condition under control. Palliative care works alongside these "active" treatments to promote comfort and well-being.

Note that when a need emerges for an episode of curative acute care, unrelated to the dependent condition, this should be considered as curative care, and not long-term care. However, in frail patients an acute health episode can often evolve into a chronic condition, and because of dependence, can result in more complex long-term needs.

The various components of long-term care can be distinguished as follows (see Figure 5.3 below):

- *Medical or nursing care* includes the management of symptoms involving medical, paramedical and nursing care services, such as relieving pain and other symptoms, administering medication, performing medical diagnoses and minor surgery, dressing wounds, health counselling to families, and providing emotional and spiritual support for the patient and their family members. Such care includes *a)* a range of preventive services, notably to avoid a greater deterioration of the patient's frail health condition, *b)* a range of chronic disease management situations, *c)* a fair amount of rehabilitative care, to recover functionality, *d)* care aimed at retarding or reducing deterioration or maintaining functionality: in short, a high level of quality of life assurance, regardless of the type of health ailment.
- *Personal care services* are provided in response to limitations in self-care primarily due to disability and illness. These services provide help with activities of daily living (ADL) such as: eating, bathing, washing, dressing, getting in and out of bed, getting to and from the toilet and managing incontinence. Most inpatient care as well as some day-care and home-based services will include personal care services as part of the package of services consumed. These services are typically administered directly or under the supervision of nursing staff. These services are included within the health care boundary because the purpose of this type of care is linked to survival and the maintenance of health status. In addition, the need for personal care services is more often than not linked to some underlying medical condition .
- *Assistance services* relate to care that enables a person to live independently in a house or apartment. They provide assistance with tasks of household management (*i.e.* instrumental activities of daily living, IADL), such as shopping, laundry, vacuuming, cooking and performing housework, managing finances, using the telephone, etc. These services are typically provided under home help services, assisted living arrangements, etc.
- *Other social care services* involve community activities and occupational support given on a continuing or recurrent basis to individuals, such as activities whose primary purpose is social and leisure.

A consistent functional approach, based on the purpose of the contact for care, would imply that care over a long or indefinite period, with nursing or personal care services as the dominant component, is the basis for inclusion within the health care boundary. On the other hand, a contact with the primary purpose of enabling independent living and interaction with the environment, as in the case of home help or assisted living, should be outside the health boundary [see Long-term care (social) HCR.1]. Figure 5.3 describes the boundary of long-term care.

Figure 5.3. **The health and social boundary of long-term care (LTC)**

<table>
<tr><th colspan="2" rowspan="2">Boundary</th><th colspan="4">Primary long-term care needs</th></tr>
<tr><th>Medical or nursing care</th><th>Personal care services (ADL)</th><th>Assistance care services (IADL)</th><th>Other social care services</th></tr>
<tr><td rowspan="4">Limited

Expanded</td><td rowspan="2">HC.3</td><td></td><td></td><td></td><td></td></tr>
<tr><td></td><td></td><td></td><td></td></tr>
<tr><td>HC.R.1</td><td></td><td></td><td></td><td></td></tr>
<tr><td>Excluded</td><td></td><td></td><td></td><td></td></tr>
</table>

Source: IHAT for SHA 2011.

In practice, what is frequently found is that nursing, personal and social care services are provided together in an integrated package of services, particularly for inpatient and day care. For home-based care, different services may be provided together, or provided and accounted for separately.

Long-term care boundaries and measurement issues

The health function (purpose of care) defines the boundary, irrespective of the provider, which in the case of long-term care can be a health professional, community worker or, in the case of home-based care, a relative. Inclusion should also be independent of the financing scheme to cover the care. However, due to differing administrative, financing and provision standards, the national boundaries of long-term care may not necessarily be aligned with the SHA-defined boundaries. Given the lack of direct records for the purpose, decisions need to be made about how to approach the measurement in a standardised way. Unless records at the individual level are available, which is not feasible in most countries, an alternative source should be progressively developed to ensure the required reporting (see suggestions for apportioning and reporting strategies in Chapter 14). Additional criteria to deal with the functional boundaries of long-term care within health care are:

- Personal care services are most frequently linked to underlying health conditions[26] and often accorded based on a medical assessment or an input from a medical professional. They are thus reported as health care;
- When, due to a higher dependency level, social assistance and other social care services are integrated into a package of care along with medical and personal care services, then they are also included as health care;
- Social long-term care services in themselves are not considered part of health care;

- When the consequences of a disease are not associated with dependency, such as hearing disabilities, then they are not included under HC.3, regardless of their length and severity;
- If there is a need for continual care to handle a dependency, *e.g.* care of persons with a mental or physical disability, then it is included within the health care boundary.

Box 5.3. **Assessing long-term care needs**

Typically an assessment of the patient or beneficiary is used in order to determine the level of care and the type of long-term care service package consumed. Within the health system there are two different models for assessing the construct "functioning/disability": the "activities of daily living (ADL)" approach (or Katz/Barthel model), and the "Functioning" (ICF) approach developed by WHO. The ICF was developed to provide a more comprehensive framework, based on the view of a health condition or disease as the interaction of body function and structures, activities and participation, which are in turn impacted on by social and environmental factors. The importance of participation as an outcome is also highlighted (WHO, 2001). Dysfunctions in ADL and IADL are considered to be activity limitations within the ICF framework.

The use of these two approaches has not been complementary in the assessment of functioning, particularly in the ageing sector, where the ADL approach has been more specifically employed. In the past, many documents related to functional dependency produced by European experts on ageing have used the ADL approach, while in most recent legislation and policy documents European countries and agencies have adopted the ICF model.[27] The use of a classification of dependency or personal functioning is itself a means to assess the need for services, rather than part of the HC classification itself. However, it should be borne in mind that the ICF is an official classification adopted by an increasing number of countries (Salvador-Carulla and Gasca, 2010).

The "length" of care can often invoke a specific mode of financing, *i.e.* once the care continues beyond a threshold period, for example, six months. In some countries, payments may start on day one but be restricted to certain conditions. Other country's records would allow measurement only based on the primary purpose of the provider– that is, whether the facility is primarily a medical or social facility. In other systems, insurance protection typically covers only part of the LTC, and sometimes carer relatives receive some compensatory transfers, which may include training.

In many cases, particularly middle- and low- income countries, long-term care is provided by relatives at home without any type of compensation, either in-kind or cash transfers. The value of informal carers is, however, outside the SHA boundary due to the absence of a valued transaction.

In a few higher-income countries there is a trend to formalise assistance, notably among the eldest sections of the population. Records and reporting strategies are, however, quite limited on LTC household consumption. Although some programmes support carers' skills and compensate them for their work, these may not be specific to health and may be recorded under social care.

Long-term care (health) by mode of provision

Different modes of provision can result from the structure of the health system as well as from the epidemiological profile of the beneficiary. Modes of coping with long-term care needs are also evolving over time. In principle the greater the dependency, the more specialised and intensive are the services that are likely to be consumed.

HC.3.1 Inpatient long-term care (health)

This item comprises long-term care (health) services provided in a health care facility (hospital, nursing home) and requiring an overnight stay with medical supervision. The package of services covers nursing and/or personal care, usually provided together, along with a range of other components such as accommodation and support services.

- *Includes*: nursing and personal care typically for moderate or severe dependent needs, such as quadriplegic or end-of-life care, delivered in a range of nursing homes and other specialised long-term care facilities. Inpatient long-term care for mentally disabled and substance abuse patients is included where the care is due to chronic or recurrent psychiatric conditions and a prolonged degree of functional limitations and/or a need for help or surveillance. It includes long-term care services provided to inpatients in long-stay hospital wards or other hospital care settings. Accommodation services are considered part of long-term health care provision.
- *Excludes*: residents of establishments where little or no medical or nursing care is provided on site. Acute care contacts in long-term care patients should be included under HC.1: Curative care.
- *Clarifying cases*: key to this category is the purpose, *e.g.* psychiatric hospital services are classified as curative inpatient care when they aim at dealing with acute needs through medical and nursing care; whereas psychiatric long-term care involves dependent patients with little or no recovery expectation who are institutionalised predominantly for nursing care and periodic medical visits.

HC.3.2 Day cases of long-term care (health)

This item comprises planned long-term care (health) services in a health care facility but without an overnight stay. Services may be provided in a hospital or nursing home or in a dedicated or stand-alone day centre facility.

Often neglected in formal statistical treatment are night cases, which are reported as day cases *e.g.* elderly patients with a disturbed sleeping pattern but normal behaviour during the day, living with relatives during the day, but admitted into an institution at night. A parallel form concerns mentally unstable persons, who may even pursue a profession during normal business hours, but stay in a psychiatric institution at night. Another case is respite care for LTC patients who live with relatives during much of the year but are "admitted" to a facility during the family's vacation period.

HC.3.3 Outpatient long-term care (health)

This comprises long-term care (health) services that have the purpose of managing damaged health conditions and the associated clinical difficulties. Dependent patients with a chronic condition may require periodic verification of medication doses and of the evolution of their condition, and advice on how to handle symptoms that emerge as the disease evolves. These services may refer to regular outpatient visits or to the increasing provision of remote monitoring services for LTC patients.

This category may represent a reporting challenge at present, because health statistics may currently have difficulty distinguishing between different types of outpatient care services and other home-based services. More detailed records would be required to facilitate this reporting. In the absence of such data, estimates based on human resources, utilisation rates or unit cost information may be useful.

HC.3.4 Home-based long-term care (health)

This comprises long-term care (health) services provided to persons within their own home, or in residential settings such as adapted housing that can be considered as their home, rather than in an "institution". Such residential facilities include community-based settings, such as adapted housing, which provide an individual housing environment in combination with certain services, such as health protection and surveillance, often for elderly people who are becoming more dependent. It can involve specialised health care at home and services to support informal (family or community) care. Note that long-term care services of a lower-level social care nature (such as home help) may be included as part of a package of home-based care. If such services cannot be separately accounted for and are not the dominant component of the package, they should be included under HC.3.4; if, however, they are the dominant feature, the complete package of care services should be included under HCR.1 Long-term care (social).

HC.4 Ancillary services (non-specified by function)

This includes the **health care or long-term care services, non-specified by function and non-specified by mode of provision, which the patient consumes directly, in particular during an independent contact with the health system, and that are not integral part of a care service package**, such as a laboratory or imaging services of patient transportation and emergency rescue.

Ancillary services are frequently an integral part of a package of services whose purpose is related to diagnosis and monitoring. Ancillary services do not, therefore, have a purpose in themselves: the purpose is to be cured, to prevent disease, etc. The ancillary service is aggregated within the first-digit purpose class and the second-digit MoP in which it was consumed. For inpatient, day care and hospital outpatient services, they are not usually identified as separate categories.

Therefore, only a part of the total consumption of ancillary services is made explicit by reporting the consumption of such services in the "non-specified by function" category, such as when the patient consumes the service directly, in particular during an independent contact with the health system.

The independent consumption of ancillary services may be associated with either early case detection as a part of prevention (HC.6), monitoring a treatment or a health condition – cure (HC.1), rehabilitation (HC.2) or long-term care (HC.3). These services are also related to consumption that has no identified mode of provision. For example, laboratory tests or an interpretation of imaging can be purchased as a result of the consumer's own initiative, or a medical test could be used for a second opinion for inpatient or outpatient cases or home-based care.

The content of ancillary services related to diagnosis and monitoring is split at the second-digit level between laboratory services (HC.4.1) and imaging services (HC.4.2). It also includes patient transportation and emergency rescue (HC.4.3).

HC.4.1 Laboratory services

This item comprises a variety of tests of clinical specimens aimed at obtaining information about the health of a patient. Laboratory tests are an integral part of the consumption of any patient, and constitute a guide for diagnosis and treatment choice.

Laboratory services (HC.4.1) includes the areas of:

- Anatomic pathology (*e.g.* histopathology, cytopathology);
- Clinical microbiology (*e.g.* bacteriology, virology, immunology and mycology);
- Clinical biochemistry (*e.g.* enzymology, toxicology and endocrinology);
- Haematology (*e.g.* blood coagulation tests);
- Cytology (*e.g.* cervical smear or PAP tests);
- Genetics (*e.g.* cytogenetics).

Clinical and other functional tests focus on specific organs and require additional technology to measure activity and are usually linked to medical specialties – cardiovascular: *e.g.* electrocardiographic diagnosis; allergy: *e.g.* allergy test, food sensitivity tests; audiology, etc. Other diagnostic services include tests such as electrocardiographic diagnosis and effort assessment.

The operation of banks for blood, semen, embryo, tissue and transplant organs, including the storing and cataloguing of available specimens, the matching of donated specimens and potential recipients, etc., are classified as part of ancillary services, whether or not they are free-standing areas. These services are not typically independent but components of a health care package, and thus are usually intermediate consumption goods and services. By convention in SHA, their value is not disaggregated: final consumption includes the value of the intermediate consumption components. Here, they should be recorded only if they relate to direct consumption.

HC.4.2 Imaging diagnosis

This item comprises a variety of services that employ imaging technology, such as X-rays and radiation for the diagnosis and monitoring of patients. The class includes an array of imaging technologies to diagnose and treat diseases, such as:

- Plain X-ray, bone and soft tissue imaging;
- Contrast X-rays or photo-imaging;
- Diagnostic ultrasound;
- Computed tomography (CT);
- Computer-assisted tomography (CAT);
- Nuclear medicine;
- Nuclear magnetic imaging; nuclear scanning;
- Positron emission tomography (PET);
- Magnetic resonance imaging (MRI);
- Other miscellaneous diagnostic imaging (arteriography using contrast material, angiocardiography, phlebography, thermography, bone mineral density studies).

HC.4.3 Patient transportation

This item comprises the transportation of patients to a health care facility on medical recommendation or as a necessary inter-facility transfer to complement a package of health care services. Examples are emergency transportation to a hospital and transfer between health facilities for additional imaging diagnosis or rehabilitative treatment. The transportation can be delivered in a specially-equipped surface vehicle or in a designated air or water ambulance and takes place to and from facilities for the purposes of receiving medical and surgical care. It also includes transportation in conventional vehicles, such as a taxi, when justified by medical recommendation and there is a transaction involved *e.g.* in the case of an inter-hospital diagnosis imaging procedure. The boundary should correspond to the criteria set out in Chapter 4.

The transport service may be specialised and may or may not involve resuscitation equipment or medical personnel. It can be billed as part of the related benefits (*e.g.* imaging diagnosis, etc.).

- *Includes*: all types of transportation services through any means as long as they fit the purpose criteria, *e.g.* emergency transport services of public fire rescue departments or defence departments that operate on a regular basis for civilian emergency services (not only for catastrophe medicine) are included.
- *Excludes*: transport costs of accompanying persons, except when the patient is dependent. See Chapter 12 regarding transport costs of travelling abroad for health care.

HC.5 *Medical goods (non-specified by function)*

This comprises **pharmaceutical products and non-durable medical goods intended for use in the diagnosis, cure, mitigation or treatment of disease, including prescribed medicine and over-the-counter drugs, where the function and mode of provision are not specified.**

Medicines and other medical goods are frequently a component of a package of services with a preventive, curative, rehabilitative or long-term care purpose. In inpatient, outpatient and day care consumption, they are not usually identified separately, except possibly at a more detailed level.

Medical goods can also be consumed as a result of being prescribed as part of a health care contact or independently in the case of self-prescription. Dispensing may take place within a health care establishment, such as a hospital, or by a free-standing retailer of medical goods. However, the diversification of distribution channels has increased the need to recognise the mixed role of independent consumption within the various modes of health care provision in many countries. The diversity of distribution mechanisms is shown in Figure 5.4. In particular, in many low- and middle-income countries, due to the lack of availability of medicines, both in hospitals and outpatient units, often the relatives or patient need to purchase medicines themselves. This category aims to include all consumption of medical goods where the function and mode of provision is not specified.

- *Includes*: medical goods acquired by the beneficiary either as a result of prescription following a health system contact or as a result of self-prescription.
- *Excludes*: medical goods consumed or delivered during a health care contact that are prescribed by a health professional.

Figure 5.4. **Distribution mechanisms of medicines**

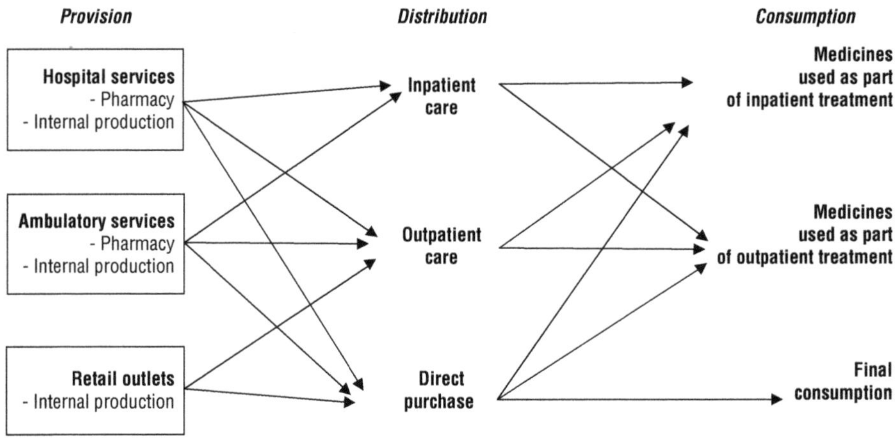

Source: IHAT for SHA 2011.

- *Clarifying cases*: as medical goods do not conform to a health purpose in themselves, they should be included as far as possible in the purpose to which they pertain, *e.g.* in the case of anti-malaria bed nets, they should be accounted for within the malaria programme when they are distributed during malaria interventions. Because their use is only preventive, they should in theory be allocated to prevention. However, by convention they are recorded in HC.5 when consumers acquire them from retail sellers, because the purpose is not usually identified.

Medical goods are broken down at the second level into pharmaceuticals and other medical non-durables (HC.5.1) and therapeutic appliances and other medical goods (HC.5.2).

HC.5.1 Pharmaceuticals and other non-durable goods

This comprises pharmaceutical products and non-durable medical goods intended for use in the diagnosis, cure, mitigation or treatment of disease. This includes medicinal preparations, branded and generic medicines, drugs, patent medicines, serums and vaccines, and oral contraceptives. Fluids required for dialysis, as well as gases used in health care, such as oxygen, should also be included when the patient or relatives purchase them directly. This class is further divided into the following sub-classes:

HC.5.1.1 Prescribed medicines. Comprises all pharmaceuticals, including branded and generic pharmaceutical products, which are provided in response to a prescription issued by a licensed medical practitioner or pharmacist.

HC.5.1.2 Over-the-counter drugs (OTC). Comprises all pharmaceuticals, including branded and generic pharmaceutical products which may or may not be available without prescription but have been purchased independently. Inclusions on this category should be linked to the health purpose.[28]

HC.5.1.3 Other medical non-durable goods. Includes adhesive and non-adhesive bandages, hypodermic syringes, first-aid kits, hot-water bottles and ice bags, medical hosiery items such as elastic stockings and knee supports, condoms and other mechanical contraceptive devices. This sub-category also includes medical non-durable goods that have been prescribed by a licensed medical practitioner.

All goods acquired by a patient, regardless of whether purchased in an independent pharmacy or a pharmacy within a medical establishment, hospital or ambulatory setting, or through any other distribution channel, are to be included.

Further breakdowns may also be of interest (and these may evolve subsequently into sub-categories), such as branded and generic medicines and hospital own-manufactured supply. Sub-categories such as "essential medicines" are operational distinctions that are already institutionalised in some countries for routine monitoring, which could be also included in a detailed breakdown. Eventually, a therapeutic breakdown based on the Anatomic Therapeutic Chemical Classification may also be feasible. For some countries the relevant split could involve procurement. A detailed compilation would be required to establish appropriate price and volume indices.[29]

- *Excludes*: veterinary products; articles for personal hygiene, such as medicinal soaps.
- *Clarifying cases*: TCAM medical goods should be included, except those products not identified as medical goods, such as "healthy food". See Table 4.1 of Chapter 4 on borderline cases for further guidance.

HC.5.2 Therapeutic appliances and other medical goods

This item comprises medical durable goods, such as glasses, hearing aids, other orthopaedic appliances, prosthetics and other medical-technical devices, where the function and the mode of provision are not specified.

- Orthotic devices that support or correct deformities and/or abnormalities of the human body, *e.g.* corrective eye-glasses and contact lenses, hearing aids, orthopaedic appliances such as orthopaedic shoes, orthopaedic braces and supports, surgical belts, trusses and supports;
- Prostheses or artificial extensions that replace a missing body part, *e.g.* artificial limbs and other prosthetic devices, including implants: an implant is a medical device made to replace (or supplement the functionality) of a missing biological structure;
- A variety of medico-technical devices such as powered and unpowered wheelchairs and invalid carriages, "special" beds, and electronic and other devices for monitoring blood pressure.

Therapeutic appliances can be further identified by type at a third-digit level:

HC.5.2.1 Glasses and other vision products. Glasses and other vision products should have a health purpose. This item comprises corrective eye-glasses and contact lenses as well as the corresponding cleansing fluid and the fitting by opticians.

- *Excludes*: sunglasses not fitted with corrective lenses.

HC.5.2.2 Hearing aids. This item comprises all kinds of removable hearing aids (including cleaning, adjustment and batteries).

- *Excludes*: audiological diagnosis and treatment by physicians (HC.1.3); hearing implants (HC.1, curative care); and audiological training (HC.1.3).

HC.5.2.3 Other orthopaedic appliances and prosthetics (excluding glasses and hearing aids). This item comprises orthopaedic appliances and other prosthetics: orthopaedic shoes, artificial limbs and other prosthetic devices, orthopaedic braces and supports, surgical belts, trusses and supports, neck braces.

- *Excludes*: glasses and vision products (HC.5.2.1) and hearing aids (HC.5.2.2).
- *Clarifying cases*: implants with a non-health primary purpose, *e.g.* aesthetic use, should be excluded. Canes for the blind and dogs for the blind should be included.

HC.5.2.9 All other medical durables including medical technical devices. This item comprises a wide variety of medico-technical devices, such as wheelchairs (powered and unpowered) and invalid carriages, as well as miscellaneous durable medical products not elsewhere classified such as blood pressure instruments. In this class, household final consumption involves the acquisition of consumer durables, meaning goods that may be used for health primary purposes of consumption repeatedly or continuously over a period of a year or more (SNA 2008, 9.42).

- *Includes*: specialised telematic equipment for emergency calls from the patient's home and/or for the remote monitoring of medical parameters.
- *Excludes*: protective goggles, belts and supports for sport. Household improvements are to be accounted for as investment: automatic staircase lifts for patients with mobility limitations; bathtub lifts and similar devices for adapting the housing situation of patients with transitory or chronic impairments, and hire of therapeutic equipment. For information on whether the fixed equipment described here is to be accounted as capital formation or current expenditure see Chapter 11.
- *Clarifying cases*: see Table 4.1 of Chapter 4 for particular borderline cases.

HC.6 Preventive care

Prevention is any measure that aims to avoid or reduce the number or the severity of injuries and diseases, their sequelae and complications (Pomey *et al.*, 2000). Prevention is based on a health promotion strategy that involves a process to enable people to improve their health through the control over some of its immediate determinants. This includes a wide range of expected outcomes, which are covered through a diversity of interventions, organised as primary, secondary and tertiary prevention levels.

- Primary prevention involves specific health measures aimed at avoiding diseases and risk factors in order to: reduce the onset of a disease, diminish the number of new cases, and anticipate the emergence and lessen the severity of diseases. The goal of primary preventive measures is the reduction of risks before they generate some effect, *e.g.* via vaccination.
- Secondary prevention involves specific interventions aimed at the detection of disease and then therapy as early as possible, *e.g.* via screening. Secondary prevention thereby increases opportunities for less costly and invasive interventions in order to prevent the progression of the disease and the emergence of symptoms, or the "stock of illness".[30] Examples include screening for diseases such as TB, diabetes and breast cancer. One characteristic of secondary prevention is that it occurs before the diagnosis has been made. Often these early case detections involve laboratory and imaging services.
- Tertiary prevention aims at reducing the negative impact of an already established disease or injury by an attempt to avoid worsening and complications, such as early surgery on a joint damaged by burns. In this example, a tertiary prevention would involve reconstructive surgery to allow for full extension and movement recovery of the joint.

In SHA 2011, preventive care (HC.6) is limited to primary and secondary prevention. Once a diagnosis has been made, a therapeutic or tertiary preventive path is established.

The rationale for excluding tertiary prevention is that it overlaps with the curative and rehabilitative purposes, which are aimed at reducing disease-related complications.

Boundary-setting considerations

The determinants of health involve a wide range of factors and action mechanisms. To set the health care accounting boundary, the criteria presented in Chapter 4 have to be considered; once the health care boundary has been established, the primary purpose principle should then be applied to set the functional classes. This is important to keep in mind because the intervention of the multiple determinants of health can also involve many different purposes. A classic example is education, which intervenes directly and indirectly in many risk-health status mechanisms. However, general education, rather than specific health-related education, has such a significant role that it constitutes a purpose in its own right; thus it does not comply with the boundary criteria and so is not included within the health accounting boundary.

The primary purpose of "health promotion" is key to defining the boundary, notably because health determinants often have a social and economic primary purpose. The same risks can be the subject of a social control policy with an economic or safety purpose, and thus not a health purpose. The health boundary for "preventive services" is defined as having the primary purpose of risk avoidance of acquiring diseases or suffering injuries, which can frequently involve a direct and active interaction of the consumer with the health care system. The spectrum of factors to be considered is wide, but the type of services included in the health prevention boundary is restricted to those components with a primary health purpose. Interventions that go beyond the health care boundary but are policy relevant can be reported as health care-related items.

Some examples of these boundary issues are preventive interventions to avoid immediate risks, such as:

- IEC (health information, education and communication) messages with a health focus regarding substance abuse and alcohol consumption, *e.g.* special warnings to pregnant women about the secondary effects of overconsumption, as well as information about appropriate healthy behaviour related to diet, smoking and sedentary life styles and about self-protection to avoid injuries due to road accidents. These messages would be prepared by communication experts and disseminated in mass media health campaigns.
- Monitoring and surveillance of health risks and disease control programmes, notably related to risks prevalent in a country, *e.g.* the gathering of epidemiological information by health offices to analyse trends in diseases and disease risks. It also involves the laboratory testing of the quality of human drinking water, food-borne risks and the personal monitoring of persistent organic pollutants[31] in the breast milk of women living in risk areas.

These are examples of components within the boundary of health expenditure. However, part of the control of alcohol abuse, road safety and environmental control interventions can be made with a primary purpose that is not health, but rather social and/or economic, *e.g.* the design of roads, the enforcement of traffic regulation, etc. Any interventions that do not have a primary health purpose lie outside the health care accounting boundary,[32] as further explained in the following examples:

The *environmental* field in the economy has a primary focus on all elements, factors and conditions that have some impact on growth and development, on ensuring sustainability and on lowering risks to society. Policy development involves legal as well as technical content. The relevance of particular environmental policies to health is clear in general. However, not all policy formulation has a primary health purpose, nor does its implementation usually have the immediate purpose of improving health. *Excluded* are all services whose primary purpose is linked to the collection, treatment and remediation of environmental risks. *Included* within the health boundary are environmental health components that are part of specific health regulations (under HC.7). Also included are the monitoring and surveillance of demonstrated environmental risks with a health purpose, in particular geographical areas that are part of early case detection (HC.6); IEC on environmental health issues, such as warnings about risk exposure during pregnancy (HC.6); and the treatment of environmental effects to reduce the sequelae and damage in affected human groups, through curative health care (HC.1).

Public safety involves the prevention of, and protection from, events and factors that might endanger the safety of the general public and cause injury, harm or damage. Interventions where health does not represent the main focus are excluded from the health care boundary. Examples of *excluded* cases include: preventing crimes and disasters (natural or man-made) through the use of specific non-health system interventions; ensuring the safety of transportation systems, roads and the social behaviour associated with them; and to police, fire and disaster fields where health does not represent the main focus. Also *excluded* are interventions through the criminal justice system that seek to prevent, control and manage the risk of injuries, through legal, judicial, police and other sector interventions focused on weapons, drugs and violence control. These interventions have a purpose that goes beyond health care, although it is relevant to health care. *Included* as health care components are: IEC measures to prevent injuries caused by individuals and to reduce drug and alcohol consumption among young people and pregnant women (HC.6). Also included are programmes to guide health services during epidemics and disasters (HC.6), and the treatment within the curative health care system of cases that arise due to public safety risks (HC.1).

Transport services. Transportation and traffic policies that involve a primary focus on transportation, but which are related but external to health prevention, are excluded, as they lie outside of the health boundary. Compliance with regulations may involve a non-health purpose, *e.g.* to avoid a fine. Thus, the implementation of such measures is counted neither as health nor as prevention. *Included*: IEC components that promote healthy behaviour on transportation (HC.6), *e.g.* information and programmes to promote self-care by the use of crash helmets. Also *included* are epidemiological studies on injuries and accidents to inform health programmes, *e.g.* studies on setting the legal limits for blood alcohol levels while driving (HC.6).[33]

Second-digit preventive classes

The design of preventive programmes target at-risk population groups. These may be based on age, sex or income level; or groups of risks based on people's environment, such as the roadway, home, workplace or residential area. Thus, selected individuals or groups of individuals exposed to similar risks are targeted by preventive programmes to help them to avoid these risks or to detect specific conditions at an early stage. Although some risks are related to specific health conditions, the same or similar types of risks may lead to various health conditions, thus overlaps may exist in the coverage of programmes, depending on their structure at the national level. The structure of the programmes reflects the epidemiological and operational conditions in the country; for example, HIV/AIDS may represent a distinct programme or be part of a joint programme with malaria and tuberculosis or be a component of an overall programme on communicable diseases.

The prevention classification in SHA 2011 is based on the type of services.[34] As in other classifications, countries with more detailed analytical needs are able to generate breakdowns according to their national characteristics. When doing so, labels should be explicit about the programmes contained and about any comprehensive metadata provided so as to allow international comparison of categories. The classes by type of service have a strategic focus more than a disease focus, which can be obtained through ICD classes in the distribution by beneficiary (see Chapter 10[35]). To ensure continuity of reporting, SHA 1.0 classes have been kept as memorandum items.

Prevention may in most cases generate positive externalities. This is clear in communicable diseases and in environmental classes as well as in non-communicable diseases. Examples include waterborne diseases such as cholera; food-borne diseases such as agro-toxics and other biological and non-biological contaminants; and airborne diseases related to PM10 (particulate matter[36]) and indoor pollutants.

The breakdown of prevention involves the following classes:

HC.6.1 *Information, education and counselling programmes*

Information, education and communication (IEC) combines strategies, approaches and methods to enable individuals, families, groups, organisations and communities to play active roles in achieving, protecting and sustaining their own health. Embodied in IEC is a process of learning that empowers people to make decisions, modify behaviours and change social conditions, including through improvements in knowledge, beliefs, attitudes, use and interaction with the health system. This is a key component of the strategy to overcome organisational and communication barriers to using the health system. The focus is on primary and secondary prevention. This covers individual as well as collective consumption, delivered through a variety of formats, such as mass media and personal advice. This can vary according to the consumer's cultural characteristics. This expenditure may involve information dissemination as well as the time and skills of the specialised personnel providing the advice.

Information and counselling programmes are usually part of control programmes, in which case they are disease-oriented, informing individuals about specific health problems, their conditioning factors and their particular risks. They can be related to risk avoidance strategies, self-protection, medication adherence, self-management guidelines for diseases, pre-operative education, or discharge plans. They can also be related to self-applied tests to monitor health conditions, orienting individuals on how to stay well if the results are negative, and orienting and referring them for follow-up, if positive. Examples include information about the health consequences of smoking, diet, physical activity or salt consumption; special warnings to pregnant women about drug abuse and alcohol consumption; information on risk protection effectiveness through the use of crash helmets and seat belts; and information on vaccination or screening programmes.

HC.6.2 *Immunisation programmes*

In order to prevent the development of a disease, before or after exposure, through the use of pharmaceutical products, such as vaccines. This is primary prevention. It can involve consumption by specific individuals in a campaign or in continued programme operations. Examples include immunisation for diphtheria, hepatitis, herpes zoster, HPV, influenza, measles, meningococcal infections, mumps, pertussis (whooping cough), pneumococcal infections, polio, rabies, rubella, tetanus, varicella (chicken pox) and yellow fever. The expenditure involved in the consultation, both for the time and skills of the personnel and the purchase of the vaccine itself, should be accounted for.

HC.6.3 Early disease detection programmes[37]

This item concerns the active search for a disease early in its course, before symptoms appear, within the risk groups, as organised programme activities. This can involve screening, diagnostic tests and medical examinations. These are directed to specific diseases, such as breast cancer, cervical cancer, colon rectal cancer, diabetes, HIV/AIDS, malaria, tuberculosis, prostate cancer and so on. According to the criteria set for prevention, it would involve only early disease detection before a diagnosis is made. According to the boundaries of health care, a self-examination performed without a transaction involved would not be accounted for. Self-examination can generate expenditure when it involves the purchase of tests to be self-performed, *e.g.* levels of sugar in blood or urine, which are to be reported as HC.5. Control and follow-up exams after diagnosis should be considered as part of curative care (HC.1).

HC.6.4 Healthy condition monitoring programmes

This item concerns the active monitoring of healthy conditions and is not focused on specific diseases. These can target specific conditions such as pregnancy (antenatal and postnatal care) or specific age groups such as children (*e.g.* child growth and development) or ageing groups, or specific health domains, such as dental and general health check-ups.

HC.6.5 Epidemiological surveillance and risk and disease control programmes

This class involves technical operations to manage knowledge and resources with a preventive and control focus. This is done through the planning, monitoring and evaluation of interventions, including measures to inform decision-making, such as accessing information and support services. This includes information systems related to epidemiology and health and management to track cases, records and health system responses;[38] support measures such as operational activities aimed at immediate improvement of the programme; and hands-on training and operational research.[39]

The generic content includes[40]: conducting surveillance of outbreaks and patterns of communicable and non-communicable diseases and of injuries and exposure to environmental agents harmful to health, as well as investigating appropriate responses.[41] Examples include: epidemiological surveillance and research by health systems to identify and diagnose cases; the measurement of selected health conditions and diseases with a community impact, such as tuberculosis; analysis of the accuracy of health records and information systems; monitoring samples of human drinking water and food in relation to water and food-borne disease; epidemiological studies of other environmental risks, such as testing human breast milk in areas at risk for persistent organic pollutants (POP); hands-on training to ensure that procedures and treatment protocols set for the various health programmes are followed; and overcoming barriers to the access of health services by individuals and population groups. This includes the appropriate assessment of programme operations so as to identify required operational improvements related to any health system

Table 5.2. **Preventive and public health components in SHA 1.0 and SHA 2011**

Content: mostly as described in SHA 1.0	Programme Code SHA 2011	New item	Programme Code SHA 1.0	Content: mostly as described in SHA 1.0	Programme Code SHA 2011	New item	Programme Code SHA 1.0
Maternal and child health; family planning and counselling			HC.6.1	**Prevention of non-communicable diseases**			HC.6.4
Genetic counselling	HC.6.1		HC.6.1	Health education	HC.6.1		HC.6.4
Identification of genetic abnormalities	HC.6.3		HC.6.1	Disease prevention	HC.6		HC.6.4
Prenatal and postnatal medical care	HC.6.4		HC.6.1	Health promotion	HC.6.		HC.6.4
Baby health care	HC.6.4		HC.6.1	Programmes of risk avoidance	HC.6.1		HC.6.4
Pre-school and school child health	HC.6.4		HC.6.1	Improvement of health status not directed specifically towards communicable disease	HC.6.4		HC.6.4
Programme design, monitoring and evaluation		HC.6.5		Interventions against smoking, alcohol and substance abuse	HC.6.1		HC.6.4
Regulation linked to basket of services and population coverage on MCH, FP		HC.7.1		Activities by community workers	HC.6		HC.6.4
School health services			HC.6.2	Services provided by self-help groups	HC.6.1		HC.6.4
Education	HC.6.1		HC.6.2	General health education and health information	HC.6.1		HC.6.4
Screening	HC.6.3		HC.6.2	Health education campaigns	HC.6.1		HC.6.4
Disease prevention	HC.6		HC.6.2	Campaigns in favour of health promotion (life style, sex, etc)	HC.6.1		HC.6.4
Health promotion	HC.6		HC.6.2	Information exchanges (alcoholism, drug addiction)	HC.6.1		HC.6.4
Basic medical treatment (including dental care)	HC.1		HC.6.2	Public health environmental surveillance	HC.6.5		HC.6.9
Interventions against smoking, alcohol and substance abuse (in school)	HC.6.1		HC.6.2	Public information on environmental conditions	HC.6.1		HC.6.9
Vaccination programmes	HC.6.2		HC.6.3	Programme design, monitoring and evaluation		HC.6.5	
Programme design, monitoring and evaluation		HC.6.5		Regulation linked to basket of services and population coverage on non-communicable diseases		HC.7.1	
Regulation linked to basket of services and population coverage on school health		HC.7.1		**Occupational health care**			HC.6.5
Prevention of communicable diseases			HC.6.3	Surveillance of employee health	HC.6.4		HC.6.5
Compulsory reporting and notification of diseases	HC.6.5		HC.6.3	Routine medical check up	HC.6.4		HC.6.5
Epidemiologic enquiries of communicable diseases	HC.6.5		HC.6.3	Therapeutic care, including emergency services	HC.1		HC.6.5
Trace contacts and origin of disease	HC.6.5		HC.6.3	Ergonomy, safety	HC.6 (health part)		Excluded
Prevention of tuberculosis	HC.6		HC.6.3	Health and environmental protection at work	HC.6 (health part)		Excluded
Tuberculosis control (screening)	HC.6.3		HC.6.3	Accident prevention at work	HC.6 (health part)		Excluded
Immunization/vaccination (compulsory and voluntary)	HC.6.2		HC.6.3	Programme design, monitoring and evaluation		HC.6.5	
Vaccination under maternity and child care	HC.6.2		HC.6.3	Regulation linked to basket of services and population coverage on occupational health		HC.7.1	
Vaccination for occupational health	HC.6.2		Exc HC.6.5	**All other miscellaneous public health services**			HC.6.9
Vaccination for travel and tourism on patient's initiative	HC.1		HC.1	Operation and administration of blood and organ banks	HC.4.1.2		HC.6.9
Programme design, monitoring and evaluation		HC.6.5		Public health environmental surveillance	HC.6.5		HC.6.9
Regulation linked to basket of services and population coverage on communicable diseases		HC.7.1		Public information on environmental conditions	HC.6.1		HC.6.9

Source: IHAT for SHA 2011.

component, such as the schedule of delivery of services, information to users, and the analysis of coverage of the delivery area by health establishments.

Records on expenditures for this class are usually linked to the technical areas organising the preventive programmes with a collective approach, *e.g.* HIV/AIDS, tuberculosis and cancer programmes, etc. Thus they may be available from technical and co-ordination areas that are related to programme components not directly involved in the operation of health care services, such as the Ministry of Health, district and regional offices, NGOs and so on. See Chapter 14 on accounting rules for more detail on the selection of allocation keys to apportion expenditure.

HC.6.6 *Preparing for disaster and emergency response programmes*

Includes preparations for an appropriate response in case of humanitarian emergencies, whether of human or natural origin. The aim is to protect health and to reduce mortality and morbidity due to health hazards through in particular field epidemiology as well as training in technical standards. This would involve *e.g.* the capacity to acquire or expand resources very quickly, and preparations for changing the handling and referencing of patients, such as patient triage and restructuring coverage in line with the nature of the emergency.

This class can be adjusted to country-specific needs, as the health risks can vary in different areas. However, in all cases health rules and a health infrastructure should be prepared to cope with emergency health care needs.

HC.7 Governance, and health system and financing administration

These services focus on the health system rather than direct health care, and are considered to be collective, as they are not allocated to specific individuals but benefit all health system users. They direct and support health system functioning. These services are expected to maintain and increase the effectiveness and efficiency of the health system and may enhance its equity.

These expenditures are incurred mostly but not exclusively by governments. Included are the formulation and administration of government policy; the setting of standards; the regulation, licensing or supervision of producers; management of the fund collection; and the administration, monitoring and evaluation of such resources, etc. However, some of these services are also provided by private entities, including by civil society (NGOs) and private medical insurance. Clear examples of such civil participation are health advocacy, health observatories and health user/consumer associations.

HC.7.1 Governance and health system administration

Although these cover more than a single function, one class is proposed at the second-digit level due to its relatively low share of spending and the difficulty in distinguishing it.

Governance[42] has been defined as "the careful and responsible management of the well-being of the population" (WHO, 2003), and comprises three broad tasks: providing vision and direction, collecting and using intelligence and exerting influence through regulation and other means. It includes planning, policy formulation and information intelligence for the entire health system, such as:

- The monitoring of health needs (WHO, 2002, EPHF 1) and health care interventions;
- Health accounting and specific resource monitoring (EPHF 6) and auditing;

- Development of policies and planning (EPHF 3);
- Health promotion partnerships, social participation and empowerment (EPHF 7);
- Research, development and implementation of innovative interventions to set standards (EPHF 9).

SHA 2011 includes in this category the *general public service* component, which is part of the government function through the overall planning and statistical services (as expressed in COFOG 01.3).

Administration involves a management focus, including to design regulatory measures, to generate incentives, and to control organisations and resources in the system, such as general and specialised medical establishments, including dental services, hospitals and clinics, nursing and convalescent home services and independent practices. Directive and operational roles as well as the resources involved in such operations are to be included.

- Strategic management of health systems and services to improve the population's health;
- Regulation to protect public health, including accreditation and quality assurance;
- Human resources development and planning.

Excludes: any overhead expenses connected with the administration or functioning of health providers, including hospitals or other providers, which are to be included in the expenditures by service consumed (HC.1-HC.6). For example, if a group of public or private hospitals has a central unit that provides certain common services, such as purchasing, laboratories, ambulances, or other facilities, the value of these common services would be taken into account as part of the value of those individual services.

Clarifying cases: the regulatory function is part of the governance function and includes the setting of modalities to enforce regulations. However, each programme's technical board has the responsibility to ensure enforcement at the operational level. Thus the formulation of regulations and their enforcement mechanisms are part of governance, and the implementation of regulatory enforcement within specific programme controls is part of the relevant function. The operational level is likely to be separable through specific programme-focused bodies.

HC.7.2 Administration of health financing

This class involves a subcomponent specific to health financing, regardless of its public and private origin or its public and private provision, *e.g.* budgeting and fund-raising (Poullier, 1992; Nicolle and Mathauer, 2010). It contains the management of the collection of funds and the administration, monitoring and evaluation of such resources. Among the specific services linked to resource mobilisation are the identification of members of the schemes; their enrolment; the billing and collection of contributions; and the management of exemptions. Within the pooling function, risk equalisation is one important service. As for the purchasing function, the services included are selecting, negotiating, purchasing and contracting with health providers, as well as the claims processing system, which includes gate-keeping, making payments to providers, and patient reimbursement.

A further optional split at the third-digit level is proposed by public and private financing schemes.

Administration of private health insurance essentially means the health insurance service and the service charge[43] for this. This covers expenditure on sales, enrolment and policy service, claim adjudication, actuarial functions, legal support services, investment functions, corporate overheads and risk charges.

For public agencies it is expected to also involve the administrative costs of Federal, State and local government health programmes.

Excludes: the administrative costs of the health providers and the health care goods and services they provide. Also excluded are the opportunity costs of paperwork for consumers and the associated general revenue tax collection.

HC.9 Other health care services not elsewhere classified (n.e.c)

This item includes any other health care services not classified in HC.1 to HC.7.

HC.RI Reporting items

HC.RI.1 Total pharmaceutical expenditure (TPE)

Pharmaceuticals are one of the most frequently used technological products for all health care purposes. Total pharmaceutical expenditure has been estimated to constitute around one-third of current health expenditure. However, the consumption may follow different paths; for example, those typically used as part of an inpatient contact are included as intermediate consumption and thus not accounted for independently. The functional classification accounts only for the direct purchase of medical goods by consumers in retail sales (HC.5), regardless of whether or not it is the result of a contact with the health system. A further sub-classification allows the identification of the prescribed consumption (HC.5.1.1). Pharmaceutical policies require information on the total pharmaceutical consumption expenditure as well as the various channels, prices, composition, etc. A comprehensive measurement of the pharmaceutical consumption is of major relevance in a health care functional approach.

An estimate of total pharmaceutical consumption expenditure is important for planning and decision-making. The total figure for expenditure on pharmaceutical consumption is obtained by adding the explicitly reported part (HC.5.1.1 + HC.5.1.2) and the other components of pharmaceutical consumption regardless of the consumption path. This is the case of the pharmaceutical component within treatment packages, notably as part of the interaction within the contact for curative care (HC.1), which is expected to be the largest amount, but also part of rehabilitative care (HC.2) and long-term care (HC.3). There may also be amounts incorporated as part of outpatient care from prescribing physicians (part of HC.1.3).

Within health facilities, notably those for inpatient care, part of the service may sometimes involve complementary efforts to produce some medicines and to integrate and deliver the "pill boxes". This would imply that the consumption of pharmaceuticals involves not only the cost of the products (directly) purchased but also the cost of the complementary distribution services. To generate an accurate amount, a stepwise approach is recommended, as in other cases.[44]

A further subclass could be *inpatient pharmaceutical consumption*. Some other partial classes, such as pharmaceuticals under procurement, generics and ATC classes, may also be of interest for national purposes.

HC.RI.2 Traditional, Complementary and Alternative Medicines (TCAM)

TCAM has been identified as policy relevant in many countries due either to its cultural importance or its high growth rate, both in high- and middle-per capita income countries. Policies related to TCAM are emerging and need to be monitored. Due to the mix of purposes and practices and financing profiles, TCAM systems, therapies and disciplines (including the related medical goods) are a *de facto* sub-class of hospitals, ambulatory care services and retailers.

The scope and boundary of traditional, complementary and alternative medicine (TCAM). Broadly stated, health care can be divided into modern (mainstream, conventional, orthodox, Western or allopathic[45]) and traditional (indigenous, complementary, alternative or integrative), with the division differing across countries.

Non-allopathic care includes all services from any practice that have a health intent but do not fall within the realm of allopathic medicine. The generic term in use is Traditional, Complementary and Alternative Medicines (TCAM). As defined by WHO, "Traditional medicine" is an amorphous concept that comprises a range of long-standing and still-evolving practices based on diverse beliefs and theories. These services involve medical knowledge systems, developed over centuries within various societies before or during the development of modern medicine. "Complementary and alternative" services are those that are used together with or instead of allopathic health care but which are not yet incorporated into the established international medical system, even when at national level they are extensively used.

TCAM[46] are common in most countries and prevalent in countries representing more than half of the world's population (WHO, 2005b; Bodeker *et al.*, 2005). The reporting of TCAM does not contravene the legislative and regulatory control advocated in countries where allopathic medicine is the dominant form. The TCAM class is included in the functional (HC) classification to describe, monitor, analyse and classify financing flows, related resource mobilisation, the use of production factors and consumption patterns. TCAM is intrinsically challenging to monitor because of its linkage to informal markets, notably in the low- and middle-income countries (LMIC). An approach based on effective institutional neutrality is needed to track TCAM in order to ensure the comparability of data between countries. There is a wide diversity within this class, and new practices are continuing to emerge. Differences in TCAM provision between countries therefore complicate the tracking of comparable information. The most common types are summarised as (Kristoffersen *et al.*, 2008):

- Alternative health systems, among which the most disseminated are acupuncture, homeopathy, chiropractics, osteopathy;
- Complementary therapies, such as Alexander therapy, aromatherapy, Bach therapy and other flower therapies, body therapy, Ayurvedic, herbal medicine, naturopathy, nutritional therapy, yoga and spa therapy;
- Alternative disciplines, such as crystal therapy, iridology, kinesiology and radionics;
- Spiritual and esoteric practices.

Essentially, the difference between traditional medicine systems and traditional medicine therapies is in the exhaustiveness of the reach. For example, traditional Chinese medicine is a system that includes the use of Chinese traditional therapies, such as needling, herbal medicines, tuina and so on. Chiropratics is in itself a system and may include therapies such as manual joint manipulation, nutritional therapy and exercise prescription. Herbal medicine, on the other hand, is a therapeutic ingredient that any system can include, when the practitioners are trained to do so.

Spiritual and esoteric components, such as religious and astrological practices, are related to an individual holistic sphere of self for which health knowledge and practice is difficult to identify and isolate from other purposes, *e.g.* spiritual and esoteric practices to promote well-being, spiritual development, social success or sport or educational performance. Thus, although they are part of the TCAM scope, spiritual and esoteric practices are not part of health care components. Some therapies, like yoga, can also be consumed with a well-being purpose, in which case they are also external to the health care boundary (see Chapter 3).

The range of purposes of TCAM services is similar to that observed for allopathic practice:

- Preventive, curative, rehabilitative or maintenance in nature;
- Diagnostic, surgical and prescriptive procedures.

Non-allopathic goods include a huge diversity of products and can be acquired during treatment and from both specialised and non-specialised retailers (WHO, 2005b):

- Types of herbal medicines;
- Prescription medicines: medicines that can be provided only in response to a prescription issued by a licensed medical practitioner or pharmacist;
- Over-the-counter medicines: medicines that may or may not be available without prescription but have been purchased independently;
- Dietary supplements: products intended to increase the total daily intake of a concentrate, a metabolite, constituent, extract or combination of these ingredients; substances that contain, for instance, a vitamin, a mineral, an herb or other botanical element or an amino acid;
- Health food: a food believed to be highly beneficial to health, especially a food grown organically and free of chemical additives. It is regulated differently from other foods;
- Functional foods: foods or food ingredients that have been shown to affect specific functions or systems in the body (*e.g.* yogurt, which promotes beneficial microflora in the gut).

The primary purpose of food, both healthy and functional, is alimentary, which puts it outside of the health care boundary.

As TCAM lies at the centre of many systems that deal with health by enhancing energy more than by treating each ailment individually, it can be difficult to define a boundary with well-being. This problem is not exclusive to TCAM, but also affects allopathic practices (*e.g.* recommendations on diet and physical activity for prevention in the cardiovascular field can be difficult to isolate and report).

Although the purpose of TCAM practice is in principle the same as for allopathic practice, some of the components can be difficult to separate from other purposes of consumption, such as well-being in the case of yoga, or alimentary in the case of food products. Measurement is also complex. In many countries, TCAM is integrated with allopathic practice. In the absence of specific records, it is neither identified nor accounted for. SHA 1.0 recommended the exclusion of illegal or non-certified health interventions (SHA 1.0 paragraph 5.15). Social and regulatory stigma reflected in survey and administrative recording should be progressively adjusted so as to improve comparability and reduce the "statistical gap". To sum up, boundaries between TCAM and allopathic practices are not easy to set and monitor, and in practice will be fixed according to national conventions.

The resources needed to produce TCAM estimates are not negligible. Some criteria to produce fairer accountability are:

- *Effectiveness*. The health benefits of TCAM have so far not been fully assessed in ways that can be universally accepted as being evidence-based. That said, many of the procedures and technologies used in allopathic medicine also continue to lack a valid assessment. Moreover, health accounts aim to measure neither the impacts on welfare nor the effectiveness of health services. Thus, the effectiveness criterion is not valid for ranking TCAM.
- *Provision*. Although TCAM practice has the same purpose as allopathic practice, the technology employed is different and the personnel in charge can have different qualifications. Thus, an analysis by provider (public and private) would also be appropriate to measure expenditure on TCAM. One difficulty already identified is the cohabitation of TCAM and allopathic practices, which may hamper a distinction. Hospitals may have a specific TCAM department, or services may be mixed with allopathic provision. The situation of outpatient offices can be similar. Direct provision by ministerial services can also mix allopathic and non-allopathic services. Thus, in countries with mixed practices, expenditures may be better allocated to specific personnel rather than to facility-type structures. Such a breakdown has already been said to be desirable, *e.g.* to highlight traditional birth attendants. This could be reflected in the classification of health care providers.
- *Qualifications*. Within most individual TCAM professions there are defined minimum standards, but many TCAM schools are not yet able to meet these standards due to limited resources.[47] In spite of the lack of qualifications, such services are expanding and are increasingly socially accepted, and official health care programmes are enlarging the coverage for specific interventions by these practitioners.
- *Registration and legislation*. In 2010, around two-thirds of WHO Member States still did not have a specific national policy on TCAM, though in more than half of them, regulations were under development. Procedures to register TCAM providers are similar to those for allopathic practitioners.[48]
- *Registration of TCAM products*. Product registration can also be set in place. For most countries, laws or regulations are the same or partly the same as for conventional pharmaceuticals, but are not yet developed for most functional foods, health foods and herbal medicines; *e.g.* in South Africa, a list of products has been compiled by technical specialists representing each of the complementary medicine modalities. Substances that have been rigorously tested for safety and efficacy in other parts of the world will not have to be re-tested in South Africa. As long as a product contains substances from accepted pharmacopoeia, at safe dosages, the product will undergo testing to ascertain that it is produced under good manufacturing procedures and to verify the contents (Robinson and Zhang, 2011a).[49]
- *Mode of financing* should not define TCAM inclusion. Financing schemes or payments for TCAM may not be different from those for allopathic medicine. Current reporting practices already include these classes in most countries without any specific marker, *e.g.* they are partially reimbursed by public and private insurance schemes and regularly

reported as aggregates by those schemes, with acupuncture, spa treatment and chiropractics being the most common.

- *Data availability* does not represent a criterion to include or exclude TCAM. Household surveys in many countries include questions about these types of consumption and they are reported as part of out-of-pocket payments (OOPS). COICOP (Classification of Individual Consumption by Purpose) includes TCAM explicitly as part of outpatient care (COICOP class 06.2.3 – Paramedical services).[50] In many countries, household payments may also involve in-kind transactions for which a record system may not be set up. Notably, the valuation criteria should be made explicit.

Towards a classificatory scheme for TCAM . Although services are to be classified as a single ***Reporting item (RI)*** category, a further breakdown could be made.[51] Table 5.3 shows TCAM aggregated into MoP major categories.

Table 5.3. **TCAM entries as a reporting item class HC.RI.2**

HC.RI.2	Traditional, Complementary and Alternative Medicines (TCAM)
HC.RI.2.1	Inpatient TCAM
HC.RI.2.2	Outpatient and home based TCAM
HC.RI.2.3	TCAM goods

Source: IHAT for SHA 2011.

HC.RI.3 Prevention and public health services (according to SHA 1.0)

The content of HC.6 Prevention and public health services in SHA 1.0 was organised by either type of programme or beneficiary group or by the setting of consumption. The main problems identified included: *a)* a potential overlap of classes, depending on the country's programme structure, *b)* the inclusion of some curative services and exclusion of some preventive services reported under HC.R 3 and HC.R 4, *c)* the exclusion of some prevention services that result from an individual initiative, *d)* some components of prevention have been difficult to disaggregate from administration, and *e)* blood banks were reported as public health services.

The classification in SHA 2011 involves the following changes: *a)* organisation by type of service, *b)* a focus on prevention, which allows for a clear boundary setting, *c)* individual preventive care is excluded and to be reported within HC.1, *d)* integration of certain health preventive components with an unclear description that were previously allocated under HC.R.3 and HC.R.4, and *e)* blood banks are relocated as an ancillary service, complementary to preventive, curative or rehabilitative care. The main barrier to reporting prevention that is integrated into curative, rehabilitative or LTC services is the lack of appropriate records. Thus, a clear definition is not yet enough to ensure a comprehensive class of prevention.

As a result, in principle the reported amount on prevention remains close to but different from that of SHA 1.0. The SHA 1.0 classification is therefore retained and a progressive refinement over time is expected. With that aim, Reporting Item (HC.RI.3) equates to HC.6 in SHA 1.0, and is within the boundary of health care. The proposal is to keep them as is, so as to promote a continued reporting practice, notably during the transition to SHA 2011 (see Table 5.2 for a mapping of these categories).

HC.RI.3.1 Maternal and child health; family planning and counselling (according to SHA 1.0)

Maternal and child health covers a wide range of health care services, such as genetic counselling and the prevention of specific congenital abnormalities, prenatal and postnatal medical attention, baby health care, pre-school and school child health, and vaccinations.

HC.RI.3.2 School health services (according to SHA 1.0)

This item comprises a variety of health education and screening services (for example, by dentists), disease prevention, and the promotion of healthy living conditions and lifestyles in the school. This includes basic medical treatment, such as dental treatment, if provided as an integral part of the public health function.

- *Includes*: interventions against smoking and alcohol and substance abuse.
- *Excludes:* vaccination programmes (HC.6.1).

HC.RI.3.3 Prevention of communicable diseases (according to SHA 1.0)

This item comprises the compulsory reporting and notification of certain communicable diseases and epidemiological enquiries into communicable disease; efforts to trace possible contacts and origins of disease; the prevention of tuberculosis and tuberculosis control (including systematic screening of high-risk groups); immunisation/vaccination programmes (compulsory and voluntary); and vaccination under maternity and child health care.

- *Excludes*: vaccination for occupational health (HC.6.1); vaccination for travel and tourism on the patient's own initiative (HC.6.1).

HC.RI.3.4 Prevention of non-communicable diseases (according to SHA 1.0)

This item comprises public health services involving health education, disease prevention, and the promotion of healthy living conditions and lifestyles such as services provided by centres for disease surveillance and control, and programmes for the avoidance of risks and the improvement of the health status of nations, even when not specifically directed towards communicable diseases.

- *Includes*: interventions against smoking and alcohol and substance abuse, such as anti-smoking campaigns; activities of community workers; services provided by self-help groups; general health education and health information of the public; health education campaigns; campaigns in favour of healthier lifestyles, safe sex, etc.; and information exchanges: e.g. on alcoholism or drug addiction.
- *Excludes*: public health environmental surveillance and public information about environmental conditions.

HC.RI.3.5 Occupational health care (according to SHA 1.0)

Occupational health care comprises a wide variety of health services such as surveillance of employee health (routine medical check-ups) and therapeutic care (including emergency health care services) on or off business premises (including government and NPISH). It excludes, however, remuneration-in-kind of health care goods and services that constitute household actual final consumption rather than intermediate consumption of business.

HC.RI.3.9 All other miscellaneous public health services (according to SHA 1.0)

This item comprises a variety of miscellaneous public health services, such as the operation and administration of blood and organ banks, and the preparation and dissemination of information on public health matters not elsewhere classified.

- *Includes*: public health environmental surveillance and public information on environmental conditions.

HCR Health care-related classes

HCR.1 Long-term care (social)

This item comprises the expenditure on lower-level social care services to assist with instrumental activities of daily living (such as home-help, meals on wheels, transport and day centres, etc.). As the health care components of long-term care are contained in HC.3, the complementary social components are included as a health care-related category that is further subdivided into in-kind and in-cash components. The health and social care components, HC.3 and HC.R.1, can be summed up to obtain a total value of long-term care (LTC). The social care components of LTC may be provided and remunerated as a package of services along with long-term nursing and personal care services. If such services cannot be separately accounted for, and are not the dominant component of the package, they should be included under HC.3; otherwise the complete package should be under HC.R.1: Long-term care (social).

- *Includes*: subsidies to residential services (as well as expenditure on accommodation) in assisted living arrangements and other kinds of protected housing for persons with functional limitations (as well as residential services for people who suffer from mental retardation, mental illness or substance abuse problems as well as homes for physically and mentally disabled people); housekeeping services, day-care social services for dependent persons; and transport to and from day-care facilities or similar social services for persons with functional limitations.
- *Excludes*: all services that are predominantly related to providing long-term health and personal care which are included in the function HC.3: Long-term care (Health). Also excluded are services involving surveillance of persons with mental deficits such as dementia patients, and medical assessment and services involving case management and co-ordination between medical and long-term health care (which are also included under HC.3).
- *Excludes also*: special schooling for disabled people and vocational rehabilitation.

HCR.1.1 In-kind long-term social care. This item comprises long-term social care services in kind as described above that are provided to persons with health problems and functional limitations or impairments, where the primary purpose is to enable independent living and interaction with the environment.

HCR.1.2 Long-term social care cash-benefits. This item comprises the provision of long-term social care benefits in the form of transfers provided to individual persons and households. It mainly covers informal care services of a social nature provided by family members or the remuneration of formal social support providers to assist in instrumental activities of daily living to enable independent living. It does not cover cash benefits for income protection in the case of sickness or disability, such as paid sickness leave or income protection in the case of disability.

HCR.2 Health promotion with a multi-sectoral approach

Health is the result of the interaction of a wide range of determinants. To improve health outcomes, health systems as well as global geopolitical, socio-economic, informational, technological and climatic interventions are required. Comprehensive coverage is sought for health promotion by including the total expenditure of joint efforts within multi-sectoral and multi-partner services and programmes that can be of policy relevance. In most cases, the multi-sectoral approach has joint interests, and expenditure that is beneficial to health care may overlap with that of other social functions. The aim of having a multi-sectoral measurement balances the restricted boundaries of health care with responsibility for accountability of the resources underlying the health system, as well as those beyond the health system, involved in health promotion efforts.

The aim of this class is to account for health promotion resources that may go beyond the health care boundary, though nevertheless clearly involved with a health interest.

HCR.2.1 Food and drinking water interventions. This item comprises a variety of activities of a collective health concern, such as the inspection and operation of health regulations covering various industries, notably those linked to food and drinking water for human consumption. The extent to which the content is covered may vary with country practices and needs. Examples include the control of human drinking water and the control of food within the food production and distribution process. The expenditure to be included may refer to communications with technical health officers external to the MoH and joint interventions with other health promotion agencies, based in particular on the evidence of existing risks associated with water and food safety issues.[52]

- *Includes*: food and water security measures, such as agro-cultural interventions to avoid toxicological pollution of food and water to be used for nutritional purposes and the enhancement of quality control measures regulating the generation and distribution of food and drinking water products.
- *Excludes*: expenditure on direct health regulations (HC.7) as well as on the monitoring and surveillance programme components, such as the quality control performed by public health laboratories (HC.6.5).

HCR.2.2 Environmental interventions (excluding those related to food and drinking water). This item comprises a variety of environmental control interventions with a specific focus on a public health concern, such as waste management (safety measures connected to these services), waste water management (safety measures and quality norms), pollution abatement (prevention, monitoring, abatement and control of noise and the pollution of air, water bodies and soil), R&D in environmental protection (R&D in public health issues related to environmental protection).

A subclass could be advisable to account for the expenditure on environmental issues related to the health system, such as the destruction of nuclear items, dangerous equipment and supplies.

Excludes: expenditure on direct health environmental regulations (HC.7), as well as on the monitoring and surveillance programme components, such as the monitoring of persistent organic pollutants in human milk in geographic risk areas performed by public health laboratories (HC.6.5).

HCR.2.3 Other multi-sectoral health promotion. This class aims at collecting expenditure that involves a heavy public health interest, but is not necessarily within the health boundaries: this is the case both of the tobacco control initiative, for which some interventions go beyond health, as well as of road safety, where there is a strong interest in injury prevention but which also involves a primary interest in transportation and other branches. It would be advisable that each of the components remains labelled and also well documented in the metadata so as to facilitate inter-country comparisons.

Interventions in such a diverse range of areas involve to some extent a systematic approach: strengthening surveillance systems, improving risk assessments, assessing new technologies for safety and risk reduction, enhancing risk communication and advocacy, enhancing the health system role in co-ordinating with other partners, and improving international and national co-operation.

The proposed breakdown for this category is by type of risk:

- Individual behaviour;
- Household risks;
- School risks;
- Work place risks;
- Road risks;
- Urban risks.

Notes

1. However, there is no intuitive global understanding of the term "function". In national accounts, this can refer to groups of goods and services or products, to the primary purpose of institutional units, to the purpose of the activities of production units or even to the purpose of financing.
2. By convention, households are the final consumers, who are also allocated the benefits of government and NGOs, in what is termed as actual final consumption in SNA.
3. Statistical systems may have limitations in generating functional expenditure distributions with the data available. Classifications, which are relevant for decision-making, promote the search for a progressive refinement in reporting systems, which can be in parallel to the use of prorating through allocation keys. Separation is then made based on shares of human resources, utilisation and cost information, and so on. Also, a reporting strategy has been used that aggregates curative-rehabilitative data. This aggregate also contains preventive components.
4. The characteristics of individual and collective consumption are explained in more detail in Chapter 3.
5. Two examples can be used to illustrate this challenge. A typical grouping, such as the diagnostic-related groups (DRG), comprises several hundred hospital products embracing only a third of total hospital activity. Pharmaceuticals may number several thousand different entries, grouped in 14 different chapters when using the Anatomic Therapeutic Chemical (ATC) Classification. Therefore, the aggregation into groupings of health care functions may follow different paths.
6. In health accounts, tri-axiality involves the equivalence of consumption, provision, financing. The advantages of this approach include an optimal use of the data sources to ensure that neither double-counting nor omissions occur.
7. This follows SNA rules: "R&D that does not provide an economic benefit to its owner should be treated as intermediate consumption" (SNA 2008, 10.103).
8. "When training is given by an employer to enhance the effectiveness of staff, the cost is treated as intermediate consumption" (SNA 2008, 1.54).

9. Instead of an episode, the tracking proposal is the contact or encounter. The difference is that a contact refers to each visit of the individual to the health system, whereas an episode can cover a series of contacts *e.g.* with various components of the health system in a single or multiple visit.

10. A specific description or "natural history of a disease" may exist per disease, which is adjusted in conjunction with the causal understanding of, in importance, the prevention and control of the disease. One example of such an adjustment concerns a neurological disease that was considered to be non-communicable until technological developments identified viral infections as the origin. It was no longer a genuine non-communicable disease, so its natural history of disease was modified.

11. In most countries each visit during chronic disease management is treated as a separate contact.

12. Prevention is also delivered by MoP. However, for HC purposes, preventive care is reported by type of service. This is because most prevention initiated by the consumer is not properly recorded, while in most countries services delivered within an organised preventive programme are registered.

13. *Information asymmetry* between the health provider and the consumer is in most cases the main reason why consumers accept the therapeutic package indicated by the provider.

14. There are usually different types of separated records for each contact for care. When the person is discharged and sent home from the emergency department, the initial record is reported as an outpatient visit (including the emergency services, if the visit occurred there); when the patient is transferred to the hospital in the same establishment or to a different hospital, the service is recorded as inpatient. When a formal admission to inpatient care follows treatment in an emergency department, there will be two records: outpatient and inpatient. When a separation of the expenditure in such situations is not possible, then the whole of the expenditure should be counted as inpatient care.

15. It may be the case that the growing occurrence of non-face-to-face encounters will lead to a new specific MoP in the future.

16. Direct consumption can also be related to inpatient and day care, such as in the case of a second opinion consultation (see Figure 5.4).

17. In SHA 1.0 and SHA 2011, Ancillary services have the same connotation, referring to complementary services to health care. However, in the SNA ancillary refers to basic, routine services to support production activities that are required by all enterprises. When they are provided in-house, they are called ancillary activities, *e.g.* cleaning premises, running the staff payroll or providing the information technology infrastructure for the enterprise, etc.

18. Health care classes involve final consumption and include all cost components, *e.g.* e-medicine is expected to be included in the resources accounted for. E-medicine is the use, in the health system, of digital data – transmitted, stored and retrieved electronically – in support of health care, both at the local site and at a distance. Support to health care involves information-intensive means for management, for hospital care, day care, outpatient care, home-based care, the retailing of medical goods, immunisation & other programmes, monitoring and evaluation, clinical information, surveillance and epidemiological work, know-how and knowledge, health education, cross-border trade, or the analysis and dissemination of medical data. It includes diverse services, *e.g.* tele-radiology, the transmission of radiographic images from one location to another for interpretation by a radiologist. It is most often used to allow rapid interpretation of emergency room, ICU and other emergency examinations after the hours of usual operation, at night and on weekends. The images are then often sent across time zones (Spain, Australia, India), with the receiving radiologist working his normal daylight hours. Tele-radiology can also be utilised to obtain a consultation with an expert or sub-specialist.

19. See earlier comment on a mental health night stay, which is usually also recorded as a day case.

20. As defined by the World Confederation for Physical Therapy: *www.wcpt.org/node/27545*.

21. Disabilities are not necessarily a permanent condition; for example, the sequelae of a stroke can be fully recovered after rehabilitation.

22. Rather than a pure classification based on the purpose of the goods and services, long-term care services also need to take into account some of the patient characteristics and level of dependency (severity-based). The labelling of the category also reflects this by the use of "long-term care (health)" rather than "long-term health care" to distinguish between services for beneficiaries suffering from certain conditions requiring treatment over a long period of time, but without a significant effect on their dependency, *e.g.* asthma, the majority of diabetes cases, etc. That said,

disease complications can in turn lead to physical dependency. It has been estimated that 15% of the cost of treatment of diabetes in the United States is on nursing care due to kidney, retina and macula, neurologic and other complications (*www.worlddiabetesday.org; www.idf.org*).

23. In 2010, it was estimated that approximately 35 million people die every year from chronic life-limiting illnesses, of which less than 8% have access to LTC (Connor, 2010).

24. Long-term care needs increase significantly with age, with typically around 50% of the population aged over 65 requiring some form of long-term care (Bulletin Luxembourgeois des Questions Sociales, 2005).

25. An effort to collect systematic and comprehensive information for the European countries is presented in Salvador-Carulla and Gasca (2009).

26. There is a complex relationship between disability (help with one or more ADL), frailty and co-morbidity, which can be seen as distinct but inter-related concepts. As part of the Cardiovascular Health Study in 2001, a US community-dwelling population were classified as disabled or frail or as having co-morbidity. Of those categorised as frail and disabled, 79% also had co-morbidity. See Fried *et al.* (2001).

27. An example is Spain's Personal Autonomy and Dependent Care Law, which is based on the ICF model in theory but uses the ADL approach in the official assessment scale.

28. *Inclusions* involve a diversity of products, such as allergy/antihistamines, analgesics, antacids/heartburn, anti smoking, anti fungal, cold and flu, eye drops, nutrition and diet (dietary supplements, laxatives). *Excluded* are components of personal care such as those stated in COICOP 12.1 and notably in the 12.1.3 class with articles for personal hygiene: toilet soap, medicinal soap, cleansing oil and milk, shaving soap, shaving cream and foam, toothpaste, etc.; beauty products: sunbathing products, etc.; other products: sanitary towels, etc.

29. Essential medicines are medicines that address the priority health care requirements of a population. These medicines are selected through an evidence-based process with due regard to public health relevance, quality, safety, efficacy and comparative cost-effectiveness. The WHO Essential Drugs List was first published in 1977 and is updated every two years. It has proved to be a powerful tool for the promotion of primary health care by rationalising the selection and use of medicines as well as their cost (Hogerzeil, 2004).

30. The provision of an effective treatment in secondary prevention means not the provision itself, but all the measures supporting the provision in the system, notably measures such as the enforcement of regulations and quality assurance of the services. Pomey *et al.* (2000), pp. 339-344.

31. Environmental health components are related to regulatory enforcement and monitoring that concerns any agent posing an evidence-based immediate risk to humans, *e.g.* persistent organic pollutants and heavy metals, which are associated with air, water and food-borne diseases and transferred across borders and generations.

32. Safety involves all activities that seek to minimise or to eliminate hazardous conditions that can cause bodily injury. Occupational safety is concerned with risks in areas where people work: offices, manufacturing plants, farms, construction sites, and commercial and retail facilities. Public safety is concerned with hazards in the home, in travel and recreation, and in other situations that do not fall within the scope of occupational safety. Although safety involves a risk relationship that can be linked to health and to prevention, its uses are not universally included in that boundary but have to do with a collective nature in such a way that specialised principles, structures and social involvement generate a field that itself deals with each of those risks. Health-related management is thus restricted to components with an implicit mention of a health purpose.

33. An example of the health approach to these problems is found in the Global Status Report on Road Safety released by WHO in 2009.

34. The change from SHA 1.0 is considered to reflect a more accurate approach. Aggregation of types of preventive services allows a better taxonomy and flexible grouping. Among other taxonomic problems, several so-called "non-communicable" diseases have now been identified as communicable and are covered by vaccines that have been or are in the process of being produced.

35. Further breakdowns by population characteristics are discussed in Chapter 10, *e.g.* by population group by age and sex, by socioeconomic status, as well as by type of epidemiological group and by geographic area.

36. PM10 is used to describe airborne particulate matter with particles of 10 micrometers or less.

37. The approach by type of service is also considered better to identify opportunities to improve prevention in the field. Early case detection can also cover both communicable and non-communicable diseases.

38. WHO (2002), WPRO WPR/RC53/10. EPHF 1.

39. WHO (2002), WPRO WPR/RC53/10. Mainly tasks associated with EPHF 2, Epidemiological surveillance/disease prevention and control.

40. WHO (2002), EPHF 2, Epidemiological surveillance/disease prevention and control and EPHF 8, Ensuring the quality of personal and population-based health services. WPRO WPR/RC53/10.

41. Comparability between countries would require a detailed set of metadata since advances in aetiology have shifted some diseases from one class to another, *e.g.* as in the case of neurological and cancer cases that are now identified as due to viral infections or in cases where the geographical distribution of certain communicable diseases has been modified due to environmental factors.

42. Governance is the careful and responsible management of something entrusted to one's care. In the context of health systems, it involves influencing policies and actions in all sectors that may affect the health of the population. The governance function therefore implies the ability to formulate strategic policy direction, to ensure good regulation and the tools for implementing it, and to provide the necessary intelligence on health system performance in order to ensure accountability and transparency. (WHO Europe)

43. SNA 2008 defines the value of an insurance service or insurance output in paragraph 6.185 as insurance output = total premiums earned plus premiums supplements less adjusted claims incurred.

44. Chapter 9 discusses inputs by provider, the sum of which ought to be equivalent to this aggregate.

45. Modern medicine has also been called mainstream medicine (MM), allopathic medicine, conventional medicine, modern medicine, orthodox medicine, traditional medicine, Western medicine or clinical medicine. It involves the approach to health care practiced in developed nations, based on scientific data for diagnosing and treating disease; MM assumes that all physiologic and pathological phenomena can be explained in concrete terms; MM tools include non-human model systems, blind studies and statistical analysis to ensure reproducible results.

46. Examples of TCAM are: Acupuncture, Ayurveda, Chiropractics, Herbal Medicines, Homeopathy, Naturopathy, Osteopathy, Traditional African medicines (Muti, Yoruba Ifa), Traditional Chinese medicine (Tuina, Unani), Shiatsu, Mind-Body Intervention, Biologically-Based Therapy, Manipulative and body-based methods and Energy Therapy. The various therapies also include Qi Gong, Tai ji, Thermal therapy, Yoga, Magnetic Therapy, Reiki, Therapeutic Touch, Aromatherapy, Art/Msic therapy, Biofeedback, Hypnosis, Meditation, Mental imagery, Prayer and Spiritual healing.

47. For example, within chiropractics, out of the several hundred schools that claim to teach these practitioners, only 34 meet the minimum standards set out in the WHO Guidelines on Basic Training and Safety in Chiropractics (WHO, 2005c).

48. In South Africa a qualified registered health care practitioner must have achieved a minimum standard of training at an institution accredited by the relevant council set up by the Department of Health (DoH). Out of 190 000 traditional health practitioners, there were about 3 600 registered Allied Health Care Professionals in 2007 (Gqaleni *et al.*, 2007).

49. So far, it is estimated that about 25 000 complementary medicines, including traditional medicines, have been submitted for registration in South Africa. The global market for TCAM products has been estimated at USD 83 billion annually in 2008.

50. In the United States, for example, 83 million adults spent USD 33.9 billion out-of-pocket on TCAM in 2007, representing 11.2% of total out-of-pocket expenditures on health care (NIH, 2009).

51. Countries in which this practice has been reported such as Indonesia, include an aggregate for Modern care and another for Traditional care. See BPS-Statistics Indonesia (2007, p. 133).

52. See for example the cases of the European Union (*http://efsa.eu.int*) and the WHO Regional Office for Europe (*www.who.dk/Nutrition*) and "Food and Health in Europe: A New Basis for Action", *who.dk/eprise/main/who/progs/FOS/Home*.

A System of Health Accounts 2011: Revised edition

PART I

Chapter 6

Classification of Health Care Providers (ICHA-HP)

Introduction

Health care providers encompass **organisations and actors that deliver health care goods and services as their primary activity, as well as those for which health care provision is only one among a number of activities.** They vary in their legal, accounting, organisational and operating structures. However, despite the huge differences that exist in the way health care provision is organised, there is a set of common approaches and technologies that all health care systems share and that helps to structure them. The classification of health care providers (ICHA-HP) therefore serves the purpose of classifying all organisations that contribute to the provision of health care goods and services, by arranging country-specific provider units into common, internationally applicable categories.

The principal activity exercised is the basic criterion for classifying health care providers. This does not mean, however, that providers classified under the same category perform exactly the same set of activities. Hospitals, which are major health care providers, usually offer not only inpatient health care services, but, depending on specific country arrangements, may also provide outpatient care, rehabilitation, long-term care services and so on. For the purpose of international comparisons, the value added of the ICHA-HP classification lies in two advantages: first, its connection with the functional classification, which gives an insight into the variety of country-specific settings for the provision of health care services, and second, its combination with the financing classification, which sheds light on the variety of health care funding mechanisms that exist across countries.

This chapter introduces the classification of health care providers (ICHA-HP) and describes its main elements. It traces health care expenditure by provider categories to address the question: *What is the organisational structure that is characteristic of the provision of health care within a country?* Together with the classification of health care functions (ICHA-HC) and the classification of financing schemes (ICHA-HF), the HP classification shapes the accounting space of the core health care expenditure accounts.

Concept of the classification of health care providers

Objectives

The main objective of the classification of health care providers is to be comprehensive and complete, which means capturing all the organisations and actors involved in the provision of health care goods and services. Second, all providers should be structured by their main characteristics into categories that enable linkages with the related structures of health care functions (HC) and health care financing (HF). And third, the classification should be described in a way that will help both data compilers and data users to match national organisations and actors with HP categories.

The classification of health care providers introduced by SHA 1.0 used the North American Industry Classification System (NAICS) as a starting point.[1] The provider classification under SHA 2011 follows that of SHA 1.0, though there are certain modifications that have been driven by countries' experiences with SHA implementation, on the one hand, and the recommendations of the International Standard Industrial Classification (ISIC Rev. 4), on the other. Both factors reflect trends in health care provision, contribute to greater comparability with other national and international classifications, and preserve continuity with the previous SHA version.

The universe of health care providers

Comprehensiveness with respect to the classification of health care providers means that all organisations in the field of interest should be covered, while completeness means that all activities in the field of interest should be compiled, irrespective of the type of organisation. Therefore, since many organisations within the domestic economy can provide some form of health care, the classification of health care providers must be able to capture all of them, regardless of whether health care is their primary or secondary activity.

Primary providers are those whose principal activity is to deliver health care goods and services as defined in the core functional classification (ICHA-HC). Typical primary providers are offices of general and specialised physicians, units of emergency ambulance services, acute and psychiatric hospitals, health centres, laboratories, nursing care facilities, pharmacies and so on. Within the ICHA-HP classification, primary health care providers are grouped under six categories (HP.1-HP.6).[2] *Secondary providers* are those that deliver health care services in addition to their principal activities, which might be partially or not at all related to health. Examples of secondary providers include: residential care institutions, whose main activities might be provision of accommodation, with other social services in addition to nursing supervision provided as secondary activities; supermarkets that sell over-the-counter pharmaceuticals; and health care facilities/professionals that provide health care services to a restricted group of the population, such as in the case of in-house occupational medicine services for employees, or prison health services (HP.8.2).

There are two special categories of secondary providers, namely: *i)* providers of health care system administration and financing (HP.7), and *ii)* households as providers of home health care (HP.8.1). The former plays an important role in the governance and management of health care systems by carrying out a type of collective service related to the provision and financing of health care (for example, activities of the Ministry of Health),[3] while the latter often provides home health care services directly to family members. The scope of activities under both of these categories is defined by the functional classification and fits within the health care boundary under the proposed criteria and circumstances (see Chapters 4 and 5). Within the ICHA-HP classification, all secondary health care providers that deliver goods and services directly to consumers (either individuals or population groups) for the purpose of its final consumption are recoded under two categories (HP.7 and HP.8, except item HP.8.9).

In order to complete the picture, any industries that perform health-related activities but are not involved in the provision of health care goods and services directly to patients (either as primary or secondary activities) can be recorded under the category HP.8.9 Other industries *n.e.c.* There are two reasons for introducing this subcategory, which comprises industries that are outside of the universe of health care providers. First, it allows the classification of establishments that are involved in the provision of health care-related activities as defined by the functional classification, *i.e.* long-term social care and health promotion with a multi-sectoral approach. Second, it enables the linking of the HP classification with the classifications of the extended accounts, the capital account in particular. Consequently, industries involved in the provision of medical equipment or in health research and development or in the education and training of health care professionals can be recorded under HP.8.9 Other industries *n.e.c.*[4]

Figure 6.1 presents an overview of primary and secondary providers as encompassed by the ICHA-HP.

Figure 6.1. **Overview of primary and secondary providers encompassed by ICHA-HP**

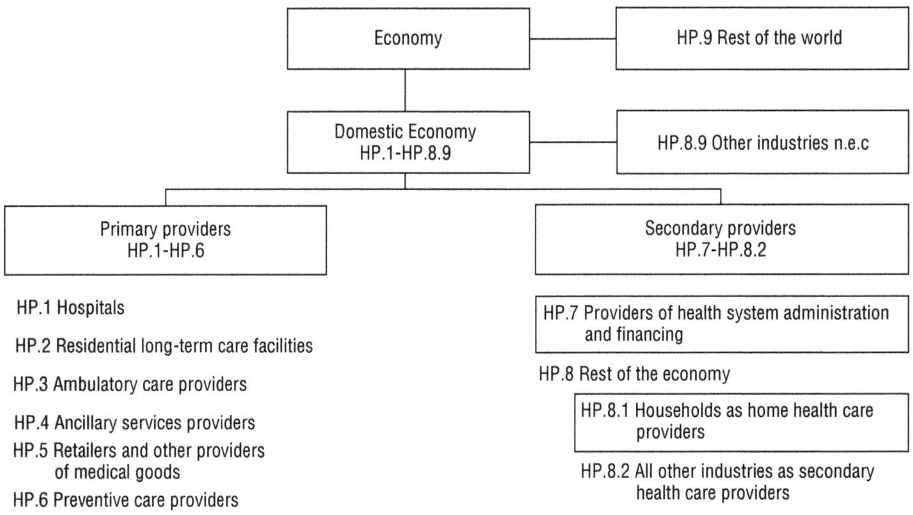

Source: IHAT for SHA 2011.

SHA focuses on the final consumption (see Chapter 3) of health care goods and services by residents. This approach has consequences for both data compilation and the provider classification itself. First, it delimits the universe of health care providers to those that deliver final health care goods and services directly to consumers. As a result, producers of intermediate health products, such as fluids for dialysis, which are further transformed or used in the provision of health care services, are not taken into consideration (unless they also deliver some products directly to patients, for example, for the purpose of home dialysis). Second, the health care goods and services consumed by non-residents should be excluded and those consumed abroad by residents should be included.[5] Therefore, if it is the case that a medical goods retailer or health professional is solely servicing non-residents, then they should not be considered part of the health provider universe. On the other hand, health care providers abroad who service patients resident in the country in question should be included. As a result, in addition to domestic health care providers, the classification also includes an entry for all health care providers abroad, recorded under the category *rest of the world* (HP.9).

The structure of health care providers

The categories of the provider classification must be *mutually exclusive*. Consequently, the HP classification tries to structure health care providers into meaningful, homogeneous groups of providers within categories and at the same time to ensure heterogeneity between categories. The criterion *type of health care activity* is relevant when providers are grouped into certain categories of the HP classification. When classifying an actor or organisation, the first question should be: does the economic unit provide health care? If the answer is yes, the next step is the identification of its main characteristics. This can be derived from the activities that it performs and the legal requirements for the provision of these activities. Examples are national standards for performing inpatient services as hospitals. Most countries keep registers of various health care providers because of the special conditions which these units must fulfil to provide quality health care. These conditions are usually related to requirements on medical professionals and on the equipment and technology involved, but also consider other factors such as sanitation regimes. The registers are one of the main information sources used to structure primary providers into categories of SHA.

In general, a precondition for grouping national health care providers into primary and secondary providers is an ability to distinguish between the health and non-health activities that they perform; a functional approach is then used to quantify those falling within the SHA health care boundary. With respect to the health care activities performed, the operational rules that follow NACE Rev. 2 (Eurostat, 2008a) and ISIC Rev. 4 (UN, 2008a) are that:

- An organisation with health care outputs for which more than 50% of the value added results from health care activities is to be classified and allocated – based on the type of the principal health care activity – into one of the HP.1-HP.6 categories;
- Those with less than 50% output of health care activities are to be classified under HP.8.2 All other industries as secondary providers of health care.

In the case that value added is not available, the ISIC/NACE proposes that other criteria related to output or input be used as a substitute for value added:

- Substitutes based on output, such as the production value or the turnover that is attributable to the goods or services associated with each activity. Examples are the revenue shares of hospitals from the sale of inpatient and outpatient services.
- Substitutes based on input, such as wages and salaries or hours worked that are attributable to the different activities; or employment according to the proportion of people engaged in the different activities of the unit. Examples are staff ratios of labour working in inpatient and outpatient departments.

Regarding the inclusion or exclusion of certain activities, reference is made to the classification of health care functions (ICHA-HC). It delimits the type of health care goods and services included in the health care boundary for the purpose of international data comparison. Under the functional classification, these health care goods and services are structured into aggregated groups of functions. Some of them, such as curative and rehabilitative services, can be directly allocated to individuals, while others, such as preventive programmes or health care system administration, are allocated to society at large. Individual health care functions are subsequently classified by mode of provision (inpatient, day care, outpatient and home care). The mode of provision underlines the technical and managerial organisation of health care provision. Together, the types of function and their mode of provision, by referring to certain characteristics of the health care goods and services delivered, offer guidance for the structure of the HP classification and for grouping the various national health care providers into more homogeneous categories. For example, providers like hospitals and long-term nursing care facilities provide services in the inpatient mode as their principal activity, but they differ due to the level of care intensiveness (acute versus nursing care), the medical personnel employed (specialised physicians versus nurses) and the level of technological support (operating theatre versus nursing room).

The interrelation between the functional classification and the provider classification requires that the latter should be complete, in the sense that all functions included are to be covered by providers. This implies, for example, that long-term nursing home care, which can be provided either by a nurse, or in some cases by family members, has to be exhibited in the providers' classification. Therefore, although the principal activity attributed to households would be consumption rather than health care provision, households are identified as a special category of secondary providers of health care goods and services (HP.8.1). Another example is the function consisting of the governance, management and administration of the health care system. Although the primary purpose of these activities is not the provision of health care goods and services directly to the patients, its role in pursuing these goals cannot be neglected. Respectively, providers such as Ministries of Health and Health Insurance Funds are captured under the provider classification as secondary health care providers, as their principal activities are related to administration and/or financing health care activities in the system as a whole (HP.7).

Table 6.1. **Classification of actors/organisations in health care provision and health system dimensions**

Health system dimensions	Activities within the functional classification	Provision of health care goods and services				Provision of health-related services
		As principal activity		As secondary activity		Other industries
		HP.1-HP.6	HP.7	HP.8.1	HP.8.2	HP.8.9
Provision						
Modes of provision: • *Inpatient* • *Day care* • *Outpatient* • *Home care*	Curative services Rehabilitative services Long-term nursing care services	Hospitals HP.1 Residential long-term care facilities HP.2 Ambulatory health care providers HP.3		Households as home health care providers HP.8.1	All other industries as secondary providers of health care HP.8.2	
	Ancillary services	Ancillary services providers HP.4				
	Medical goods	Retailers HP.5				
	Preventive care services	Preventive care providers HP.6				
Governance/ administration	Governance management and health care system administration		Principal activity of Providers of health care system administration and financing HP.7			
Health-related provision	• Long-term social care, • Multi-sectoral prevention					Principal activity of other industries *n.e.c.* under category "rest of economy" HP.8.9

Source: IHAT for SHA 2011.

In practice, all industries with principal activities other than health care can be classified as secondary providers in the ICHA-HP, so long as they do provide some health care goods and services directly to individuals or population groups. Included are social care facilities with some elements of medical care provision, prison health care facilities and research institutes involved in health promotion campaigns (HP.8.2). However, in contrast, even if the principal activity of a research institute is related to health, *i.e.* study and research on the development of new-generation antibiotics, and is thus important for the purpose of resource generation for health care in the future, this activity lies outside the core health care accounts, as it does not fall within the consumption boundaries. Table 6.1 shows the relation between different functions and health care providers, both primary and secondary, with, in addition, reference to the dimensions of health systems.

Description and guidelines for compilers

In the following section of this chapter, the main changes in the HP classification of SHA 2011 as compared to SHA 1.0 are highlighted. Furthermore, specific issues relevant for compilation are outlined.

Changes from SHA 1.0

For almost all provider categories at both the first-digit level and second-digit level, the HP classification of SHA 2011 keeps continuity with that of SHA 1.0. The majority of categories are retained, although partly under different codes.

a. Under HP.1 Hospitals, the structure of the classification has been kept the same as SHA 1.0. The subcategory Mental and substance abuse hospitals has been renamed into HP.1.2 Mental health hospitals.

b. Under HP.2 Residential long-term care facilities, the two subcategories Community care facilities for the elderly and All other residential care activities have been replaced by the category Other residential long-term care facilities. This is reserved for special residential facilities not elsewhere classified, as for example geriatric rehabilitation clinics. The reason is that in general only a part of residential care facilities can be qualified as health care establishments. Often the expenditure share for long-term health care in these residential care facilities is less than 50 per cent, in which case these facilities have to be classified under HP.8.2 All other industries as secondary providers of health care. As a result, the category HP.2 Residential long-term care facilities consists of three sub-categories: long-term nursing care facilities, Mental health and substance abuse facilities and Other residential long-term care facilities.

c. Under HP.3 *Providers of ambulatory health care*, the SHA 1.0 subcategory *Offices of physicians* is split into *General medicine* and *Medical specialists*, following the revision of the NACE.[6] As most countries have implemented some form of primary care system, it would be useful to show this explicitly in health accounts. The HP classification offers a breakdown of medical practices into *Offices of general medical practice, Offices of medical specialists* and *Offices of mental medical specialists* at the three-digit level.

d. Under HP.4 *Providers of ancillary services* have been separated from HP.3 because of the special characteristics of their services. Providers of ancillary services comprise organisations that provide specific ancillary services (*e.g.* blood tests) directly to outpatients (with or without medical prescription or supervision of health professionals) that are not covered by hospitals, nursing care facilities, ambulatory care providers or other providers. The HP.4 category is further broken down into *Providers of patient transportation and emergency rescue, Providers of medical and diagnostic laboratories* and *Other providers of ancillary services.*

e. The categories under HP.5 *Retailers and other providers of medical goods* have been restricted to three categories: *pharmacies, retail sellers and other suppliers of durable medical goods and appliances* and *all other miscellaneous retail sellers and other suppliers of pharmaceuticals and medical goods.* This means that retail sellers of hearing aids, vision products and orthopaedic prostheses that were classified separately in SHA 1.0 are captured now by a single class, because the breakdown by products is available by the functional classification.

f. The category HP.6 *Providers of preventive care* is retained as in SHA 1.0. It encompasses all providers such as Institutes of Public Health and of Occupational Medicine or Sanitary agencies for water control whose primary activity concerns various types of health preventive services. Note, however, that the total value of health care preventive programmes (targeting both individuals and population groups) can be captured only by the functional classification HC.6 *Preventive health care,* which may encompass, as well, some activities of other providers, such as *Providers of ambulatory care* (HP.3).

• The category HP.7 *Providers of health care system administration and financing* follows SHA 1.0 in that the structure of the subcategories at the second-digit level refers to the institutional structure of the financing agents, and not to the structure of the financing schemes (Chapter 7).

g. The category HP.8 *Rest of economy* comprises *Households as providers of home health care* (HP.8.1) and *All other industries as secondary providers of health care (HP.8.2)* as well as the separate subcategory *Other industries n.e.c.* (HP.8.9). Under the HP.8.2 subcategory, all secondary providers of health care are included except HP.7 and HP.8.1. Establishments of in-house occupational health care providers are no longer separated from all other industries as secondary providers of health care thus recorded under (HP.8.2). The subcategory HP.8.9 *Other industries n.e.c.* – is reserved for all industries not providing health care as primary or secondary activities. Although this category comprises industries with activities that go beyond the SHA health care boundary, it can be used to link the health care provider classification with health care-related functions.

h. The category HP.9 *Rest of world* has been kept the same as in SHA 1.0, although in SHA 2011 it is explicitly recommended that both the health care providers as well as establishments outside the health care boundary (as with HP.8.9) be recorded under this item. This is to identify and cross-classify with functional classification all foreign units with activities related either to health care goods and services or health-related functions.

Specific compilation issues

University hospitals. The experience from the compilation of hospital expenditure data by SHA 1.0 shows that most countries allocate hospital expenditures to general hospitals at the second-digit level. University and teaching hospitals are usually classified as general hospitals, except those which provide highly specialised services dedicated to patients with specific diseases or health conditions. In some countries, these specialised university hospitals constitute the so-called third level of inpatient/hospital care. Countries might wish to separate university hospitals for the purpose of further analysis of expenditures on education and research, which are often closely connected to expenses for treatment, or due to the medical high-technology involved, by adding such categories at the third-digit level.

Independent doctors working in hospitals. One particular issue in the provision of services in hospitals concerns individual doctors performing a specific service to patients in the hospital framework as subcontractors (integrated as offices in hospitals). In SHA 2011, offices of self-employed doctors working in hospitals are recorded under hospitals in the same way as services of employed doctors. Only if the provision is clearly independent of the hospital's activities (*i.e.* the physician rents a room or equipment for his own outpatient practice) should it be separately accounted as a provider of ambulatory care.

Long-term care providers. Here SHA 2011 is closely related to SHA 1.0. Providers of long-term care encompass establishments that are primarily engaged in the provision of residential care with medical or nursing care in combination with personal care as the dominant activities (as defined under the HC classification). Providers of long-term care should be classified either as *Residential long-term care facilities* (HP.2) or as *Providers of home health care services* (HP.3.5) if provided at home. Institutions with dominant social care services that provide health care only to a limited extent are classified under HP.8.2 *All other industries as secondary providers of health care, e.g.* residential care homes for the elderly, or providers of meals-on-wheels (providers of IADL services), if these organisations also provide some nursing and/or personal care.

Health care providers with less extensive medical knowledge. In ambulatory care, a wide variety of informal and less-than-fully-qualified health care providers might exist in many countries. SHA 2011 recommends that these categories should be recorded in line with their qualifications according to the ISCO 08 rules. In SHA 2011, HP.3.3 *Other health care practitioners* offers the possibility of including paramedical practitioners that provide different forms of traditional medicine. This item, however, should be restricted to providers with a certain level of medical education and/or skills (*e.g.* similar or equal to the level of nurses, midwives and physiotherapists; see ISCO 08: 3221 Nursing associate professionals, 3222 Midwifery associate professionals, 3230 Traditional and complementary medicine associate professionals, 3255 Physiotherapy technicians and assistants, 3259 Health associate professionals not elsewhere classified[7]).

Public versus *private ownership.* The ICHA-HP classification of SHA 2011 does not distinguish between public and private ownership and the legal status of establishments. A separation according to ownership (with application of SNA rules) might be useful for monitoring the efficiency and quality of health care provision of public vs. private owners of health care settings; it is thus primarily suggested for national purposes.[8]

Statistical units. The statistical unit is the entity from which the recommended items of data are collected. Different types of statistical units meet different needs, but each unit is a specific entity, which is defined in such a way that it can be recognised and identified and not confused with any other unit. It may be an identifiable legal or physical entity or, as for example in the case of the unit of homogeneous production, a statistical construct.[9] However, one has to be sure that all health care activities, especially those provided as secondary activities, are covered in the health accounts. As a consequence, one has to investigate whether establishments not classified by ISIC/NACE as corresponding to health care providers do deliver any health care goods or services, as defined by the functional

Table 6.2. **Classification of health care providers**

Code	Description	SHA 1.0 codes
HP.1	**Hospitals**	**HP.1.0**
HP.1.1	General hospitals	HP.1.1
HP.1.2	Mental health hospitals	HP.1.2
HP.1.3	Specialised hospitals (other than mental health hospitals)	HP.1.3
HP.2	**Residential long-term care facilities**	**HP.2**
HP.2.1	Long-term nursing care facilities	HP.2.1
HP.2.2	Mental health and substance abuse facilities	HP.2.2
HP.2.9	Other residential long-term care facilities	HP.2.3, 2.9
HP.3	**Providers of ambulatory health care**	**HP.3**
HP.3.1	Medical practices	HP.3.1
HP.3.1.1	Offices of general medical practitioners	HP.3.1
HP.3.1.2	Offices of mental medical specialists	HP.3.1
HP.3.1.3	Offices of medical specialists (other than mental medical specialists)	HP.3.1
HP.3.2	Dental practice	HP.3.2
HP.3.3	Other health care practitioners	HP.3.3
HP.3.4	Ambulatory health care centres	HP.3.4
HP.3.4.1	Family planning centres	HP.3.4.1
HP.3.4.2	Ambulatory mental health and substance abuse centres	HP.3.4.2
HP.3.4.3	Free-standing ambulatory surgery centres	HP.3.4.3
HP.3.4.4	Dialysis care centres	HP.3.4.4
HP.3.4.9	All other ambulatory centres	HP.3.4.5, 3.4.9
HP.3.5	Providers of home health care services	HP.3.6
HP.4	**Providers of ancillary services**	
HP.4.1	Providers of patient transportation and emergency rescue	HP.3.9.1
HP.4.2	Medical and diagnostic laboratories	HP.3.5, 3.9.2
HP.4.9	Other providers of ancillary services	HP.3.9.9
HP.5	**Retailers and other providers of medical goods**	**HP.4**
HP.5.1	Pharmacies	HP.4.1
HP.5.2	Retail sellers and other suppliers of durable medical goods and medical appliances	HP.4.2, 4.3, 4.4
HP.5.9	All other miscellaneous sellers and other suppliers of pharmaceuticals and medical goods	HP.4.9
HP.6	**Providers of preventive care**	**HP.5**
HP.7	**Providers of health care system administration and financing**	**HP.6**
HP.7.1	Government health administration agencies	HP.6.1
HP.7.2	Social health insurance agencies	HP.6.2
HP.7.3	Private health insurance administration agencies	HP.6.3, 6.4
HP.7.9	Other administration agencies	HP.6.9
HP.8	**Rest of economy**	**HP.7**
HP.8.1	Households as providers of home health care	HP.7.2
HP.8.2	All other industries as secondary providers of health care	HP.2.3, 2.9, 7.1, 7.9
HP.8.9	Other industries *n.e.c.*	
HP.9	**Rest of the world**	HP.9

Source: IHAT for SHA 2011.

classification. Examples are pharmaceuticals distributed by supermarkets or medical care delivered in residential facilities by employed health professionals. In both cases, the statistical units would be single establishments, parts of larger enterprises (a pharmacy within a drugstore chain or a nursing unit in a home for the elderly), that provide goods and services directly to consumers, and thus recorded as HP.8.2 *All other industries as secondary providers of health care*. In general, the classification of health care providers follows the ISIC/NACE approach as far as possible.[10] In practical terms, the situation with data availability may vary from country to country, and between groups of providers depending on institutional structures and the legal framework for activities in the health care sector. This might also be determined by the level of development of statistical systems, traditions, national priorities in data collection or the resources available.

Household own accounts. The own-account provision of home health care services by members of the household for their own final consumption is excluded from measured production in conventional national accounting practice.[11] In contrast to SNA, SHA explicitly recognises in specific cases that the work devoted to the home care of household members has an economic value, which is measured in monetary terms. Cash allowances granted to households for home health care, such as nursing allowances, are considered as "paid" household provision.[12]

Explanatory notes to the ICHA-HP classification of health care providers

HP.1 Hospitals

Hospitals comprise **licensed establishments that are primarily engaged in providing medical, diagnostic and treatment services that include physician, nursing and other health services to inpatients and the specialised accommodation services required by inpatients.** Hospitals provide inpatient health services, many of which can be delivered only by using specialised facilities and professional knowledge as well as advanced medical technology and equipment, which form a significant and integral part of the provision process. Although the principal activity is the provision of inpatient medical care **they may also provide day care, outpatient and home health care services.** The tasks of hospitals may vary by country and are usually defined by legal requirements. In some countries, health care facilities need in addition a minimum size (such as a number of beds and medical staff to guarantee 24-hour access) in order to be registered as a hospital. SHA 2011 distinguishes between general hospitals, mental health hospitals and specialised hospitals other than mental health hospitals depending both on the scope of medical treatments provided and the specificity of diseases or medical conditions of inpatients.

HP.1.1 *General hospitals*

This category encompasses licensed establishments that are primarily engaged in providing general diagnostic and medical treatment (both surgical and non-surgical) to inpatients *with a wide variety of medical conditions*. These establishments may provide other services, such as outpatient services, anatomical pathology services, diagnostic X-ray services, clinical laboratory services or operating room services for a variety of procedures and/or pharmacy services, that are usually used by internal patients (intermediate outputs within the hospital treatment) but also by outside patients.

Illustrative examples

- General acute care hospitals;
- Community, county and regional hospitals (other than specialised hospitals);
- Army, veterans, prison and police hospitals if settled in a separate establishment[13] (other than specialised hospitals, *e.g.* forensic hospitals);
- Teaching hospitals, university hospitals (other than specialised hospitals);

- Company general hospitals (*e.g.* hospitals owned by oil companies) if set up as a separate independent establishment;
- General hospitals of private non-profit organisations (such as the Red Cross or Red Crescent) (other than specialised hospitals).

Note: Included are integrated community health care centres providing both inpatient and outpatient services but which are primarily engaged in inpatient services.

Cross-references

- University hospitals comprise licensed tertiary hospitals that are engaged in academic medical education, clinical research and patient care as teaching hospitals. In case there are specialised university hospitals where activities relate to certain types of treatment or disease, they should be recorded respectively under HP.1.2 *Mental health hospitals* or HP.1.3 *Specialised Hospitals (other than mental health hospitals)*;
- Forensic hospitals should be classified under HP.1.2 *Mental health hospitals*.

HP.1.2 Mental health hospitals

This item comprises licensed establishments that are primarily engaged in providing diagnostic and medical treatment and monitoring services to inpatients who suffer from severe mental illness or substance abuse disorders. The treatment often requires an extended stay in an inpatient setting, including intensive pharmaceutical treatment. Depending on the specificity of the hospital's various therapies, psychiatric, psychological or physical therapies are available at the facilities as well as other types of services including educational and vocational services in order to ensure comprehensive treatment, leading at the end to patient recovery. To fulfil the complexity of these tasks, mental health hospitals usually provide services other than inpatient services, such as outpatient mental health care, clinical laboratory tests, diagnostic X-rays and electroencephalography services, which are often available for both internal and outside inpatients but also for outpatients. Mental health hospitals exclude community-based psychiatric inpatient units of general hospitals.

Illustrative examples

- Psychiatric hospitals;
- Forensic hospitals;
- Substance abuse hospitals.

Cross-references

- Establishments that are primarily engaged in providing treatment for mental health and substance abuse illnesses on an outpatient basis are classified under HP.3.1.2 *Offices of mental medical specialists* or HP.3.4.2 *Ambulatory mental health and substance abuse centres*;
- Establishments referred to as hospitals that are primarily engaged in providing residential care for persons diagnosed with mental retardation or engaged in providing inpatient services of mental health and substance abuse illness with the emphasis on longer stay/care and counselling rather than on medical treatment are classified under HP.2.2 *Mental health and substance abuse facilities*.

HP.1.3 Specialised hospitals (other than mental health hospitals)

This item comprises licensed establishments that are primarily engaged in providing diagnostic and medical treatment as well as monitoring services to inpatients *with a specific type of disease or medical condition.*

Illustrative examples

- Specialised hospitals or university hospitals with a focus on specific disciplines (oncology, gastroenterological, paediatric, orthopaedic, cardiology, etc.);
- Specialised emergency centres;
- Maternity clinics;
- Orthopaedic hospitals;
- Specialised sanatoriums (primarily engaged in medical post-acute, rehabilitative and preventive services);
- Thermal health care centres and spa hospitals that focus on medical rehabilitation;
- Specialised hospitals for infectious disease (tuberculosis hospitals; hospitals for tropical diseases);
- Aesthetic clinics; and
- Traditional, Complementary and Alternative Medicine (TCAM) hospitals or inpatient centres/clinics (*e.g.* hospitals specialising in Oriental medicine).

Cross-references

- Establishments licensed as hospitals that are primarily engaged in providing diagnostic and therapeutic inpatient services for a variety of medical conditions, both surgical and non-surgical, are classified under HP.1.1 *General hospitals*;
- Mental health hospitals, hospitals providing inpatient acute care for the mentally ill, are to be classified under HP.1.2 *Mental health hospitals;*
- Establishments referred to as hospitals but primarily engaged in providing inpatient long-term nursing and rehabilitative services to persons requiring convalescence are classified under HP.2.1 *Long-term nursing care facilities*;
- Facilities specialising in the long-term care of persons diagnosed with mental retardation or mental health problems or in substance abuse programmes are classified under HP.2.2 *Mental health and substance abuse facilities*.

HP.2 Residential long-term care facilities

The category of *Residential long-term care facilities* comprises **establishments that are primarily engaged in providing residential long-term care that combines nursing, supervisory or other types of care as required by the residents.** In these establishments, a significant part of the production process and the care provided is a mix of health and social services, with the health services being largely at the level of nursing care, in combination with personal care services. The medical components of care are, however, much less intensive than those provided in hospitals.

HP.2.1 Long-term nursing care facilities

This subcategory comprises establishments that are primarily engaged in providing inpatient nursing and rehabilitative services for long-term care patients. The care is generally provided for an extended period of time to individuals requiring nursing care. These establishments have a permanent core staff of registered or licensed practical nurses that, along with other staff, provide nursing care in combination with personal care. They provide predominantly long-term care, but also occasionally acute health care and nursing care in conjunction with accommodation and other types of social support, such as assistance with day-to-day living tasks and assistance towards independent living. Included are various establishments that provide long-term care involving regular basic nursing care to chronically ill, frail, disabled or convalescent persons or senile persons placed in an inpatient institution. The exact classification in the corresponding types of institutions (skilled nursing care facilities, residential mental retardation facilities, other residential long-term care facilities) depends on the country-specific division of labour in the care process, especially in long-term care and rehabilitation.

Illustrative examples

- Convalescent homes or convalescent hospitals (other than mental health and substance abuse facilities);
- Homes for the elderly with nursing care;
- Inpatient care hospices;
- Palliative care establishments for the terminally ill;
- Nursing homes;
- Rest homes with nursing care;
- Skilled nursing facilities (*e.g.* in the United States);
- Teaching nursing homes.

Cross-references

- Institutions where nursing care interventions are more of an incidental character or are performed by non-permanent staff such as visiting nurses are probably social care institutions and should be classified as HP.8.2 *All other industries as secondary providers of health care*. This should also apply to organisations with a physician acting as director, for example, in a home for handicapped persons, where medical and nursing health care services account for only a small share of the institution's overall activity. Another example of this type of institution is residential homes for the elderly with visiting nurses. Nurses visiting these institutions should be reported separately as a corresponding category of ambulatory health care, in this case, *Other health care practitioners* HP.3.3;
- Hostels with only limited medical assistance, such as supervision of compliance with medication, should be classified under HP.8.2 *All other industries as secondary providers of health care*.

HP.2.2 Mental health and substance abuse facilities

This item comprises establishments (*e.g.* group homes, intermediate care facilities) that are primarily engaged in providing, in an inpatient setting, domiciliary services for persons diagnosed with mental retardation. These facilities provide mental health care, though the focus is on room and board, protective supervision and counselling. Residential mental health and substance abuse facilities comprise establishments that are primarily engaged in providing residential care and treatment for patients with mental health and substance abuse illnesses. Although health care services may be available at these establishments, they are incidental to the counselling, mental rehabilitation and support.

Illustrative examples

- Residential mental retardation facilities;
- Mental health and substance abuse facilities;
- Alcoholism or drug addiction rehabilitation facilities (other than licensed hospitals);
- Mental health convalescent homes or hospitals;
- Day and night care institutions providing, for a limited time, long-term nursing, including personal care for persons with mental illness such as dementia, etc.

Cross-references

- Hostels with only limited medical assistance, such as supervision of compliance with medication or continuing-care retirement communities and homes for the elderly without nursing or health care are classified under HP.8.2 *All other industries as secondary providers of health care*;
- Day-care centres with curative or rehabilitative care focusing on individuals other than those diagnosed with mental retardation are classified under HP.3.4.9 *All other ambulatory centres;*
- Establishments that are primarily engaged in providing residential nursing and rehabilitative services for individuals other than those diagnosed with mental retardation, for example, for oncology rehabilitation or geriatric rehabilitation, are classified under HP.2.1 *Long-term nursing care facilities* or HP 2.9 *Other residential long-term care facilities*.

HP.2.9 Other residential long-term care facilities

This category includes the provision of residential and health care services in organisations classified neither as long-term nursing care facilities HP.2.1, nor as mental health and substance abuse facilities HP.2.2. This includes specialised non-mental residential facilities, as, for example, geriatric rehabilitation facilities that do not fulfil the criteria for geriatric hospitals.

HP.3 Providers of ambulatory health care

This item comprises **establishments that are primarily engaged in providing health care services directly to outpatients who do not require inpatient services. This includes both offices of general medical practitioners and medical specialists and establishments specialising in the treatment of day-cases and in the delivery of home care services.** Health practitioners in ambulatory health care primarily provide services to patients who visit the health professional's office, or the practitioners visit the patients at home. Consequently, these establishments do not usually provide inpatient services. This item has five subcategories, including: medical practices, dental practices, other health care practitioners, ambulatory health care centres and providers of home health care services.

HP.3.1 *Medical practices*

This subcategory comprises both offices of general medical practitioners and offices of medical specialists (other than dental practice) in which medical practitioners holding the degree of a doctor of medicine (Code 2210 ISCO-08, ISCED-97 level 5 and 6) are primarily engaged in the independent practice of general or specialised medicine, including psychiatry, cardiology, osteopathy, homeopathy, surgery and others. This group also includes the practices of TCAM professionals with a corresponding medical education. These practitioners can operate as individual practitioners or in a group practice in their own or rented offices (*e.g.* centres, clinics) or independently in the facilities of others, such as hospitals or health maintenance organisations (HMO)-type medical centres.

HP.3.1.1 Offices of general medical practitioners. This item comprises establishments of health practitioners who hold the degree of a doctor of medicine or a corresponding qualification and are primarily engaged in the independent practice of general medicine. Although in some countries "general practice" and "family medicine" may be considered as medical specialisations, these occupations should always be classified here.

Illustrative examples

- General/family practitioners in private offices;
- Physician walk-in offices/centres;
- Paediatricians providing general medicine in private offices (general practitioner for children and adolescents);
- District medical doctors; family medical practitioners; medical doctors (general); medical officers (general); resident medical officers specialising in general practice; physicians (general); primary health care physicians;
- Independent practising general practitioners and general paediatricians within the public system.

Note: The role of a paediatrician varies considerably across countries; therefore their appropriate classification under offices of general medicine – primary care physicians – or specialists has to be decided by the country.

Cross-references

- Free-standing medical centres that are primarily engaged in providing emergency health care for accident or catastrophe victims and free-standing ambulatory surgical centres are classified under HP.3.4.3 *Free-standing ambulatory surgery centres*,
- Offices of psychotherapists and psychoanalysts without a degree of medical doctor are to be recorded under HP.3.3 *Other health care practitioners*.

HP.3.1.2 Offices of mental medical specialists. This item comprises establishments of independent mental health practitioners holding the degree of a doctor of medicine with a specialisation in mental medicine or a corresponding qualification.

Illustrative examples

- Practices of independent psychiatrists;
- Offices of medical doctors of mental health;

- Offices of mental health physicians;
- Offices of mental health paediatricians;
- Offices of psychoanalysts (medical doctors);
- Offices of psychotherapists (medical doctors).

Cross-references

- Providers of ambulatory mental health services in combination with other health and social professions have to be classified under HP.3.4.2 *Ambulatory mental health and substance abuse centres.*

HP.3.1.3 Offices of medical specialists (other than mental medical specialists). This item comprises establishments of health practitioners holding a degree of medical doctor with a specialisation other than general medicine or mental health (equivalent to ISCO-08 Code 2212).

Illustrative examples

- Offices of surgeons, aesthetic surgeons, anaesthetists, cardiologists, dermatologists, emergency medicine specialists, gynaecologists, endocrinologists, ENT (ear, nose, throat), gastroenterologists, infection specialists, nephrologists, obstetricians, ophthalmologists, orthopaedists, pathologists, paediatricians for specialised care (*e.g.* oncological treatment), pathologists, preventive medicine specialists, radiologists and radiotherapists, rheumatologists, specialist physicians (internal medicine), urologists, offices of medical specialists practicing TCAM, etc.;
- Establishments that are known as medical clinics other than multi-specialist centres, which are primarily engaged in the treatment of outpatients (Korea, Japan);
- Self-employed and independent specialists who rent a room or equipment for the purpose of their own outpatient practices on-site in hospitals or residential long-term care facilities.

Cross-references

- Paediatricians and other physicians working in primary care are classified under HP.3.1.1 *Offices of general medical practitioners;*
- Offices of nephrologists with dialysis units are classified under HP.3.4.4 *Dialysis care centres;*
- Offices of surgeons who operate with colleagues and anaesthetists as well as other medical staff and are primarily engaged in providing surgical services (*e.g.* orthoscopic and cataract surgery) in specialised facilities are to be reported under HP.3.4.3 *Free-standing ambulatory surgery centres;*
- Offices of midwives, physiotherapists and other paramedical practitioners are included under HP.3.3 *Other health care practitioners;*
- Doctors of dental medicine with a specialisation (*e.g.* dentist surgery) are to be recorded under HP.3.2 *Dental practices.*

HP.3.2 Dental practices

This subcategory comprises independent establishments of health practitioners who hold a university-level degree in dental medicine or a qualification at a corresponding level

(Code 2261, ISCO-08) and are primarily engaged in the independent practice of general or specialised dentistry or dental surgery. These practitioners operate private or group practices in their own offices (*e.g.* centres, clinics) and either provide comprehensive preventive, reconstructive or emergency care or specialise in a single field of dentistry. They can provide dental practice activities of a general or specialised nature, *e.g.* dentistry, endodontics, paediatric dentistry, oral pathology and orthodontic activities.

Illustrative examples

- Dental practitioners; dentists; endodontists;
- Dental surgeons; oral and maxillofacial surgeons;
- Oral pathologists; orthodontists; paedodontists; periodontists; and prosthodontists.

Cross-references

- Dental laboratories that deliver services directly to patients and are primarily engaged in making dentures, artificial teeth and orthodontic appliances for dentists are classified under HP.4.2 *Medical and diagnostic laboratories* (including dental laboratories);
- Establishments of dental hygienists who are primarily engaged in cleaning teeth and gums or establishments of denturists primarily engaged in taking impressions for and fitting dentures are classified under HP.3.3 *Other health care practitioners*; *e.g.* denturists in the Netherlands and dental prosthetists in Australia are allowed to provide full dentures.

HP.3.3 Other health care practitioners

This subcategory comprises the group of paramedical and other independent health practitioners (other than medical professions: general or specialist physicians, and dentists), such as chiropractors, optometrists, psychotherapists, physical, occupational, and speech therapists and audiologist establishments who are primarily engaged in providing care to outpatients. These practitioners operate as individual or group practices in their own offices (for example, centres and clinics) or independently in the facilities of others, such as hospitals or HMO medical centres. Some form of legal registration and licensing (implying a minimum of public control over the contents of the care provided) is regarded as a necessary condition in order to be reported as a paramedical practitioner in many countries.

Illustrative examples

- Nurses and midwifes offices;
- Offices of acupuncturists (other than physicians);
- Chiropractors (other than physicians);
- Physiotherapists and physical therapists;
- Occupational and speech therapists;
- Audiologists;
- Offices of dental hygienists;
- Offices of denturists;
- Offices of dieticians;
- Offices of homeopaths (other than physicians);

- Offices of inhalation or respiratory therapists;
- Offices of naturopaths (other than physicians);
- Offices of podiatrists;
- Practitioners with a less extensive understanding of Chinese medicine and other forms of traditional medicine based on relatively short periods of formal education and training (Code 3230 ISCO-08); in countries where these forms of medicine have been an integral part of medical practice for a long time, formal licensing may not be required as criteria for recognition as health practitioner; oriental (traditional) medicine clinics (Korea).

Cross-references

- The independent medical practice (general physician, mental or other specialist) is classified, respectively, under HP.3.1.1 *Offices of general medical practitioners*, HP.3.1.2 *Offices of mental medical specialists* or HP.3.1.3 *Offices of medical specialists (other than mental medical specialists)*;
- The independent practice of dentistry is classified under HP.3.2 *Dental practices*;
- The independent practice of home health care services is classified under HP.3.5 *Providers of home health care services*.

HP.3.4 *Ambulatory health care centres*

This item comprises establishments that are engaged in providing a wide range of outpatient services by a team of medical and paramedical staff, often along with support staff, that usually bring together several specialities and/or serve specific functions of primary and secondary care. These establishments generally treat patients who do not require inpatient treatment. They differ from HP.3.1.3 *Offices of medical specialists* by their multi-specialisations, the complexity of the medical-technical equipment used and the range of types of health professionals involved.

HP.3.4.1 Family planning centres. This subcategory comprises establishments with medical staff who are primarily engaged in providing a range of family planning services on an outpatient basis, such as contraceptive services, genetic and prenatal counselling, voluntary sterilisation and therapeutic and medically indicated termination of pregnancy.

Illustrative examples

- Pregnancy counselling centres;
- Birth control clinics;
- Childbirth preparation classes; and
- Fertility clinics.

Cross-references

- Centres involved in providing collective preventive programmes and campaigns against the transmission of HIV (including maternity health) are classified under HP.6 *Providers of preventive care*.

HP.3.4.2 Ambulatory mental health and substance abuse centres. This item comprises establishments with medical staff that are primarily engaged in providing outpatient services related to the diagnosis and treatment of mental health disorders, alcohol and other substance abuse. These establishments generally treat patients who do not require inpatient treatment. They may provide counselling staff and information regarding a wide range of mental health and substance abuse issues and/or refer patients to more extensive treatment programmes, if necessary.

Illustrative examples

- Outpatient alcoholism treatment centres and clinics (other than hospitals and mental health facilities);
- Outpatient detoxification centres and clinics (other than hospitals and mental health facilities);
- Outpatient drug addiction treatment centres and clinics (other than hospitals and mental health facilities);
- Outpatient mental health centres and clinics (other than hospitals and mental health facilities);
- Outpatient substance abuse treatment centres and clinics (other than hospitals and mental health facilities).

Cross-references

- Hospitals primarily engaged in the inpatient treatment of mental health and substance abuse illnesses with an emphasis on medical treatment and monitoring are classified under HP.1.2 *Mental health hospitals*;
- Establishments primarily engaged in the inpatient treatment of mental health and substance abuse illness with an emphasis on residential care and counselling rather than medical treatment are classified under HP.2.2 *Mental health and substance abuse facilities*;
- Practices of mental health specialists are to be recorded under HP.3.1.2 *Office of mental health specialists*.

HP.3.4.3 Free-standing ambulatory surgery centres. This subcategory comprises specialised establishments with physicians and other medical staff who are primarily engaged in providing surgical services (*e.g.* orthoscopic and cataract surgery) on an outpatient basis. Outpatient surgical establishments have specialised facilities, such as operating and recovery rooms, and specialised equipment, such as anaesthetic or X-ray equipment.

Cross-references

- Physician walk-in centres are classified under HP.3.1.1. *Offices of general medical practitioners;*
- Hospitals that also perform ambulatory surgery and emergency room services are classified under HP.1 *Hospitals*.

HP.3.4.4 Dialysis care centres. This subcategory comprises establishments with medical staff who are primarily engaged in providing outpatient kidney or renal dialysis services.

HP.3.4.9 All other ambulatory centres. This subcategory comprises establishments that are engaged in providing a wide range of outpatient services, by a medical and paramedical staff, and often support staff too, usually bringing together several specialities and/or serving specific functions of primary care and/or secondary care, *e.g.* centres or clinics of health practitioners with different degrees from more than one speciality practising within the same establishment (*i.e.* physician and dentist) are included in this item.

Illustrative examples

- Outpatient community centres and clinics;
- Chemotherapy and radiotherapy centres;
- Multi-speciality outpatient polyclinics;
- Multi-speciality HMO medical centres and clinics;
- Outsourced call centres staffed with trained call advisors or experienced nurses who are trained to answer clinical questions (*e.g.* England and United States);
- Multi-specialised TCAM providers not elsewhere classified.

Note: HMO-type medical centres comprise establishments with physicians and other medical staff primarily engaged in providing a range of outpatient health care services to HMO subscribers, with a focus generally on primary health care.

Cross-references

- Offices of medical practitioners who are primarily engaged in the independent practice of their profession are classified under HP.3.1.1 *Offices of medical practitioners*, HP.3.1.2 *Offices of mental medical specialists*, or HP.3.1.3 *Offices of medical specialists (other than mental medical specialists)* and HP.3.2 *Dental practices*; and HP.3.3 *Other health care practitioners*;
- Centres of hospitals that also perform ambulatory surgery and emergency room services are classified under HP.1.1 *General hospitals* if they are fully integrated.

Note: Mixed health and social care. In some health care systems "*integrated care*" refers to the inclusion of social care elements. It can be classified under HP.3.4.9 *All other ambulatory centres* if medical ambulatory care dominates, or otherwise under HP.8.2 *All other industries as secondary providers of health care*, if social care dominates. However, there is no common definition across countries. Countries might add categories at the third-digit level if necessary.

HP.3.5 *Providers of home health care services*

This subcategory comprises establishments that are primarily engaged in providing skilled nursing services in patients' homes, along with a range of the following: personal care services: medical social services, support in medications, use of medical equipment and supplies, counselling; 24-hour home care; occupational and vocational therapy; dietary and nutritional services; speech therapy; audiology; and high-tech care, such as intravenous therapy. The services of home nursing care providers are often substitutive for inpatient long-term services delivered by HP.2 *Residential long-term care facilities* or outpatient services provided by *HP.3.3 Other health care practitioners*.

Illustrative examples

- Community nurses and domiciliary nursing care (including child day care in the case of sickness);
- Home health care agencies;

- In-home hospice care services;
- Visiting nurse associations.

Cross-references

- Excluded are non-medical or non-paramedical providers offering help and support at home, and thus predominately engaged in providing services related to instrumental activities of daily living (IADL) such as help in cleaning, shopping, etc. These non-health care activities are outside the health care boundary, and respective providers that deliver only IADL services are captured under *HP.8.9 Other industries n.e.c.*

HP.4 Providers of ancillary services

This category comprises **establishments that provide specific ancillary type of services directly to outpatients under the supervision of health professionals and not covered within the episode of treatment by hospitals, nursing care facilities, ambulatory care providers or other providers.** Included are providers of patient transportation and emergency rescue, medical and diagnostic laboratories, dental laboratories and other providers of ancillary services. These specialised providers may charge patients directly for their services rendered or may provide these ancillary services as benefits-in-kind under special service contracts.

HP.4.1 Providers of patient transportation and emergency rescue

This subcategory comprises establishments that are primarily engaged in providing the transportation of patients by ground or air in the case of emergencies at patients' homes or outside (on the street) as well as in the case of illness as a component of the treatment process (*e.g.* transferring patients between health care providers, transportation of patients to dialysis or chemotherapy). The ambulance vehicles are usually equipped with lifesaving equipment operated by medically trained personnel. Transportation of patients might be carried out by different types of providers. The transportation in specially-equipped vehicles or in a designated air ambulance to and from facilities for the purposes of receiving medical and surgical care is often delivered by ambulance services such as the Red Cross or Red Crescent, but also in some regions by fire brigades or private suppliers, depending on national regulations. In this case, the department of fire brigades that is responsible for ambulance services is considered as a primary provider.

Illustrative examples

- Ambulance services for patients with or without emergency rescue;
- Establishments primarily engaged in providing specialised patient transportation that is not rescue service along with health care *e.g.* transport services for dialysis or chemotherapy;
- Patient transportation (by ground and air) related to specific medical services like transplantology;
- Patient transportation by conventional vehicles specially adjusted for a medical purpose;
- Ambulance services provided in peacetime or non-disaster situations by the army, police or fire brigade.

Note: Transportation of body organs/fluids or other medical products is excluded as it is treated as intermediate output within the whole episode of treatment.

Cross-references

- Transportation in conventional vehicles by non-specialised providers, such as by taxis when this is authorised and the costs are reimbursed by health insurance (*e.g.* for transportations of patients undergoing renal dialysis or chemotherapy), is classified under HP.8.2 *All other industries as secondary providers of health care.*

HP.4.2 *Medical and diagnostic laboratories*

This item comprises establishments that are primarily engaged in providing analytic or diagnostic services, including body fluid analysis or genetic testing, directly to outpatients with or without referral from health care practitioners.

Illustrative examples

- Diagnostic imaging centres;
- Dental X-ray or medical X-ray laboratories;
- Medical/clinical laboratories;
- Medical pathology laboratories;[14]
- Medical forensic laboratories;
- Genome data banks.

Note: Excluded are any providers of diagnostic services, forensic laboratories, genome data centres or blood and organ banks that deliver their services only as intermediate outputs to other health care providers within an episode of medical treatment.

Cross-references

- Establishments such as optical and orthopaedic laboratories that are primarily engaged in making lenses to prescription or making orthopaedic or prosthetic appliances to prescription are classified under HP.5 *Retailers and other providers of medical goods*;
- Establishments, such as dental laboratories making dentures, artificial teeth and orthodontic appliances to prescription usually provide their services directly to dental practices and not to patients. In this case the value of their services should be included under HP.3.2 *Dental practices*. But there are exemptions: *e.g.* in the Netherlands denturists and in Australia prosthetists are allowed to provide full dentures; they may also work in independent practices. In the latter case, they should be classified under HP.3.3 *Other health care practitioners*.

HP.4.9 *Other providers of ancillary services*

This subcategory comprises other providers of ancillary services not explicitly listed above.

Illustrative examples

- Hearing testing services (except by offices of audiologists);
- Pacemaker monitoring services;
- Physical fitness evaluation services (except by offices of health practitioners).

HP.5 Retailers and other providers of medical goods

This item comprises specialised **establishments whose primary activity is the retail sale of medical goods to the general public for individual or household consumption or utilisation.** Establishments whose primary activity is the manufacture of medical goods, such as making lenses, orthopaedic or prosthetic appliances for direct sale to the general public for individual or household use, are also included, as is **fitting and repair done in combination with sale.** This category is made up of three subcategories.

Note: Due to special medical safety and quality regulations, retailers of over-the-counter medical products and other providers of medical goods are subject to licensing and/or pharmaceutical authorisation in order to be eligible to provide their activities. Non-health care products such as cosmetics, dietetic products and natural products are excluded from health expenditures.

HP.5.1 *Pharmacies*

This subcategory comprises establishments that are primarily engaged in the retail sale of pharmaceuticals (including both manufactured products and those prepared by on-site pharmacists) to the population for prescribed and non-prescribed medicines. Pharmacies operate under strict jurisdiction/licences of national pharmaceutical supervision. Usually, either the owner of a pharmacy or its employees must be a registered pharmacist, chemist or pharmacy doctor.

Illustrative examples

- Dispensing chemists;
- Community pharmacies;
- Independent pharmacies in supermarkets; and
- Pharmacies in hospitals that mainly serve outpatients.

Cross-references

- Pharmacies integrated in hospitals that mainly serve inpatients are part of establishments classified under HP.1;
- Specialised dispensaries where the continuous monitoring of compliance and treatment plays an important role (such as for diabetes patients) are classified under HP.3.4 *Ambulatory health care centres (e.g.* HP.3.4.4 *Dialysis care centres,* HP.3.4.9 *All other ambulatory centres*);
- Dispensed medicines in doctors' offices are recorded under HP.3.1 *Medical practices;*
- Over-the-counter medicine sales in supermarkets are to be classified as HP.8.2. *All other industries as secondary providers of health care.*

HP.5.2 *Retail sellers and other suppliers of durable medical goods and medical appliances*

This item comprises establishments that are primarily engaged in the retail sale of durable medical goods and medical appliances such as hearing aids, optical glasses, other vision products and prostheses to the general public for individual or household use. This includes the fitting and repair provided in combination with sales of durable products, for example, in the case of hearing aids, cleaning, adjustment and the provision of batteries. Also included are establishments that are primarily engaged in the manufacture of medical appliances as prostheses, where the distribution to the general public, the fitting and the repair is usually done in combination with the manufacture of medical appliances.

Illustrative examples

- Retail sellers of glasses and vision products;
- Retail sellers of hearing aids;
- Suppliers of wheelchairs;
- Providers of orthopaedic shoes, artificial limbs and other prosthetic devices;
- Medical supply stores.

Note: Examples of specialised professions of suppliers of vision products are opticians, ophthalmic opticians, optometrists and orthoptists. Professions of suppliers of hearing aids include audiologists, hearing aid technicians. Usually, hearing health care professionals are an integral part of the selection and delivery of appropriate hearing instruments. The supply of prostheses involves professions like medical and dental prosthetic technicians, orthodontic technicians and orthopaedic appliance makers.

HP.5.9 All other miscellaneous sale and other suppliers of pharmaceuticals and medical goods

This subcategory includes all other principal activity retail suppliers of medical goods to the general public for individual or household consumption or utilisation not elsewhere classified.

Illustrative examples

- Cartridges, sale of fluids (*e.g.* for home dialysis);
- All other suppliers of medical goods *n.e.c.* delivering medical goods directly to consumers;
- Electronic shopping and mail-order houses specialising in medical goods.

HP.6 Providers of preventive care

This category comprises **organisations that primarily provide collective preventive programmes and campaigns/public health programmes for specific groups of individuals or the population-at-large, such as health promotion and protection agencies or public health institutes as well as specialised establishments providing primary preventive care as their principal activity.** This includes the promotion of healthy living conditions and lifestyles in schools by special outside health care professionals, agencies or organisations (see also HP.8.2).

Illustrative examples

- Institutes of Occupational Medicines;
- Local occupational health and safety networks/centres;
- Public health institutes/departments (in case of major prevention activities);
- Epidemiological surveillance and disease control centres;

- Institutes administering health registers related to disease control programmes;
- Institutes for communicable diseases;
- Health promotion agencies;
- Centres of public health education with activities involving the promotion of healthy lifestyles, healthy food and diets;
- Local health authorities operating preventive health programmes.

Cross references

- Preventive programmes provided in schools by employed health professionals are classified under HP.8.2 *All other industries as secondary providers of health care*;
- The provision of individual preventive screenings such as mammography are recorded under *e.g.* HP.3.1 *Medical practices* or HP.4.2 *Medical and diagnostic laboratories*. If services are provided to inpatients this has to be classified under HP.1 *Hospitals*;
- Provision of occupational medicine could be recorded under *Providers of ambulatory health care e.g.* HP.3.1.3 *Offices of medical specialists (other than mental health specialists)* if outsourced by enterprises to special medical providers, or under HP.8.2 *All other industries as secondary providers of health care*, if provided by enterprises in-house as an ancillary activity;
- Agencies and laboratories involved in activities related to drinking water and food control outside the health care industry (*e.g.* bottled water manufacturing) should be recorded under HP.8.9 *Other industries*;
- Vaccination programmes for children are recorded under the respective HP.3 *Providers of ambulatory health care*, but under HP.6 in the case of provision by institutes for communicable diseases.

Note: While the operative administrative costs of the preventive programmes should be recorded as a part of the function "preventive care", the general regulation of preventive programmes or related legislative measures undertaken by the Ministry of Health should be compiled under HP.7.1 *Government health administration agencies*.

HP.7 Providers of health care system administration and financing

This item comprises **establishments that are primarily engaged in the regulation of the activities of agencies that provide health care and in the overall administration of the health care sector, including the administration of health financing.** While the former relates to the activities of government and its agencies in handling governance and managing the health care system as a whole, the latter reflects administration related to fund raising and purchasing health care goods and services by both public and private agents. The main reason for inclusion of financing agents in the HP classification is to keep the balance and consistency of the compilation of the tri-axial system of transactions. Thus expenditures captured under HP.7 for health care system administration and financing cover the administrative expenses of financing schemes, presented by their institutional structure as financing agents. Financing agents can be involved in the management of several financing schemes in the HF classification.

Note: The administrative expenditure of primary health care providers (hospitals, physicians etc.) as well as part of the administrative costs related to the provision of health services of secondary health care providers should be included under the respective provider's category.

HP.7.1 Government health administration agencies

This subcategory comprises government administration (excluding social security) that is primarily engaged in the formulation and administration of government health policy, in the administration of health financing, and in the setting and enforcement of standards for medical and paramedical personnel and for hospitals, clinics and so on, including the regulation and licensing of providers of health services. Health departments of regional or municipal governments should be included. This item covers also such establishments as the statistical institutes of a ministry of health (but not institutes administering population-based health registers) and public registers of health care providers, as both are part of health care system administration.

Illustrative examples

- Ministry of Health;
- Local and regional departments of the Ministry of Health;
- Board of Health;
- Drug regulation agencies, including law enforcement;
- Agencies for the regulation of safety in the workplace;
- Institute of Health System Information and other institutes affiliated with the Ministry of Health;
- Local health authorities (in case of major administrative activities, such as law enforcement, licensing and registering providers);
- Local centres for drug control inspections;
- Local centres for medical device control;
- Health care financing administration.

Cross references

- Government health agencies mainly engaged in providing public health services, even if predominantly of a collective nature (surveillance, hygiene), are classified under HP.6 *Providers of preventive care.*

Note: *Government administration of employee schemes.* The subcategory also includes administration of compulsory employer-based health insurance covering various groups of state employees (army, veterans, railroad and other public transport, police, state officials and so on in the case of separate financing schemes for these groups). It excludes universal social health insurance administration.

HP.7.2 Social health insurance agencies

This subcategory comprises the social health insurance agencies (sickness funds) that handle the administration of social health insurance schemes. Sickness funds may also provide the administration of employer's health insurance schemes not offered by the government. Also included is the administration of compulsory social health insurance covering various groups of state employees (army, veterans, railroad and other public transport, police, state officials, etc.). Social health insurance agencies may also administer voluntary private health insurance schemes. Organisations subordinated to health insurance funds, like the Medical Advisory Boards, are also to be included.

Illustrative examples

- Administration of health insurance schemes of social insurance;
- Administration of accident insurance schemes (health care part) of social insurance;
- Administration of voluntary health insurance schemes of social insurance.

Cross references

- Compulsory medical savings accounts under government administration should be classified under HP.7.1 *Government health administration agencies,* while compulsory medical savings accounts under private insurance administration should be classified under HP.7.3 *Private health insurance administration agencies;*
- Community-based voluntary health insurance managed by NPISH should be classified under HP.7.9 *Other health administration agencies.*

HP.7.3 Private health insurance administration agencies

This subcategory comprises private insurance corporations that may manage more than one type of health insurance scheme at the same time (for example, compulsory private health insurance and voluntary health insurance). This subcategory includes establishments that are primarily engaged in activities consisting of or closely related to the management of insurance (activities of insurance agents, average and loss adjusters, actuaries and salvage administration). It covers the administration of all types of compulsory and voluntary private health insurance.

Illustrative examples

- Private insurance corporations providing the administration of compulsory health insurance;
- Private health insurance funds;
- Agencies administering complementary health insurance (for example, a French *mutualité*) in the case of non-financial corporations;
- Agencies administering employer private health insurance programmes (other than government social security and government health programmes for state employees).

Cross references

- Agencies administering complementary health insurance (for example, a French *mutualité*) in the case of NPISH are to be classified under HP.7.9 *Other health administration agencies.*

HP.7.9 Other administration agencies

This subcategory is important for organisations or administrative units that cannot be clearly classified into the above categories, for example, these involved in the generation of financial sources as in the case of medical savings accounts. This category comprises also non-profit institutions serving households (other than social insurance). The health administration of the NPISH has to be covered here only if administration of health financing or of services is not covered by the other health provider categories.

Illustrative examples

- NPISH that administer government health care financing schemes for special groups of the population, such as students.
- Community-based voluntary health insurance managed by NPISH.

Note: Excludes doctors associations; hospital associations; associations of the medical professions; and trade unions financed by fees from members, because they provide (intermediate) services to their members and not directly to patients.

Cross references

- *HMO administration units* (other than those providing health care services) primarily engaged in underwriting health and medical insurance policies are classified under HP.7.3 *Private health insurance administration agencies* or HP.7.2 *Social health insurance agencies,* depending on the institutional classification of the schemes.

HP.8 Rest of economy

HP.8.1 Households as providers of home health care

The health care boundary drawn in SHA includes personal home health services provided within households by family members, in cases where they correspond to social transfer payments granted for this purpose. This item therefore comprises private households as providers of home health care. Unpaid care by household members is not included in the core health accounts of SHA. Problems of data comparability across countries and over time may arise when households have the choice between benefits in cash or benefits in kind, in which case both kinds of care (by laypersons within the family and by specially trained nurses) are considered to be close substitutes, but are treated differently in common national accounting practice (as health care benefit in kind or social transfer in cash). However, in SHA, those parts of the cash transfers to private households for care givers of home care for the sick and disabled are treated as paid household production of health care.

HP.8.2 All other industries as secondary providers of health care

This subcategory includes organisations that offer health care as a secondary activity, *e.g.* occupational health care services provided within enterprises, providers of social care with occasional health services or patient transport services provided by taxis. This category of secondary providers varies greatly among countries, depending on accreditation and licensing rules. In these establishments, the provision of health care goods and services usually constitutes a minority share of the output value. **This item comprises all other organisations and industries that deliver health care goods and services as a secondary activity not classified above.**

Illustrative examples

- Occupational health care services provided in-house and not delivered by health care establishments;
- Taxis that provide patient transport under the supervision of health personnel;

- Prison health care services not provided in independent/separate health care establishments;
- Wholesale retailers delivering also medical goods directly to consumers;
- Schools with employed health professionals for *e.g.* treatment of ill children or providing health education;
- Social care facilities providing to a limited extent, services related to health and long-term nursing care.

Cross-references

- Establishments that are primarily engaged in providing inpatient long-term nursing and rehabilitative services are classified under HP.2 *Residential long-term care facilities.*

HP.8.9 Other industries n.e.c.

This category in the HP classification comprises establishments that are outside the health care provider universe and do not provide health care goods and services either to individuals or groups of the population, but which are specialised in health-related activities such as those identified within the functional classification: *i) long-term care (social)* and *ii) health promotion with a multi-sectoral approach.*

Establishments of *long-term social care* are those primarily engaged in providing assistance and social care type services for elderly and other persons 1) unable to fully care for themselves; and/or 2) unwilling to live independently. This category also includes organisations that focus on social services that aim predominantly to prevent and combat the social isolation of persons with body or functional limitations. Instrumental activities of daily living (IADL), such as housekeeping, laundry, shopping, preparation of meals, help with financial activities, etc., reflect the scope of long-term social care activities and can be provided both in residential settings and at home.

Illustrative examples

- Assisted-living facilities without on-site nursing care;
- Continuing-care retirement communities;
- Homes for the elderly without on-site nursing care;
- Home social care providers, *e.g.* specialised in IADL services, such as home care, meals-on-wheels, etc., with additional nursing care services.

Cross-references

- Health and long-term care services are captured by primary or secondary health care providers HP.1-HP.8.2.

Establishments involved in *health promotion with a multi-sectoral approach* might include various organisations that deal with a wide range of public safety measures, such as food and water security measures, environmental control interventions or road and travel safety measures.

Illustrative examples

- Local food control agencies;

- Waste management enterprises;
- Agencies monitoring the level of noise or pollution;
- Transport Security department/agencies.

Cross-references

- Sanitary Institutes, laboratories testing the quality of human drinking water, food-borne risks, and epidemiological surveillance and disease control centres should be recorded under HP.6 *Providers of preventive care.*

Note: Activities related to health care research and development as well as to training and education in the health care sector are no longer included under health-related items within the functional classification of SHA 2011. These expenditures which are considered a type of investment, are to be re-coded as memorandum items, respectively under Research and Development or Training of Personnel in the capital account (see Chapter 11). Consequently, establishments such as nursing schools, medical research institutes and training centres can be recorded in the capital account (*i.e.* extended account) under HP.8.9 *Other industries n.e.c.* for the purpose of cross-classifying the health care provider classification with the classification of financing agents.

HP.9 Rest of the world

This item comprises **all non-resident units providing health care goods and services as well as those involved in health-related activities.** In both cases the provision is directed for final use to country residents.[15]

Notes

1. In comparison with the International Standard Industrial Classification (ISIC) or the NACE, the NAICS is based more on a single production-oriented concept under which, in principle, the boundaries between industries demarcate differences in production processes and production technologies.
2. Some categories, such as nursing care facilities, may either provide nursing care in combination with social services or offer various social-type services as secondary activities. As these services go beyond the health care boundary, they should be identified and cross-classified with health-related functions, as appropriate.
3. Depending on the country, the Ministry of Health or health insurance might also provide some functionally defined health care goods and services directly to the patients/population along with their governance or financing activities.
4. See the memorandum items in Table 11.2 "Capital account", for the purpose of cross-classifying the health care provider classification with the classification of financing agents.
5. The expenditure for health care goods and services by the resident population (consumption) must not equal the total sales (outputs) of the health care providers. One reason is that health care goods are provided for non-residents (exports). Another reason could be that some of the services provided do not meet the criteria of health care goods and services, such as in the case of social care. In order to maintain consistency with the two other core classifications in health accounts, expenditures related both to exports and to non-health outputs should be separated.
6. NACE Rev. 2 supports this by the separation between General medical practice 86.21 and Specialist medical practice 86.22; unfortunately, the ISIC does not.
7. Occupations whose practice requires a less extensive understanding that is developed through relatively short periods of formal or informal education and training or informally through the traditions and practices of the communities where they originated are included in unit group 3230.

8. For the decision tree that data compilers should follow when classifying institutional units (the providers of health care goods and services) into private or public providers, as well as identifying those public providers that should be allocated to the government or public corporations sector, see Kawiorska (2008).
9. See Eurostat (2008a), NACE Rev. 2, Definitions and principles.
10. According to NACE Rev. 2, the following are the units that are described in the Council Regulation on statistical units: a) the enterprise group; b) the enterprise; c) the kind-of-activity unit (KAU); d) the local unit; e) the local kind-of-activity unit (local KAU); f) the institutional unit; g) the unit of homogeneous production (UHP); and h) the local unit of homogeneous production (local UHP).
11. In the SNA, the provision of services by members of the household for their own final consumption has traditionally been excluded from measured production. One main reason is that the labour force would include inactive household members if household production were considered. Entries as care of the sick, infirm or elderly are not recorded in the SNA when they are produced by household members and consumed within the same household.
12. However, not all countries have implemented this guideline because of difficulties in measuring home health care provision. Home health care provision is actually not integrated in the Spanish, UK and Swiss health accounts. According to a recent academic study in Switzerland, the costs of unpaid work for care to dependent persons can be estimated at 0.3% of GDP or nearly 3% of the total expenditure on health.
13. SHA gives priority to the classification of establishments from the view point of health care activities. In the ISIC, both prison and military hospitals are classified under code 86.10 hospital activities.
14. In NACE Rev. 2, establishments primarily engaged in collecting, storing and distributing blood and blood products are part of the pharmaceutical industry.
15. A further optional breakdown of ROW providers can be the same as for the other parts of the HP classification to give more detailed information on imports, i.e. HP.9.1 ROW *Hospitals*, HP.9.2 ROW *Nursing health care*, etc.

PART I

Chapter 7

Classification of Health Care Financing Schemes (ICHA-HF)

Introduction

This chapter presents a summary of the conceptual accounting framework for health financing and of one of its main components, the new classification of health care financing schemes (ICHA-HF). This summary also serves as an introduction to Chapter 8, in which the classification of revenue of financing schemes (ICHA-FS) is presented. Furthermore, in SHA 2011 the accounting framework for health care financing also encompasses the concept of institutional units of health financing and the related classification of financing agents (ICHA-FA) as a tool for a more detailed national analysis (see Annex D). The three classifications together provide the tools to account comprehensively for health care financing and describe the flow of financial resources in the health system. This introduction therefore provides a brief definition of all the key concepts and highlights their relationships. The relevance of the particular classifications and cross-tabulations may vary for countries that differ in the organisational structure and level of resources of their health care systems, as well as in their level of economic development and their dependency on foreign resources.

This chapter is concerned with the financing of the final consumption of health care goods and services; Chapter 11 discusses the financing of fixed capital formation. As to the main functions of health financing, Chapter 7 focuses on accounting tools for the allocation of resources; while Chapter 8 focuses on accounting tools for revenue-raising.

The aim of the accounting framework for health financing is to help health accountants and analysts obtain a clear and transparent picture of health financing systems, including information that is relevant to health policy about the structure and flows of funds (transactions). This includes indicators – comparable across countries and over time – that can contribute to the assessment of the performance of health financing systems.

Health financing systems mobilise and allocate money, within the health system, to meet the current health needs of the population (individual and collective), with a view to expected future needs. Individuals may have access to care by means of direct payment for services and goods or through third-party financing arrangements, such as with a National Health Service, social insurance or voluntary insurance.

The concept of health care financing schemes is an application and extension of the concept of social protection schemes defined by the European System of Integrated Social Protection Statistics (ESSPROS). The ESSPROS Manual emphasises: "the scheme concept of social protection [is straightforward as it] starts from the point of view of the beneficiaries". As health policy is primarily concerned with ensuring access to health care, the approach of ESSPROS is considered to be a highly relevant starting point.

ESSPROS defines social protection schemes as follows: "A social protection scheme is a distinct body of rules, supported by one or more institutional units, governing the provision of social protection benefits and their financing .... Institutional units can support more than one social protection scheme, when they administer and provide very diverse types of social benefits. On the other hand, a single social protection scheme can be supported by several institutional units .... The *body of rules* referred to in this definition may be established *de jure*, by virtue of laws, regulations or contracts, or *de facto*, by virtue of administrative practice...".

The *structure* of a health care financing system consists of two types of entities: *financing schemes* (such as national health service, social health insurance and voluntary insurance, and so on) *and institutional units* (financing agents, such as government units, a social security agency, private insurance corporations and so on) that in practice operate the financing schemes. A social insurance scheme, for example, defines who is obliged to participate in the scheme, what is the basis for entitlement to health care and what benefits the scheme offers as well as the rules on raising and pooling the social insurance contributions. The scheme may be operated by a single government agency or by specific insurance funds or by a government agency and insurance companies at the same time. *The operation* of a health financing system entails transactions by the three main functions of health financing: revenue-raising, pooling and purchasing – such as, for example, payment of social insurance contributions to a single national fund and distribution of the resources, first among the different purchasing organisations, and then among the services and their providers. The transactions are executed by the financing agents, according to the rules of the financing schemes.

The SHA framework for the accounting of health care financing makes it possible to analyse the following major issues:[1]

- How does a particular financing scheme collect its revenues? (HFxFS tables);
- From which institutional units of the economy are the revenues of a particular financing scheme mobilised? (HFxFS.RI[2]; and HFxFSxFS.RI);
- Through what kind of financing arrangements do people have access to care? The role (share) of the main financing schemes[3] in a country's health care sector (HF table);
- What kinds of services are ensured (purchased) under the different financing schemes? How are the resources of the different financing schemes allocated among the different services? [HCxHF table];
- How are the particular health care services or goods financed? For example, what share of the spending on inpatient care is covered by compulsory insurance, voluntary insurance and out-of-pocket (OOP) payments? (HCxHF table);
- How are the resources of the different financing schemes allocated among the different groups of beneficiaries, such as different groups of diseases? (BeneficiariesxHF table);
- "Where does the money go?" From which providers are the services purchased under the particular financing schemes? (HPxHF table);
- How is health care financing managed in a country? What kind of institutional arrangements govern the funds of financing schemes? What changes have occurred in the institutional arrangement of health care financing in a given period? (HFxFA table).

Main concept

Summary of the accounting framework for health care financing

The aim of the accounting framework for health care financing is to provide a clear and transparent picture of a country's key transactions (flows) and the structure of its health financing system. A comprehensive accounting of the financing flows requires tools for accounting the transactions of revenue-raising and resource-allocation, as well as the institutional units involved.

The accounting framework for health financing consists of the following main components:

- Key concepts and definitions;
- Classifications (Chapters 7 and 8 and Annex D);
- Accounts (tables): accounts for the allocation of resources; and accounts for revenue-raising (Chapter 15 and Annex D);
- Key indicators;
- Accounts for sectoral analysis of the main health care financing schemes and institutional units (Annex D).

Key concepts

The framework for health care financing under SHA 2011 does not intend to show all the complexity and all the details of a health financing system. Instead, it focuses on the most important issues from the perspective of accounting for health expenditure.

Key concepts under SHA 2011 for describing the structure of the financing system and its key transactions are as follows:[4]

- *Health care financing schemes* as the main "building blocks" of the functional structure of a country's health financing system: the main types of financing arrangements through which health services are paid for and obtained by people. Examples include direct payments by households and third-party financing arrangements, such as social health insurance, voluntary insurance, etc. Although the financing schemes in this framework are key for purchasing health care, they also include the rules for other functions, such as the collection and pooling of the resources of the given financing scheme.[5]
- *Types of revenues* of health care financing schemes: the approach used to identify, classify and measure the mix of revenue sources for each financing scheme (for example, social security contributions used to fund the purchases by social security schemes and grants to sustain the non-profit organisation schemes). Measurement of the revenue sources of each financing scheme, as well as for the system as a whole, provides essential information to policy makers, particularly on the mix of public and private expenditures (see Chapter 8).
- *Institutional units* of health care financing systems that may play the role of providers of revenues for financing schemes (such as households and corporations); and/or the role of financing agents that manage one or more financing schemes. *Financing agents* are institutional units that administer health financing schemes in practice: they implement the revenue collection and/or the purchasing of services. Examples include local governments, social insurance agencies, private insurance companies, non-profit organisations and so on. (The structure of the financing agents does not always reflect

the functional arrangements to cover the purchasing and paying strategies in health systems.)

Figure 7.1 shows the relationships between these key entities of the health financing system.

Figure 7.1. **A graphical representation of SHA 2011 financing framework**

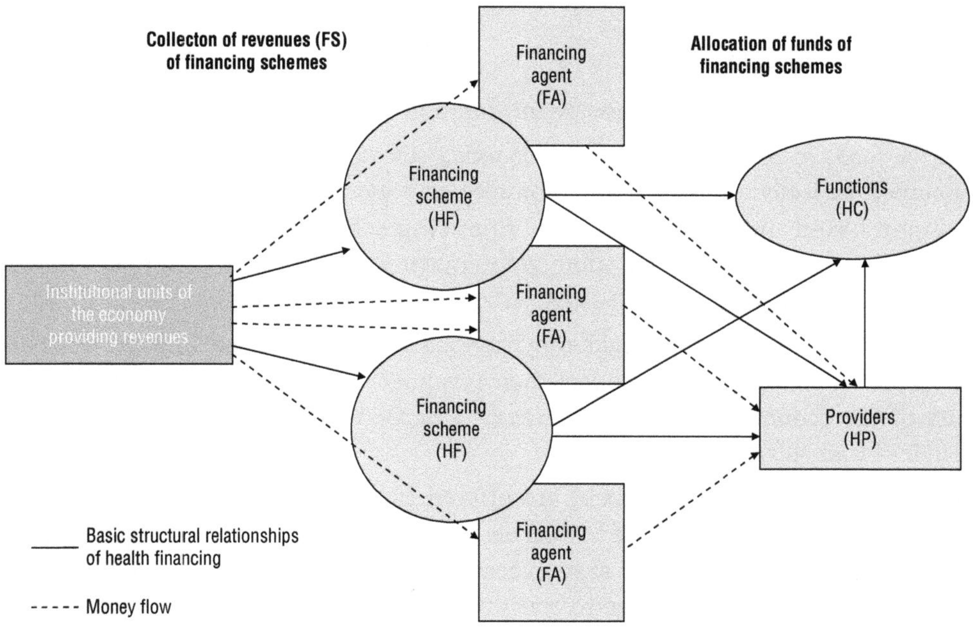

Source: IHAT for SHA 2011.

The key concepts for describing the structure of the health financing system under SHA 2011 are based on measuring *a)* the expenditure of *health care financing schemes*, under which goods and services are purchased directly from health care providers, on the one hand, and *b)* the types of revenues of health care financing schemes, on the other hand (such as government domestic revenues, social insurance contributions, voluntary prepayments and so on). Health care financing schemes are perceived here as the main "building blocks" of the structure of a country's health financing system: they are the main types of financing arrangements through which people can get access to health care, for example government schemes, social insurance and voluntary insurance. Financing agents are perceived here as the institutional units that operate the financing schemes in practice. There is not necessarily a one-to-one correspondence between financing schemes and financing agents. For example, in the Slovak Republic in 2009 the compulsory social insurance was managed by two government-owned agencies and four commercial insurance companies. In the Netherlands, private insurance companies operated compulsory private insurance schemes and voluntary insurance at the same time.[6] In this case, the insurance corporations follow two different types of regulation. For example, they have to accept everybody under the compulsory health insurance, but may apply risk-related premiums and refuse individuals under the voluntary insurance.

There is a need to clearly distinguish, on the one hand, the concepts that make it possible to analyse the financing of the consumption of health care goods and services and, on the other hand, the data collection processes. Health care financing schemes (HF) are the key units for the analysis of financing the consumption of health care goods and services, while the data concerning the relevant transactions may be collected either from financing agents operating the different financing schemes or from the providers, depending on countries' statistical systems. To put it another way: the categories of health care financing schemes are key analytical units of SHA 2011, for which data are collected from financing agents or providers (see the section on *Specific conceptual issues* later in this chapter for further details).

Classifications and tables

Health accounts tables can provide information on:

- *How the funds of particular health care financing schemes are allocated;* What services are consumed by individuals or the community as a whole, and from what providers are they purchased under the particular financing schemes? (HCxHF and HPxHF and HCxHPxHF). What institutional units are managing the purchase of services under the particular financing schemes? (HFxFA, HCxHFxFA and HPxHFxFA).
- *How the revenues of particular health care financing schemes are raised:* In what ways do the particular financing schemes collect their revenues? (HFxFS). From which institutional units of the economy are the revenues of a particular financing scheme mobilised? (HFxFS.RI; and HFxFS.RI tables).

Sectoral accounts (see Annex D) are offered as tools for country-specific analysis. Sectoral accounts make it possible to analyse the main health care financing schemes and institutional sectors of the health system separately. Sectoral accounts involve a different organisation of the data, closer to national accounting criteria. They can provide information from the perspective of a given financing scheme or institutional unit (on a national accounting basis, *e.g.* central government, households) that cannot be directly gained from any of the SHA tables.[7] For example, a sectoral account of the government presents – in the form of a T-account – the total health-specific revenues (on the right-side of the T-account) and expenses of government, including both payment to providers and transfers made by the government to other financing schemes (on the left-side of the T-account).

Table 7.1 shows the key changes in the accounting framework of health financing in SHA 2011 compared with SHA 1.0. The use of "health care financing" as the general term in SHA 1.0 proved to be too vague, as in a wider sense it may include financing schemes and their revenues, as well as financing agents. Financing agents as a concept remains largely unchanged from the *Producers Guide*. Based on the relevant health policy literature, the SNA and ESSPROS, "health care financing schemes" is regarded as a more suitable term for labelling HF.

The financing framework:

- Is based on the concept of the *financing scheme*, and is analysed through: the financing schemes, the revenue sources of each scheme; and the institutional units (financing agents) managing the schemes;
- Distinguishes between the institutional sectors of the economy providing resources to financing schemes and the flow of these resources, that is, the types of revenues of health care financing schemes (mechanisms of revenue-raising);

Table 7.1. **Key health financing concepts and classifications in SHA 2011 and SHA 1.0/*Producers Guide***

Key concepts	
SHA 2011	SHA 1.0/PG
Health care financing schemes (HF) **Financing agents (institutional units implementing/managing financing schemes) (FA)** **Revenues of health care financing schemes (FS)**	**Health care financing (HF under SHA 1.0) Source of funding (HF under SHA 1.0)** **Financing agent (HF in PG)**
Institutional units of the economy[8] providing the revenues of the financing schemes	Financing sources defined as institutional units (FS under PG)
Classifications	
SHA 2011	SHA 1.0/PG
ICHA-HF Classification of health care financing schemes **ICHA-FA Classification of financing agents**	**ICHA-HF** Classification of health care financing (SHA 1.0) Classification of financing agents (PG)
ICHA-FS Classification of revenues of health care financing schemes	ICHA-FS Classification of financing sources (PG) defined as institutional units

Source: IHAT for SHA 2011.

- Changes the focus from "financing sources" as institutions to the types of revenues of health care financing schemes (transactions), as this is more relevant for health policy analysis;
- Distinguishes between financing schemes (HF) and the institutional units (financing agents: FA) that manage them;
- Interprets financing schemes (HF) as the key functional components of the health financing system, and hence connects them to providers and health care functions in the tri-axial system of the SHA;
- Allows for a distinction between the different roles that institutional units such as the government and households play in a health system (see Figure 7.5);
- Provides possibilities for national analysis to show the relationship *i)* among the institutional units providing revenues, the types of revenues and the financing schemes; *ii)* among financing schemes and financing agents; *iii)* among financing schemes, financing agents and health care providers; *iv)* among financing schemes, financing agents and health care functions;
- Provides possibilities for national analysis to link the SHA financing analysis to other statistical systems, *e.g.* to prepare sectoral accounts of the most important financing schemes or financing agents.

In a simple health financing system, there may be one-to-one correspondence among revenues of schemes, financing schemes and financing agents. For example, the National Health Service in a country may be financed only from general government revenues and operated by government units. However, neither theoretically nor in practice is this a typical case. A financing scheme may raise its revenues from several sources, and it can be operated by more than one type of institutional unit (financing agents). For example, social health insurance may raise its revenues not only from contribution payments by employees and employers, but also from transfers from the general government budget. Furthermore, a social health insurance scheme may be operated by a government unit and private insurance companies at the same time.

The definitions of the categories of health care inancing schemes in ICHA-HF are intended to facilitate the reporting of comparable, policy-relevant expenditure data across countries and over time. It should be emphasised that the interpretation of ICHA-HF as a classification of financing schemes would *not* require major changes to the current reporting practice of most countries, in particular those with a one-to-one correspondence between the financing agent and financing scheme. In fact, the revised categories of ICHA-HF in many cases provide a better alignment with current country practices of reporting health expenditure. The revised definition and categories of ICHA-HF are relevant from a health policy point of view and are in accordance with the dominant view of health financing in the health policy literature.

The SHA 2011 HF classification provides additional detail for some of the categories, in particular for voluntary insurance. The relevance of the detailed categories to particular countries will differ according to the specific characteristics of their health care systems.

The concept and main categories of health care financing schemes

Each country's health financing system consists of several "building blocks" in the form of a set of sub-systems or financing arrangements.[9] Key characteristics of a financing sub-system are its coverage (who is entitled to which services) and the features of the basic health financing functions: the collection of funds, the pooling of funds and the purchasing/paying for health services (*i.e.* the allocation of funds to providers and services) (Kutzin, 2001; Mossialos and Dixon, 2002; WHO, 2000). A financing sub-system may involve a mix of contribution mechanisms and a mix of purchasing methods and organisations. For example, social insurance schemes may involve not only compulsory insurance contributions but also transfers from government general revenues.

The legal basis of financing schemes

It is important to consider the legal basis of financing schemes to distinguish compulsory social insurance from compulsory private insurance. Third-party financing schemes may be established and operated as follows: through public law and publically operated; through private law and privately operated; or through public law and privately operated.[10]

- A third-party financing scheme may be established by a specific public law with the purpose of providing protection against the financial risks of ill-health for the society as a whole, or for specific groups in society (employed persons, the most vulnerable groups, etc.). The operation of the financing scheme is also regulated by public law and the operating rules of the institutions involved differ in many respects from the operation of the market economy (government schemes, social health insurance).
- A third-party financing scheme may be created by private economic actors and operated under private law. An example is voluntary health insurance.
- A third-party financing scheme may be established by a specific public law with the purpose of providing protection against the financial risks of ill-health for the society as a whole, or for specific groups in society. However, whether the purchase of a contract is needed is decisive in distinguishing between compulsory private insurance and social health insurance. The day-to-day operation of the financing scheme (involving many elements of the relationship between the insuree and the insurer) is regulated under private law (*e.g.* compulsory private health insurance in the Netherlands).

Criteria for distinguishing the categories of financing schemes

The following list contains the main criteria for distinguishing the different health care financing schemes:

- Resident or non-resident (foreign) scheme with mandatory or voluntary coverage (mode of participation);
- Entitlement – contributory or non-contributory (basis for entitlement);
- Compulsory or voluntary contributions;
- Contribution prepaid or made at the time of service use;
- Pooling is interpersonal or solely for the individual or family;
- Purchase of insurance policy needed or not

The key distinguishing characteristics, from a policy perspective, are:

- Whether participation is compulsory by law (or government regulation) or voluntary; and
- Whether or not entitlement is based on a contribution (made by or on behalf of the covered individuals) or on another criterion, such as citizenship, residency, income/ poverty status, etc.

SHA 2011 uses the terms "compulsory" or "mandatory" in the sense of compulsory by law (or government regulation).

However, there are some complex financing arrangements that require further categories of participation and entitlement.

The *mode of participation* refers to the relationship between the individuals (residents of a country) and the different financing schemes, which leads to the following categories:

- Compulsory/mandatory:
  - Coverage of the population is automatic, universal for all citizens/residents (for example, national health services);
  - Participation (contribution payment) is mandatory by law for all of the population or for defined groups within the population (social health insurance or compulsory private insurance).
- Voluntary:
  - Coverage of individuals or groups is at the discretion of individuals or firms (*e.g.* individual- or group-based voluntary health insurance).

The *basis for benefit entitlement* refers to the general conditions (basic rules) for access to care under the different financing schemes. An individual's access to health services under a financing scheme may be:

- Non-contributory: defined by constitution or law (citizens/residents, or defined individuals or groups within the country) and not linked to a specific contribution payment;
- Contributory: defined by law/government regulation and requires a contribution payment made by or on behalf of the covered individual (*e.g.* social health insurance);
- Discretionary: based on the *discretion* of a private entity (charity foundation, employer, foreign entity).

The *method for raising funds* is the mechanism through which the revenues of a particular financing scheme are set and collected. The main types are: government domestic revenues, mandatory income-related insurance contributions, mandatory non-income related premiums, voluntary insurance premiums (risk-related or non-risk-related), other domestic voluntary transfers, foreign transfers and so on. The classification of revenues of health care financing schemes (see Chapter 8) provides only the main types of revenues and does not distinguish several aspects mentioned (*e.g.* between income-related or non-income related insurance premiums). The key distinctions are:

- Compulsory:
  - Taxation and other sources of general government revenues;
  - Compulsory prepayment (*e.g.* social health insurance, compulsory private insurance, compulsory Medical Savings Accounts – MSAs).
- Voluntary:
  - Voluntary health insurance and out-of-pocket payments.

The *mechanism and extent of the pooling and re-allocation of funds* are defined by the regulations of the given scheme. The main types may be income-related contributions pooled at national level; mandated community rating of premiums at national level; community rating of premiums at a local level (financing agent level); and risk-related contributions. In the case of decentralised sub-systems (both health insurance and tax-financed systems), mechanisms may exist for the re-allocation of the revenues raised. In the case of household out-of-pocket payments, no pooling is involved. The key distinctions are:

- Pooled across individuals:
  - Geographic level, such as national or sub-national;
  - Scheme level, such as by insurance fund or "programme".
- No inter-personal pooling:
  - Out-of-pocket payments, compulsory medical savings accounts.

Table 7.2 summarises the main characteristics of financing schemes according to the above criteria. Figure 7.2 presents a "criteria-tree" showing how the combination of these criteria defines the main categories of health care financing schemes. The "criteria-tree" provides a precise algorithm to help experts categorise the components of a country's health financing system.

The classification of financing schemes also fulfils the key statistical requirements of classifications, i.e. that the categories are mutually exclusive.

The label of HF.1.2.1 and the criteria tree contain some simplifications: the label HF.1.2.1 *Social health insurance schemes* does not show that Social health insurance schemes does include those social security programmes in which the payment for health services is complementary to the main types of benefits, such as pension and unemployment benefits. These social security schemes are not labelled as health insurance in the national practice of the countries concerned (for more detail, see the section on HF.1.2.1).

To facilitate the definition of a financing scheme, the criteria and the decision tree linked to them are presented below. The logic of this tree is to comply with a very relevant rule: each scheme can be classified only once. The classificatory criteria should be as clear as possible so that each scheme can be classified in only one position.

Table 7.2. **Main criteria of health care financing schemes**

	Mode of participation	Benefit entitlement	Basic method for fund-raising	Pooling
HF.1.1. Government schemes	Automatic: for all citizens/ residents; or a specific group of the population (*e.g.* the poor) defined by law/government regulation.	Non-contributory, typically universal or available for a specific population group or disease category defined by law (*e.g.* TB, HIV, oncology).	Compulsory: budget revenues (primarily taxes).	National, sub-national, or programme level.
HF.1.2.1 Social health insurance	Mandatory: for all citizens/ residents; or a specific group of the population defined by law/government regulation. In some cases, however, the enrolment requires actions to be taken by the eligible persons.	Contributory: based on payment by or on behalf of the insured person.	Compulsory: non-risk-related health insurance contribution. Insurance contributions may be paid by the government (from the state budget) on behalf of some non-contributing groups of the population, and the government may also provide general subsidies to the scheme.	National, sub-national, or by scheme; with multiple funds, extent of pooling will depend on risk-equalisation mechanisms across schemes,
HF.1.2.2 Compulsory private insurance	Mandatory: for all citizens/ residents; or a specific group of the population defined by law/government regulation.	Contributory: based upon a purchase of an insurance policy from a selected health insurance company (or other agency involved).	Compulsory health insurance premiums. Tax credits may also be involved.	National, sub-national, or by scheme; with multiple funds, extent of pooling will depend on risk-equalisation mechanisms across schemes. Also depends on the extent of regulation of premium, and standardisation of benefits across schemes.
HF.1.3 Compulsory Medical Saving Accounts (CMSA)	Mandatory: for all citizens/ residents; or a specific group of the population defined by law/government regulation.	Contributory: based upon the purchase of MSAs; persons having MSAs can, however, only use the money saved, regardless of whether the saving covers the costs of the care necessary.	Compulsory, defined by law (*e.g.* as percent share of income).	No inter-personal (except perhaps family members).
HF.2.1 Voluntary health insurance schemes	Voluntary.	Contributory: based upon the purchase of voluntary health insurance policy (usually on the basis of a contract).	Usually non-income-related premium (often directly or indirectly risk-related). Government may directly or indirectly (*e.g.* tax credits) subsidise.	Scheme level
HF.2.2 Non-profit institutions financing schemes	Voluntary.	Non-contributory, discretionary.	Donations from the general public, governments (budget of national government or foreign aid) or corporations.	Varies across programmes, but typically programme level.
HF.2.3 Enterprise financing schemes (other than employer-based insurance)	Voluntary choice of particular corporation, with coverage based on employment at such a firm (*e.g.* compulsory occupational health care).	Non-contributory, discretionary with regard to the type of services, though may sometimes be specified by law.	Voluntary: choice of the firm to use its revenues for this purpose.	At an individual enterprise level.
HF.3 Household out-of-pocket expenditure	Voluntary: willingness to pay of the household.	Contributory: service provided if individual pays.	Voluntary: household disposable income and saving.	No inter-personal pooling.
HF.4 RoW financing schemes	Compulsory or voluntary.	Criteria set by foreign entities.	Grants and other voluntary transfers by foreign entities.	Varies across programmes.

Source: IHAT for SHA 2011.

- The initial question is whether the scheme is based in the country or abroad. The rest of the world financing schemes refer to schemes set abroad (generated and regulated abroad). Resident schemes are classified regardless of the origin of their resources.
- For both cases, resident and foreign (rest of the world schemes), the next classificatory criterion is based on the mode of participation. Notably the compulsory coverage is related to government schemes and compulsory pre-paid schemes. Their further classification is based on whether the characteristics of the benefit entitlement are based on contributions.

The voluntary inclusion is classified based on the prepayment and its coverage, *i.e.* linked to contributions, and to cost-sharing.

Figure 7.2. **Criteria tree for health care financing schemes**

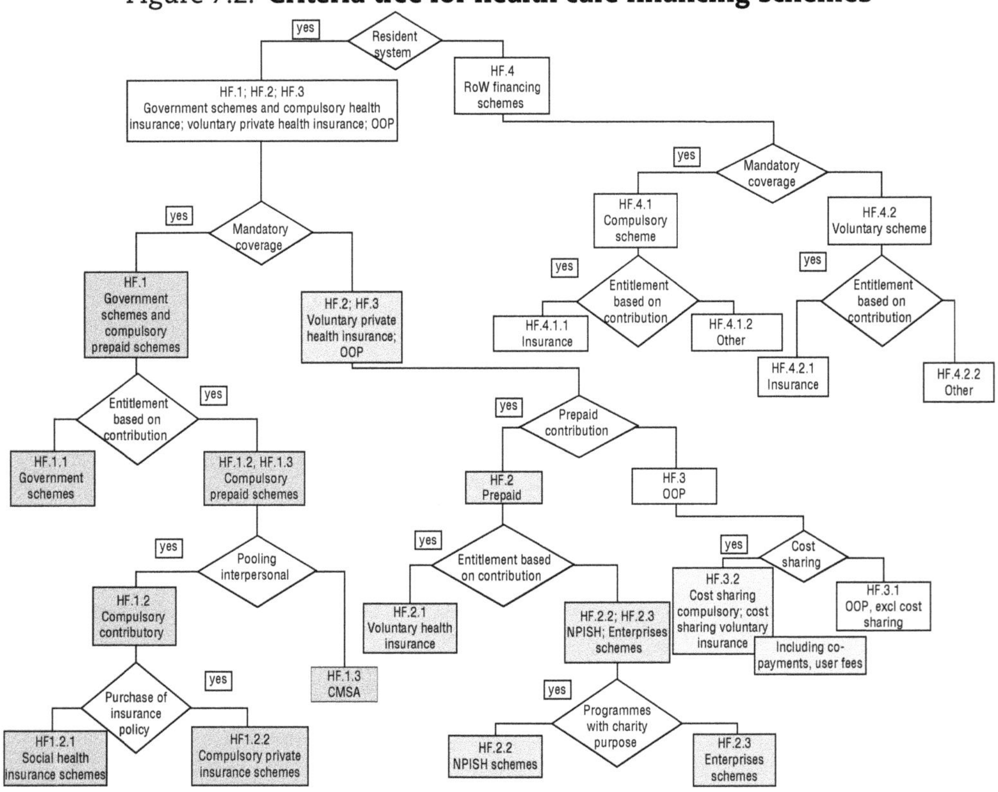

Source: IHAT for SHA 2011.

Definition of health care financing schemes[11]

> **Health care financing schemes are structural components of health care financing systems: they are the types of financing arrangements through which people obtain health services. Health care financing schemes include direct payments by households for services and goods and third-party financing arrangements.** Third party financing schemes are distinct bodies of rules that govern the mode of participation in the scheme, the basis for entitlement to health services and the rules on raising and then pooling the revenues of the given scheme.

Table 7.3 shows the full HF classification.[12]

Table 7.3. **Classification of health care financing schemes**

Code	Description
HF.1	**Government schemes and compulsory contributory health care financing schemes**
HF.1.1	**Government schemes**
HF.1.1.1	Central government schemes
HF.1.1.2	State/regional/local government schemes
HF.1.2	**Compulsory contributory health insurance schemes**
HF.1.2.1	Social health insurance schemes
HF.1.2.2	Compulsory private insurance schemes
HF.1.3	**Compulsory Medical Saving Accounts (CMSA)**
HF.2	**Voluntary health care payment schemes**
HF.2.1	**Voluntary health insurance schemes**
HF.2.1.1	Primary/substitutory health insurance schemes
HF.2.1.1.1	Employer-based insurance (other than enterprises schemes)
HF.2.1.1.2	Government-based voluntary insurance
HF.2.1.1.3	Other primary coverage schemes
HF.2.1.2	Complementary/supplementary insurance schemes
HF.2.1.2.1	Community-based insurance
HF.2.1.2.2	Other complementary/supplementary insurance
HF.2.2	**NPISH financing schemes**
HF.2.2.1	NPISH financing schemes (excluding HF.2.2.2)
HF.2.2.2	Resident foreign agencies schemes
HF.2.3	**Enterprise financing schemes**
HF.2.3.1	Enterprises (except health care providers) financing schemes
HF.2.3.2	Health care providers financing schemes
HF.3	**Household out-of-pocket payment**
HF.3.1	**Out-of-pocket excluding cost-sharing**[13]
HF.3.2	**Cost sharing with third-party payers**
HF.3.2.1	Cost sharing with government schemes and compulsory contributory health insurance schemes
HF.3.2.2	Cost sharing with voluntary insurance schemes
HF.4	**Rest of the world financing schemes (non-resident)**
HF.4.1	**Compulsory schemes (non-resident)**
HF.4.1.1	Compulsory health insurance schemes (non-resident)
HF.4.1.2	Other compulsory schemes (non-resident)
HF.4.2	**Voluntary schemes (non-resident)**
HF.4.2.1	Voluntary health insurance schemes (non-resident)
HF.4.2.2	Other schemes (non-resident)
HF.4.2.2.1	Philanthropy/international NGOs schemes
HF.4.2.2.2	Foreign development agencies schemes
HF.4.2.2.3	Schemes of enclaves (*e.g.* international organisations or embassies)
Memorandum items	
Financing agents managing the financing schemes	
HF.RI.1.1	Government
HF.RI.1.2	Corporations
HF.RI.1.3	Households
HF.RI.1.4	NPISH
HF.RI.1.5	Rest of the world
Financing schemes and the related cost-sharing together	
HF.RI.2	Government schemes and compulsory contributory health insurance schemes together with cost-sharing (HF.1 + HF.3.2.1)
HF.RI.3	Voluntary health insurance schemes together with cost-sharing (HF.2+HF.3.2.2)

Source: IHAT for SHA 2011.

The definition of health care financing schemes calls for further clarification. In correspondence with the ESSPROS, the body of rules referred to in this definition may be established *de jure*, by virtue of laws, regulation or contracts, or *de facto*, by virtue of administrative practice. *De facto* schemes include, for example, occupational health programmes set up by employers.

Table 7.4 compares HF classification under SHA 2011 with that of SHA 1.0. It is emphasised again that there is a difference between SHA 2011 and SHA 1.0 concerning the concept of HF: the HF categories under SHA 2011 are types of financing schemes, while the HF categories under SHA 1.0 were a mixture of schemes (such as private social insurance) and institutional units (such as private insurance enterprises). Table 7.4 does not show the fourth-digit or memorandum items.

Table 7.4. **ICHA-HF in SHA 2011 in comparison to SHA 1.0**

ICHA-HF classification of health care financing schemes SHA 2011		ICHA-HF classification of health care financing SHA 1.0	
HF.1	**Government schemes and compulsory contributory health care financing schemes**	**HF.1**	**General government**
HF.1.1	**Government schemes**	**HF.1.1**	**General government excluding social security funds**
HF.1.1.1	Central government schemes	HF.1.1.1	Central government
HF.1.1.2	State/regional/local government schemes	HF.1.1.2	State/provincial government
		HF.1.1.3	Local/municipal government
HF.1.2	**Compulsory contributory health insurance schemes**		
HF.1.2.1	Social health insurance	**HF.1.2**	Social security funds
HF.1.2.2	Compulsory private insurance		
HF.1.3	**Compulsory Medical Saving Accounts**		
		HF.2	**Private sector**
HF.2	**Voluntary health care payment schemes (other than OOP)**		
HF.2.1	**Voluntary health insurance schemes**		
HF.2.1.1	Primary/substitutory health insurance schemes	HF.2.1	Private social insurance
HF.2.1.2	Complementary/supplementary voluntary insurance schemes	HF.2.2	Private insurance enterprises (other than social insurance)
HF.2.2	**NPISH financing schemes**	HF.2.4	NPISH (other than social insurance)
HF.2.3	**Enterprise financing schemes**	HF.2.5	Corporations (other than health insurance)
HF.2.3.1	Enterprises (except health care providers) financing schemes		
HF.2.3.2	Health care providers financing schemes		
HF.3	**Household out-of-pocket payment**	HF.2.3	Private household out-of-pocket expenditure
HF.3.1	Out-of-pocket excluding cost-sharing	HF.2.3.1	Out-of-pocket excluding cost-sharing
HF.3.2	Cost sharing with third-party payers:	HF.2.3.2	Cost sharing: central government
HF.3.2.1	Cost sharing with government schemes and compulsory contributory health insurance	HF.2.3.3	Cost sharing: state/provincial government
		HF.2.3.4	Cost sharing: local/municipal government
HF.3.2.2	Cost sharing with voluntary insurance schemes	HF.2.3.5	Cost sharing: social security funds
		HF.2.3.6	Cost sharing: private social insurance
		HF.2.3.7	Cost sharing: other private insurance
		HF.2.3.9	All other cost sharing
HF.4	**Rest of the world financing schemes**	**HF.3**	**Rest of the world**
HF.4.1	Compulsory schemes (non-resident)		
HF.4.1.1	Compulsory health insurance schemes (non-resident)		
HF.4.1.2	Other schemes (non-resident)		
HF.4.2	Voluntary private schemes (non-resident)		
HF.4.2.1	Voluntary health insurance schemes (non-resident)		
HF.4.2.2	Other schemes (non-resident)		

Source: IHAT for SHA 2011.

Explanatory notes to the ICHA-HF classification of health care financing schemes

HF.1 Government schemes and compulsory contributory health care financing schemes

This category includes all schemes aimed at ensuring access to basic health care for the whole society, a large part of it, or at least some vulnerable groups. Included are:

government schemes, social health insurance, compulsory private insurance and compulsory medical saving accounts.

A key rationale for government intervention in health systems is to ensure access to basic health care for the whole society (or vulnerable social groups). This purpose can be pursued through different coverage schemes, which implies differing levels of redistribution between social groups and individuals. Health accounts are also expected to provide information for assessing how well health systems achieve this key policy goal. Therefore, for international comparability, it is important to have a general, aggregate category that includes all financing schemes that serve this goal.

HF.1.1 Government (health care financing) schemes

The characteristics of government health care financing schemes are **determined by law or by the government. A separate budget is set for the programme, and a government unit has an overall responsibility for it.** Usually, but not necessarily, government schemes are operated by government unit(s). The government schemes may also be managed by NPISH or by an enterprise.

Government (health care financing) schemes have the following characteristics:

- Mode of participation: automatic for all citizens/residents, or for a specific group of the population (*e.g.* the poor) defined by law/government regulation;
- Benefit entitlement: non-contributory, typically universal or available for a specific population group or disease category defined by law (*e.g.* TB, HIV, oncology);
- Basic method for fund-raising: compulsory; domestic revenues of government (primarily taxes). Foreign revenues may also play an important role in some lower-income countries.
- Mechanism and extent of pooling funds: national, sub-national, or programme level.

A government scheme does not necessarily cover the total price of the services and goods included in its benefit basket, that is, the scheme may involve cost-sharing with the patients through co-payments, or other forms of cost-sharing). The full costs of certain services are shared between two financing schemes: the government scheme and the OOP (cost-sharing). (The same holds true for the compulsory insurance and voluntary insurance schemes.) Obviously, only the costs covered by the government scheme are accounted under HF.1.1. As the full cost of these services also constitutes important information, the following memorandum items are included in the classification: government schemes and compulsory contributory health insurance schemes together with cost-sharing (HF.1 + HF.3.2.1); and Voluntary health insurance schemes together with cost-sharing (HF.2.1 + HF.3.2.2).

Country examples

Government health care financing schemes were the major financing schemes in fifteen OECD countries in 2009 (for example, Canada, Denmark, New Zealand, Spain, United Kingdom and so on), accounting for 55-85% of total health expenditure in these countries. These OECD health systems are primarily financed from the state budget (for example, the National Health Service of the United Kingdom), or under the responsibility of the local/regional governments in the Scandinavian countries). The universal entitlement of the population (or groups of the population) for a fairly comprehensive benefit package is defined by law.

Government financing schemes can take many forms. Some examples include:

- General government financing programmes that provide primary health coverage for the entire population, as in the OECD examples noted above, as well as where such programmes meet the same core criteria (*i.e.* universal non-contributory entitlement) but may cover far less than half of total health spending (in many low-income countries, for example);
- Programmes for specific groups of the population (for example, Medicaid in the United States, the Civil Servants Medical Benefits Scheme in Thailand, etc.);
- General government financing programmes in specific areas of the health sector, for example, public health, some aspects of prevention, investments, research, education, the HIV programme, the TB programme, etc.;
- Government expenditure on administration of the health system;
- Subsidies paid by the government *to health care providers* to cover persistent losses (included in health care expenditure) are classified in category HF.1.1;
- Health-specific conditional cash transfers to households.[14]

Government schemes that offer universal *entitlement* may still demand individual enrolment. For example, in Thailand *the Universal Coverage Scheme* (UCS), which covers 74.6% of the population and is financed solely from general tax revenue, is a government scheme with universal entitlement. To access health services under the UCS, entitled persons need to register at a public hospital responsible for managing the programme. Enrolment is not obligatory, and anyone still uninsured can register at any time.

Government schemes can involve a purchaser-provider split, and sometimes the names of schemes can be misleading. For example, in Latvia, the "State Compulsory Health Insurance Fund" is funded entirely by general budget transfers and provides coverage to all Latvian citizens on a non-contributory basis. It is thus a "government scheme", and not a social insurance scheme, despite the name of the government agency.

One specific accounting issue is the treatment of capital charges. In some countries – in an effort to increase efficiency – public hospitals may be required to pay charges to the government for the use of the physical assets. Although the payment of capital charges is a cost component of the hospital, and as such should be recorded together with the other factors of provisions (Chapter 9), it may be the case that capital charges are deducted directly out of the budget the hospitals receive from the state budget. In such circumstances, the capital charges should be added to the payment made by the government to the hospital in order to record the total expenditure of the government schemes.

Sub-categories of government schemes

Sub-categories of government schemes are:

- Central government schemes (HF.1.1.1);
- Regional/local government schemes (HF.1.1.2).

Countries may want to distinguish the regional and local level of government for national data reporting purposes. In this case, they can create relevant sub-categories under the "regional/local government schemes".

Countries may want to create further optional sub-categories, for example, by types of government programmes.

Government employees schemes

Government (or public) employees may have a separate arrangement: government may provide specific health programmes for its employees or buy private insurance. In some countries, the government reimburses its employees' health care bills and pays for their care while abroad. Optional sub-categories under government schemes can be used to account for these cases, as follows:

- HF.1.1.1.1 Central government schemes (excluding government employees schemes);
- HF.1.1.1.2 Government employees schemes.

The financing agent (*e.g.* government unit, private insurance corporation, etc.) will show the exact institutional form of the given government employees scheme.

It is not necessary to distinguish between government (or public) employees and other insurees in the case where government employees participate in the general social insurance scheme and the government pays a social insurance contribution in the same way that other employers do.

HF.1.2 Compulsory contributory health insurance schemes

Compulsory health insurance involves **a financing arrangement to ensure access to health care for specific population groups through mandatory participation and eligibility based on the payment of health insurance contributions by or on behalf of the individuals concerned.**

HF.1.2.1 Social health insurance schemes. Social health insurance is a financing arrangement that ensures access to health care based on a payment of a non-risk-related contribution by or on behalf of the eligible person. The social health insurance scheme is established by a specific public law, defining, among others, the eligibility, benefit package and rules for the contribution payment.

Social health insurance schemes have the following characteristics:

- *Mode of participation*: mandatory, either for all citizens/residents or for a specific population group defined by law/government regulations (*e.g.* formal sector employees);
- *Benefit entitlement*: contributory, based on non-risk-related payments made by or on behalf of the insured person. Family members may or may not be covered on the basis of the contributor's payment. The government may make contributions on behalf of certain defined categories of the population (*e.g.* pensioners).
- *Basic method for fund-raising*: compulsory non-risk-related health insurance contributions. Insurance contributions may be paid by the government (from the state budget) on behalf of some non-contributing groups of the population, and the government may also provide general subsidies to the scheme.
- *Mechanism and extent of pooling funds*: national, sub-national, or by scheme. With multiple funds, the extent of pooling will depend on risk-equalisation mechanisms across schemes. By using such mechanisms, it is possible to create pooling across schemes.

Traditionally, laws on social health insurance define the coverage of persons and the benefit basket to which the insured persons are entitled. Usually (but not necessarily) those who are entitled are also mandated. Entitlement for services originates from the law on social health insurance, which establishes the insurance automatically for all persons who meet the criteria. With some exceptions (*e.g.* non-residents), no individual contract between the insurance fund and the insured is involved on the basis of their contributions (including made on their behalf).[15] Membership may be legally assigned, usually based on two criteria: 1) professional status or employer; and 2) place of residence. In some countries insurees may have the right to choose an insurance fund.

One main characteristic of social insurance schemes is that contributions are not related to risk. Contributions are raised mainly through wage-related (and occasionally income-related) contributions that are shared between employers and employees. There are differences between countries with respect to: the uniformity of the rate; the ratio of employer contributions to employee contributions; the existence of an upper contribution ceiling; the existence of additional non-wage-related revenues; the calculation of contributions for non-waged persons; and the role of general government revenues in funding.

This category includes *all* social insurance schemes that provide health care services, even if their main activity is not health-related (*e.g.* some pension schemes would fall into this category). Of course, only the health-related spending of these schemes is reported under HF.1.2.1.

Country examples

Social health insurance schemes have been established in more than 60 countries all over the world (Gottret and Schieber, 2006). Social health insurance was the major financing scheme in thirteen OECD countries in 2009 (including Austria, France, Germany, Japan, Korea and the Slovak Republic). Social health insurance schemes exist in many other countries as well, though often with limited population coverage.

In some countries the law defines the entitled groups, but it is not mandatory for the eligible persons to enrol in the programme. An example is Medicare in the United States: it is mandatory to pay payroll taxes for Medicare, and every person aged 65 and over is entitled to enrol in Medicare, but enrolment is not compulsory.

In many countries with social health insurance schemes, the central budget pays a contribution on behalf of certain population groups (such as people without an income, children, etc.). For example, in Moldova the contribution made by or on behalf of covered persons is the basis of entitlement. In 2008, the central budget transfers to the National Health Insurance Company accounted for 55% of its revenues, while the payroll tax provided only 42%. Even though most of its revenues come from general government budget transfers, this is clearly a social health insurance scheme, because the basis for entitlement is contributory (the transfers are on behalf of specific individuals/groups of the population, while other groups are not covered).

The criteria provided in Table 7.2 and Figure 7.2 make clear how to categorise a financing scheme in an internationally comparable way, even when the names of the relevant agencies may be potentially confusing. The example of Latvia was shown above to be a government financing scheme, even though the name of the Financing Agent is the State Compulsory Health Insurance Agency. The mode of participation is universal, *i.e.* based on citizenship, and entitlement is non-contributory. In Estonia, conversely, the main revenue sources for the Estonian health insurance fund (EHIF) are social insurance contributions from employers and employees (called the "social tax" in Estonia). However, the government must approve the budget for the EHIF as part of its responsibility to keep the overall fiscal deficit within the Maastricht criteria. Despite this government involvement, the EHIF should be classified as a social health insurance scheme, because entitlement to benefits is determined on a contributory basis (paid by or on behalf of the insured persons).

Government may contribute to social health insurance schemes in its role as an employer. For example, in Tanzania, public service employees have to participate in the National health insurance fund, with a contribution of 3% of member's salaries made by the government as the employer and an equal 3% made by the employee.

In China, there are now three major schemes: i) the Urban employees' basic medical insurance scheme (UEBMI); ii) the New rural co-operative medical scheme (NRCMS) for the rural population; and iii) the Urban basic health insurance scheme (UBHI), covering elementary and middle school pupils, teenagers and young children, the elderly, the disabled and other nonworking urban residents. Under the UEBMI, employers and employees each pay a share of the premium, and enrolment is mandatory. For the NRCMS and the UBHI, participation is voluntary, with the government subsidising a substantial part of the premiums (80% at the end of the 2000s). Thus, only the first of these – the UEBMI – should be classified as social health insurance. Because their mode of participation is voluntary, the other two should be classified as voluntary health insurance (VHI) schemes, despite the substantial level of public subsidies. The ICHA-HF classification makes it possible to distinguish such schemes as a specific type of voluntary health insurance (HF.2.1.1.2 Government-based voluntary health insurance).

There are examples where the same agency manages different schemes. In Kyrgyzstan, for example, the same public agency (the Mandatory Health Insurance Fund, or MHIF) is the financing agent for both a "government scheme" and a "social health insurance" scheme. The MHIF manages a universal, population-based entitlement funded from general revenues, as well as a contributory-based entitlement funded from a mix of payroll tax and general budget transfers. The contributory social health insurance scheme is explicitly complementary to the non-contributory government scheme. In Slovenia, the compulsory health insurance fund (the Health Insurance Institute of Slovenia, HIIS) also sells complementary voluntary health insurance, which is in competition with insurance offered by private companies. Thus, the HIIS manages the social health insurance scheme and one of the voluntary health insurance schemes in the country.

HF.1.2.2 Compulsory private insurance schemes. Compulsory private insurance is a financing arrangement under which all residents (or a large group of the population) are obliged to take out health insurance with a health insurance company or health insurance fund, meaning that the purchase of private coverage is mandatory. The insurance is established by (*i.e.* entitlement for services is based on) an insurance contract/ agreement between the individual and the insurer.

Compulsory private insurance schemes have the following characteristics:

- Mode of participation: mandatory, either for all citizens/residents, or for a specific group of the population obligated by law/government regulation to purchase a health insurance policy (*e.g.* formal sector employees);
- Benefit entitlement: contributory, based upon the purchase of an insurance policy from a selected health insurance company (or other agency involved);
- Basic method for fund-raising: compulsory health insurance premiums, sometimes partially or fully subsidised by the government, including the possible use of tax credits;[16]

- Mechanism and extent of pooling funds: national, sub-national, or by scheme; with multiple funds, the extent of pooling will depend on risk-equalisation mechanisms across schemes. This also depends on the extent of regulation of the premium and the standardisation of benefits across schemes.

Country examples

In the Dutch system introduced from 1 January 2006, the government heavily regulates the market for compulsory insurance: insurers are obliged to accept anybody for the basic package of services, and the insurance premium is unrelated to individual risks. At the same time, the day-to-day operation of health insurance is now organised under private law (Netherlands Ministry of Health, Welfare and Sport, 2005). Entitlement for services is based upon a contract between the individual and the selected health insurance company. Anyone who fails to fulfil the obligation to buy insurance becomes uninsured, and insurers are allowed to remove the non-payers from their list. The number of uninsured was estimated at around 1.7% of the population in 2009 (CBS, Statline, updated 31/08/2010).

Notes

In countries where insurance companies are financing agents for compulsory insurance, insurance companies, at the same time, also offer voluntary, complementary insurance. In this case, an insurance company acts as a financing agent for two different financing schemes. These schemes operate under different regulations.

HF.1.3 Compulsory medical savings accounts

Compulsory Medical Savings Accounts (CMSAs) mean legally compulsory MSAs, whereby the basic method for fund raising and some issues concerning the use of the account to pay for health services are regulated by the government. There is no pooling across individuals, except perhaps for family members. CMSAs have the following characteristics:

- Mode of participation: mandatory for all citizens/residents, or for a specific group of the population defined by law/government regulation;
- Benefit entitlement: contributory based upon the purchase of MSAs, persons having MSAs can, however, use only the money saved, regardless of whether the saving covers the costs of the care necessary;
- Basic method for fund-raising: compulsory, defined by law (*e.g.* as percent share of income);
- Mechanism and extent of pooling funds: no pooling across individuals, except perhaps family members.[17]

Under compulsory MSAs, it is legally compulsory to take out a medical savings account; and the minimum payments and some issues concerning the use of the accounts to pay for health services are regulated by the government. Its compulsory feature justifies categorising it under HF.1.

Although CMSAs are a form of compulsory prepayment, the absence of inter-personal pooling means that they should not be considered a sub-category of compulsory insurance. The compulsory nature of the CMSA makes it different from other types of people's savings, including the non-compulsory MSAs found in some countries, such as China and the United States. Where MSAs are voluntary, they are essentially indistinguishable as a "scheme" from other types of out-of-pocket spending (under HF.3), since the "source" of funds for such spending is household savings (or borrowing), whether or not this is from something designated as a "health" or "medical" savings account.

Country example

In 1984, Singapore introduced a system of medical savings accounts, called Medisave, and it is currently the only country in the world with CMSAs. Every employed citizen is obliged to pay 6-8% of their income – according to age – into an individual account managed by the state. Savings in the individual medical savings accounts can be used to pay for hospital costs and certain selected outpatient costs for a state-approved catalogue of services (Gottret and Schieber, 2006).

HF.2 Voluntary health care payment schemes (other than Household out-of-pocket payments)

This category includes all domestic pre-paid health care financing schemes[18] under which the access to health services is at the discretion of private actors (though this "discretion" can and often is influenced by government laws and regulations). Included are: voluntary health insurance, NPISH financing schemes and Enterprise financing schemes.

The term "compulsory scheme" refers to schemes where membership is made compulsory by the government (by law). All other schemes are considered voluntary. For instance, an employer can decide to have a group insurance for all its employees: this is considered as voluntary insurance, although for each employee participation in the insurance can be imposed by the employer.

There is one important difference between these schemes and household OOP payments that is of critical policy-relevance: the presence or absence of inter-personal and/ or inter-temporal pooling, which is also reflected in the separation between the time of payment and the time of service use. In the case of OOP payments, households must pay the whole or part of the cost of care at the time of care delivery. OOP expenditures show the *direct* financial burden of medical care for the household, which may have a catastrophic effect on its financial situation. This justifies a separate first-digit level category for voluntary private schemes (other than OOPs) and Out-of-pocket payments.[19]

HF.2.1 Voluntary health insurance schemes

Voluntary health insurance schemes are based upon the purchase of a health insurance policy, which is not made compulsory by government. Insurance premiums may be directly or indirectly subsidised by the government.

Voluntary health insurance (VHI) schemes have the following characteristics:

- Mode of participation: voluntary, at the discretion of an individual or a firm;
- Benefit entitlement: contributory: based upon the purchase of the voluntary health insurance policy (usually on the basis of a contract);
- Basic method for fund-raising: usually non-income-related premiums (often directly or indirectly risk-related); may be directly or indirectly subsidised by the government (*e.g.* through tax credits);
- Mechanism and extent of pooling funds: individual scheme level.

Voluntary health insurance is taken up and paid for at the discretion of individuals or firms. Voluntary health insurance may also be purchased by the employer.

Premiums may be either risk-rated or community-rated, but in some countries (*e.g.* France) even income-related. Voluntary insurance is usually purchased from private insurance organisations (both for-profit and non-profit), although in some cases it may also be purchased from public or quasi-public bodies. In several countries enterprises may also have their own insurance arrangements.

Sub-categories of voluntary health insurance

There are several possible aspects that distinguish different types of voluntary health insurance. These aspects may overlap or may be combined when creating sub-categories of voluntary health insurance. For example, both group policies and individual policies can provide either primary or complementary coverage. The type of coverage, that is, whether the voluntary insurance provides primary coverage or complementary coverage for an individual, is the most important factor for defining the sub-categories.

HF.2.1.1 Primary/substitutive insurance schemes. Voluntary health insurance is labelled primary coverage or "substitutive" if it covers people who are excluded from or allowed to opt out of the public system, and who are not mandated to buy private health insurance, or simply if there is no publicly mandated system available to them (as for much of the population under age 65 in the United States, for example). It is important to distinguish voluntary substitutive insurance from systems where at least some people are given the choice to either join the social health insurance or buy private insurance, but are obliged to buy some form of health insurance. In Germany until 2009, higher-income persons were allowed to "opt out" of the statutory insurance arrangement and did not have to obtain any health insurance. Since 2009, health insurance has been obligatory, and opting out is hampered by new rules on income measurement. Furthermore, a privately insured person can return to social healthcare insurance only if that person is required by legislation to hold social healthcare insurance (*e.g.* if that person's income decreases under certain conditions).

HF.2.1.1.1 Employer-based insurance. One main type of group insurance is insurance purchased by employers, through a contract between the employer (the company) and the insurance entity. The premium paid by the employer is usually risk-related at the group level, but the contributions paid by the individuals are usually not risk-related.

HF.2.1.1.2 Government-based voluntary insurance. This specific type of insurance scheme is initiated and subsidised by the government in order to provide primary coverage for specific groups of the population. Such schemes may be initiated, for example, when the government does not have the administrative capacity necessary for running a compulsory insurance. For example, in China the government has set up, operates and heavily subsidises the New rural co-operative medical scheme (NRCMS) for the rural population, and the Urban basic health insurance scheme (UBHI), which covers elementary and middle school pupils, teenagers and young children, the elderly, the disabled and other nonworking urban residents.

HF.2.1.1.3 Other primary coverage schemes. This category includes primary coverage insurance taken by individuals or group insurance other than HF.2.1.1.1 and HF.2.1.1.2. For example, insurance companies can offer group insurance to patient organisations and the like.

HF.2.1.2 Complementary or supplementary voluntary insurance schemes. Health insurance can be complementary in two ways: it can cover services excluded from the public system or it can cover cost-sharing obligations (*i.e.* user charges, co-payments, etc.) required by the compulsory insurance or government health scheme. Supplementary health insurance covers the same services as the compulsory insurance, but ensures faster access and/or enhanced consumer choice of providers (Thomson and Mossialos, 2009). Complementary and supplementary VHI can exist in the same scheme, as in Ireland, where the combined scheme covers about 50% of the population. High levels of complementary VHI have been attained in Slovenia and France, where it covers over 70% and 92% of the population, respectively, to reimburse the costs of statutory user charges (*ibid.*). Examples of supplementary VHI include private insurance in countries such as the United Kingdom and Spain.

Complementary VHI that reimburses cost-sharing by the patient can create an accounting challenge. This case should be treated similarly to cases where voluntary insurance reimburses the bill for a service not covered by compulsory insurance. The payment is considered expenditure by the voluntary insurance. Consequently, the part of cost-sharing reimbursed by voluntary insurance should be accounted as expenditure by voluntary insurance, and should not be taken into consideration under OOP payment by the households. This treatment ensures a proper attribution of health expenditures.

HF.2.1.2.1 Community-based voluntary health insurance. Community-based voluntary health insurance implicitly provides complementary or supplementary coverage in some lower- and middle-income countries, often in contexts where the individuals are legally entitled to the services of government health schemes, but where such schemes are not fully effective. Key characteristics of community-based health insurance include:

- Mode of participation: voluntary;
- Benefit entitlement: based upon contribution;
- Basic method for fund-raising: defined at local level;
- Mechanism and extent of pooling funds: at scheme level, often described as being "local community" level. While schemes may operate on a local community level, some may not be geographic in nature but instead be organised on another basis (*e.g.* the health insurance scheme of the Self-Employed Women's Association of India)

Community-based health insurance is a form (subcategory) of voluntary health insurance that exists in many low- and middle-income countries, especially in Africa and Asia (Carrin, 2003; ILO, 2005). "These schemes exist within localised communities, most often in rural areas: members make small payments to the scheme, often annually and after harvest time, and the scheme covers the fees charged by local health services." (McIntyre, 2007, p. 4)

Most community-based health insurance schemes in Sub-Saharan Africa are based on the voluntary participation of individuals and have fewer than 500 members. The population covered by these schemes is still relatively small in most low-income countries (Gottret and Schieber, 2006).

Community-based voluntary health insurance may be subsidised by the central government, as is currently the case in Rwanda.

HF.2.1.2.2 Other complementary or supplementary schemes. This includes complementary or supplementary schemes other than HF.2.1.2.1. It is possible to split this category according to the characteristics of insurance premium, such as Other complementary voluntary insurance: risk-rated premiums (HF.2.1.2.2) and Other complementary voluntary insurance: non-risk-rated premiums (HF.2.1.2.3). Such schemes may be employment/group-based or individually based.

Voluntary insurance offered by the government as an employer to its employees (civil servants) should be included here. [Note: It should be distinct from government employees schemes (HF.1.1.1.2.)].

HF.2.2 Non-profit institutions financing schemes

Non-profit institutions (NPISH) financing schemes means non-compulsory financing arrangements and programmes with non-contributory benefit entitlement that are based on donations from the general public, the government or corporations.

NPISH financing arrangements or financing programmes consist of a "quasi-set" of rules that define the mode of participation, entitlement and methods of fund-raising, and hence they can be treated as categories of financing schemes.

International institutions that have representation in the country are considered resident NPISHs and any schemes linked to these institutions are included under HF.2.2. Such institutions may include resident representations of bilateral agencies, international organisations or international NGOs (see HF.4 for further details).

NPISH financing schemes have the following characteristics:

- Mode of participation: voluntary;
- Benefit entitlement: non-contributory, discretionary;
- Basic method for fund-raising: donations from the general public, governments (budget of national government or foreign aid) or corporations;
- Mechanism and extent of pooling funds: varies across programmes but typically programme-level.

This category is proposed as a replacement for SHA 1.0 item "HF.2.4. Non-profit institutions serving households (other than social insurance)". The category of non-profit institutions has proved rather ambiguous during SHA implementation. The definition in SHA 1.0 was taken from SNA 1993: "Non-profit institutions serving households (NPISH) consist of non-profit institutions which provide goods or services to households free or at prices that are not economically significant." This definition does not allow for a clear distinction between non-profit institutions as third-party payers of health care and non-profit institutions as providers of care. For example, hospitals may have a non-profit legal status and provide services to households free of charge under a social insurance scheme, in which case, of course, the social insurance is the financing scheme and the hospital (HP.1) is the provider. The unambiguous way in which the ICHA-HF interprets financing schemes provides a starting point.

A qualitative analysis of an NGO's activity is always required in order to decide whether the given activity can be regarded as the operation of a financing scheme. A few examples are given for the different NPISH functions.

- An NPISH organisation may provide – besides their non-health activity – resources for other NPISH that carry out the financing of special health programmes. The NPISH in question does not have a direct relationship with providers of care. In this case NPISH is a provider of resources and the programme of the NPISH is the financing scheme.
- A non-profit institution may create a special fund, usually through donations to finance special types of health services, for example, to operate special facilities for the homeless, or to provide care for households affected by natural disasters or war. Donations may be provided in cash or in kind from the general public, corporations or governments. During implementation, the NPISH may pay for its own staff and also for health care providers and other entities. (For example a charity organisation may pay for a special operation for a child abroad that is not available in the home country.) In these cases the NPISH programme is a financing scheme.
- The "non-profit" institution may be the legal form through which providers receive payment, for example, from a social health insurance scheme as compensation for the services they provide. In this case the NPISH is a provider and the social health insurance is the financing scheme.

HF.2.3 Enterprise financing schemes

This category includes **primarily arrangements where enterprises directly provide or finance health services for their employees (such as occupational health services), without the involvement of an insurance-type scheme.** Therefore, this excludes employer-based insurance schemes.

Enterprise financing schemes have the following characteristics:

- Mode of participation: voluntary choice of particular enterprise/corporation, with coverage based on employment at the firm (*e.g.* compulsory occupational health care);
- Benefit entitlement: non-contributory, discretionary with regard to the type of services, though may sometimes be specified by law;
- Basic method for fund-raising: voluntary choice of the firm to use its revenues for this purpose;
- Mechanism and extent of pooling funds: at an individual enterprise level.

Compared to SHA 1.0, the change is in the label (and hence the definition) so that it better reflects the content of the data. The label in the SHA 1.0 Manual is: "Corporations (other than health insurance)". This label is not accurate, as corporations may provide revenues to other financing schemes, for example, they may pay insurance contributions or voluntary insurance premiums. The revised category better reflects the actual role of the enterprises accounted under this category (as financing schemes).

A distinction between two sub-categories is proposed: enterprise financing schemes (except health care providers); and Health care providers..

Under the special category of Health care providers financing schemes (HF.2.3.2) health care providers finance part of the services they provide to their patients from their own sources (that are additional sources to the payment they receive from the financing schemes). These are "imputed" expenditures included in health accounts in order to obtain an adequate estimation of the value of the services consumed by individuals. In fact, payments are made for the factors of health care provision by the providers or suppliers of these factors (*e.g.* pharmaceuticals), as the payment by the purchasers does not cover the full costs of providing the services concerned. For an adequate estimate of the value of the services concerned, these specific items are estimated and accounted as expenditure by Health care providers financing schemes (HF.2.3.2), and the revenues are accounted as FS. 6.2. Other revenues from corporations *n.e.c.* These specific sources may be as follows:

- Health care providers may have special revenues from economic activities other than the provision of health services (for example, lending premises, providing laundry or catering services for other institutions, or private hospitals may have revenues from interest, etc.) and they may use these revenues to cover the costs of health services they provide.
- A private hospital may incur a loss in one year. To balance revenues and expenditure, the hospital may take out a loan from a commercial bank to be repaid in subsequent periods.
- In some countries, a public hospital may accumulate arrears (unpaid bills) towards suppliers of pharmaceuticals (or other material resources). The increase in these arrears in the given accounting period can, in fact, be interpreted as additional financing raised by the provider,

Country examples

Occupational health services in several countries (*e.g.* in Hungary) are excluded from the benefit package of social health insurance, and employers are obliged to finance occupational health examinations specified by law.

HF.3 Household out-of-pocket payment

Households' out-of-pocket expenditure by definition is regarded as a financing scheme. Its distinguishing characteristic is that it is **a direct payment for health care goods and services from the household primary income[20] or savings (no third-party payer is involved): the payment is made by the user at the time of the purchase of goods or use of services.** Included are cost-sharing and informal payments (both in cash and kind).

Out-of-pocket payments (OOP) show the direct burden of medical costs that households bear at the time of service use. (This is the reason for categorising OOP as a first-digit level category of ICHA-HF.) OOP play an important role in every health care system. In lower-income countries, out-of-pocket expenditure is often the main form of health care financing.

OOP expenditure (schemes) is characterised by:

- Mode of participation: voluntary, based on the willingness and ability to pay of the individual or household, though the government or voluntary insurance scheme may specify the amount of payment that is required;
- Benefit entitlement: contributory: the service is provided if the individual pays;
- Basic method for fund-raising: voluntary, based on the decision of the household to use the services, and therefore to pay for them.[21] The government may indirectly subsidise some OOP expenditures through tax deductions or credits;

- Mechanism and extent of pooling funds: no inter-personal pooling.

From a health policy perspective, it is important to distinguish *three main types of out-of-pocket expenditure* (OOP): OOP excluding cost-sharing (HF.3.1); OOP cost-sharing with government schemes and compulsory contributory health insurance schemes (HF.3.2.1); and OOP cost-sharing with voluntary insurance schemes (HF.3.2.2). The role (share) of each of these sub-categories and the changes in the share over time provide a more detailed picture of the burden of health financing on households than does just total OOP. Furthermore, the three types may provide important information about the effect of government intervention in health financing.

Informal payments are considered as out-of-pocket-payments and reported under HF.3.1. Note: only formal cost-sharing is reported under HF.3.2 (Cost sharing with third-party payers).

Notes

A payment by the individual is not always accounted as OOP, because it may be reimbursed by voluntary insurance or covered by the government (conditional cash transfers) or a domestic or foreign NGO. In these cases, the payment for the health care is technically made by the household, but not from the household's "pocket", *i.e.* not from the household's primary income or savings. Therefore, the first step is to deduct those items that should be accounted as other than OOP, such as government schemes (conditional cash allowances), voluntary insurance, NPISH financing schemes and RoW financing schemes. Also tax credits and income tax deductions generated by health spending should be taken into account when estimating OOP.

The only possible sources of OOP are the household's income (including remittances) or savings or loans that it has taken out. (Chapter 8 provides a table for distinguishing OOP from payments made by households but not accounted as out-of-pocket payment.)

The payments from Voluntary Medical Saving Accounts for health care services or goods in the given accounting period are regarded as a special type of out-of-pocket payment, but not accounted separately from OOP. *Note*: The payments into Voluntary Medical Saving Accounts in the given accounting period are not included in the HF tables, as they are not payments for health care services or goods.

Households as an institutional sector are defined as the financing agent for household out-of-pocket payments.

It is important to distinguish households as an institutional sector and household OOP as a financing scheme. Households, as an institutional sector, play several roles in the health system: as beneficiaries, as providers of sources to third-party financing schemes (by paying taxes and/or insurance contributions and/or insurance premiums); as informal providers of care; and last but not least, as a financing agent for OOP.

The special case of household cost-sharing covered by voluntary insurance has been discussed above under complementary voluntary health insurance.

HF.4 Rest of the world financing schemes

This item comprises **financial arrangements involving institutional units (or managed by institutional units) that are resident abroad, but who collect, pool resources and purchase health care goods and services on behalf of residents, without transiting their funds through a resident scheme.** For example, a person resident in country A can buy a voluntary insurance in country B and can use that insurance to pay for services in either Country A or B. US citizens of Mexican origin, for instance, may buy health insurance in Mexico that gives them emergency cover in the United States but pays for elective treatment in Mexico.

A resident scheme has the predominant economic interest in the country for which the accounts are drawn up. It has a physical presence in the country and is under the jurisdiction of the local government (*e.g.* compulsory reporting activities). Non-resident (RoW) schemes may also operate in the country for which the health accounts are produced, but these schemes originate with and are controlled by agencies subject to foreign government jurisdiction, including, for example, aid agencies and military agencies.

Rest of the world financing arrangements are defined according to the following characteristics:

- Mode of participation: 1) mandatory, *e.g.* based on the conditions of employment (such as foreign insurance), or 2) voluntary;
- Basis for entitlement: 1) a contract between an insurance carrier and the individual, or 2) discretion of a private entity (charity foundation, employer, foreign entity);
- Method for fund raising: funds are collected and pooled abroad;
- Coverage: foreign entities usually have the freedom to design the benefits.

Note that the rest of the world usually contributes to the financing of health care in the example of a typical model economy, as international aid and other flows, by channelling the funds via government or resident NPISH agencies. This is a typical case of RoW revenue for resident financing schemes, and could thus be classified as HF.1 or HF.2 spending and RoW revenue.

International agreements strive to ensure that external funding agencies work with resident health care agencies to ensure that external resources (financing revenues) are directed towards national priorities in a co-ordinated way. There is a need for reporting to national authorities and co-ordinating with national efforts to achieve that goal and foster complementary health actions. Agencies managing external funds for aid would then be acting as residents (resident units and schemes). If SHA adjusts for international aid agreements, the external resources would be recorded as external sources (revenues) and would in most cases be executed by resident schemes, grouped as NGOs and corporations.

It is not always clear whether a foreign assistance programme should be accounted as *i)* a financing RoW source (FS), or *ii)* both as a financing RoW source and a financing RoW scheme.

In the case of enclaves, these are non-resident units that are physically located in the host territory but have immunity from the host country laws (*e.g.* international organisations and embassies). When health care for the personnel of enclaves does not require any allowance or jurisdiction of the resident country, then the foreign health scheme should be classified as a RoW financing scheme (HF.4). However, an entity created by a government under the laws of another jurisdiction is a resident unit in the host jurisdiction, and not part of the general government sector in either economy (SNA 2008, 26.43). Thus, a foreign aid programme set up by an external aid organisation to handle resources in a foreign country is to be considered as a resident NGO or corporation in that country.

Foreign assistance may be given for a specific purpose (*e.g.* an AIDS programme), and a separate organisation, also part of the foreign entity, may be established to manage the fund, which is not necessarily involved in the provision of the service.

When the scheme is part of a global or multinational entity but is operated in the country as a "branch", it is considered resident, *e.g.* an insurance agency having a local setting is resident. The key feature is that it shares permanent economic interests with local entities, as well as a physical presence; individual accounting and linkages to the rules of local governments, such as reporting, are also features of resident schemes.

However, when the scheme cannot be differentiated as a specific "branch" but is kept as a unique scheme because it is run as an indivisible operation with no separate accounts, then it is treated as a RoW scheme. The value of multinational schemes reported as RoW schemes cannot be taken as the entirety of multinational schemes, but would be based prorata on the volume of activity in the country.

Specific conceptual issues

The interpretation of "public" and "private"

In accounting for health financing, it is possible to calculate aggregate "public" and "private" expenditures using either the classification of financing schemes or the classification of revenues of financing schemes. In either case, there is some ambiguity about whether to classify revenues for or expenditures by "compulsory private" schemes as public or private.[22] SHA 2011 groups them with public expenditures:

- The calculation of expenditures by financing schemes will yield the following two major expenditure aggregates:
  - Expenditure by government schemes and compulsory contributory health care financing schemes; and
  - Expenditure by voluntary health care financing schemes.
- The calculation of expenditures by the revenues of financing schemes will yield the following two major aggregates:
  - Health spending by public and compulsory private funds;
  - Health spending by voluntary funds.

Which approach is to be taken depends on the purpose of the analysis. The main distinction between the two is that in the first approach the division is performed on the level of the schemes, and follows the HF division. This approach does not account for the sources of the funds but gives information about the extent of public regulation of the healthcare system. The second approach, on the contrary, focuses on dividing the sources that feed into the financial schemes. It thus provides information about the publicly or privately regulated revenue. In other words, if the first approach answers the question, who manages the health funds, the second approach answers the question, who pays them. The second approach (public and private calculated according to the *type of revenue*) is clearly superior for meeting the objective of reporting the share of government versus non-government expenditure in the health sector. This would, for example, ensure that the large increases in spending by the Chinese government to subsidise the NCRMS, a voluntary insurance scheme, would indeed be counted as public expenditure.

Showing "compulsory private" in a separate category allows the analyst to calculate public and private shares by either including these with government spending, or not. Within the expenditure by government schemes and compulsory contributory health care financing schemes, it is possible to separate two sub-aggregates: 1) expenditure by government and social health insurance; and 2) expenditure by compulsory private schemes (see Table 7.5).

Tables 7.5 and 7.6 provide explanations for the recommended approaches and show the relevant categories.

The categories used (instead of "public" and "private") provide a more adequate picture of the structure of spending by the current complex financing arrangements.

The categories (expenditure aggregates) of "Expenditure by government schemes and compulsory contributory health care financing schemes" and "Expenditure by voluntary health care financing schemes", however, do not take into consideration that voluntary health care financing schemes may receive revenues from government. For example, total spending by NPISH financing schemes is accounted as private expenditure – although the revenue of NPISH financing schemes may partly come from government transfers. Under the other approach (Table 7.6), all spending from government general revenues on health is accounted as spending from public funds, including transfers to private financing schemes.

Table 7.5. **Expenditure by social, compulsory private and private health care financing schemes**

	Financing schemes	Major expenditure aggregates
HF.1	**Government financing schemes and compulsory contributory health care financing schemes**	**Expenditure by government schemes and compulsory contributory health care financing schemes**
HF.1.1	Government financing schemes	Expenditure by government and social health insurance
HF.1.2.1	Social health insurance	
HF.1.2.2	Compulsory private health insurance	Expenditure by compulsory private schemes – analyst can choose whether to include these as part of aggregate public or private spending
HF.1.3	**Compulsory Medical Saving Accounts (CMSA)**	
HF.2	**Voluntary health care payment schemes (other than OOP)**	
HF.2.1	Voluntary health insurance	
HF.2.2	NPISH- financing schemes	**Private expenditure**
HF.2.3	Enterprise financing schemes	
HF.3	**Household out-of-pocket payment**	
HF.4	**Rest of the world financing programmes**	

Source: IHAT for SHA 2011.

Under the above approach, the following categories are defined:

- *Public funds* include: *i)* funds allocated from general revenues of government for government schemes; *ii)* funds created from social insurance contributions; *iii)* transfers allocated from general revenues of government to health care financing schemes other than government schemes (grants, subsidies and transfers to NPISH, etc.); and *iv)* foreign revenues of government allocated to health care;
- *Compulsory/Mandatory private funds* are funds created from compulsory private insurance premiums and payment for compulsory MSAs. The explicit identification of these types of funds enables the analyst to classify them as either public or private. The decision

Table 7.6. **Health spending from public, compulsory private and private funds**

	Revenue of financing schemes	Major expenditure aggregates
FS.1	Transfers from government domestic revenue	**Public and compulsory private funds spent on health care**
FS.2	Transfers distributed by government from foreign origin	
FS.3	Social insurance contributions	
FS.4	Compulsory prepayment (other than FS.3)	
FS.7.1.1/FS.7.1.2	Bilateral and multilateral financial transfers	
FS.7.2.1.1/FS.7.2.1.2	Bilateral and multilateral aid in kind	
FS.7.2.2.1	Foreign aid in kind: services (technical assistance (TA) by governments and international organisations	
FS.5	Voluntary prepayment	**Voluntary private funds spent on health care**
FS.6	Other domestic revenues *n.e.c.*	
FS.7.1.3	Other foreign financial transfers	
FS.7.2.1.3	Other foreign aid in goods	
FS.7.2.2.2	Foreign aid in kind: services (including TA) by private entities	
FS.7.3	Other foreign transfers (*n.e.c.*)	

Source: IHAT for SHA 2011.

about which approach (compulsory/public or private) is considered more appropriate will depend on the nature of the analysis to be performed;

- *Voluntary private funds*, including all other funds.

As already noted, the main difference between the two recommended approaches to the revised interpretation of "public" versus "private" expenditure is the treatment of transfers allocated from general revenues of government to health care financing schemes (other than government schemes). In order to determine total public spending on health, all government transfers including those to private entities need to be included.

Treatment of cost-sharing

There are three components of coverage by a third-party financing scheme (insurance or government scheme): population coverage, the service package covered and the share of the costs of the given services covered by the scheme. Cost-sharing by the patients should be considered as a component of out-of-pocket payment and should not be considered as expenditure by a third-party financing scheme. The concept, the monitoring and the assessment of financial protection require a clear distinction between the share of the costs covered by compulsory insurance (or a government scheme) and the share of the costs paid by the patients. Obviously, a high level of cost-sharing by the patients jeopardises financial protection. Thomson and Mossialos (2009) emphasised that: "Several countries have made efforts to expand population coverage ... However, the scope and depth of coverage are as important as its universality, and the trend in some countries to lower scope and depth undermines financial protection" (p. xxi).

Voluntary insurance may reimburse cost-sharing by the patient. This case should be treated similarly to the case when voluntary insurance reimburses the bill of a service not covered by compulsory insurance. The payment is considered expenditure by the voluntary insurance. Consequently, the part of cost-sharing reimbursed by voluntary insurance should be accounted as expenditure by voluntary insurance, and should not be considered as OOP payment by the households. This treatment ensures that a proper picture of financial protection is provided. It should, however, be noted that the characteristics of the coverage by the government scheme or insurance determine the household cost-sharing, which is a component of household out-of-pocket payment (OOP). The full cost of the services or goods concerned accounts for its two payer components: the third-party payer and the OOP. As the full costs of the services or goods concerned are also important information, the following memorandum items are included in the classification: government schemes and compulsory contributory health insurance schemes, together with cost-sharing (HF.1+HF.3.2.1); and Voluntary health insurance schemes, together with cost-sharing (HF.2+HF.3.2.2).

Relationship between financing schemes and financing agents

Financing agents are institutional units that manage one or more financing schemes: they collect revenues and/or purchase services under the rules of the given health care financing scheme(s). This includes households as financing agents for out-of-pocket payments.

SHA 2011 interprets financing schemes as the key components of the health financing system from the point of view of access to care, and hence connects them to providers and health care functions in the SHA's tri-axial system.

At the same time, from the point of view of the accountability of institutions in the health financing system, it is also important to consider the financing agents. Increasing accountability at the country level through improved governance and efficiency is a key policy issue. This requires an understanding of who manages the financial schemes (financial resources) and how well they do this. In other words, at the country level financing agents may be a critical element of the analysis. Table 7.7 provides a tool to illustrate the institutional arrangements of a country's financing schemes.

As already mentioned, financing agents (FA) serve as key statistical units in producing national health accounts. While financing schemes are the key units for analysing how the consumption of health care goods and services is financed, the data concerning the relevant transactions are collected either from the financing agents (FA) that operate the different financing schemes or from the providers, depending on the national statistical system. To put it another way, the categories of health care financing schemes are key analytical units of SHA 2011 with respect to which data are to be collected from financing agents (FA) or providers. Annex D provides a classification of financing agents. Table 7.7 shows the possible financing agents for the main types of financing schemes.

As already discussed, there are wide variations in the organisational settings of the basic health care financing schemes across countries. In the case of countries with complex institutional settings, it is of great importance to distinguish clearly between financing schemes and financing agents, and to clarify unambiguously the different possible roles of key institutional units involved in health financing (*e.g.* the government, the rest of the world).

In several countries there is a one-to-one correspondence between financing schemes and financing agents (Figure 7.3). For example, in Country A with a simple organisational arrangement, all government-financed care may be operated by local government units, voluntary insurance is offered by insurance companies, and households pay out-of-pocket for certain services.

The one-to-one correspondence is, however, not necessary from a theoretical point of view. Moreover, in reality, there are many countries where the relationship between

Table 7.7. **Possible financing agents for the main categories of financing schemes**

Financing schemes	Financing agents	
	Revenue-collecting agencies	Purchasing agents
Government schemes	Government unit(s)	Government units: ministries, local governments NPISH Corporations
Social health insurance schemes	Government unit National Health Insurance Agency Social health insurance funds Private insurance corporations	National Health Insurance Agency Social health insurance funds Private insurance corporations
Compulsory private insurance schemes	Government units Private insurance corporations	Private insurance corporations Public corporations
Voluntary health insurance schemes	Private insurance corporations Social health insurance funds NPISH	Private insurance corporations Social health insurance funds NPISH
NPISH financing schemes	NPISH	NPISH
Enterprise financing schemes	Corporations	Corporations
Rest of the world financing schemes	RoW	RoW NPISH Government units

Source: IHAT for SHA 2011.

financing schemes and financing agents is rather complex and has changed considerably over the past few years (Figure 7.4). For example:

- The same actor can serve as a financing agent for more than one financing scheme (*e.g.* private insurance corporations, besides offering voluntary insurance, may be involved in managing the social insurance scheme);
- Actors belonging to different institutional sectors of the economy can serve as financing agents for the same financing scheme (*e.g.* the compulsory social insurance scheme can be managed – at the same time in a given country – by both a social insurance agency and private insurance corporations);
- The same actor (*e.g.* the tax office) can act as a collecting organisation for more than one financing scheme (*e.g.* central government scheme and social insurance, etc.).

Expenditure by health care financing schemes and financing agents

While for international comparison the HCxHF and the HFxHP tables provide adequate information, for national purposes expenditure by both financing schemes and financing agents may be required. It may be possible to create sub-categories of financing schemes according to the financing agents that operate the given scheme, for example, "Central government financing schemes operated by NPISH"; "Social health insurance operated by social security funds"; or "Social health insurance operated by private insurance corporations". (A separate set of guidelines for the implementation of classifications of health care financing under SHA 2011 will provide concrete examples for this.)

This kind of table would present important information about the institutional arrangements of the particular financing schemes. The total spending by a financing scheme would be aggregated across all institutional units. When more than one type of institutional unit is involved in the operation of a given financing scheme, the table would show the role of each institutional unit.

Figure 7.3. **The relationship between financing schemes and financing agents: one-to-one correspondence**

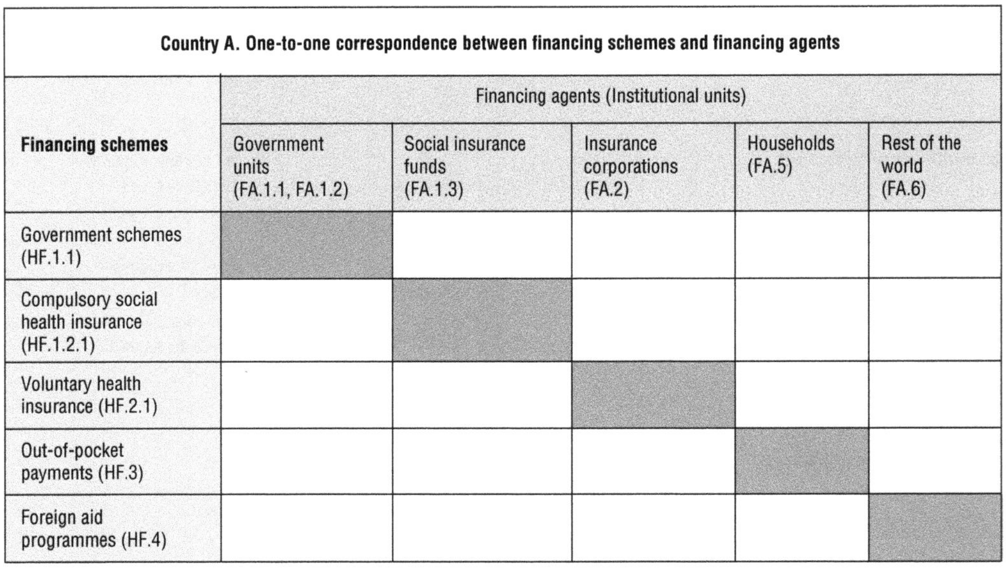

Source: IHAT for SHA 2011.

Figure 7.4. **The relationship between financing schemes and financing agents: example of a more complex institutional setting**

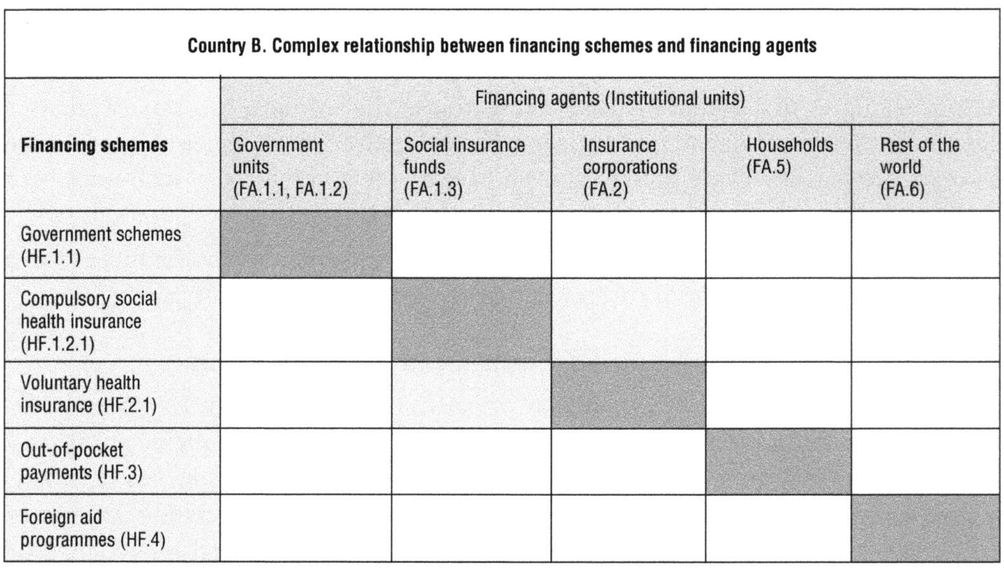

Source: IHAT for SHA 2011.

The expenditure of a financing scheme includes the spending on health care goods and services and the administration of the given financing scheme. The administration of a given financing scheme includes expenses related to revenue collection and purchasing. Therefore, if two different institutional units are involved in the revenue collection and purchasing, the administrative costs of both institutional units should be included.

This table may be used for cross-country comparison of the institutional characteristics of health financing and also for monitoring changes in the institutional arrangements of health financing schemes in countries with complex institutional arrangements, for example, changes in the institutional arrangement of compulsory insurance, or changes in the involvement of NGOs in managing government health programmes. Countries with simple institutional arrangements for health financing do not need such a table.

The relationship between financing schemes and financing agents from a data collection viewpoint

As already noted, in a statistical sense, HF is an analytical unit (similar to HC). The data collection units are the establishment units of financing agents or providers (depending on the country's statistical system) – similar to the data collection for HC, which is also collected from providers (or financing institutions).

In some countries (for example, the Netherlands), commercial health insurance companies operate both compulsory health insurance, which is heavily regulated by the government, and voluntary health insurance, which is regulated by EU regulations that allow only very limited government intervention. Units of the insurance company managing the compulsory insurance and units managing the voluntary health insurance should be considered as separate establishment units, in much the same way as inpatient and outpatient units within a hospital (despite the fact that there are units of the insurance company serving both activities).

For example, in Portugal, the main financing scheme is the National Health Service (HF.1.1 Government schemes). However, the data for preparing the table HCxHF are collected from several sources: for example, from the ACSS, which is a body of the Ministry of Health operating the National Health Service and retail sale surveys for pharmaceuticals.

Distinguishing between government schemes and government as an institutional unit

Government is involved in the operation of the health financing system – in revenue-raising, pooling and purchasing – in several different ways. Figure 7.5 provides an example of the relationship between government schemes and the involvement of government as a provider of revenues and as a financing agent. The marked boxes in the second column indicate the government financing schemes (HF.1.1.1 and HF.1.1.2); the marked boxes in the first column indicate the revenues provided by the government; and the marked boxes in the third column indicate the government units acting as financing agents for HF.1.1.1 and HF.1.1.2.

Figure 7.5 shows that:

- The government provides revenues from domestic origin (FS.1) not only for the government schemes (HF.1.1), but also for other financing schemes (*e.g.* compulsory social insurance: HF.1.2.1, voluntary health insurance HF.2.1, etc.);
- The government schemes may receive revenues from sources other than the general revenues of the government (*e.g.* foreign aid: FS.7.2);
- The central government schemes (HF.1.1.1) may be managed by different government units (FA.1.1.2; FA.1.2; FA.1.9) and have NGOs as financing agents (FA.4);
- Local government schemes (HF.1.1.2), besides the general revenues of the local government, may receive grants from the central government (FS.1.1) and grants from foreign entities (FS.7.1);
- Local government financing schemes (HF.1.1.2) may be managed by local government units (FA.1.2), other government units (FA.1.9) and NGOs (FA.4).

Figure 7.5. **An example of the relationship between government schemes, government as a provider of financial resources and government as a financing agent**

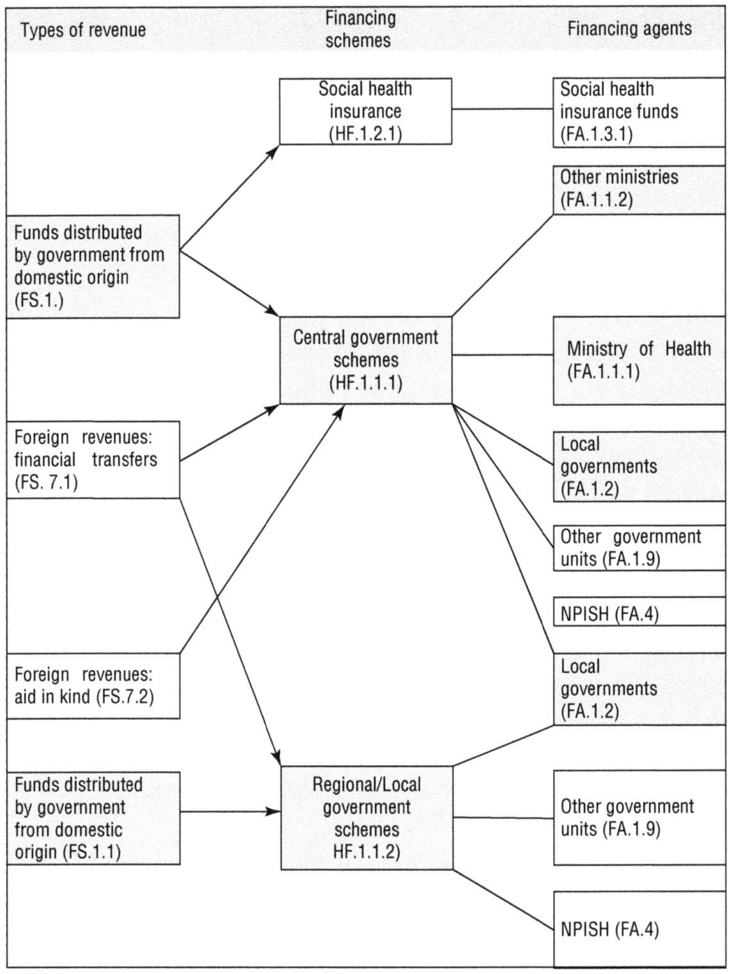

Source: IHAT for SHA 2011.

Distinguishing between rest of the world financing schemes, foreign entities as providers of revenues and foreign entities as financing agents[23]

The role of foreign resources (from international agencies, foundations, etc.) in the financing of health care may be of great importance in lower-income countries. Here only the complex relationships between the health care financing schemes, their revenue and the institutional units are discussed. The shaded boxes in Figure 7.6 indicate the different types of rest-of-the-world involvement. Figure 7.6 illustrates:

- Foreign entities are involved mainly in providing financial resources and aid in kind for domestic health care financing schemes. The rest of the world (as a provider of revenues) may include international organisations, foreign governments and other foreign entities (including family living abroad – remittances). Figure 7.6 shows only the types of revenue (and does not indicate the institutional units from which the given revenue is collected).
- RoW may provide revenues for government schemes (HF.1.1) or NPISH health programmes (HF.2.2), or a foreign entity (*e.g.* a foundation) may set up a separate health programme that – if meeting certain criteria – could be regarded as a financing scheme (HF.4).

- A foreign (non-resident) institutional unit (FA.6) may be involved in managing RoW financing schemes (for example, a foreign NGO may implement a prevention programme that is financed from foreign aid).
- In some cases providers receive external funds directly. These cases refer to RoW as sources (revenues).

Figure 7.6. **The possible roles of foreign resources and foreign (non-resident) institutional units in health financing**

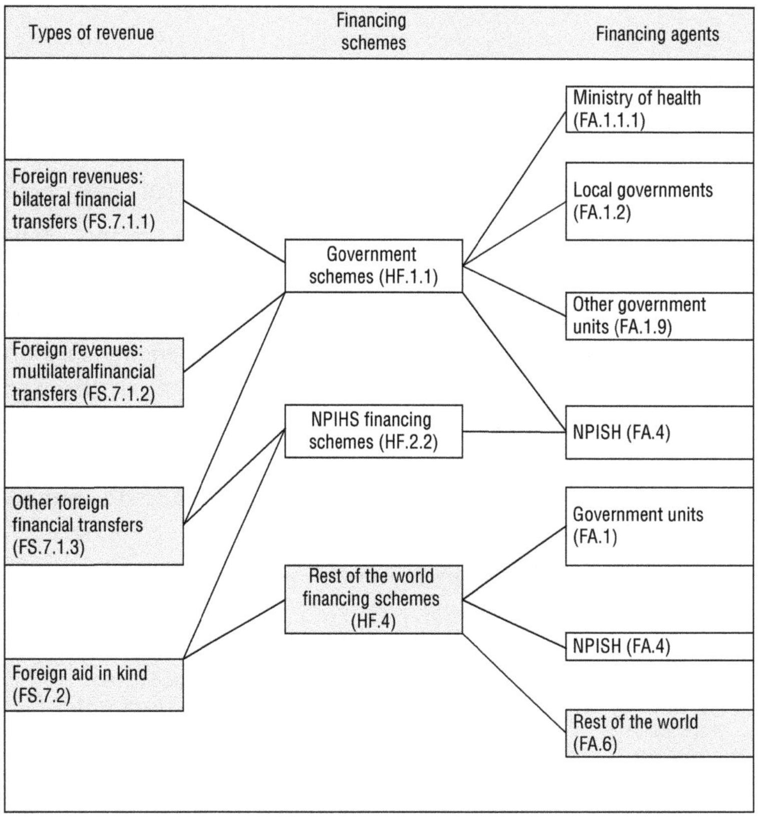

Source: IHAT for SHA 2011.

The treatment of surplus funds or deficits under SHA 2011[24]

The HCxHF and HPxHF tables show the spending by health care financing schemes in a given accounting period, while the HFxFS table refers to all revenues of health care financing schemes raised in the given period. A scheme's revenue may be greater or smaller than the expenditure on health care goods and services by the given scheme.[25] Therefore, the total expenditure in the HCxHF and HPxHF tables does not necessarily equal the total revenue in the HFxFS table. The differences between the sub-totals in HFxFS and HCxHF (revenue minus expense of each financing scheme) shows the surplus or deficit of the particular financing schemes in a given accounting period.

Social insurance schemes in several countries finance not only health care goods and services but other social services as well. In such cases, only "*health-relevant revenues*" and health-related expenditures should be taken into account. As revenues may not be fully separated between the different spending components of such social insurance schemes, a number of assumptions may be needed. It is possible to analyse the deficits and surpluses of such health insurance schemes, but this may be highly influenced by assumptions about how to calculate "health-related revenues".

An alternative tool for presenting the surplus or deficit is the table of sectoral accounts discussed in Annex D.

Relationship to other statistical systems

Figure 7.7 shows the concept of the financing scheme in the context of SHA 2011 and SNA 2008.

Main steps in adjusting SHA 1.0 or *NHA Producers Guide* of a country to SHA 2011 accounting of health financing

A *qualitative analysis* can be a good basis for the adjustment of a country's national health accounts to the SHA 2011 health financing framework. This may include:

- As a first step, clarifying the types of *health care financing schemes* (sub-systems) the country has (for example, based on Table 7.3 and the criteria tree in Figure 7.2);
- Defining the *types of revenues and financing agents for each financing scheme*. The clarification of all types of revenues and institutional units involved may require additional qualitative analysis in the case of government schemes and the rest of the world financing programmes (see Figures 7.5 and 7.6).

Figure 7.7. **Financing schemes in the context of SHA 2011 and SNA 2008**

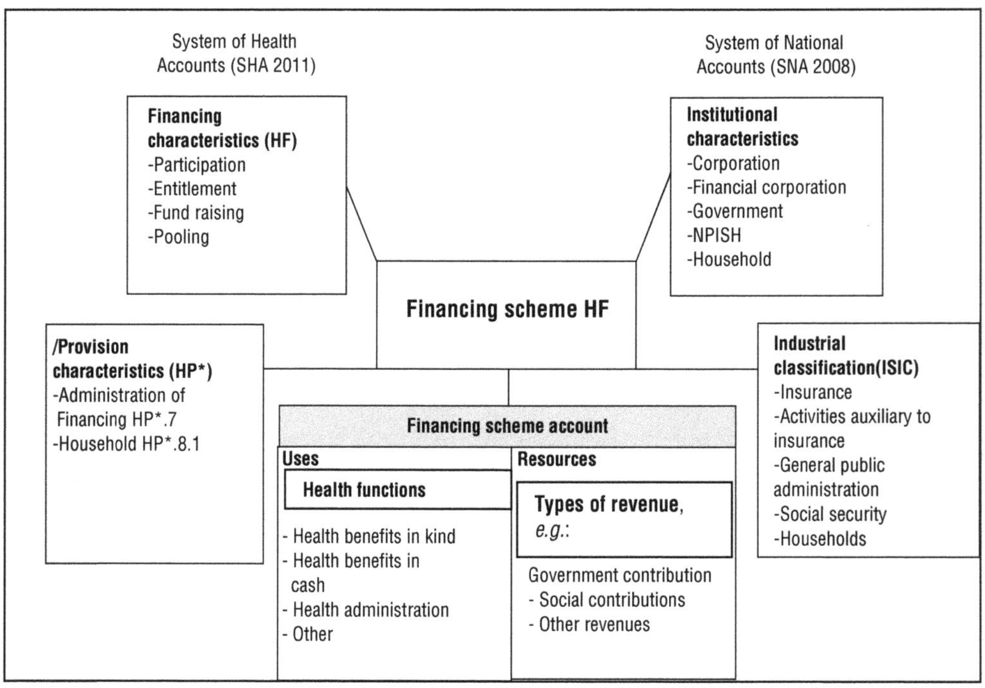

Source: IHAT for SHA 2011.

Based on this qualitative description:

- The correspondence between the SHA 1.0/PG categories of ICHA-HF used in the NHAs of the given country and the SHA 2011 categories of ICHA-HF can be made (see Table 7.4). In many cases this requires only changes in the naming;
- The country-relevant categories of the proposed classification for financing agents and classification of revenues of health financing schemes can be identified;
- Any optional tools that may be relevant to the further development of the NHAs of the given country can be chosen (see proposed optional tables and sectoral accounts);
- It can be decided whether a specific analysis of foreign assistance is desirable.

Notes

1. For countries that have found it useful to identify who is purchasing the various production factors, the HFxFP table may also be relevant. An example of this is where some non-resident entities in the rest of the world (RoW) may supply in kind (or finance) specific inputs. A central government may concentrate on the payment of human resources.
2. FS.RI refers to the institutional units providing revenues to financing schemes. These are reporting items under the FS classification. See Chapter 8 for further detail.
3. Government financing programmes, compulsory social insurance, voluntary insurance, out-of-pocket payments, foreign aid programmes, etc.
4. Definitions of these concepts are provided in the next section of the Manual.
5. Financing schemes are a flexible approach to functional financing structures, *e.g.* they can include mixed functional arrangements such as public-private partnerships.
6. Traditionally in the Netherlands, private insurance companies could execute the social health insurance, just as the health insurance funds were allowed to execute private supplementary insurance. To do so separate legal structures were mandatory for each activity. Since the change in the financing structures in 2006, this is no longer the case, although separate accounts are required for each activity.
7. The HFxFS matrix provides aggregate information about revenue collection in the whole health care sector. There may be a need for more in-depth information about the collection and use of resources (including information on deficits/surpluses) concerning the major financing schemes separately. Sectoral accounts provide a tool for this.
8. The categories of the institutional sectors in SNA (such as households, corporations, government, rest of the world) are used to represent institutional units as providers of revenues in the relevant SHA tables.
9. Gottret and Schieber (2006) proposed the following financing arrangements, which involve different risk-pooling mechanisms: Ministry of Health/National health service systems, Social health insurance systems, Community-based health insurance and Private or voluntary health insurance.
10. Generally speaking, public law governs the relationship between individuals (citizens, companies) and the state. Private law is the area of law that affects the relationships between individuals or groups without the intervention of the state or government. This distinction is often conflated.
11. The word *scheme* is widely used in different areas, including mathematics, linguistics and management, with different meanings, including: an elaborate and systematic plan of action; a system: a group of independent but interrelated elements comprising a unified whole; or a systematic or organised configuration. The term *health care financing scheme* is widely used in the health policy literature as a synonym for a health financing arrangement or a health financing sub-system.
12. Table 7.4 compares the structure of the ICHA-HF classification in SHA 2011 with that in SHA 1.0.
13. This category includes informal payments. *De facto* the cost-sharing would include informal payments. However, usually informal or under-the-table payments are not seen as cost-sharing but as genuine out-of-pocket payments.
14. Conditional cash transfers by the government (CCT) are payments that are conditioned on specific action by the recipients, *i.e.* requiring individuals receiving cash payments to undertake a specific action, for example, attendance at primary care centres for preventive interventions (childhood

immunisation and pregnancy care, such as perinatal visits and nutrition). Over the past few years, several Latin American and African countries have introduced CCT programmes to encourage health care utilisation and health-seeking behaviour. For more detail, see WHO (2008c).

15. Insured people enrol with a fund.
16. Tax credits are amounts deductible from the tax that otherwise would be payable.
17. The savings account may cover, besides the owner of the account, dependent family members, and hence, there is pooling only within this very small group. Because the savings account can be maintained over many years, it provides for inter-temporal pooling.
18. Voluntary health care payment schemes (HF.2) do not have to come from a private initiative. For example, the Thai government initiated a voluntary health insurance scheme, and the current Chinese NRCMS is also a voluntary insurance scheme that was initiated by the government.
19. While out-of-pocket expenditures are the leading cause of potentially catastrophic and impoverishing levels of health payments globally, the text here should not be read to imply that other forms of contributions do not impose a financial burden on households.
20. According to SNA, primary income is the income that resident units receive by virtue of their participation in the production process, along with income receivable by owners of financial or other assets in return for placing those assets at the disposal of other institutional units.
21. The use of the word "voluntary" here is debatable, as the government or insurance scheme may impose the obligation to co-pay for the services.
22. The current practice in using the terms "public" and "private" in health financing has some ambiguity. This is in part because the terms "public" and "private" can be (and are) used with different meanings in health statistics. SHA 1.0 defined the private sector as follows: "This comprises all resident institutional units which do not belong to the government sector." If this definition were strictly applied, compulsory private insurance and social insurance schemes executed by private insurance companies would be reported under private expenditure, together with voluntary insurance and OOP. (This obviously would not be appropriate.)
23. The arrows show the flows of revenues and the solid lines show the relationships between financing schemes and financing agents.
24. The arrows show the flows of revenues and the solid lines show the relationships between financing schemes and financing agents.
25. Under SHA 1.0/NHA tables, total current health expenditure is required to be equal in the HCxHF and HFxFS tables. The HFxFS table is expected to show the sources of the expenditure used for final consumption in the given accounting period. SHA 2011 has a different interpretation of the HFxFS table.

PART II

Further Classifications, Applications and Methodology Concerning Health Accounts

A System of Health Accounts 2011: Revised edition

PART II

Chapter 8

Classification of Revenues of Health Care Financing Schemes (ICHA-FS)

Introduction

This chapter presents the concept of the revenues of health financing schemes (FS) and their classification. The accounting framework for health financing presented in Chapter 7 provides the conceptual basis for this chapter.

Main concept

A key set of information for policy analysis is *i)* how much revenue is collected; *ii)* in what ways is it collected; *iii)* from which institutional units of the economy are revenues raised for each particular financing scheme; and *iv)* which financing schemes receive those revenues. Health accounts should therefore provide information both about *i)* the contribution mechanisms the particular financing schemes use to raise their revenues, and *ii)* the institutional units of the economy from which the revenues are directly generated. As a consequence, financing sources could be interpreted in two ways: as types of revenues, and as institutional units.

For the analysis of revenue-raising, three viewpoints can be taken: where the flows originate; where the flows go; and what is the nature of the flows. Understanding the nature of the flows is of importance from the perspective of both health and public finance policy. For example, the classification of the FS should make it possible to distinguish between public and private funding of health care finance. Understanding how resources are raised by financing schemes is important for many countries, as many health systems are struggling with the issue of funding. They either want to increase total funding or to use it in a better way, keeping in mind that an increase in funding needs to be both sustainable and equitable. There is a growing need for policy makers to inform their decision-making with respect to both existing and advocated mechanisms for financing the health care system. The classification of revenues of financing schemes is suitable for tracking the collection mechanisms of a financing framework. Furthermore, the new classification makes it possible to analyse the contribution of the institutional units to health financing.[1]

The classification of revenues also makes an adequate interpretation of public and private finance possible. It has been recognised that *there is no one-to-one correspondence* between the public-versus-private split regarding *institutional units* of the health system and the public-versus-private split regarding the *funds used for financing health care*. This is a source of ambiguity for the interpretation of public and private. For example, "households", as an institutional sector, belongs to the private sector, while households contribute to both public and private funds (*e.g.* the funds of social health insurance and the funds of voluntary health insurance, and, of course, households are the main source of government revenues more generally). Social health insurance contributions paid by households are considered as elements of public finance, and voluntary health insurance fees paid by households are considered as elements of private finance.[2] This is consistent with public finance logic, as "social security taxes" are considered part of public finance for the purposes of public deficit/surplus calculations. In other words, social insurance contributions are part of a government's "fiscal space".

Nevertheless, understanding the total contribution of each institutional sector of the economy is also key information, as this indicates the respective financial burden of each sector. For this reason, it is proposed to include institutional sectors (using the SNA categories) as memorandum items in the classification of FS, which would sum up the revenues for each institutional sector from the types of revenues.[3]

Table 8.1. **Comparison of FS in SHA 2011 with the *Producers Guide***

	Revenues of financing schemes under SHA 2011	Financing sources under the *Producers Guide* (PG)
Definition of ICHA-FS	*Revenues of financing schemes* (*e.g.* government revenues, social insurance contributions, etc.).	*Institutional units of the economy* whose resources are mobilised and managed by financing schemes (government, corporations, etc.)
Key information provided by the FS classification	"How" revenues are mobilised by financing schemes (type of transactions)	"From whom" revenues are collected by financing schemes
Additional informationneeded	"From whom" revenues are collected (sub-categories of the proposed classification)	"How" revenues are mobilised

Source: IHAT for SHA 2011.

Comparison of the concept of revenues of financing schemes with financing sources under the Producers Guide

The main advantages of the revenue of schemes classification are as follows:

- It provides comprehensive information about revenue-raising (how and what type of revenues are raised by the financing schemes and – in combination with information on institutional units – from which institutional sectors of the economy).
- It allows for a sound interpretation of the structure of "public" and "private" finance; more precisely, by modifying the major expenditure aggregates in a way that better reflects the current health financing arrangements. The proposed aggregates are: "Public and compulsory private funds spent on health care" and "Voluntary private funds spent on health care" (see Chapter 7[4]).
- It makes it possible to analyse the issue of multiple layers of financing and the issue of who bears the burden of financing the schemes (see Table 8.4).

Definition of revenues of health care financing schemes

Revenue is an increase in the funds of a health care financing scheme, through specific contribution mechanisms. The categories of the classification are the particular types of transaction through which the financing schemes obtain their revenues.

The objective of this classification is to group types of revenues[5] of health financing schemes into mutually exclusive classes. If appropriate, the revenue category has sub-categories that are defined according to who (or which institutional sector) provides the given revenue. (For example, voluntary prepayment as a category of Revenues of financing schemes has the sub-categories: voluntary prepayments from households, voluntary prepayments from employers and so on.)

Revenues can also be in-kind transfers (for example, in-kind foreign assistance to government financing schemes).

In several countries, social security agencies or private insurance companies act as financing agents not only for health insurance but also, for example, for pensions, unemployment and housing. In these cases, *only their health-relevant revenues should be taken into account*. This requires different adjustment procedures, and hence the development of guidelines. In particular, when such complex institutions serve as financing agents, analyses of their deficits and surpluses require careful examination,. The deficits and surpluses of health financing schemes may be highly influenced by the assumption of how to calculate "health-related revenues".

Table 8.2 presents the classification of revenues of financing schemes, and the following paragraphs provide explanations of some of the major categories.

Explanatory notes to the ICHA-FS classification of revenues of health care financing schemes

FS.1 *Transfers from government domestic revenues*

This item refers to the funds allocated from government domestic revenues for health purposes. Countries with decentralised public administration (and decentralised collection of public revenues) may want to show the role of central and local government in providing revenues of health financing schemes. These countries may wish for national purposes to create sub-categories under FS.1.1 to FS.1.4 (see Table 8.5).

FS.1.1 *Internal transfers and grants*

This item refers to transfers within the central government and – in countries with decentralised tax system (where regional/local government also collects taxes) – transfers within regional/local governments, as well as grants from central to local government. Internal transfers are the key components of the budget of the government health financing schemes (HF.1.1). As Table 8.3 shows, government schemes may have other types of revenues, such as other domestic revenues (FS.6, for example, donations) and foreign revenues (FS.7).

- *Includes*: revenues allocated to government schemes (FS.1.1), which may be an internal transfer within the same level of government or a transfer between central and local governments. Includes: the budget of national health services; funds allocated to central government health programmes in countries with social insurance; etc.

This item includes grants received from another domestic government unit.

- *Includes*: grants by central government to local government financing schemes; revenues allocated to specific government employees schemes (see definition of government health financing schemes in Chapter 7); etc.
- *Excludes*: social insurance contributions paid by government as an employer. (This is accounted under FS.3.2).

FS.1.2 *Transfers by government on behalf of specific groups*

This item refers mainly to payments to social health insurance. In several countries, the government pays on behalf of certain population groups (for example, children, the elderly, certain groups of the unemployed and so on) to guarantee insurance coverage for these groups.

Table 8.2. **Classification of revenues of health care financing schemes**

Code	Description
FS.1	**Transfers from government domestic revenue (allocated to health purposes)**
FS.1.1	Internal transfers and grants
FS 1.2	Transfers by government on behalf of specific groups
FS.1.3	Subsidies
FS.1.4	Other transfers from government domestic revenue
FS.2	**Transfers distributed by government from foreign origin**
FS.3	**Social insurance contributions**
FS.3.1	Social insurance contributions from employees
FS.3.2	Social insurance contributions from employers
FS.3.3	Social insurance contributions from self-employed
FS.3.4	Other social insurance contributions
FS.4	**Compulsory prepayment (other than FS.3)**
FS.4.1	Compulsory prepayment from individuals/households
FS.4.2	Compulsory prepayment from employers
FS.4.3	Other compulsory prepaid revenues
FS.5	**Voluntary prepayment**
FS.5.1	Voluntary prepayment from individuals/households
FS.5.2	Voluntary prepayment from employers
FS.5.3	Other voluntary prepaid revenues
FS.6	**Other domestic revenues *n.e.c.***
FS.6.1	Other revenues from households *n.e.c.*
FS.6.2	Other revenues from corporations *n.e.c.*
FS.6.3	Other revenues from NPISH *n.e.c.*
FS.7	**Direct foreign transfers**
FS.7.1	**Direct foreign financial transfers**
FS.7.1.1	Direct bilateral financial transfers
FS.7.1.2	Direct multilateral financial transfers
FS.7.1.3	Other direct foreign financial transfers
FS.7.2	**Direct foreign aid in kind**
FS.7.2.1	Direct foreign aid in goods
FS.7.2.1.1	Direct bilateral aid in goods
FS.7.2.1.2	Direct multilateral aid in goods
FS.7.2.1.3	Other direct foreign aid in goods
FS.7.2.2	Direct foreign aid in kind: services (including TA)
FS.7.3	Other direct foreign transfers (*n.e.c.*)
Memorandum items	
Reporting items	
FS.RI.1	Institutional units providing revenues to financing schemes
FS.RI.1.1	Government
FS.RI.1.2	Corporations
FS.RI.1.3	Households
FS.RI.1.4	NPISH
FS.RI.1.5	Rest of the world
FS.RI.2	Total foreign revenues (FS.2 +FS.7)
FS Related items	
FSR.1	Loans
FSR.1.1	Loans taken by government
FSR.1.2	Loans taken by private organisations
FSR.2	Aid in kind at donor value

Source: IHAT for SHA 2011.

The government may buy voluntary insurance covering the co-payments for the poor. In this case, voluntary insurance fees paid by the government are also accounted under this category.

- *Excludes*: contributions paid by the government as employer.

FS.1.3 *Subsidies*

This item refers to the funds allocated from government domestic revenues to financing schemes operated by institutional units other than government units or NPISH.

- *Includes*: subsidies for compulsory or voluntary health insurance schemes (managed by private insurance companies). Tax allowances provided to households who buy private health insurance may be accounted under this category.

FS.1.4 *Other transfers from government domestic revenues*

This item includes government transfers to NPISH financing schemes. These transfers usually are intended to cover the costs of NPISH activities or to provide the funds out of which NPISH may make current transfers to households (*e.g.* for foreign treatment of sick children). This category also covers transfers in kind.

FS.2 *Transfers distributed by government from foreign origin*

Transfers originating abroad (bilateral, multilateral or other types of foreign funding) that are distributed through the general government are recorded here. For the financing scheme receiving these funds, the provider of the fund is the government, but the fund itself is from a foreign origin. The origin of the revenue can only be registered at the level of the transaction of the revenue.

Transactions involving revenues from foreign entities channelled via government may take the following major forms:

- *Foreign financial revenues earmarked for health*. These revenues are usually grants by international agencies or foreign governments donated to the government, or voluntary transfers (donations) by foreign NGOs or individuals to the government. Governments may use these donations to fund governmental or NPISH health financing schemes.
- *Non-earmarked foreign revenues*. These revenues are grants and voluntary transfers (other than grants) received by the government without detailed specification of their use by the foreign agency.

FS.3 *Social insurance contributions*

Social health insurance contributions are receipts either from employers on behalf of their employees or from employees, the self-employed or non-employed persons on their own behalf that secure entitlement to social health insurance benefits. Sub-categories of social insurance contributions are classified by the type of institutional units that pay the social insurance contribution on behalf of the insuree.

This category *excludes* social insurance contributions paid by the government on behalf of specific groups (which are recorded in FS.1.2). It also excludes "imputed social insurance contributions" (which are under FS.6).

FS.3.1 *Social insurance contributions from employees*

This item covers the social health insurance contributions received from households. In a technical sense, employees' contributions are either paid directly by employees or are deducted from employees' wages and salaries and transferred on their behalf by the employer.

FS.3.2 *Social insurance contributions from employers*

This item comprises the social health insurance contributions received from employers. Employers' contributions are paid directly by employers. This includes insurance contributions by the government *as an employer, if public employees participate in the general social health insurance scheme* (if there is no specific scheme for government employees).

For national purposes, countries may want to create sub-categories by distinguishing the different institutional types of employers, such as government units, public and private corporations, and NPISH. In this case, similar sub-categories under FS.3.1 should be created.

In a macroeconomic sense, both employees' and employers' social insurance contributions are part of the compensation of employees (elements of labour costs). However, for health policy analysis, it is useful to make a distinction between them.

FS.3.3 *Social insurance contributions from self-employed*

This item covers the social health insurance contributions received from self-employed persons.

FS.3.4 *Other social insurance contributions*

This item refers to revenues of social health insurance schemes (HF.2) other than those classified under FS.1.2 and FS.3.1 to 3.3. It includes, for example, health insurance contributions paid by pension insurance funds on behalf of retired persons.

FS.4 *Compulsory prepayment (other than FS.3)*

This includes compulsory private insurance premiums and payments to compulsory MSAs. Compulsory private insurance premiums are payments received from the insuree or other institutional units on behalf of the insuree that have been mandated by government and secure entitlement to benefits of compulsory health insurance schemes. Under compulsory private health insurance, all residents (or defined groups of residents) are obliged to purchase a health insurance policy. The law may also define the rules for insurance premiums, for example, to oblige insurance companies to apply community rating.

Sub-categories of compulsory prepayment (other than FS.3) are classified by the type of institutional units paying the revenues, as follows:

- Compulsory prepayment from individuals/households (FS.4.1);
- Compulsory prepayment from employers (FS.4.2);
- Other compulsory prepaid revenues (FS.4.3), for example, compulsory private insurance premiums received from institutional units other than households and employers.

FS.5 Voluntary prepayment

This includes voluntary private insurance premiums. Voluntary insurance premiums are payments received from the insuree or other institutional units on behalf of the insuree that secure entitlement to benefits of the voluntary health insurance schemes. Sub-categories of voluntary prepayment are classified by the type of institutional units paying the revenues, as follows:

- Voluntary prepayment from individuals/households (FS.5.1);
- Voluntary prepayment from employers (FS.5.2);
- Other voluntary prepaid revenues (FS.5.3) (for example, received from institutional units other than households and employers).

Methodological note

As already discussed, there exists a variety of types of voluntary health insurance across countries. Accordingly, the rules for setting their premiums also differ. The main types are: risk-rated individual premiums; group-rated premiums; and community-rated premiums. While there is no intention to use such detailed categories for international data collection, countries may find it useful for their national health accounts to define sub-categories of voluntary insurance premiums according to these types.

FS.6 Other domestic revenues n.e.c.

This category includes domestic revenues of financing schemes not included under FS.1 to FS.5. Sub-categories are defined according to the institutional units that provide the voluntary transfers:

- Other revenues from households *n.e.c.* (FS.6.1);
- Other revenues from corporations *n.e.c.* (FS.6.2);
- Other revenues from non-profit institutions *n.e.c.* (FS.6.3).

FS.6.1 Other revenues from households n.e.c.

This category includes the sources of households' out-of pocket payments, as well as any voluntary transfers from households to health financing schemes, other than those classified under FS.5, for example, donations to NPISH health programmes.

FS.6.2 Other revenues from corporations n.e.c.

This category includes the resources of corporations devoted to health purposes, other than those included in FS.3 to FS.5. This category is the main financing source of the Enterprise financing schemes (HF.2.3). Enterprise financing schemes primarily include arrangements where enterprises provide or directly finance health services for their employees (such as occupational health services), without the involvement of an insurance-type scheme.

The SNA uses the term "Imputed social contributions" for social benefits that are provided directly by employers without creating a special fund. These revenues are accounted under this category of SHA 2011.

This also includes voluntary donations from corporations. A special example is as follows. Some health care providers (*e.g.* hospitals) may earn money (interest) by keeping their funds in banks. The health care providers may spend this extra income on providing health care. In this case, the financing scheme is: HF.2.3.2 Health care providers financing scheme (which is a sub-category of Enterprise financing schemes); the revenue category is: FS.6.2 Other revenues from corporations.[6]

Similarly, private insurance corporations may use interest revenue for activities related to the provision of health insurance. These receipts have to be included as revenues for health care only when they are used to fund health services (including the administration of health insurance). SHA does not explicitly distinguish between funded and unfunded systems, because funded systems could be characteristic of various types of schemes including social insurance. The recording of revenues from interest should always be part of FS.6.2.

FS.7 Direct foreign transfers

The main ways that revenues from foreign entities directly (via transfers) received by health financing schemes may be transacted are:

- Direct foreign financial revenues earmarked for health. These revenues are usually grants by international agencies or foreign governments, or voluntary transfers (donations) by foreign NGOs or individuals that contribute directly to the funding of domestic health financing schemes;
- Direct foreign aid in kind (health care goods and services).

Current transfers for international co-operation in cash or in kind include emergency aid after natural disasters. This should be distinguished from capital transfers of a similar kind, which would fall under capital formation.

Two subcategories of direct foreign revenues are defined:

- Financial transfers or foreign aid in kind (goods or services);
- Bilateral, multilateral or other transfers.

The detailed sub-categories of foreign revenues are as follows: direct bilateral financial transfers, direct multilateral financial transfers, other direct foreign financial transfers; direct bilateral aid in goods, direct multilateral aid in goods, other direct foreign aid in goods; and direct foreign aid in services (including TA).

Note: If donations or types of assistance from a foreign source are channelled through government or government agencies, these flows are recorded under FS.2 and not under FS.7. FS.7 is restricted to the direct foreign contributions received by the various schemes. [Direct (earmarked) foreign transfers to governmental health financing schemes are also recorded as FS.7.]

Memorandum items

Loans

See the section on the "Treatment of loans". Countries may want to report sub-categories of loans, such as their origin, domestic or external, according to Table 8.3. Other breakdowns could be by maturity (one year, more years) or by instruments, taking into account the total net borrowing (currency and deposits, securities other than shares, excluding financial derivatives and loans).

Table 8.3. **Suggested reporting of loans as memorandum items to the FS classification**

Code	Description
FSR.1	Loans
FSR.1.1	Loans taken by government
FSR.1.1.1	Loans from international organisations
FSR.1.1.1.1	Concessional
FSR.1.1.1.1	Non-concessional
FSR.1.1.2	Other loans taken by government
FSR.1.2	Loans taken by private organisations

Source: IHAT for SHA 2011.

Institutional units

The second group of memorandum items consists of the institutional units that provide revenues to financing schemes. Included are:

- Government;
- Corporations;
- Households;
- NPISH;
- Rest of the world.

These categories allow the estimation and analysis of the revenue collection transactions from the perspective of the institutional units of the economy from which the health financing schemes receive their revenues. (The section "SHA tables on revenue collection" provides a more detailed discussion.)

This (revenue-provider) role of the institutional units should be distinguished from the role of institutional units as agencies that collect funds. For example, social insurance contributions provided by households and corporations to social insurance schemes may be collected by a government agency, for example, the National Tax Authority in a country. In this case the National Tax Authority is the institutional unit collecting the funds. However, it does not appear explicitly in the classification of revenues of health financing schemes. The revenues concerned are accounted under FS.3 and also recorded under Households and Corporations.

Specific conceptual issues

Transfers from government revenues

The role of government in revenue-raising requires special consideration. In a macroeconomic sense, there are two main ways that financing schemes raise their revenues:

- Revenues are directly received from the primary owners of income: households, corporations and the rest of the world. The amount of revenues is decided by regulation, contracts or decisions made by the primary owners of income;
- Revenues are received as the result of the allocation of the general revenues of the government. First, the government raises general revenues for their overall activities from the primary owners of income, then it allocates the revenues among the different public spending areas, including health financing schemes.

In the case of non-earmarked revenues of the state budget, there is no direct link between the types of government revenues[7] (income tax, VAT, corporate taxes, grants, sales, etc.) and the types of spending area (education, health, etc.). It is the budget decision that determines the revenues for the government health financing schemes. Therefore FS.1 "Transfers from government domestic revenues" refers to government domestic revenues allocated to health purposes and FS.2 to transfers by government from foreign sources.

It is clear that the main primary owners of income are households, corporations and the rest of the world.[8] However, due to its decision-making role concerning the allocation of its general revenues, it is important to show the role of the government as the institutional unit that allocates revenues to health financing schemes.

In order to provide a transparent picture of the role of government, the sub-categories of FS.1 distinguish between internal transfers (for example, allocations from the central government budget to the Ministry of Health and grants to local governments); a contribution by government on behalf of specific groups (for example, on behalf of the children, the elderly, the inactive poor, etc.); subsidies (*e.g.* to employers buying health insurance for their employees); and other transfers from government domestic revenues (such as for NPISH). The information on social insurance contributions paid by the government on behalf of certain non-active population groups is increasingly important for policy analysis in countries where the social insurance scheme plays the major role in financing the health services.

Figure 8.1 displays the allocation of domestic and foreign revenues of government to financing schemes and subcategories of FS.1.

Figure 8.1. **A simplified display of transfers from government revenues to financing schemes**

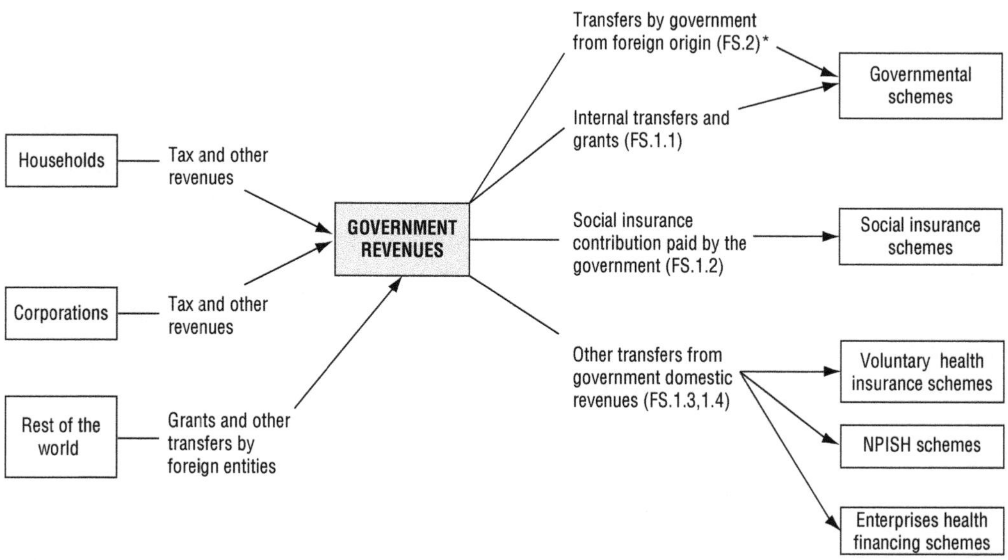

* It is assumed that FS.2 is used for governmental schemes but other schemes are not excluded for receiving transfers from foreign origin via government.

Source: IHAT for SHA 2011.

In some countries, tax earmarked for health may play a considerable role. In this case, it is possible first to distinguish general tax, earmarked tax and other government revenues as sub-categories of FS.1, and then under each of these to create the following sub-categories: internal transfers and grants; transfers by government on behalf of specific groups; and subsidies and other transfers.

FSR.1 *Treatment of loans*

By definition, loans are changes in financial assets or liabilities (that is, loans are not included in revenues). Loans are generally taken to cover the state budget expenditure that is not balanced by domestic revenues. There are also health sector specific loans, usually for investments in the health sector. It is proposed to present the amount of loans "used" in the given accounting period as memorandum items. (This amount obviously may be different from the loans "taken" in the same period.) For some lower-income countries it may be important to show the role of foreign loans in financing the health system. In these cases, it is proposed to apply the "Statement of Government Operation" presented in GFS for the health sector; that is to prepare a Statement of Government Health sector-related Operation. (Separate guidelines on implementation will provide more details.)

This Manual does not address general public finance issues, such as, for example, debt cancellation or debt relief. Those issues can be analysed using the GFS Manual. However, countries involved in debt cancellation, either as a debtor or creditor, may need to track those resources. Further analysis of this issue is discussed at the end of this chapter.

As already discussed in Chapter 7, sectoral accounts provide possible tools to account for the deficits or surpluses of health financing schemes (and financing agents) and for any loans or other financial instruments taken to balance the deficit. Sectoral accounts show how deficits or net borrowing are covered by the net lending of other sectors of the economy or by the rest of the world. Deficits and surpluses with institutional units of the same sector are consolidated.[9]

Households may also take loans to pay for health care. This is, however, disregarded and not included in the memorandum item, as estimating it does not seem feasible.

Valuation of in kind assistance and technical support

According to the GFS, grants in kind should be valued at current market prices. If market prices are not available, then the value should be the explicit costs incurred in providing the resources or the amounts that would be received if the resources were sold. In some cases, the donor and the recipient may view the value quite differently. SHA 2011 deviates from the GFS and records the value applied by the recipients as the health expenditure. In these cases, the valuation from the viewpoint of the donor is, however, included as a memorandum item (FSR.2), in order to make the difference between the valuation by the donor and the recipient transparent.

SHA tables on revenue collection

Revenues of health financing schemes by types of revenues (HFxFS table)

The table "Revenues of health financing schemes by types of revenues" (HFxFS) shows the revenue structure of the health financing schemes: the types of transactions through which resources are channelled from the institutional units of the economy to financing schemes (see Table 15.4 in Chapter 15).

Revenues of health financing schemes by institutional units and types of revenues

The appropriate presentation of the revenues of financing schemes by the types of revenues and by the institutional units of the economy (providing the revenues) requires a double-entry accounting. This also makes it possible to show the final burden of health financing on institutional units (the last line "Net contribution" in the upper part of Table 8.4).

Table 8.4. **Revenues of health financing schemes by Institutional units and types of revenues**

		Health-specific revenues and expenses of institutional sectors of the economy													
Institutional sectors of the economy		General government		Corporations		Households		NPISH		Rest of the world		Total			
		R	E	R	E	R	E	R	E	R	E	R	E		
FS.1.1	Internal transfers and grants	200	–150				–200					200	–350	150	**Public and compulsory private funds**
FS.1.2	Contribution payment on behalf of specific groups		–30										–30	30	
FS.1.4	Other transfers from government domestic revenues		–20					10				10	–20	10	
FS.3	Social insurance contributions		<		–100		–100					0	–200	200	
FS.4	Compulsory prepayment (other than FS.2)											0	0		
FS.5	Voluntary prepayment						–10					0	–10	10	**Private funds**
FS.6	Other domestic revenues *n.e.c.*				–5		– 50		–10			0	–65	65	
FS.7	Foreign revenues										–50	0	–50	50	
	Total	200	–200	0	–105	0	–360	10	–10	0	–50	210	–725		
	Net contribution		**0**		**–105**		**–360**		**0**		**–50**		**–515**		
	Revenues of financing schemes														
Financing schemes HF.1.1	Government financing schemes		150								20		170		
HF.1.2	Social health insurance		30		100		100						230		
HF.1.3	Compulsory private health insurance												0		
HF.2.1	Voluntary health insurance						10						10		
HF.2.2	Non-profit Institutions schemes		10						10		30		50		
HF.2.3	Enterprises schemes				5								5		
HF.3	Household out-of-pocket payments						50						50		
	Total		**190**		**105**		**160**		**10**		**50**		**515**		

Source: IHAT for SHA 2011.

The upper part of Table 8.4 presents simplified T-accounts for the institutional units of the economy. These T-accounts show the revenues (R) and expenses (E) of institutional units related to health financing.

The table contains an important simplification: the resources provided by the RoW (that is to say, expenses of RoW) are accounted as revenues of the "final destination", even if the fund goes through the government budget. However, if necessary, it is possible to prepare a table that shows all government revenues (domestic and foreign together) and distinguishes funds by RoW that go through the government budget as well as the other RoW funds.

The numbers in the bottom part of the table present the revenues of financing schemes. For example, the bottom part shows that the social health insurance scheme collects 30 units from the government, and the upper part (-30) shows that the government paid this as an insurance contribution (on behalf of certain groups of the population).

An institutional unit may provide resources:

- Directly to a health financing scheme, *e.g.* social insurance contribution by corporations to social health insurance (100 in Table 8.4); and
- Indirectly contribute to the revenues of a health financing scheme. In this case, the institutional unit provides resources to another institutional unit from which a health financing scheme collects revenues. (As mentioned, however, the table provides this information only for domestic revenues.) For example, the government provides transfers of 20 units to NPISH, of which 10 units go directly to NPISH financing schemes, while 10 units go to NPISH that do not purchase health services, but only collect resources and transfer them to NPISH purchasing services.

The total in the bottom part of the table shows the last phase of revenue collection, *i.e.* from which institutional units the financing schemes directly raise their revenues. For example, the general government provides 190 units to the different financing schemes together.

The total in the upper part of the table shows the primary sources of health finance. It can be seen that the government only redistributed its general domestic revenues to the different health financing schemes and to other institutional units that provide revenues to health financing schemes. Hence, this table is appropriate to show the multiple layers of domestic revenues.

Furthermore, based on the types of revenues, it is possible to distinguish the domestic public and compulsory private funds and private funds and foreign revenues used for health finance (see the last two columns).

Additional tools

Sub-categories of government domestic revenue

As already mentioned, countries with decentralised public administration (and decentralised collection of public revenues) may, for national purposes, wish to show the role of the central and local governments in providing the revenues of health financing schemes. These countries may create sub-categories under FS.1.1 to FS.1.4 (see Table 8.5).

Tool for the analysis of the sources of household out-of-pocket payments

Countries with very large proportions of OOP payments, such as many countries in Africa and Asia, may be interested in identifying the sources of OOP in detail.

A payment by the individual should not always be accounted as OOP, because it may be reimbursed by voluntary insurance or covered by the government (conditional cash transfers) or by an NGO. In these cases, the payment for the health care is technically made by the household, but not from the household's "pocket", nor from the household's primary income or savings. Therefore, the first step is to deduct those items that should be accounted as other than OOP, such as government schemes (conditional cash transfers), voluntary insurance, NPISH health financing schemes and RoW financing schemes.

The sources of OOP can only be the household's income (including remittances) or savings, or loans taken out by the household.

Table 8.5. **Sub-categories of transfers from government domestic revenue**

Code	Description
FS.1	**Transfers from government domestic revenue (allocated to health purposes)**
FS.1.1	Internal transfers and grants
	Internal transfers within central government
	Internal transfers within regional/local government
	Grants from central government
	Grants from regional/local government
FS.1.2	Payment by government on behalf of specific groups
	Payment by central government
	Payment by regional/local government
FS.1.3	Subsidies from government
	Subsidies from central government
	Subsidies from regional/local government
FS.1.4	Other transfers from government domestic revenue
	Other transfers from central government
	Other transfers from regional/local government

Source: IHAT for SHA 2011.

The item "Conditional cash transfers" is perceived as a specific government health financing scheme (HF.1.1) and *not* as a source of OOP (see Chapter 7 for more detail).

Table 8.6 provides a possible tool for distinguishing household out-of-pocket payments as a financing scheme from total household payments for health care. *Note*: Countries obviously have to consider, on the one hand, the usefulness of this information, and on the other hand, whether the necessary information is available or can be made available at a reasonable cost.

Table 8.6. **Accounting payments made by households for care under SHA 2011**

Possible sources of payment for health care by households	Accounting under SHA 2011	
Household's primary income (from employment or assets)	FS.6.1. Other revenues from households	HF.3 Household out-of-pocket payments
Remittance	FS.6.1	HF.3
Savings	FS.6.1	HF.3
Health savings accounts	FS.6.1	HF.3
Micro savings (for health)	FS.6.1	HF.3
Non-health-specific savings	FS.6.1	HF.3
Selling of goods/barter of goods	FS.6.1	HF.3
Loans	FS.6.1	HF.3
Bank loans	FS.6.1	HF.3
Micro-credit loans	FS.6.1	HF.3
Loans from traditional societies (co-operatives) other than micro-credit	FS.6.1	HF.3
Loans from friends/families	FS.6.1	HF.3
Transfers		
Conditional cash transfers from government	FS.1.1.	HF.1.1. Government schemes
Transfers from national NGOs	FS.1.4.Other transfers from government, FS.6.Other domestic revenues	HF.2.2 NPISH financing schemes
Transfers from foreign philanthropic sources	FS.7.1.Foreign financial transfers	HF.4.2.2. Other voluntary RoW financing schemes

Source: IHAT for SHA 2011.

Further analysis of external resources distributed by governments

Health accounts expenditure does not include transactions in financial instruments; for certain types of analysis, such as development aid, loans that are given or received under preferential conditions must be accounted for.[10] Any countries concerned may wish to analyse the use of specific classes of earmarked and non-earmarked funds. The main classes to highlight are the use of budget support, debt forgiveness or debt cancellation[11] resources and the use of loans by health care government programmes. An additional table should be developed by countries to show how external resources are channelled through government funds to health care schemes. Specific guidelines to further analyse external resources distributed by governments are to be developed separately.

Notes

1. Whereas the interpretation of the FS as a set of institutional units does not allow an analysis of the types of health financing flows.
2. The FS categories, as presented in the *Producers Guide* (PG), do not show the types of transfers through which resources are channelled from institutional units to financing schemes. This can lead to a lack of transparency about important information, such as different forms of household finance. It does not provide a full picture of household involvement in health care financing. For example, classifying compulsory and voluntary household premiums separately provides useful information, as these imply different contribution and pooling/prepayment mechanisms. A classification of institutional units would not distinguish between a) a household's compulsory contributions (*e.g.* social insurance contributions of employees), which are part of the "fiscal space" and a government's public finance accounts, and hence should be treated as public expenditure, and b) voluntary prepayments (*e.g.* voluntary health insurance premiums), which are clearly private expenditure.
3. For example, all contributions by households (social insurance contributions, voluntary prepayments and other revenues from households (*n.e.c.*) would be added to evaluate total household contributions to the health system.
4. As noted in Chapter 7, by accounting separately for compulsory prepayments (for compulsory private insurance), analysts can in fact decide whether or not to count these as part of total public or total private health spending.
5. According to the GFS Manual, revenue is an increase in net worth resulting from a transaction, including both monetary and non-monetary transactions. Every transaction is either an exchange or a transfer. A transaction is an exchange if one unit provides a good, service, asset or labour to a second unit and receives a good, service, asset or labour of the same value in return. A transaction is a transfer if one unit provides a good, service, asset, or labour to a second unit without receiving simultaneously a good, service, asset, or labour of any value in return.
6. As the health care providers generate the extra resource – from the interest – and voluntarily decide to use it on patient care. In fact, the "transfer" is an internal transfer within the health care providers.
7. It is beyond the scope of this Manual to examine the different types of general government revenues (*e.g.* the share of personal income tax, VAT, etc.). However, separate guidelines may be important for national analysis, in particular lower-income countries.
8. Here it is disregarded that government may also be the primary owner of certain income, *e.g.* from selling properties.
9. Consolidation is a method of presenting statistics for a set of units as if they constituted a single unit.
10. Financial transactions are not part of expenditure in the SNA; however, the need of specific analysis is also recognised in SNA 2008, 29.72.
11. It should be verified that the part of the debt recorded is related to the health care schemes. See definition and details in SNA 2008, 22.107 and related paragraphs: debt cancellation is the voluntary cancellation of all or part of a debt obligation within a contractual arrangement between a creditor and a debtor by the agreement between the parties and with the intention to convey a benefit. Debt forgiven may include all or part of the principal outstanding, inclusive of any accrued interest arrears and any other interest costs that have accrued.

PART II

Chapter 9

Classification of Factors of Health Care Provision (ICHA-FP)

Introduction

Knowing how much health providers spend on the inputs needed to produce health care goods and services (factors of provision)[1] can have many policy uses. This information is typically tracked at national aggregate levels to meet the need to ensure an efficient, appropriate allocation of resources in the production of health care services. Specific policy needs may require information regarding total payments for human resources, expenditure on pharmaceuticals, and other significant inputs. Furthermore, the financial planning of health programmes and services often relies on information about the volume and mixture of factor spending.

Key to this chapter is the grouping together of variables so as to offer a global insight into the factors of provision used by health care providers, as these represent the valued inputs used in health care delivery for the resident population. Thus, factors of provision are to be determined by all the domestic providers in the system. The total of the distribution of expenditure by factors of provision is expected to equal the current expenditure on health. Clearly, for operational reasons, imported services are not disaggregated by factor, but, as far as possible, the inputs used for exported services should be excluded.

The classification of factors of provision was not identified as an explicit item in SHA 1.0. However, for the internal estimation process, separate accounts for both non-market and market production were recommended as an essential tool (SHA 1.0: 5.21). Such estimations for cost data are essential. The *Producers Guide* (PG) proposed a classification of resource costs based on the Government Finance Statistics Manual.[2] The factors of health care provision (FP) classification presented here is a revised version of the PG resource cost classification. Explanatory notes on selected factors and provision units are also included.

In terms of data sources, most government reports include audited values with a "line item" approach frequently found for the governmental sector of the health system. A classification of factors is also part of other public reporting systems, and it is a standard tool of analysis for government finance statistics at the international level.[3] For private providers, enterprises also have certain obligations to report costs for internal accounting purposes. A factors of provision classification is also needed for reports to the tax authorities (*e.g.* in the case of VAT and income tax). Thus, to develop more comprehensive health care accounts some countries might consider the implementation of FP.

Main concept

The scope of the factor classification

Factors of provision are defined in SHA as the valued inputs[4] used in the process of provision of health care.[5] The boundary of health care (as set out in Chapter 4) determines the boundary of health care provision and by implication the factors of provision by provider. Provision involves a mix of factors of production – labour, capital and materials and external services – to provide health care goods and services. It refers not only to health-specific resources but also to the non-health specific inputs needed to generate health services, all of them equally important for efficiency purposes. Some examples are:

- Labour involved in health care, security, maintenance and other services;
- Capital consumed, including buildings and medical and office equipment;
- Medical materials such as sutures and syringes, as well as non-medical inputs such as electricity, water and cleaning supplies;
- Externally purchased services, which may include laboratory services, legal services and any outsourced support services, such as food preparation for patients, cleaning and security or garden services, administration and so on.

To be able to function, providers also have to cover other expenditure on inputs, such as the payment of taxes (*e.g.* VAT). Thus, the factors of health care provision account for the total value of the resources, in cash or in kind, used in the provision of health care goods and services. It is equal to the amount payable to health care providers by the financing schemes for health care goods and services consumed during the accounting period. Spending on factors of provision is related to the current spending for the provision of goods and services. The spending for capital to be used in the provision of future periods should be separated from the use of resources for the current provision of health care, as in the other ICHA classifications.

Factors of provision can be cross-classified with different axes to illustrate the shares of current health expenditure allocated to resources of labour, pharmaceutical supplies, use of equipment and buildings, and so on. For example, the cross-classifications can show providers by factors of provision (HPxFP), where the focus is more on differences across production patterns (providers).

If the financing axes are cross-classified with the factors of provision (FS/HFxFP), the data facilitate an assessment of how different financing and allocation strategies affect mixes of "inputs" (see PG 5.20). The factors of provision can be purchased through various revenue sources and means for each provider, which makes it relevant to identify the various funding strategies to cope with financing needs.

The table of factors of provision by function (HCxFP) allows a measurement by production factor mix according to the purpose of consumption (Table 9.1). The profile of inputs is frequently used to monitor and plan scaling-up processes by type of service.

Notes related to the classification and selected types of classes

The boundary of Factors of health care provision

Health care providers deliver not only health care but also some products that are outside the health care boundary. For ICHA classifications, the goal is to identify and restrict the core component of all classifications to the health care boundary. This is also the case for the classification of factors of provision, which thus has the aim of assigning all types of resources to health care activities. The inputs used to provide activities outside the health care boundary, for example, cosmetic surgery or social services, or any exported health services, should – as far as possible – be separated and reported below the line if this is of interest for national policy analysis. These could be displayed as Factor of Provision-related components.

Table 9.1. **Classification of factors of health care provision**

Code	Description
FP.1	**Compensation of employees**
FP.1.1	Wages and salaries
FP.1.2	Social contributions
FP.1.3	All other costs related to employees
FP.2	**Self-employed professional remuneration**
FP.3	**Materials and services used**
FP.3.1	Health care services
FP.3.2	Health care goods
FP.3.2.1	Pharmaceuticals
FP.3.2.2	Other health care goods
FP.3.3	Non-health care services
FP.3.4	Non-health care goods
FP.4	**Consumption of fixed capital**
FP.5	Other items of spending on inputs
FP.5.1	Taxes
FP.5.2	Other items of spending

Source: IHAT for SHA 2011.

There may be clear differences in the structure of factors of provision between market and non-market production (for example, the remuneration of human resources can differ for public and private health providers). This information can also be displayed if there is a national interest in analysing it in detail.

Households as providers

An important starting point is that the totality of spending on the factors of provision is equal to the amount spent on the consumption of health care goods and services for each provider category. Furthermore, to be included within the health care boundary, a transaction is required: in principle, only payments linked to health care provision should be included. Households (HP 8.1) mostly provide health care for own consumption. Within the health care boundary, this provision is included only when a transaction is documented, *e.g.* when some compensatory payment for LTC services and/or when reimbursement for in-kind provision is received. These transactions should be accounted for explicitly to facilitate a matching of totals with the financing axis. Transactions on inputs linked to own consumption normally have no accounting records. If it is important for national policy reasons to account for the inputs used for own-produced health care services, it is recommended to report them as memorandum items. To do that, the majority of these factors may need to be imputed.

Providers of governance and administration of health care financing

The providers of administration of health financing (HP.7) also require special treatment. The category of administrators of health financing schemes, notably health insurance, is often a category that consists of providers of health care services as a secondary activity. This can be the case for both government as well as private organisations engaged in activities related to the management of health insurance. The planning, management, regulation and collection of funds and the handling of delivery system claims are performed not only for the private health system but also for other (non-health-related) insurance packages. The health share within the total output of institutions such as insurance companies can be very small, as could the use of inputs for the provision of these services. For example, social security can have total costs covering more than just the operation of the health insurance funds. In some countries this can represent a minor component, but in other countries it can be the largest. This is also the case in private insurance companies, which operate much more than health care insurance.

Governance of health care services is clearly a primary activity of government ministries of health and agencies with a major role in the health system. The units involved in governance and administration are primarily engaged in formulating policy, co-ordinating and monitoring plans, programmes and budgets, and administering, operating and supporting the social security funds that cover the health services. They are involved as well in the setting and enforcement of standards for medical and paramedical personnel and for hospitals, clinics and so on. This includes the regulation and licensing of providers of health services. The sum of factors of provision involved in governance and administration should equal the total expenditure amount presented in the provider classification category on administration (HP.7).

Explanatory notes to the ICHA-FP classification of factors of health care provision

FP.1 *Compensation of employees*

The compensation of employees refers to the total remuneration, in cash or in kind, paid by an enterprise to an employee in return for work performed by the latter during the accounting period. It includes wages and salaries and all forms of social benefits, payments for overtime or night work, bonuses, allowances, as well as the value of in-kind payments such as the provision of uniforms for medical staff.

The compensation of employees measures the remuneration of all persons employed by providers of health care irrespective of whether they are health professionals or not.[6]

Importantly, any services contracted, such as cleaning and restaurant services in hospitals, are considered as purchases, and the wages and salaries of the staff involved should not be reported under this item.

When shareholders also work for the corporation and receive paid remuneration other than dividends, the shareholders are treated as employees. The owners of any type of corporations who work in that corporation and receive paid remuneration other than the withdrawal of earnings from the corporation are also treated as employees.

Students who contribute their labour as an input into an enterprise's process of production, for example, as worker trainees, student nurses and hospital interns, are treated as employees, whether or not they receive any remuneration in cash for the work they do in addition to the training received as in-kind payment.

FP.1.1 *Wages and salaries of employees*

The wages and salaries of employees include remuneration, both in-cash and in-kind, either as regular interval payments or as pay for piecework, overtime, night work, work on weekends or other unsocial hours, allowances for working away from home or in disagreeable or hazardous circumstances, as allowances linked to housing, travel or sickness benefits, ad hoc bonuses, commissions, gratuities, and in-kind provision of goods and services required to carry out the work or as meals and drinks, uniforms[7] and transportation. It excludes social security paid by the employer. Social contributions paid on behalf of employees are the actual or imputed payments to social schemes to secure their entitlement to social benefits such as social security.

FP.1.2 *Social contributions (see SNA 2008 7.56 for more detail)*

Social contributions are payments, actual or imputed, to social insurance schemes to obtain entitlement to social benefits for employees, including pensions and other retirement benefits. Included are payments to social security/insurance on behalf of the employees (as well as contributions for pensions).

As employers' social contributions are made for the benefit of their employees, their value is recorded as one of the components of compensation of employees. The social contributions are then recorded as being paid by employees as current transfers to the social security schemes or other employment-related social insurance schemes.

FP.1.3 *All other costs related to employees*

Retention policies have been developed in many countries to ensure service delivery by health personnel under hardship conditions. These conditions can vary with social situations, geography and disease conditions, such as communicable diseases like HIV/AIDS, and with extreme weather conditions, low salaries, etc. Specific incentives in monetary terms and in kind can be recorded here.

Fringe benefits are also to be recorded here, such as the provision of a car to employees,[8] or the provision of benefits so that the employee obtains a car with a major discount.

FP.2 *Self-employed professional remuneration*[9]

The class FP.2 is meant to be used for independent self-employed professionals carrying out health care activities. This class refers to the remuneration of the independent health professional practice, to the income of non-salaried self-employed professionals and to the complementary or additional income generated through the independent practice of salaried health personnel, which is common in most countries' health systems. Despite the frequency, relevance and importance of the work performed by qualified independent practitioners in health care, full measurement standards have not been proposed and reached in most guides. Measurement has been approached through surveys and through records from providers, notably related to the SNA. In fact, this type of income is involved in all practitioners' offices[10] and quasi-corporations.

Self-employed income refers to final consumption payments made by patients or health care beneficiaries to independent professionals. The income resulting from the operation of an independent medical practice usually refers to the sole owners or to the joint owners of the organisations in which they work. It includes the remuneration for work performed by the health care professional (and other household members, if applicable) and their profit as the owner or entrepreneur. The income of households, as providers of paid long-term care, is recorded as mixed income under FP.2 after deduction of the cost of delivering home care.

The income of non-salaried self-employed health professionals is the remuneration for their work less the other cost items of their work. These other costs include payments for leasing, interest payments, capital consumption and other inputs used in their practice.

Frequently the remaining income cannot be identified separately from the profits earned as the owner or entrepreneur. In many cases, though, the element of remuneration may dominate the value of the total income.[11] In national accounts it is estimated as a residual or "balancing item".[12] Profits/losses exist after deduction of capital costs but before income taxes.

In case the household is treated as a quasi-corporation and provides a complete set of accounts, the income component of the owner can be separated from the profits earned as entrepreneur and is to be classified as compensation of employees. The remaining balance (total earnings minus total cost) is in this case treated as gross operating surplus, as would be the case in corporations.

The acquisition of supplies (FP.3) and capital consumption (FP.4) should not be included, neither the cost of capital (financial and non-financial). The cost of financial capital is recorded under the item FP.5.2: other items of spending on inputs.

FP.3 *Materials and services used*

This category consists of the total value of goods and services used for the provision of health care goods and services (not produced in-house) bought in from other providers and other industries of the economy.[13] All the materials and services are to be fully consumed during the production activity period.

Materials refer to all the health care and non-health care inputs required for the multiple production activities to be carried out in the health system. They rank from highly specific ones, such as pharmaceuticals and inputs for clinical laboratory examinations, to those with a more universal purpose, such as paper and pens. Materials deteriorated, lost, accidentally damaged or pilfered are included. Materials used over more than one production period are classified as capital (equipment and the like) and are thus excluded from this classification. Usually materials are cheaper than capital goods such as machinery and equipment.

Services used involve the purchase of services produced by another agent. They can be defined as outsourced or external services purchased by the provider and involved in their own production process. Services consumed usually refer to general services provided by non-health industries, such as security, and payments for the rental of buildings and equipment as well as their maintenance, and cleaning. They can also include health care services such as laboratory work, imaging and patient transportation.

From a policy perspective, one of the most important types of materials is pharmaceuticals, for which a subcategory has been specifically created.

FP.3.1 *Health care services*

One reason that health care services delivery is so complex is that it may involve a considerable amount of subcontracting of health care services, such as diagnosis and monitoring services as imaging and laboratory services, or direct provision of health care by specialised personnel, such as rehabilitation, long-term care (health), renal dialysis and some cancer therapy.

Health care services purchased by a provider to complement the package of services offered by that health provider can be offered within the same unit or in a different one. The purchased service can imply the movement of the patient to the other unit where the purchased service is provided, such as when the patient is taken to another hospital or unit to get a specialised treatment or test, as in the case of imaging services. Another example is when services are moved between provider locations, such as when test interpretations and imaging results are delivered through electronic means from other units. These movements can involve samples for laboratory tests that are actually developed and interpreted in another unit. It can also imply that the provider of the service is moving to the patient's location (see Box 9.1 for more details on intermediate consumption).

FP.3.2.1 Expenditure on pharmaceuticals and FP.3.2.2 Other health care goods

Pharmaceuticals are defined as any chemical compound used in the diagnosis, treatment or prevention of a disease or other abnormal condition. They include reactive and other chemical products used in laboratory tests.[14]

The share of pharmaceuticals and other medical goods in total health use is one topic of particular interest to policy makers. Medicines and medical goods, together with human resources, represent at least two-thirds of current spending in most health systems. No standard measurement has been set in many countries. This expenditure item[15] is partially covered by the functional classification, with a display for medical goods independently consumed (HC.5.1 in SHA 1.0 and SHA 2011) and for inpatient consumption, not separately described but contained in the service provision (the same is possible in day-care services and in outpatient care too). In the factors of provision classification, this item is expected to cover the totality of use of medicines and other medical goods, regardless of their mode of provision. Thus, services supplied to hospital patients using medicaments, prostheses, medical appliances and equipment and other health-related products should also be detailed here.

Donations of materials and supplies should be treated to reflect purchaser values, so the amounts recorded should be at market prices and net of subsidies minus indirect taxes. When a donation of material or supplies lacks a purchaser price because there is no availability in the local market, the price to be used is the one paid by the entity that has offered the donation. An example is medicines or supplies for the treatment of cancer or HIV/AIDS, such as antiretroviral medicines.

- *Includes*: all medicines and pharmaceutical products such as vaccines and serum and other consumable goods, such as cotton, wound dressings and tools used exclusively or mainly at work, for example, clothing or footwear worn exclusively or mainly at work (such as protective clothes and uniforms).
- *Excludes*: all goods acquired to increase stocks should not be included, such as medicines to be stored for future use. Excluded are also equipment and tools to be repeatedly used, which are part of capital.

FP.3.3 Non-health care services and FP.3.4 Non-health care goods

These classes involve goods and services used for health care production, but of a non-specialised health nature. They are of a general nature such as those required in the operational activities of the provider, as in management offices (*e.g.* software, pens and paper), kitchens (in hospitals and to supply to overnight patients if they are not outsourced services), transport (*e.g.* oil and tools to operate vehicles) or other types of more general usage, such as electricity, water and the like.

Some countries may want to have a more detailed classification of these non-health care materials and services, *e.g.* for the calculation of multi-factor productivity (*e.g.* KLEMS

Table 9.2. **Further breakdown of non-health care goods**

Code	Description
FP.3.4	Non-health care goods
FP.3.4.1	Energy
FP.3.4.2	Water
FP.3.4.3	All other non-health care goods

Source: IHAT for SHA 2011.

multi-factor measurement: capital, labour and inputs (see also Box 9.1) of energy, supplies and services). In that case, additional codes could be introduced in FP.3.4, at the third-digit level as presented in Table 9.2 below.

In SNA 2008 and the *Eurostat Manual of Supply, Use and Input-Output Tables* (Eurostat, 2008c) both electricity as a component of energy products and water are treated as goods. This is the convention followed in this Manual.

Non-health care services such as services for infrastructure are also required (*e.g.* maintenance of buildings and equipment). Typically, any services purchased, such as staff training, operational research, transport, housing, meals and drinks, and payment for the rental of equipment and buildings, are included here. Services used as employees' compensation are excluded.

Maintenance is one of the services that is frequently of interest. The distinction between maintenance and repairs and gross fixed capital formation (see Chapter 11) is not clear-cut. The ordinary, regular maintenance and repair of a fixed asset used in production constitutes a normal cost item and is recorded under material and services used. Ordinary maintenance and repair, including the replacement of defective parts, are typical activities provided in-house, but such services may also be purchased from other enterprises. Whether these maintenance and repair services are provided in-house or purchased from other enterprises, they should be included as factor costs. However, the valuation in both cases is different, depending on the way charges are made:

- In-house maintenance would allow a separate bill for human resources (under FP.1) and any materials used (*e.g.* FP.3.4);
- Outsourced maintenance usually gets a full bill, including both factors.

The practical problem is to distinguish ordinary maintenance and repairs from major renovations, reconstructions or enlargements that go considerably beyond what is required simply to keep the fixed assets in good working order. Major renovations, reconstructions or enlargements of existing fixed assets may enhance their efficiency or capacity or prolong their expected working lives. They must therefore be treated as gross fixed capital formation, as they add to the stock of fixed assets in existence.

Ordinary maintenance and repairs are distinguished by two features:

- They are activities that owners or users of fixed assets are obliged to undertake periodically in order to be able to utilise such assets over their expected service lives. They are current costs that cannot be avoided if the fixed assets are to continue to be used. The owner or user cannot afford to neglect maintenance and repairs, as the expected service life may be drastically shortened otherwise;
- Maintenance and repairs do not change the fixed asset or its performance, but simply maintain it in good working order or restore it to its previous condition in the event of a

breakdown. Defective parts are replaced by new parts of the same kind without changing the basic nature of the fixed asset.

FP.4 Consumption of fixed capital

The consumption of fixed capital is a cost of production. It may be defined in general terms as the cost, in the accounting period, of the decline in the current value of the producer's stock of fixed assets as a result of physical deterioration, foreseen obsolescence or normal or accidental damage. It excludes losses associated with damage caused by war or natural disasters (see SNA 2008, 6.244). In accounting, the consumption of fixed capital is an economic construct that should be distinguished from depreciation, which is a legal construct. In many cases the two constructs lead to different results.[16] The consumption of fixed capital should reflect underlying capital use as a factor of production at the time the production takes place. For further details see Chapter 11 "Capital formation in health systems".

Included are estimates on the use of buildings, equipment and other capital goods such as vehicles. Excluded are rentals paid on the use of equipment or buildings, and fees, commissions, royalties, etc., payable under licensing arrangements. These are included as the purchase of services. In theory the benefits of the use of own capital[17] should be considered. This estimate would require difficult imputations that are not justified due to the relatively low values involved.

FP.5 Other items of spending on inputs

This item includes all the financial costs, such as interest payments on loans, taxes and so on.

FP.5.1 *Taxes*[18]

Following the definition of the SNA, taxes are compulsory, unrequited payments, in cash or in kind, made by economic agents to government units. They are described as unrequited because the government provides nothing in return to the economic agent making the payment, although governments may use the funds raised in taxes to provide goods or services to other units, either collectively to the community as a whole or individually. The item FP.5.1: Taxes in the factor cost account comprise taxes on production and taxes on products. As the name implies, taxes on products are payable per unit of the product. The tax may be a flat amount that depends on the physical quantity of the product or it may be a percentage of the value at which the product is sold, *e.g.* VAT. Taxes on production are taxes imposed on the producer that are neither applied to products nor levied on the producer's profits. Examples include taxes on the land or premises used in production or on the labour force employed.

FP.5.2 *Other items of spending*

Other spending items include all transactions related to items not elsewhere classified. Transactions recorded here include *e.g.* property expenses, fines and penalties imposed by government; interest rates and costs for the use of loans; and non-life insurance premiums and claims.

Interest payments accruing to loans made by different entities are not negligible. Interest is defined as payment on top of the amount of the principal borrowed that has to be paid to the creditor by the debtor over a given period of time and that does not reduce

Box 9.1. **Relevant facts related to intermediate consumption in the health system**

Intermediate consumption in the macroeconomic accounts of the SNA relates to the interaction between the analysed branch (in this case health care) and the rest of the economy, and consists of the goods and services used up in the course of production in that branch (health care goods and services). Several issues need to be considered when the concept of intermediate consumption is applied to a functional health approach, which aims to comprehensively account for and analyse expenditure for the health purpose. Below are some of the main features of intermediate consumption:

- ❖ Health care goods and services can be provided by a range of establishments whose primary activity is not necessarily the production of health care services. In macroeconomic accounting, occupational health care, *i.e.* the provision of health services to employees by an enterprise, which leads to its economic benefit, is recorded as intermediate consumption. It is thus not recorded as a health product except when a detailed record is made, as in a supply and use table. From a health accounts point of view, all resources used with a direct health purpose should be included, and in this case, health care offered to employees as beneficiaries involves the consumption of these services. Many other services obtained from secondary providers involve health consumption by households.
- ❖ When in the macroeconomic accounts an activity is allocated to a branch, there is no loss for the measurement of the total economy, but for health accounts some functions may be relatively undervalued and some others overvalued. Some health services are linked to business requirements, such as eye tests and blood alcohol tests for airline pilots. Current recording procedures do not permit a fine reallocation of the few services that essentially benefit the enterprise and are of limited benefit to households. On the basis of general accounting principles, a complete allocation of these services to household consumption is needed.
- ❖ Some health needs are satisfied by a bundling of inpatient and outpatient services, such as diagnostic procedures (laboratory and imaging) and the prescription/provision of medical goods. Two situations may arise with respect to intermediate consumption:
  - Health services are consumed as part of a "package", produced and provided in a single health contact to the patient in a health establishment. Any typical case-mix in services involves resources of one establishment, which are included both in the production and in the costing schedule. Production value and final consumption value match one another. The value of final consumption equals the sum of the value of the inputs used, which equals the value of the goods and services consumed. For all providers, the remunerations of employees are included. For market services, entrepreneurial income is added to that value. The total value is already supplied in the commodity's bill.
  - When an establishment outsources part of the service, for example, some ancillary services are purchased from another establishment, domestic or foreign, the total value of the final use is reflected in the bill, but they are reflected in an aggregate of intermediate services purchased. A risk of double-counting exists as well as a risk of omission, depending on the data sources used in the establishment, and according to the way accounts are generated.

Box 9.1. **Relevant facts related to intermediate consumption in the health system** *(cont.)*

- Within the health system, a considerable amount of intermediate consumption is generated in the total product consumed by households. Hospital billing not only includes the services provided by the hospital itself but may also include purchases from the pharmaceutical industry, transport industry, food industry and so on. The intermediate purchases need to be distinguished[19] because they are included in the final consumption expenditure, but they may not be disaggregated on the production side. This fact could potentially undervalue health production compared to other branches of the economy.

the amount outstanding. Interest may be a predetermined sum of money or a percentage of the outstanding principal. Interest is added to the principal. When government units pay interest on debts on behalf of another unit, as the government incurring the debt as the primary obligor (debtor), the interest paid on the existing debt of another unit should be recorded as a subsidy (when the other unit is an enterprise) or a transfer (if it is a government unit).

Cross-classification of functional and economic classifications of expenses (GFSM)

Table 9.3 cross-classifies the economic and functional classifications of expenses. The table includes a column for acquisitions of non-financial assets, in addition to columns for each type of expense. The table is relevant for reporting the expenses of financing schemes (see Chapter 7).

Table 9.3. **Cross-classification of functional and economic classifications of expenses**

	Compensation of employees [GFS]	Use of goods and services	Consumption of fixed capital [GFS]	Interest [GFS]	Subsidies	Grants	Social benefits [GFS]	Other expense	Acquisition of non-financial assets
General public services									
Defense									
Public order and safety									
Economic affairs									
Environmental protection									
Housing and community amenities									
Health									
Recreation, culture, and religion									
Education									
Social protection									

Source: IMF (2001), Table 6.3, p. 78.

Notes

1. Factors of provision are all the inputs used in the process of producing health care goods and services. In national accounts terminology, part of the factors of provision are treated as value added components (*e.g.* compensation of employees), while another part is treated as intermediate consumption (*e.g.* materials and services used).
2. See for example Providers Guide, Table 4.8, p. 47, and IMF (2001), Table 6.1, p. 63.
3. Table 6.3 of the GFSM cross-classifies the economic and functional classifications of expenses. The table includes a column for acquisitions of non-financial assets in addition to columns for each type of expense. The table is relevant for reporting the expenses of financing schemes (see Chapter 7).
4. Included in the FP classes are taxes. Although, technically speaking, taxes are not an input, they represent an important factor in expenditure.
5. Factors of provision spending in SHA are the uses of the providers and are presented on the left-hand side of the T-account, which on the right-hand side shows the revenues (payments by financing schemes).
6. In order to be classified as employed, that is, either as an employee or self-employed, the person must be engaged in an activity that falls within the production of health care provision. Non-employed persons consist of the unemployed and persons not in the labour force (SNA 2008, 7.29). Employees are workers in a relationship with an employer: this involves a written or oral agreement, formal or informal, between an enterprise and a person, normally entered into voluntarily by both parties, whereby the person works for the enterprise in return for remuneration in cash or in kind. The remuneration is normally based directly, or indirectly, on the amount of work done, on either the time spent at work or labour contributed to some process of production, or some other objective indicator of the amount of work done, and is paid at a previously agreed fixed amount. The self-employed are persons who work for themselves and whose self-owned enterprises are distinguished neither as separate legal entities nor as separate institutional units in the SNA. They may be persons who are the sole owners, or joint owners, of the unincorporated enterprises in which they work or a member of a producers' co-operative or a contributing family worker (that is, a family member who works in an unincorporated enterprise without pay). The self-employed are remunerated as a function of the value of the outputs from some process of production for which that person is responsible, regardless of how much is contributed to it.
7. Uniforms provided by the employer are part of intermediate consumption. According to SNA 2008, "when the goods or services are used by employees in their own time and at their own discretion for the direct satisfaction of their needs or wants, they constitute remuneration in kind. However, when employees are obliged to use the goods or services in order to enable them to carry out their work, they constitute intermediate consumption" (SNA 2008, 6.220). The latter is generally the situation for health workers.
8. Although fringe benefits should be included, valuing them can sometimes be problematic. The valuation of a car or the use of a car could be easy, but other things such as the use of a mobile phone could be more difficult. It could also mean that benefits have to be estimated when they are covered in a government budget under an item such as housing, for instance if employees are living in a house for free. This is frequently the case of health personnel located in rural areas.
9. Self-employed professional remuneration is an item that includes more than simply the cost of an independent professional. The separation of the salary part of the self-employed from his profit is very difficult. This profit part is usually included in this "cost" item.
10. In national accounts, when households engage in production they can be treated like corporations. Household "unincorporated" market enterprises are created for the purpose of producing goods or services for sale or barter on the market as a small enterprise. They can be engaged in virtually any kind of productive activity, including health care services. They can range from single persons working in health care with virtually no capital or premises of their own up to *e.g.* large specialist practices with employees (derived from SNA 2008, 4.155). Private practices in health care that have employees are treated as corporations and include a type of salaried employees (even the owner can keep a salary from his enterprise). Non-salaried private practices involve small enterprises with self-employed workers, represented in national accounts within the household sector. See HP classification. An unincorporated corporation can be treated as a quasi-corporation also when it refers to a small enterprise but it has a complete set of accounts.

11. Operating surplus and mixed income are two alternative names for the same balancing item used for different types of enterprises in the SNA. Mixed income is the term reserved for the balancing item of the generation of income account of so-called unincorporated enterprises owned by members of households. For example, private practitioners as providers of paid long-term care are unincorporated organisations, and their balancing item after the deduction of the cost of delivering health care would be recorded as mixed income FP.2 in the factors of provision account.
12. In the SNA, this terminology refers to the net operating surplus, which measures the surplus or deficit accruing from production after taking account of any interest, rent or similar charges payable on financial or tangible non-produced assets borrowed or rented by the enterprise, or any interest, rent or similar receipts receivable on financial or tangible non-produced assets owned by the enterprise. That is to say, excluding operation and capital costs.
13. This class is comparable to "intermediate consumption". Following the SNA, intermediate consumption consists of the value of the goods and services consumed as inputs by a process of production, excluding fixed assets, as costs associated with these are recorded in the consumption of fixed capital (an imputed cost). The goods or services may be either transformed or used up by the production process.
14. See Chapter 5 for a full description of the content of the category pharmaceuticals.
15. The expenditure on medical goods for outpatient services and the expenditure on medical goods for inpatient services together are presented as total spending on medical goods in the functional classification only as a memorandum item. In theory, the value of the medical goods used in the production process of health provision (FP) should equal the purchasing value of these goods by the providers.
16. For the European Union countries, on average approximately one-third of the output of the health branch is absorbed as input in the production of other health services (*i.e.* as intermediate consumption) by the health branch itself (*Source*: Eurostat website SUT data for 2000, extracted on 9 March 2011).
17. The consumption of fixed capital is the economic value of the use of capital goods in the production used by national accounts. In business accounts, the term depreciation is used, which usually reflects the legally allowed amounts of the capital goods to be included in the cost structure of the companies.
18. There might be national regulations concerning the reimbursement of services by public agencies, in which case it would be difficult to exclude this component. In such cases the remuneration of the use of capital is included in the factors of provision.
19. Taxes in essence are not a resource but paid from revenues. Taxes are part of the cost structure of the provider and as such are of interest in the expenditure.

A System of Health Accounts 2011: Revised edition

PART II

Chapter 10

Health Spending by Beneficiary Characteristics

Introduction

This chapter provides an illustrative example of how SHA data can be used in conjunction with other data sources to further develop health accounts, in this case the allocation of current health expenditure for specific analyses according to classifications of beneficiary characteristics, such as disease, age, sex, region and economic status.

The chapter starts by reviewing the original recommendations in SHA 1.0 and the *Producers Guide*, and summarises some of the recent developments in this field, as well as some potential uses of such analyses. It outlines the possible approaches for developing a framework to organise such analyses for both international and national purposes and makes some broad recommendations for the different types of beneficiary classifications. There is also a discussion of some of the remaining methodological issues, which often have to be kept in mind when developing standard classifications.

Background

As the use of the System of Health Accounts has increased the availability of comparable data on national health expenditures, there has been a growing interest in analysing the distribution of national expenditures across different population groups. This is being driven by three general motivations, namely concerns about social disparities in health outcomes, political and societal interest in the allocation of health care resources, and the need to improve the sustainability and planning of health care systems.

Health inequality is a concern for rich and poor countries alike. The existence of disparities in health outcomes naturally generates interest in knowing how these relate to disparities between population groups both in access to health care resources and in health care spending. This motivation is underlined by the Final Report of the World Health Organisation's Commission on Social Determinants of Health (WHO, 2008a), which stressed the need for countries to measure and monitor disparities in social determinants of health outcomes, such as health spending.

The distribution of resources within health care systems is a matter of political and social interest in all countries, whether it is related to issues such as fairness and equity, or other political, legal or administrative requirements. Ensuring the appropriate distribution of resources requires reliable information on how health care spending is being distributed. Such data are particularly relevant in a policy context where achieving universal coverage by health systems or improving social solidarity is guiding strategic goals, which is common in many countries.

Many analytical and planning activities also require data on the disparities in spending on individuals and different population groups. For example, data on the variation in spending by age group is a critical input into most exercises that attempt to project future health care expenditures or health care resource requirements (Rannan-Eliya and Wijesinghe, 2006). Such analyses are acquiring increasing importance as both developed and developing nations focus their attention on the financing and sustainability of health care systems.

Disparities in health care spending are found within populations along many different social dimensions that are potentially of policy and analytical interest. Dimensions of particular interest include the type of disease or health care condition, age, gender, geographic area and socioeconomic status.

There have been efforts since at least the mid-1960s to estimate variations in health care expenditures within national populations. Rice (1967) made the first attempts to measure the variations in spending by disease, age and gender in the United States. In developing countries, Meerman (1979) and Alailima and Mohideen (1983) pioneered the tracking of expenditures by socioeconomic groups with their estimations of how government and private health care spending varied by income and other groupings in Malaysia and Sri Lanka. However, few of these analyses linked their estimates to health accounts data, with the notable exceptions of the studies on Cost of illness performed in the Netherlands by the RIVM.[1] The most recent versions by RIVM also take account of the dimensions presented in SHA. In its most recent report (Poos *et al.*, 2008), the data are reported according to six dimensions: health care provider, health care function, source of finance, age, gender and disease. For this exercise a mapping is made between the diseases on the one hand and the detailed data on expenditure on the other.

Despite the proliferation of similar studies in the past two decades, these analyses have generally produced results that are not comparable between countries or even between individual studies. Such comparisons are increasingly needed and requested. An important reason for the lack of comparability has been the lack of standardised statistics and definitions of health expenditures, but this problem could be largely resolved by the development and institutionalisation of SHA.

SHA 1.0 and the Producers Guide

SHA 1.0 included two tables that present personal health expenditures cross-classified by patient condition or characteristics: firstly, by the chapters of the International Classification of Disease (ICD-10); and secondly, by broad age classes (0-4, 5-14, 15-44, 45-64, 65-74, 75-84 and 85+ years) and by gender.

The *Producers Guide* proposed some other distributions of expenditure on health in addition to those based on disease, age and gender. It looked at the possibility of allocating expenditures by household expenditure quintile, and by region. It pointed out the importance of socioeconomic inequalities in health spending. Tables 5.6 to 5.9[2] in the *Producers Guide* proposed matrices of financing agents crossed by the above-mentioned population groups. For expenditure by disease, it suggested using the Global Burden of Disease (GBD) classification for cross-classifying with financing agents. GBD[3] is a disease classification based on the detailed International Classification of Disease (ICD-10), and with the major cause subcategories of GBD closely aligned with the chapters of the ICD (Mathers *et al.*, 2004).

International comparisons

Although health accounts expenditures were already applied to studies on diseases over the past two decades, the use of standard classifications on expenditure has given an additional dimension to the value of the results (Heijink *et al.*, 2006). A number of significant projects since 2000 have explored the feasibility of analysing health spending by beneficiary characteristics. In particular, Eurostat and OECD have jointly collaborated on projects to develop a set of guidelines, based on the pioneering work by RIVM, for the distribution of spending by disease, age and gender, which were subsequently tested in a selection of member countries. WHO has also sponsored a number of such studies across developing countries. These have demonstrated that the general framework is feasible and able to generate broadly comparable data. In most of these country pilots, the age classifications used have been more detailed than those initially proposed in SHA 1.0, especially at the upper age limits. Moreover, in allocating spending by disease, most studies have been more successful in inpatient care settings than in outpatient or other settings. Such a distinction, particularly between estimations of inpatient and outpatient expenditures, appears to be both of policy interest and feasible. However, the work has also shown that there is a need for further methodological development in certain areas where allocation is more problematic, such as collective consumption (*e.g.* health promotion and administration), over-the-counter purchases and household spending more generally.

In addition to the studies of expenditure by disease, age and gender, several projects in recent years have also focused on the distribution of health spending by the socioeconomic characteristics of beneficiaries, and in particular income level. Few, if any of these studies have explicitly linked their estimates to health accounts data. Given the growing policy interest in such analyses, there is a need to provide guidelines for the future development of such estimates on a standardised basis linked to SHA and national health accounts statistics. One of the benefits of such SHA-linked estimates would be that they would be consistent with the overall estimates of national health expenditure, which is often not the case.

If SHA is to provide a basis for standardised comparisons of the distribution of expenditure by beneficiaries, a framework for such presentations must be provided. Comparability of results between different studies and estimates would require consistency in the following:

- The scope and types of health expenditures that are included in the comparisons;
- The schemes for classifying recipient or beneficiary groups along different social dimensions;
- The rules or basis by which expenditures are apportioned to individuals of different characteristics.

Analytical uses

Breakdowns of expenditure by beneficiary characteristics are intended to provide policy-related information on variations in spending between population groups that are differentiated by their characteristics. In itself, these breakdowns depict differences between groups (*e.g.* expenditures on health between men and women, between different age groups, between income level groups, etc.). It is important to note that such data on inequalities in spending do not, by themselves, imply any unfairness in the distribution of expenditure, but merely report current resource allocations, and act as one of the inputs for analysis. Equity in spending must be determined by reference to some normative framework of what constitutes fairness and requires other information on relevant factors, such as health needs, disease burdens, or capacity to pay. Details on expenditure by beneficiary characteristics can provide real support for policy makers, who need to allocate scarce resources and to evaluate how resources are reaching various groups of the population. In order to plan for the future, it is imperative that policy makers understand the present, including how resources are currently distributed.

Expenditure breakdowns by beneficiaries, while important for meeting national needs, can also benefit from being comparable at the international level. There is no agreed normative framework that allows definitive assessment of the appropriateness or optimality of a given expenditure distribution, so in practice comparison between countries is an important means by which policy makers can assess whether expenditures should, or even could, be changed.

Expenditure by disease

Depending on the approach and scope of the studies, information on expenditure by disease can serve a number of purposes, such as monitoring and providing information about resource allocation by disease/priority area. Linked with health accounts, the information gained can help address the following questions for both temporal and spatial analyses:

- What diseases/conditions are consuming health care resources, and how much?
- Which schemes pay for the services that address these diseases or conditions, and how much?
- How is spending on certain diseases broken down according to types of care?

Health accounts contribute a useful input for the planning of resource allocation. However, expenditures per disease or per condition alone cannot evaluate or justify the allocation of resources for a disease/condition, and additional information is needed, such as on needs and costs.

There are important caveats that should be considered when measuring expenditure by disease or condition and analysing the results, or comparing results internationally. Because expenditure by disease is mainly estimated using information on reported cases by disease, the difference in reporting practices between countries affects the potential for comparability. For example, a patient could return to a provider for a follow-up visit related to the same disease for which the patient was earlier treated. Depending on the allocation methodology, this second visit could be recorded under the same disease case in one country, or as an additional disease case in another country. Such discrepancies could be large enough to explain variations in expenditure by disease between countries. Another cause for concern when using contact-based information is the lack of a full linkage between disease and spending, and more particularly the different allocation methods in cases of co-morbidity. Depending on whether spending is allocated solely to the primary diagnosis or pro-rated across diseases, then the effect on estimating the spending on certain underlying diseases or conditions, such as diabetes and mental health, can be significant and may lead to unfounded conclusions.

It has been suggested that expenditure by disease/condition analyses should be produced regularly, possibly every three to five years (BASYS *et al.*, 2006). Analyses of expenditure by disease or condition are highly resource-intensive and should preferably be more than ad-hoc studies or research initiatives so that they can serve as a regular monitoring tool for policy makers to assess expenditure levels and trends (trends should be linked to changes in disease burdens or epidemiological profiles).

Expenditures by socioeconomic categories

Estimating expenditure by socioeconomic categories addresses the issue of inequalities, in particular by exposing differences in the level and pattern of spending by the poorer and the richer. This provides a better understanding of the possible reasons for, or consequences of, inequalities. In theory, expenditure distributions by socioeconomic (SE) groups could provide information on inequalities in sources of funding (for example, whether a contribution system is progressive or regressive), as well as on inequalities in payments (such as whether households' out-of-pocket spending is proportionate to ability to pay). In turn, expenditures on providers and functions per SE group would help design or monitor policies. For example, the data could inform as to what type of care is driving high household spending or how the allocation of public expenditures could be adjusted to better support the poorer sections of the population. In many low- and middle-income countries, data by socio-economic categories are of high policy relevance. These data can be used in studies on catastrophic spending and the impoverishment of certain population groups.

Policy indicators for expenditure by beneficiary characteristics

The following provides an illustration of the type of indicators that have been used to report expenditure distributions used by policy makers.

- Average per person expenditure in each region by provider (for example, per capita expenditure on health in each region for hospitals, ambulatory care providers, etc.);
- Expenditure by schemes in each socioeconomic group (for example, expenditure by government schemes, health insurance schemes, households out of pocket, and other, in the five income quintiles);
- Expenditure by disease for different types of care (for example, inpatient, outpatient and pharmaceutical expenditures for cardiovascular diseases, for respiratory diseases, for injuries, for neoplasms, etc.).

In addition, trends in expenditure by beneficiary characteristics such as age or disease are useful for projections of spending levels. Per capita spending in constant prices is best for comparisons of expenditure distributions and levels across time (comparison of volumes).

Finally, the following examples of beneficiary expenditure indicators, combined with other non-financial indicators, have also proven to be policy relevant:

- Expenditure per prevalence of a disease, over time;
- Expenditure per person at risk of a disease, over time;
- Expenditure per person correlated to unmet health care needs, by income quintile.

Possible framework for analysing expenditures by beneficiaries

Concept and definition of beneficiaries

The analysis of variations in health spending explicitly recognises that health expenditures are not uniform across the population. When considering the possibility that expenditures do vary non-uniformly and there is an attempt to measure that variation, what this implies is that expenditures are measurably different between different units of the population. If such expenditure differences exist between different units and such units can be classified according to some criteria, then the possibility of breaking down expenditures according to some social dimension arises. This implies that for the classification of expenditure by beneficiary characteristics or population groups, the minimum requirements are that:

- Variations in health expenditure exist across units of the population;

- It is possible and feasible to measure differences in expenditure of different units of the population;
- The different units of the population can be distinguished and classified according to some measurable, definable and meaningful set of criteria.

The smallest statistical unit of the population is the individual. A beneficiary might be defined as an individual to whom health expenditures can be assigned individually or collectively, as definable groups, on the basis that they are deemed to benefit from such expenditures.

The basis for assigning expenditures to an individual should be that the individual concerned is the direct recipient or beneficiary of the particular good or service, either as an individual or as a member of a (small, selective) group of individuals. This would cover most individual patient treatment services that are given to individual patients. The receipt of services as a (large, impersonal) group arises when expenditures are incurred to provide collective or non-personal services that benefit groups of individuals. An example of this would be health education campaigns to discourage smoking that are targeted at a particular demographic group or the population as a whole. It would also include activities undertaken to administer the health system, since these are intended to improve the health of the population overall.

Although the identification of individual beneficiaries provides a clear basis for allocating expenditures, the concept of a beneficiary needs further elaboration to deal with all the likely dimensions of analysis. Most such dimensions are consistent with the mutually exclusive categorisation of all individuals, but not all are. For example, an individual cannot have more than one age or one gender at a time. However, when expenditure concerns characteristics of individuals that are not mutually exclusive or that can be coincident in the same individual, the individual is not ultimately the unit of analysis. This is the case when allocating expenditures by type of illness or disease. Although all illnesses are a personal or individual phenomenon, it is possible for individuals to experience more than one type of illness at the same time. Thus, in the expenditure by disease category, it is not possible to separate the population into mutually exclusive categories of individuals. It is meaningful in this situation to allocate expenditures by individual according to the diseases that each individual suffers from, and to sum these expenditures by type of disease, but it is not feasible or meaningful to sum these expenditures by groups of individuals.

Considering this issue, it is proposed that for the purpose of distributional analyses linked to SHA framework, beneficiaries are defined as consisting either of mutually exclusive groups of individuals each categorised by some unique individual characteristic or of non-mutually exclusive groups of recipients who benefit from mutually exclusive types of expenditures that can be each assigned to individuals. In the latter case, an individual can be a recipient of more than one type of expenditure, and in each instance can be assignable to a different group in relation to each type of expenditure.

Scope of health expenditures considered in analyses by beneficiary characteristics

This illustrative framework is intended for use in extending the SHA framework to analyse variations in spending across beneficiaries in different population groups, with the ultimate objective being to facilitate comparisons between countries and between studies.

This requires that the scope of expenditures considered in the analyses be clearly articulated in relation to the overall SHA framework. At the same time, the expenditures must be of a type that can be assigned or allocated to beneficiaries along the possible dimensions of analysis. Finally, considerations of feasibility, reliability and reproducibility must be taken into account.

The boundary of what constitutes health care expenditures is defined in SHA according to the functional purposes of the spending, with the exact boundaries being based on the categories set out in the ICHA-HC functional classification. It follows that any analysis of health expenditure by beneficiary that is elaborated as an extension of SHA be also limited in its scope to expenditures falling within such boundaries. That being noted, it is still necessary to further narrow the scope of expenditures that are considered in analyses of expenditure by beneficiary. Since SHA itself defines the boundary of health care expenditures using a functional approach, it is sensible and appropriate to do this in a similar manner.

All expenditures according to the functional classification relate to the provision of health care services to individuals or groups of individuals (except parts of prevention and administration), and can therefore be considered as being potentially available for the distribution of expenditure by beneficiary characteristics.

Most health care goods and services benefit individuals as opposed to groups or society as a whole, and the receipt of a service by one individual usually means that the benefit cannot benefit another. This naturally lends itself to a breakdown of expenditure by beneficiary, since the recipient individual can be identified.

Expenditures recorded in the capital account (capital formation and related memorandum items) pose a different set of issues, as they consist of expenditures whose purpose is to finance the inputs that the health care system needs for the future provision of health care. The benefits of the services created with these inputs typically cannot be assigned to specific individuals or groups of individuals, since the inputs will be utilised for producing many different services. For example, capital formation includes investment in new hospitals, which will benefit a wide range of individuals over a long period of time. At the same time, some of these expenditures might be partially assignable to specific groups of individuals. For example, the building of a clinic for diabetes treatment will specifically benefit individuals with diabetes, although in many instances it might not be known whether the facility might be converted in the future to some other purpose.

Expenditures in health care reporting items and the health care-related functional categories (HC.RI and HCR categories) can usually be assigned to groups of individuals and could be presented in the distribution of expenditure. However, it is important to note that the majority of these are not routinely measured or reported in current SHA implementations. It is therefore not recommended that these be systematically analysed.

Consequently, it is recommended that analyses of expenditures per beneficiary be restricted in scope to current health care expenditures (HC.1-HC.9), with the option to also analyse and present separately capital expenditures per beneficiary. Some analyses will indeed need to consider the allocation of expenditures on investments for those investments that can be easily separated and assigned to specific beneficiary groups.

Health accounts-based analyses of the distribution of expenditure by disease should be distinguished from costing studies. A disease costing study might seek to analyse the full impact of a disease, including economic impact or impact on the quality of life. These dimensions would not be included under expenditure by disease, as explained in earlier paragraphs. Expenditures broken down by beneficiaries, as by disease, will distribute current spending for health functions HC.1 through to HC.9. Expenditures related to a person can always be attributed to an individual with a specific condition or disease. Expenditures on groups whose health status can either be related to a disease (*e.g.* preventive care for diabetes) or to the whole population can be distributed equally across all persons. Therefore, expenditure by disease in this framework only classify direct medical costs, and exclude indirect and intangible costs that are also sometimes included in costing studies.

Linkage to main SHA estimates

Calculating expenditure by beneficiary characteristics involves a consideration of the use and receipt of the associated services or goods. Ideally, this necessitates that expenditures be analysed at a detailed level of individual transactions at the point of provision. All such transactions can then be described according to the type of service involved, the provider generating the service and the type of financing used to cover the service. Consequently, the transactions can in theory be directly mapped or assigned to a provider, a function and a financing scheme. It would therefore be helpful to link analyses to at least one of the main SHA classifications (HC, HP, HF) to produce a matrix, rather than simply distributing current expenditure on health care according to the beneficiary characteristics. In particular, linking expenditure by patient characteristics to the functional classification facilitates comparability between health systems by ensuring neutrality from the point of view of provision and financing (even if data sources come from financing or provider sides).

The revenues of financing schemes (FS) classification provides information on the contribution mechanisms (premiums, social contributions, etc.) of the financing schemes (HF). The transactions involved with revenues and financing schemes normally do not occur at the same time as the transactions that take place between providers and patients, and, in fact, typically take place at a different level within the health care financing system. For example, the payments of premiums or social contributions by private enterprises and households to health insurance schemes take place at separate times than the use of the scheme funds to pay providers and involves separate transactions (in fact, the collection of funds by the scheme is administered separately both in time and space from the payments of benefits). In most cases, when a scheme's funds are used to pay a provider, the payment takes place only after the funds received have been pooled, thus making it impossible to directly identify the revenue source of the money spent to pay for service provision, unless it was targeted funding. This means that the distribution of expenditures by revenues of schemes can only be imputed by making a number of arbitrary assumptions about how pooled spending should be assigned, and as such, the validity of such a distribution is questionable. However, countries may be interested in making such estimations. For example, retracing the revenues of schemes' expenditure on health by region could be particularly interesting for countries that rely heavily on external funding.

Classifications of beneficiaries

Taking recent experience into account and in light of the perceived demand for analyses by patient characteristics in an international context, the following are the principal types of characteristics that a standard framework for a beneficiary classification might require:

- Age and gender;
- Type of disease or condition;
- Socioeconomic status;
- Geographical region.

Countries may wish to adopt other classifications based on their need for information and their particular policy needs. For example, some countries may be interested in comparing expenditures on health between the insured and non-insured populations. For each of the four proposed groupings, the guidelines below provide further details.

Age and gender

Expenditures by age and gender are probably the most established form of distributional or beneficiary expenditure. Expenditures in relation to age and gender have acquired increasing importance owing to the growing attention being given to the implications of population ageing for health care systems and health care financing. Such analyses require that expenditures be classified with sufficient detail in the age categorisation to show the significant variations in spending that exist, and to permit adequate modelling of the impact of future changes in age structure.

In recent years, several studies[4] have attempted to extend the health accounts framework to look at spending by age and gender. Many of these also incorporate expenditure by disease. These studies have demonstrated the general feasibility of estimating expenditures by age and gender in a wide range of national settings and data contexts.

Because of the importance of the impact of ageing and disease at opposite ends of the scale, it is suggested to include smaller age classes for the very young and the older population. Thus, when reporting expenditures by age and gender at the international level, it is suggested that 5 year age groups[5] up to 95 (with the 0 year age group separated) would allow for full coverage of most types of policy relevant groupings across the world. However, countries or regions are obviously free to aggregate these classes, or to break them down further, as is most relevant to their policies or corresponds best to the non-expenditure information with which the produced results may be used. This classification is primarily for use in inter-country comparisons, but countries or groups of countries should use other classifications that respond to country-specific policy needs or feasibility issues, or to facilitate comparison with particular countries, where appropriate.

Disease

Considerable work has been done in recent years on estimating expenditures by type of disease within SHA framework, both at a national level and in comparative analyses of countries.[6]

The OECD guidelines for the estimation of health accounts by age, gender and disease correspond closely to approaches also implemented outside the OECD – in Sri Lanka, for example – demonstrating their general applicability. These guidelines and country experiences provide a rich basis from which to develop a standard classification for analyses of expenditure by disease.

The internationally accepted standard for classifying diseases is the WHO-published International Classification of Disease (ICD), which is currently in its tenth revision (WHO, 2004). All recent work in the area of expenditure by disease utilises disease categorisations based on the ICD-10 (or the earlier ICD-9) classifications. The ICD has been developed to categorise diseases by diagnosis in order to collect mortality and morbidity information (*i.e.* on prevalence, incidence, etc.), which is used in a wide range of public health policy areas. This information supports decision makers with regard to disease prevention, public health programmes, treatment and reimbursement schemes. The ICD framework helps compare information across time and between countries. While ICD-10 is more frequently used in hospital settings than in outpatient settings, the 11th revision (in development) is seeking to adjust the classification to provide a better framework for primary care purposes.

However, the ICD-10 system in its full implementation defines more than 30 000 different disease classes and about 1000 agreed levels of classes for international reporting. The production of estimates according to this agreed level is impractical in terms of actual final presentation and often is not feasible given the sample sizes and level of disease coding of many primary data sources. These constraints necessitate the use of a more aggregated grouping of ICD classes. Countries that produced expenditure by disease have restricted themselves to expenditures by broad ICD-10 chapters (BASYS *et al.*, 2006), or have adopted nationally-specific groupings of ICD codes, as in the United States (Roehrig *et al.*, 2009), or they have used WHO Global Burden of Disease (GBD) categorisations (or a modified version of it), as in Australia or Sri Lanka. The GBD is itself a grouping or meta-classification of ICD classes.

A variety of other international classifications have also been used by countries to estimate specific areas of expenditure by disease. Some countries – mainly EU Member States – have used the International Shortlist for Hospital Morbidity Tabulation (ISHMT) to collect information on inpatient cases by disease (WHO, 2005d updated in 2008). The list, while very extensive, does not seek to be exhaustive. The ISHMT system is not widely used outside Europe, and reflects a bias that arises from its primary use in hospital settings.

Another major classification that is better adapted to health service transactions in the primary care setting is the International Classification of Primary Care (ICPC), currently in its second version (ICPC-2). The ICPC was developed to classify diseases, symptoms, conditions and reasons for a patient's encounter (including non-medical ones) with the general/family practice and primary care setting, as the ICD-9 system was found to be deficient in its descriptive scope owing to its focus on diseases and its roots in the classification of mortality statistics.[7] However, the ICPC, although WHO-endorsed, has not been universally adopted at the global level. Recent efforts have produced mappings of the ICPC to ICD-10, overcoming the problem of comparability (Lamberts and Wood, 2002). The ICPC may be useful as an intermediary classification when processing data for producing a full distribution of expenditure by disease, but is not recommended for purposes of international reporting of the full distribution.

One other classification that should also be mentioned is the Anatomical Therapeutic Chemical Classification (ATC), developed by WHO to classify medicines. Although it would lend itself for classifying expenditures on medicines, it cannot be mapped to the ICD, since it conceptually refers to quite different domains of analysis, and cannot easily be used for classifying expenditure by disease.

Any classification used in comparative analyses of the distribution of expenditure by disease/condition will inevitably be based on the ICD system, as it serves as a unique reference point for international classification to which almost all other international and national classifications are mapped (or can potentially be mapped). However, for reporting and comparative purposes, an international classification must provide a level of aggregation that is both feasible in a wide range of countries and useful from a policy perspective.

In the absence of a single international standard classification for collecting data, two alternatives are recommended: the GBD classification (slightly adapted) at a high level of aggregation and the ICD-10 main chapters. A categorisation of disease based on the GBD classification system is found to be most appropriate for international comparisons of expenditure by disease. While the ICD framework seeks to illustrate mortality and morbidity statistics, the GBD classification is geared towards epidemiological information and the reasons for disabilities or deaths. The WHO GBD classification also has the advantage of having primarily been developed for comparison of disease burdens in a wide range of both developed and developing countries. That said, it is important to reiterate that the GBD is an aggregated grouping of ICD classes, and so can be fully mapped to ICD classes.

In case the use of the adapted GBD is not possible (due to lack of detailed ICD second and third-digit level information), an alternative for international comparison can be found in the use of the ICD-10 at main chapter level. The prime advantage is the availability of data at chapter level and the widespread use of this classification, as well as the comparability across countries and over time.

In the tables below, the two classifications are presented: Table 10.1 presents the GBD two-digit groupings; Table 10.2 presents the ICD-10 main chapters. More information on the classifications of the GBD and the ISHMT can be found in Annex F.

A significant number of health system contacts and therefore expenditures are not linked to specific diseases, but to undefined conditions or to general health screening or investigations. An additional category should thus be introduced to the GBD to capture expenditures related to *Unspecified abnormal clinical and laboratory findings, symptoms, signs and ill-defined conditions and contacts with health services*; *factors influencing health status and contacts with health services* (GBD.nsk).

Ill-defined conditions refer to expenditures allocated to symptoms for which no diagnosis classifiable elsewhere is recorded. This "includes the more ill-defined conditions and symptoms that point with perhaps equal suspicion to two or more diseases or to two or more systems of the body, and without the necessary study of the case to make a final diagnosis. Practically all categories in this group could be designated as "not otherwise specified". The conditions and signs or symptoms consist of: *a)* cases for which no more specific diagnosis can be made even after all facts bearing on the case have been investigated; *b)* signs or symptoms existing at the time of initial encounter that proved to be transient and whose causes could not be determined; *c)* provisional diagnoses in a patient who failed to return for further investigation or care; *d)* cases referred elsewhere for investigation or treatment before the diagnosis was made; *e)* cases in which a more precise diagnosis was not available for any other reason; and *f)* certain symptoms which represent important problems in medical care and which it might be desired to classify in addition to a known cause."

Table 10.1. Classification of disease/condition by Global Burden of Disease (GBD) category

GBD code	Cause	ICD-10 code
GBD.1	**Communicable, maternal, perinatal and nutritional conditions**	A00-B99, G00-G04, N70-N73, J00-J06, J10-J18, J20-J22, H65-H66, 000-099, P00-P96, E00-E02, E40-E46, E50, D50-D53, D64.9, E51-64
GBD.1.1[8]	Infectious and parasitic diseases	A00-B99, G00, G03-G04, N70-N73
GBD.1.2	Respiratory infections	J00-J06, J10-J18, J20-J22, H65-H66
GBD.1.3	Maternal conditions	000-099
GBD.1.4	Perinatal conditions	P00-P96
GBD.1.5	Nutritional deficiencies	E00-E02, E40-E46, E50, D50-D53, D64.9, E51-E64
GBD.1.9	All other communicable, maternal, perinatal and nutritional conditions	
GBD.2	**Non-communicable conditions**	C00-C97, D00-D48, D55-D64 (minus D 64.9) D65-D89, E03-E07, E10-E16, E20-E34, E65-E88, F01-F99, G06-G98, H00-H61, H68-H93, I00-I99, J30-J98, K00-K92, N00-N64, N75-N98, L00-L98, M00-M99, Q00-Q99
GBD.2.1	Malignant neoplasms	C00-C97
GBD.2.2	Other neoplasms	D00-D48
GBD.2.3	Diabetes mellitus	E10-E14
GBD.2.4	Endocrinal disorders	D55-D64 (minus D64.9), D65-D89, E03-E07, E15-E16, E20-E34, E65-E88
GBD.2.5	Neurospsychiatric disorders	F01-F99, G06-G98
GBD.2.6	Sense organ disorders	H00-H61, H68-H93
GBD.2.7	Cardiovascular diseases	I00-I99
GBD.2.8	Respiratory diseases	J30-J98
GBD.2.9	Digestive diseases	K20- K92
GBD.2.10	Diseases of the genitourinary system	N00-N64, N75-N98
GBD.2.11	Skin disorders	L00-L98
GBD.2.12	Musculoskeletal diseases	M00-M99
GBD.2.13	Congenital anomalies	Q00-Q99
GBD.2.14	Oral diseases	K00-K14
GBD.2.99	All other non-communicable conditions	
GBD.3	**Injuries**	V01-Y89
GBD.3.1	Unintentional	V01-X59, Y40-Y86, Y88, Y89
GBD.3.2	Intentional	X60-Y09, Y35-Y36, Y870, Y871
GBD.3.9	All other injury conditions	
GBD.nsk.	Unspecified abnormal clinical and laboratory findings and other ill-defined conditions and contacts with health services; factors influencing health status and contacts with health services	R00-R99, Z00-Z99
Reporting items		
GBD.RI.1	Injuries to the head	S00-S09
GBD.RI.2	Injuries to the neck	S10-S19
GBD.RI.3	Injuries to the thorax, Injuries to the abdomen, lower back, lumbar spine and pelvis	S20-S39
GBD.RI.4	Injuries to the shoulder and upper arm, Injuries to the elbow and forearm, Injuries to the wrist and hand	S40-S69
GBD.RI.5	Injuries to the hip and thigh, Injuries to the knee and lower leg, Injuries to the ankle and foot	S70-S99
GBD.RI.6	Injuries involving multiple body regions, Injuries to unspecified part of trunk, limb or body region	T00-T14

Source: Global Burden of Disease 2008 Study, forthcoming.

Contacts with health services are not restricted to the treatment or investigation of current illness or injury. Episodes may also occur when someone who may not currently be sick requires or receives limited care or services.

Table 10.2. **International statistical classification of diseases and related health problems (ICD-10) 10th revision**

ICD Chapter	Blocks	Description
I	A00-B99	Certain infectious and parasitic diseases
II	C00-D48	Neoplasms
III	D50-D89	Diseases of the blood and blood-forming organs and certain disorders involving the immune mechanism
IV	E00-E90	Endocrine, nutritional and metabolic diseases
V	F00-F99	Mental and behavioural disorders
VI	G00-G99	Diseases of the nervous system
VII	H00-H59	Diseases of the eye and adnexa
VIII	H60-H95	Diseases of the ear and mastoid process
IX	I00-I99	Diseases of the circulatory system
X	J00-J99	Diseases of the respiratory system
XI	K00-K93	Diseases of the digestive system
XII	L00-L99	Diseases of the skin and subcutaneous tissue
XIII	M00-M99	Diseases of the musculoskeletal system and connective tissue
XIV	N00-N99	Diseases of the genitourinary system
XV	O00-O99	Pregnancy, childbirth and the puerperium
XVI	P00-P96	Certain conditions originating in the perinatal period
XVII	Q00-Q99	Congenital malformations, deformations and chromosomal abnormalities
XVIII	R00-R99	Symptoms, signs and abnormal clinical and laboratory findings, not elsewhere classified
XIX	S00-T98	Injury, poisoning and certain other consequences of external causes
XX	V01-Y98	External causes of morbidity and mortality
XXI	Z00-Z99	Factors influencing health status and contact with health services
XXII	U00-U99	Codes for special purposes

Source: WHO (2004).

There also needs to be some consideration regarding the classification of injuries. While the GBD framework proposes only a class by cause of injury (*e.g.* Road traffic accidents, Poisonings, Falls, Fires, Drowning, Self-inflicted injuries, Violence, War), the ICD offers both reporting by cause (ICD Chapter XX) and by nature or body region (ICD Chapter XIX; for example, injuries to the head, to the neck, to the thorax, to the abdomen, to the shoulder and upper arm, to the hip and thigh, and so on). It is important to understand this distinction. It is suggested that for policy information relating to public safety and prevention it is preferable that injuries be classified by cause (road traffic and others), but countries may choose to break down Injuries by body regions as Reporting Items, if that is more commonly used in their statistical reporting and analysis.

Co-morbidity

Many patient contacts from which the necessary primary data are generated can also be related to secondary or underlying diseases and conditions, such as diabetes or mental disorders. The problem of co-morbidity and the allocation of expenditure by disease to the primary diagnostic approach is that it could underestimate the spending on some of these underlying diseases. In analysis of HIV/TB, allocation of resources by primary diagnosis may give an expenditure distribution that is misleading, depending on the policy perspective. For example, expenditures for an HIV patient treated for TB, and external resources allocated to HIV, which might cover spending on HIV patients with TB, would all fall under HIV. This would lead to an underestimate of TB expenditures.[9]

There are three potential options for dealing with this issue: *i)* to classify expenditures according to the primary diagnosis, *ii)* to equally pro-rate the expenditures over the applicable diagnoses and *iii)* to distribute expenditures across the applicable diagnoses using disease-specific weights that reflect the relative resource intensity involved.

Although the third is conceptually the most ideal and provides a clear link between disease and total spending, in practice the data requirements to support such an approach are immense and in most countries will not be currently met. The second option is more feasible, but in many situations the available data will only have recorded the primary diagnosis, and not all co-morbidities. Given this, it is generally agreed that the standard approach should follow the first option.[10] That is, to classify expenditures according to the primary diagnosis,[11] except in those instances where the primary diagnosis cannot be differentiated from other diagnoses in the available data, in which case the expenditures should be pro-rated equally across all relevant conditions.

Socioeconomic status

Health outcomes vary in all countries by level of the socio-economic status of individuals, and such disparities are a major policy concern both within countries and at a global level. Consequently, policy makers and others are interested in understanding how health care resources and expenditures are distributed across people at different socioeconomic levels. The WHO Commission on Social Determinants of Health (WHO, 2008a) has called on all governments to routinely measure such disparities.[12]

Generally speaking, the results of such exercises can be presented either in the form of tables or as single statistics, such as the concentration index, that summarise the overall level of inequality in spending. However, in the context of extending SHA framework to analyse the distribution of spending by socioeconomic status, an approach that directly apportions health expenditure by different population groups and presents this in tabular form is desirable. To do this, beneficiaries need to be ranked and grouped according to their relative socioeconomic status, including potentially the levels of their living standards.

Taking into account the experience gained in past studies and their relative conceptual merits, as well as the frequently expressed needs of policy makers, it is recommended, in international reporting of the distribution of expenditure by socioeconomic status, that beneficiaries be classified according to quintiles of their relative socioeconomic level, as represented by levels of living standards.[13]

However, several alternative approaches are available and commonly used to measure relative affluence: income, expenditure and consumption, or wealth (stock concept as opposed to flow), or even a combination of several indicators such as income, education and occupation. In general, economic theory prefers consumption, as it is most correlated with long-term economic well-being and resources. However, consumption is often hard to measure, as it requires the imputation of the value of goods and services consumed which are not paid for or associated with measurable financial transactions, such as living in a self-owned house. In the absence of data to compute consumption, the next best alternative would in most cases be expenditure, and then income. In certain settings, where the relevant data sources do not permit computation of either household consumption or expenditure, a wealth index based on ownership of assets can be used. A wealth index correlates well in many surveys with consumption and expenditure measures, and wealth is also correlated with long-term living standards, so in practice it can be considered a better measure than income measures.

Income, expenditure and consumption are commonly measured in household surveys, which are the primary data source for this type of distributed expenditures. It should be noted at this point that these measures typically will require the use of household survey data and are not generally feasible using provider-generated data.

Household surveys typically provide a measure of the consumption of a household. The total aggregate consumption of a household is not by itself a good measure of the relative well-being of household members, since this also depends on how many individuals share this consumption. This points to the need to adjust household consumption for household size. Several approaches are available in the literature to do this. One is simply to take the value of per capita consumption, which is derived by dividing total household consumption by the size of the household. The weakness of this approach is that it takes into account neither the different consumption needs of adults and children, nor any economies of scale that households can achieve by pooling household consumption. In response, economists have proposed equivalence scales to adjust household consumption to take into account the actual size and age composition of the household. There is no standard equivalence scale that is widely used across different organisations or in the literature. Some equivalence scales are also specific to individual countries, and must be estimated separately by each. More detailed discussion of the different statistical computation methods that can be used and the issues involved is provided in recent World Bank guidelines (O'Donnell *et al.*, 2008).

So the first and preferred option to use as an instrument for classifying personal socio-economic status per person is consumption, followed by expenditure, income[14] and finally a wealth index. However, in view of the difficulties in estimating personal consumption, spending or income data, groupings per household are used instead.

Geographical region

WHO has produced detailed guidelines for the estimation of the distribution of expenditure by geographical region (WHO, 2008b). In practice, the classification of areas must be done separately in each country, taking into account both policy needs and data availability and feasibility. Consequently, no standard classification of regions is feasible.

Nevertheless, two important issues are noted. The first concerns the basis on which expenditure should be assigned to an individual. Two alternatives are available. The first is to assign expenditures to regions according to the location where the medical service is provided, and the second is to assign expenditures according to the region of residence of the beneficiary. These guidelines recommend the latter for consistency with overall health accounts boundaries and principles (more information can be found on the former in the WHO guidelines). However, in practice, the data sources that are used to apportion expenditures often relate to where the expenditures were incurred, making this second approach not feasible. In these situations, it is often necessary to compromise and take a pragmatic approach.

The second issue is the treatment of collective health services expenditures. In most studies, collective services are ignored. It might be thought that this would have little effect on the expenditure by region of the beneficiary, since these expenditures can only be pro-rated across all individuals. However, in practice there can be variation in such expenditures across national regions, since in most countries the budgets for such services are to some extent separate for different regions. It is recommended that all such studies fully analyse such expenditures (HC.6-HC.7), apportioning them equally within relevant geographical populations.

All health account dimensions might be considered when building regional accounts. Policy makers might be interested in understanding the financing mechanisms in place in each region in order to focus policies on the regions with more inequalities. Some regions may find that their households bear the largest share of funding or health care payments, or that financing schemes may be used more in some regions than in others. Where the resources are being spent also informs policy makers about the patterns of spending in regions, such as variations in providers or in functions (*e.g.* pharmaceutical goods), which can lead to creating policy incentives for a more efficient use of resources or a better redistribution of funds.

When developing expenditure by regions, actual accounts can be built. We would call these regional accounts. Health accounts dimensions are computed for each region and matrices are built per region (for example, crossing revenues by schemes, schemes by functions, etc.). These matrices are recommended for expenditure by regions, while they are not feasible for other beneficiary expenditure breakdowns.

Expenditure by regions can also be expanded to expenditure on the production of each region. This is particularly interesting when governments need to understand the production capacities of their regions, especially in relation to subsidies.

Possible methodological approaches

In all cases, regardless of the type of classification, the estimation of expenditure by beneficiary characteristics requires additional data sources, beyond those used to construct the health accounts. Detailed guidelines on how different distributional analyses can be conducted are available in complementary guides on how to produce health accounts in various contexts/regions. Nevertheless, some basic principles and issues are described here. They serve to give indications on how to proceed in estimating expenditure by beneficiaries, for each type of beneficiary.

In contrast to studies that are not linked to the health accounts, SHA-based expenditure by beneficiary constrains estimates to the overall estimates of national health spending. Thus, SHA-based beneficiary analyses must generally adopt what is known as a top-down approach. In a top-down approach, the major components of spending in a health system are first identified (cost units), and then other data sources are used to distribute each component of spending across the population according to the beneficiary classification being used. The top-down approach can be contrasted with a bottom-up approach, which is usually used in specific disease cost-of-illness studies. The bottom-up approach depends on the availability of detailed patient-level data, which are used to directly estimate the expenditure by different patient characteristics. Such an approach may be desirable or even necessary in some situations, and should be adapted to support a top-down approach. This can be done by using the patient-level data to build up a picture of overall spending by patient characteristics, and then applying the resulting distribution to the estimates of national spending, thus combining a bottom-up approach with a top-down approach.

The general strategy adopted should proceed through the following steps:

- Identification of major spending areas or components within national health spending as reported in SHA accounts;
- Identification of suitable data sources that permit the breakdown of each identified major spending area by beneficiary characteristics;
- Use of the identified data sources as distribution keys to distribute spending across different beneficiary characteristics, for example, disease, age and gender, concurrently.

A spending area or component can be defined from a provider, a functional or a financing perspective. The choice of spending areas in this approach depends on the beneficiary characteristic and the availability of data. It will thus vary between countries, and no general recommendations are made here. For example, most of the countries participating in the Eurostat study of expenditure by age, gender and disease reported that estimates by type of provider were most feasible (BASYS *et al.*, 2006) . This was because most relevant data consisted of patient records generated at the provider-level. However, in a comparable US study (Roehrig *et al.*, 2009), a large proportion of the estimates were developed by analysing person-based expenditures generated in a household survey, which allowed direct mapping to conditions and other personal characteristics.

In general, studies of expenditure by disease will mostly rely on provider-generated data, since these tend to be coded at the necessary level of detail with respect to diagnoses. However, analyses of expenditure by different socioeconomic status will generally rely on household survey data, as typically only household surveys collect and report data that allow the status of a household to be assessed.

Once a spending area is identified, a data source must be used to distribute the expenditure by beneficiary characteristics. Suitable data sources will act as distributional keys, which provide information on the proportionate distribution of spending. For example, if inpatient expenditures are the spending area, large samples of patient records can be used to distribute expenditure by diagnosis. In an ideal situation, these patient records would contain details of the actual expenditures incurred, but in other instances they will not. In the latter cases, the cost contribution of each patient might need to be estimated on the basis of other data, such as length of stay, medicines dispensed and other hospital facilities utilised.

The basic approach outlined above lends itself to expenditure by beneficiary characteristics and one ICHA dimension. Although desirable, in practice estimating a tri-axial distribution of spending by provider, function and financing scheme is more difficult and requires more detailed data. Specifically, it requires that the patient-level data used allow the coding of each transaction by all three dimensions. Certainly, at the current time this is often not feasible at the full level of detail used in the major ICHA classifications,[15] even in OECD economies (BASYS *et al.*, 2006). Nevertheless, this should be seen as the ultimate objective.

In situations where the primary data source does not support the coding of expenditure by all three dimensions of provider, function and financing scheme, an alternative approach is to use a second data source to impute the distribution of spending along the additional dimensions.

Estimation of expenditure by disease

Most studies to date have used a prevalence-based method, in which all costs due to prevalent cases of disease in a given period are aggregated to total costs. This is the approach recommended here when reporting at the international level. There are various approaches to the allocation of expenditure to disease which, for example, may use different units of analysis, and thus are best adapted for different uses (Rosen and Cutler, 2009).

As soon as a definition study has been completed and utilisation data are obtained, the direct medical cost calculations by disease, using a prevalence-based method with a top-down attribution of costs, is a fairly straightforward procedure. It can be divided into four steps:

1) Selection of a suitable year for analysis and assessment of national health expenditure;
2) Partition of national health expenditure into homogeneous cost-units – *i.e.* displaying similar characteristics across provider and function dimensions, for example;
3) Construction of a detailed probability map (that is, the proportional distribution across all combinations of all dimensions) based on health care utilisation data retrieved from the collected data sources;
4) Multiplication of health expenditure for a homogeneous unit (from step 2) with the probability map (from step 3) to establish a partial cost of illness table for this unit, and aggregate partial tables for each unit to establish the total cost of illness (OECD, 2008).

Estimation of expenditure by geographical region

The methodology described here is to be used for distributing expenditure on health by region of residence. It is taken from the WHO *Guide to Producing Regional Health Accounts* and it is proposed for expenditures that are made by national agencies, and which should be apportioned to regions using a top-down approach. However, where expenditures are made by sub-national agencies and where the data are generated at the sub-national level, it is recommended to use bottom-up approaches to compile the necessary estimates.

When data are not available on a sub-national basis, the expenditures under consideration can be distributed using proxy variables (sometimes called "keys") as indicators of the likely distribution. In some cases, the sum of region-based estimates does not equal the national total, which is presumed to be more accurate. Typically, one can assume that the "error" – the difference between the regional sum and the national total – is proportionate across the regions, and the regional figures can be adjusted accordingly. For example, a one-off survey of household spending on health in Mexico was calibrated to national estimates produced from other data, producing state-level figures consistent with the national total and reflecting regional variations as found in the survey itself. In other cases, a closely related expenditure figure can serve as a proxy. For example, in Sri Lanka, provincial governments have their own budgets for medical supplies. At the same time, the central health ministry, which purchases supplies and distributes them to the provinces, accounts for a large part of public spending on medical supplies. The central ministry does not maintain clear records of how its centrally procured supplies are distributed, so Sri Lanka's health accountants distribute the central ministry spending among provinces by assuming that the ratio between provincial and central spending on supplies is identical across all provinces. In other cases, the proxy will be some measure of inputs or outputs. For example, because labour accounts for a large share of expenditure, regional estimates of spending on health personnel (preferably wages but, failing that, work hours) might be used to allocate a national total among regions. The number of inpatient days might be used to allocate a national estimate of ministry hospital spending if facility level costs are not known. Some proxy measures can be more elaborate than a single indicator. For example, if information exists regarding the prices of multiple inputs into a cell in the health accounts, a sort of market basket can be developed as a distribution tool.

Distributing spending equally on a population basis should be a last resort, except in the case of population health measures intended to protect the population on a collective basis. In practice, most health resources are not distributed according to the population to be served, so the assumption of equal distribution per capita is unlikely to produce meaningful conclusions in terms of the equity, efficiency, or effectiveness of the financing flows. However, if no better proxy measure is available, this method can be used as a temporary solution, pending discussions with sub-national authorities about spending in their jurisdiction and the development of a more relevant tool for monitoring and assessment. Of course, using proxy measures limits the conclusions that can be drawn from the results. For instance, when per capita data are used to construct one of the dimensions, nothing can be concluded about per capita distributions. When resource indicators are used, a productivity analysis may be meaningless. In any case, the proxy measure must be chosen carefully, as an inappropriate proxy can distort the regional accounts to such an extent that they become meaningless (WHO, 2008b, 5.17-5.22).

Estimation of expenditure by socioeconomic status

The following approach is based on work by the EQUITAP network and on analyses by the ECuity network. Health accounts statistics should be used to derive the total aggregates of spending by financing scheme, or by provider and function. Household survey data should then be used to distribute these expenditures by socioeconomic status (SES).[16] The main aggregates to distribute are the expenditures of households, government, insurance, NGOs and firms on health care.

- Household survey data are typically used for allocating health expenditure by quintile of socioeconomic status.
- Distribution of public subsidies for health care (using the benefit incidence analysis) is computed from estimates of government subsidies to outpatient and inpatient care. Where possible, the distribution is done at provincial or regional level using household data and hospital unit costs data. Only health services that potentially receive a subsidy from the state-controlled budget should be included (usually all publicly provided health care services).

Notes

1. Polder was one of the first to try to link the data on disease, age and gender to the health accounts data. See Polder *et al.* (2002); Polder and Achterberg (2004).
2. Table 5.6 "Personal health expenditure by type of financing agent and by age and sex of the population"; Table 5.7 "National health expenditure by type of financing agent and by per capita household expenditure quintile"; Table 5.8 "National health expenditure by type of financing agent and by disease group"; Table 5.9 "National health expenditure by type of financing agent and by region".
3. The GBD 1990 Study (1) classified disease and injury causes using a tree structure. The first level of disaggregation comprised three broad cause groups:

   - Group I: Communicable, maternal, perinatal and nutritional conditions;
   - Group II: Non-communicable diseases;
   - Group III: Injuries.

   Group I causes consist of the cluster of conditions whose mortality typically declines at a faster pace than all-cause mortality during the epidemiological transition. In high-mortality populations, Group I dominates the causes of death, whereas in low-mortality populations, it accounts for only a small proportion of deaths. Each group is divided into major subcategories. For example, cardiovascular diseases and malignant neoplasms (cancers) are two major cause subcategories of Group II. Beyond this level, there are two further disaggregation levels. The major cause subcategories are closely based on the chapters of the International Classification of Diseases (ICD) (2), with some important differences. Whereas the ICD classifies chronic respiratory diseases and acute respiratory infections into one chapter, the GBD classification included acute respiratory infections in Group I. Similarly, infectious diseases such as meningitis and cystitis included in the ICD chapters – neurological conditions and genito-urinary conditions, respectively – have also been moved to Group I.

4. Of particular relevance are national studies in Australia (AIHW, 2010), the Netherlands and the United States (Roehrig *et al.*, 2009), the Eurostat Feasibility Study of Health Expenditures by Patient Characteristics (BASYS, CEPS and IGSS 2006), WHO-sponsored pilot studies in Sri Lanka and Thailand, and the OECD Guidelines on Estimating Expenditure by Disease, Age and Gender under SHA Framework (OECD, 2008).

5. Five-year age groups: 0, 1-4, 5-9, 10-14, etc., up to 94, and finally adding 95+. An alternative can be a distinction in 10 year age groups: 0, 1-9, 10-19, etc., up to 99 and adding 100+.

6. See the Australian and US studies referred to in the footnote above. In addition, the Eurostat study of EU member states demonstrated the feasibility of distributing expenditure by disease categories, whilst two WHO-supported pilot studies have demonstrated the feasibility of comparable estimates in two developing countries.

7. "Recognising the problems of the ICD, and the need for an internationally recognised classification for general practice, the WONCA Classification Committee [now the Wonca International Classification Committee (WICC)] designed the International Classification of Health Problems in Primary Care (ICHPPC), first published in 1975, with a second edition in 1979 related to the 9th revision of ICD. Although this provided a section for the classification of some undiagnosed symptoms, it retained the basic ICD structure and was still inadequate. A third edition (ICHPPC-2-Defined) in 1983 had added to it criteria for the use of most of the rubrics, greatly adding to the reliability with which it could be used, but not overcoming its deficiencies for primary care. A new classification was needed for both the patient's reason for an encounter and the provider's record of the patient's problems. (...) A small working party was formed under the auspice of WHO (...). Over several years of work, this working party developed the Reason for Encounter Classification (RFEC), which, after extensive field trials involving many members of WICC, eventually evolved into ICPC." *www.globalfamilydoctor.com/wicc/icpcstory.html*. N.B. The World Organisation of National Colleges, Academies (Wonca) and Academic Associations of General Practitioners/Family Physicians or in short World Organisation of Family Doctors is an international organisation of national colleges, academies and organisations concerned with the academic aspects of general family practice. Wonca was founded in 1972.

8. Infectious and parasitic diseases includes diseases such as tuberculosis, HIV/AIDS and malaria at the third-digit level, for which expenditure estimates are highly policy relevant in a large number of countries.

9. This touches upon the difference between expenditure by diseases and disease-specific accounts. In the example here, the same joint spending on HIV/TB would be accounted for under both disease-specific accounts. However, when distributing spending by diseases, double-counting is not possible, and either spending is allocated to one disease (risking over- and under-estimations), or a special combined class is created.

10. This is also the solution recommended in the OECD guidelines.

11. Here in the adapted GBD classification used in this chapter it is proposed to follow the convention that the primary cause is the leading cause in which the data should be classified, which is opposite to the choice made in the GBD classification.

12. There is a long history of analysing expenditures by the socioeconomic status of beneficiaries, and methods for the analysis of micro-data for this purpose are well developed. Of particular note is the work sponsored by the European Commission since the early 1990s to examine equity in health care financing and delivery in European countries, with a similar effort in the following decade in Asian countries. This work, led by the ECuity network in Europe has been examining disparities in health care spending in different European countries (van Doorslaer, 1993) for two decades, and in Asia the EQUITAP network, which has emulated ECuity in Asia since 2000, has been supporting similar work (Rannan-Eliya and Somanathan, 2006). At the same time, these efforts have rarely been directly linked to estimates of national spending as derived from the health accounts, although EQUITAP has done this in countries where the data permit.

13. Note that what is presented in subsequent paragraphs is only one dimension of socioeconomic status. SES is in fact a wider concept, potentially involving many dimensions other than income or consumption, such as education or work status.

14. Equivalence or economies of scale issues apply equally to the use of expenditure or income measures.
15. Sri Lanka's disease accounts project does estimate by three dimensions plus disease, however, there was a need to aggregate the classifications in at least one or two ICHA dimensions. See *www.ihp.lk/research/project.html?project_id=HA-009*.
16. Where possible, aggregates should be at the sub-national level if there are significant variations in spending between regions.

A System of Health Accounts 2011: Revised edition

PART II

Chapter 11

Capital Formation in Health Systems

Introduction

Knowing how much a health system is investing in infrastructure, machinery and equipment is very relevant for policy making and analysis. Although health systems remain a highly labour-intensive sector, capital has been increasingly important as a factor of production of health services over recent decades. Consider, for example, the growing importance of diagnostic and therapeutic equipment or the expansion of information, computer and telecommunications technology in health care over the last few years. The availability of statistics on capital are essential to the analysis of the health system's production capacity (that is, whether capacity is appropriate, deficient or excessive), which is needed in turn to inform policy implementation (for example, if excess capacity exists, the marginal cost of expanding coverage will be lower than if the health care system is already straining to fill current demand). Information on capital could also assist with the estimation of productivity, capital intensity and rates of return.

The remainder of this chapter presents the definition of the capital aggregates in health systems, the identification of their boundaries and the criteria for valuation, with a short section illustrating some guidelines for the estimation of capital formation. The chapter provides an example of a capital account for SHA. Research and development in health and the Education and training of health personnel are included as memorandum items to the capital account.

Definition of gross capital formation in SHA

The aggregate "Gross[1] capital formation" is measured by the sum of three components:

- Gross fixed capital formation (*e.g.* hospital buildings or ambulances);
- Changes in inventories (*e.g.* vaccinations kept in stock); and
- Acquisitions less disposals of valuables (*e.g.* artworks).

Gross fixed capital formation is generally the most relevant component. It is defined as follows:

Gross fixed capital formation

Gross fixed capital formation in the health care system is measured by the total value of the fixed *assets* that health providers have *acquired* during the accounting period (less the value of the disposals of assets) and that are used repeatedly or continuously for more than one year in the production of health services.

Assets are defined as "a store of value", or a means of carrying forward value from one period to another. By holding or using the assets, the owner can accrue benefits. Fixed assets have come into existence as outputs from a production process. Assets qualify as "fixed" only if they can be used repeatedly or continuously in production for more than one year. Goods that can be used once only (*e.g.* coal), even if physically highly durable, are not considered as fixed assets. Examples of fixed assets in the health sector include, among other things, hospital buildings, ambulances and medical imaging machines.

Health care providers, as defined in Chapter 6, can acquire fixed assets by purchase or barter or as transfers in kind. Symmetrically, health providers can dispose of the assets by selling them, surrendering them in barter or as transfers in kind.

Note that it is possible for gross fixed capital formation to be negative. This would occur if the value of the disposed assets exceeds the value of those acquired.

Boundaries

Ownership

The guiding principle for the recording of gross capital formation in health accounts is the legal ownership of the assets by health care providers. Only assets legally owned by the health care providers are included under capital formation.[2]

SHA records the value of assets acquired, and disposed of, by all health care providers except health care providers classified under the rest of the world. The exclusion of the rest of the world avoids recording the same assets in two countries.[3,4] Particular attention should be paid to the assets acquired by those health care providers whose principal activity is not the provision of health services. Assets used repeatedly or continuously for the provision of health services should be included regardless of the fact that the provision of health services is the principal activity of the owner. For example, road ambulances used repeatedly or continuously for the transportation of patients should be included regardless of the fact that the principal activity of the owner of the ambulance is to operate taxis. However, a taxi used occasionally, but not repeatedly or continuously, by the same owner for the transportation of patients should be excluded. Similarly, air-ambulances should be included even if the owner is primarily engaged in the air transportation of passengers. The net acquisition of capital assets made by retail sellers of medical goods are also included, since retail sellers are considered as health care providers in a number of countries. For example, in Switzerland, pharmacists can recommend and even prescribe medicines. In other countries, pharmacists also offer advice on common complaints such as coughs, colds, aches and pains and other health issues, such as healthy eating and giving up smoking. Health capital goods acquired by households are included only if their costs are reimbursed. For example, financing schemes can reimburse households that purchase a hospital-type bed or can cover completely or partially the cost of adapting vehicle access for people with reduced mobility. Some difficulties might arise in recording the value of the assets owned by "Providers of health care system administration and financing" (HP.7) and "Other health care providers" (HP.8) that can also be used for the production of services other than health. For example, buildings owned by insurance companies might well be used indistinctively for the production of both health and non-health insurance services. In such cases, only a part of the value of the assets should be recorded. To do that, it would be advisable to use a pragmatic approach in which only the proportion of the value of the assets that can be identified through a relatively inexpensive effort should be recorded.

Assets owned by non-health care providers are not accounted for in SHA. Therefore, assets owned by banks and leased (operational leasing) to health care providers are not recorded in SHA. For example, an MRI machine bought by a bank (which is the legal owner) and leased to a hospital with no intention of transferring the ownership will not be recorded in SHA, as the bank is not a health care provider.[5]

Time of recording

Acquisitions and disposals of fixed assets are recorded when the ownership is transferred to the health care provider that intends to use them in production (in the case of acquisitions) or from the health care provider who has previously used them in production (in the case of disposals). In general, this is not the same as the time at which the fixed assets are produced. Nor is it necessarily the time at which the assets are put into use in the production of health care goods or services.

Exceptions

Exceptions to the ownership and change of legal ownership principles are possible in the case of financial leasing or when the construction of the fixed assets spans a long period of time, as is often the case for hospital buildings (typically several years).

Financial leasing is a form of contract that allows one party (the lessee) to use the asset in exchange for rental payments. During the leasing period, it is the responsibility of the lessee to repair and maintain the asset. At the end of the leasing period the lessee can buy the asset. In this case, the asset is recorded as gross fixed capital formation of the lessee at the beginning of the leasing period and not at the end of the leasing period when the legal ownership is acquired (see Box 11.3 for the distinction between financial and operating leasing).

An exception is made when the construction of the fixed assets spans a long period of time, and the two following conditions are met: the future owner is known and stage payments are made during the construction period. The future owner can be identified before the construction is finished if the asset is produced under a contract of sale agreed in advance between the producer and the future owner. The contract of sale can foresee stage payments to be made on a regular basis during the construction period. In these circumstances, the stage payments can be regarded as the purchase of a part of the fixed asset and recorded as gross capital formation of the future owner. This can also be done in the case when the value of the stage payment exceeds the value of the incomplete asset put in place. In that case, the excess part of the stage payment can be seen as a trade advance.

Valuation

The value of the various components of gross capital formation is given by the sum of acquisitions less disposals. Acquisitions include the whole value of fixed assets purchased, acquired through barter or received as capital transfers in kind plus the value of fixed assets produced by health care providers and retained for their own use (such as software). Disposals include the value of existing fixed assets sold or surrendered in barter and capital transfers in kind. The value of fixed assets purchased or produced by health care providers and retained for their own use include new assets, existing assets, the value of improvements to assets and the cost of ownership transfers in respect of these assets. Disposals include assets that may cease to be used as fixed assets by their new owners (for example, a hospital sold by local government to central government[6]), assets that are scrapped or demolished by their new owners (*e.g.* obsolete ambulances) and assets that are exported.

Box 11.1. **Terminology**

Difference between gross capital formation (GCF) and gross fixed capital formation (GFCF)

Gross capital formation is the sum of the value of the following three components:

1. Gross fixed capital formation;
2. Changes in inventories; and
3. Acquisitions less disposals of valuables.

Therefore gross fixed capital formation is one of the three elements included in the wider aggregate called gross capital formation.

Consumption of fixed capital (CFC)

As time goes by, capital goods progressively lose their value. This could be due either to physical use or obsolescence. Consider for example a personal computer bought at a certain point in time for EUR 1 000: after three years its market value would be greatly reduced, and after five years it would be almost negligible. The loss of the value of the capital goods due to their normal wear and tear or obsolescence is called *Consumption of fixed capital* or *capital consumption*. Capital consumption is an *imputed*, not an actual cost. In other words it is a non-cash expense. Capital consumption is added to all other production costs to indirectly estimate the value of the non-market production. The indirect measure is an approximation required to overcome the lack of economically significant prices for the non-market sector.

Difference between capital formation and consumption of fixed capital (CFC)

Capital formation identifies the value of the assets acquired in the accounting period (*e.g.* new ambulances purchased or new hospitals built in that period), while the consumption of fixed capital refers to the loss in value (due to normal wear-and-tear or obsolescence) of the whole existing stock of capital (which includes not only the assets newly acquired, but all those still available regardless of the moment they were initially acquired).

Difference between gross and net capital formation

A refined measure of how much value has been added to the existing capital stock in the accounting period should take into account the loss of value of the existing capital goods that has been lost due to use or obsolescence. Such a refined measure, called net capital formation, is obtained by subtracting the value of capital consumption from gross capital formation.

Investment

While gross capital formation is an investment, not all investments can be classified as gross capital formation. For example, the purchase of a financial product is an investment, although it is not included in gross capital formation.

Assets acquired (or improvements carried out) are valued at purchasers' prices, which include all transport and installation charges as well as all costs of the transfer of ownership.

Type of asset

A fundamental question for national compilers is, "what assets are to be included in health accounts?" For example, are road ambulances included or not? And buildings? And what about computers? A clear identification of the assets might help national compilers, and also enhance the international comparability of the data. To address this issue, a list of categories of assets whose value should be included in the aggregate gross fixed capital formation is given in Table 11.1. The classification of type of assets is meant to be used primarily for the identification of the capital goods and services to be reported.

The classification of health capital goods by type of asset provides policy makers with relevant information on the nature of equipment, machinery, buildings and so on. One reason this is useful to know is that the technology embedded in the assets will affect their expected service life. For example, investments in hospital buildings are likely to last longer than investments in transport equipment, and transport equipment are expected to serve longer than ICT devices. A classification by assets could also serve policy analysts by enhancing the international comparability, and also by facilitating the linkage to non-expenditure statistics (*e.g.* number of beds, number of scans). Indeed, as with current health expenditure, for which the functional classification allows the identification of comparable aggregates, the classification by assets of gross fixed capital formation would allow categories to be set that are more directly comparable. For example, the amount spent on medical equipment is more comparable than how much was spent on investment by hospitals.

Table 11.1. **Classification of gross fixed capital formation in health systems by type of asset**

HK.1.1.1 Infrastructure
HK.1.1.1.1 Residential and non-residential buildings
HK.1.1.1.2 Other structures
HK.1.1.2 Machinery and equipment
HK.1.1.2.1 Medical equipment
HK.1.1.2.2 Transport equipment
HK.1.1.2.3 ICT equipment
HK.1.1.2.4 Machinery and equipment *n.e.c.*
HK.1.1.3 Intellectual property products
HK.1.1.3.1 Computer software and databases
HK.1.1.3.2 Intellectual property products *n.e.c.*

Source: IHAT for SHA 2011.

HK.1.1.1 Infrastructure

Infrastructure in the health care system includes two components: "Residential and non-residential buildings" and "Other structures".

HK.1.1.1.1 Residential and non-residential buildings. Residential and non-residential buildings acquired (less those disposed) by the health care providers are included in this category. Examples include nursing and residential care facilities, hospital settings, ambulatory facilities and so on. Health providers' residential and non-residential buildings are included in the subclasses Multi-dwelling residential buildings (53112 in CPC ver.2.), Commercial buildings (53122) and Other non-residential buildings (53129).

HK.1.1.1.2 Other structures. Other structures include structures other than buildings acquired (less those disposed) by the health care providers, for example, emergency helicopter landing facilities (Airfield runways 53213 in CPC ver.2.), aircraft hangars and so on, whenever they are not incorporated in the building.

HK.1.1.2 Machinery and equipment

Machinery and equipment covers medical equipment, transport equipment, information, communication and telecommunications (ICT) equipment, and other machinery and equipment not elsewhere classified. As explained above, leased machinery and equipment is recorded under capital formation of the health providers in the case of financial leases only (that is, the provider will eventually become the owner of the assets). On the contrary, assets used by health care providers under operational lease are not recorded as capital formation of the user, as the ownership of the assets is the guiding principle for inclusion or exclusion of the assets. Tools that are relatively inexpensive and purchased at a relatively steady rate, such as hand tools, are considered as intermediate consumption and are therefore excluded from capital formation. Also excluded are machinery and equipment integral to a building.

HK.1.1.2.1 Medical equipment. Medical equipment consists of assets employed for the diagnosis, monitoring or treatment of medical conditions. Examples include: diagnostic equipment (*e.g.* ultrasound and MRI machines, PET and CT scanners, and X-ray machines), therapeutic equipment (*e.g.* infusion pumps, medical lasers and LASIK surgical machines), life support equipment (*e.g.* medical ventilators, heart-lung machines, ECMO and dialysis machines), medical monitors (for example, ECG, EEG, blood pressure) or miniature robots employed to perform complex surgery; laboratory equipment (blood test devices) and hospital-type beds can also be included in this category.

HK.1.1.2.2 Transport equipment. Transport equipment consists of equipment for moving patients, organs and health personnel. Examples include road vehicles (road ambulances, patient transport vehicles, patient transport cars, rapid response cars and cars used by health personnel in the framework of vaccination provision programmes) and air ambulances (either fixed or rotary wing). In a few specific cases this could also include water ambulances (boat) or special rapid-response motorbikes and bicycles in urban areas. Mobile health clinics are also included in this item. In CPC ver.2, the health providers' transport equipment would be classified under the subclasses Motor cars and other motor vehicles principally designed for the transport of persons (49113), Special-purpose motor vehicles *n.e.c.* (49119), Aeroplanes and helicopters (4962) and Other floating structures (49390).

HK.1.1.2.3 ICT equipment. Information, computer and telecommunications (ICT) equipment consists of devices using electronic controls as well as the electronic components incorporated in these devices. In the health system, ICT devices can be used to deliver health care services where distance is a critical factor, such as when health care professionals exchange information for the diagnosis, treatment and prevention of diseases and injuries, for research and evaluation, and for the continuing education of health care providers. In addition, ICT devices can be employed in the administration of health providers. Relevant subclasses of the CPC ver.2 for ICT equipment are: from 4522 to 4525, from 45261 to 45269, 4527, 45281 and 45289.

HK.1.1.2.4 Machinery and equipment not elsewhere classified. Other machinery and equipment not elsewhere classified includes, for example, kitchen equipment used in hospital for the preparation of meals for patients and personnel or closed-circuit television (CCT) used for the security of health care facilities.

Box 11.2. **Difference between gross capital formation (GCF) and intermediate consumption**

Health care providers require an array of goods and services that are used as inputs for the provision of health care services. Some goods and services are entirely used up (*e.g.* electricity, water, fuel, surgical masks, protective wear). Other goods are transformed or incorporated into the final service provided to the users (*e.g.* bandages). Those categories of goods and services whose economic life ends within the accounting period are classified as intermediate consumption. As such they are recorded in the factors of provision (see Chapter 9).

Those goods and services differ significantly from other inputs that are used repeatedly or continuously for more than one year in the production of health services, for example, hospital infrastructure, road ambulances or MRI machines. Only this category is classified as capital formation.

HK.1.1.3 Intellectual property products

Intellectual property products are the result of research, development, investigation or innovation leading to knowledge that the developers can market or use to their own benefit in production, because use of the knowledge is restricted by means of legal or other protection.

Intellectual property products could be produced by health care providers on their own account. Examples of intellectual property products are computer software and databases, and the results of research and development.

HK.1.1.3.1 Computer software and databases. Computer software consists of computer programmes, programme descriptions and supporting materials for both systems and applications software. Databases consist of data files organised in such a way as to permit resource-effective access to and use of the data.

Due to the specific nature of research and development and to the methodological difficulties related to the estimation of this specific item, SHA 2011 does not consider expenditure on R&D as an investment, and it is therefore not included in health capital formation. Health R&D is to be reported separately as a memorandum item. This represents a departure from SNA 2008.

Treatment of specific cases

In general, the bulk of capital goods acquired by health care providers are produced outside the health care sector (either by other sectors of the national economy or abroad). The main exception is the production of specific software. In this case, if the software produced by the health provider is acquired by units that cannot be classified as health care providers, then that production should be seen as secondary non-health production activity and thus outside SHA boundaries. Otherwise, the value of the software will be recorded under the acquiring health care provider.

For practical reasons, it would be advisable to exclude capital formation of Providers of health system administration and financing whenever their activity is embedded in larger units for which health administration is not the predominant activity and/or it would be impossible to identify the capital goods used specifically for health administration. For example, consider the purchase of a new building by an insurance company that deals with all sorts of personal insurance and not just health insurance. It would be advisable to record the value of the portion of the assets used for the provision of health insurance services only so long as such estimations could be made. A similar principle should be applied to recording the capital formation of health care providers classified under "Other health care providers" (see Chapter 6), as the provision of health services is not the predominant activity. To clarify this point, consider two airline companies: the first company has as its sole activity patient transportation, while the second airline company's main activity is regular and charter passenger transportation, but its secondary activity is transport for medical emergencies and organ transportation. If both companies purchase the same specially-equipped new helicopter to operate the same health services, both acquisitions should be recorded in SHA, regardless of the fact that patient transportation is the main activity in one company and the secondary activity in the other. In other words, the guiding principle for the economic units included under HP.8 is to record the acquisition of those assets used to provide health services only, even if the provision of health services is a secondary activity of the provider.

Immovable assets owned by non-residents

Capital formation by foreign providers (that is, providers included in the rest of the world) is recorded in the accounts of the country of residence of the provider. For example, despite the fact that some French citizens use health services provided by hospitals in Luxembourg, France does not record the acquisition of assets made by the Luxembourg hospitals, as those acquisitions are already recorded in Luxembourg.

Furthermore, by convention, immovable assets such as hospital buildings are considered as belonging to the economic territory regardless of the residence of the owner. If the legal owner (or lessee under a financial lease) of an immovable asset does not qualify as a resident, an artificial statistical unit is specifically created in the economic territory. For example, the building of the American Hospital in Paris is an immovable asset on French economic territory which by convention generates a statistical unit (a SHA health provider) in France, regardless of whether the owner of that building is resident in France or not.

Relatively inexpensive tools

Tools such as medical instruments that are relatively inexpensive and purchased at a steady rate, such as hand tools, may be excluded from gross capital formation and considered as intermediate consumption (*e.g.* stethoscopes, thermometers). In a number of statistical systems a threshold value is set to discriminate between intermediate consumption and capital formation.[7] Although such a strategy would be recommendable for the compilation of SHA too, no threshold value is proposed in this Manual, and its determination is left to national compilers. In the event of the start-up of a new activity, the costs for the acquisition of large quantities of relatively inexpensive tools might be relevant. In such a case this should be recorded as capital formation.[8]

Machinery and equipment integral to buildings

Machinery and equipment integral to buildings is not reported separately from the value of the building itself. For example, if a new hospital is recorded, the value of the lifts installed is normally included in the value of the structure.

Existing fixed assets

Capital goods acquired by a health care provider are not necessarily newly produced. Since assets have a long life, they may change hands but continue to function as fixed assets for their new owners, for example, a hospital that is converted into a hotel, or vice-versa. Thus, when the ownership of an existing fixed asset is transferred, the value of the asset sold, bartered or transferred is recorded as negative gross fixed capital formation by the former owner and as positive gross fixed capital formation by the new owner. The value of the positive gross fixed capital formation recorded for the purchaser usually exceeds the value of the negative gross fixed capital formation recorded for the seller by the value of the costs of ownership transfer incurred by the purchaser (*e.g.* taxes). Generally speaking, two cases can be distinguished which are relevant:

- Both units exchanging the assets belong to the health care system. Consider, for example, the case of a hospital sold by a municipality to the central government. In this case, a negative entry would be recorded under the health care provider selling the asset (the municipality); and an equivalent value would be recorded as a positive entry for the provider purchasing the hospital (the central government). The purchasing provider will also register an additional entry to account for the costs of ownership (e.g. taxes occasioned by the change of ownership of the item) incurred in the purchasing process. As a consequence, the overall value of gross capital formation for the whole health sector increases only by the costs of ownership, as the sum of the positive and negative entries mentioned above is null.
- One of the units belongs to the rest of the economy or the rest of the world: the value of the asset acquired or disposed of by the health care provider will be recorded as above. However, the value of overall gross capital formation for the health sector increases or decreases by the same amount. It is worth noting that, in the case of immovable assets (i.e. buildings), sold by a resident unit to a unit resident abroad, by convention a new statistical unit is created in the economic territory where the immovable asset is located – in order to represent the foreign unit.

Improvements to existing fixed assets

Health care facilities have service lives of up to 50 years or more. However, in order to maintain a fixed asset in working order or to increase its performance or productive capacity, renovations and refurbishments are often required. Depending on their nature, some of the expenditure on these can be considered as ordinary maintenance and therefore recorded as intermediate consumption, while other expenditure could be recorded as gross fixed capital formation. Drawing the distinction between ordinary maintenance and capital formation is not clear-cut. Ordinary maintenance and repairs can be identified by two features:

- They are activities that must be undertaken regularly in order to maintain a fixed asset in working order over its expected service life. The owner or user of the asset has no choice about whether or not to undertake ordinary maintenance and repairs if the asset in question is to continue to be used in production.
- Ordinary maintenance and repairs do not change the fixed asset's performance, productive capacity or expected service life. They simply maintain it in good working order, if necessary by replacing defective parts by new parts of the same kind.

Box 11.3. **Owners and users of fixed assets**

Every asset has both an owner and a user, though in many cases the two roles coincide. The **owner** is the economic unit that has property of the asset in law, whereas the **user** is the unit with the right to use the asset in its production process although the asset legally remains the property of the owner. The distinction is relevant when assets are leased or rented. For example, a helicopter air-ambulance could be owned by a financial corporation that leases it to a health care provider who uses it in rescue operations. The distinction is important, as it implies the inclusion or exclusion of the assets from the System of Health Accounts.

Two types of leasing are usually identified: operating leasing and financial leasing.

In *operating leasing* the lessee (user) acquires the right to use the asset for a certain period of time, which is not necessarily defined in advance. To acquire the right to use the asset the lessee pays a rental to the lessor (owner). The rental needs to be large enough to cover *i)* any direct costs incurred by the owner, including the costs of maintaining the asset, *ii)* any reduction in the value of the asset over that period, and *iii)* the interest costs on the value of the asset at the start of the period. The leasing period normally does not cover the whole economic lifetime of the asset. During the leasing period it is the responsibility of the lessor (owner) to provide any necessary repair and maintenance of the asset. When the leasing period expires, the asset is returned to the lessor (owner) in the same condition as when it was hired, apart from normal wear and tear. The lessor is then likely to hire out the asset to another lessee or to use it otherwise. The asset is recorded in the lessor's balance sheet during its entire economic life. In this case, the asset is recorded as gross fixed capital formation of the lessor.

The second type of leasing is *financial leasing*. In this form of contract, the lessee acquires the right to use the asset in exchange for rental payments over a predetermined and protracted term. However, in this case the leasing period covers all, or most of, the economic lifetime of the asset. At the end of the leasing period the lessee often has the option to buy the asset. All risks and rewards of ownership are, de facto though not de jure, transferred from lessor to lessee. In particular it is the responsibility of the lessee (user) to carry out any necessary repair and maintenance of the asset. In this case, when acquired, the asset is recorded as gross fixed capital formation of the lessee.

In the SNA, a distinction is made between the concepts of legal and economic ownership. The legal owner of an asset is the institutional unit entitled in law, on grounds that can be legally sustained, to claim the benefits associated with the asset. By contrast, the economic owner of assets is the institutional unit entitled to claim the benefits associated with the use of the asset in question in the course of an economic activity by virtue of accepting the associated risks. Therefore, in the SNA, the economic property is transferred from the lessor to the lessee in the case of financial leasing but not in operating leasing. Some confusion might arise about the meaning of the term user: some authors see the renting activity of the lessor as usage of the asset and therefore employ the term "user" to identify the lessor. In this context, the term user identifies exclusively the economic unit using the assets in its production process (the lessee).

To constitute gross fixed capital formation, improvements to existing fixed assets must produce significant changes in some of the characteristics of existing fixed assets. The following criteria should be met:

- The decision to renovate, reconstruct or enlarge a fixed asset is a deliberate investment decision that may be taken any time, even when the good in question is in good working order and not in need of repair.

- Major renovations, reconstructions or enlargements increase the performance or productive capacity of existing fixed assets, or significantly extend their previously expected service lives, or both.

Box 11.4. **Cost of use, maintenance, consumption and return to capital**

The full cost of using a fixed asset in production can be measured by the cost of renting the asset. The rental can be either actual, if the asset is rented, or imputed, if the asset is owned by the user (see SNA 2008, 6.245). The rental (actual or imputed) needs to be large enough to cover:

- Any direct costs incurred by the owner, including the costs of maintaining the asset;
- The capital services rendered by the asset, which in turn include two categories:
  - The consumption of fixed capital: the decline, during the course of the accounting period, in the current value of the fixed assets as a result of physical deterioration, normal obsolescence or normal accidental damage:
  - The return to fixed capital: the interest costs on the value of the asset at the start of the period. The interest costs may consist either of actual interest paid on borrowed funds or the loss of interest incurred as a result of investing own funds in the purchase of the fixed asset instead of a financial asset.

Therefore the cost of use of the capital asset is larger than the consumption of fixed capital alone.

Note: The actual rental is the amount payable by the user of a fixed asset to its owner, under an operating lease or similar contract, for the right to use that asset in production for a specified period of time. When the asset is actually rented under an operating lease or similar contract, the rental is recorded under intermediate consumption as the purchase of a service produced by the lessor.

Costs incurred on acquisition and disposal of assets

Purchasing a fixed asset often involves the use of lawyers or the payment of taxes. Highly complex machinery might require significant costs associated with delivery and installation that were not included in the purchase price. All the costs associated with acquiring and disposing of assets are considered as costs of ownership transfer and also treated as gross fixed capital formation.

Financial leases

A financial lease (also called capital lease) is a contract between two parties: the lessee (in this case, the health care provider) and the lessor (for example, a finance company or a bank). The terms of the lease are such that the lessor (*e.g.* finance company or bank) purchases the assets (such as an MRI machine) and therefore is legally the owner, but the lessee takes over both the economic risks and rewards of using the asset in production. In return, the lessee pays a series of rentals or instalments for the use of that asset. Rentals paid by the lessee cover a large part or all of the cost of the asset incurred by the lessor plus a mark-up. At the end of the duration of the lease, the lessee has the option to acquire ownership of the asset (for example, paying the last rental, or bargain option purchase price). The lessee becomes the economic owner of the asset even if the lessor remains the legal owner. In SHA, the asset (*e.g.* the MRI machine) is recorded as being acquired by the lessee (*e.g.* a hospital). This means that the value of the asset is recorded as capital formation of the lessee at the beginning of the lease. The payments due under the lease arrangement are treated as if they were repayments of the principal of a loan, of the interest and possibly of the service charge. Therefore the payments are not recorded in the capital account.

Assets produced by public-private partnerships or similar arrangements

The term public–private partnership includes a wide variety of different forms and schemes. In the health system, the term public–private partnership often refers to a concession contract. A concession awards a company full responsibility for the delivery of services from an asset, including the operational activities, although in health care this does not usually include clinical services. A typical public–private partnership example in the health system would be a hospital building financed and constructed by a private developer and then leased to the hospital authority. The private developer then acts as landlord, providing housekeeping and other non-medical services, while the hospital itself provides clinical services. Similar schemes are the private finance initiative (PFI) or the Build, Own, Operate, Transfer (BOOT) scheme, originally used in the United Kingdom and now also adopted in some other countries. Another form of public–private partnership is so-called "energy performance contracting (EPC)". The EPC is an arrangement whereby a company is contracted by a health provider to upgrade existing energy equipment (such as heating boilers and lighting systems) with more efficient and technologically advanced devices. The contracted company finances the modernising of equipment, which then becomes the property of the health care providers. The savings in energy bills resulting from the more efficient equipment are shared between the health care provider and the company under the terms of the agreement.[9] Under such schemes it is not always straightforward to establish which unit is the legal owner of the asset during the contract period. This is currently the subject of a wider accounting debate, with experts trying to identify the best possible solution to record those assets. While waiting for a conclusion, a possible temporary solution for SHA 2011 is proposed, *i.e.* that one of the following conditions should be met:

- If the owner qualifies as a health provider the asset is recorded in SHA;
- If the acquisition of the asset can be interpreted as a form of financial lease made by a health provider and then can be treated as such, the whole value of the asset is recorded at the beginning of the contract period.

Changes in inventories and acquisitions less disposals of valuables

Although gross fixed capital formation constitutes the most important component of capital formation in health systems, the two additional components making up the aggregate gross capital formation should also be considered: namely, change in inventories and acquisitions less disposals of valuables.

Changes in inventories

Changes in inventories are measured by the value of the entries into inventories less the value of withdrawals and less the value of any recurrent losses of goods held in inventories during the accounting period.

Inventories are produced assets that came into existence in the accounting period or in an earlier period, and that are held by health providers for sale, use in production or other use at a later date. For practical reasons, we would recommend that in SHA 2011 only expenditure on inventories of considerable value be considered, such as the storage of medical goods and equipment to be used in the event of a catastrophic occurrence. Change in inventories of health care providers for their ordinary activities (*e.g.* the value of pharmaceuticals stored in hospitals) can be ignored, assuming for simplicity that the value at the beginning of the accounting period equals the value at the end of the same period.

Work-in-progress

Work-in-progress consists of output produced by an enterprise that is not yet sufficiently processed to be in a state in which it is normally supplied to other institutional units. Work-in-progress is recorded under inventories for any output that is not complete at the end of the accounting period. The only exceptions to recording incomplete work as work-in-progress are for partially completed projects for which the ultimate owner is deemed to have taken ownership, either because the production is for own use or as evidenced by the existence of a contract of sale or purchase. Consider for example the construction of a hospital, which may take years to complete: if the ultimate owner is deemed to have taken ownership, then the partial value of the asset will be recorded as capital formation rather than change in inventories.

Acquisitions less disposals of valuables

Valuables are produced goods of considerable value (for example, works of art) usually held as a store of value over time. Whilst artwork is not a central element in the provision of healthcare services, they have been acquired by some health care providers, as they seem to have an impact in the treatment of certain conditions or pathologies.

In some countries (such as the United Kingdom), art work is increasingly being displayed in long-term care facilities for older people as well as in settings dealing with physically disabled young people, mental health and outpatients, rheumatology patients, renal dialysis patients and those in need of palliative care.

Different approaches to the estimation of gross capital formation

Three perspectives on the analysis of capital formation in health

As current health expenditure can be analysed from at least three view-points (functions, financing and provision), capital formation can also be analysed from at least three perspectives (see Chapter 11): the providers who acquire the capital goods, the financing agents who fund the acquisition of the assets and the type of assets (for example, machinery, medical equipment, buildings, transport equipment).

However, the following differences are of note:

- As mentioned above, when dealing with current health expenditure, health care providers represent the supply side; when capital formation is analysed, they represent the demand side.
- The boundaries of current health expenditure and those of capital formation aggregates are different, in that the products included in one aggregate are not included in the other.
- The products included in current health expenditure are classified using the functional classification of the health care goods and services consumed by the resident

Figure 11.1. **Current health expenditure and gross capital formation in SHA**

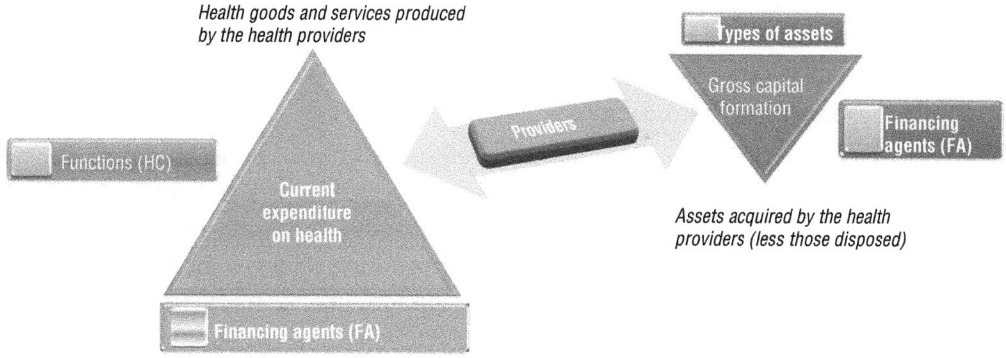

Source: IHAT for SHA 2011.

population, while it is more relevant to classify capital goods by type of assets (see Table 11.1).

- The agents financing current health expenditure do not necessarily finance capital formation, and vice-versa. Some might, but not all of them. Consider, for example, the case of European Union (EU) Structural Funds, which can provide grants for the purchase of capital goods (such as the building of a new hospital) but are not used for current health expenditure. The most important difference is that health care providers can fund the purchase of capital goods using their own resources (*i.e.* savings). Depending on the institutional setting in place in each country, savings could be a source of funding for capital formation both for private and public providers. Consider, for example, the case of those countries where health services provided to households are paid by the financing agent through a product-based price system that reimburses both current and capital expenditure incurred by providers, and then it is up to the provider to save a part of the income received to then purchase the capital goods. The consequence is that health care providers will then also appear among the financing agents whenever a part or all of the value of the capital goods and services they have purchased is funded out of savings. In that case, providers would be included under corporations or non-profit institutions serving households (NPISH), depending on their status.
- Finally, households might play a role in funding capital formation through donations, as might the Rest of the economy and the rest of the world, which can fund the acquisition of non-financial assets through capital transfers either in cash or in kind.

Estimation

Different approaches can be used to estimate the value of gross capital formation. In principle, each of the three main dimensions mentioned above (financing agent, provider and type of assets) can represent a valid starting point to estimate capital formation. Among OECD countries currently reporting capital formation, the majority seem to rely essentially on information coming from the financing agents. A few countries have direct access to providers' annual accounts from which they can retrieve the value of capital formation acquired in the accounting period. As the "type of assets" is a new categorisation, it remains to be seen whether countries have access to sources (*e.g.* national registries) that could be used to estimate capital formation.

Depending on the institutional setting in place in each country, and consequently on the way data sources are organised, a blend of the three approaches could be employed to estimate the value of capital formation or its components. However, each approach has its strengths and weaknesses. The following paragraph briefly describes the three approaches and highlights some of their limitations.

- The *financing agent* approach relies essentially on the information on capital transfers made by the financing agents to the providers (*e.g.* capital grants awarded by public bodies to health care providers, the EU structural funds). The main shortcoming of this approach is that while the estimation of capital formation refers to the total value of the goods and services acquired in the accounting period, capital transfers may represent only a part of the value of the assets. This can occur whenever the transfer is just one of many instalments made over several accounting periods by the financing agent. In addition, this approach is limited in that it provides no information about the providers receiving the funds and, most importantly, is unable to detect the "savings" made by the providers nor the donations providers receive from households, NPISH and corporations. Often countries employing this approach alone confront difficulties in reporting capital formation for the private sector.
- The *provider* approach aims at estimating gross capital formation using the providers' balance sheet for successive accounting periods. In practice this method consists of taking the "Book value" of "fixed assets" reported in the balance sheet at the end of the reference period t, and subtracting the corresponding "Book value" of "fixed assets" reported in the balance sheet at the end of the period t-1. The difference between the two should equal the actual amount paid for the acquisitions, less disposals, of fixed assets during the accounting period. Similarly, the change in inventories can be estimated by subtracting the values for "Stocks and work in progress" also reported in the accounts of the providers. The main shortcoming of this approach is that it provides no information about financing agents.
- The *type of assets* approach uses direct data on the value of the fixed assets purchased by providers (*e.g.* using information from the commodity flow method[10]). As some of the capital assets are registered in public registers (*e.g.* building, transport means), the latter can represent an additional source of information. However, this approach, like the previous one, provides no information on financing agents.

To conclude, as none of the three approaches can be regarded as the "perfect" approach, a blend of the three methods (sometimes called "integration of sources") would appear to be the best option. The national availability of data will determine the extent to which one method should be preferred for the estimation of the different components of gross capital formation.

The consumption of fixed capital in SHA

The consumption of fixed capital is an essential variable in SHA. As shown in Chapter 3, the estimation of consumption of fixed capital is required to value the non-market services produced by government units and NPISH. In the absence of economically significant prices, non-market services are valued by the sum of the costs incurred in their production: that is, by the sum of intermediate consumption, compensation of employees, taxes (less subsidies) on production, and the consumption of capital. Hence, the omission of the consumption of fixed capital in countries where non-market services represent an extensive component of the health provision can result in a serious under-estimation of overall health expenditure.

The consumption of fixed capital is defined as the decline, during the accounting period, in the current value of the stock of fixed assets owned by health care providers. The consumption of fixed capital is the result of physical deterioration, normal obsolescence or normal accidental damage. It is sometimes also called capital consumption.

Figure 11.2. **Consumption of fixed capital in SHA**

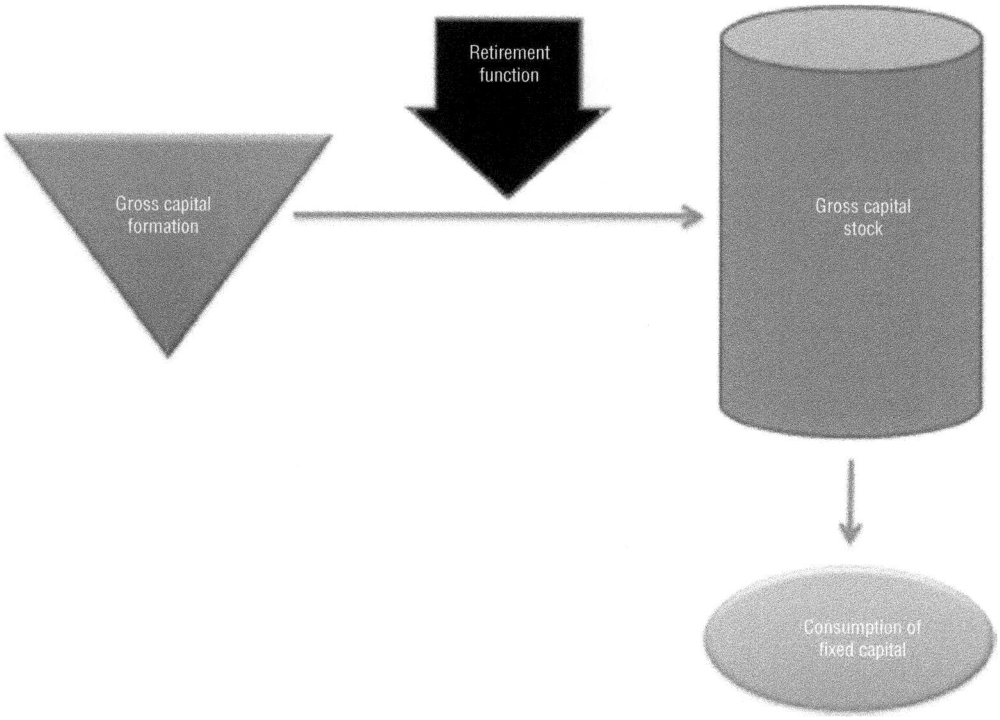

Source: IHAT for SHA 2011.

To derive a measure of the consumption of fixed capital (see Figure 11.2), it is necessary to know the current value of health care providers' gross capital stock. The gross capital stock is basically estimated by cumulating gross fixed capital formation (GFCF) year by year and deducting retirements.[11]

Retirements, in turn, are calculated by applying a retirement function[12] to the gross capital formation flows. As various types of capital assets have different service lives (for example, buildings are likely to last longer than transport equipment), to apply specific retirement functions it would be advisable to identify cohorts of assets of similar ages and cluster them by type of asset.

Finally, to calculate the consumption of fixed capital, a pattern of decline in value over time (an age-price profile) is applied to the capital stock (for a complete overview, see the OECD 2009 "Measuring capital" and SNA 2008).

Capital account

Besides information on how much has been spent to acquire the health capital assets, it can be of interest to policy makers and stakeholders to know which financing mechanisms have been used to cover the capital costs. For example, it could be of interest to know whether the construction of a new hospital has been funded out of transfers from government or through public-private partnerships, as well as the extent to which the costs were covered with donations from philanthropic organisations, households, or from abroad, or indeed whether providers' own accumulated resources have been used. In other words, it could be of interest to explicitly record all the transactions underlying the acquisitions of the assets (*e.g.* capital transfers, grants, capital transfers in kind). Such information can be recorded in the capital account (see Table 11.2), which reports the transactions to acquire and dispose of the non-financial assets and shows the change in net worth due to savings and capital transfers as a balancing item.

The top part of the capital account reports the value of gross capital formation, possibly broken down by type of assets, plus the acquisition (less disposals) of non-produced non-financial assets (*e.g.* land[13] acquired to build health structures). The sum of the latter two components is called the "Change in assets". The acquisitions (purchases, barters or production for own use) are reported as positive entries, while the resources coming from the disposal of existing assets are registered as negative entries in the same side of the account. Consumption of fixed capital is also recorded, as a negative change in assets in the top part of the capital account, to calculate the net change in non-financial assets (acquisitions less disposals of produced and non-produced non-financial assets, less the consumption of fixed capital).

The bottom part of the capital account reports the "Changes in liabilities and net worth". This aggregate represents the amount available to the providers for the acquisition of non-financial and financial assets. The amount, which could be positive or negative, results from the sum of two components: net savings and capital transfers.

Net savings

Net savings is the first item recorded on the bottom part of the capital account and could be either positive or negative. When positive, it means that during the accounting period income available to health providers exceeded expenditure for recurrent costs. The excess income is then necessarily used to acquire either non-financial or financial assets, including cash, or to repay liabilities. Negative net savings represents the amount by which expenditure on recurrent costs has gone beyond disposable income. That amount needs to be financed by disposing of assets or incurring new liabilities.

Capital transfers

A transfer is defined as a transaction in which one institutional unit provides a good, service or asset to another unit without receiving any direct counterpart from the latter. Transfers may be either current or capital. Wherever required, a breakdown by financing agents can be employed to break down capital transfers received by health care providers. To be considered as capital, a transfer needs to meet at least one of the following two conditions:

- The party receiving the transfer is obliged to acquire an asset (other than cash);
- The party making the transfer realises the funds involved by disposing of an asset (other than cash or inventories), relinquishing a financial claim (other than accounts receivable).

Transfers may take place in cash or in kind. A capital transfer in kind necessarily concerns the change of ownership of a product previously recorded as a non-financial asset in the accounts of the donor.

Investment grants

Investment grants are of particular importance in the health sector. These consist of capital transfers made to health care providers to finance all or part of the costs of the acquisition of their assets. The health care providers receiving the grants are obliged to use them for the purpose of gross fixed capital formation (often represented by specific investment projects, such as the construction of hospitals). If the investment project continues over a long period of time, investment grants in cash may be paid in instalments. Payments of instalments continue to be classified as capital transfers even though they may be recorded in a succession of different accounting periods.

For example, the US Hill-Burton Programme awarded hospitals, nursing homes and other health facilities grants for construction and modernisation (between 1946 and 1997). Similarly, NHS trusts can allocate grants to fund completely, or in significant proportions, the refurbishment of hospitals, hospices, medical practices and so on. The Scottish Dental Access Initiative makes grants of up to GBP 100 000 to establish a new NHS dental practice or to purchase or relocate an existing NHS dental practice.

Investment grants may also be made in kind, for example, transfers of transport equipment like ambulances, machinery and other health equipment made to health care providers. Investment grants in kind may also include the direct provision of buildings.

Other capital transfers

The item "All other capital transfers" includes all other funds received by health care providers to finance the acquisition of assets. Of particular importance are the donations received from households, enterprises and NPISH. For example, philanthropists and religious groups can play a major role in financing capital in some countries.

Net lending/borrowing

The difference between "Change in assets" and "Changes in liabilities and net worth" is the "Net lending (+)/net borrowing (–)" which represents how much can be lent or needs to be borrowed.

Memorandum items: loans, accumulated savings and public-private partnerships

Other financing methods available to health providers include loans, accumulated savings and public-private partnerships, which are separately recorded as memorandum items, as they differ in nature from the financing mechanisms mentioned above. Loans and accumulated savings in fact imply that savings were either put aside in the past (accumulated savings) or will be realised in the future to repay the loans (principal plus interest and expenses). As the implementation of a full financing account is beyond the scope of SHA 2011, those transactions are reported below the capital account in the form of memorandum items.

Loans

Loans to health care providers are recorded as memorandum items of the capital accounts. The category includes all the funds (*i.e.* overdrafts, instalment loans, hire-

Table 11.2. **Capital account**

	SHA Capital account		Health care providers								
			HP.1	HP.2	HP.3	HP.4	HP.5	HP.6	HP.7	HP.8	**Total**
			Hospitals	Residential long-term care facilities	Providers of ambulatory health care	Providers of ancillary services	Retailers and other providers of medical goods	Providers of preventive care	Providers of health care system administration and financing	Rest of economy	
Changes in assets (Acquisitions less disposals)	**HK.1 Gross capital formation**										
	HK.1.1 Gross fixed capital formation										
	HK.1.1.1 Infrastructure										
	HK.1.1.1.1 Residential and non-residential buildings										
	HK.1.1.1.2 Other structures										
	HK.1.1.2 Machinery and equipment										
	HK.1.1.2.1 Medical equipment										
	HK.1.1.2.2 Transport equipment										
	HK.1.1.2.3 ICT equipment										
	HK.1.1.2.4 Machinery and equipment *n.e.c.*										
	HK.1.1.3 Intellectual property products										
	HK.1.1.3.1 Computer software and databases										
	HK.1.1.3.2 Intellectual property products *n.e.c.*										
	HK.1.2 Changes in inventories										
	HK.1.3 Acquisitions less disposals of valuables										
	HK.1.1.c Consumption of fixed capital										
	HK.1.1.n Net capital formation										
	HK.2 Non-produced non-financial assets										
	HK.2.1 Land										
	HK.2.2 Other non-produced non-financial assets										
Changes in net worth	HKF.1 Saving, net										
	HKF.2 Capital transfers — HKF.2r Receivable — HKF. 2.1 Investment grants from:	FA.1									
		FA.2									
		....									
		FA.6									
	HKF.2.2 Other capital transfers										
	HKF.2p Payable										
Net lending (+) /net borrowing (–)											
	Memorandum Items										
	HKR.1 Loans										
	HKR.2 Accumulated savings										
	HKR.3 Public-private partnership										
	HKR.4 Research and development in health (Funded by)	FA.1									
		FA.2									
		....									
		FA.6									
		Total									
	HKR.5 Education and training of health personnel (Funded by)	FA.1									
		FA.2									
		....									
		FA.6									
		Total									

Source: IHAT for SHA 2011.

purchase credit and loans to finance trade credit) lent by creditors to health care providers to purchase non-financial assets (they must be evidenced by documents that are not negotiable).

Accumulated savings

"Accumulated savings" refers to the sum of savings that have been put aside over past accounting periods.

Public-private partnerships

Although the whole value of assets acquired by health providers through public-private partnerships is included in the capital account together with all other assets acquired (less disposed) by health care providers, it may be of interest to policy makers and stakeholders to know the extent to which investment in the health system has been financed using public-private partnership mechanisms. Therefore, a memorandum item is included below the line in the capital account to separately record the value of the assets that have been acquired by health care providers using public-private partnership programmes.

Other memorandum items

In SHA 2011, expenditure on "Research and development in health" and "Education and training of health personnel" are considered as investments and as such are recorded as additional memorandum items to the capital account. In SHA 1.0 these items were included as health care-related expenditure under the functional classification (HC.R.3 and HC.R.2 respectively).

The approach used in SHA 2011 diverges from SNA 2008 where R&D is included in the capital account while "Education and training of health personnel" is regarded as an input in the production process of health care providers and thus recorded as intermediate consumption. The exclusion of R&D from the capital account in SHA is guided exclusively by practical considerations. At the time of the preparation of SHA 2011, information on R&D in the health systems was available only for a few countries, so its inclusion would likely impair international comparability of the data. The health policy relevance of expenditure on "Education and training of health personnel" has instead guided the need to report this item separately from other production inputs (see Chapter 9).

Explanatory notes for tackling the boundary problems arising from health-related functions are given below.

Research and development in health

The *Frascati Manual* (OECD, 2002a) provides detailed guidelines for the estimation of expenditure on research and development, which are also deemed appropriate for R&D in health according to the functional boundaries described in Chapter 5. Where R&D is an ancillary activity in medical industries that cannot be assigned to a separate institutional unit of homogeneous production, a serious double-counting problem arises from the definition of national totals on expenditure in health accounting that adds R&D to health care goods and services.

A major innovation introduced in the 2008 edition of the SNA is the capitalisation of research and development. Although there seems to be a wide consensus on the theoretical motivation guiding this choice, the practical implementation of reporting that aggregate remains an issue for a number of countries.

Therefore, SHA 2011 has opted to suggest a pragmatic approach that keeps a separate recording of expenditure on R&D as a memorandum item "below the line", without capitalising expenditure on health R&D.

Explanatory notes

The *Frascati Manual* provides detailed guidelines for the estimation of expenditure on research and development for R&D in health according to the functional boundaries (OECD, 2002, Annex A4). Further information on international comparisons and examples of national efforts can be found in Measuring expenditure on Health-related R&D (OECD, 2001). The separate recording of expenditure on R&D as a component of capital formation is suggested.

This item defines R&D in health as follows:

> *"R&D programmes directed towards the protection and improvement of human health. It includes R&D on food hygiene and nutrition and also R&D on radiation used for medical purposes, biochemical engineering, medical information, rationalisation of treatment and pharmacology (including testing medicines and breeding of laboratory animals for scientific purposes) as well as research relating to epidemiology, prevention of industrial diseases and drug addiction."* (OECD, 1994, *Frascati Manual*, p. 122)

Note: Government involvement in health R&D is classified in the COFOG (UN, 1999) as part of the health function (COFOG, 07.5 R&D Health).

The *Frascati Manual* (OECD, 1994) provides detailed definitions of R&D in business and government activities, including non-profit institutions and institutions of higher education. The *Frascati Manual* is the joint product of national experts on R&D in OECD Member countries, the OECD Secretariat and other international organisations. These guidelines are consistent with UNESCO recommendations.

The *Frascati Manual* discusses boundary problems between R&D, education, health care and other industries. It provides guidelines for standard reporting in these and other fields and draws the boundary line that distinguishes the field from health care and from the education and training of health personnel.

The *Frascati Manual* provides a basic definition of R&D:

> *"Research and experimental development (R&D) comprise creative work undertaken on a systematic basis in order to increase the stock of knowledge, including knowledge of man, culture and society and the use of this stock of knowledge to devise new applications. R&D covers three distinct activities: basic research, applied research and experimental development. Basic research is experimental or theoretical work undertaken primarily to acquire new knowledge of the underlying foundation of phenomena and observable facts, without any particular application or use in view. Applied research is also original investigation undertaken in order to acquire new knowledge. It is, however, directed primarily towards a specific practical aim or objective. Experimental development is systematic work, drawing on existing knowledge gained from research and/or practical experience that is directed to producing new materials, products or devices, to installing new processes, systems and services, or to improving substantially those already produced or installed."* (OECD, 1994, *Frascati Manual*, p. 29)

The basic criterion for distinguishing R&D from related activities is "the presence in R&D of an appreciable element of novelty and the resolution of scientific and/or technological uncertainty, *i.e.* when the solution to a problem is not readily apparent to someone familiar with the basic stock of commonly used knowledge and techniques in the area concerned." "... In the field of medicine, routine autopsy on the causes of death is simply the practice of health care and not R&D; special investigation of a particular mortality in order to establish the side effects of certain cancer treatments is R&D. Similarly, routine tests, such as blood and bacteriological tests carried out for doctors are not R&D but a special programme of blood tests in connection with the introduction of a new drug is R&D." (OECD, 1994, p. 33)

The following recommendation regarding the borderline between specialised health care and R&D from the *Frascati Manual* on R&D statistics should be adopted for the collection of health care statistics: "In university hospitals where, in addition to the primary activity of health care, the training of medical students is of major importance, the activities of teaching, R&D and advanced as well as routine health care are frequently very closely linked". "Specialised health care" is an activity which normally is to be excluded from R&D. However, there may be an element of R&D in what is usually called "advanced health care", carried out, for example, in university hospitals. It is difficult for university doctors and their assistants to define that part of their overall activities which is exclusively R&D. If, however, time and money spent on routine health care are included in the R&D statistics, there will be an over-estimate of R&D resources in the medical sciences. Usually such advanced health care is not considered R&D and all health care not directly linked to a specific R&D project should be excluded from the R&D statistics" (OECD, 1994, p. 37). R&D in health, when measured according to the rules of the *Frascati Manual*, excludes outlays by pharmaceutical firms, shown separately. For data collection on R&D, international standards exist. More details on data collection and international standards for reporting in R&D are documented in the *Frascati Manual*. Activities of R&D in health care should exclude all education and training of health personnel in universities and special institutions of higher and postsecondary education. However, research by postgraduate students carried out at universities and university hospitals in medical sciences should be counted, wherever possible, as part of R&D in health care. R&D outlays by pharmaceutical firms have to be distinguished from other related scientific and technological activities (OECD, 1994, pp. 30-33), such as, for example, patent and licence work.

Education and training of health personnel

Estimation strategies for expenditure on the education and training of health personnel in general are provided in the UNESCO/OECD/Eurostat (1995) guidelines. For education and training, similar problems of double-counting are encountered whenever national totals of expenditure on health are calculated that include education and training. A separate reporting constitutes an adequate way of handling the question.

Explanatory notes

This item comprises government and private provision of education and training of health personnel, including the administration, inspection or support of institutions providing education and training of health personnel. This corresponds to post-secondary and tertiary education in the field of health (according to ISCED-97 code) run by central and local government, and private institutions such as nursing schools run by private hospitals.

Note: If properly accounted for, the education and training of health personnel is not an overlapping function between health and education. In teaching hospitals, for example, it would be desirable to have separate budgets for care provision, R&D and training. Where detailed accounts are missing, an alternative option would be the statistical practice designed for UNESCO/OECD/Eurostat data collections on education and training (UNESCO/OECD/Eurostat, 1995).

The education and training of health personnel takes place mainly at ISCED-levels 5 (non-university degree tertiary level) to 7 (university tertiary level of education, leading to a second or further university degree or equivalent). The following institutions are involved:

- Paramedical schools (ISCED 5);
- Undergraduate schools, in medical/paramedical departments (ISCED 6);
- Graduate schools, in medical/biomedical departments (ISCED 7).

In the list of fields of study (at the tertiary level of education) provided by the ISCED Manual (UNESCO, 1996), medical education and training corresponds to the category Medical science and health-related (ISCED code 50). The ISCED Manual, furthermore, has a category Health-related auxiliary programmes (ISCED 50) at the upper secondary level of education for vocational and technical programmes. Complete costs would include expenditure for universities and other training institutions. Salaries of medical interns and residents or trainee nurses are reported under expenditure on health, for the services rendered. Training expenditure is also reported in the educational accounts. The intent of this SHA category is to include expenditure for the training of personnel already operational in the patient care. The following recommendation for university hospitals is taken from the UNESCO/OECD/Eurostat Manual: "Expenditure of or for teaching hospitals (sometimes referred to as academic hospitals or university hospitals) should not be included in education expenditure, except to the limited extent that they are directly and specifically related to the training of medical personnel. In particular, all costs of patient care other than general expenses of academic hospitals should be excluded from the education figures, even if the education authorities must pay such expenses. Expenditure for research in academic hospitals should also be excluded, except that no attempt should be made to distinguish between the research and non-research portions of the time of teaching staff whose compensation is otherwise considered part of education expenditure" (UNESCO/OECD/Eurostat, 1995).

Notes

1. The term "gross" indicates that the loss of value due to use or obsolescence is not taken into account. A more refined measure called "net" capital formation can be obtained by subtracting the value of capital consumption from Gross capital formation.
2. An exception to the principle of legal ownership is represented by financial leasing. In that case, the value of the capital goods is recorded as capital formation of the lessee at the beginning of the leasing period, although the lessee could became the legal owner of the asset only at the end of the leasing period (see Box 11.3).
3. For example, if a hospital in Luxembourg acquires diagnostic equipment that is used to provide diagnosis to patients from France, Belgium or Germany, the acquisition of the assets is recorded in Luxembourg only.
4. By convention, all infrastructures within the economic territory are owned by the resident unit regardless of whether the economic owner (or lessee under a financial lease) is resident abroad. For example, if the construction of a new building (*e.g.* a new hospital) is completely funded by transfers from abroad, a resident health provider is automatically established in the economic territory for statistical purposes.

5. The availability of the MRI machine is important information that can be recorded in health on-expenditure statistics.

6. When the transfer occurs, the value of the asset originally attributed to the local government is cancelled from the local government accounts by a negative capital transfer in kind made to the government unit (and registered as a positive entry in its account).

7. ESA95 suggests using a threshold to discriminate between capital formation and intermediate consumption (see ESA95 10.9). Therefore, tools and appliances are recorded as fixed capital formation if their purchaser's expenditure exceeds EUR 500 (at 1995 prices) per item (or, when bought in quantities, for the total amount bought). If their value does not exceed the threshold, they are recorded as intermediate consumption.

   Another example is the thresholds set by the Scottish Government for the Scottish NHS reporting. The Scottish Executive adopted a GBP 5 000 capitalisation threshold for individual assets, although assets of lesser value may be capitalised if they form part of a group, with a group value in excess of GBP 20 000, including VAT where this is not recoverable (SEHD, 2008).

8. For example, the glasses used in laboratories are regarded as small, inexpensive tools and are therefore usually recorded as intermediate consumption even if they are used repeatedly, or continuously, in production over many years. However, if glasses are purchased in quantity, say at the start-up, the total value of the acquisition is recorded as capital formation.

9. The upgrade of the central heating system in the Bulovka Teaching Hospital in Prague is an example of "energy performance contracting" (EPC).

10. The term "commodity flow method" refers to the compilation of goods and services accounts for detailed product groups. The method relies on the accounting identity Supply=demand (Uses) which can be further broken down:

    Output + Import = Intermediate cons. + Final consumption + Gross capital formation + Export.

    Using the above equation, all goods and services are traced from different sources of supply to different categories of use. If a component in the equation has no data but the other components do, the unknown data can be derived through this equation. For example, if the value of the MRI machine acquired in the accounting period is unknown but data on the value of the MRI produced is known as well as the value of those imported and exported, it is possible to estimate the missing information as:

    Gross capital formation in MRI= MRI produced (output) + MRI imported – MRI exported.

11. Retirement refers to the removal of an asset from the capital stock, when the asset is exported, sold for scrap, dismantled, pulled down or simply abandoned.

12. The retirement function expresses the probability that an asset is removed during its life length.

13. There are at least two reasons to treat land differently from other assets that are owned by the health providers and included in gross fixed capital formation. Firstly, land is not the outcome of a production process. Secondly, land is not usually "used up" in the production process, and therefore capital consumption is not accounted for land. An exception is contaminated land, in which case the loss in its value should be considered.

PART II

Chapter 12

Trade in Health Care

Introduction

As defined in Chapter 4 "Global boundaries of health care", the System of Health Accounts focuses on final consumption of health care goods and services by the *resident* population, irrespective of where this takes place. As a further qualification, this should also be irrespective of who is financing the goods or services consumed. Therefore, current health expenditure should include all final consumption by residents, both in the economic territory and abroad. This means the explicit inclusion of imports (health care goods and services provided by non-resident units, HP.9) and the exclusion of exports (those goods and services provided to non-residents by resident providers, HP.1-8) in order to correctly determine total health spending.

Past experience from international data collections[1] has shown that the consideration of the exports and imports of health care goods and services in the estimation of overall health spending has generally been weak, and the issue was not covered sufficiently in the first SHA Manual. At the same time, the changing face of delivery and payment mechanisms (for example, e-health, tele-diagnosis and Internet pharmacies) has also led to increased challenges in monitoring and tracking the great variety of transactions, as the traditional data sources used in the estimation of imports and exports (*i.e.* in the Balance of Payments) are less and less adequate.[2] A further factor complicating data collection for trade in health services is the widespread existence of third-party payments from public sources and private health insurance.

This chapter first considers the globalisation of health care and recent trends as a rationale for the need to improve the measurement of trade in this area. In order to meet the new requirements, the chapter sets out concepts and definitions of external trade in relation to health expenditure and, where applicable, the implications beyond this boundary. Where possible, links to existing concepts developed in the domains of international trade statistics and trade negotiations are exploited to ensure close synergy. There is discussion of the reporting of imports and exports as part of SHA tables, including supplementary trade tables, and their relation to other economic statistics. Finally, some preliminary ideas on guidelines and possible data sources for producing and improving estimates of trade in health care goods and services are discussed.

Background and policy issues

The increasing importance of the health sector, together with the trend towards globalisation, which is being reinforced by the reduction of regulatory obstacles to economic activities, has fuelled a steady growth in international trade in health care goods and services, albeit from relatively low levels. Improved communications and transportation have also facilitated the movement of people, both as patients and independent service suppliers. While for the most part, individuals prefer to receive health care in their home country, under certain circumstances it may be more beneficial for a patient to receive treatment in another country, for example, when the nearest health facility may be across a border, or when there is more expertise available, or if the same care can be provided sooner or at lower cost.

Travelling for health care is nothing new – since early times people covered long distances to seek cures and healing. Health care goods and services have traditionally been viewed as non-tradable commodities – amid national concerns regarding the sovereignty of public health provision – or in most cases as negligible in value and volume. In recent years, however, there has been a growing body of evidence that in many countries an increasing number of patients have been travelling across international borders specifically for the purpose of receiving treatment (commonly termed "medical or health tourism"), *e.g.* Thailand reported that over one million foreign patients were treated there in 2006 (Thai Board of Investment, 2008). Independent studies have provided wide-ranging estimates of the global level of activity. A report by Deloitte (2008) estimated that in 2008 the value of the world medical tourism market was around USD 60 billion, and it expected this figure to continue to grow at a double-digit pace over subsequent years. In this context, a number of countries have actively promoted their comparative advantage as medical travel destinations, hoping to attract patients from both neighbouring countries and further afield through the promise of high-quality, technologically-advanced and competitively-priced health services. Individual hospitals and clinics or clusters of health care providers have also sought international accreditation in order to put themselves on the map of the international health insurance and purchaser networks.

There have also been examples, particularly in the European Union, of cross-border contracting between health care purchasing authorities and foreign providers. One example of this was an agreement in 2003 between the NHS in England and various Belgian hospitals that aimed to reduce some of the waiting lists in England at that time (Glinosa *et al.*, 2010). Other regional contracting arrangements and cross-border co-operation have existed in various border regions, *e.g.* between the Netherlands and Belgium, France and Spain, and among the Nordic countries.

However, the consumption of health care goods and services abroad goes beyond planned care. Much of the activity between non-resident providers and residents can be of an unplanned nature, that is, the use of a country's health system while temporarily in the country on business or leisure travel. In addition, the movement of short-term, seasonal or border workers is another important area to be considered. For some smaller countries or border regions that experience large flows of persons and workers across their borders, the import and export of health care goods and services can be significant. Increasing levels of travel and tourism can put strains on the health system of a country or region. For example, past agreements between the UK and Spanish governments resulted in lump-sum payments that were linked to the number of UK tourists travelling to Spain and were intended to cover their use of Spanish health care services (Legido-Quigley and McKee, 2006).

Rising health care costs at home and a lack of health insurance cover are among the major incentives for patients to seek treatment abroad, where procedures and treatments sometimes cost only a fraction what they would at home. But technological advances, market openings and obstacles to accessing health care treatment at home (for example, waiting times, quality of treatment and legal/ethical obstacles) have all been cited as factors behind the increase. Continuing economic and political co-operation between states is likely to lead to the increased movement of patients and health care professionals.

Indeed, past ambiguities regarding the right of European Union citizens to seek treatment in other Member States have helped to push the issue of cross-border health care towards the top of the European health agenda in recent years.[3] In summary, the flow of patients from one country to another has been increasing, sometimes as a matter of individual choice, sometimes organised through contracting abroad by purchasing authorities.

The regulatory liberalisation of health services may have important effects on a country's health system, offering new opportunities, but also posing risks. For example, foreign patients can provide considerable revenues for the receiving country, but they may also draw critical resources away from local patients, leading to a two-tier health service. Blouin *et al.* (2006) analysed in detail the possible implications of trade in health services on public health systems.

For exporting countries, there may be a risk that there exists high-quality richly resourced care for foreign patients in contrast to low-quality poorly resourced care for nationals, or that scarce public funds in the form of tax breaks, incentives and subsidies for private providers are diverted away from primary care needs. Another possible concern is the possible brain drain of trained health professionals from the domestic public health system to private providers, and from rural to urban areas.

Public health issues in the patients' countries have also been well documented. In addition to the possible indication of an inadequate domestic health system that is unable to meet the needs of its own population, there are questions over equity, as patients who can afford the expense are able to access certain services abroad or to jump waiting lists, and care sought abroad may be a substitute for needed health care reforms or investment in the domestic health system. There may also be concerns over the lack of controls or regulations on certain treatments abroad as well as question marks over the quality of treatment and aftercare, with the domestic system left to deal with any resulting complications or malpractice.

On the other side, there can be potential benefits of medical travel for both sides. For the recipient (exporting) country, there are foreign earnings from increased health and tourist flows and increased employment and improved infrastructure resulting from health provider investment. With the diffusion of new technologies and treatments, a "seepage" effect may be envisaged that helps raise the health standards of the local population. Some anecdotal evidence has also pointed to a "reverse brain drain" whereby health professionals return to their country of origin. For the importing country, there may be important economies of scale and cost savings to be made, and rather than a substitute for reform, it can be seen as a catalyst or a necessary introduction of external price competition in the domestic market.

Apart from the physical movement of patients between countries, trade in health services can also take other forms, notably the cross-border delivery of health care goods and services directly to patients or other health care providers. Technological advances, in particular the widespread use of the Internet, mean that individuals are able to seek out health information and to purchase medical goods and services remotely. A study of Internet use for health purposes in Norway over the period 2000-2007 showed a dramatic rise in usage, with 67% of the population using the Internet for health information in some way, and this is forecast to rise to more than 80% by 2010 (Wangberg *et al.*, 2009). While much of the on-line activity is to gather supplementary information regarding illness and health, there was also a tendency towards purchasing medicines or health-related products, with almost a quarter of those who used the Internet for health purposes reporting this in 2007. Diagnostic services and health administrative services are also increasingly being outsourced, including to overseas organisations. The increase in the number of medical websites and Internet pharmacies has highlighted current gaps with respect both to existing legislation on the purchasing of prescription medicines and to the lack of data to monitor this trade.

Finally, trade can also involve the movement of health care personnel rather than the patient across borders. This can come under the scope of direct foreign aid in kind from governments or international organisations with the provision of medical teams to needy areas, but can also be linked to individuals or groups of health professionals who move independently across borders to provide health services to patients.

While much of the trade in health care goods and services remains marginal – for the most part, a direct patient-provider contact close to home is still the norm for most treatments – there are areas where consumption abroad or cross-border supply may account for an increasing part of care, such as in the area of dental care or fertility treatments. There is also a growing awareness in some countries that parts of domestic health service demand are increasingly being met by foreign providers of health care or *vice versa* – part of domestic health care provision is satisfying the health care needs of non-residents.

There is also a wider policy interest in trade in health services from the viewpoint of trade negotiations and the World Trade Organisation General Agreement on Trade in Services (GATS).[4] The interest from a number of countries in developing health service exports as a potential currency earner has also contributed to the need to better assess levels and trends in this trade. Policy makers and trade negotiators need reliable data to better understand the dynamics of trade liberalisation and the impacts on public health. This data would enable analysts to gauge trade flows as well as a country's openness to trade in health services. Most importantly, it would make it possible to assess the risks and opportunities related to liberalisation commitments on public health, and thus to craft appropriate policies in order to move towards coherent health and trade objectives.

Basic concepts and definitions

The System of Health Accounts requires a conceptual basis for the reporting of imports and exports of health care goods and services that is in line with the boundaries of health expenditure. To ensure that SHA statistics are compiled on a basis that is in line with other macroeconomic statistics as much as possible, it is reasonable for SHA to take its lead from the standard definitions and concepts already developed within the System of National Accounts (SNA) and in the Balance of Payments and International Investment Position Manual of the International Monetary Fund (IMF), known as BPM6. The different perspectives can lead to different definitions of trade: on the one hand, trade that falls within the core framework of SHA, and on the other, trade in health care products in a wider economic sense.

In addition, reference is also made to the concepts and definitions outlined in Tourism Satellite Accounts (TSA), with an assessment of the existing survey instruments and methodologies employed in developing estimates of tourist consumption of health care goods and services.

Within the central accounting framework of SHA, health care goods and services are defined according to a clear set of criteria (Chapter 4) and delineated according to the functional classification (Chapter 5). The same boundary considerations and treatment of borderline cases should therefore be applied in estimating the value of imports and exports of health care goods and services. Furthermore, in the interests of completeness, the universe of health care providers must include all providers irrespective of whether the provision of health care is a primary or secondary activity. One of the challenges, which is not limited solely to matters of external trade, is to adapt existing product and activity classifications to the functional classification of SHA. Additional consideration of extended boundaries so as to analyse the part of non-resident consumption in areas such as health education and training may also be of interest.

Key to being able to determine the level of international trade in health care goods and services are the concepts of economic territory and residence. The following definitions are for the most part in accordance with those set out in the BPM6,[5] where further detail and clarification can be sought.

Economic territory

In its broadest sense, an economic territory refers to any geographic area or jurisdiction for which statistics are required. In the case, for example, where health systems are organised and financed at a regional level and the interest is in building regional health accounts, it could be desirable to define the territory as a sub-national region. On the other hand, the economic territory may consist of more than one country, for example, the Economic Union of Belgium and Luxembourg, or supra-national territories such as the European Union (EU). The definition of economic territory is important in determining resident and non-resident entities with respect to the consumption and provision of health services, and therefore what should be included or excluded in an estimate of health expenditure.

Residence

The concept of residence is subsequently determined by the delimitation of the economic territory. A unit is said to be resident in a country when its "centre of economic interest" is situated within that country's economic territory. BPM6 further defines: "The residence of each institutional unit is the economic territory with which it has the strongest connection, expressed as its centre of predominant economic interest." Each institutional unit is therefore a resident of one and only one economic territory determined by its centre of predominant economic interest.

Households

A household's centre of economic interest is determined based on "when members of that household maintain, within a country, a dwelling or succession of dwellings that the members treat and use as their principal residence". All individuals belonging to the same household must be residents of the same economy. It is important to make the distinction between the concept of residence in economic terms and concepts based on nationality or legal criteria. An individual considered to be a resident of a particular economy may not necessarily be a citizen of that country. A differentiation between the resident population and the covered or insured population is also of particular relevance to health care. Public health care insurance coverage may not cover the whole population or may extend beyond the resident population, *e.g.* cross-border workers who work in Luxembourg but reside outside the economic territory may be included in the insured population of Luxembourg, or retired EU citizens who are still covered under their national insurance scheme but are resident in another EU country (see resident versus covered population).

The criterion for residence is nominally based on a period of one year, which can be seen as an objective, if arbitrary, benchmark for determining a person's status. Therefore, a member of a resident household who leaves the economic territory and returns to that same household after a limited period of time (*i.e.* less than a year) continues to be a resident even if that individual makes frequent journeys outside the economic territory. On the other hand, if an individual stays or *intends* to stay in an economy for a year or longer, he or she is considered a resident of that economy. If not, he or she is considered a non-resident. All such individuals are classified as being in travel status and as having their centres of interest outside the economies to which they have travelled. In the most obvious case, foreign tourists who visit for a short period (generally a few weeks) are not counted as resident. Similarly, seasonal workers coming from another country to work for a few months a year in a country are not regarded as resident.

Certain categories, such as diplomatic representatives, members of the armed forces, students and – of particular relevance here – patients undergoing medical care abroad, do not change their centres of interest and therefore remain residents of their home economies. Border workers – persons who cross the border between two economies on a regular, frequent basis because they work in one economy but have homes in the other – are classed as residents of the economy in which they have their homes and not of the economy in which they are employed. Persons living in Belgium but crossing daily into and out of France for work would continue to be regarded as residents of Belgium rather than residents of France.

Refugees are considered residents if they stay or, importantly, *are expected to stay* for one year or more in their host countries. Persons taking refuge in another country for only a short period remain residents of their home economies.

As stated, an exception to the one-year rule is made in determining the resident status of students and long-stay medical patients, because application of the one-year rule could lead to problems with the interpretation and availability of data. Students are generally expected to return to their home economies upon completion of their studies. However long they study abroad, students should be treated as residents of their countries of origin if they maintain economic attachments to their countries. The factors to be considered in determining whether such an attachment has been maintained includes whether a student is dependent on funds from his/her country of origin to finance his or her studies; whether he or she is funded by the host country under foreign aid or similar programmes; and whether he or she plans to return home upon completion of study. This is important to note regarding expenditure on health education and training of medical professionals abroad.

The same rules regarding residence apply to patients who are expected to return home after the period of treatment. That is, they are considered – regardless of the length of stay in the economies in which they are receiving treatment – to be residents of their economies of origin. While this is likely to be of significance only to a very small minority of medical patients, consideration should be given to the residential status of Long-term care patients in nursing care homes abroad, in light of the inclusion of such care boundaries of health under SHA. This is of relevance where persons from one country have retired to another country but continue to be covered under their "home" social security system. This is considered in the following section.

Resident versus covered population

Confining the boundary of health expenditure to that of the resident population has a number of direct consequences on the inclusion or exclusion of certain groups of the population, in particular, with respect to the financial obligations of social security and government spending. In some cases, the differences between the resident population and the insured population can be significant.

It may be the case, such as in the European Union, that persons receiving a state pension or other long-term benefit who reside in another country may still depend on their "home" nation for paying for their health care. This is also the case for those living abroad, but dependent on someone working in another member country. In this case the obligation of the home social security system covers a part of the non-resident population and *vice versa* – a portion of the resident population may be covered by a foreign government. In this case, adjustments may have to be made to conform to the definitions of residence above, which may not be wholly desirable in measuring the financial obligations of a country regarding their health spending.[6] Any deviations in this respect should be made transparent in reporting.

Another issue concerns refugees as well as those who may be defined as residents from the point of view of the Balance of Payments definitions but are not legally entitled to the benefits of public health insurance. This raises the question of where their consumption of health services is being captured. Given sizeable temporary flows of people between countries, both legal and illegal, the expenditure may also be sizeable. Coupled with the fact that in these cases the moral obligation and therefore the cost of providing health services falls onto the host country, it may be arguable whether such expenditure should in fact be deducted from the country's health accounts as an export.

BPM6 provides further detail on the status of other categories of persons, such as diplomats, employees of international organisations, military personnel, etc., which are also adopted by the System of Health Accounts.

To classify a provider of health care – whether government agencies, enterprises or non-profit institutions – as resident generally requires that they have undertaken activity in the territory over a period of time, usually interpreted as one year. Classifying a provider as resident or non-resident is synonymous with deciding whether or not the final expenditure by resident households on goods or services from these providers is classed as imports.

For the most part, the classification into resident and non-resident providers poses few problems, such as in the case of residents receiving care from hospitals or buying medical goods from pharmacies whilst abroad. The short-term provision of services to residents abroad, by health care professionals or as part of foreign government or international aid efforts may be less straightforward. Similarly, foreign-owned institutions and the use of commercial agents require careful consideration.

Enterprises

An enterprise has a centre of economic interest and is therefore a resident unit of a country (or economic territory) when the enterprise is engaged in a significant amount of production of goods and/or services there. This means that it maintains at least one establishment in the country and plans to operate that establishment indefinitely or over a long period of time (that is, one year or more). Other considerations – such as whether there is a complete and separate set of local accounts, whether taxes are paid to the host government, or whether funds for the local operation are locally managed – must also be considered in determining the residence of an enterprise. In practice, these additional conditions are generally satisfied for enterprises engaged in longer-term activity.

The term enterprise includes 1) corporations, which are entities engaged in production for profit and recognised as legal entities separate from the owners, and 2) quasi-corporations, which are unincorporated entities owned by resident or non-resident institutional units and managed as separate entities, which is the case for many self-employed doctors and dentists.

Commercial agencies

Agencies representing non-resident principals should be treated as resident in the economies in which they are located. For example, new burgeoning areas include health tourism facilitators and medical travel agents as well as commercial offices that have been set up abroad to represent medical institutions. Most agents charge the providers a fee for each client sent abroad based on a commission percentage of the package price or a set fee per patient. Other models are also possible, including a service fee direct to the client (patient) or a payment from a third-party payer as a share of the cost savings, *i.e.* the difference between the cost of the procedure at home and the cost abroad (Stephano and Cook, 2010). If the agent is a resident of the same economy as the patient, then the margin or commission is a resident-to-resident transaction. The net amount payable to service providers resident in other economies (after the margin or commission receivable by the agent is deducted) should be recorded as a resident-to-non-resident transaction. However, in other cases, the gross amount is payable to the non-resident provider, who subsequently pays the resident agent's commission.

Non-profit institutions

Like enterprises, non-profit bodies are resident entities of the economic territories in which they are located or conduct their affairs. Non-profit bodies generally provide health and other social and community services free of charge or at prices that do not fully cover the costs of production. Examples of non-profit bodies can be private hospitals, churches, foundations, universities, colleges and charities such as the Red Cross.

In practice, the residence of the vast majority of non-profit institutions can be determined without ambiguity. However, when such an institution is engaged in charity or relief work on an international scale, it is necessary to specify the residence of any branches the institution may maintain in individual countries. In this case, it is appropriate to use the guideline of length of time to determine the residence of such branches. If a non-profit institution maintains a branch, or similar unit, for a year or more in a particular country, that branch should be considered a host country resident that is, however, financed largely or entirely by transfers from abroad. On the other hand, short-term medical emergency work or specific health campaigns in another country may be classified as being provided by non-resident units.

Government

The general government agencies of an economy include all central, state and local government departments, establishments and bodies located in the economic territory and all general government embassies, consulates, entities and military establishments located elsewhere. In the case of imports and exports of health services, the provision of medical treatment to residents abroad in foreign government health facilities and the provision of services by public health institutions to non-residents in the territory are the most obvious examples of imports and exports, respectively.

In the case of government agencies involved in foreign aid programmes, this type of expenditure comprises goods and services provided by foreign governments to resident units and *vice versa*. It should be reiterated that it is the provision of goods and services, and not the financing by the foreign government, that is important in determining whether this is an import or export. For example, if a government donates money to other countries or to international organisations, this amounts only to a transfer of funds. If, however, the government provides health care goods and services for final use directly to a foreign country, this will be a health export for the country and a health import for the foreign country (and should be reflected in that foreign country's health accounts). The core of this type of expenditure is represented by government aid programmes for enhancing health in foreign countries. It should be noted that if the provision is led by the military, for example, only health expenditures should be taken into account.

International organisations

International organisations and enclaves, limited to those created by governments (such as embassies), are resident in an economic territory of their own, and not of the economy in which they are physically located. This treatment applies to both international organisations located in only one territory and those located in two or more territories. Therefore any transactions with an international organisation or enclave should be treated as international trade.

Rest of the world and trade in health care

Having determined the residence status of all units, the rest of the world is thus composed of all non-resident units carrying out transactions with the reference country. Regarding trade in health accounts, the rest of the world comprises all non-resident units that provide health care goods and services to resident units (these transactions being imports) and the non-resident units that consume health care goods and services provided by resident units (these transactions being exports).

Valuation

In the case of transactions between residents and non-residents, the values of exports and imports denominated in foreign currencies should be converted into national currency using market rates of exchange. In principle, the most appropriate exchange rate to be used in converting transaction values from the currency of transaction to the currency of compilation is the market rate prevailing at the time that the transaction takes place. The use of a daily average exchange rate for daily transactions provides a very good approximation. If daily rates cannot be applied, average rates for the shortest period should be used.

With regard to the provision of non-market services to non-residents by general government or non-profit institutions,[7] such services should be valued consistently using the methodology in SHA Manual, *i.e.* by their total cost of production and not by the subsidised price (see Chapter 3).

SHA records expenditure on goods and services in purchasers' prices. It should be noted that total figures for imports and exports in the national accounts are normally reported at FOB ("free on board") prices, and detailed foreign trade statistics are valued at CIF (cost, insurance, freight) for imports and FOB for exports (see Box 12.1). The difference between the two can vary widely, but can be up to 10% (Eurostat, 2004). From this it would be expected that the import value would exceed the export value, but even this cannot be guaranteed. One reason is timing differences, whereby a basket of goods cleared as exports from one country in a particular year need not be cleared as imports into the receiving country in the same year.

Transactions in health services, for example between governments, should be recorded on a gross basis, that is, total claims and reimbursements should be separately compiled, rather than recorded net. One issue relates to the valuation of externally provided goods and services when there is a large differential between the valuation of the recipient (importing) and donor (exporting) country, *e.g.* health system consultancy services provided by a higher-income country in a lower-income country. In this case, in a departure with BPM6 (para. 3.75), the valuation should be made in terms of the recipient country's market prices. However, a memorandum item based on the donor country's market valuation is also deemed to be appropriate.

Box 12.1. **The CIF/FOB adjustment in trade statistics**

Imported goods registered by trade statistics are valued CIF (cost, insurance and freight) which includes three different components:

- Imported goods FOB;
- Transport services rendered by both resident and non-resident transporters;
- Insurance services rendered by both resident and non-resident insurers.

The two latter components represent services that can be rendered by either resident or non-resident units. If rendered by residents, this is domestic output and thus should not be treated as imports. If no adjustment is introduced, imports are obviously higher than they should be according to the total value of transport and insurance services rendered by both residents and non-residents. One must be careful about the treatment of the value of transport and insurance services rendered by residents on imports. If these services are bought and paid for by non-resident exporters to resident carriers and insurers, their value will be recorded as the export of services in the balance of payments, and therefore must be excluded from the export of services.

Timing

In line with national accounting rules, exports and imports are to be recorded on an accrual basis, that is, at the time when a service is delivered or, in the case of medical goods, when the change in ownership occurs. There may be practical issues of data collection in that for the most part the movement of goods is a reasonable proxy for the change of ownership. However, in the case of patients travelling abroad to receive treatment, the fees may be paid in part or in full either before or some period after the service is consumed. Moreover, concerning bilateral agreements, there are often significant delays – sometimes a couple of years – between the time of treatment and the time of payment or claim for reimbursement.

Imports and exports under the *System of Health Accounts*

The SHA Manual establishes a conceptual basis for statistical reporting rules that is compatible with other economic and social statistics and that uses the International Classification for Health Accounts (ICHA), which covers three dimensions: health care by functions of care; providers of health care services; and health care financing. The System of Health Accounts (SHA) therefore follows a different logic than the one proposed in international trade statistics (that is, according to the type of service industry and mode of supply) (see Annex G).

In the System of Health Accounts, a category related to non-resident units exists in both the provider and financing schemes classifications. Both classifications refer to the "rest of the world". However, with respect to the imports and exports of health care goods and services, it is important to clarify that it is the provision by non-resident units that is of relevance to trade, rather than the financing. For example, if a foreign government or NGO pays for services for residents, then these services are financed by the rest of the world but may still be provided by a domestic provider and are therefore not imported. If, however, the service is also provided by a foreign government to a resident (irrespective of who pays for it), then this is indeed an import.

The primary classifications of imports and exports under the System of Health Accounts are by function (purpose of consumption) and provider. The classification of functions distinguishes *inter alia* the different services of care[8] (*e.g.* curative, rehabilitative and long-term care), medical goods dispensed to outpatients as well as services delivered collectively to the population, such as health promotion campaigns and the governance of the health system. The main reconciliation of this definitional classification with the System of National Accounts at an aggregate level is via the "functional" or "purpose" classifications (COICOP, COFOG and COPNI). The corresponding provider classification is linked to the International Standard Industrial Classification (ISIC, Rev. 4). This is important in terms of source data since the ISIC provides the basis for business, survey, employment and census statistics. International trade statistics are more aligned with the analysis of production and as such, classifications are based on the standard classification of products (CPC).

Examples of trade in health care goods and services under SHA

Imports and exports cover a wide range of health care goods and services for final consumption; coverage extends beyond the standard provision of medical treatment abroad, in line with the boundaries of the functional classification. It may be useful to consider the following examples, using the different modes of supply applied to both goods and services.

Individual health care services

Regarding the provision of health care services to individuals, this could be remote health counselling (which comes under many names, such as telemedicine, e-health, e-medicine, etc.) provided over the phone or Internet by a doctor in one country directly to a patient in another. This type of remote patient monitoring may involve a patient who has undergone surgery abroad and then returned to their home country. Note, however, that health care goods and services delivered from a provider in one country to a provider in another are considered as intermediate consumption and as inputs to a resident-to-resident service (*e.g.* diagnostic tests or blood products sent from a laboratory abroad to a hospital in the patient's country) and are therefore not recorded as imports under SHA.

However, most of the relevant transactions relating to international trade in health care under SHA concern the consumption by patients who are abroad either due to planned treatment (*e.g.* dental treatment, knee surgery, rehabilitative stay, etc.) or as a result of an unplanned need while abroad. This could be a patient from Country A receiving planned medical treatment in a hospital in Country B. This would be an entry in the total health spending of Country A – treated as an export for Country B and an import for Country A. Similarly, the cost incurred by a tourist who purchases medicines while abroad or falls sick and visits a GP should also be included in the health spending of the tourist's home country.

The temporary movement of health professionals from one country to another is also an example of international trade in health services. This could be an individual health care professional or a team of doctors or specialists working for a non-resident provider fulfilling a short-term contract to deliver services in another country. This is also relevant in the domain of foreign aid programmes, where goods and services may be provided directly to residents by foreign governments or NGOs. Again, it is the provision and not the financing that is of importance here.

The temporary presence of health professionals can also lead to some grey areas regarding inclusion under trade due to the employment and/or resident status of the provider. This may be particularly difficult to establish in areas of personal care, for example, when non-resident caregivers may be providing long-term care services.

Medical goods

With respect to medical goods, this could simply be the provision of health goods (pharmaceuticals, other medical non-durable and durable goods) directly to the patient/consumer from a non-resident provider by telephone, mail order or, increasingly, via the Internet. The rise of Internet pharmacies and the increased recognition of prescriptions and reimbursements across borders, *i.e.* in the European Union (Schmidt and Pioch, 2003), are likely to expand the range of delivery mechanisms for medical goods beyond the traditional local pharmacy.

Otherwise, the consumption of medical goods abroad is the main channel for trade. Much of this will be incidental purchases of tourists and visitors while abroad (which in terms of international trade statistics are reported under the "travel" category). Large price differentials and the liberalisation of prescription regulations between countries can also lead to large cross-border movements to purchase pharmaceuticals in neighbouring countries (Byrd and Law, 2009).[9]

Collective health care services

The provision of health insurance to residents by non-resident insurance companies and *vice versa* should also be considered as examples of foreign trade under SHA. However, in line with the general SHA treatment of health administration and insurance, this includes only the service charge element of the premium paid by households. Any payments made by a non-resident insurer to or on behalf of residents for health care services would only be treated as foreign trade if the care is also provided by non-resident health-care providers. For example, if a US resident takes out health insurance with a Mexico-based health insurance company and receives dental care from a Mexico-based dentist, then both the insurance service charge and dental care are regarded as imports.

In the realm of public health, and for certain aspects of health system governance and administration, it may be that some areas are outsourced or provided by non-resident entities. For example, health system planning and reform may be provided as consultancy services or may directly involve international organisations in public health and prevention measures. Similarly, part of in-kind technical assistance (TA) provided by a foreign entity would be considered as an import to the recipient country.

Borderline issues relevant to trade in health care goods and services

There are a number of borderline cases that may be gaining in importance for trade in health services. It may be that a greater proportion of the treatments being received while abroad or delivered by foreign providers arise due to legal restrictions in the home country or the non-availability of certain specialist treatments or stigmas attached to them.

A higher proportion of *cosmetic surgery* may be performed abroad, partly to preserve anonymity. Cosmetic or plastic surgery may be for reconstructive purposes or purely for aesthetic reasons in special clinics. Even though treatments for aesthetic purposes are provided by health professionals using medical technology, they are considered outside the health boundary since the main purpose is not health (see Chapter 4). However, when it is not possible to separate the types of cosmetic surgery or there is a doubt about the purpose, it is recommended that all services of this nature be included under health spending and thus reflected in estimates of total imports and exports.

Another treatment area that tends to attract consumers from overseas is *assisted reproductive technologies* (ART). This is usually provided by *bona fide* institutions and professionals and the main purpose is for health reasons, therefore, it is recommended that this be included under health spending.

One major driver of "medical tourism" is the borderline area of *well-being* and health. Many tourists visit a country to take advantage of establishments that promote wellness. These can range from spa/fitness centres to hotel/resort spas to traditional-type spas linked to a country's natural resources to more medical-type institutions employing healthcare professionals (SRI International, 2008). Often the distinction between health and well-being is not made in tourist surveys, but generally inclusion should be restricted to cases in which a clear curative, rehabilitative or preventive purpose can be identified.

Similarly, many visitors may be drawn to a country to take advantage of alternative therapies and *traditional medicine* unavailable in their home country. Reference should also be made to the section on TCAM in Chapter 5 regarding inclusion or exclusion in health spending and as a health-related item.

In terms of the consumption of medical goods, the same boundaries set out in Chapters 4 and 5 should be applied for trade in medical goods, whether these are purchased directly while abroad or delivered from overseas. This refers to recommendations regarding nutritional products and other "health" products, which should only be included on a restrictive basis – *i.e.* on the advice of health professionals, and vitamins and minerals in the case of prescription and distribution by health care providers. The exclusion of sun creams, for example, is a particular case, given the special link with holiday tourism.

Travel abroad for the specific purpose of receiving treatment incurs other costs that may or may not be linked to health care. One example is the linked *transport costs*, which may be particularly high if air travel is included. When travel is an integral part of the medical care "package" (for example, some UK residents are sent abroad by the National Health Service for certain operations) and covered by private or social insurance, then it should be included in the overall spending. However, the transport of a resident patient, if it can be separately identified, should not be regarded as an import if the service is provided by a resident carrier. In the case of private travel, or travel without the specific purpose of receiving medical treatment, then it is proposed that the transport costs should be excluded from health spending. Other costs may also be attached to medical travel that is organised through a medical travel agent or facilitator, as is often the case in the United States. Since such agents are normally resident in the patient's own country, any fee or commission paid to arrange a medical travel package is a resident-to-resident transaction and should not be included as international trade.

In certain cases, patients travelling abroad may be accompanied by one or more persons (especially in the case of children requiring treatment). Often the costs involved will also be covered by public budgets or health insurance. Unless there is a particular medical role of the *accompanying persons*, it is suggested that such expenditure should not be included under health care but rather under a health care-related item – non-health travel-related services.

One area of growth in medical travel abroad has been *illegal or unethical trade* (*e.g.* organ transplantation). While such trade may be undesirable or illegal, if it meets the criteria of the health care boundaries then it should in principle be recorded in the accounts in the same way as legal actions. For example, although the provision of abortion may be illegal in certain countries, it is still provided, albeit illegally. In such circumstances, whenever the service is paid, which is most likely the case, the payment should be recorded in SHA. Other activities could be deliberately concealed from the public authorities, even though they clearly fall within SHA boundaries and are also legal.

Intermediate use versus final use of health care goods and services

The *final consumption* approach adopted within the SHA framework highlights a notable difference between the scope of external trade that is of primary interest to health accounts and the broader measure of trade in the balance of payments and national accounts. Even though international trade statistics do not make a distinction for imported health care goods and services destined for intermediate use (*e.g.* provided by a foreign provider as an input to a service provided to a patient by a domestic provider), they should be excluded in the case of health accounts.

The distinction between final and intermediate use becomes relevant only for goods and services delivered across borders, which currently forms a minor although expanding part of trade in health (through the development of e-health, Internet pharmacies, etc.). For the direct consumption by residents abroad (considered as imports of health services) and by non-residents within the country (considered as exports of health services), these are for all intents and purposes provided directly to patients (*e.g.* a planned visit by a non-resident to a specialist or hospital) and are thus considered as final consumption.

For health services delivered across borders, the situation may be different. Some of the recent growth in cross-border trade of health services has been in the provider-to-provider category *e.g.* the provision of diagnostic services from foreign laboratories to resident hospitals, instead of delivery directly to the patient. For one country, the imports of medical services may be primarily destined for intermediate consumption, whereas for another, perhaps smaller country, the imports of health services for final use may well be relatively high. The difference in approaches between SHA and national accounts highlights two different concepts that may be relevant to imports of health services:

First, in SHA, occupational health is included in the national totals of health care spending. In SNA, this item is recorded as ancillary services and as part of the intermediate consumption of enterprises. Therefore, the use of non-resident health services by resident businesses for their employees (or the use of health services abroad by employees on business travel) would be counted under intermediate consumption in national accounts, whereas it should be included as final consumption and as an import under SHA.

Secondly, the view of consumption in SHA requires a different approach than the view of production in national accounts. National accounts make no distinction between medical goods imported by wholesalers and pharmacies and destined for sale and medical goods imported directly by households for own use. This approach contrasts with SHA, whereby only household purchases of medical goods from overseas retailers for personal consumption are treated as imports – imports by wholesalers and pharmacies are treated as inputs into the function of health care provision of medical goods and services of pharmacies and other medical goods retailers (Figure 12.1) (see Chapter 4).

Figure 12.1. **The treatment of imports under SHA**

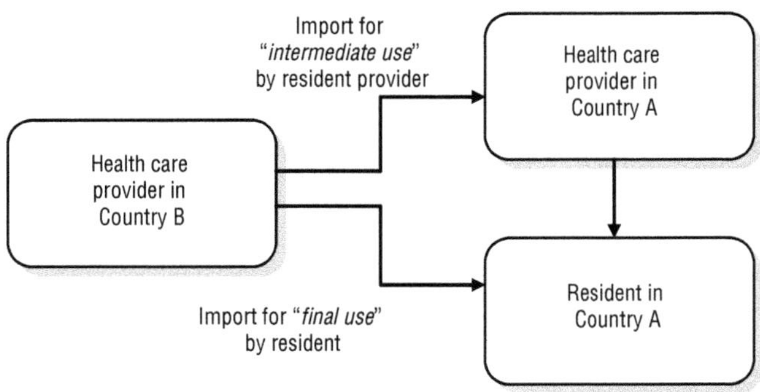

Source: IHAT for SHA 2011.

These differences should be taken into account with regards to comparisons with import and export figures in the balance of payments and national accounts. However, in any further analysis it may be of interest to examine the total imports and exports within the health care system and reconcile the figures with international trade figures.

Data sources for estimating international trade in health services under SHA

For the most part, the data sources used to compile international trade and balance of payments statistics will be the principal sources of information for health accountants to estimate flows of health care goods and services between countries, despite the minor conceptual differences outlined above. Indeed, the "health-related travel" and "health services" components of the EBOPS classification (see Annex G) theoretically provide a good starting point to estimate a large part of the trade under SHA. Moreover, EBOPS 2010 future reporting recommendations will further group together and isolate "health services" from other travel-related consumption, which will help to further harmonise the definitions with SHA.

That said, current data on trade flows in health services remain quite sparse, with gaps in country coverage and likely under-reporting. The quality of existing data varies considerably from country to country and according to the mode of delivery. One of the main purposes of this section is therefore to give guidance on how to collect and improve data on trade in health services by reviewing existing standard sources of information and identifying new potential sources. Improving trade statistics in the health area should be viewed not just in terms of how this benefits health accountants, but instead as a collaborative venture aimed at improving the measurement of international trade in general, so as to assist compilers of balance of payments and health accounts alike. That said, for the most part the value of the imports and exports of health services is still relatively marginal for most countries and for most types of health care, which means that the investment of resources to identify or develop new data collection tools and instruments needs to be considered carefully. This also has to be reviewed in the light of international reporting obligations and perceived trends.

The compilation and data sources for the EBOPS health categories and for imports and exports under SHA share many common features, but as has been seen, there are also some differences in concepts and boundaries that should be kept in mind. Health accounts require additional information and detail over and above that needed for balance of payments, but one of the guiding principles should be to show the clear links and correspondence between the different systems for their mutual benefit.

As in many areas of health accounts compilation, the measurement of international trade in health services presents many challenges. The choice of the best data sources is very much linked to the organisation of the health care system. No one data source will fit all needs. In addition, different approaches will be required to estimate imports and exports. In the case of exports, generally, but not always, information from foreign providers will not be available. Typically, estimates of imports and exports are compound statistics that do not come from single sources but rely on a number of different sources, and in many cases on assumptions and hypotheses.

One of the initial tasks in compiling estimates of imports and exports of health care goods and services should be to inventory the current and available data sources and to assess whether they are suitable and sufficient. In an ideal situation, they should match the definitional, geographical and/or temporal (*i.e.* period of residency) scope outlined in this chapter and elsewhere in the Manual. In reality, however, existing data is unlikely to be fully concordant with the compiler's needs. For example, tourist surveys may not make the necessary distinction between "tourists" and other non-resident categories, such as border or seasonal workers, or they may include medical care and well-being within the same activity. As a minimum requirement, differences should be well-documented. Otherwise, it may be necessary to adjust or calibrate data using other information and sources, including non-financial data. However, there is a need for care in handling the trade-off between forcing a breakdown into detailed categories and the resulting validity and quality of the estimates.

In the first instance, no separation by the mode of supply is made, although this may be desirable as an additional reporting item for national purposes. The structure of SHA requires in the first instance a breakdown of imports by function (HC) and by financing scheme (HF) and then if possible by mode of supply. From the point of view of exports, the primary dimension may be by function (HC) and provider (HP), with mode of supply again secondary.

Different compilation approaches can be taken, reflecting the different data sources, so as to achieve a full disaggregation between functions and providers. In some cases this might involve a top-down approach, so that there is a degree of confidence in the overall estimate, but with a distribution applied, using information from a different source or year to allocate across other categories. In other cases, where there are a number of different valid data sources covering the components, the total can be built up using a bottom-up approach. Finally, the most likely outcome is a mixed approach, where some parts of the puzzle might be available from detailed administrative data and other parts may be missing.

Enterprise and business surveys

From the point of view of services provided by domestic health care providers to non-residents, enterprise or business surveys can be useful. These can vary from small irregular sample surveys to more exhaustive annual administrative data collections with mandatory reporting by providers.[10] One could conduct a short intensive study on a sample of representative providers, find out how many foreign patients have been treated and how much their treatment has cost, how it has been paid, etc. An estimate for the national level could be obtained from this sample. Alternatively, if the provision of health care goods and services is concentrated in a few providers, the results of a study of these few providers would constitute the national estimates. Non-monetary information, such as numbers of non-resident admitted patients, may be all that is available. In some cases, it may be valid to assume that the cost per treatment does not vary between resident and non-resident patients, thus allowing for an estimation of the total cost.

In most cases, designing a new questionnaire or study may not be a viable option, which means that the use of existing surveys and data collections may need to suffice. While such data may be available for large providers such as hospitals and clinics, it may be more problematic to obtain data for smaller and individual health care providers, such as private dentists[11] and specialists – often people travelling for health reasons buy goods and services from specialised private health clinics. Some information may be available on an ad-hoc basis through umbrella and trade organisations, charity groups, etc. This may be the case regarding health and travel insurance services provided to non-residents for the estimation of administrative services provided to non-residents.

Other specific surveys may focus on obtaining data from NGOs and charities that perform a role in providing health services to persons in irregular situations, such as refugees and immigrants. Data will typically be of a non-financial nature (Médecins du Monde UK, 2007).

Retail industry and e-commerce (see OECD, 2009)

Information on the total revenue from dispensing chemists and the retail sale of suppliers of optical glasses, hearing aids and other medical appliances may be available from administrative tax statistics. However, these data sources do not normally include any hints about the share of revenues stemming from the purchases of non-residents. Any use of pharmacy sales data should also take account of increasing parallel imports and exports of medical goods.

Significant pharmaceutical price differentials between countries belonging to free trade systems, such as in the EU, have led to a rapid increase in what are called "parallel" imports and exports. Intermediaries, such as wholesalers, pharmacies and other traders, can take advantage of these price differences to buy up prescription medicines from pharmacies in countries where they are cheaper and then resell them still below the official price in the countries to which they import. In the EU, it has been estimated that this accounts for a tenth of the European medicine trade (FT.com, 7 June 2010).

Much of the information on purchases of goods abroad will come from visitor and tourist surveys and perhaps be applied to information on the total revenues of retailers.

For individual members of households, e-commerce presents an alternative method of purchasing (and increasingly selling) goods and services for private use. The statistical and policy interest for the household sector concerns the use of the Internet for such transactions, with particular interest in purchase rather than sale transactions. Surveys of ICT use in households typically collect information on individual purchasing activity via the Internet, with details often including the nature of the goods and services purchased, the value of those purchases, the value of online payments and/or the barriers to purchasing over the Internet.[12]

The reliability of the reported value of online sales has long been a concern to statisticians. As with purchasers, the split of Internet commerce transactions by the customer's location (international versus domestic) is similarly problematic. Evidence indicates that businesses have trouble reporting these splits as, firstly, they will not necessarily know the destination of their sales, and secondly, even if they did, they would not necessarily record this information in a way that is readily retrievable.

Since, for the most part, information from foreign providers regarding health care goods and services will not be available, the main source of information will be linked to the financing of consumption abroad – notably, reimbursements by public and private insurance.

Government administrative sources (liaison offices)

Government sources may maintain data and records on services provided both to non-residents by resident health providers and to residents (or insured persons) by non-resident providers. In countries where bilateral or regional agreements are in place, data may be available on the numbers and expenditures both of residents abroad and of non-residents in the country. Where lump-sum transfers are made between countries based on waiver agreements, these should be taken as the gross payments and not the net transfer. Where bilateral or regional agreements exist (such as EU citizens' entitlements to benefits in kind during a stay in another EU Member State), administrative data may be obtained by the various ministries (Ministry of Finance or Health or another relevant ministry that keeps track of the health care imports and exports, as specified by regulations). In some countries, data may be available from the health insurance funds (both public and private) where reimbursements for foreign-provided health care have occurred.

Social security schemes and international liaison offices

The records of the social security liaison offices are a potentially rich source of information about the health care goods and services consumed by the *insured* population. The information available is increasingly detailed in terms of type of treatment and country for both insured persons abroad and non-residents in the country.[13] However, these institutions handle only the claims based on certain international legislation and bilateral agreements. Claims for reimbursement by patients addressed to health insurance funds based on national legislation are not recorded by the liaison offices, and this will need to be supplemented with information from the health insurance funds themselves. However, an important qualification is needed regarding the records in both cases, in that at the base level the information reflects the insured population rather than the resident population. The insured population is not necessarily identical with the resident population as defined under SHA.[14] Without controlling for expenditure caused by non-residents, the use of the financial records will lead to an overestimation of the consumption of health care goods and services abroad.

Another point to bear in mind is that the information relates to the reimbursement of treatment abroad rather than to the full cost. In optimal cases, additional information may be available on the total cost of services allowing assumptions to be made regarding the cost-sharing or direct out-of-pocket element. In most cases though, travel and household surveys may need to be used to obtain more information about private insurance reimbursement and out-of pocket payments.

Other administrative sources

In some countries, public health care purchasing authorities and ministries of health have organised contracts with non-resident health care providers, under which patients are sent for certain treatments abroad. Annual reports at an individual purchasing authority level or nationally should be available to give patient numbers and costs.

Further administrative information may also be held in various ministries on the "free" treatment of some particular population groups, such as refugees, and of other non-residents in countries with universal health care systems and no payment at the point of delivery. Expenditures abroad for military personnel, overseas embassy staff,[15] etc., may be collected separately. Data on overseas assistance may also be available from development agencies and ministries.

Private health insurance

The financial records of private health insurance companies that provide primary or complementary insurance (including travel insurance) may be a potential source of information on the number of claims by insured persons abroad. This depends very much on the statutory obligations to provide data, and the detail of the data regarding a split into type of treatment and country will vary accordingly. The national association of private insurers may have the responsibility for collating and publishing data from its members.[16]

Household and tourist surveys

The basic data sources for private out-of-pocket payments are usually household surveys. These surveys can be institutionalised household budget surveys or specialised household surveys that rely on self-reported information and are typically provided on a voluntary basis.

Caution must be exercised when analysing self-reported data on expenditure as to whether the reported amount spent is the gross or net value. People with primary private health insurance typically have to cover the costs of medical treatment upfront and get the total costs or parts of the costs reimbursed by their insurance company. Not deducting reimbursement by other schemes is a potential source of double-counting and overestimation of private out-of-pocket payments. What makes correct accounting even more challenging is the fact that usually some time passes between the payment of the bills and their reimbursement, *i.e.* the two payments can occur in different accounting periods. Furthermore, information on health spending abroad may not systematically be requested or may result in unrepresentatively low samples. The addition of new questions to existing surveys (*e.g.* Health expenditure surveys, Household budget surveys, etc.) would be more cost-effective and easier than building a whole new questionnaire. Additional questions may only need to be asked fairly infrequently, as an add-on module, which would reduce extra costs further.

Travel or tourist surveys are conducted in various forms by many countries to measure the activities of travellers.[17] Some surveys may be designed purely to meet balance of payments requirements for measuring travel and, possibly, other forms of expenditure and income. In most cases the information is unlikely to meet the needs of SHA exactly and should be adjusted or noted. Travellers can be surveyed when they arrive or depart or sometimes after they have returned to their home countries, thus providing the possibility for information on both imports and exports. Surveys of arrivals measure actual expenditures abroad of residents returning home and anticipated expenditures of non-resident visitors. Conversely, surveys of departures measure actual expenditures of departing non-resident visitors and anticipated expenditures of departing resident visitors. Some surveys of returned travellers collect data from residents some time after they return. Surveys often include a category for purpose, including for "health and medical" reasons, and for how much was spent on treatment. Again, care should be taken in analysing spending to avoid double-counting with later reimbursements.

Additional information can also be found from patient surveys conducted by health insurance groups. In a prime example, TK (Techniker Krankenkasse), one of the main insurers in Germany with over 7 million insured persons in 2009, carries out a regular annual survey of its patients that provides detailed information on cross-border care (Techniker Krankenkasse, 2009).

Other sources

In some cases, data published by other countries (mirror statistics) may be used, possibly to reconcile or validate other data, or as a source for exports. This may be the case for some of the claim and reimbursement data compiled under international and bilateral agreements.

Health services provided by professionals abroad could be delivered by either non-migrants (going abroad for less than one year) or short-term migrants (admitted in another country for at least three months, but less than 12 months). In order to fall within the boundary of imports or exports, the health service professionals need to supply a health service abroad without seeking access to the employment market of the host country. The data collected should include the number of health service providers, the type of health services delivered, the occupation of the health professionals, and their length of stay. Helpful sources to collect this data could be professional registers, hospitals, industry surveys or government agencies that issue working permits.

The supply and use tables of national accounts describe in detail the sale and purchase relationships, both final and intermediate, between producers and consumers, either in terms of industry or product outputs. A supplementary table that on the face of it could be of use to the compiler of health accounts is the use table for imports, which is compiled to separate the use of imported goods and services from domestically-produced goods and services. Such a table is not necessarily a core feature of the input-output framework and therefore is likely to be available only for a reduced number of countries.[18] A number of important points need to be taken into consideration when assessing information from supply, use and input-output tables:

- First, the difference in the concepts and definitions of imports in national accounts and SHA. As noted in the previous section, with regard to goods, SHA has a much narrower definition of imports, which is restricted to medical goods imported directly by households for own use. Thus, information on total imports of pharmaceuticals and the split between intermediate and final use from import matrices will be of limited value. In the case of health services, the different treatment of imported occupational health needs to be considered, in that in the national accounts this will typically be treated as intermediate consumption, whereas under SHA this should be accounted for as final consumption.
- There is a separate treatment for the direct purchases of goods and services abroad by residents on personal trips. In practice, most countries are not able to break these expenditures down into product types without using stylised assumptions that preserve input-output balances that are of questionable analytic value – and so they are often shown in a single adjustment row in the supply table to arrive at total imports and are added to household final consumption in the use table.[19] Any spending on health services by business travellers is treated as intermediate consumption and in theory is allocated to the branch of activity as *imported* intermediate consumption, rather than final consumption.
- Similarly, purchases in the domestic territory by non-residents are treated as exports and deducted from households' final consumption expenditure. Thus the corresponding total is entered in the exports column with a positive value and deducted in the same amount in the column of final consumption expenditure of households. Methodologies vary considerably on how to break down this total spending by non-residents amongst products. For example, the expenditure of foreign visitors to the United Kingdom was analysed in a special survey. Although this gave only broad expenditure headings, it was possible to sub-divide them further using the expenditure patterns of UK residents on similar groups of products, although the results therefore had a relatively weak basis (UK Input-Output Balances: Methodological Guide, 1997).
- Directly collected information for compiling import use tables is rare. Thus, in most cases assumptions must be made and various modelling techniques may be used to populate the tables. Very small values may be estimated in certain cells, but the statistical accuracy of these data cannot be verified. Often countries will make use of the import proportionality assumption in the construction of their import matrices. This technique assumes that, for any product, the share of total expenditure on that product that is made up of imports is the same for all consumers, whether final demand or intermediate – with the share determined by the contribution imports make to the total supply of the product in the economy. For example, if 10% of all health services sold within an economy is imported, it is assumed that the share of expenditure on health services that is made up by imports is 10% for any consumer.

- Finally, the set of supply and use tables may sometimes, albeit infrequently, be available only at basic prices, whereas SHA tables require purchasers' prices.

Other balance of payments data sources

Compilers of balance of payments statistics use many of the data sources and methods listed above, some of which can be particularly relevant to compilers of health accounts. However, the conventional information coming from International Trade Statistics and International Transactions Reporting Systems are unlikely to provide the sufficient detail necessary for health accounts purposes.

International trade statistics. The traditional source of information for international trade statistics (ITS) regarding the movement of goods between countries has been the custom records. For the European Union, procedures have been developed for enterprises to make direct declarations for intra-union trade. ITS provides little information of direct use to SHA, since it covers in principle the movement of all goods in and out of a country and conforms to the wider concept of trade. In principle, this should include postal items. However, for the most part individual consignments of, for example, mail-order pharmaceuticals are generally not considered significant and are not subject to declaration and will be neither recorded nor separately identifiable.

Individuals arriving in a country are also required to complete a customs declaration for ITS purposes. Again, individual purchases of pharmaceuticals or medicals goods are unlikely to be captured in such statistics and in any case would be recorded under the travel services item of the balance of payments.

Detailed as trade statistics might be, there still remain some serious shortcomings that will affect their usability for estimating exports and imports of health care goods in the SHA framework:

- Imports are valued with their CIF-price, which excludes taxes. SHA requires goods and services to be valued at the purchaser's price, which includes value added taxes.
- With regard to intra-community (*e.g.* within the EU) trade, private households are exempt from the obligation to provide information about exports and imports for trade statistics purposes. Likewise businesses are exempt from this obligation, if their exports and imports do not exceed a volume of EUR 400 000 per year.
- The available information from trade statistics do not allow for splitting the traded commodities based on use in final consumption or intermediate consumption.

International transactions reporting systems. An ITRS includes individual cash transactions between resident and non-resident banks. Data is collected from forms submitted to banks and forms submitted directly from enterprises. The forms will likely include information on the value and purpose of the transaction and the country. However, a number of problems arise. Firstly, the classification conforms to the BOP classification and is therefore insufficient for SHA needs. The data will cover transactions involving intermediate goods and services, and again certain thresholds apply such that many private transactions are not considered separately but are part of a sample survey. There is also a question of the timing since payment may not coincide with the timing of service delivery.

Reporting of trade in health care goods and services under the SHA framework

In SHA table HCxHP, the classification of health care providers (ICHA-HP) contains a category HP.9 Rest of the world for "non-resident units providing health care for final consumption to resident units".[20] Thus, health care goods and services from non-resident providers are explicitly recorded and can be classified according to the various functions – since the same boundary of health care applies for those goods and services consumed by residents abroad (Figure 12.2). Similarly, cross-classification of the provider and financing classifications provides a breakdown of who is paying for the function (*e.g.* government, private insurance, out-of-pocket, etc.).

Exports are not included, since the health expenditure of an economy is restricted to consumption by its residents only. In practice, from the provision perspective the direct purchase of health care goods and services by non-residents will need to be explicitly excluded from domestic provider revenues. For reasons of transparency and to allow the compiler and user to report consumption by non-residents, such exports should also be recorded. Therefore, goods and services consumed by non-residents could be reported under a supplementary table.

Figure 12.2. **Health care goods and services from non-resident providers in the HCxHP table**

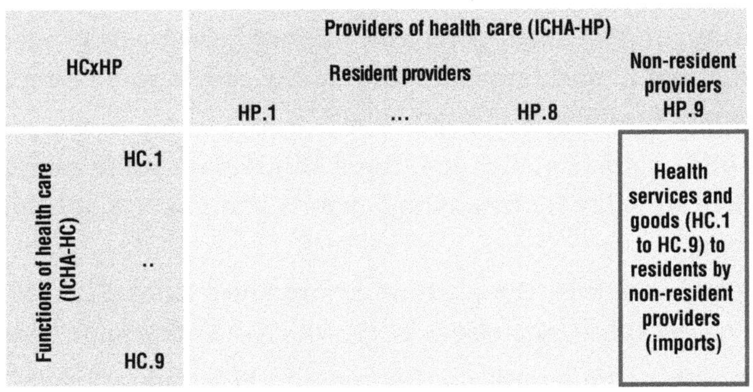

Source: IHAT for SHA 2011.

Supplementary tables and reporting

The supplementary tables on trade provide further information on health care goods and services consumed by residents abroad and the provision of health care goods and services to non-residents (Tables 12.1 and 12.2). For imports, there is a cross-classification of imported health care goods and services by the financing scheme. For exports, since the prime source of information is resident health care providers, a table cross-classifying the function of health care by provider is recommended.

To reflect the areas of main policy interest as well as possible data limitations, the HC categories are limited to the main categories of individual health care services (HC.1-4), medical goods (HC.5), preventive care (HC.6) and governance and health system and financing administration (HC.7), with selected categories for inpatient, outpatient and dental care, as defined in Chapter 5.

Table 12.1. **Expenditure on health care imports by function and financing scheme**

Functions	Financing schemes Million of national currency	HF.1 Governmental schemes and compulsory contributory health financing schemes	HF.1.1 Governmental schemes	HF.1.2 Compulsory contributory health insurance schemes	HF.1.3 Compulsory Medical Saving Accounts (CMSA)	HF.2 Voluntary health care payment schemes	HF.3 Household out-of-pocket payment	HF.4 Rest of the world financing schemes (non resident)	TOTAL
HC.M.1-4	**Curative/rehabilitative/long-term care (health) and ancillary services**								
	Of which:								
HC.M.1.1/2.1/3.1	Inpatient care								
HC.M.1.3/2.3/3.3	Outpatient care								
	Of which:								
HC.M.1.3.2	Dental care								
HC.M.5	**Medical goods (non specified by function)**								
HC.M.6	**Preventive care**								
HC.M.7	**Governance, management and health system administration**								
HC.M.9	**Other health care services not elsewhere classified (*n.e.c.*)**								
	TOTAL								
Memorandum items:									
HC.RI.M.2	Traditional, Complementary and Alternative Medicines (TCAM)								

Source: IHAT for SHA 2011.

Because of the relative importance of some health-related items in imports and exports, it may be of interest to report expenditure on TCAM as a reporting item, possibly supplemented by additional items, such as "spa and well-being" and "non-health travel-related services".

Spas encompass a myriad of different services and providers, making international comparisons difficult, but in general they can be defined as "establishments that promote wellness through the provision of therapeutic and other professional services aimed at renewing the body, mind and spirit" (SRI International, 2008). However, where a clear curative, rehabilitative or preventive nature can be identified, either through a prescription and/or provision by a health professional then this should be included in health spending. For example, some "medical spas" operate under the full-time on-site supervision of a licensed health care professional.

"Non-health travel-related services" refers to expenditure that is incurred as part of travel abroad to seek care but is not directly related to the patient's health. This may include additional travel and accommodation costs of the patient plus the expenses of accompanying persons such as relatives.

On a national level, it may also be desirable to produce tables according to the mode of supply, specific trading partners or regions (*e.g.* in the case of EU countries – separating intra-EU and extra-EU trade) or sub-national regions.

Table 12.2. **Expenditure on health care exports by function and provider**

Functions	Providers / Million of national currency	HP.1 Hospitals	HP.2 Residential long-term care facilities	HP.3 Providers of ambulatory health care	HP.4 Providers of ancillary services	HP.5 Retailers and other providers of medical goods	HP.6 Providers of preventive care	HP.7 Providers of health care system administration and financing	HP.8 Rest of economy	TOTAL
HC.X.1-4	**Curative/rehabilitative/long-term care (health) and ancillary services**									
	Of which:									
HC.X.1.1/2.1/3.1	Inpatient care									
HC.X.1.3/2.3/3.3	Outpatient care									
	Of which:									
HC.X.1.3.2	Dental care									
HC.X.5	**Medical goods (not specified by function)**									
HC.X.6	**Preventive care**									
HC.X.7	**Governance, management and health system administration**									
HC.X.9	**Other health care services not elsewhere classified (*n.e.c.*)**									
	TOTAL									
Memorandum items:										
HC.RI.X.2	Traditional, Complementary and Alternative Medicines (TCAM)									

Source: IHAT for SHA 2011.

Notes

1. For example, the Joint OECD, Eurostat and WHO Health Accounts (SHA) Data Collection – JHAQ (2006-2010).
2. The main data sources for Balance of Payments statistics are traditionally the International Transactions Reporting System (ITRS) and Enterprise surveys. Other sources used in country estimations include tourism and visitor surveys, household expenditure surveys and government administrative sources, *e.g.* information on government health services provided to non-residents.
3. A proposal for cross-border healthcare in the European Union was first discussed by the College of Commissioners on 25 June 2008 as part of the social agenda package, and it is hoped that the report will provide a new legal framework for the area in order to meet European Court of Justice rulings (Kohll-Decker Ruling C-120/95 [1998] and C-158/96 [1998] European Court of Justice) on cross-border access to care, as well as to ensure that e-Health or telemedicine services can be supplied from one country to another safely and efficiently.
4. See Annex G "International standards and classifications of trade and tourism".
5. The same concepts and definitions are adopted in the System of National Accounts.
6. When the health spending of certain groups of the population (*e.g.* those retired or living abroad) is still covered by their country of origin, then the transfers made from the country of origin to the country of residence will be shown in the table HFxFS of the receiving country; the revenue of the financing scheme will be either FS.2 or FS.7.1 (see Chapter 8). From the point of view of the reimbursing country, the sectoral account of the "Total health-related revenues and expenses of government" can detail the payments made to foreign governments for non-residents (see Annex D).
7. In the absence of any reimbursement of this cost/expenditure, this may result in reported deficiencies in the providing country, as the consumption of resources does not match the capacity and consumed resources. Hence it will be under-reported or not reported at all.
8. In addition, the basic functions of care can also be classified by the mode of production (*e.g.* inpatient, day care, outpatient and home care).
9. The study by Byrd and Law highlights the practice of US residents crossing the border to purchase antibiotics, which are available without prescription in Mexico.

10. In Korea, for example, Article 27-2 of the Medical Affairs Act stipulates that a medical institution intending to treat foreign patients should register with the Minister of Health and Welfare and report to the same on the results for the previous year by the end of March each year, providing detailed information on each treatment, including nationality, age, sex, type of treatment, period of treatment and cost.

11. To compile the Austrian balance of payments, a survey of dentists near the Austrian border with Hungary was used to model cross-border flows. *Source*: Balance of payments country notes (*www.esds.ac.uk/international/support/user_guides/imf/bops.asp*).

12. The collection efforts of OECD countries vary in this area. In particular, because of changes to Eurostat's model household survey, fewer European countries are collecting the value of purchases over the Internet. The 2005 OECD model survey has nominal value of purchases as a non-core question reflecting the low priority and difficulty respondents have in recalling the value of purchases. In addition to purchasing activity, the model questionnaire asks individuals whether they have sold over the Internet, for example, using auction sites. It also asks about the types of products purchased over the Internet and about barriers to Internet purchasing.

13. For example, the EU liaison offices CLEISS in France and DVKA in Germany provide information on the claims of the health insurance funds for the treatment of non-residents on behalf of where the person is insured (export of services) and claims from international liaison offices for the treatment of persons insured in Germany abroad on behalf of the German health insurance funds (import of services).

14. In the case of the German statutory health insurance scheme, close to 300 000 people who are covered under it and therefore cause expenditures borne by it are non-residents (*e.g.* a German pensioner spending his retirement in Spain). Unfortunately, expenditure caused by non-residents cannot be separated from expenditure caused by residents.

15. The Balance of Payments Compilation Guide includes a model collection form to collect expenditure information from embassies and international institutions on various services.

16. For example, in Germany the PKV, the association of private health insurance companies that organises 46 private health insurers. It provides the combined financial results of the primary and complementary health insurance branches of the organised insurers and can provide information on claims abroad for categories such as inpatient, ambulatory and dental services.

17. For an example of a Household Travel Survey for Ireland, see Ireland Central Statistics Office (2009).

18. The OECD Input-Output Database provides input-output tables for an increasing number of OECD and non-OECD countries on a harmonised basis, that is, industry-by-industry, basic prices and industry classifications. See OECD (2006a), document DSTI/DOC(2006)8.

19. ESA 1995 recommends that direct purchases abroad should be broken down by product.

20. The distinction between the "rest of the world" category under the financing scheme classification should also be made. For example, if a foreign government or NGO pays for health services consumed by residents, then these services are financed by these non-resident units but may still be provided by a resident entity and therefore not an import.

A System of Health Accounts 2011: Revised edition

PART II

Chapter 13

Price and Volume Measures

Introduction

Getting more value for money is a common interest of policy makers and consumers. While progress has been made since the release of the first edition of the SHA Manual, there remains concern among policy makers and statisticians that the difficult task of price and volume measurement in health care needs more attention. This chapter provides a methodological discussion and several illustrative examples of the developmental work related to health care prices and volumes.

Health care poses basic conceptual difficulties for price and volume measurement that are common to other service industries, for instance, communications, and computer and information services. Some of these are partly due to well-known fundamental measurement problems in service industries, such as the definition of output, the appropriate choice of unit of measurement, and the monitoring of quality changes.

The study of impacts of health care services on the growth of service industries, overall economic productivity trends and relative prices also depends on the availability of reliable measures for price and volume in health care goods and services. Weaknesses in measuring the price and volume of health care also have implications for the measurement of total GDP growth in real terms. Growth of real private household income might also be underestimated in countries where health care is an important component in the consumer price index (Boskin *et al.*, 1996).

This chapter outlines some of the difficulties in the calculations of the constant-price output of health care industries – services and goods – both for market and non-market production, and discusses methodological problems of international price comparisons in this field. This chapter skips the more technical parts of index numbers and focuses on proposals to improve the measurement of price and volume changes in health care.

The chapter presents an overview of the methods tested in several countries that have carried out projects to improve their countries' price and output measurement in health care, mainly using directly-measured output indicators. Results from these studies indicate that, where elaborate health information systems are in place, improved indicators for price and output measurement are feasible. It is thus important that some agreements are reached on how to advance the information systems in such a way that relevant and desirable indicators can be progressively built.

Measurement of changes in price and volume in the SHA framework

The SHA Manual focuses on the final consumption of health care goods and services, with valuation at purchasers' prices. The aggregate "current health expenditure" combines in a single figure the monetary value of the final consumption of all health care goods and services by residents of a given country during a given period.

Another key indicator of interest to stakeholders is the growth in the value of health spending over time. This change in the observed monetary aggregate can be separated into the part of growth that stems from a change in volume and the part that is due to a change in price. Growth in volume controls for changes in the price level between two periods in order to identify whether changes in expenditure reflect only an increase in the prices of health services or instead an increase in production, and consequently, improved services, more coverage and the like.

Volume is associated with quantities. In a time series, a volume index summarises the proportionate changes in the quantities of a specified set of goods or services between two periods of time. The quantities compared over time must be for homogeneous items, and the resulting quantity changes for different goods and services must be weighted by their economic importance, as measured by their relative values in one or other, or both, periods. For this reason, volume is a more correct and appropriate term for comparisons in time than is quantity (SNA 2008, 15.13). Similarly, for inter-country comparisons, differences in price levels between countries are removed from the expenditure values to provide a comparison between the volumes in the countries concerned.

The first part of this chapter will focus on this *temporal* volume/price breakdown. For this time series type of analysis, a framework for compiling a consistent and integrated set of price and volume measures covering all flows of goods and services is suggested. In this chapter it will be argued that the basic estimation strategies for measuring prices of market health products also provide an adequate starting point for measuring output and prices for a significant share of non-market services in health care.

Besides, the principles of trend analysis can also be used to measure output across countries while holding time constant, that is, to carry out "cross-country" comparisons. Measurement of changes in price and volume can be analysed from a perspective of change in purchasing power across countries over some basket of final consumption goods and services (*spatial* volume/price breakdown).

A cross-country comparison should show that two countries producing the same number of identical items of a given quality would be measured as having the equivalent volume of output. The similarity with the method used for time series should be quite obvious: a time series comparison within the same country can easily be viewed as comparing two countries. In other words, the method used to compare prices in Denmark in 2000 with Denmark in 2010 should be consistent with the method used to compare Denmark in 2010 with France in 2010. This similarity will be heavily used in this chapter: the quantity and quality indicators that are recommended for use in a time series analysis will be, at least conceptually, the same as the quantity and quality indicators to be used in cross-country comparisons, and vice-versa.

Volume time-series are generally calculated by deflating current price time series by adequate temporal price indices. Similarly, appropriate spatial price indices ("Purchasing power parities") are used to deflate current price aggregates (typically in different currencies) in order to compare the volume of output (or consumption) between countries.

It is important to clarify that a time series of volumes and volumes derived using PPP estimates as deflators are two different measures. In a time series of volumes, the effects of price changes from one period to another are removed to produce volume measures from which rates of economic growth are calculated. In the case of an inter-country comparison, the effects of differences due to exchange rates and those due to different price levels within each country are removed from the expenditure values to provide a comparison between the volumes in the country concerned (SNA 2008, 15.228).

Inter-temporal indexes of price and volume

To use an analogy from the whole economy, much effort is spent on measuring the value of GDP at current prices, but often a more important objective is to derive a measure of the growth of GDP and its components in volume. Growth in volume controls for changes in the price level between two periods.

To express a flow in volume terms, each of the goods and services that are the counterparts of money spent must, in principle, be identified. This is because quantities are additive only for a single homogeneous product: if a hospital carries out 200 (expensive) hip replacement operations and 400 (less expensive) cataract surgeries, it is not informative in economic terms to add these together and say that 600 treatments were carried out. Inevitably, the question therefore arises of how are the 200 hip replacement operations and the 400 cataract surgeries to be added in a meaningful way. This question will arise for all the thousands of goods and services that populate the global concept of health services. The answer traditionally draws on the knowledge that the relative prices of the different goods and services bought and sold reflect both their relative utilities to purchasers and their relative costs for the producers. However, is this relevant, in particular, for non-market services where, by definition, there is no market price that reflects the interaction of consumers and producers?

In the simple market situation, index numbers are designated to decompose changes in value aggregates into their overall change in price and volume components. A price index can be used to deflate the value of products that have been transacted on the market, and this yields a volume measure of the goods or services transacted. Instead of deflating values with a price index, one could also set up an index of volumes or quantities produced and consumed directly.

A price index can be calculated as a weighted average of the proportionate changes in the prices of a specified set of goods and services between two periods of time. Similarly, a volume index can be calculated as a weighted average of the proportionate changes in the volume of a specified set of goods and services between two periods of time.

The two most commonly used indices are those of Laspeyres and Paasche. The former is used mainly to calculate changes in volumes while the latter is used to calculate changes in prices.[1]

Three things are worth noting about these indices:

- First, price or quantity changes of the products are weighted with expenditure shares and these expenditure shares – measured by market observation – reflect the joint, equilibrium valuation of each product by consumers and producers. Thus, market prices and quantities reveal the interaction of consumer preferences and producer costs.
- Second, in the simple model at hand, changes in quantities Y_i^t/Y_i^{t-1} and in prices P_i^t/P_i^{t-1} are simply measured by comparing them between periods – implying that the units of measurement for Y_i^t are the same as the units of measurement for Y_i^{t-1} and that the set of products is stable – product i has to exist in both periods to be compared.
- Third, the simple presentation here also makes the implicit assumption that there is exactly one measured unit of quantity that constitutes Y_i or one measured price that constitutes P_i. In practice, this is rarely the case. The P_i's are un-weighted averages of individual items which constitute an elementary price index. Similarly, the Y_i's for a volume index are actually product counts. How individual products ("items") are

Box 13.1. Laspeyres and Paasche indexes

Volume indices of the Laspeyres type are shown below where P_i^t stands for the price of product i in period t and Y_i^t for its quantity:

$$Y^{L,t} = \sum^{N} \left(\frac{P_i^{t-1} \times Y_i^{t-1}}{\sum^{N} P_i^{t-1} \times Y_i^{t-1}} \right) \frac{Y_i^t}{Y_i^{t-1}} \qquad [1]$$

In the formula [1] above, quantity changes Y_i^t/Y_i^{t-1} for elementary commodity groups are aggregated by weighting them by their value shares in period t-1. The index can be interpreted as the change in value at constant prices of a basket of products whose composition is kept fixed as it was in the reference period.

The Paasche price index is defined as follows:

$$P^{P,t} = \frac{\sum_{i=1}^{N} P_i^t Y_i^t}{\sum_{i=1}^{N} P_i^{t-1} Y_i^t},$$

which can be written in terms of the price changes of the individual commodities, as follows:

$$P^{P,t} = \left[\sum_{i=1}^{N} \frac{P_i^t \times Y_i^t}{\sum_{j=1}^{N} P_j^t \times Y_j^t} \left(\frac{P_i^t}{P_i^{t-1}} \right)^{-1} \right]^{-1} \qquad [2]$$

Similarly to [1], the price index written in [2] can be defined as the change in the price of a basket of products whose composition every period is updated and the quantities of the new period t are applied to the prices in t and t – 1.

The volume index [1] can also be obtained indirectly, by dividing the change in value by the Paasche price index (so-called deflation method):

$$Y^{L,t} = \left(\frac{\sum_{i=1}^{N} P_i^t Y_i^t}{\sum_{i=1}^{N} P_i^{t-1} Y_i^{t-1}} \right) \Big/ P^{P,t}$$

grouped is a question that has to be answered with respect to the purpose of the price or volume index. A useful criterion for grouping individual items is that they potentially satisfy the same or similar consumer needs or that they are substitutes from a consumer perspective. Conversely, if different items are not interchangeable from a consumer perspective, they should be treated as different products.

The considerations above already indicate that in a non-market context, prices for goods or services are not in general observable. It could be argued that this may also be the case for market services, where a price mechanism is observable but not necessarily a price per unit of output. For example, if health services are defined as completed cycles of treatment, the price for a particular completed treatment may not be directly observable, because the observable pricing mechanism may be geared to individual activities or providers rather than to a complete treatment. There is also the issue of health insurance: prices that are observed in the health services market may not be indicative of consumers' willingness to pay if these are covered by health insurance. This leads us to conclude that differences in measurement between the "market" and "non-market" provision of health services may be less pronounced than is sometimes assumed.

In the literature, deflation procedures are often exclusively associated with market producers. This reflects the idea that constructing a price index requires the presence of market prices and that the latter are directly associated with market production. While this argument is correct, things are less clear-cut if one allows for a more comprehensive meaning of "deflation". In particular, "deflation" can be understood as applying a true market price index, but it can also be understood as applying a unit cost or "quasi price index" (Schreyer, 2008).

In some countries, hospitals and other providers of medical services are considered market producers because they receive reimbursement that, on average, covers their costs. In such cases, a quasi price index consists of average revenues per treatment. One notes, however, that the fact that there are revenues does not imply that there is a competitive market where prices necessarily carry signals about consumer preferences.

Market and non-market measures for health care

Market output is output that is sold at prices that are economically significant. Thus, for market health services, the value of output in current prices can be measured by the value of sales of these services. However, health is one of the most common examples of services provided by government free of charge or at prices that are not economically significant and thus constitute non-market output. A price which is not economically significant is deliberately fixed well below the equilibrium price that would clear the market. It is defined as a price which has little or no influence over how much the producer is willing to supply and which has only a marginal influence on the quantities demanded.

The measure of the volume of health care goods and services consumed by patients should not be affected at all by the status, whether market or non-market, of the provider of the service. Thus one objective is to encourage the compilation of consistent measures of health output, whether these services are provided by market or non-market producers. Hill (1975) formulated this idea as follows:

"*It is proposed as a matter of principle that the basic methodology used to measure changes in the volume of real output should always be the same irrespective of whether a service is provided on a market or on a non-market basis. This is not to say that the actual numerical measures would not be affected by whether the service is market or non-market, because different weighting systems would be involved, but at least the methods of measurement should be conceptually similar*" (page 19).

To achieve such convergence, an obvious first approach would be to try to find out whether components of the consumer price index (CPI)[2] could be used to adjust the weights (value shares) in a volume index for the non-market sector. Indeed, the existence of expenditure by households implies that there should be a CPI calculated for these flows, and thus it seems there already exists some experience in calculating a volume/price split. The question then arises as to whether this experience cannot be directly applied to the non-market sector.

The extension from the market sector to the non-market sector, while possible in some cases, is generally more complicated. A problem occurs when the services provided by the market sector are different from those provided by the non-market sector. For example, in some countries, the hospital market sector may be mainly dealing with standard interventions, for which it is easier to calculate a volume measure, while public hospital services also cover more complicated interventions, for which volume calculations are also more difficult. Thus, the market sector may not be representative of the entire sector. Even if many outputs of non-market producers are equivalent to those of market producers, the efficiency of these types of providers may differ.

Another reason for this is that the expenditures on social transfers in kind to individual households by government or non-profit institutions are excluded from the scope of the index, as they are not incurred by households. In the health sector, many of the goods and services consumed by households are financed and paid for by government units or non-profit institutions. This is why the CPI is of limited use to deflate health expenditures whenever social transfers in kind represent an important proportion of health spending.

The United States is a case in point. A large part of expenditures on health in the United States is directly attributed to household expenditure and provided by "market producers". These expenditures are therefore covered in the CPI. The volume of health services in the national accounts is then obtained by applying a mixture of the relevant CPI and Producer Price Index (PPI)[3] deflators to health expenditure (US Bureau of Economic Analysis, 2009). The choice is based on which deflator provides the best coverage. However, the extensive literature on the difficulty of quality adjustment for health services in CPIs and PPIs shows that the basic problems with price indices are the same as with volume indices in other countries.

The basic measurement methods used for both the market and the non-market sector should be consistent. Consistency concerns in particular the aggregation method, where the same type of weights should be used to combine quantities or prices of services into volume or price indices. The main issue is to ensure that the quantities, prices, or unit costs refer to a unit of output, and not to units of inputs. Otherwise, the objective of measuring volumes of outputs cannot be achieved.

Products classification for price and volume measures

The objective of this section is to provide guidance on the measurement of the volume of health services provided by the health care industry. Ideally, the unit of output would capture complete treatments, and would take into account quality change in the provision of treatments. This measurement of health care output would then be able to differentiate among price, quantity and quality changes. In practice, rather than quantifying "complete treatments", it is common practice to define output in the health sector by counting the amount of each type of activity[4] that is undertaken in each health care setting.

A complete treatment refers to the pathway that an individual takes through different health providers in order to receive full and final treatment for a disease or condition. This definition of the target measure, otherwise known as a disease-based estimate of health care output, is similar to that used in the *Eurostat Handbook on Price and Volume Measures* (2001), Berndt *et al.* (2001), Aizcorbe and Nestoriak (2008) and Triplett (2003). We note, however, that the notion of a complete treatment is not always applicable.

A first limitation arises with regards to measuring complete treatments. Conceptually, "complete" is understood as a complete treatment pathway across the health care system. As an example of a complete treatment pathway, consider a hip replacement operation. The pathway approach would imply aggregating all services or procedures associated with the intervention on the condition, whether these are received from primary care services such as a general practitioner, specialists, at hospitals, or at rehabilitation centres. Thus, using the pathway approach would entail collecting data on outputs from a number of health care providers and aggregating them in a meaningful way. This is very challenging.

There are additional reasons why the principle of complete treatment is difficult to implement:

- The total output of an industry is based on summing up outputs of various service providers (establishments), and therefore a complete treatment is hard to capture if service provision cuts across several establishments. Even if it were possible to observe complete treatments, if there are several service providers involved (*e.g.* hospitals and outpatient services), there would be no simple way to allocate the overall service to the different participating units, and yet this is a requirement for national accounts purposes.
- Most data retrieval systems do not have the capacity to link the treatment of an individual across institutions to enable measurement of the complete treatment. Data would be required on both expenditures (value of inputs) and the services received. Thus a health care pathway approach imposes demanding data requirements, as patient records have to be linked across activities and institutions. Even within institutional settings, data may not be appropriately linked.
- The beginning and end point of a treatment pathway is observable in the case of acute health conditions, but unclear for chronic health problems or for medical conditions that give rise to long-term care and services provided in nursing homes. Many of the diseases associated with ageing and most psychiatric conditions are chronic, long-term conditions, and the patient may be treated for more than one illness or problem within a period. Thus, the boundaries of the complete treatment would be unclear.

Given the difficulty with compiling complete treatments, estimates of health care output usually occur at the institutional level. Thus a narrower view of a treatment is that defined by the type of health service. This measure captures the full treatment only within an institution and generally by function or type of service. Norway and the United Kingdom have, for instance, adopted this practice. Dawson *et al.* (2005) compiled an output index with 1700 categories of NHS activity, including primary care. This aligns with standard practice in national accounting.

Thus, rather than reasoning in terms of complete pathways of treatment across the health system, the output measures proposed in what follows are best thought of as episodes of treatment of particular diseases provided by a given institutional unit. Furthermore, this measurement objective will mainly be applicable for curative care, whereas other measures will have to be targeted for long-term care and other specialised services where it is difficult to establish when an episode of treatment is complete. For example, inpatients in nursing homes do not generally receive treatment for a specific illness or illnesses that have an obvious start and end point. For such institutions, a strong case can be made that the output is defined by the processes of the institution of care, not by a treatment. The same applies to chronic and progressive health conditions where the patient faces a slow, variable and unpredictable progression of a disease.

Direct measures of output in these units will have to rely on measures such as the number of particular processes (procedures, consultations, etc.) or the number of patients treated in various institutional settings. There are advantages in continuing within this framework until the linkage of patient treatment across institutions becomes available.

The present considerations suggest that it is best to treat the measurement of output of medical services by type of health care provider. A limitation of this approach is that it is not able to capture substitution effects between providers. For instance, if treatment of a disease moves from inpatient treatment to outpatient treatment at the same facility, this shift and the ensuing consequences for the unit costs of output will not be captured.[5]

Measurement by provider industry

For practical reasons, the following discussion is organised by health care provider. Firstly, as already emphasised in the previous section, data may not be available to measure health volume by disease across health care providers.[6] Secondly, some health care institutions produce quite different products from others (for example, curative treatments of an acute problem versus ongoing treatment for a chronic condition), which makes it natural to discuss output measurement for each type of provider separately.

The discussion will distinguish between hospitals, residential long-term care facilities and providers of ambulatory health care, following the HP categorisation. For each type of provider, the measurement of health volume output requires identifying a set of homogeneous products and a set of weights (value shares) that can be used to aggregate changes in these products (direct volume measurement) or to aggregate unit cost changes in these products (deflation approach – see above).

Hospitals

Typically, hospitals provide inpatient as well as outpatient treatments. Within a hospital, different outputs can be captured by the identification of treatments. Although this may not always be possible in practice, it is desirable from a conceptual viewpoint to separate inpatient and ambulant treatments of the same disease so as to be able to capture effects of substitution between inpatient and outpatient treatments provided by the same hospital.

To measure treatments, there are two common patient classification systems, both of which attempt to deal with the heterogeneity of hospital output while making comparisons between hospitals possible. The first system is the International Classification of Diseases (ICD) which was originally developed as a basis for mortality statistics, and which thus refers to diagnoses. It is used to classify diseases and other health problems recorded on many types of health and vital records, including death certificates and hospital records. The ICD underlies the development of diagnosis-related groups (DRG) categories. Responsibility for updating the ICD lies with the WHO; ICD-10 was endorsed in 2004.

The most widely available categorisation of hospital inpatient services is provided by DRGs (Fetter, 1991). They were developed with the explicit objective of creating relatively cost-homogeneous groups in order to compare hospital performance. Instead of providing a cost for each component of a hospitalisation, DRGs give a composite bundle of hospital services a single predetermined cost or reimbursement rate. This amount includes all activities from which the patient benefits in the process of the treatment, including nursing care, drugs, imaging and the hotel amenities of care.

DRG systems are attractive for the measurement of volume output because they provide information on (unit) costs per type of treatment and on the number of treatments carried out: in other words, the basic ingredients for a (quasi) price or a volume index.

A typical DRG system comprises a large number (500-1000) of categories. By construction, each category stands for a relatively homogeneous service and thus, in principle, construction of a unit cost or of a volume index from the most detailed level of categories is desirable. This is, however, not always possible. One main reason is that DRG systems are updated on an ongoing basis, with some categories being aggregated and others disaggregated, making comparisons between periods difficult.[7]

Given cost weights and the number of treatments, either a unit cost (quasi-price) index or a direct volume index can be constructed. The choice between these alternatives is often governed by data availability. When indices are constructed such that the weight reference period proceeds the latest period for which (quasi) price changes are to be measured, it is easier to construct a unit cost index than a direct volume index.

The matching of services has its limits when comparable products do not exist in comparison periods or when new services only gradually diffuse in practice. This is the case even when using relatively sophisticated output measures such as DRGs. One possible way to deal with the problem of categorisation changes in the output indices involves imputing values – by deflation or inflation – where cost data are missing for any particular period of time (Castelli *et al.*, 2008).

Residential long-term care facilities

For residential long-term care providers, the notion of a complete treatment is not very meaningful. Elderly and other long-term stay patients tend to have complex clinical presentations characterised by disability, dependency and multiple pathologies. The start and end point of the condition is not clear, and the fact that the condition is chronic means that incentives for reducing the length of stay as under a DRG system would be inappropriate. A classification for nursing home patients, Resource Utilisation Groups (RUGs),[8] has been developed (Carpenter *et al.*, 1995), as DRGs are of little value for chronic care patients and those without straightforward clinical conditions.

Where countries do not have an RUG-type system, the number of occupant days differentiated by the level of care can be used. Many countries have their own care classifications based on an assessment of a patient's care needs, and thus the intensity (and cost) of the care received. If information on costs per level of intensity of care is available, it can be combined with data on the number of occupant days to derive either an approximate direct volume index of output or an approximate unit cost index.

This is, for instance, the case in Denmark. Data on unit costs for different types of residential facilities (nursing homes, sheltered housing, day centres and social centres) exist, if only for the city of Copenhagen. Combined with the evolution of the number of care places, grouped in the same way, this is used to construct a unit cost index for residential and care places.

Providers of ambulatory health care

Medical and dental practices

Medical and dental practice activities are considered market production in many countries. Persons receiving dental services in particular are more likely to be charged an economically significant price. Medical and dental practice activities each provide both general and specialist services. In the case of both types of services, an appropriate deflator for market output would be a price index such as a CPI component that accounts for the different types of services received and captures – to the extent possible – quality changes.

As a rule, the definition and measurement of hospital-based outpatient treatments remain rudimentary (Castelli *et al.*, 2007). A limited number of countries have developed and used outpatient classification systems. Ideally, all outpatient activity related to one treatment episode would be combined into one measure of output, in the same way as for inpatient activity. The episode would include all consultations, pathology tests, imaging and prescriptions. Developing outpatient DRGs requires a capacity to track patients across outpatient services for the same treatment. To do so, it would be necessary to be able to identify the start and end point of the complete treatment and to have an appropriately supportive legal and information technology framework. There have been limited developments in outpatient DRGs.

Until an international classification system for outpatient care is developed and implemented or national systems become more widespread, basic quantity measures such as number of doctor visits will have to be used in the construction of volume measures, in particular for non-market providers. The *Eurostat Handbook on Prices and Volumes* in the national accounts suggests that outputs should be classified into medically meaningful groups that are as homogeneous as possible. The stratification may take into account the medical content of the output as well as a time dimension. For example, a visit to a general practitioner could be a measure of output. Other quantity indicators would be patient transfers by ambulance, number of pathology tests by broad category of type of test, or the number of prescriptions filled by type. Generally, these data are collected as part of the process of public or private reimbursement.

The *Eurostat Handbook* suggests that general practitioner consultations are measured by the number of visits, but specialist consultations are measured by the first visits only. The reason given for this differentiation is that specialists' visits are more likely to be follow-up visits, *i.e.* ongoing treatment for the same medical condition. This distinction seems arbitrary, as many GP visits are also follow-up visits. In addition, while this recommendation may be applicable to some specialties, it may not be applicable to all. Specialties to which the notion of ongoing treatment would not usually apply include many diagnostic specialties such as pathology, radiology, nuclear medicine, etc.

Offices of other health care practitioners

This category refers to a range of diverse activities such as activities of nurses, midwives, physiotherapists or other paramedical practitioners in the fields of optometry, hydrotherapy, medical massage, occupational therapy, speech therapy, chiropody, homeopathy, chiropractics, acupuncture, etc. Many of these services are provided by market producers. In cases where some of those activities do not have significant prices, it will be necessary to aggregate the output by using relatively basic methods such as the number of consultations, visits or tests.

Other health care providers

This category includes ambulatory health care centres and providers of home health care services. Most likely, output will be aggregated by using relatively basic methods such as the number of consultations, visits or tests.

Overview of measures

To complete the discussion above, Table 13.1 provides a summary of suggested output measures by provider category. The proposed methods are in principle output-based, although the degree to which they constitute fully-fledged measures of output varies and sometimes depends on the level of stratification in implementation.

Table 13.1. **Overview of indicators for volume output of health service providers (HP.1-HP.3)**

HP code	Providers	Output-based methods
HP.1	**Hospitals**	(Quasi) Price index based on DRGs (cost or revenue-weighted) Direct volume index based on DRGs (cost or revenue-weighted) Direct volume index based on ICD categories (*e.g.* number of discharges by category with quantity-weights such as shares in hospital days) Number of days of care* Number of cases/discharges*
HP.2	**Residential long-term care facilities**	(Quasi) Price or unit cost index based on Resource Utilisation Groups (RUGs) or equivalent (cost-weighted) Direct volume index based on RUGs or equivalent (cost-weighted) Direct volume index based on number of days of care by level of care (cost-weighted) Direct volume index based on number of cases by level of care (cost-weighted) Number of days of care* Number of cases/discharges*
HP.3	**Providers of ambulatory health care ****	
HP.3.1	Medical practices	(Quasi) Price index based on number and type of service (cost or revenue-weighted) Direct volume index based on number and type of service (cost or revenue-weighted) Relevant component of the consumer price index if applicable** (Quasi) Price index based on average costs/revenues per service (cost or revenue-weighted) Direct volume index based on number of services (cost or revenue-weighted) Number of services*
HP.3.2	Dental practices	Relevant component of the consumer price index (if applicable) Direct volume index based on number of services (cost or revenue-weighted) Number of services*
HP.3.3	Offices of other health care practitioners	Direct volume index based on number of consultations by type of consultation (cost or revenue-weighted) (Quasi) Price index based on average cost or revenue per consultation (cost or revenue-weighted) Relevant component of the consumer price index (if applicable) Number of consultations* Number of cases treated*
HP.3.4	Ambulatory health care centres	
HP.3.5	Providers of home health care services	

* proxy index.
** services are defined as consultation/visit/treatment depending on the typology of the country.
Source: IHAT for SHA 2011.

Measurement of quality changes

Price and volume measures of output should reflect quality changes in the health services provided. In other words, only prices, unit values or quantities of the same quality, that is, with the same characteristics, should be compared over time.

A first and important step towards capturing quality change is the correct stratification, *i.e.* a comparison of products with the same or at least similar characteristics. In this way, stratification keeps quality constant if the products included in a particular stratum are relatively homogeneous.

A second way of incorporating the quality of services into output indices would require an adjustment factor that reflects the compliance rate with established procedures by country and disease group. Changes in the proportion, either positive or negative, would indicate where medical practice and procedures have changed to reflect the introduction of new treatments and improvements in the existing practices. There is a limited literature reporting such proportions. For example, by averaging the findings from US preventive care studies, Schuster *et al.* (2005) found that 50% of people received recommended care, and for acute care studies they found that 70% of patients received recommended care and 30% received contraindicated acute care. It is important to note that the achievement of full compliance with guidelines, that is, a rate of 100%, is not necessarily a public health goal. In industrial production processes, uniformity ensures the highest quality of outcomes. The same does not hold in health care, as individual differences and preferences need to be accommodated.

There is a wealth of information on clinical practice guidelines by country but insufficient summary information at this stage on the rate of compliance with best practice. In the United States, the National Guideline Clearinghouse maintains a catalogue of high-quality guidelines published by various organisations (mostly professional physician organisations). In the United Kingdom, clinical practice guidelines are published primarily by the National Institute for Health and Clinical Excellence (NICE). In the Netherlands, the Dutch Institute for Healthcare Improvement (CBO) and the Dutch College of General Practitioners (NHG) have guideline development programmes that use an evidence-based approach. In Germany, the Agency for Quality in Medicine co-ordinates a national programme for disease management guidelines. All these organisations are members of the Guidelines International Network, an international not-for-profit association of organisations and individuals involved in clinical practice guidelines.

A third aspect of quality relates to the impact/contribution of health services on health outcomes. Obviously there is a strong connection between process and output, as treatment guidelines are based on medical evidence about what is efficacious. Health services researchers recommend using both process and outcome indicators for two reasons. First, there is a difference between evidence in research (efficacy) and outcomes in real life (effectiveness). Second, there is frequently a considerable time lag between a process and its impact on the outcome. For example, studies have examined family doctors' compliance with guidelines for hypertension treatment. The outcome associated with this treatment is a reduction in heart attacks and strokes (as an intermediate outcome) and mortality related to cardiovascular diseases (as an ultimate outcome). Reductions in the incidence of these diseases occur over a very long time period, and hypertension treatment is only one factor involved in the ultimate outcome. Among other things, the hypertensive patients themselves have to comply with a lifestyle that includes healthy nutrition and adequate exercise.

This discussion emphasises the use of quality adjustment using process and outcome indicators. It is also noted that there is an "industry of quality measures", but at this stage none appear appropriate for quality adjustment of health volume output. The main reasons for this lack of applicability is that many of the available process and outcome indicators are specific to a country or even institution.

Since quality is multidimensional, it would be ideal to be able to subsume several characteristics of quality into a single indicator that reflects the contribution of the product to outcome. Alternative means have been suggested to derive a single indicator. The first is to choose the most important dimension only, *e.g.* 30-day survival rate. The second is to use indicators from more than one quality dimension and weigh them as equally important. Third, indicators from a number of quality dimensions can be used but expert opinion should be sought on the appropriate weights (UK ONS, 2008). Finally, measures such as quality-adjusted life years (QALYs) can be used that reduce modifications in health outcomes due to medical care to one dimension, the quality-adjusted gain in time. However, many of these empirical methods are still in a research stage and are normally not robust enough to be applied in the System of Health Accounts.

There are a number of desirable characteristics of indicators that could be used for quality adjustment for volume output for determining the marginal contribution of the health industry to outcome. These are outlined below.

- The quality measure should be aligned with the processes sought by consumers, which would generally be a complete treatment of the disease;
- The adjustment in output should reflect the marginal contribution of the health industry to an outcome. It should not be affected by any other factors that influence health outcomes such as genetic background, income or lifestyle;
- Consumers are ultimately concerned to achieve an improvement in their health outcome. Waiting times and comfort are secondary to improvements in health status. This points to the conclusion that different dimensions of quality should not be given the same weight;
- In many health treatments or processes, there is a time lag before the improvements in health status. Quality adjustment needs to address in a realistic manner the impact of lifetime effects of health expenditures;
- The quality measure should reflect as closely as possible the normal, average or expected effect of the activity on the state of health. Individual capacities to benefit from treatment, or what is known as co-production, should not be counted in the measure of quality-adjusted health volume output;
- International comparison is important, and the indicators and methods of output adjustment should be standardised across countries to facilitate comparisons (Smith and Street, 2007).

To sum up, methods for quality adjustment of output are still under development. Some headway towards capturing quality can be made by using detailed product specifications and following the associated costs and treatments over time. The importance of explicit quality adjustment is undeniable, but until there is a consensus on techniques for adjustment, it will be difficult to put forward a recommendation for an explicit quality adjustment of health volume output in the System of Health Accounts. A similar conclusion has been reached by the United States Bureau of Economic Analysis (BEA), who note that the "BEA will not attempt to account for potential changes in the quality of treatments, a problem where no clear consensus exists on a solution" (Aizcorbe and Nestoriak, 2008, p. 25).

Inter-country indexes of price and volume

Purchasing Power Parities (PPP) are used to compare levels of price and volume between different regions or countries in the same period of time. These allow for a *spatial* price/volume breakdown (*i.e.* a price/volume breakdown among countries for a given point in time).

Conceptually, PPPs are very similar to consumer price indexes. PPPs are measures of price level differences across space or, in their most popular form, across countries. Because the prices of goods and services in different countries are expressed in national currencies, the purchasing power parity between currencies of two countries, say A and B, is the number of units of currency of country B (or A) that has the same purchasing power as one unit of currency of country A (or B). Though the PPPs are similar to price index numbers in spatial comparisons, they assume special significance because the PPPs can be used as a conversion factor, in place of exchange rates, in converting various economic aggregates from different countries into a common currency unit (a statistical construct).

PPPs are regularly measured for all components of GDP in the International Comparison Programme (see Box 13.4 below) and in the Eurostat-OECD PPP comparison.[9] In their simplest form PPPs are nothing more than price relatives that show the ratio of the prices in national currencies of the same good or service in different countries. PPPs are calculated in three stages. The first is at the product level, where price relatives are calculated for individual goods and services. The second is at the product group level (*i.e.* basic heading), where the price relatives, which are calculated for the products in the group, are averaged to obtain unweighted PPPs for the group. And the third is at the aggregation levels, where the PPPs for the product groups covered by the aggregation level are weighted and averaged to obtain weighted PPPs for the aggregation level. The weights used to aggregate the PPPs in the third stage are the expenditures on the product groups.[10]

In the ICP and Eurostat-OECD PPP comparison programmes, expenditure on health appears in three parts in GDP expenditure: household consumption expenditure, expenditure of non-profit institutions serving households (NPISH) and government expenditure on health, and they are classified according to 25 basic headings (20 in the case of the ICP).[11]

PPPs for medical goods and services under household consumption expenditure and social benefits in kind are based on a "normal" price collection. This means that the estimation of PPPs starts by selecting a sample of products in each expenditure category to compare their prices in different countries. Prices to be collected should be average prices for the whole country.

For inpatient services, an input method is applied for public but also for private hospitals. This follows national accounts conventions that recommend that the value of the output of institutional units in the health industry is measured by the sum of the costs of production in the case of non-market products (SNA 2008, 6.130). In the input method, PPPs for the compensation of employees are based on a wage comparison of employees, that is, wages are used in the PPP estimation in the same way as normal product prices. PPPs for other inputs are based on proxy PPPs extracted from other parts of the comparison.[12]

A PPP between two countries for a particular expenditure category is a geometric average of all price relatives (parities) formed from a set of product prices belonging to the category. In the ICP and OECD-Eurostat comparison programmes, countries also indicate whether or not products they have priced are representative (so-called starred products). In the averaging, parities based on products that are representative in both countries, get a higher weight, and parities based on non-representative products (but included in the product list because of their importance for some third countries) are excluded.

In a multilateral comparison, PPPs are derived for all pairs of countries whenever prices are available in both countries. If all countries price the same products and the products are representative everywhere, geometric averages of the price relatives provide directly transitive PPPs (that is, for countries A, B and C, PPP relatives for A/B and B/C are consistent with A/C) for a given basic heading. On the other hand, if a full set of representative prices is not available for all countries, comparisons between pairs of countries will be based on different sets of products, resulting in intransitivity. To make results transitive, an EKS procedure, due to Elteto and Koves (1964) and Szulc (1964), is applied where the final parity for a pair of countries is based on a geometric average of all direct and indirect (via all other countries) parities.

Box 13.2. **PPP indexes**

If there are M countries in the comparison, then a price index between country j and country k is derived as:

$$I_{jk}(EKS) = \prod_{s=1}^{M} \left[I_{js} \times I_{sk} \right]^{\frac{1}{M}}$$

where:

$$I_{js} = \left\{ \prod_{i \in M(s)}^{M} \left[\frac{p_{is}}{p_{ik}} \right]^{\frac{1}{n(s)}} \times \prod_{i \in M(j)}^{M} \left[\frac{p_{is}}{p_{ik}} \right]^{\frac{1}{n(j)}} \right\}^{\frac{1}{2}}$$

where n(s) and n(j) are the number of starred items in countries s and j; M(s) and M(j) are the sets of commodities that are starred in countries s and j.

Despite a long tradition of work in the area, three main problems have to be addressed in the measurement of PPPs. The first issue is to identify products that are comparable across countries: while simple in some cases (*e.g.* a particular type of washing machine), this can be complicated in many other cases, because products are not identical, because there are differences in quality or because products simply do not exist in all countries. The second issue is to ensure the representativeness of the products: whatever price is compared, it has to be the price of a product that is widely and typically purchased in each country. The third issue arises when there is a product, but no meaningful market price for comparison. Issues one and two arise in the comparison of all prices, while issue three arises in the comparison of non-market products. In many countries, health services count among these products.

When goods or services are supplied by a non-market producer such as the government, the prices charged to consumers are significantly below the price that a market producer would charge. In some cases, the price may even be zero. It would make no sense to compare such prices charged to patients or consumers across countries, as they reflect administrative decisions and not the value of products. It has therefore not been customary in PPP compilations to compare costs of producing non-market goods and services.

There are two possibilities for comparing costs, one based on *inputs* and one based on *outputs*. The input-based method, traditionally applied in PPP comparisons of non-market products, consists of comparing the prices of inputs in the production process of non-market services. In the case of health services, an input-based method would, for example, compare the wage rate of a surgeon in different countries. In other words, the price comparison is approximated through a comparison of wages or values per unit of inputs. Apart from the fact that it is notoriously difficult to compare wages across countries (even for the same type of occupation: qualifications may be different, it is hard to control for experience and seniority payments, etc.), the main drawback of this method is that it ignores any productivity differences between countries. In other words, if health services are provided more efficiently in one country than in another, this would go unnoticed in a PPP comparison that is based on the price of inputs.

Box 13.3. **The International Comparison Programme**

The International Comparison Programme (ICP) is a worldwide statistical operation that produces internationally comparable price and volume measures for gross domestic product (GDP) and its component expenditures. The measures are based on purchasing power parities (PPPs). To calculate the PPPs, the ICP holds surveys every five years to collect price and expenditure data for the whole range of final goods and services that comprise GDP, including consumer goods and services, government services and capital goods.

The ICP was first established in 1968 as a joint venture of the UN and the International Comparisons Unit of the University of Pennsylvania, with financial contributions from the Ford Foundation and the World Bank. Starting with a modest project to undertake comparisons in 10 countries in 1970, further ICP rounds have been conducted in 1975, 1980, 1985, 1990 (only partial), 1993, and 2005. The 2005 ICP was the largest ICP round to date, covering 146 economies from five geographic regions: Africa, Asia and the Pacific, the Commonwealth of Independent States, Latin America, and Western Asia, and the countries of the regular PPP programme managed by the OECD and the Statistical Office of the European Union (Eurostat).

The ICP is being implemented as a true global initiative for the second time, with the reference year 2011. It will build on well-programmed activities of a wide network of national and bi- and multi-lateral institutions that will engage in methodological research and review, survey activities and data processing and analysis in the areas of price statistics and national accounts and related fields, with a view to estimating the PPPs of the world's principal economies.

The second option for comparing costs is based on *outputs*. Here PPPs are measured by comparing the costs per unit of output; in the case of medical services, this is typically the *cost per treatment*. The comparison of quasi-prices per unit of output is – in principle – capable of reflecting productivity differences between countries. It is thus conceptually preferable to input-based approaches (SNA 2008, 15.122).

In the health domain, costs per unit of output are not generally readily observable, but there is an alternative source of information that provides valuations of outputs: in many countries, health services are managed through reimbursement schemes, where health providers and health administrations or insurance companies either negotiate reimbursements per treatment or where the government administers reimbursements per treatment. Reimbursement values per treatment or per episode of illness can be used to emulate the role that prices play for other goods and services. We label negotiated or administered rates as "*quasi-prices*" to signal that they are not necessarily the result of market transactions, that they are not prices that apply to transactions between producers and consumers of health services, and that they are not observed.

An OECD Working Paper (Koechlin, Lorenzoni and Schreyer, 2010) reports on the pilot work on PPPs at the OECD that aims to develop an output-based measurement of hospital services PPPs.

Notes

1. For a discussion of index number formulae for consumer and producer prices, see ILO *et al.* (2004a, 2004b).
2. The Consumer Price Index measures changes over time in the prices of consumption goods and services acquired, or used, by households.
3. The Producer Price Index measures average changes in prices received by domestic producers for their output. The output of the services sector and other sectors that do not produce physical products is conceptually within the PPI universe.
4. An activity might be a consultation with a general practitioner, a hip replacement involving a stay in hospital or a visit to an outpatient clinic.
5. See Aizcorbe and Nestoriak (2008) for a discussion about the effect on costs (and real expenditure growth) of treatment substitution among providers.
6. See the discussion on expenditure by disease in this Manual.
7. This is true to a larger extent for cross-country comparisons, given that the DRG classification logics may differ.
8. RUG-III is a hierarchical classification system with a structure that has forty-four groups. Each group is assigned an index score that represents the amount of nursing time and rehabilitation treatment associated with caring for residents who qualify for that group. The forty-four groups fall into seven major categories: rehabilitation (14 final RUG-III groups), extensive services (three groups), special care (three groups), clinically complex (six groups), impaired cognition (four groups), behaviour problems (four groups), and reduced physical function (ten groups). Across most RUG-III categories, patients are divided into a final classification group based on their performance on an index of four activities of Daily Living: eating, toileting, bed mobility and transferring.
9. For a full description of the methods used, the reader is referred to World Bank (*www.worldbank.org/ICP*) and Eurostat-OECD (2006).
10. This methodological description is greatly simplified. Further information can be found in Eurostat-OECD (2006), *Eurostat-OECD Methodological Manual on Purchasing Power Parities*.
11. A detailed description of the basic headings can be found in Annex II of the methodological manual (see note 229). Government expenditure on health is classified according to 17 basic headings, Household consumption according to seven basic headings, and spending by NPISH to a single heading.
12. As an example, PPPs for pharmaceutical products are used as proxy PPPs for intermediate consumption, although the relative difference between prices paid by hospitals and pharmacy prices is not necessarily the same in all countries.

A System of Health Accounts 2011: Revised edition

PART II

Chapter 14

Basic Accounting and Compilation Guidance

Introduction

The System of Health Accounts provides a toolkit for describing and summarising health consumption expenditure that enables an analysis of the consumption, provision and financing dimensions of health care goods and services, both over time and between countries. This chapter describes some of the basic accounting guidelines for SHA and provides some initial assistance on compilation processes, including practical guidance on good accounting practice in relation to selected measurement issues.

The accounting principles are in addition to the SHA accounting concepts discussed in Chapter 3, such as coverage, timing of recording, cash versus accrual accounting, residents, valuation and the treatment of subsidies and non-market provision. The practical guidance on compilation processes presented here is not intended as a complete compilation guide, but merely outlines some of the main steps in creating health accounts, such as understanding the national health system, making an inventory of data sources, identifying data gaps, creating a health accounts database and ultimately filling the tables and presenting data.

Finally, the chapter provides practical assistance on some selected measurement issues across the function, providers and financing dimensions, introducing techniques such as prorating and discussing particular problematic areas such as the estimation of components of private health expenditure. More thorough guidelines are, or will become, increasingly available in some of these more complex areas of compilation as implementation experience improves.

The guidelines draw on and summarise material from the SHA guidelines, the *Producers Guide* and various OECD project reports, and, where necessary, update them in the context of SHA 2011.

Basic accounting criteria

SHA provides a framework that seeks to provide comprehensive coverage and consistent, internationally comparable estimated data that are as far as possible compatible with international economic statistical frameworks, in particular the SNA, and that are sufficiently accurate and timely to be useful for health policy analysis. Selected criteria on general data quality in relation to the main concepts of the SHA framework are addressed below.

Comprehensiveness of coverage

SHA seeks to account for the whole set of health system transactions, determined by the functional boundary set out in Chapters 4 and 5, that is, involving the health care consumption of the resident population irrespective of where the consumption takes place or who is paying for it. That means that it is not limited to government-financed or government-provided health programmes, but includes private transactions, either directly financed out of pocket by households or via third-party payers. In principle, it includes formal as well as informal transactions, provided that the health care criteria set out in Chapter 4 are met. The triangular nature at the core of the basic SHA accounting framework requires that the aggregate of these functional transactions is equal to the provision of these health care goods and services, and is equal in turn to the total financing by financing schemes. Beyond this set, totals may be different.

Consistency and comparability of data

SHA, by referring to common health care boundaries and classifications, enables the reporting of health expenditure estimates that are consistent over time. The internal consistency of the SHA's accounting rules and the consistency between components are important in cross-checking and validating estimates from different health dimensions.

The SHA's common boundary and categories for health systems may differ in some respects from those used in national health accounts for national purposes in a particular country. The purpose of a common boundary and sub-categories is to facilitate comparisons between countries as well as to track changes over time within countries.

International compatibility

The consumption-based accounting framework of SHA, with its set of expenditure tables, is designed to be methodologically compatible in basic terms with the System of National Accounts. This methodological compatibility with the SNA enables the calculation of a number of expenditure ratios that compare health expenditure aggregates with appropriate aggregates of the economy as a whole so as to facilitate international comparisons. For examples of such ratios, see Chapter 15.

Timeliness and accuracy

Health accountants must consider two other quality criteria when preparing the accounts. The criteria of timeliness and accuracy are both essential, but are also in conflict. It is necessary to establish a minimum level of detail and accuracy for regular reporting, while respecting a reasonable timeliness to address users' needs for data in order to inform, for example, any budgetary or policy adjustment process.

Relevance

The health expenditure data produced by SHA needs to be able to respond to the health policy questions and issues of the day, particularly at times of frequent changes in public policy in health care. In the past, for example, the monitoring of the economic consequences of health care reform was often obstructed by the inability of existing reporting systems to distinguish between changes in coverage and the mode of financing and actual change. The data framework should be flexible enough to adapt to current and future analytical requirements.

Summary introduction to SHA compilation processes

This section provides summary guidance on the main steps in building SHA accounts. It draws extensively on the EU SHA guidelines (and the *Producers Guide*), updating them for SHA 2011. This may be of assistance both for countries that do not yet have national health accounts (NHA) and more generally for those readers who are relatively new to health accounting. There is also a need for guidelines for the transition from SHA 1.0 to SHA 2011 for those countries that already have SHA-based NHAs. Such guidelines are expected to be developed separately.

Before any health accounting work begins, preliminary work will be necessary to gain a mandate, establish the project, involve the key institutions, fund and staff the project, and develop a plan with a timetable. From a value-for-money perspective, there are many advantages to planning for a regular production of health accounts, perhaps annually or every two years. This will in due course yield trend information as well as snapshots of the health system, and it will spread out the initial one-off start-up costs for the operation. In general, a stepwise approach is recommended for the whole process, with a few of the milestones described below:

Step I. Understanding the national health care system under study

Before considering data collection and calculation methods, it is worthwhile spending some time to understand how the national health care system works. This includes the preparation of a list of the financing schemes and the institutional actors (enterprises, government units, NPISH, households, rest of the world), along with their roles in allocating financial resources (collecting, pooling and purchasing) as well as of a list of providers of health care. The preparation of a chart on the financial flows can be useful, particularly if the units responsible for the flows are identified.

It might take some time initially to develop an overall view of the system, but achieving this will save lots of time and misunderstandings in the future. The national health system may be broken down into various sub-systems based on their relationship to public or private health care provision and financing arrangements, or into particular subsets of the population; this will help to identify the principal actors in the system. Examples may be found in the *Producers Guide*, Table 2.1 for Lebanon and, for a considerable number of countries, descriptive summaries of national health systems may be found at the website of the European Observatory on Health Systems and Policies, and more detailed information may be gathered from national sources.

A clear picture of the health care system should be drawn up that takes SHA definitions into account in order to avoid missing out on important parts of expenditure. As a starting point, it is worth looking for existing models put together by academics or other health care experts. Diagrammatic models of the national system may have to be remodeled according to SHA requirements based on consultation with a wide variety of colleagues, such as analysts from ministries, boards, trade associations and academic researchers, since the health care system is usually complex and in general no single person has a comprehensive understanding of all of its parts.

The initial model should show the flows of funds circulating within the health care sector and between the health care sector and the rest of the economy. This overview of the system is meant to outline all the major actors in the health care system and to link them according to the way funds flow between them. It should be noted that the same entity may appear more than once in the chart. Households, for example, can act both as providers of health care (household provision) and as the financing scheme (they buy health care goods and services out-of-pocket). Flows of funds should be identified at all levels, *i.e.* one should trace not only the payments made by financing schemes to health care providers but also the flow of funds to the financing schemes. In this initial view, the emphasis is on the identification of the flows and their direction rather than on the assignment of any monetary value to the flows.

Step II. Setting the boundaries of NHA and clarifying any differences between the national boundaries of the health care system and SHA boundaries

The SHA definition and boundary of health care is likely to be different to varying extents from the definitions and boundaries of health care used in national systems of health accounting due to differences in institutional arrangements, payment systems and country traditions. It is therefore important to identify the points of divergence between the two systems. For example, for those countries whose estimates of health spending are based on the national accounts, the main boundary difference will be that the national accounts place domestic *production* within the boundary, whilst SHA puts all domestic *consumption* within the boundary. Other key differences are the inclusion in SHA of items such as household provision of health care services and occupational health care.[1] Experience from implementation in different countries has shown that the adoption of SHA definitions can make significant changes in estimates of current health expenditure as compared with national estimates, in some cases by as much as 1% of GDP or more (see Orosz and Morgan, 2004).

Even before embarking on SHA-based health accounts, many countries already have existing estimates of health care expenditure, and they use various national classifications to break down existing estimates. If there are national standards for classifying health care expenditure using the function, provider or financing dimension, then it would make sense to start from these and undertake a mapping exercise to construct correspondence tables to SHA classifications.

Identifying the existing national concepts and classifications is therefore one of the first steps in any health accounts compilation, and this can be very useful for spotting where there may be large differences between a national system and SHA. For example, health policy in some countries targets not only health care but also social care, and both types of expenditures may be included in existing estimates of health care expenditure. In other countries, expenditure related to long-term care activities may not be considered as health expenditure at all. If the difference between the national and SHA boundaries of the health system is not clearly understood, then there is a risk that some components of the health system as defined by SHA 2011 are not included in the national concept and therefore might be not taken into account.

Other examples are some of the activities related to environmental protection or hygiene that in some countries may come under the responsibility of the health care system and therefore be counted as health expenditure, whereas in SHA they are health-related functions and do not form part of total health expenditure.

In countries where the majority of health care expenditure is financed publicly, either through government finance (primarily from taxes) or social security funds, depending on the country, the first point of contact for establishing a working definition of what is considered to be health at the national level is likely to be the Ministry of Health or the Social Security Fund authorities.

Step III. Investigating and evaluating data sources

It is essential to identify and catalogue the available data sources along with their main characteristics, and make some assessment of their quality that can potentially provide information on the dimensions that they might serve. This stage should also see the construction of an exhaustive list of actors in the health care system identified in the previous step. These various health system actors and institutions may possess reports or records that could be useful. If some kind of national health accounts have been previously produced that may not have the same coverage and structure as SHA, the data sources used could still serve as a valuable starting point.

At this stage, the inventory of data sources is unlikely to be exhaustive. In the process of compiling health accounts, the investigation of potential data sources forms an important part of the development work. These may include the national accounts, any non-SHA health accounts, government records (for example, Ministry of Health budgetary information, regional government data) and Social Security data. These should then be complemented with other data and metadata obtained from, for example, insurance umbrella organisations, trade associations or NPISH financial accounts.

When making the inventory, each data source should be examined with the aim of finding out what the main content is, what information is provided, what questions are answered and what the original purpose of the source is. The aim here is to record all relevant metadata that will be of use when dealing with data for SHA compilation.

Bottom-up or top-down?

A *top-down* approach is used when most of the health accounts data are taken directly from pre-existing aggregate health expenditure classifications and recording systems. This often involves an extensive system of proxies and estimates to break down the aggregates. The technique of estimating through prorating is discussed in the section on measurement issues. An example of the use of aggregate estimates is where health accountants attempt to migrate directly from national accounts.

A *bottom-up* approach is used when most of the health accounts information is obtained using detailed information and data sources, for example, the internal reports of health insurance that describe both the scope and the values of services contracted with particular health care providers, and reports on the detailed activity of the Ministry of Health or NPISH that can be linked with financial information or budget data. Aggregate data may still be used and reconciled in the system.

This Manual recommends the advantages of a *bottom-up* approach under which various information sources, of both a monetary and non-monetary nature, can be used or combined either directly or using allocation keys for the purpose of data compilation. The advantage of a bottom-up approach is that it lowers the risk of double-counting of the same expenditure item, while enhancing provision of a mutually exclusive and exhaustive counting of expenditure. This is not to say that national accounts or other aggregate data are not useful, but the health accountant should as far as possible try to use detailed sources. This should be contrasted, however, with the top-down methods of allocation, once health expenditure aggregates have been estimated, for example, allocating hospital spending among the various functions (see Estimation through Prorating).

Identifying the core data sets

When compiling the inventory, each data source should be examined for: its original purpose, the main content, what information it provides, and what questions it answers. Some basic assessment of data quality would also be useful, including potential bias, accuracy and timeliness. All this will provide valuable metadata (information about the data) for SHA compilation and analysis. It is of vital importance to show the links of a particular database to the basic classifications of SHA 2011. The following items might be used to describe the data (IRDES and BASYS, 2007):

- Name of the data source;
- Administrator/Institution;
- Type of data source (registers, business surveys, etc.);
- Method of collection (*e.g.* administrative source, statistical full-scope or sample survey; national source versus standardised international survey);
- Availability of data (for which years data is available/data is used for SHA);
- Concept of the measuring units (costs, expenditures, turnover);
- Breaks in time (main methodological changes);
- Coverage of health actors (*i.e.* which categories of providers or financiers by HP and HF are covered; whether public or private institutions; national accounts sectors);
- Configuration of data (*i.e.* what dimensions of data are available: by HP, HC, HF, age, gender, diagnosis, geography, ownership, etc.).

Health accounts compilers need to deal with multiple data sources that primarily come from the financing or provider perspective, and they need to reconcile these sources continually. They also tend to use both basic data sources and aggregate information. Nonetheless, a generalisation can be made about the two approaches that health accounts developers tend to adopt when compiling health accounts.

- Financing approach: health accounts developers who follow this approach use data from the financing perspective as their main data source. The core data are financial data on expenditure by the different financing schemes. This information is then integrated with provider data sources where possible.
- Provider approach: health accounts developers who predominantly follow this approach use data from health care providers as their main data source. The core data are financial data on the receipts of the providers, but also data on the inputs used by the providers (mainly staff costs and intermediate consumption) and on their outputs (activities and their prices/costs). This information is then integrated with data from the financing side where possible.

Generally, when the information on the data sources has been collated, in particular on the availability, quality and timeliness of the data, a decision should be made as to whether the basic datasets will come primarily from the database of financing institutions or the database of providers. It may also be the case that different databases will be identified as core datasets for different functions (such as for pharmaceuticals and inpatient care). That said, all the relevant datasets needed to get a complete set of core accounts must be included.

If the databases of financing schemes (or agents) are the core data set, the first step is to make a qualitative analysis. This should include distinguishing the different types of government transactions: transfers from government revenues to financing schemes other than government schemes and the expenditure by government schemes. Another key issue is to clarify whether a financing agent (such as a social insurance agency or insurance company) operates more than one financing scheme. In such cases, expenditure by the different financing schemes should be treated separately. One special issue may be to estimate the administrative costs separately. It will be necessary to ensure that all spending on health care functions by financing schemes are included and that transactions for other purposes (*e.g.* government transfers to voluntary financing schemes) are excluded. The information from databases of financing institutions will then be integrated with information from provider and functional information, for example, but the benchmark figure for current health expenditure will be that based on the total health care expenditure of financing schemes.

If the databases of providers form the primary approach, the data from providers usually relates to their revenues. Exhaustiveness is again important, as the benchmark figure for current health spending will represent the total revenue of providers for the provision of health care goods and services to the resident population.

Ideally, health expenditure and its sub-aggregates are estimated according to both approaches, that is, using the databases of both the financing institutions and providers, and the relevant data are compared and the differences are analysed and reconciled.

Government agencies may play various roles in SHA – as a provider of revenues of financing schemes, a financing agent and a provider of health care – and some of those agencies not obviously involved in health may still hold useful information. Ministries of health, health system agencies, ministries of finance, national statistics agencies (likely to hold an array of relevant data sources), ministries of social services, social security agencies, central banks, regional or local government departments, financial regulators and business registries may all have relevant data sources. How much access national health accounts have to the data sources of these agencies may be another issue. These sources should be complemented by other sources, such as health insurance companies,[2] trade associations, commercial market information and NPISH accounts data.

Step IV. Creating a health accounts database[3]

After the inventory of data sources and an initial list of health system institutional actors and financing schemes, data should start to be compiled and recorded in a database or spreadsheets. The eventual structure of the database will be important, but at the outset a simple structure based on providers or functions, and which allows ample space for metadata descriptions, might be sufficient.

The following may be the main steps of the process:

- Deciding the structure of the database and the data-records;
- Deciding which data to acquire; entering existing data into the database;
- Allocating SHA classification codes to all data entries;
- Further investigation of gaps and data sources; and
- Finally, preparing the SHA tables.

An iterative approach is recommended so that initial estimates can be improved, data gaps addressed and data from different sources reconciled.

Which data are to be collected? In principle the more data the better, but there are cost considerations to bear in mind in acquiring data, both in terms of time and money. Some datasets may require a fee to be paid, which can be substantial. For other datasets, the burden on data providers in tailoring the dataset, or the time and other resources required of the team to acquire the data, should be considered. Of particular importance in the early stages of development will be to focus on the acquisition of data on expenditure. Other, non-expenditure datasets can be acquired at a later date when a view has been taken on the extent to which expenditure sources are sufficient. Some priorities may need to be established in the early stages, when expenditure data on the main health care functions may be most important. The data acquired are to be entered in the database and a provisional allocation by SHA classification made, a simple illustrative example is given in Tables 14.1, 14.2 and 14.3. The organisation of the database should be constructed while bearing in mind the nature of the health system and the availability of information.

Table 14.1. **Provider example: hospital activity information**

Hospital activity code	Description	HC Function
HOSP1	Accident and emergency department	Curative (HC.1)
HOSP2	Orthopaedic Surgery	Curative (HC.1)
HOSP3	Physical therapy services	Rehabilitative (HC.2)
HOSP4	Mammography (breast cancer screening programme)	Prevention (HC.6)
....	...	...

Source: IHAT for SHA 2011.

Table 14.2. **Source of funding example: Ministry of Health budgetary information**

Code for budget item	Description	HC Function
1	Diagnostic procedures not specified by function	Ancillary services (HC.4)
2	Vaccination programmes	Prevention (HC.6)
3	Purchase of MRI machines	Not HC but Capital Formation
4	Civil servants pay	Health system administration (HC.7)
...	...	...

Source: IHAT for SHA 2011.

Examples of initial allocation to SHA tables

A note on national and SHA health care boundaries and codes

As indicated in Step II, it is necessary to identify significant divergences between national health accounts concepts and SHA 2011 concepts. Usually, all administrative data and data from business and household surveys are nationally coded as defined by national statistical classifications, which need to be mapped, as well as possible, to SHA 2011 codes. It is recommended to revisit these correspondence tables annually because of annual revisions of titles in the government health care budgets.

The SHA database should be integrated with the national health accounts database using dual coding that will allow simultaneous reporting according to national and international requirements. This also allows the presentation of health accounts for national purposes in a way that is different but consistent with international reporting.

A more detailed allocation of SHA classification codes

If dealing with detailed data records, in order to be able to achieve equality in total expenditure across the basic dimensions of functions, providers and financing schemes or agents, it would be useful to set up a database that allows for the simultaneous coding of data entries across several SHA classifications (see the example in Table 14.3). Further columns could be added as appropriate in the database, such as one for a sub-national regional identifier.

Resolving issues

Following the initial allocation of data according to SHA classifications, a number of questions about the data source may arise. It is imperative to get into contact with the data providers and/or experts involved in the data source in order to discuss the use to which the health accounts compiler is putting the data. This will allow the expert to advise accordingly.

It is important to keep a record of issues related to the data, which may concern individual datasets or multiple data sets. What kind of issues may be encountered? These might include: no data available for some actors known to have expenditure on health care; insufficient health care functional information; a difficulty in splitting health care from, say, social care; a lack of information on cross-classification; contradictory results; and information on health care activities without the associated expenditure data.

These issues may lead to the need to acquire additional data, make assumptions on allocations, or use proxy variables and estimations for the reconciliation of contradictory results.

Step V. Background calculations and filling the tables

When the database is deemed to be as complete as possible and a final iteration and/or checking have been done, the output of the process is the cross-classification of current health expenditure, initially by function, provider and financing scheme, and then any other tables that may be feasible. An important element of the work is to clarify whether background/working tables are to be prepared. For example, it may be useful first to prepare a separate HC x HF table for each financing scheme in order to reconcile sub-aggregates from databases of financing institutions and databases of providers separately for each financing scheme.

Finally, it is important to audit the compilation process for quality in terms of data, methods and data manipulation before the work is approved for publication. For this, descriptive information explaining the methods used in order to obtain the figures should also be presented. In particular, the relative quality of different parts of the table should be flagged and the reasons for this given. This also promotes the improvement of information, as data suppliers begin to understand how their information is used and to strive to make improvements in it.

Step VI. Preparing a detailed documentation of the health accounts work

It will be necessary in systematising the health accounts work for regular production to record the detailed data sources, calculation methods, adjustments and estimation procedures that are used in the production of SHA. This information may later be published in a more summary format to help users understand the results better.

Step VII. Quality check of the results

In addition to quality checks that should be built into the various steps of the production of health accounts, specific checks should also be performed on the final results. These checks will most likely include the confrontation of data from different sources, the validation of the latest year's data points with corresponding data points from the previous year and the investigation of any significant but unexplained changes.

Table 14.3. **Detailed representation of how data entries might be stored in a database**

Line item	Year	Description	National area of expenditure	Data source	SHA 2011				Amount (Millions NCU)	Comments
					HC	HP	FA	HF		
1	2009	Radiation oncology services	Public hospital services	Central government scheme (FA: government unit)	1.1.1	1.1	1.1.1	1.1.1	50	This government funding was limited to public hospitals in 2009
2	2009	Ambulance services	Patient transport services	Private health insurance funds	4.3	4.1	2	2.1.1	40	
3	2009	Breast cancer screening	Preventive health	Central government scheme (FA: non-profit institution)	6.1.3	6	1.1.1	1.1.1	100	
4	2009	Dental services paid by workers compensation insurers	Dental services	Voluntary insurance (FA: injury compensation insurers)	1.3.2	3.2	2	2.3	5	
5	2009	Departmental costs of Ministry of Health	Administration	Central government scheme (FA: MoH)	7.1	7.1	1.1.1	1.1.1	1000	
…	…									

Additional columns could be added for metadata, calculations, adjustments or estimation methods.

Source: IHAT for SHA 2011.

Step VIII. Presentation of the results (output tables, key indicators, analysis for different audiences, etc.)

The final step relates to the presentation of the results, giving key indicators and summary information about the data, such as any significant divergences from accepted standards or information on coverage. The presentation may also include some particular analyses for a particular target audience. Chapter 15 provides a further discussion of this step, with some examples of tables and indicators that health accountants can use or adapt, if they wish to do so.

General measurement issues

This section sets out some general measurement issues to bear in mind regarding the key concepts of the functional, provider and financing dimensions of the SHA accounting framework as well as certain specific parts of it, and it discusses the use of prorating as an estimation technique. It also considers the particular issue of estimating private health expenditure.

Timing

As stated in Chapter 3, this Manual recommends the accrual method, in which expenditures are attributed to the time period during which the activity took place, rather than the cash method, in which expenditures are registered when the transaction that paid for the activity took place. Recording on a cash basis can lead to a distorted picture; for example, budget or wage negotiations or health reform measures may entail spill-over effects from one fiscal year to another. Cash accounting is in many instances not compatible with the recording of non-monetary flows and with other economic statistics.

However, it is recognised that cash accounting may still be applied in some countries or in some parts of the health system. Health accountants may find a variety of accounting practices in their data sources, some accrual and some cash. Good practice should involve converting everything to an accrual basis to the extent possible.

For international purposes, this Manual recommends compiling health accounts on a calendar year basis. However, data are often reported according to different time frames; for example, government data may be on an alternative fiscal year basis. The easiest way to convert fiscal years to calendar years is to assume that expenditures occur equally in each month. It then follows that a portion of each fiscal year total can be allocated to a given calendar year. However, if price inflation or some other mechanism is believed to affect spending in each month, then a constant spending assumption is not a good one. In this case, a sort of indicator can be created that permits a change in the constant/ proportions adjustment. For example, in the case of price inflation, a monthly price index can be derived either from published sources or by decomposing annual inflation into monthly figures. The sum of those monthly figures can then be used to determine into what proportions to split the fiscal year total.

HC The functional classification

HC.1 and HC.2 Curative and rehabilitative care

In order to distinguish between the medical service functions (curative, rehabilitative and long-term care), it is the type of episode of care provided that is key. While the types of functions may have different cost profiles, particularly in hospitals, the difficulty many countries face in distinguishing between the first two medical services – curative and rehabilitative care – is acknowledged in the SHA tables, such that expenditure on these two functions may be combined into a single reporting item.

The broad definition of curative care in particular, with its consequent inclusion of a set of rather disparate activities, contrasts with the narrower definitions of other functions, which consequently tend to have more homogeneous sets of activities. In some countries, this contrast has led to this function being estimated by a residual: as total health expenditure (or medical services) less the other relevant functions.

Mode of provision and administration and hotel costs. At the two-digit level, cure and rehabilitation (as well as long-term care) are subdivided into the four types of mode of provision of care, *i.e.* inpatient, outpatient, day cases and home-based care. The subdivision of functions into these modes of provision is important for health policy purposes, and it is very useful to have data on totals by mode of provision in a country. Given the importance of this topic, a separate guideline has been written on modes of production in hospitals.

The concept of a mode of provision summarises a number of separate dimensions: *i)* whether or not the care is provided on the premises of the provider; *ii)* whether or not the patient is formally admitted for care on the premises of the provider (or formally discharged); and *iii)* whether or not the patient stays overnight on the premises of the provider.

In order to avoid repetition, this guideline focuses on modes of provision in hospitals, but the principles are general and can be applied equally to other providers.

Where the care is provided at a patient's home, this is clearly home care. Where the care is provided on the premises of the provider, the modes of production are summarised in Table 14.4.

Table 14.4. **Allocation of institutional care to mode of provision**

	Formal admission or discharge	No formal admission
No overnight stay	Day care	Outpatient
Overnight stay	Inpatient	Not applicable

Source: IHAT for SHA 2011.

Inpatient care. For inpatient care, the "hotel costs" – cooking, cleaning, accommodation, but also the hosting of patients' relatives (if it is indispensable) – associated with the overnight stay of the patient should be included as part of the cost of health care where the main reason for institutionalisation is health care. This borderline poses a particular difficulty for mixed providers, that is, typically HP.2 Residential long-term care facilities. Inpatient care occurs mainly in hospitals, but also in other providers, for example, residential and ambulatory care, prisons and army hospitals. The term "inpatient" in SHA has a relatively wider meaning compared to some national reporting systems (where this term may be limited to inpatient care in hospitals).

Day care. Usually the stay (formal admission) lasts between 3 and 8 hours and often takes place in institutions or wards specialised for this kind of care, for example, elective surgery.

Outpatient care. Outpatient care is provided, for example, in a physician's office, hospital outpatient centres, ambulatory care centres and so on. It can also include tele-health services. Again, outpatient care in SHA may be defined more broadly than in some national reporting systems.

Home-based care. Home-based care excludes the consumption of medical goods dispensed in pharmacies as part of private household consumption. Examples of the type of services provided at home are obstetric services, dialysis, services provided by mobile nurses and health visitors, and long-term care (health and social).

HC.4 Ancillary services

HC.4: Ancillary services to health encompass a variety of services, mainly performed by paramedical or medical technical personnel with or without the direct supervision of a medical doctor. There are three sub-categories for ancillary services: HC.4.1: Laboratory services; HC.4.2: Imaging services; and HC 4.3: Patient transportation. The only ancillary services to be reported separately are those that are directly requested by patients and not intermediate services. Diagnostic services within outpatient departments are usually part of the bundle of activities of treatment and are therefore not to be excluded.

HC.4.3: Patient transportation comprises all such services – irrespective of the mode of production – even though these services are related to medical services that do have a mode of production dimension.

These ancillary services are supporting activities rather than medical interventions, and do not necessarily require medical training or knowledge. In the inpatient and day-care modes of production, the costs of these services are difficult to separate out from the other costs of the medical services, and as such are not separately identified in SHA. In outpatient and home-care settings, SHA requires the ancillary services to be recorded separately. As delivery of health services differs across countries in terms of their mode of production, the relative proportion of ancillary services separately identified in SHA framework will also differ. Some countries have therefore found it useful for national purposes to collect information on ancillary services delivered in all settings. The "total" ancillary services figure, if compiled, could appear in national health accounts as a Reporting item.

Ancillary services may be provided in two main ways. Firstly, they may be provided by a different institution than are the medical services to which they relate. Secondly, they may be provided by the same institution. The availability of data and the corresponding methods for accounting for ancillary services provided may be different.

For ancillary services that are carried out in a separate institution, it is usually not difficult to find information about these activities and their costs. Regardless of whether one uses a demand or a supply approach, financial flows or output data of this type are clearly identifiable. If a hospital, for example, contracts out ancillary services to an independent laboratory, the financial flow will generally be easy to trace. The more difficult cases involve ancillary services that are provided in the same institution as the medical services.

There appear to be basically two current methods available to the compiler. In summary, the first method involves searching for information on financial flows. The second involves the commissioning of a specific study to examine expenditure on ancillary costs.

HC.5 *Medical goods*

The compilation of information on this item may be relatively straightforward, as medical goods are tangible and thus more easily accounted for. As several countries reported difficulty in distinguishing between goods associated with different modes of production, this aspect is abandoned in SHA 2011 and all medical goods sold directly to patients are included in this category of HC.5.

HC.5 is divided into two groups: *i)* pharmaceuticals and other non-durable goods, and *ii)* therapeutic appliances and other medical goods (Table 14.5).

Table 14.5. **Consumption of medical goods non-specified by function**

HC.5 Medical goods (non-specified by function)
HC.5.1 Pharmaceuticals and other non-durable goods
HC 5.1.1 Prescribed medicines
HC 5.1.2 Over-the-counter medicines
HC 5.1.3 Other medical non-durable goods
HC 5.2 Therapeutic appliances and other medical durable goods
HC 5.2.1 Glasses and other vision products
HC 5.2.2 Hearing aids
HC.5.2.3 Other orthopaedic appliances, orthesis and prosthetics (excluding glasses and hearing aids)
HC.5.2.9 All other medical durables, including medical technical devices non-specified by function

Source: IHAT for SHA 2011.

It may be possible in some countries to find data from the provider side HP.5, such as retailers (pharmacies or supermarket sales of medical goods) and other providers of medical goods. It is also to be noted that there are strong links between HC.5 and COICOP 6.1 (for more details see the annexes).

Information about private expenditures for medical goods can be found in business surveys. In surveys of pharmacies, total sales may be greater than sales of medicines, as they may also sell other products such as food, groceries and stationery. In these cases, adjustments may be required to exclude items that fall outside the scope of the health accounts concept of final expenditures for health, and additional supplementary data may be needed to adjust the primary data (see Rannan-Eliya and Lorenzoni, 2010).

Additional areas to be tackled cover such issues as how to apportion the different health care functions, e.g. administration in health insurance or integrated curative-rehabilitative-preventive services, and how to separate health care functions from other activities, such as research. Some guidance in these areas can be gained from the section on prorating.

HP The provider classification

The provider approach is used by compilers who use "provider-based data" as their core dataset. Expenditure on health care when derived from this approach will mainly be based on information obtained from the financial receipts of providers. Examples of the key data sources used when following this approach are: business surveys, surveys on financial activities, accounting information submitted to statistical offices and tax offices, and market information, such as information on supply and demand collected by market research companies. When this type of information is unavailable or incomplete, an estimation of receipts may be obtained by using information on inputs and their costs (staff wages and intermediate consumption) as well as output or activity information (number of activities performed and their respective prices or costs). However, attention should be paid to the possibility of double-counting. As described in Chapter 6, when a hospital contracts laboratory services from an independent ancillary service provider, the health accounts compiler must ensure that this expenditure is not counted twice; once when analysing hospital accounts, and a second time when looking at the ancillary service providers' accounts. In addition, when using this approach care must be taken to exclude non-health expenditure borne by the provider (*e.g.* expenditure on social care).

In terms of the general process: first, the health accounts compiler organises the database comprising the universe of health care providers to include both primary and secondary providers for all activities that are identified as health care within the functional classification. To estimate the value of health care goods and services provided, it can be particularly important to separate providers into market and non-market providers. The second step comprises an estimation of the health care-specific provision value, to equal the revenues from financing schemes. The HPxHF cross-classification table helps to estimate and reconcile the money flows of current health spending from the financing schemes to providers as well as supporting further reconciliation with a functional breakdown.

HF, FS and FA The financing classifications

The original sources of detailed data on financing will come from some of the institutional units involved in the health financing system. These may include government ministries, government agencies, health insurance agencies, NGOs, health providers, households, enterprises and foreign donors.

As funds may pass through one or more intermediate agencies, it is important to ensure that there is no double-counting and that all the funds made available for the provision of health care goods and services are identified.

This Manual identifies financing schemes as of interest for international comparison and policy monitoring over time. However, the core information on schemes and their revenues are typically derived from the data coming from the financing agents who manage the schemes or from the institutional units that provide revenues to financing schemes, as each financing agent or institutional unit that funds schemes may either manage or participate in one or more schemes. For further information, see Chapters 7 and 8. Guidelines separate from this Manual will provide detailed assistance to compilers for the implementation of classifications of health financing under SHA 2011.

Box 14.1 provides a far from exhaustive list of compilation issues that concern some of the other chapters of the Manual, and which could be considered in the development of additional guidelines and good practice.

Estimation using prorating

This section aims to guide the data generation of expenditure under a top-down approach, which involves distributing an aggregate among components. In many endeavours the data can be too aggregated to be broken down into specific services. This methodological approach has been validated in the field as feasible and convenient for general health accounts, but guidance on how to distribute the expenditure is required. The usual approaches followed are:

a) *Allocation using the main activity principle of an industry classification.* This approach can lead to major distortions of spending and is thus not recommended except when it refers to minor components of health spending. One difference with the SNA is that for the total economy, eventual distortions are not as relevant because the important point is to have all resources integrated. However, for a functional exercise, where the aim is to have an idea of levels by class, distortions can potentially damage the data credibility. Nonetheless, this approach could be useful as the starting point for both the provider divisions and the linkages to ISIC/NACE on production.

b) *The development of specific studies.* These can vary largely in scope as well as in the accuracy of their results. It can include anything from focal groups or expert opinions, to measuring actual activities through "time and motion" studies. These studies involve resources and time that can be adapted based on country conditions. The recommendation is to analyse previous experiences and to the extent possible, to draw on closely related examples. If more accurate estimation methods are needed, then a more bottom-up approach is suggested.

c) *Allocation using keys.* The allocation of aggregates usually involves the use of reference values or allocation keys. The process is to identify an available value that can reliably reflect the amount of resources and expenditure involved in the various components included in the aggregate to be divided. The basic information can refer to service unit costs or the human resources involved and/or the quantity of specific services provided. Composite indexes that account for various inputs and costs have also been generated, according to the available information in the field.

d) *Case-by-case adjustment.* Some adjustments can be decided on a case-by-case basis. For example, the expenditure on the administration of insurance companies could be distributed in proportion to total expenditure in the class.

Box 14.1. **Other selected compilation issues**

Factors of provision

- How to identify and estimate expenditure on intermediate consumption
- How to estimate income of non-salaried self-employed professionals
- How to estimate capital consumption

Beneficiaries

- How to identify appropriate distribution keys
- How to split expenditure by disease group
- How to estimate income/expenditure groups

Capital formation

- How to estimate investment on R&D and E&T
- How to estimate values on household improvements with a health purpose
- How to handle foreign investment

External trade

- How to deal with illegal or unethical trade (*e.g.* of organs)
- How to handle major differences between the resident and covered population
- How to handle major differences on valuation in origin and destination pricing
- How to determine when medical tourism is important and needs more consideration

This type of prorating is commonly used to fill the gaps when expenditure tracking records are insufficient to estimate the specific outlays. The general overview can be applied to further split the expenditure on health on the selected services in a top-down approach: inpatient care, nursing homes, outpatient care, pharmaceutical provision and prevention.

A brief description of this approach is included in the Guide to Producing National Health Accounts (PG) and can be applied to the distribution of expenditure by beneficiary for age, gender and disease in paragraphs 14.74-14.93 (WHO, World Bank and USAID, 2003).

The underlying principle for prorating

The underlying principle is the equation:

Value = price * quantity

Boundary setting. A definition of the components to be estimated has to be clearly established to set the boundary of the estimation.

Partition of current expenditure into homogeneous cost blocks. The data to be distributed are taken from the health accounts aggregates: those handled frequently appear to be, in particular, inpatient care/outpatient care in hospitals; nursing homes: for health care and social care; outpatient care: for curative and rehabilitative care; and some components of prevention. Whenever possible, each component should be disaggregated into smaller units to ensure a better cost linkage.

Distribution of current expenditure through utilisation keys. Distribution keys are estimates of the distribution of health care use over distinct combinations of all dimensions, and they are linked to each cost block or cost group. Every key receives a fraction of total utilisation within the group. Some requirements of the use of keys have to be fulfilled: all together they have to add up to 100% of the care delivered, with no double-counting of the services, as the distribution refers to indicators of the health care utilisation and the cost unit. Thus, the nature of such indicators should reflect a relationship to the resource cost of the associated health care services: unit costs, human resources or services consumed.

The utilisation keys (percentage shares) by cost group are multiplied by the total spending or an aggregate to be allocated, and are then added up. The results should be analysed and validated through per capita values, obtained by dividing the expenditure by subclass by the population.

Some examples of utilisation keys

For inpatient care: hospital days, admissions, patients, procedures. This is preferably adjusted by type of hospital.

For providers of ambulatory health care: contacts, visits, treatment sessions.

For preventive services: covered population.

This type of approach, although imperfect, can be performed with limited cost and has been progressively refined, *e.g.* to distribute expenditure using available data, such as for costs. The closer the costing studies relate to the type of service consumed, the more appropriate the information for expenditure purposes, *e.g.* costing studies should reflect medical units stratified according to the level of care and the technological complexity and/or size of the unit. Cost analysis may be linked to services and to cost centres. The distribution of cost centre costs can also be made using human resources, *e.g.* ward costs, bed-days, IP drugs – actual drug costs/numbers, theatre costs, radiology. In fact, an indirect use of the cost is made to estimate intermediate values, then the distribution profile is identified and then applied to "weight the component".

The basic method

Service A Expenditure	=	Total Expenditure	X	No. of patients receiving service A *Divided by* the number of all patients

As data that can directly provide the expenditure by service are generally not available, there is a need to identify a way to allocate the expenditure, which, again, is linked to other data availability. A mix of data and of keys may finally be used. There is a need for periodic quality verifications to ensure that the best approach has been taken.

Each set of expenditures may pose additional problems to be solved, for example, in practice, units may be either non-market providers or market providers, requiring different measurement methods in the two cases.[4]

1) Non-market provider units

The basis of measurement is **cost** (not price). The data available include budgetary spending and user charges, which should be distributed according to the cost of production. In countries where hospital budgets do not differentiate inpatient from outpatient inputs, an estimate of inpatient share could be needed.

2) Market provider units

The basis of measurement is **price** (not cost). In most countries, obtaining the data may be difficult. Possible alternatives are household surveys data or insurance claims data. Caution is advised when the insured population is not representative.

Measurement issues in a special case

Private health expenditure

Incomplete sources and estimation methods for components of private expenditure on health are widely thought to be a major limitation for international comparisons.

The principal source of problems in the measurement of private health expenditures is the inherent tendency both for much private health care financing to occur without the generation of linked, reliable and comprehensive routine data, and for private providers, who are more likely to be financed by private expenditures, to tend to operate without reporting routine data to statistical agencies. The frequent lack of suitable registration data for private providers reinforces the difficulties, since this limits the potential for comprehensive and representative surveys. As a result, in the absence of routine, administrative or transactional data, an estimation of private health expenditures must often rely on the use of survey data. The production of reliable estimates thus requires considerable care in the selection of appropriate methods, in the assessment of the available data, and in combining information from multiple data sources.

The data sources currently used to estimate private expenditure components such as household budget surveys and data reported in national accounts have been developed for other purposes. A mapping of national categories to the International Classification of Health Accounts (ICHA) is therefore often difficult due to differences in concepts and definitions and in the exhaustiveness of classifications.

The OECD guidelines (2010) on measuring private health expenditure present a set of recommended approaches to measuring private health expenditure. These are based on a review of known problems in private expenditure estimation and on consideration of the reliability, reproducibility and feasibility of current and potential methods. As such, they provide a platform for ongoing work to develop improved methods.

Private health expenditures are expenditures whose final purpose is health care and which are financed by all resident institutional units other than those belonging to the government or compulsory insurance schemes. Expenditures that mainly cover voluntary health insurance and out-of-pocket expenditures are categorised as HF.2 and HF.3 by the ICHA-HF classification.

The guidelines provide advice on the general approach to be taken in measuring private health expenditures, in particular how a measurement strategy should be formulated, and how data sources and methods should be identified. They also provide a tool for a national self-assessment of existing methodology. They review in detail potential methods for estimating private expenditure flows, with those specific to financing agents presented before those specific to providers. The specific methods for estimating household out-of-pocket expenditures are only presented afterwards, as these require consideration of when and how household survey data can be used. Finally, the guidelines discuss how the different estimation methods and data sources can be combined to produce overall and final estimates in an integrative approach.

The measurement strategy:

- Foresees the decomposition of the HF.2 and HF.3 measurement problem into separate and independent estimation problems:
  - Segregation of financing flows in practice;
  - Variation in data sources by financing flow;
  - Independence of errors in individual components.
- Considers each financing flow as three elements:
  - Level;
  - Trend;
  - Composition.
- Suggests that the optimal strategy may be to estimate an aggregate first, and then to estimate distribution by providers/functions

This measurement strategy also suggests using an integrative approach, which foresees the use of information from different perspectives on each set of transactions to triangulate best estimates of actual financing flows from three perspectives: financing; provider; and consumption (in terms of composition of expenditures).

Usually, a variety of methods are potentially available for estimating any specific expenditure flow. Some are more reliable than others. To indicate this, the guidelines classify methods into three groups based on quality and reliability:

- Methods that are reliable and ideal, which are most appropriate;
- Methods that are less reliable, but are acceptable if ideal methods cannot be used; and
- Methods that are not acceptable except as a last resort.

Health accountants are encouraged to evaluate the quality of the data sources for private health expenditure and use integrative triangulation methods to confront the data sources.

Further information can be found in the OECD guidelines on measuring private health expenditure.

Notes

1. See Annex B for a full description of the links and differences between SHA and National Accounts.
2. In addition, other insurers, for example, injury compensation insurers, may have some relevant information.
3. Steps IV together with various other steps are to be considered an iterative process. There will be an initial compilation of the database using identified data sources. It is then important to consider whether there are any gaps or problem areas in the database, which should lead to a search for additional data sources. These should be confronted with the database and estimations made as necessary. This iterative procedure is repeated until the database achieves a sufficient stability and quality.
4. For more discussion of measuring non-market provision, see Chapter 3, 9 and 13.

A System of Health Accounts 2011: Revised edition

PART II

Chapter 15

Presentation of Results, Tables and Basic Indicators

Introduction

Health expenditure is the object of measurement in health accounts. A country's health accounts (HA) provide the measurements for a given time period and present these in a set of tables in which various aspects of the nation's health expenditure are arrayed. The tables themselves are simply a means to display the financial flows related to a country's consumption of health care goods and services. The data contained are intended for use by analysts and national policy makers to assist in assessing and evaluating a country's health system. Reporting the data and estimates in a comparative way allows for evaluations between countries and is thus useful for international comparisons.

While it is important to understand that tables provide a systematic way to report health accounts data, policy makers will often request that information be presented in a form that is concise and immediately meaningful in terms of its relation to policy questions. Key results will often need to be extracted from the tables, as well as linked to non-expenditure data, such as on outputs and outcomes, in order to explicitly inform decision makers about specific emerging issues or about the progress of policies already implemented and their observed impacts.

Three main ways that a country's health accounts for each time period are disseminated and systematically archived are, first, through the regular dissemination of selected indicators, and, second, through periodic reporting via national, regional and international databases. The third method would be a report summarising the health accounts prepared each time a round of estimates is produced.

- Health accounting indicators represent the most frequent way that health accounts data are disseminated. They usually cover a Minimum Data Set for which (current) expenditure on health as a total is presented, *e.g.* as a share of GDP, and in per capita values, among others.
- HA results of countries are also reported and tracked in national, regional and international databases. These databases generally maintain historical data for countries, but can sometimes provide less detail compared to country HA reports.
- A summary report should present HA results in a systematic manner. The contents of the report should be useful to different audiences and for various purposes, but, more importantly, relevant to national policy issues. It should also contain any necessary information on data sources and methods.

This chapter contains a discussion of the suggested content of an HA report. It also discusses the issue of harmonising country data across databases. One objective of this chapter is thus to bring about some degree of comparability in future HA reports across countries to facilitate, not only national, but also international use of country data. Another objective of the chapter is to emphasise the need for HA records to provide careful documentation of sources and methodological information so that observed differences, say, for one country over time and between countries, can be understood and put into proper context.

The health accounts report

The basic content of an HA report should ideally include the following: a number of tables and indicators that will inform sound national policy and good governance; country background information to provide the context to better understand the HA findings, including reference information for computing indicators; and brief documentation of the HA data sources and any methodological information that is important to properly interpret the HA results. Among the basic set of tables in an HA report the tables on HCxHP, HCxHF, HFxHP as well as HFxFS could be considered. Each of these topics is discussed further. Additionally, HA time series, the use of HA combined with other health-related data and quality checks of HA results are also discussed.

Health accounts tables

The rows and columns of the HA tables incorporate the various classifications presented in this Manual. The classifications or dimensions of health expenditure include the following:

- *Functions (HC)*: the types of goods and services provided and activities performed within the health accounts boundary;
- *Providers (HP)*: entities that receive money in exchange for or in anticipation of producing the activities inside the health accounts boundary:
- *Financing schemes (HF)*: components of a country's health financial system that channel revenues received and use those funds to pay for, or purchase, the activities inside the HA boundary;
- *Financing agents (FA)*: institutional units that manage health financing schemes;
- *Financing sources (FS)*: the revenues of the health financing schemes received or collected through specific contribution mechanisms;
- *Factors of provision (FP)*: the types of inputs used in producing the goods and services or activities conducted inside the HA boundary;
- *Beneficiary characteristics* of those who receive the health care goods and services or benefit from those activities (beneficiaries can be categorised in many different ways, including their age and gender, their socio-economic status, their health status and their location);
- *Capital formation (HK)*: the types of the assets that health providers have acquired during the accounting period and that are used repeatedly or continuously for more than one year in the production of health services;
- *Trade in health*: imports of health care goods and services provided to residents by non-resident providers, and exports of health care goods and services provided to non-residents by resident providers;
- *Products*: the various goods and services provided by the providers, including the non-health care goods and services produced and consumed.

The classifications can be applied to health expenditures individually to produce expenditure tabulations by a single dimension. Although this type of data presentation can be very useful as a starting point, and it can be used for specific issues of high relevance within the health system, there is additional information to be gained from cross-classifying expenditures using two or more classifications.

HA tables basically involve cross-classification. Although many combinations of tables can be created using all the dimensions listed above, only a selection of tables that are typical of tables that might be included in an HA report are presented. A number of these tables are of particular interest for international comparisons. For national purposes, the list of proposed tables can represent a "menu" from which health accountants can choose, while always bearing in mind that these tables are not the only ones of potential value. Each country's policy makers have their own information needs that must be addressed using health accounts data. Producing any tables at all is certainly better than producing none. Producing more will often be preferable to producing fewer, although it may be better to concentrate on a few key tables when faced by resource constraints. The choice of which tables to produce should be linked to their potential usefulness as well as to the feasibility of their construction.[1]

SHA revolves around a tri-axial approach to estimation where it is expected that the value of health care goods and services estimated from the consumption side should coincide with the values estimated from the provision and the financing sides. Thus, the cross-classification of the three axes or dimensions defines a basic set of tables with credible HA estimates that countries might expect to produce and report. Experience in countries where health accounts have been created indicates that the application of the three classifications (functions, providers and financing schemes) is critical to obtaining a realistic estimate of total current health spending. The HA tables that cross-tabulate these dimensions are important tools for creating consistent aggregate totals and subtotals across HA tables.

Most of the HA tables described in this chapter are two-dimensional tables. Each table represents a specific type of health financial transaction or resource flow, where the flows have on one side the origins of the funds and on the other side the recipients or the uses of those funds. By convention, the columns of the HA tables show the "origins", and the rows the recipients or "uses" of the resource flows. The labels of HA tables refer first to the row classification (uses) and then the column classification (origin), *e.g.* the table showing the resource flow from financing schemes (HF) to providers (HP) is referred to as the HPxHF table. The sequence of transactions or resource flows through the health care system can be captured through a series of HA tables: from financing sources and types of revenues to financing schemes, from financing schemes to providers, and from providers to the health care goods and services consumed, and, finally, to how these are distributed among beneficiaries.

The tables that illustrate what may be included in the HA report are described below, together with generic depictions of the tables. The first three tables cross-classify expenditures according to the three main dimensions of the tri-axial approach of the SHA.

Health expenditure by type of financing scheme and by function (HCxHF)

The table showing health expenditure by type of financing scheme and type of function (see Table 15.2) describes the overall and specific allocation of resources to the major types of health care services by the financing schemes. This table highlights the resource paths that are key for informing health analysts. It addresses the question of "who funds what" and allows the identification of both these functions where resources are concentrated and their main funding paths. Experience shows this table to be important for validating estimates of the demand side of current health spending.

Health expenditure by type of provider and by function (HCxHP)

The table showing current health expenditure by type of provider and by function (see Table 15.3) shows how expenditures on different health functions are channelled through the various types of providers. That is, it tells the user "who provides what". This table provides a summary perspective of the health market in a country, *i.e.* what is the structure of its health care needs and who are the providers involved. This table has been shown to be valuable for validating the supply side of the CHE estimate.

Health expenditure by financing scheme and by type of provider (HPxHF)

This table shows the structure of current health expenditure according to the financing arrangements (financing schemes) for providing the financial means to the providers (see Table 15.4). It describes how funds are distributed across different types of providers and addresses the question, "who funds who". The table allows the user to identify those providers where resources are concentrated and their funding paths. Experience with health accounting has shown that the HPxHF table is an important tool for estimating total current health spending, and it should be an early focus in the initial work.

Types of revenues by revenues of the financing scheme (HFxFS)

This table shows the financing path to fund the various schemes (see Table 15.5). Actually, the institutional units collect the funds used to finance the schemes. The table addresses the question "where does the money come from" by showing the types of revenue of each financing scheme. The table also displays the relative importance of each type of revenue in the financing of each financing scheme and in total current spending overall.

Health expenditure by financing agent and by financing scheme (HFxFA)

The table shows each scheme and how much of its expenditure is managed by each agent (see Table 15.6). This table displays the institutional structure of health financing by indicating the relationship between the schemes and agents. The table addresses the question of "who manages which payment scheme". Financing agents are usually the starting point in the construction of the tables of financing schemes, as they are the origins of the data for this exercise.

Factors of provision by type of provider (HPxFP), by type of function (HCxFP) and by financing scheme (HFxFP)

The information on the mix of factors of provision is a key monitoring tool in determining overall system performance, and it provides a basis for the analysis of the efficiency of production and resource use. Factors of provision can be cross-classified against three other classifications: HP, HC and HF. The first table shows the allocation of factors by provider on different types of resources used to produce health care goods and services (see Table 15.7). The question addressed by this table is, "what are the various inputs used in the provision process and by which specific provider groups". The second option shows the allocation of different types of factors among the various types of health care goods and services (grouped by functions). The question addressed by this table is "what are the various inputs used for provision of specific goods and services". The third possible table shows how the different factors used in health care provision are financed. The question addressed by the HFxFP table is, "who pays for the various inputs used in the provision".

Expenditure by type of provider and capital goods (HKxHP)

This table (see Table 11.2 in Chapter 11) shows the net value of the capital goods by type of asset acquired by the various providers. It shows "who is investing" to expand physical capacities to provide health care and the types of investments. It gives insight into the future capacity of the various providers.

Expenditure by financing agent and by capital goods (HKxFA)

This table provides an overview of how the acquisition of the capital goods is financed. The question addressed by the table is "who pays for investment". Investment is displayed by type of asset or durable goods. It gives an insight into the way the investments of health providers are funded and whether this financing structure can be sustained.

Trade in health care: exports and imports (HC.XxHP and HC.MxHF)

These kinds of tables (Tables 12.1 and 12.2 in Chapter 12) show the two components of trade: imports of health care goods and services by types of health function provided to non-residents by different resident providers; and exports of health care goods and services by type of health function provided to residents by non-resident providers, as well as how these functions are paid for. The basic data on imports are also shown in the HCxHP table – the entries in the column for Rest-of-the-world providers (HP.9) are the values of imports, but the values of exports are implicitly excluded from the domestic health providers columns (HP.1 to HP.8). Trade in health care has seen significant growth in many countries for several reasons, including, among others, technological advances, ease of movement of patients and medical professionals, the portability of insurance, and differentials in the prices of health care service across countries. While there is an increasing interest in measuring and reporting the extent of such trade because of its implications on regulation and investment in health in a country, nonetheless for many countries it remains a marginal phenomenon in the overall health accounts.

Expenditures on health care by disease/condition

These tables can show health expenditure by major GBD group (or ICD-10 chapter) cross-classified by health care function, provider and financing scheme. These are some of the more challenging tables to produce, as this requires reliable health conditions data or diagnostic data from providers and/or patients that can be linked to expenditure data. With the function dimension, the table can show the types of health care services used to treat different disease groups, and how each service is allocated (in financial terms) between the different disease groups. With the provider dimension, the table shows who provides the health activities that address each type of disease or condition and what share of their total revenues relates to each disease. With the financing scheme dimension, the table shows who pays for the health activities that address different health conditions and what share of each scheme's spending relates to each disease group. These questions are important as an input to how health financial resources may be allocated to various uses, and to provide information for policy formulation and for the design and implementation of health programmes.[2]

Expenditure on health care by age and gender

The table shows health expenditure by age and gender of the beneficiary, cross-classified by health care function, provider or financing scheme. Health care requirements vary with age, with the young, the elderly and women of childbearing age generally requiring more health care. The table provides information that can be used to assess the age/gender targeting of expenditures of specific financing schemes; for example, is the government scheme successful in increasing support for child health, elderly health and women's reproductive health programmes? The same holds for questions about the functions and providers classification: which health care services and providers are reaching specific age groups of the population?

Expenditure on health care by income quintile

The table shows health expenditure by income group of the beneficiary of expenditure, cross-classified by health care function, provider and financing scheme. The portion of the table cross-classified with functions and providers can help to assess access (in financing terms) to specific types of health care services and to providers according to beneficiaries' capacity to pay. The portion of the table cross-classified with financing schemes shows: how the composition of financing for health care varies with income class; what share of health spending is being borne by different income groups; and how well specific schemes, such as the government scheme and social health insurance, target vulnerable groups.

Multi-dimensional tables

Three dimensions can also be used in a single table. For example, revenues of schemes could be crossed with financing schemes, and then crossed further with providers or functions. The information from the table helps link the origin of the funds funnelled into the health system to their final uses. For example, in countries with high external funding or with a high level of government transfers, a three-dimensional table can help identify whether government revenues or foreign aid are addressing key needs (for example, prevention vs. curative; hospitals vs. district ambulatory services).

Selected HA indicators

In addition to the tables, a health accounts report should also summarise key results in the form of indicators. An indicator is defined as a measurable variable that is used as a representation of an associated phenomenon. Health accounts indicators are measurements in reduced form that represent the different aspects or attributes of a country's health expenditures and health financing system. If health accounts are to be viewed as a measuring tool, the indicators are the measurements or readings derived from this tool.

A modest selection of indicators, as listed below in Table 15.1, is provided as an example of what may be included in countries' health accounts reports. The indicators in the list are computed either using purely HA results or in combination with additional macro-economic and non-expenditure data. Indicators of the first type include absolute expenditure levels, percentage shares to total and ratios of one health accounts component to another. Indicators of the second type include share of GDP, per capita values and values converted using exchange rates or PPPs.

In general, indicators for policy analysis can be created from the most important cross-tabulations. Examples are the share of prevention in hospital services; the ratio of inpatient and outpatient spending financed by government; and the level of capital spending targeted in publicly owned hospitals.

The levels of detail in these cross-tabulations may be specified differently in the regions of the world. The focus in the European Union relates to concerns among the Member States.[3] Some regional communities, such as the Commonwealth of Independent States (CIS), the Caribbean Community (CARICOM) and the MERCOSUR[4] have their own specific needs, which may make the reporting of certain HA tables a priority. As a result of this situation, some indicators that are feasible in one region may not be feasible in another one.

However, in all countries where HA have been established, health expenditure estimates classified according to only one key would generally be available, especially expenditures classified by function, provider and financing scheme. These data also provide information that address specific policy issues. Examples include the total amount of out-of-pocket health expenditures, the amount paid to hospitals, and the amount spent for prevention. Aggregates such as total spending on pharmaceuticals (adding inpatient use of pharmaceuticals to outpatient use) have also been of interest to policy makers. Another example is the amount spent on long-term care, summing both the health care part and the social part. Traditional medicine is also a topic of special policy interest in some parts of the world.

The indicators that a country decides to adopt do not have to be limited to the proposed list. Many more can be created, usually to meet national or even local needs. For example, the additional indicators that some countries have expressed an interest in include the following: total contributions of households to financing schemes through the different contribution mechanisms; expenditures of government schemes and compulsory financing schemes as a percentage of general government expenditures; expenditures on communicable diseases; expenditures supporting the Millennium Development Goals (MDGs); and health expenditures in specific geographic areas. The calculation of these additional indicators may require the use of reporting items of classifications (*e.g.* reporting item for functions for expenditures on communicable diseases and preventive health programmes). Other indicators may require the creation of new aggregates that need to be reported as memorandum items of the appropriate tables. For example, to calculate expenditures supporting MDGs, an aggregate consisting of expenditures for specific diseases (named in the MDG) needs to be constructed from either of the sets of tables showing disease breakdown, ICD-10 chapter or Global Burden of Disease category. Also, total contributions of households to financing schemes include the social health insurance contributions of employees and self-employed, voluntary pre-payment from households/individuals and other revenues from households.

Table 15.1 shows examples of some of the more frequently requested values, but those not included and considered to be useful can also be calculated. See Box 15.1 below for one example on levels of care.

HA time series

The use of commonly-agreed classifications and boundaries as set out in the SHA Manual should result in data that can be better compared across countries, and nationally should provide more consistent data over time. For example, a standard definition of health care based on the functional boundary can avoid sudden changes in national aggregates due to a change in responsibilities of the various ministries and the resulting reorganisation of various programmes. This makes it possible both to monitor and follow

Table 15.1. **Selected examples of indicators used in health care analysis**

Axis	Indicator	Million NCU	Million of USD or EUR	PPP	% GDP	Per capita NCU	Per capita USD or EUR	Per capita PPP	Percentage of CHE
General	Total current health expenditure	X	X	X	X	X	X	X	
	Total current health expenditure plus capital spending[5]	X	X	X	X	X	X	X	
Health functions	Preventive spending								X
	Curative spending								X
	Inpatient spending								X
	Outpatient spending								X
	Health expenditure on long-term care	X	X	X					X
	Total LTC spending	X	X	X	X	X	X	X	
	Total pharmaceutical spending	X	X	X	X	X	X	X	X
Financing schemes	Government health schemes								X
	Compulsory contributory health insurance schemes								X
	Voluntary health insurance schemes								X
	Out-of-pocket expenditure on health								X
Providers	Hospital health spending								X
	Ambulatory health spending								X
Revenue of schemes	Externally funded expenditure on health								X
	Domestic public and compulsory private funded expenditure on health								X
	Privately funded expenditure on health								X
Factors	Expenditure on human resources								X
Beneficiaries	Expenditure on health on non-communicable diseases	X	X	X	X	X	X	X	X
	Expenditure on health on injuries	X	X	X	X	X	X	X	X
	Expenditure on health age 65 and over	X	X			X	X		X
Capital formation	Total public spending on capital formation	X	X						X
	Total private spending on capital formation	X							X
	Spending on capital formation by hospitals	X							X

changes in functional financing within the system and to facilitate the possibility of forecasting and the use of simulation models.

Many countries have now developed time series of health accounts. Therefore, any HA report should present total expenditures and selected aggregates over time where these are available. To complete the tables, one can also include other useful reference data for computing selected indicators. The additional data usually reported include population size, GDP and a price index (preferably a medical/ [health] price index) over time.

When viewing a time series of health expenditures, it is commonly remarked that these have grown continuously through time. To properly analyse the time series data, it is important to determine first whether the increase was due to changes in the price, the content of the service or the quantity of the services provided. The effect of price increases can be removed through "deflating" health expenditure by converting to values in real terms or in constant prices, also referred to as "volumes" (see Chapter 13 for more detail). Then, to better appreciate the health expenditure trends over time, per capita real health expenditures, health expenditures as percentage of GDP, and average annual real growth rates may also be computed. Health expenditure values may be reported in national currency units and in PPP values.

Box 15.1. **An example of an indicator on levels of care**

National needs for information vary extensively both between countries and over time. Health accounts provide a flexible toolkit to support analysis, and can be enlarged with minimal additional information requirements. Also, the analysis can use a variety of axes to explore the expenditure process under scrutiny. One example is the model of health care that considers the complexity of the health system and the structure of health needs in the population.

For example, levels of care can be separated into general and specialised types of services, which are introduced in the functional and provider classification of SHA 2011. In the following table, an example is presented in which the functions that deal with general and specialised care at the third-digit breakdown are included. Similarly, the provider classification can also be separated into general and specialised care providers. Functions and providers components without any special relevance to either area have been omitted from the table. The table then shows the amount of general care services consumed from providers of general care, and similarly the share of specialised services from providers of specialised care. Finally, the financing agents that pay for the services consumed are included in the example to identify the path for funding those matching profiles.

Expenditure on health care by financing schemes and a selection of providers of care and functions

Functions Million of national currency Financing schemes - Providers			HC.1 **Curative care**	HC.1.1.1, HC.1.2.1, HC.1.3.1, HC.1.3.2 General curative care	HC.1.1.2, HC.1.2.2, HC.1.3.3 Specialised curative care	HC.2 **Rehabilitative care =**	HC.6 **Preventive care**	Total **Total**
HF.1	**Governmental schemes and compulsory contributory health financing schemes**							
	HP.1 Hospitals							
	HP.1.1	General hospitals						
	HP.1.2 + HP.1.3	Mental health hospitals and other specialised hospitals						
	HP.3 Providers of ambulatory health care							
	HP.3.1.1 + HP.3.2	Offices of general medical practitioners + Dental practice						
	all other HP.3	All other providers of ambulatory health care = specialised						
	HP.6 Providers of preventive care							
HF.2	**Voluntary health care payment schemes**							
	HP.1 Hospitals							
	HP.1.1	General hospitals						
	HP.1.2 + HP.1.3	Mental health hospitals and other specialised hospitals						

Box 15.1. **An example of an indicator on levels of care** *(cont.)*

Expenditure on health care by financing schemes and a selection of providers of care and functions *(cont.)*

Functions				HC.1			HC.2	HC.6	Total
					HC.1.1.1, HC.1.2.1, HC.1.3.1, HC.1.3.2	HC.1.1.2, HC.1.2.2, HC.1.3.3			
Financing schemes - Providers			Million of national currency	Curative care	General curative care	Specialised curative care	Rehabilitative care =	Preventive care	Total
	HP.3	Providers of ambulatory health care							
		HP.3.1.1 + HP.3.2	Offices of general medical practitioners + Dental practice						
		all other HP.3	All other providers of ambulatory health care = specialised						
	HP.6	Providers of preventive care							
HF.3	Household out-of-pocket payment								
	HP.1	Hospitals							
		HP.1.1	General hospitals						
		HP.1.2 + HP.1.3	Mental health hospitals and other specialised hospitals						
	HP.3	Providers of ambulatory health care							
		HP.3.1.1 + HP.3.2	Offices of general medical practitioners + Dental practice						
		all other HP.3	All other providers of ambulatory health care = specialised						
	HP.6	Providers of preventive care							
HF.4	Rest of the world financing schemes (non resident)								
	HP.1	Hospitals							
		HP.1.1	General hospitals						
		HP.1.2 + HP.1.3	Mental health hospitals and other						
	HP.3	Providers of ambulatory health care							
		HP.3.1.1 + HP.3.2	Offices of general medical practitioners + Dental practice						
		all other HP.3	All other providers of ambulatory health care = specialised						
	HP.6	Providers of preventive care							
Total	Total								

Source: IHAT for SHA 2011.

If a series of HA reports already exist, the current report should highlight any new patterns observed from the updated HA results.

Using HA with other health system information

In addition to GDP, population and prices data, health accounts may also be reported together with other health system information to explore particular policy questions. For example, total expenditure on specific types of providers can be linked to measures of the service throughput of those providers in order to estimate average expenditure per unit of service delivered. More specifically, if a country's health accounts can separate hospital spending into government and non-government acute hospitals and if the total admissions into each type of hospital are known, then the average expenditure per admission for each type of hospital can be computed. Such comparisons may provide a useful first look at efficiency, although obviously further analysis is needed to explain any differences adequately.

These kinds of analyses or studies can be extensive in nature, and it is suggested that full accounts of these studies be reported in separate research or policy papers. Papers that have a specific policy focus can be more effective in communicating and informing concerned stakeholders of the facts about an existing situation and about what possible actions may be needed. The health accounts report can then present highlights or relevant findings extracted from these research or policy papers.

Country background

The health accounts report requires relevant background information to be sure that the results can be interpreted in their proper context. It is suggested that a summary description of the health care system be included. It should discuss the main financing flows, the actors involved, some contextual elements (*e.g.* the role of NGOs, of the private sector, of the external sector) and major policy issues (*e.g.* recent reforms, reforms under discussion, reforms required).

As indicated previously, it would be useful to have price index data in the HA report. Other data that may be valuable for interpreting HA results include statistics on providers and on health care utilisation and services provision, such as hospital bed-days, medical consultation visits, surgeries, immunisations and other key services, the volume of medicines and other health goods, and health outcomes data.

If a series of HA reports already exist, the current report should highlight new trends in health status, health facilities, health financing arrangements and health policies.

Metadata and data sources

The collection of the basic input data and the construction of the health accounts tables is a time-consuming effort. However, the effort will be much less worthwhile if the metadata behind the data are not properly documented. Solid, comprehensive metadata facilitates an appropriate interpretation and use of the HA results. For example, trends in health expenditures can be analysed better when there is knowledge about, say, changes in the accounting system. At a minimum, background information should include the sources of data, how data were validated (especially in the case of multiple data sources), the reasoning behind the selection of the data used in the estimation, the procedures applied to make the data usable, and more.

Quality checks

A final set of checks on the quality of the HA data should be performed before publication in any report. These consist of checking for 1) the consistency of totals across tables, 2) consistency in the value of similar expense items across tables, and 3) the plausibility of percentage shares, per capita values, and growth rates. Checks on the quality of HA estimates are to be described further with some examples.

In the tri-axial approach, it is expected that the same total expenditures observed for consumption of health care should hold in the other axes of provision and financing. Basic quality checks include ensuring that the totals reported agree with the sums of the constituent parts. Identical items with identical classifications that appear in different tables should have the same value. Another set of quality checks should look into the plausibility of the various indicators in relation to the totals, in relation to the population (per capita data), in relation to GDP and in relation to historical values (percentage change from year to year, growth rates). Although the percentage shares and growth rates considered reasonable vary across countries, the relative changes should be within pre-determined ranges of acceptability. For example, if private insurance is replaced by a government mandatory insurance scheme, then the relative change from one year to another in these two items would be significant, but in conformity with a real change.

National, regional and international databases

National, regional and international databases that report HA data have different purposes, scopes, and types of information and levels of detail available. All databases would contain time series, but different ranges or types of HA information. National databases primarily address data needs for country-level analysis, while regional and international databases provide data for examining cross-country issues and concerns.

National databases, being the repository of the country's HA estimates, tend to contain the most detailed information and estimates of specific health expenditure aggregates or components that may be memorandum items to the standard classifications, but which are of special interest to the country's policy makers. It is the responsibility of the national health accountants to include basic information that would help users to interpret the HA estimates properly as part of the databases; and these basic information should include definitions, data sources, computational procedures and other relevant information about the raw data used in the HA estimation.

Regional and international databases are constructed from information collected regularly from countries, using a standard table or questionnaire. The types of the information collected and the levels of detail are well-defined in the data collection instrument. The data sources and other relevant information used to arrive at the estimates being reported by countries in the standard questionnaire should be entered as explanatory notes. Steps have been taken to harmonise HA data collection efforts (for databases) of the different international agencies through the use of a jointly developed standard questionnaire.

The HA data of countries that is collected and reported in different regional and international databases are expected to be comparable, since countries presumably are using the same SHA methodology to generate their results and the data are collected for regional/international databases using a similar data collection instrument. Even so, differences between regional vs. international and national vs. international databases have been noted particularly for indicators. One important reason for differences has generally been the use of different sources for reference information. In the country database, national official data for GDP and population, for example, would be used, while some international databases use compilations of GDP and population by, say, the United Nations or the International Monetary Fund. Such differences can be put in a proper context so long as there is systematic documentation of the data sources and other relevant information in the databases.

For comparative purposes, however, it would be beneficial to ensure harmonised data reporting nationally and internationally for a given country. Reporting strategies and collaborative efforts between involved agencies are required to achieve that aim. Notably, one principle would be:

- To standardise categories and their expected content so that the values under one label would refer only to one single boundary and type of expenditure;
- To state clearly the reported coverage in time and in geographical area;
- To state clearly the reference values used and their source, time and coverage, *e.g.* gross domestic product (GDP), general government expenditure (GGE), population and exchange rates, etc.

The selection of tables presented in this chapter

In the section below, examples of the tables (at the second-digit level) mentioned above are presented. The presentation of this particular set of tables does not mean that any of them is mandatory or that the level of detail shown and the number of categories mentioned is recommended for country adoption.

Notes

1. It is important to understand that health accounts information will become routine information, and thus produced at a lower cost, if policy makers find the results useful and request the information regularly.
2. Expenditures targeted at some of the Millennium Development Goals can be monitored through this table.
3. See, for example, the European Community Health Indicators Monitoring (ECHIM), or the Health and Long-term care indicators under the EU Open Method Co-ordination Framework.
4. MERCOSUR: *Mercado Comun del Sur* (Trade agreement of the Southern-cone countries).
5. Although total health expenditure is no longer proposed in SHA 2011, the indicator current health expenditure plus capital spending is included here for continuity reasons with respect to SHA 1.0.

Table 15.2. **Expenditure on health care by financing schemes and functions of care**

Functions		Financing schemes Million of national currency	HF.1 Governmental schemes and compulsory contributory health financing schemes	HF.1.1 Governmental schemes	HF.1.2 Compulsory contributory health insurance schemes	HF.1.3 Compulsory Medical Savings Accounts (CMSA)	HF.2 Voluntary health care payment schemes	HF.2.1 Voluntary health insurance schemes	HF.2.2 NPISHs financing schemes	HF.2.3 Enterprises financing schemes	HF.3 Household out-of-pocket payment	HF.3.1 Out-of-pocket excluding cost sharing	HF.3.2 Cost sharing with third-party payers	HF.4 Rest of the world financing schemes (non-resident)	HF.4.1 Compulsory schemes (non-resident)	HF.4.2 Voluntary schemes (non-resident)	All HF All financing schemes	Memorandum items – Reporting items HF.RI.1 Government	HF.RI.1 Corporations	HF.RI.1 Households	HF.RI.1 Non-profit institutions serving households (NPISHs)	HF.RI.1 Rest of the world	Reporting items HF.RI.2 Governmental schemes and compulsory contributory health insurance schemes together with cost sharing (HF.1 + HF.3.2.1)	HF.RI.3 Voluntary health insurance schemes together with cost sharing (HF.2.1+HF.3.2.2)
HC.1		**Curative care**																						
	HC.1.1	Inpatient curative care																						
	HC.1.2	Day curative care																						
	HC.1.3	Outpatient curative care																						
	HC.1.4	Home-based curative care																						
HC.2		**Rehabilitative care**																						
	HC.2.1	Inpatient rehabilitative care																						
	HC.2.2	Day rehabilitative care																						
	HC.2.3	Outpatient rehabilitative care																						
	HC.2.4	Home-based rehabilitative care																						
HC.1+HC.2		**Curative care and rehabilitative care**																						
	HC.1.1+ HC.2.1	Inpatient curative and rehabilitative care																						
	HC.1.2+ HC.2.2	Day curative and rehabilitative care																						
	HC.1.3+ HC.2.3	Outpatient curative and rehabilitative care																						

Table 15.2. **Expenditure on health care by financing schemes and functions of care** *(cont.)*

Functions		Financing schemes / Million of national currency	HF.1				HF.2				HF.3			HF.4			All HF	Memorandum items: Reporting items					Reporting items	
			HF.1 **Governmental schemes and compulsory contributory health financing schemes**	HF.1.1 Governmental schemes	HF.1.2 Compulsory contributory health insurance schemes	HF.1.3 Compulsory Medical Savings Accounts (CMSA)	HF.2 **Voluntary health care payment schemes**	HF.2.1 Voluntary health insurance schemes	HF.2.2 NPISHs financing schemes	HF.2.3 Enterprises financing schemes	HF.3 **Household out-of-pocket payment**	HF.3.1 Out-of-pocket excluding cost sharing	HF.3.2 Cost sharing with third-party payers	HF.4 **Rest of the world financing schemes (non-resident)**	HF.4.1 Compulsory schemes (non-resident)	HF.4.2 Voluntary schemes (non-resident)	All financing schemes	HF.RI.1 Government	HF.RI.1 Corporations	HF.RI.1 Households	HF.RI.1 Non-profit institutions serving households (NPISHs)	HF.RI.1 Rest of the world	HF.RI.2 Governmental schemes and compulsory contributory health insurance schemes together with cost sharing (HF.1 + HF.3.2.1)	HF.RI.3 Voluntary health insurance schemes together with cost sharing (HF.2.1+HF.3.2.2)
	HC.1.4+ HC.2.4	Home-based curative and rehabilitative care																						
HC.3		**Long-term care (health)**																						
	HC.3.1	Inpatient long-term care (health)																						
	HC.3.2	Day long-term care (health)																						
	HC.3.3	Outpatient long-term care (health)																						
	HC.3.4	Home-based long-term care (health)																						
HC.4		**Ancillary services (non specified by function)**																						
	HC.4.1	Laboratory services																						
	HC.4.2	Imaging services																						
	HC.4.3	Patient transportation																						
HC.5		**Medical goods (non specified by function)**																						
	HC.5.1	Pharmaceuticals and other medical non durable goods																						
	HC.5.2	Therapeutic appliances and other medical durable goods																						

Table 15.2. **Expenditure on health care by financing schemes and functions of care** *(cont.)*

Functions		Financing schemes	HF.1				HF.2				HF.3			HF.4			All HF	Memorandum items						
				HF.1.1	HF.1.2	HF.1.3		HF.2.1	HF.2.2	HF.2.3		HF.3.1	HF.3.2		HF.4.1	HF.4.2		Reporting items					Reporting items	
																		HF.RI.1	HF.RI.1	HF.RI.1	HF.RI.1	HF.RI.1	HF.RI.2	HF.RI.3
		Million of national currency	**Governmental schemes and compulsory contributory health financing schemes**	Governmental schemes	Compulsory contributory health insurance schemes	Compulsory Medical Savings Accounts (CMSA)	**Voluntary health care payment schemes**	Voluntary health insurance schemes	NPISHs financing schemes	Enterprises financing schemes	**Household out-of-pocket payment**	Out-of-pocket excluding cost sharing	Cost sharing with third-party payers	**Rest of the world financing schemes (non-resident)**	Compulsory schemes (non-resident)	Voluntary schemes (non-resident)	All financing schemes	Government	Corporations	Households	Non-profit institutions serving households (NPISHs)	Rest of the world	Governmental schemes and compulsory contributory health insurance schemes together with cost sharing (HF.1 + HF.3.2.1)	Voluntary health insurance schemes together with cost sharing (HF.2.1+HF.3.2.2)
HC.6		**Preventive care**																						
	HC.6.1	Information, education and counseling programmes																						
	HC.6.2	Immunisation programmes																						
	HC.6.3	Early disease detection programmes																						
	HC.6.4	Healthy condition monitoring programmes																						
	HC.6.5	Epidemiological surveillance and risk and disease control programmes																						
	HC.6.6	Preparing for disaster and emergency response programmes																						
HC.7		**Governance and health system and financing administration**																						
	HC.7.1	Governance and health system administration																						
	HC.7.2	Administration of health financing																						

Table 15.2. **Expenditure on health care by financing schemes and functions of care** *(cont.)*

Financing schemes		**HF.1**	HF.1.1	HF.1.2	HF.1.3	**HF.2**	HF.2.1	HF.2.2	HF.2.3	**HF.3**	HF.3.1	HF.3.2	**HF.4**	HF.4.1	HF.4.2	All HF	**Memorandum items** Reporting items HF.RI.1	HF.RI.1	HF.RI.1	HF.RI.1	HF.RI.1	Reporting items HF.RI.2	HF.RI.3
Functions	Million of national currency	**Governmental schemes and compulsory contributory health financing schemes**	Governmental schemes	Compulsory contributory health insurance schemes	Compulsory Medical Savings Accounts (CMSA)	**Voluntary health care payment schemes**	Voluntary health insurance schemes	NPISHs financing schemes	Enterprises financing schemes	**Household out-of-pocket payment**	Out-of-pocket excluding cost sharing	Cost sharing with third-party payers	**Rest of the world financing schemes (non-resident)**	Compulsory schemes (non-resident)	Voluntary schemes (non-resident)	All financing schemes	Government	Corporations	Households	Non-profit institutions serving households (NPISHs)	Rest of the world	Governmental schemes and compulsory contributory health insurance schemes together with cost sharing (HF.1 + HF.3.2.1)	Voluntary health insurance schemes together with cost sharing (HF.2.1+HF.3.2.2)
HC.9	**Other health care services not elsewhere classified (*n.e.c.*)**																						
All HC	All functions																						
Memorandum items																							
Reporting items																							
HC.RI.1	Total pharmaceutical expenditure (TPE)																						
HC.RI.2	Traditional, Complementary and Alternative Medicines (TCAM)																						
HC.RI.3	Prevention and public health services (according to SHA1.0)																						
Health care related items																							
HCR.1	Long-term care (social)																						
HCR.2	Health promotion with multisectoral approach																						

Source: IHAT for SHA 2011.

Table 15.3. **Expenditure on health care by health care providers and functions of care**

Functions	Providers Million of national currency	HP.1 Hospitals	HP.1.1 General hospitals	HP.1.2 Mental health hospitals	HP.1.3 Specialised hospitals (other than mental health hospitals)	HP.2 Residential long-term care facilities	HP.2.1 Long-term nursing care facilities	HP.2.2 Mental health and substance abuse facilities	HP.2.9 Other residential long-term care facilities	HP.3 Providers of ambulatory health care	HP.3.1 Medical practices	HP.3.2 Dental practices	HP.3.3 Other health care practitioners	HP.3.4 Ambulatory health care centres	HP.3.5 Providers of home health care services	HP.4 Providers of ancillary services	HP.4.1 Providers of patient transportation and emergency rescue	HP.4.2 Medical and diagnostic laboratories	HP.4.9 Other providers of ancillary services	HP.5 Retailers and other providers of medical goods	HP.5.1 Pharmacies	HP.5.2 Retail sellers and other suppliers of durable	HP.5.9 All other miscellaneous sellers and other suppliers	HP.6 Providers of preventive care	HP.7 Providers of health care system administration and financing	HP.7.1 Government health administration agencies	HP.7.2 Social health insurance agencies	HP.7.3 Private health insurance administration agencies	HP.7.9 Other administrative agencies	HP.8 Rest of economy	HP.8.1 Households as providers of home health care	HP.8.2 All other industries as secondary providers of health care	HP.8.9 Other industries *n.e.c.*	HP.9 Rest of the world	All HP All providers
HC.1	**Curative care**																																		
HC.1.1	Inpatient curative care																																		
HC.1.2	Day curative care																																		
HC.1.3	Outpatient curative care																																		
HC.1.4	Home-based curative care																																		
HC.2	**Rehabilitative care**																																		
HC.2.1	Inpatient rehabilitative care																																		
HC.2.2	Day rehabilitative care																																		
HC.2.3	Outpatient rehabilitative care																																		
HC.2.4	Home based rehabilitative care																																		
HC.1+ HC.2	**Curative care and rehabilitative care**																																		
HC.1.1+ HC.2.1	Inpatient curative and rehabilitative care																																		
HC.1.2+ HC.2.2	Day curative and rehabilitative care																																		
HC.1.3+ HC.2.3	Outpatient curative and rehabilitative																																		

Table 15.3. Expenditure on health care by health care providers and functions of care (cont.)

Functions	Providers / Million of national currency	HP.1 Hospitals	HP.1.1 General hospitals	HP.1.2 Mental health hospitals	HP.1.3 Specialised hospitals (other than mental health hospitals)	HP.2 Residential long-term care facilities	HP.2.1 Long-term nursing care facilities	HP.2.2 Mental health and substance abuse facilities	HP.2.9 Other residential long-term care facilities	HP.3 Providers of ambulatory health care	HP.3.1 Medical practices	HP.3.2 Dental practices	HP.3.3 Other health care practitioners	HP.3.4 Ambulatory health care centres	HP.3.5 Providers of home health care services	HP.4 Providers of ancillary services	HP.4.1 Providers of patient transportation and emergency rescue	HP.4.2 Medical and diagnostic laboratories	HP.4.9 Other providers of ancillary services	HP.5 Retailers and other providers of medical goods	HP.5.1 Pharmacies	HP.5.2 Retail sellers and other suppliers of durable	HP.5.9 All other miscellaneous sellers and other suppliers	HP.6 Providers of preventive care	HP.7 Providers of health care system administration and financing	HP.7.1 Government health administration agencies	HP.7.2 Social health insurance agencies	HP.7.3 Private health insurance administration agencies	HP.7.9 Other administrative agencies	HP.8 Rest of economy	HP.8.1 Households as providers of home health care	HP.8.2 All other industries as secondary providers of health care	HP.8.9 Other industries *n.e.c.*	HP.9 Rest of the world	All HP All providers
HC.1.4+ HC.2.4	Home-based curative and rehabilitative care																																		
HC.3	**Long-term care (health)**																																		
HC.3.1	Inpatient long-term care (health)																																		
HC.3.2	Day long-term care (health)																																		
HC.3.3	Outpatient long-term care (health)																																		
HC.3.4	Home-based long-term care (health)																																		
HC.4	**Ancillary services (non specified by function)**																																		
HC.4.1	Laboratory services																																		
HC.4.2	Imaging services																																		
HC.4.3	Patient transportation																																		
HC.5	**Medical goods (non specified by function)**																																		
HC.5.1	Pharmaceuticals and other medical non durable goods																																		

Table 15.3. **Expenditure on health care by health care providers and functions of care** *(cont.)*

Functions	Providers Million of national currency	HP.1 Hospitals	HP.1.1 General hospitals	HP.1.2 Mental health hospitals	HP.1.3 Specialised hospitals (other than mental health hospitals)	HP.2 Residential long-term care facilities	HP.2.1 Long-term nursing care facilities	HP.2.2 Mental health and substance abuse facilities	HP.2.9 Other residential long-term care facilities	HP.3 Providers of ambulatory health care	HP.3.1 Medical practices	HP.3.2 Dental practices	HP.3.3 Other health care practitioners	HP.3.4 Ambulatory health care centres	HP.3.5 Providers of home health care services	HP.4 Providers of ancillary services	HP.4.1 Providers of patient transportation and emergency rescue	HP.4.2 Medical and diagnostic laboratories	HP.4.9 Other providers of ancillary services	HP.5 Retailers and other providers of medical goods	HP.5.1 Pharmacies	HP.5.2 Retail sellers and other suppliers of durable	HP.5.9 All other miscellaneous sellers and other suppliers	HP.6 Providers of preventive care	HP.7 Providers of health care system administration and financing	HP.7.1 Government health administration agencies	HP.7.2 Social health insurance agencies	HP.7.3 Private health insurance administration agencies	HP.7.9 Other administrative agencies	HP.8 Rest of economy	HP.8.1 Households as providers of home health care	HP.8.2 All other industries as secondary providers of health care	HP.8.9 Other industries *n.e.c.*	HP.9 Rest of the world	All HP All providers
HC.5.2	Therapeutic appliances and other medical durable goods																																		
HC.6	**Preventive care**																																		
HC.6.1	Information, education and counseling programmes																																		
HC.6.2	Immunisation programmes																																		
HC.6.3	Early disease detection programmes																																		
HC.6.4	Healthy condition monitoring programmes																																		
HC.6.5	Epidemiological surveillance and risk and disease control programmes																																		
HC.6.6	Preparing for disaster and emergency response programmes																																		

Table 15.3. **Expenditure on health care by health care providers and functions of care** *(cont.)*

Functions	Providers Million of national currency	HP.1 **Hospitals**	HP.1.1 General hospitals	HP.1.2 Mental health hospitals	HP.1.3 Specialised hospitals (other than mental health hospitals)	HP.2 **Residential long-term care facilities**	HP.2.1 Long-term nursing care facilities	HP.2.2 Mental health and substance abuse facilities	HP.2.9 Other residential long-term care facilities	HP.3 **Providers of ambulatory health care**	HP.3.1 Medical practices	HP.3.2 Dental practices	HP.3.3 Other health care practitioners	HP.3.4 Ambulatory health care centres	HP.3.5 Providers of home health care services	HP.4 **Providers of ancillary services**	HP.4.1 Providers of patient transportation and emergency rescue	HP.4.2 Medical and diagnostic laboratories	HP.4.9 Other providers of ancillary services	HP.5 **Retailers and other providers of medical goods**	HP.5.1 Pharmacies	HP.5.2 Retail sellers and other suppliers of durable	HP.5.9 All other miscellaneous sellers and other suppliers	HP.6 **Providers of preventive care**	HP.7 **Providers of health care system administration and financing**	HP.7.1 Government health administration agencies	HP.7.2 Social health insurance agencies	HP.7.3 Private health insurance administration agencies	HP.7.9 Other administrative agencies	HP.8 **Rest of economy**	HP.8.1 Households as providers of home health care	HP.8.2 All other industries as secondary providers of health care	HP.8.9 Other industries *n.e.c.*	HP.9 **Rest of the world**	All HP **All providers**
HC.7	**Governance and health system and financing administration**																																		
HC.7.1	Governance and health system administration																																		
HC.7.2	Administration of health financing																																		
HC.9	**Other health care services not elsewhere classified (*n.e.c.*)**																																		
All HC	All functions																																		
Memorandum items																																			
Reporting items																																			
HC.RI.1	Total pharmaceutical expenditure (TPE)																																		
HC.RI.2	Traditional, Complementary and Alternative Medicines (TCAM)																																		

Table 15.3. **Expenditure on health care by health care providers and functions of care** *(cont.)*

Functions	**Providers**	HP.1	HP.1.1	HP.1.2	HP.1.3	HP.2	HP.2.1	HP.2.2	HP.2.9	HP.3	HP.3.1	HP.3.2	HP.3.3	HP.3.4	HP.3.5	HP.4	HP.4.1	HP.4.2	HP.4.9	HP.5	HP.5.1	HP.5.2	HP.5.9	HP.6	HP.7	HP.7.1	HP.7.2	HP.7.3	HP.7.9	HP.8	HP.8.1	HP.8.2	HP.8.9	HP.9	All HP
	Million of national currency	**Hospitals**	General hospitals	Mental health hospitals	Specialised hospitals (other than mental health hospitals)	**Residential long-term care facilities**	Long-term nursing care facilities	Mental health and substance abuse facilities	Other residential long-term care facilities	**Providers of ambulatory health care**	Medical practices	Dental practices	Other health care practitioners	Ambulatory health care centres	Providers of home health care services	**Providers of ancillary services**	Providers of patient transportation and emergency rescue	Medical and diagnostic laboratories	Other providers of ancillary services	**Retailers and other providers of medical goods**	Pharmacies	Retail sellers and other suppliers of durable	All other miscellaneous sellers and other suppliers	**Providers of preventive care**	**Providers of health care system administration and financing**	Government health administration agencies	Social health insurance agencies	Private health insurance administration agencies	Other administrative agencies	**Rest of economy**	Households as providers of home health care	All other industries as secondary providers of health care	Other industries *n.e.c.*	**Rest of the world**	**All providers**
HC.RI.3	Prevention and public health services (according to SHA1.0)																																		
Health care related items																																			
HCR.1	Long-term care (social)																																		
HCR.2	Health promotion with multisectoral																																		

Source: IHAT for SHA 2011.

Table 15.4. Expenditure on health care by financing schemes and health care providers

Providers		Financing schemes — Million of national currency	HF.1 Governmental schemes and compulsory contributory health financing schemes	HF.1.1 Governmental schemes	HF.1.2 Compulsory contributory health insurance schemes	HF.1.3 Compulsory Medical Savings Accounts (CMSA)	HF.2 Voluntary health care payment schemes	HF.2.1 Voluntary health insurance schemes	HF.2.2 NPISHs financing schemes	HF.2.3 Enterprises financing schemes	HF.3 Household out-of-pocket payment	HF.3.1 Out-of-pocket excluding cost sharing	HF.3.2 Cost sharing with third-party payers	HF.4 Rest of the world financing schemes (non resident)	HF.4.1 Compulsory schemes (non-resident)	HF.4.2 Voluntary schemes (non-resident)	All HF All financing schemes	Memorandum items – Reporting items HF.RI.1.1 Government	HF.RI.1.2 Corporations	HF.RI.1.3 Households	HF.RI.1.4 NPISHs	HF.RI.1.5 Rest of the world	Reporting items HF.RI.2 Governmental schemes and compulsory contributory health insurance schemes together with cost sharing (HF.1 + HF.3.2.1)	HF.RI.3 Voluntary health insurance schemes together with cost sharing (HF.2.1+HF.3.2.2)
HP.1		**Hospitals**																						
	HP.1.1	General hospitals																						
	HP.1.2	Mental health hospitals																						
	HP.1.3	Specialised hospitals (other than mental health hospitals)																						
HP.2		**Residential long-term care facilities**																						
	HP.2.1	Long-term nursing care facilities																						
	HP.2.2	Mental health and substance abuse faciltites																						
	HP.2.9	Other residential long-term care facilities																						
HP.3		**Providers of ambulatory health care**																						
	HP.3.1	Medical practices																						
	HP.3.2	Dental practices																						
	HP.3.3	Other health care practitioners																						
	HP.3.4	Ambulatory health care centres																						
	HP.3.5	Providers of home health care services																						
HP.4		**Providers of ancillary services**																						
	HP.4.1	Providers of patient transportation and emergency rescue																						
	HP.4.2	Medical and diagnostic laboratories																						
	HP.4.9	Other providers of ancillary services																						
HP.5		**Retailers and other providers of medical goods**																						
	HP.5.1	Pharmacies																						
	HP.5.2	Retail sellers and other suppliers of durable medical goods and medical appliances																						

Table 15.4. **Expenditure on health care by financing schemes and health care providers** *(cont.)*

Providers	Financing schemes Million of national currency	HF.1				HF.2				HF.3			HF.4			All HF	Memorandum items						
			HF.1.1	HF.1.2	HF.1.3		HF.2.1	HF.2.2	HF.2.3		HF.3.1	HF.3.2		HF.4.1	HF.4.2		Reporting items HF.RI.1.1	HF.RI.1.2	HF.RI.1.3	HF.RI.1.4	HF.RI.1.5	Reporting items HF.RI.2	HF.RI.3
		Governmental schemes and compulsory contributory health financing schemes	Governmental schemes	Compulsory contributory health insurance schemes	Compulsory Medical Savings Accounts (CMSA)	**Voluntary health care payment schemes**	Voluntary health insurance schemes	NPISHs financing schemes	Enterprises financing schemes	**Household out-of-pocket payment**	Out-of-pocket excluding cost sharing	Cost sharing with third-party payers	**Rest of the world financing schemes (non resident)**	Compulsory schemes (non-resident)	Voluntary schemes (non-resident)	All financing schemes	Government	Corporations	Households	NPISHs	Rest of the world	Governmental schemes and compulsory contributory health insurance schemes together with cost sharing (HF.1 + HF.3.2.1)	Voluntary health insurance schemes together with cost sharing (HF.2.1+HF.3.2.2)
HP.5.9	All other miscellaneous sellers and other suppliers of pharmaceuticals and medical goods																						
HP.6	**Providers of preventive care**																						
HP.7	**Providers of health care system administration and financing**																						
HP.7.1	Government health administration agencies																						
HP.7.2	Social health insurance agencies																						
HP.7.3	Private health insurance administration agencies																						
HP.7.9	Other administrative agencies																						
HP.8	**Rest of the economy**																						
HP.8.1	Households as providers of home health care																						
HP.8.2	All other industries as secondary providers of health care																						
HP.8.9	Other industries *n.e.c.*																						
HP.9	**Rest of the world**																						
All HP	**All providers**																						

Source: IHAT for SHA 2011.

Table 15.5. Expenditure on health care by revenues of financing schemes and financing schemes

Financing schemes	Revenues of financing schemes Million of national currency	FS.1	FS.1.1	FS.1.2	FS.1.3	FS.1.4	FS.2	FS.3	FS.3.1	FS.3.2	FS.3.3	FS.3.4	FS.4	FS.5	FS.6	FS.7	FS.7.1	FS.7.2	All FS			Memorandum items: FSR.1.1	Memorandum items: FSR.1.2	Memorandum items: FSR.2	Revenues by institutional units: FSRI.1.1	Revenues by institutional units: FSRI.1.2	Revenues by institutional units: FSRI.1.3	Revenues by institutional units: FSRI.1.4	Revenues by institutional units: FSRI.1.5
		Transfers from government domestic revenue	Internal transfers and grants	Transfers by government on behalf of specific groups	Subsidies	Other transfers from government domestic revenue	**Transfers distributed by government from foreign origin**	**Social insurance contributions**	Social insurance contributions from employees	Social insurance contributions from employers	Social insurance contributions from self-employed	Other social insurance contributions	**Compulsory prepayment (other than FS.3)**	**Voluntary prepayment**	**Other domestic revenues *n.e.c.***	**Direct foreign transfers**	Direct foreign financial transfers	Direct foreign aid in kind	All revenues of financing schemes	Total current expenditure by financing schemes	Operating balance	Loans taken by the government	Loans taken by private organisations	Aid in kind at donor value	Government	Corporations	Households	Non-profit institutions serving households (NPISHs)	Rest of the world
HF.1	**Governmental schemes and compulsory contributory health financing schemes**																												
HF.1.1	Governmental schemes																												
HF.1.2	Compulsory contributory health insurance schemes																												
HF.1.3	Compulsory Medical Savings Accounts (CMSA)																												
HF.2	**Voluntary health care payment schemes**																												
HF.2.1	Voluntary health insurance schemes																												
HF.2.2	NPISHs financing schemes																												
HF.2.3	Enterprises financing schemes																												
HF.3	**Household out-of-pocket payment**																												
HF.3.1	Out-of-pocket excluding cost sharing																												
HF.3.2	Cost sharing with third-party payers																												
HF.4	**Rest of the world financing schemes (non resident)**																												

Table 15.5. **Expenditure on health care by revenues of financing schemes and financing schemes** *(cont.)*

	Revenues of financing schemes / Million of national currency																				Memorandum items			Revenues by institutional units				
Financing schemes		**FS.1** Transfers from government domestic revenue	FS.1.1 Internal transfers and grants	FS.1.2 Transfers by government on behalf of specific groups	FS.1.3 Subsidies	FS.1.4 Other transfers from government domestic revenue	**FS.2** Transfers distributed by government from foreign origin	**FS.3** Social insurance contributions	FS.3.1 Social insurance contributions from employees	FS.3.2 Social insurance contributions from employers	FS.3.3 Social insurance contributions from self-employed	FS.3.4 Other social insurance contributions	**FS.4** Compulsory prepayment (other than FS.3)	**FS.5** Voluntary prepayment	**FS.6** Other domestic revenues *n.e.c.*	**FS.7** Direct foreign transfers	FS.7.1 Direct foreign financial transfers	FS.7.2 Direct foreign aid in kind	All FS All revenues of financing schemes	Total current expenditure by financing schemes	Operating balance	FSR.1.1 Loans taken by the government	FSR.1.2 Loans taken by private organisations	FSR.2 Aid in kind at donor value	FSRI.1.1 Government	FSRI.1.2 Corporations	FSRI.1.3 Households	FSRI.1.4 Non-profit institutions serving households (NPISHs)	FSRI.1.5 Rest of the world
HF.4.1	Compulsory schemes (non-resident)																												
HF.4.2	Voluntary schemes (non-resident)																												
All HF	All financing schemes																												
Memorandum items																													
Reporting items																													
HF.RI.1.1	Governmental schemes and compulsory health insurance combined with cost sharing (HF.1 + HF.3.2.1)																												
HF.RI.1.2	Voluntary health insurance schemes together with cost sharing (HF.2.1+HF.3.2.2)																												
Related items																													
HF.RI.2.1	Government																												
HF.RI.2.2	Corporations																												
HF.RI.2.3	Households																												
HF.RI.2.4	Non-profit Institutions Serving Households (NPISHs)																												
HF.RI.2.5	Rest of the world																												

Source: IHAT for SHA 2011.

Table 15.6. **Expenditure on health care by financing agents and financing schemes**

Financing agents			FA.1	FA.1.1	FA.1.2	FA.1.3	FA.1.9	FA.2	FA.2.1	FA.2.2	FA.3	FA.3.1	FA.3.2	FA.4	FA.5	FA.6	FA.6.1	FA.6.2	FA.6.3	All FA
Financing schemes		Million of national currency	**General government**	Central government	State / Regional / Local government	Social security agency	All other general government units	**Insurance corporations**	Commercial insurance companies	Mutual and other non-profit insurance organisations	**Corporations (other than insurance corporations)**	Health management and provider corporations	Corporations (other than providers of health services)	**Non-profit institutions serving households (NPISHs)**	**Households**	**Rest of the world**	International organisations	Foreign governments	Other foreign entities	All financing agents
HF.1		**Governmental schemes and compulsory contributory health financing schemes**																		
	HF.1.1	Governmental schemes																		
	HF.1.2	Compulsory contributory health insurance schemes																		
	HF.1.3	Compulsory Medical Savings Accounts (CMSA)																		
HF.2		**Voluntary health care payment schemes**																		
	HF.2.1	Voluntary health insurance schemes																		
	HF.2.2	NPISHs financing schemes																		
	HF.2.3	Enterprises financing schemes																		
HF.3		**Household out-of-pocket payment**																		
	HF.3.1	Out-of-pocket excluding cost sharing																		
	HF.3.2	Cost sharing with third-party payers																		
HF.4		**Rest of the world financing schemes (non-resident)**																		
	HF.4.1	Compulsory schemes (non-resident)																		
	HF.4.2	Voluntary schemes (non-resident)																		
All HF		All financing schemes																		
Memorandum items																				
Reporting items																				
	HF.RI.1.1	Government																		

Table 15.6. **Expenditure on health care by financing agents and financing schemes** *(cont.)*

Financing agents / Million of national currency / Financing schemes		FA.1	FA.1.1	FA.1.2	FA.1.3	FA.1.9	FA.2	FA.2.1	FA.2.2	FA.3	FA.3.1	FA.3.2	FA.4	FA.5	FA.6	FA.6.1	FA.6.2	FA.6.3	All FA
		General government	Central government	State / Regional / Local government	Social security agency	All other general government units	**Insurance corporations**	Commercial insurance companies	Mutual and other non-profit insurance organisations	**Corporations (other than insurance corporations)**	Health management and provider corporations	Corporations (other than providers of health services)	**Non-profit institutions serving households (NPISHs)**	**Households**	**Rest of the world**	International organisations	Foreign governments	Other foreign entities	All financing agents
HF.RI.1.2	Corporations																		
HF.RI.1.3	Households																		
HF.RI.1.4	NPISHs																		
HF.RI.1.5	Rest of the world																		
HF.RI.2	Governmental schemes and compulsory contributory health insurance schemes together with cost sharing (HF.1 + HF.3.2.1)																		
HF.RI.3	Voluntary health insurance schemes together with cost sharing (HF.2.1+HF.3.2.2)																		

Source: IHAT for SHA 2011.

Table 15.7. Expenditure on health care by factors of provision and health care providers

Providers		Factors of provision Million of national currency	FP.1 Compensation of employees	FP.1.1 Wages and salaries	FP.1.2 Social contributions	FP.1.3 All other costs related to employees	FP.2 Self-employed professional remuneration	FP.3 Materials and services used	FP.3.1. Health care services	FP.3.2 Health care goods	FP.3.3 Non-health care services	FP.3.4 Non-health care goods	FP.4 Consumption of fixed capital	FP.5 Other items of spending on inputs	FP.5.1 Taxes	FP.5.2 Other items of spending	All FP All factors of provision
HP.1		**Hospitals**															
	HP.1.1	General hospitals															
	HP.1.2	Mental health hospitals															
	HP.1.3	Specialised hospitals (other than mental health hospitals)															
HP.2		**Residential long-term care facilities**															
	HP.2.1	Long-term nursing care facilities															
	HP.2.2	Mental health and substance abuse faciltites															
	HP.2.9	Other residential long-term care facilities															
HP.3		**Providers of ambulatory health care**															
	HP.3.1	Medical practices															
	HP.3.2	Dental practices															
	HP.3.3	Other health care practitioners															
	HP.3.4	Ambulatory health care centres															
	HP.3.5	Providers of home health care services															
HP.4		**Providers of ancillary services**															
	HP.4.1	Providers of patient transportation and emergency rescue															
	HP.4.2	Medical and diagnostic laboratories															
	HP.4.9	Other providers of ancillary services															
HP.5		**Retailers and other providers of medical goods**															
	HP.5.1	Pharmacies															
	HP.5.2	Retail sellers and other suppliers of durable medical goods and medical appliances															
	HP.5.9	All other miscellaneous sellers and other suppliers of pharmaceuticals and medical goods															

Table 15.7. **Expenditure on health care by factors of provision and health care providers** *(cont.)*

Providers	Factors of provision / Million of national currency	FP.1 Compensation of employees	FP.1.1 Wages and salaries	FP.1.2 Social contributions	FP.1.3 All other costs related to employees	FP.2 Self-employed professional remuneration	FP.3 Materials and services used	FP.3.1. Health care services	FP.3.2 Health care goods	FP.3.3 Non-health care services	FP.3.4 Non-health care goods	FP.4 Consumption of fixed capital	FP.5 Other items of spending on inputs	FP.5.1 Taxes	FP.5.2 Other items of spending	All FP All factors of provision
HP.6	**Providers of preventive care**															
HP.7	**Providers of health care system administration and financing**															
HP.7.1	Government health administration agencies															
HP.7.2	Social health insurance agencies															
HP.7.3	Private health insurance administration agencies															
HP.7.9	Other administrative agencies															
HP.8	**Rest of the economy**															
HP.8.1	Households as providers of home health care															
HP.8.2	All other industries as secondary providers of health care															
HP.8.9	Other industries *n.e.c.*															
HP.9	**Rest of the world**															
All HP	All providers															

Source: IHAT for SHA 2011.

References

Abel-Smith, B. (1963), "Paying for Health Services: A Study of the Costs and Sources of Finance in Six Countries", *Public Health Papers*, No. 17, World Health Organisation, Geneva.

Abel-Smith, B. (1967), "An International Study of Health expenditure and its Relevance for Health", *Public Health Papers*, No. 32, World Health Organisation, Geneva.

AIHW – Australian Institute for Health and Welfare (2010), "Health System Expenditure on Disease and Injury in Australia, 2004-05", Catalogue No. HSE 87, AIHW, Canberra.

Aizcorbe, A. and N. Nestoriak (2008), "The Importance of Pricing the Bundle of Treatments", BEA Working Paper, Bureau of Economic Analysis, Washington D.C.

Alailima, P.J. and F. Mohideen (1983), "Health Sector Commodity Requirements and Expenditure Flows", National Planning Department, Colombo, Sri Lanka.

Anand, S. and M. Ravallion (1993), "Human Development in Poor Countries: On the Role of Private Incomes and Public Services", *Journal of Economic Perspectives*, No. 7, pp. 133-150.

Auerbach, H., J. Gokhale and L.J. Kotlikoff (1994), "Generational Accounting: A Meaningful Way to Evaluate Fiscal Policy", *Journal of Economic Perspectives*, Vol. 8, pp. 73-94.

BASYS, CEPS and IGSS (2006), "Feasibility Study of Health Expenditures by Patient Characteristics", Augsburg, Germany.

Berman, P. (1997) "NHA in Developing Countries: Appropriate Methods and Recent Applications", *Health Economics*, Vol. 6, pp. 11-30.

Berman, P., A. Banerjee, T. Bossert, A. Mahal, M. Mitchell, N.S. Kumar, S. Kappagantula and L. Limgam (2003), "A Medium Term Strategy and Expenditure Framework for Health in Andhra Pradesh: Final Report", Department for International Development and the Government of Andhra Pradesh, New Delhi.

Berndt, E.R., D.M. Cutler, R.G. Frank, Z. Griliches, J.P. Newhouse and J.E. Triplett (2001), "Price Indexes for Medical Goods and Services: An Overview of Measurement Issues", in Cutler, D.M. and Berndt, E.R. (eds.), *Medical Care Output and Productivity*, University of Chicago Press, Chicago.

Blouin, C., N. Drager and R. Smith (2006), "International Trade in Health Services and the GATS - Current Issues and Debates", World Bank, Washington D.C.

Bodeker, G., C.K. Ong, C. Grundy, G. Burford and K. Shein (2005), "WHO Global Atlas of Traditional, Complementary and Alternative Medicine", World Health Organization, Centre for Health Development, Kobe, Japan.

Boskin, M.J., E. Dulberger, R. Gordon, Z. Griliches and D. Jorgenson (1996), "Toward a More Accurate Measure of the Cost of Living", Final Report to the U.S. Senate Finance Committee, Commission to Study the Consumer Price Index, Washington, D.C.

BPS-Statistics Indonesia (2007), "Statistical Yearbook, 2007", BPS-Statistics Indonesia, Jakarta, p. 133.

Brændvang, A.-K. (2008), "Norwegian Health Accounts", Eurostat project report, Statistics Norway, Oslo, available at *www.ssb.no/english/subjects/09/90/doc_200809_en/doc_200809_en.pdf*

Bulletin luxembourgeois des questions sociales (2005), "Long Term Care for Older People", Vol. 19, Conference organized by the Luxemburg Presidency of the European Union, with the Social Protection Committee of the European Union, Luxembourg, 12-13 May 2005.

Busse, R. and A. Riesberg (2004), "Health Care Systems in Transition: Germany", European Observatory on Health Care Systems, Copenhagen.

Byrd, T.L. and J.G. Law (2009), "Cross-border Utilisation of Health Care Services by United States Residents Living Near the Mexican Border", *Rev Panam Salud Publica*, Vol. 26, No. 2, pp. 95-100.

Carpenter, G.I., A. Main and G.F. Turner (1995), "Case-mix for the Elderly Inpatient: Resource Utilization Groups (RUGs) Validation Project", *Age and Ageing*, Vol. 24, No. 1, pp. 5-13.

Carrin, G. (2003), "Community-based Health Insurance Schemes in Developing Countries: Facts, Problems and Perspectives", Discussion Paper No. 1, Department of Health System Financing, Expenditure and Resource Allocation (FER), World Health Organisation, Geneva.

Castelli, A., D. Dawson, H. Gravelle and A. Street (2007), "Improving the Measurement of Health System Output Growth", *Health Economics*, Vol. 16, No. 10, pp. 1091-1107.

Castelli, A., L. Mauro and A. Street (2008), "Measuring NHS Output Growth", *CHE Research Paper*, No. 43, available at *www.york.ac.uk/inst/che/publications/publicationsbyyear.htm*.

CBS – Statistics Netherlands (2010), Statline, available at *http://statline.cbs.nl/StatWeb/?LA=en*.

Centre for Medicare and Medicaid Services (2010), "National Health Expenditures Accounts: Definitions, Sources, and Methods, 2009", available at *www.cms.gov/NationalHealthExpendData/downloads/dsm-09.pdf*.

Chawla, M., D. Kawiorska and G. Chellaraj (1997), "The Impact of Economic and Demographic Factors on Government Health Expenditure in Poland", DDM, Harvard School of Public Health.

Connor, S. (2010), "Caring for People Suffering from Life-limiting Conditions", WHO Seminar, 4 March 2010, available at *www.thewpca.org/about-hospice-and-palliative-care/the-need/*.

Dawson, D., H. Gravelle, M. O'Mahony, A. Street, M. Weale, A. Castelli, R. Jacobs, P. Kind, P. Loveridge, S. Martin, P. Stevens and L. Stokes (2005), "Developing New Approaches to Measuring NHS Outputs and Productivity: Final Report", Research Paper No. 6, Centre for Health Economics, York.

D'Cruz, P. and S. Bharat (2001), "Which Way To Turn: Inadequacies in the Health Care System in India", *Journal of Health Management*, Vol. 3, pp. 85-125.

De, S., T. Dmytraczenko, D. Brinkerhoff and M. Tien (2003), "Has Improved Availability of Health Expenditure Data Contributed to Evidence-Based Policymaking? Country Experiences with National Health Accounts", PHRplus.

Deloitte Center for Health Solutions (2008), "Medical Tourism – Consumers in Search of Value", available at *www.deloitte.com/centerforhealthsolutions*.

DermNetNZ (accessed 05/2011), "Synthetic Wound Dressings", available at *http://dermnetnz.org/procedures/dressings.html*.

Doorslaer, E. van, A. Wagstaffe and F. Rutten (1993), "Equity in the Finance and Delivery of Health Care: An International Perspective", Oxford University Press, Oxford.

Eggleston, K. and W. Yip (2004), "Hospital Competition under Regulated Prices: Application to Urban Health Sector Reforms in China", *International Journal of Health Care Finance and Economics*, Vol. 4, No. 4, pp. 343-368, Springer.

Elteto, O. and P. Koves (1964), "One Index Computation Problem of International Comparisons" (in Hungarian), *Statisztikai Szemle*, Vol. 7, pp. 507–518.

European Commission (2009), "Ageing Report: Economic and budgetary projections for the EU-27 Member States (2008-2060)", Office for Official publications of the EU Communities, Luxembourg.

EC, IMF, OECD, UN and World Bank (2009), "System of National Accounts 2008", European Commission, International Monetary Fund, Organisation for Economic Co-operation and Development, United Nations and World Bank, New York, Dec. 2009.

Eurostat (2001), "Handbook on Price and Volume Measures in National Accounts", Office for Official publications of the EU Communities, Luxembourg.

Eurostat (2003), "Household Production and Consumption: Proposal for a Methodology of Household Satellite Accounts", Office for Official publications of the EU Communities, Luxembourg.

Eurostat (2004), "Differences between Balance of Payments and Foreign Trade Statistics", Office for Official publications of the EU Communities, Luxembourg.

Eurostat (2008a), "Statistical Classification of Economic activities in the European Community NACE Rev.2", Office for Official publications of the EU Communities, Luxembourg.

Eurostat (2008b), "ESSPROS Manual. 2008 edition. The European System of Integrated Social Protection Statistics (ESSPROS)", Office for Official publications of the EU Communities, Luxembourg.

Eurostat (2008c), "Eurostat Manual of Supply, Use and Input-Output Tables", Office for Official Publications of the EU Communities, Luxembourg.

Eurostat (2008d), "CPA Revision 2, Classification of Products by Activity", Office for Official Publications of the EU Communities, Luxembourg.

Eurostat and Office of National Statistics UK (2003), "SHA Guidelines: Practical Guidance for Implementing a System of Health Accounts in the EU", available at *http://circa.europa.eu/Public/irc/dsis/health/library?l=/methodologiessandsdatasc/systemsofshealthsaccount/sha_guidelinespdf/_EN_1.0_&a=d.*

Eurostat and OECD (2006), "Methodological Manual on Purchasing Power Parities", OECD Publishing, Paris, available at *www.oecd.org/document/3/0,3746,en_2649_34357_37961859_1_1_1_1,00.html.*

Fetter, B. (2006), "Origins and Elaborations of the National Health Accounts, 1926-2006", *Health Care Financing Review,* Vol. 28, No. 1, pp. 53–67.

FT.com (2010), "European Drug Groups Fear Parallel Trade", *Financial Times*, published 7 June 2010.

Frenk, J., J. Sepúlveda, O. Gómez-Dantés and F. Knaul (2003), "Evidence-based Health Policy: Three Generations of Reform in Mexico", *The Lancet*, Vol. 362, No. 9396, pp. 1667-1671.

Fried, L.P., C.M. Tangen, J. Walston, A.B. Newman, C. Hirsch, J. Gottdiener, T. Seeman, R. Tracy, W.J. Kop, G. Burke and M.A. McBurnie (2001), "Frailty in Older Adults: Evidence for a Phenotype", *Journal of Gerontology*, Medical Sciences, Vol. 56a, No. 3, pp. 146-156.

Gerdtham, U., J. Sogaard, F. Andersson and B. Jonsson (1992), "An Econometric Analysis of Health Care Expenditure: A Cross-section Study of the OECD Countries", *Journal of Health Economics*, Vol. 11, No. 1, pp. 63-84.

Glinosa, I.A., R. Baetenb and H. Maarsea (2010), "Purchasing Health Services Abroad: Practices of Cross-border Contracting and Patient Mobility in Six European Countries", *Health Policy*, Vol. 95, No. 2, pp. 103-112.

Gottret, P.E. and G. Schieber (2006), "Health Financing Revisited: A Practioner's Guide", World Bank, Washington D.C.

Government of Turkey (2003), "National Health Accounts", Ministry of Public Health, Ankara.

Gqaleni, N., I. Moodley, H. Kruger, A. Ntuli and H. McLeod (2007), "Traditional and Complementary Medicine: Health Care Delivery", *South African Health Review.*

Hartman, M.B., R.J. Kornfeld and A.C. Catlin (2010), "A Reconciliation of Health Care Expenditures in the National Health Expenditure Accounts and in Gross Domestic Product", *Survey of Current Business*, BEA, US, available at *www.bea.gov/scb/pdf/2010/09%20September/0910_healthcare.pdf.*

Hartman, M.B., R.J. Kornfeld and A.C. Catlin (2010), "Health Care Expenditures in the National Health Expenditures Accounts and in Gross Domestic Product: A Reconciliation", BEA Working Paper, Washington, DC.

Heijink, R., M. Koopmanschap and J. Polder (2006), "International Comparison of Cost of Illness", National Institute for Public Health and the Environment, Bilthoven, available at *www.rivm.nl/bibliotheek/rapporten/270751016.html.*

Hill, P. (1975), "Price and Volume Measures for Non-Market Services", *Statistical Office of the European Communities*, Brussels, available at *http://siteresources.worldbank.org/ICPINT/Resources/Price_and_Volume_Measures.pdf.*

Hogerzeil, H.V. (2004), "The Concept of Essential Medicines: Lessons for Rich Countries", *British Medical Journal*, Vol. 329, pp. 1169-1172.

Huber, M. and R. Rodrigues (2008), "A Framework for Measuring Long-term Care Expenditure in Europe", Presentation to the International Association for Research on Income and Wealth.

ILO – International Labour Organisation (2005), "Health Micro-insurance Schemes: Feasibility Study Guide", ILO, Geneva, available at *www.ilo.org/manila/whatwedo/publications/lang--en/docName--WCMS_124889/index.htm.*

ILO (2008). "International Standard Classification of Occupations, ISCO-08", available at *www.ilo.org/public/english/bureau/stat/isco/isco08/index.htm.*

ILO, IMF, OECD, Eurostat, United Nations and World Bank (2004a), "Producer Price Index Manual, Theory and Practice", Washington D.C.

ILO, IMF, OECD, Eurostat, United Nations and World Bank (2004b), "Consumer Price Index Manual, Theory and Practice", Washington D.C.

IMF – International Monetary Fund (2001), *Government Finance Statistics Manual* (GFSM).

IMF (2009), "Balance of Payments and International Investment Position Manual, 6th Edition (BPM6)", IMF, Washington, D.C.

IRDES and BASYS (2007), "Tools for Data Collection on Health Care Statistics", *EUROSTAT Project*, Final report.

Ireland Central Statistics Office (2009), "Household Travel Survey for Ireland", available at *www.cso.ie/surveysandmethodologies/surveyforms/documents/transport_tourism/pdf_docs/household_travel_q3_2009.pdf*.

ISPO – International Society for Prosthetics and Orthotics (2005), available at *www.ispoint.org/images/docs/education/WHOGuidelines.pdf*.

Izazola-Licea, J.A., C. Avila-Figueroa, D. Arán, S. Piola, R. Perdomo, P. Hernández, J.A. Saavedra-López and R. Valladares-Cardona (2002), "Country Response to HIV/AIDS: National Health Accounts on HIV/AIDS in Brazil, Guatemala, Honduras, México and Uruguay", AIDS 2002, Vol. 16, Suppl. 3, pp. 566-575

Kamp-Nielsen, I. (2002), "The Danish Health Account 1997-1999", Ministry of Interior and Health, available at *www.oecd.org/dataoecd/0/49/15781505.pdf*.

Kawiorska, D. (2008), "Guidelines for the Delineation into Public and Private Units", available at *www.oecd.org/dataoecd/38/14/40191715.pdf*.

KITH (2011), "International Classification of Primary Care", rev 2, available at *www.kith.no/templates/kith_WebPage____1111.aspx*.

Koechlin, F., L. Lorenzoni and P. Schreyer (2010), "Comparing Price Levels of Hospital Services Across Countries: Results of a Pilot Study", OECD Health Working Paper, No. 53, OECD Publishing, Paris, available at *www.oecd.org/els/health/workingpapers*.

Kristoffersen, A.E., V. Fønnebø and A.J. Norheim (2008), "Use of Complementary and Alternative Medicine Among Patients: Classification Criteria Determine Level of Use", *Journal of Alternative and Complementary Medicine*, Vol. 14, No. 8, pp. 911–919.

Kutzin, J. (2001), "A Descriptive Framework for Country-level Analysis of Health Care Financing Arrangements", *Health Policy*, Vol. 56, No. 3, pp. 171-204, Elsevier.

Kutzin, J. (2008), "Health Financing Policy: A Guide for Decision-makers", *Health Financing Policy Paper*, World Health Organization.

Lamberts, H. and M. Wood (2002), "The Birth of the International Classification of Primary Care (ICPC): Serendipity at the Border of Lac Léman", *Family Practice*, Vol. 19, No. 5, pp. 433-435.

Legido-Quigley, H. and M. McKee (2006), "Patient Mobility in the European Union – Drivers of Patient and Professional Mobility", Europe for Patients.

Lequiller, F. and D. Blades (2007), "Understanding National Accounts", OECD Publishing, Paris.

Lozano, R., C. Murray, A. Lopez and T. Satoh (2001), "Miscoding and Misclassification of Ischaemic Heart Disease Mortality", *Global Program on Evidence for Health Policy*, Discussion Paper No. 12, WHO, Geneva.

Mathers, C.D., A. Lopez, C. Stein, D. Ma Fat, C. Rao, M. Inoue, K. Shibuya, N. Tomijima, C. Bernard and H. Xu (2004), "Deaths and Disease Burden by Cause: Global Burden of Disease Estimates for 2001 by World Bank Country Groups", Disease Control Priorities Project, Working Paper No. 18.

McIntyre, D. (2007), "Learning from Experience: Health Care Financing in Low- and Middle-Income Countries", Global Forum for Health Research, Geneva, available from: *www.globalforumhealth.org/Site/000__Home.php*.

Mattoo, A., R.M. Stern and G. Zanini (2007), "A Handbook of International Trade in Services", Oxford University Press.

Médecins du Monde (2007), "Report and Recommendations, Improving Access to Healthcare for the Community's Most Vulnerable", Project London, UK.

Medscape Reference (accessed 05/2011), "Surgical Dressings", available at *http://emedicine.medscape.com/article/1127868-overview*.

Meerman, J. (1979), "Public Expenditure in Malaysia: Who Benefits and Why", Oxford University Press for the World Bank, New York.

Mosseveld, C.J.P.M. van (2003), "International Comparison of Health Care Expenditure, Existing Frameworks, Innovations and Data Use", Statistics Netherlands, Voorburg.

Mosseveld, C.J.P.M. van and J. M. Smit (2005), "Statistics Netherlands", Working Paper Health and Social Care Accounts 1998-2003.

Mossialos, E. and A. Dixon (2002), "Funding health care in Europe: Options for Europe", Open University Press, Buckingham, UK.

Murray, C.J.L. and D.B. Evans (2003), "Health Systems Performance Assessment. Debates, Methods and Empiricism", WHO, Geneva.

Netherlands Ministry of Health, Welfare and Sport (2005), "Health Insurance in the Netherlands. The new health insurance system from 2006".

Newhouse, J.P. (1992), "Medical Care Costs: How Much Welfare Costs", *Journal of Economic Perspectives*, Vol. 6, No. 3, pp. 3-21.

Nicolle, E. and I. Mathauer (2010), "Where and What Do They Hide?", WHO Discussion Paper, WHO, Geneva.

NIH – National Institutes of Health (2009), "The Use of Complementary and Alternative Medicine in the United States: Cost Data", US DHSS, available at *www.nccam.nih.gov*.

Nordic Innovation Centre (2009), "Nordic Collaboration in Health Services: A Feasibility Study on the Potentials and Barriers towards an Open Market for Health Services in the Nordic Countries", Copenhagen, available at *www.nordicinnovation.net/_img/nordic_collaboration_in_health_services_summary_report_web.pdf*.

Norman, G. (2003), "New Strategies in Disease and Utilization Management", Society of Actuaries, Spring Meeting, 22-24 June, San Francisco.

O'Donnell, O., E. van Doorslaer, R.P. Rannan-Eliya, A. Somanathan, S.R. Adhikari, B. Akkazieva, D. Harbianto, C.C. Garg, P. Hanvoravongchai, A.N. Herrin, M.N. Huq, S. Ibragimova, A. Karan, S.M. Kwon, G.M. Leung, J.F. Lu, Y. Ohkusa, B.R. Pande, R. Racelis, K. Tin, K. Tisayaticom, L. Trisnantoro, Q. Wan, B.M. Yang and Y. Zhao (2008), "Who Pays for Health Care in Asia?", *Journal of Health Economics*, Vol. 27, pp. 460-475.

O'Donnell, O., E. van Doorslaer, A.Wagstaff and M. Lindelow (2008), "Analyzing Health Equity Using Household Survey Data: A Guide to Techniques and Their Implementation", *WBI Learning Resources Series*, World Bank, Washington, D.C.

OECD (1977), "Public Expenditure on Health", OECD Studies in Resource Allocation No. 4, OECD Publishing, Paris.

OECD (1985), "Measuring Health Care 1960-1983, Expenditure, Costs and Performance", OECD Social Policy Studies No. 2, OECD Publishing, Paris.

OECD (1990), "Health Care Expenditure and Other Data", *Health Care Systems in Transition*, OECD Publishing, Paris.

OECD (1994), "The Measurement of Scientific and Technical Activities, Proposed Standard Practice for Surveys of Research and Experimental Development", *Frascati Manual*, OECD Publishing, Paris.

OECD (2000), *A System of Health Accounts*, OECD Publishing, Paris.

OECD (2001), *Measuring Expenditure on Health-related R&D*, OECD Publishing, Paris.

OECD (2002a), *Frascati Manual. Proposed Standard Practice for Surveys on Research and Experimental Development*, OECD Publishing, Paris.

OECD (2002b), *Measuring the Non-observed Economy: A Handbook*, OECD Publishing, Paris.

OECD (2004), *Towards High-performing Health Systems. Policy Studies*, OECD Publishing, Paris.

OECD (2006a), "The OECD Input-output Database", STI Working Paper No. 2006/8, OECD Publishing, Paris.

OECD (2006b), *OECD Reviews of Health Systems. Switzerland*, OECD Publishing, Paris.

OECD (2008), *Estimating Expenditure by Disease, Age and Gender under the System of Health Accounts (SHA) Framework*, unpublished, Paris.

OECD (2009), *Guide to Measuring the Information Society*, OECD Publishing, Paris.

OECD (2010), "Guidelines for Improving the Comparability and Availability of Private Health Expenditures Under the System of Health Accounts Framework", OECD Health Working Paper No. 52, OECD Publishing, Paris.

Orosz, E. and D. Morgan (2004), "SHA-based National Health Accounts in Thirteen OECD Countries: A Comparative Analysis", OECD Health Working Paper, No. 16, OECD Publishing, Paris.

PAHO – Pan American Health Organization (2005), "Satellite Health Account (SHA) Manual. Version 1", Health Policies and Systems Unit (HP) Strategic Health Development Area (SHD), Office of the Director of Program Management (DPM), PAHO, Washington D.C., available at *www.paho.org/spanish/ad/ge/chile06-background15.pdf.*

Pollack, A. (2003), "Who's Reading Your X-Ray?", *New York Times*, Published 16 November.

Peeples, L. (2009), "Following the Money; Where Do the Billions in Global Health Funds Come from, and Where Do They Go?", *Scientific American*, 19 June 2009 available at *www.scientificamerican.com/article.cfm?id=global-health-fund-tracking-philanthropy*.

Petrera, M. and A. Vicente (2008), "Conceptual and Practical Boundaries in Health Accounting", *Observatory of Health of Peru*, OECD Publishing, Paris.

Polder, J.J. (2001), "Cost of illness in the Netherlands: Description, Comparison and Projection", PhD. Thesis, Erasmus University, Rotterdam.

Polder, J.J., J. Takkern, W.J. Meerding, G.J. Kommer G.J. and L.J. Stokx (2002), "Cost of Illness in the Netherlands", RIVM, Bilthoven.

Polder, J.J. and P.W. Achterberg (2004), "Cost of Illness in the Netherlands", RIVM, Bilthoven.

Polder, J.J., J.J. Barendregt and J.A.M. van Oers (2007), "Health Care Costs in the Last Year of Life. The Dutch Experience", *Social Science and Medicine*, Vol. 63, No. 7, pp. 1720-1731.

Pomey, M.P., J.P. Poullier and B. Lejeune (2000), "Quel avenir pour le système de soins canadien?", *Santé Publique*, Paris, France.

Poos, M.J.J.C., J.M. Smit, J. Groen, G.J. Kommer and L.C.J. Slobbe (2008),"Cost of Illness in the Netherlands 2005", RIVM, Bilthoven.

Poullier, J.P. (1992), "Administrative Costs in Selected Industrialised Countries", *Health Care Financing Review*, Vol. 13, No. 4, pp. 167-172.

Poullier, J.P., P. Hernandez and K. Kawabata (2002), "National Health Accounts: Concepts, Data Sources and Methodology", WHO/EIP/02.47, WHO, Geneva.

Rannan-Eliya, R.P. and R. Wijesinghe (2006), "Global Review on Health and Social Care Expenditure and Resources for Older Persons in Developing Countries", WHO Kobe Centre, Kobe, Japan.

Rannan-Eliya, R.P. and A. Somanathan (2006), "Equity in Health and Health Care Systems in Asia", Elgar Companion to Health Economics, edited by A.M. Jones, Cheltenham, UK.

Rannan-Eliya, R.P. and L. Lorenzoni (2010), "Guidelines for Improving the Comparability and Availability of Private Health Expenditures Under the System of Health Accounts Framework", OECD Health Working Papers, No. 52, OECD Publishing, Paris.

Rice, D.P. (1967), "Estimating the Cost of Illness", *American Journal of Public Health*, Vol. 57, No. 3, pp. 424-440.

Robinson, M. and X. Zhang (2011a), "Traditional Medicines, Self-Medication, and OTC", *World Medicines Situation*, WHO, Geneva.

Robinson M. and X. Zhang (2011b), "Traditional Medicines: Global Situation, Issues and Challenges", *World Medicines Situation* 2011, WHO, Geneva, available at *www.who.int/medicines/areas/policy/world_medicines_situation/WMS_ch18_wTraditionalMed.pdf.*

Roehrig, C., G. Miller, C. Lake and J. Bryant (2009), "National Health Spending By Medical Condition, 1996–2005", *Health Affairs* (Millwood), Vol. 28, No. 2, pp. 358-367.

Rosen, A. and D. Cutler (2009), "Challenges in Building Disease-Based National Health Accounts", *Medical care*, Vol. 47, No. 7, Suppl. 1.

Salvador-Carulla, L., M. Poole, M. Bendeck, C. Romero and J.A. Salinas (2009), "Coding Long-term Care Services: eDESDE-LTC", *International Journal of Integrated Care*, Vol. 9, available at *http://ukpmc.ac.uk/abstract/PMC/2707571*.

Salvador-Carulla, L. and V. I. Gasca (2010), "Defining Disability, Functioning, Autonomy and Dependency in Person-centered Medicine and Integrated Care", *International Journal of Integrated Care*, Vol. 10, Suppl. 25.

Schieber, J.G. and J.P. Poullier (1989), "International Health Care Expenditure Trends: 1987", *Health Affairs* (Millwood), Vol. 8, No. 3, pp. 169-77.

Schneider, M. (1995), "Framework for the International Comparison of Health Expenditures and Financing", in C. Van Mosseveld and P. Van Son (eds.), *International Comparison of Health Care Data, Methodology Development and Application*, Kluwer Academic Publishers, Dordrecht, Netherlands, pp. 263-278.

Schneider, M., D. Kawiorska *et al.* (2002), "A System of Health Accounts in Poland", Office for Foreign Aid at the Ministry of Health, Warsaw.

Schreyer, P. (2008), "Output and Outcome – Measuring the Production of Non-market Services", Paper presented at the 30th meeting of the International Association for Research in Income and Wealth, Portoroz, Slovenia, available at *www.iariw.org*.

Schuster, M.A., E.A. McGlynn and R.H. Brook (2005), "How Good Is the Quality of Health Care in the United States?", *Milbank Quarterly*, Vol. 83, No. 4, pp. 843-895.

Scottish Executive Health Department (2008), "NHS Scotland Capital Accounting Manual 2007/08", Edinburgh, available at *www.fpma.scot.nhs.uk/manuals/cap_acc_manual_2007.pdf.*

Schmidt, R.A. and E.A. Pioch (2003), "Pills by Post? German Retail Pharmacies and the Internet", *British Food Journal*, Vol. 105, No. 9, pp. 618-633.

Smith, P.C. and A. Street (2007), "Measurement of Non-Market Output in Education and Health", CHE Research Paper No. 23, Centre for Health Economics, University of York.

SRI International (2008), "Global Spa Economy 2007", Global Spa Summit, May 2008.

Stache, D., T. Forster, M. Kuschel, C. Meißmer and P. Schmidt (2007), "Ausgaben des Staates nach Aufgabenbereichen – Datenbasis zur Beurteilung der Qualität der Staatsausgaben?", *Wirtschaft und Statistik*, Vol. 12/2007, pp. 1180-1197.

Stephano, R.-M. and W. Cook (2010), "The Medical Tourism Facilitator", Global Health Insurance Publications.

Swedish Association of Local Authorities and Regions and the National Board of Health and Welfare, Quality and Efficiency (2007), *Swedish Health Care; Regional Comparisons*, Stockholm.

Swiss Federal Statistical Office (2008), "Tourism Satellite Account for Switzerland, 2001 and 2005", FSO, Neuchatel.

Szulc, B. (1964), "Indices for Multiregional Comparisons", *Przeglad Statystyczny*, Vol. 3, pp. 239-254.

Techniker Krankenkasse (2009), "TK Europe Survey 2009: German Patients en Route to Europe", Corporate Development Department (UE) and the Scientific Institute for Benefit and Efficiency in Healthcare (WINEG).

Thai Board of Investment (2008), "A Medical Trade Valued at US$40 billion with a 20% Annual Growth",available at *www.boi.go.th/english/why/Medical.pdf.*

Thomson, S. and E. Mossialos (2009), "Private Health Insurance in the European Union", European Commission, Brussels.

Tomqvist, L. (1936), "The Bank of Finland's consumption price index", *Monthly Bulletin*, Vol. 10, Bank of Finland, pp. 1-8.

Triplett, J.E. (2003), "Integrating Cost-of-disease Studies into Purchasing Power Parities", *A Disease-based Comparison of Health Systems. What is Best and at What Cost?*, OECD Publishing, Paris.

UK ONS – United Kingdom Office of National Statistics (1997), "UK Input-Output Balances: Methodological Guide".

UN (1999). COFOG, United Nations Statistical Division, available at *http://unstats.un.org/unsd/cr/registry/regcst.asp?Cl=4.*

UN (2000), "Classifications of Expenditure According to Purpose: COFOG, COICOP, COPNI, COPP", Series M, No. 84, United Nations Statistical Division.

UN (2008a), "International Standard Industrial Classification of All Economic Activities", Rev.4, ISIC, United Nations Statistical Division.

UN (2008b), CPC Ver.2, Central Product Classification, Department of Economic and Social Affairs, Statistics Division, New York.

UN (2010), *Manual on Statistics of International Trade in Services 2010* (MSITS 2010), United Nations Statistical Division. Available at *http://unstats.un.org/unsd/statcom/doc10/BG-MSITS2010.pdf*

UN, OECD, Eurostat and UNWTO (2008), "Tourism Satellite Account: Recommended Methodological Framework".

United Nations Economic Commission for Europe (2008), "Non-observed Economy in National Accounts. Survey of Country Practices", United Nations, New York, Geneva.

UNESCO (1996), "International Standard Classification of Education (ISCED) 1997", UNESCO, Paris, available at *www.uis.unesco.org/TEMPLATE/pdf/isced/ISCED_A.pdf.*

UNESCO, OECD and Eurostat (1995), "Data Collection on Educational Statistics".

UNGASS – United Nations General Assembly Special Session, available at *www.unaids.org/en/dataanalysis/monitoringcountryprogress/.*

US Bureau of Economic Analysis (2009), "Updated Summary NIPA Methodologies", Washington.

Waldo, D.R. (1996), "Creating Health Accounts for Developed and Developing Countries", Human Development Department, World Bank, Washington D.C.

Wangberg, S., H. Andreassen, P. Kummervold, R. Wynn and T. Sørensen (2009), "Use of the Internet for Health Purposes: Trends in Norway 2000-2010", *Scandinavian Journal of Caring Sciences*, Vol. 23, pp. 691-696.

WCPT – World Confederation for Physical Therapy (2007), "Description of Physical Therapy", WCPT, London, available at *www.wcpt.org.*

WHO (2000), "World Health Report 2000: Health Systems: Improving Performance – Strengthened Health Systems Save More Lives", WHO, Geneva, available at *www.who.int/whr/2000/en/whr00_en.pdf.*

WHO (2001), "International Classification of Functioning, Disability and Health (ICF)", WHO, Geneva.

WHO (2002), "Essential Public Health Functions: The Role of Ministries of Health", WHO, Geneva.

WHO (2003), *Health Systems Performance Assessment: Debates, Methods and Empiricism*, C. Murray and D. Evans (eds.), WHO, Geneva, pp. 289-295.

WHO (2004), "International Statistical Classification of Disease and Related Health Problems: 10th Edition", WHO, Geneva, version for 2007 available at *http://apps.who.int/classifications/apps/icd/icd10online/.*

WHO (2005a), "Strengthened Health Systems Save More Lives. An Insight into WHO's European Health Systems' Strategy", WHO, Geneva, available at *www.euro.who.int/__data/assets/pdf_file/0011/78914/healthsys_savelives.pdf.*

WHO (2005b), "National Policy on Traditional Medicine and Regulation of Herbal Medicines", *Report of WHO Global Survey*, WHO, Geneva.

WHO (2005c), "Guidelines on Basic Training and Safety in Chiropractic ", WHO, Geneva, available at *http://apps.who.int/medicinedocs/en/m/abstract/Js14076e/.*

WHO (2005d), "International Shortlist for Hospital Morbidity Tabulation (ISHMT)", WHO, Geneva, available at *www.who.int/classifications/icd/implementation/morbidity/ishmt/en/index.html.*

WHO (2008a), "Closing the Gap in a Generation: Health Equity through Action on the Social Determinants of Health", Commission on Social Determinants of Health, Final Report, WHO, Geneva, available at *www.who.int/social_determinants/thecommission/finalreport/en/index.html.*

WHO (2008b), "Guide to Producing Regional Health Accounts", WHO, Geneva, available at *www.who.int/nha/developments/Guide%20to%20Producing%20Regional%20Health%20Accounts.pdf.*

WHO (2008c), "Conditional Cash Transfers", WHO, Geneva, available at *http://apps.who.int/rhl/effective_practice_and_organizing_care/Support3/en/.*

WHO (2009), "Global Status Report on Road Safety", WHO, Geneva, available at *http://whqlibdoc.who.int/publications/2009/9789241563840_eng.pdf.*

WHO (2011a), "The World Medicines Situation 2011; Medicines Prices, Availability and Affordability", WHO, Geneva, available at *www.who.int/medicines/areas/policy/world_medicines_situation/WMS_ch6_wPricing_v6.pdf.*

WHO (2011b), "Guidelines for ATC classification and DDD assignment", available at *www.whocc.no/atc_ddd_publications/guidelines/.*

WHO, World Bank and USAID (2003), "Guide to Producing National Health Accounts with Special Applications for Low-income and Middle-income Countries", WHO, Geneva, available at *www.who.int/nha/docs/English_PG.pdf*.

WICC (2011), "Wonca International Classification Committee: International Classification of Primary Care", available at *www.globalfamilydoctor.com/wicc/edu.html*.

Yip, W. and A. Mahal (2008), "The Health Care Systems of China and India: Performance and Future Challenges", *Health Affairs* (Millwood), Vol. 27, No. 4, pp. 921-932.

Yip, W. and P. Berman (2001), "Targeted Health Insurance in a Low Income Country and its Impact on Access and Equity in Access: Egypt's School-health Insurance", *Health Economics*, Vol. 10, No. 3, pp. 207-220.

Zida, A., M.P. Bertone and L. Lorenzetti (2010), "Using National Health Accounts to Inform Policy Change in Burkina Faso", Policy Brief, Health Systems 20/20, Bethesda, MD.

Zweifel, P., S. Felder and A. Werblow (2004), "Population Aging and Health Care Expenditures: New Evidence on the Red Herring", *Geneva Papers on Risk and Insurance*, Vol. 29, No. 4.

ANNEX A

Relationship of the ICHA to Other Classifications

Introduction

Annex A aims to support the mapping of categories of the three core classifications of SHA 2011 with international economic classifications used within the frameworks of the System of National Accounts (SNA) and the European System of Social Protection Statistics (ESSPROS). Each of the three core classifications of SHA 2011 – ICHA-HC, ICHA-HP and ICHA-HF – focuses on specific characteristics of actors (organisations) and transactions that differ from those of the other classifications. This annex briefly discusses some of the conceptual issues involved and then presents correspondence tables with the classification categories of the SNA and ESSPROS. Despite similar terms and some overlap with the main categories, there is no one-to-one relationship between the classifications of SHA and those of the two other statistical systems. Both users and compilers should also be aware that the international classifications undergo regular revisions and can be differently applied by countries. The same holds for the actors (organisations) used as statistical units in SHA and the economic entities (institutional units) used in SNA. The cross-tables of this annex, therefore, can only serve as a tentative guide to map the different classifications. Furthermore, the classifications discussed are not the only available classifications in the statistical systems of the countries.

The classifications of SNA occupy a central position in economic statistics because activities of the whole economy are either classified according to the industries and sectors of the economy, or structured by the goods and services produced and their uses by purpose, which includes the production and consumption of the health care sector. In addition, health activities captured in some of the more specialised statistical systems, such as the balance of payments statistics, or employment in health care classified by labour force statistics, are themselves integrated into the System of National Accounts data. Not only are the general aggregates of SNA, such as gross domestic product (GDP), of interest to SHA compilers, but also specific health care aggregates of SNA. The analysis of health accounts data used in conjunction with SNA often refers to the share of GDP devoted to health expenditure as one of the key indicators of health accounts. Current health care expenditure of SHA, presented as a percentage of GDP, exhibits the share of consumption of health care by the resident population in relation to national income. Another indicator is the share of public expenditure on health care as a percentage of total government spending. This shows the financial burden of health care expenditures on total government funds. In the following, specific health care aggregates of SNA are outlined and discussed from the perspective of the boundary of SHA, while the accounting links to the aggregates of SNA are presented in Annex B.

The correspondence tables outlined in this annex follow the structure of the SHA 2011 Manual and are built around the tri-axial relationship between health care functions, provision and financing. They distinguish between:

- The functional approach used in SHA (Chapter 5) and that of SNA related to the consumption of health care (description and demarcation in relation to the classification used in ESA/SNA[1], including COFOG, COICOP and COPNI);
- The functional approach used in SHA and ESSPROS (description and demarcations in relation to the classification of health risks/health benefits of ESSPROS;
- The classification of health care providers ICHA-HP (Chapter 6) and the activity classification of the ISIC/NACE related to health care;
- The structure of financing schemes of health care ICHA-HF (Chapter 7) and the institutional sectors of the SNA that correspond with the financing agents (FA) of SHA.

Figure A.1.1 shows in an illustrative way some of the potential linkages that can be made between classifications of the core accounting framework of SHA and international classifications used by other statistical systems that encompass information related to health care expenditure. From SNA perspective, the top of the triangle represents final demand for health care goods and services by residents, while the bottom right illustrates the supply side of health care. Supply and demand are balanced in SNA in the goods and service accounts from the perspective of the whole economy to include imports, exports, accumulation and intermediate use. To balance these flows, the classification of products is used (see Annex E). The second classification used in SNA to structure supply and use is the Industrial classifications of economic activities (ISIC), which classifies enterprises and establishments into groups of industrial branches. Furthermore, to analyse economic behaviour, these enterprises and establishments are classified as mutually exclusive "institutional units" and grouped into "institutional sectors" in the sector accounts of the SNA. The providers in SHA and the institutional sectors of SNA could be linked by grouping the providers according to SNA rules. However, one should note that SHA classifies each financing organisation (except households) into two separate statistical units – providers of administration (HP.7) and financing schemes (HF) – while SNA classifies each organisation as only one institutional unit grouped into one of the five institutional sectors and further subsectors (see the explanation to Table A.1.12).[2]

The bottom left of the triangle shows the potential relationship of the financing interface with the SNA Classification of Institutional Sectors and the Government Finance Statistics (GFS) Classification of Revenues. As outlined later in this annex, the financial schemes (HF) and financing agents (FA) used in SHA are not identical to the financial corporations used in the SNA sector classification (see Table A.1.11). The international guidelines on the GFS (IMF, 2001) are harmonised as much as possible with those of the SNA. Both the GFS and SNA define economic entities in terms of institutional units that are capable of owning assets, incurring liabilities, and engaging in economic activities and transactions with other entities in their own right. These characteristics render institutional units a subject of economic and statistical interest that can be satisfied by the compilation of a full set of accounts, including balance sheets (see Annex B).

The correspondence tables presented in this annex draw attention to international classifications, which can be considered as a minimum structure of expenditures. National statistical systems translate and/or adapt structures from international systems into the national statistical environment in practice. However, while in certain statistical domains

Figure A.1.1. **Correspondence between classifications of the SNA/ESSPROS and SHA**

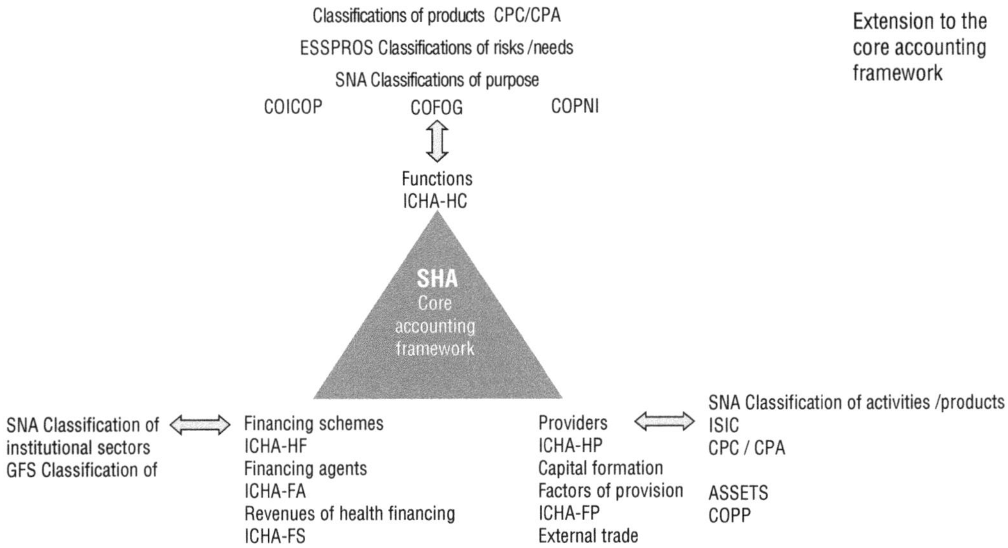

Source: IHAT for SHA 2011.

national systems may offer more detailed structures than those required within the international classifications framework, in others data feasibility might be more limited for various reasons, including the historical development of statistical systems, different economic and social structures or policy priorities. Therefore, the correspondence tables presented give only a rough guide that might be further developed depending on national conditions.

Health care aggregates of the SNA and ESSPROS and their relation to SHA

Health care aggregates of other statistical systems such as SNA and ESSPROS differ from those of SHA due to the scope of health care goods and services included, the types of transactions selected and the estimation methods used. In the following, a short overview is given about the main deviations between SNA aggregates and SHA. More detailed information is available in the correspondence tables presented later in this annex.

Ten aggregates of SNA and ESSPROS are presented, which show health care consumption, provision and financing based on the compilations of these other two statistical systems. The aggregates are not necessarily different; however, their interpretation varies depending on the chosen perspective. For example, SNA aggregates (1) and (2) of Table A.1.1 present the same SNA aggregate from different perspectives of consumption. The two ESSPROS aggregates (5) of Table A.1.1 and (10) of Table A.1.4 are also identical, except that in the first case the interpretation is related to consumption and in the second case to financing. As the classifications vary according to the perspective or purpose of the classification, the respective aggregates express these different approaches.

SNA *and* ESSPROS *health care aggregates by function (purposes)*

Based on the classifications by purpose, SNA allows the compilation of several aggregates related to health care consumption. Table A.1.1 presents four of them: (1) Final consumption expenditure on health, (2) Actual final consumption of health care, (3) Actual final individual consumption of health care and (4) Actual final collective consumption of health care. Any reflection about the comparability of these SNA aggregates with SHA aggregates should always consider the objectives of the accounts (final consumption vs. actual consumption), the types of transactions involved (purchase of consumption goods and services vs. purchases of capital goods) and the definition of health care (health care vs. non-health care).

Two of them, *i.e.* **(1) Final consumption expenditure of health care** and **(2) Actual final consumption of health care,** are compiled from different perspectives: "who spends" (final consumption expenditure, which relates to the use of disposable income account) and "who consumes" (actual final consumption, which relates to the use of adjusted disposable income account). The aggregates of the two concepts are the same (see Box B.1.1 of Annex B). However, in the first case all health care expenditures incurred by general government are presented as consumption of government. In the second case, all those general government expenditures that are by nature services delivered to individuals are presented as consumption of households. As a consequence, the breakdown of expenditures by purpose remains the same in both aggregates, but they differ in the breakdown of consumption by the institutional sectors (Households, NPISH, General Government). Government and NPISH expenditures of individual consumption are also named "social transfers in kind".[3]

Both aggregates (1) Final consumption expenditure of health care and (2) Actual final consumption of health care deviate from the SHA aggregate "Current health expenditure" due to a different health care boundary, which results in several activities not being covered under the COFOG and COICOP. Besides occupational health care and "remunerated" unpaid household production, the SHA borderlines in relation to social care have to be considered (see Table A.1.1).

The aggregates **(3) Actual individual consumption of health care** and **(4) Actual collective consumption of health care** are sub-aggregates[4] of (2) Actual final consumption of health care. National statistics usually provide further information about the breakdown of (3) Actual individual consumption of health care based on COICOP and actual collective consumption of health care based on COFOG. One should note that some social transfers in kind, accounted under (3), may be receivable by non-residents, for example, emergency medical treatment in a public hospital for a non-resident tourist, but SNA assumes that the figures involved are likely to be very small compared with total social transfers in kind and that all social transfers in kind can be shown as payable to resident households.[5] SHA departs from this assumption and considers as actual individual consumption of households only those transfers in kind that are actually provided to residents and consumed by residents. Therefore, from the viewpoint of the SHA: the aggregates of actual final consumption and final consumption expenditures as well as the sub-aggregates are not identical.[6]

The SNA aggregate P.42 Actual collective consumption of health care covers collective health care services as part of HC.6 Preventive care and HC.7 Governance and health system & financing administration. One should note that some countries classify social health insurance administration under COFOG 10 Social protection, and some under COFOG 01 General administration.

The last health care aggregate discussed here is **(5) In-kind social protection expenditures on Sickness/Health care** based on ESSPROS. This aggregate also differs from

Table A.1.1. **SNA and ESSPROS health care aggregates related to consumption**

No	Aggregate	Statistical system	Compilation	Deviation from SHA
(1)	Final consumption expenditure on health care	SNA	P.31 Individual consumption expenditure on health + P.32 Collective consumption expenditure on health = P31-Housholds individual consumption of health + P31-NPISH* individual consumption of health + P31-Government individual consumption of health (part of COFOG 07) P32-Government collective consumption of health (part of COFOG 07)	SHA additionally includes *a)* Occupational health care (intermediate consumption within establishments) minus an estimated share of occupational health in the net administration of health providers and other medical industries. *b)* "Remunerated" unpaid household production in the form of transfer payments (social benefits in cash) for home care of sick, disabled and elderly persons provided by family members for the purpose of LTC. *c)* "Health care activities" not classified as health care in SNA, *e.g.* health care in social care institutions, or administration of social insurance. The borderlines in the SNA are determined by COICOP and COFOG.
(2)	Actual final consumption of health care	SNA	P.41 Actual individual consumption of health care + P.42 Actual collective consumption of health care = 06 COICOP Households +13.2 COICOP NPISH +14.2 COICOP Government + COFOG 07.5 and 07.6	The SNA aggregate on health does not comprise expenditures covered in categories captured by other purposes, *e.g.* expenditures for private insurance administration. See Tables A.1.5 and A.1.6 for detailed correspondence between HC and COICOP, COFOG.
(3)	Actual individual consumption of health care	SNA	06 COICOP Households +13.2 COICOP NPISH +14.2 COICOP Government	The SNA aggregate includes expenditures reimbursed by private insurance (excluding administration). It includes social transfers in kind as consumption of households while final consumption expenditures cover social transfers in kind under government consumption.
(4)	Actual collective consumption of health care	SNA	COFOG 07.5 and 07.6	The SNA aggregate on collective consumption might deviate from collective consumption in SHA, which encompasses health preventive programmes (part of HC.6), and health system financing/administration (HC.7). Research and development in health (COFOG 07.5) is not recorded under the SHA core framework but as memorandum items in the capital account.
(5)	In-kind social protection expenditures on Sickness/ Health care	ESSPROS	Sickness/Health care benefit in kind	ESSPROS aggregate covers in-kind benefits related to direct provision and reimbursement of health care goods and services although due to different health care boundary, the scope of health care goods and services in ESSPROS is limited as compared to SHA 2011 (*e.g.* SHA includes expenditure related to collective preventive programme, long-term care (health) services provided at home by family members, the latter being recorded under Sickness/Health care benefit in cash. Other ESSPROS functions may comprise expenditure that is included as health care goods and services in SHA 2011.

* SNA 2008 allows P32-NPISH* collective consumption of health. See SNA 2008, p. 598: "It has been recognized that it is possible for NPISHs to have collective consumption though no excessive efforts should be made to try to identify such instances."

Source: IHAT for SHA 2011.

SHA 2011 in the scope of health care goods and services included, as it covers only expenditure directed – via social benefits in kind – to individuals. Consequently, by definition neither out-of-pocket expenditure of households nor expenditure on collective services related to preventive care are covered. Furthermore, it excludes care allowances (cash benefits) in the case of long-term care (health) to households as providers of home care. The breakdown of health care expenditure and the level of information details in both statistical systems vary significantly, so there is not a one-to-one relationship. Both SHA and ESSPROS use the statistical information of financing schemes, although the scope of the schemes is not the same. In ESSPROS, benefits are made through collectively-organised schemes by government and/or any collective agreements, irrespectively of whether they are publicly or privately administered. [See correspondence between the functional classification (ICHA-HC) of SHA and ESSPROS.] Therefore any individual agreements, *i.e.* private households or individuals who insure themselves solely on their own initiative (*e.g.* voluntary private health insurance, out-of-pocket expenditures) are not taken into account by ESSPROS. A later section of this annex describes in greater detail the correspondence between ICHA-HC and ESSPROS.

The health aggregate of COFOG classifies all types of government outlays for the purpose of health.[7] It comprises the complete set of different public expenditures, like local government expenditures for employees, waste management, energy, depreciation, etc. in public hospitals, purchases of social health insurance funds for private hospital treatment, central government expenditures for gross capital formation, subsidies, property income, securities and shares or equity, loans, capital transfers, as well as social benefits in cash and other current transfers, pharmaceutical expenditures and expenditures for types of medical durables, non-durables and equipment (see Table A.1.2). The expenditure amount exhibited under the category 07 Health of COFOG is bigger than that exhibited under category 14.2 COICOP Government, because the latter captures only expenditures for individual final consumption (see Table A.1.2, "Government outlays on health (COFOG 07)" and "Final consumption expenditure on health (COICOP Government)".

SNA health care aggregates by provider industry

From the perspective of health care provision, the SNA compiles several aggregates based on the ISIC (rev. 4) classification of economic activities, in particular those recorded under category 86 Human health activities, *i.e.* **(6) Output of production of human health activities** at basic prices and **(7) Gross value added of human health activities**. The measure of output presented by the SNA for human health activities according to the borderlines of division 86 of the ISIC encompasses 8610 Hospital activities, 8620 Medical and dental practice activities and 8690 Other human health activities, although each of these items may include non-health activities (provided as secondary activities) or certain services such as cosmetic surgery provided with an aesthetic purpose, which in both cases are excluded from the health care boundary of SHA 2011. On the other hand, the SHA concept is broader than that of the ISIC (division 86), as it relates to several other ISIC classes, *e.g.* 8710 Residential nursing care facilities, 4772 Retail sale of pharmaceuticals, 8412 Regulation of activities of providing health care and 6512 Non-life insurance. In general, the estimate for the human health activities aggregate as defined by ISIC division 86 is less than SHA current health expenditures. Table A.1.10 presents the correspondence between the classification of health care providers ICHA-HP (Chapter 6) and the ISIC activity classification related to health care.

Other deviations result from the fact that the aggregate "Output of production" of SNA includes production for non-residents, while SHA focuses on the consumption of residents. Furthermore, there are different price concepts. Intermediate inputs and final consumption are measured at purchasers' prices, whereas output is measured at either basic prices or producers' prices. In contrast, SHA focuses on purchasers' prices, with some adjustments.

The aggregate **(7) Gross value added of human health activities** at basic prices is the central measure in the SNA, derived as the balancing item in the production account. Gross value added is itself equal to output (valued at basic prices) minus intermediate consumption (valued at purchasers' prices).[8] Gross value added represents the

Table A.1.2. **Government outlays on health (COFOG) according to categories in Austria, 2009 (in million EUR)**

Code	ESA 1995 (general government)	7.0 Health	7.1 Medical products, appliances and equipment	7.2 Outpatient services	7.3 Hospital services	7.4 Public health services	7.5 R&D Health	7.6 Health *n.e.c.*
P.5 +	Gross capital formation +	142.6	–	25.0	63.5	3.5	24.4	26.2
K.2	Acquisitions and disposals of non-financial non-produced assets							
D.1	Compensation of employees	2117.7	0.0	406.0	514.4	178.3	309.5	709.4
D.3	Subsidies	4665.0	23.9	133.9	4456.5	0.8	49.8	
D.4	Property income							
D.62 +	Social benefits other than social transfers in kind	142.6	–	25.0	63.5	3.5	24.4	26.2
D.6311 +	Social security benefits, reimbursements	13769.6	3281.5	3999.3	6328.1	160.7		
D.63121 +	Other social security benefits in kind, for which the service is produced by market producers and purchased by general government units							
D.63131	Social assistance benefits in kind, for which the service is produced by market producers and purchased by general government units							
P.2	Intermediate consumption	836.8	2.3	109.0	244.1	161.3	112.7	207.4
D.29 +	Other taxes on production, payable +	60.9	–	11.4	17.7	4.3	9.3	18.2
D.5 +	Current taxes on income and wealth, payable +							
D.8	Adjustment for the change in the net equity of households in pension funds reserves							
D.7	Social benefits other than social transfers in kind	293.0	12.8	114.8	114.6	42.8	4.3	3.7
D.9	Capital transfers	636.0	–	16.6	615.5	1.1	2.9	
	Government outlays (expenditure =TE) on health (COFOG 07)	22521.6	3320.4	4816.0	12354.5	552.8	512.9	964.9
TE	Total government expenditure (all COFOGs)	143526.7						
P.3	**Final consumption expenditure on health care (COICOP – government)**	15541.2	3283.8	4115.0	6359.4	448.2	368.3	966.6
P.31	Individual government consumption expenditure on health care	13758.2						
P.32	Collective government consumption expenditure on health care	1334.9						
P.3	Final consumption expenditure (COIPCOP - government)	54610.7						

Source: Eurostat database.

Table A.1.3. **SNA health care aggregates by provider industry**

No	Aggregate	Statistical system	Compilation	Deviation from SHA
(6)	Output of production of human health activities at basic prices (or producers' prices)	SNA	86 ISIC	This SNA aggregate does not cover several activities included in health, *e.g.* retail sales of pharmaceuticals; see Table A.1.10 for detail correspondence between the ICHA-HP and ISIC. Included are health care services utilised by non-residents (exports); not included are imported health care services.
(7)	Gross value added of human health activities at basic prices	SNA	86 ISIC	This SNA aggregate does not cover the value added of several activities included in health, *e.g.* retail sales of pharmaceuticals; see above. See also Chapter 10 and Annex B.

Source: IHAT for SHA 2011.

contribution of labour and capital to the production process. Although the core account of the SHA does not provide any measure of value added, one should be aware that the measure of final consumption in the SNA is also a measure of value added created by economic activities.

The specific SNA health care aggregates, shown in Table A.1.3, are not defined by the classification of purpose, but by the classification of activities. At the level of activities and products, usually the most detailed information can be found in the SNA. Table A.1.7 presents the correspondence between the functional classification of the SHA and the Central Product Classification (CPC) of the SNA.

SNA *and* ESSPROS *health care aggregates by financing side*

A further set of specific SNA health care aggregates can be derived for the financing side. To do this, the classifications of purpose in combination with the classification of institutional sectors are relevant.

The SNA exhibits the structure of health care financing ("who spends?") in the breakdown of final consumption expenditures by institutional sectors, households, NPISH and government, together usually expressed as private consumption[9] and the consumption of government.

The SNA aggregate **(8) Household final consumption expenditure on health** corresponds to a large extent with expenditure recorded under several categories of the financing schemes under the SHA 2011 classification, that is. HF.1.1.2 Compulsory private insurance + HF.1.3 Compulsory medical savings accounts + HF.2 Voluntary health care payment schemes + HF.3 Household out-of pocket payment. As by definition, corporations in the SNA do not record consumption, the expenditures of private insurance and medical savings accounts are handled as reimbursements.[10]

Reimbursements[11] of private health insurance are the settlement of a claim by the insurance company, which is treated as a current transfer to the claimant, and as a consequence is included in the SNA aggregate of the individual consumption of households. Therefore, out-of-pocket-financed health expenditures in SHA form a less comprehensive aggregate than household expenditures in SNA. In SHA, the term "Household out-of-pocket payment (HF.3)" includes direct expenditures, excluding cost-sharing and cost-sharing with third-party payers.

The SNA aggregate **(9) Government outlays on health** derived from COFOG 07 is a comprehensive measure of publicly-financed health expenditures. It exhibits all government outlays with the function "health". However, it does not correspond to current health care expenditures financed by governmental schemes (HF.1.1) and social health insurance schemes (HF.1.2.1). This is for three reasons: *i)* the health consumption boundary of COFOG differs from that of SHA, *e.g.* in the personal care services to be included; *ii)* the specific focus of SHA is on the consumption of the resident population; and *iii)* COFOG comprises outlays for transactions of non-consumption purposes as *e.g.* capital formation.

The aggregate (10) In-kind social protection financing of Sickness/Health care of ESSPROS is equal to (5) In-kind social protection expenditures on Sickness/Health care.

Table A.1.4. SNA and ESSPROS health care aggregates related to financing

No	Aggregate	Statistical system	Compilation	Deviation from SHA
(8)	Household final consumption expenditure on health	SNA	06 COICOP Households	06 COICOP includes expenditures of households not covered in Household out-of-pocket payment (HF.3) as pre-payments for medical care or pharmaceuticals that are reimbursed by private insurance companies. COICOP 06 is therefore a more comprehensive aggregate. In SNA, the compilation of household expenditures sometimes includes NPISH (02 COPNI).
(9)	Government outlays on health	SNA	07 COFOG	07 COFOG aggregate relates to governmental schemes (HF.1.1) and social health insurance schemes (HF.1.2.1), but includes transactions for non-consumption purposes as capital formation, outlays for non-residents, and scope of services covered.
(10)	In-kind social protection financing of Sickness/Health care	ESSPROSS	1. Sickness/Health care (benefit in kind)	ESSPROS includes governmental schemes (HF.1.1) and social health insurance schemes (HF.1.2.1) as well as compulsory private insurance schemes (HF.1.2.2). ESSPROS aggregate does not include voluntary private insurance (only compulsory) and out-of-pocket payments.

Source: IHAT for SHA 2011.

Correspondence between the functional classifications of SHA and SNA

Overview

The SNA applies several "functional" classifications to the basic transactions of consumption in order to classify these transactions by purpose, as health, education, defence, etc. The main classifications by purpose are:

- The Classification of the Individual Consumption by Purpose (COICOP);
- The Classification of the Functions of Government (COFOG);
- The Classification of the Purposes of Non-profit Institutions Serving Households (COPNI);[12] and
- The Classification of Outlays of Producers by Purpose (COPP).

The first three classifications can be used for partial analysis of consumption of health care. These three classifications are compatible with each other with respect to the health care services and goods covered. However, they refer to different institutional sectors (households, government and NPISH), meaning that the calculation of a total for the whole economy has to consider these differences (SNA 2008, 2.154). The last of these four classifications (COPP) of transactions by purpose of the SNA is used for the classification of expenditures for intermediate consumption, and therefore not presented here. To identify all transactions related to a particular "functional" activity, such as, for example, health, the SNA recommends developing this classification further, outside the central framework in a satellite account. Table A.1.5 gives a general overview of the correspondence between categories of health care in SHA and in the first three SNA classifications mentioned above.

The health parts of the three classifications, COICOP, COFOG and COPNI expenditures, follow similar patterns by structuring expenditures into classes of health care goods and classes of health care services, although they use different codes and levels of detail. It is also important to note the overlapping between the classifications in Table A.1.5. This is because COICOP has to be able to serve the compilation of consumption following the two approaches: final consumption expenditures and actual final consumption. In the case of final consumption expenditures, the columns (1), (4) and (5) are used, and in the case of actual final consumption expenditures, the columns (1), (2) and (3) and the collective consumption part of column (4). Please note that the intention of Table A.1.5 is to present the relationship between HC and these international classifications of the SNA, but not the relationship of these international classifications with each other. For example, HC.6.1 Preventive care relates to 14.2.8 Public health services with reference to "individual services" (IS), as specified in COFOG 07.4.0, but one also has to consider in the compilation of HC.6.1 the part of expenditure classified under the COFOG Code 07.6.0 Health *n.e.c.* as a preventive type of "collective services" (CS) that can then be mapped with the collective part of the information, education and counselling programmes (IEC).

The COICOP is used to classify the *individual* consumption expenditure not only of households, but also of Non-profit Institutions Serving Households (NPISH) and of General Government:[13]

- Divisions 01 to 12: Individual consumption expenditure of households;
- Division 13: Individual consumption expenditure of NPISH;
- Division 14: Individual consumption expenditure of general government.

The purpose breakdowns within Divisions 13 and 14 of the COICOP replicate the purposes in the classifications for NPISH and general government, that is to say, in COPNI and COFOG respectively. Thus, once the consumption expenditures of NPISH and general government have been classified according to the COPNI and COFOG, the individual consumption expenditures in these two classifications can be transferred directly into Divisions 13 and 14 of the COICOP.

In the health division, the COICOP broadly distinguishes between three groups: medical goods, outpatient services and hospital services. The same holds for the COFOG and COPNI. But the COFOG distinguishes three additional groups: Public health services, R&D Health and Health *n.e.c.*; the COPNI includes three additional groups: Public health services, R&D Health and Other health services.

In all three classifications, there is a quite good correspondence between medical products for outpatients (HC.5) and medical products listed under 06.1 COICOP (households), 02.1 COPNI and 07.1 COFOG, although there is not a perfect match between the HC and the COICOP, COPNI and COFOG.[14] With regard to outpatient and inpatient medical services, the three classifications do not provide subcategories of curative, rehabilitative and preventive services, and are still too aggregated for the purposes of SHA.

COFOG (Health 07)

In the COFOG, government outlays on health are grouped into six groups and 14 classes including expenditure on goods and services provided to *individual* persons and services provided on a *collective* basis. Expenditures on individual services are allocated to groups (07.1) through (07.4); expenditures on collective services are assigned to groups (07.5) and (07.6). Collective health services are concerned with matters such as administration and operation of government agencies engaged in applied research and experimental development

Table A.1.5. **Cross-check of the classification of health care functions (ICHA-HC) with SNA classifications**

ICHA-HC	Title of headings	COICOP Households (1)	COICOP NPISH (2)	COICOP Government (3)	COFOG (4)	COPNI (5)
HC.1	**Curative care**					
HC.1.1	Inpatient curative care	06.3	13.2.7	14.2.7	07.3	02.3
HC.1.2	Day curative care	06.3	13.2.7	14.2.7	07.3	02.3
HC.1.3	Outpatient curative care	06.2	–	–	07.2	02.2
HC.1.3.1	General curative outpatient care	06.2.1	13.2.4	14.2.4	07.2.1	02.2.1
HC.1.3.2	Dental curative outpatient care	06.2.2	13.2.5	14.2.5	07.2.3	02.2.2
HC.1.3.3	Specialised curative outpatient care	06.2.1	13.2.6	14.2.4	07.2.2	02.2.1
HC.1.4	Home-based curative care	06.2.1, 06.2.3	13.2.4, 13.2.6	14.2.4, 14.2.6	0.7.2.1, 0.7.2.3, 07.2.4	02.2.1, 02.2.3
HC.2	**Rehabilitative care**					
HC.2.1	Inpatient rehabilitative care	06.3	13.2.7	14.2.7	07.3	02.3
HC.2.2	Rehabilitative day care	06.3	13.2.7	14.2.7	07.3	02.3
HC.2.3	Rehabilitative outpatient care	06.2.3, 06.2.1	13.2.6, 13.2.4	14.2.6, 14.2.4	07.2.2, 07.2.4	02.2.1 02.2.3
HC.2.4	Rehabilitative home-based care	06.2.3	13.2.6	14.2.6	07.2.4, 07.3.4	02.2.3
HC.3	**Long-term care (health)**					
HC.3.1	Long-term inpatient care (health)	06.3, 12.4.0	13.2.7	14.2.7	07.3, 10.1.2	02.3
HC.3.2	Day cases of long-term care (health)	06.3, 12.4.0	13.2.7	14.2.7	07.3	02.3
HC.3.3	Outpatient long-term care (health)	06.3, 12.4.0	13.2.7	14.2.7	07.2.4	02.2.3
HC.3.4	Home-based long-term care (health)	06.3, 06.2.3, 12.4.0	13.2.7, 13.2.6	14.2.7, 14.2.6	07.2.4, 10.1.1, 10.2.0	02.2.3, 02.3
HC.4	**Ancillary services non-specified by function**					
HC.4.1	Laboratory services	06.2.3	13.2.6	14.2.6	07.2.4	02.2.3
HC.4.2	Imaging services n.s.f.	06.2.3	13.2.6	14.2.6	07.2.4	02.2.3
HC.4.3	Patient transportation n.s.f.	06.2.3, 06.3	13.2.6, 13.2.7	14.2.6, 14.2.7	07.2.4 ,7.3	02.2.3, 02.3
HC.5	**Medical goods non-specified by function**					
HC.5.1	Pharmaceuticals and other medical non–durable goods					
HC.5.1.1	Prescribed medicines	06.1.1	13.2.1	14.2.1	07.1.1	02.1.1
HC.5.1.2	Over-the-counter drugs (OTC)	06.1.1	13.2.1	14.2.1	07.1.1	02.1.1
HC.5.1.3	Other medical non durable goods	06.1.2	13.2.2	14.2.2	07.1.2	02.1.2
HC.5.2	Therapeutic appliances and other medical goods					
HC.5.2.1	Glasses and other vision products	06.1.3	13.2.3	14.2.3	07.1.3	02.1.3
HC.5.2.2	Orthopaedic appliances and other prosthetics	06.1.3	13.2.3	14.2.3	07.1.3	02.1.3
HC.5.2.3	Hearing aids	06.1.3	13.2.3	14.2.3	07.1.3	02.1.3
HC.5.2.4	All other medical durables including medical technical devices	06.1.3	13.2.3	14.2.3	07.1.3	02.1.3
HC.6	**Preventive care**					
HC.6.1	Information, education and counselling programmes		13.2.8	14.2.8	07.4, 07.6	02.4
HC.6.2	Immunisation programmes		13.2.8	14.2.8	07.4, 07.6	02.4
HC.6.3	Early disease detection programmes		13.2.8	14.2.8	07.4, 07.6	02.4

Table A.1.5. **Cross-check of the classification of health care functions (ICHA-HC) with SNA classifications** *(cont.)*

ICHA-HC	Title of headings	COICOP Households (1)	COICOP NPISH (2)	COICOP Government (3)	COFOG (4)	COPNI (5)
HC.6.4	Health condition monitoring programmes		13.2.8	14.2.8	07.4, 07.6	02.4
HC.6.5	Epidemiologic surveillance and risk and disease control programmes		13.2.8	–	07.6	02.4
HC 6.6	Preparing for disaster and emergency response programmes		13.2.8	–	07.6	02.4
HC.7	**Governance and health system & financing administration**					
HC.7.1	Governance and health system administration:	–	13.2.8	–	07.6.0	02.6
HC.7.2	Administration of health financing	12.5.3	13.2.8	–	07.6.0	02.6
HC.9	**Other health care services not elsewhere classified (*n.e.c.*)**					
HC.RI	**Reporting items**					
HC.RI.1	Total pharmaceutical expenditure (TPE)					
HC.RI.2	Traditional, Complementary and Alternative Medicines (TCAM)					
HC.RI.2.1	Inpatient TCAM					
HC.RI.2.2	Outpatient and home-based TCAM					
HC.RI.2.3	TCAM goods					
HC.RI.3	Prevention and public health services					
HC.RI.3.1	Maternal and child health, family planning and counselling	–	13.2.8	14.2.8	07.4	02.4
HC.RI.3.2	School health services	–	13.2.8	14.2.8	07.4	02.4
HC.RI.3.3	Prevention of communicable diseases	–	13.2.8	14.2.8	07.4	02.4
HC.RI.3.4	Prevention of non-communicable diseases	–	13.2.8	14.2.8	07.4	02.4
HC.RI.3.5	Occupational health care	–	–	–	–	–
HC.RI.3.6	All other miscellaneous public health services	–	13.2.8	14.2.8	07.4 ,07.6.0	02.4
HC.R	**Health care-related classes**					
HC.R.1	Long-term care (social)	12.4.0	13.5.0	14.5.0	10.1.1, 10.1.2 10.2.0, 10.7.0 10.9.0	05.1
HC.R.1.1	In-kind long-term social care	12.4.0	13.5.0	14.5.0	10.1.1, 10.1.2 10.2.0, 10.7.0 10.9.0	05.1
HC.R.1.2	Long-term social care cash benefits			14.5.0	10.1.2	
HCR.2	Health promotion with multi-sectoral approach	–	13.6.3	–	05	08.1.0

n.e.c.: not elsewhere classified; n.s.f.: non-specified by function; n.s.k.: not specified by kind.
Source: Updated version of SHA 1.0 Table 9.5 Cross-classification of ICHA-HC and SNA 93 classifications.

related to health (07.5) and those related to formulation, administration, co-ordination and monitoring of overall health policy; plans, programmes and budget, preparation and enforcement of legislation and standards for the provision of health services, including the production and dissemination of general information, technical documentation and statistics on health (07.6). Activities recorded under COFOG 07.5 R&D Health are not covered by the SHA core account. But, as in SHA, overhead expenses connected with the administration of a group of hospitals, clinics, surgeries, etc., are considered to be individual expenditures and are classified to groups (07.1) through (07.4), as appropriate.

In the following, an overview is given about the six health groups of the COFOG. Information on the correspondence between the functional classification of the SHA (HC) and COFOG as well as possible deviations from SHA is given in Table A.1.6.

The COFOG category 07.1 *Medical products, appliances and equipment,* which comprises three classes 07.1.1 *Pharmaceutical products* (IS), 07.1.2 *Other medical products* (IS) and 07.1.3 *Therapeutic appliances and equipment* (IS), corresponds closely to SHA category HC.5 Medical goods non-specified by function. This COFOG group covers both prescribed and non-prescribed medical goods. They are intended for consumption or use outside a health facility or institution. Such products, when dispensed directly to outpatients by medical, dental and paramedical practitioners or to inpatients by hospitals and the like, are included in *Outpatient services* (07.2) or *Hospital services* (07.3). The COFOG does not distinguish between curative, rehabilitative, long-term care and ancillary services. The compilation of the corresponding SHA subcategories of HC therefore requires additional information.

The category of 07.2 *Outpatient Services* comprises four classes 07.2.1 *General medical services* (IS), 07.2.2 *Specialised medical services* (IS), 07.2.3 *Dental services* (IS) and 07.2.4 *Paramedical services* (IS). These outpatient services may be delivered at home, in individual or group consulting facilities, in dispensaries or the outpatient clinics of hospitals and the like. Outpatient services include the medicaments, prostheses, medical appliances and equipment and other health-related products dispensed directly to outpatients by medical, dental and paramedical practitioners and auxiliaries. Co-payments for public services are not included. Therefore, additional information on the procedures governing these payments is necessary for SHA data compilation of HC.1.3 and HC.2.3 Outpatient curative and rehabilitative care.

Medical, dental and paramedical services provided to inpatients by hospitals and the like are included in *Hospital services* (07.3), which comprises four classes: 07.3.1 *General hospital services* (IS), 07.3.2 *Specialised hospital services* (IS), 07.3.3 *Medical and maternity centre services (IS)* and 07.3.4 *Nursing and convalescent home services* (IS). The focus is on the corresponding curative and rehabilitative inpatient services (HC1.1) and (HC.2.1) of SHA, rather than on long-term care inpatient services (HC.3.1). In the COFOG, hospitals are defined as institutions that offer inpatient care under the direct supervision of qualified medical doctors. Hospitalisation is defined as occurring when a patient is accommodated in a hospital for the duration of the treatment. It covers the services of military base hospitals, the services of institutions serving old people in which medical monitoring is an essential component, and the services of rehabilitation centres providing inpatient health care and rehabilitative therapy where the objective is to treat the patient rather than to provide long-term support. Hospital day-care and home-based hospital treatment is included in COFOG 07.3, as are hospices for terminally ill persons. Medical centres, maternity centres, nursing homes and convalescent homes also providing inpatient care

are recorded under COFOG 07.3.3 and 07.3.4, even if their services are supervised and frequently delivered by staff with lower qualifications than medical doctors. In SHA, nursing homes and convalescent homes are not classified as hospitals, but as long-term care facilities. COFOG 07.3 does not cover facilities for providing long-term services such as institutions for disabled persons and rehabilitation centres that primarily provide long-term support (10.1.2) and facilities usually out of the SHA boundary, like retirement homes for elderly persons (10.2.0). Neither does it cover payments to patients for loss of income due to hospitalisation (10.1.1). Social long-term care expenditures are reported in COFOG 10 *Social protection*.

Hospital services include medicaments, prostheses, medical appliances and equipment and other health-related products supplied to hospital patients. As under SHA, this COFOG item also includes the non-medical expenditure of hospitals on administration, non-medical staff, food and drink, accommodation (including staff accommodation) and so on.

The group 07.4 *Public health services* of the COFOG comprises only one class 07.4.0 *Public health services* (IS), which includes individual services in the provision of public health services, including: administration, inspection, operation or support of public health services, such as blood bank operation (collecting, processing, storing, shipping), disease detection (cancer, tuberculosis, venereal disease), prevention (immunisation, inoculation), monitoring (infant nutrition, child health), epidemiological data collection, family planning services and so forth; as well as the preparation and dissemination of information on public health matters. In general, this group includes: public health services delivered by special teams to groups of clients, most of whom are in good health, at workplaces, schools or other non-medical settings; public health services not connected with a hospital, clinic or practitioner; public health services not delivered by medically qualified doctors; and public health service laboratories. It excludes: medical analysis laboratories (07.2.4) and laboratories engaged in determining the causes of disease (07.5.0). As a result, this group is not directly comparable with HC.6 *Preventive care* of SHA, as on the one hand it comprises part of administrative services related to overall administration recorded in SHA under HC.7 *Governance and health system & financing administration,* and on other hand it may not include some of the collective preventive services that are recorded under COFOG 07.6 *Health n.e.c.*

The group 07.5 *R&D Health* with the only class 07.5.0 *R&D Health* (CS) is not part of current health expenditures and should not be included in the core accounts, but can be included in the memorandum item R&D in the Capital formation account. Definitions of basic research, applied research and experimental development are given under (01.4) and (01.5) of the COFOG.

The group 07.6 *Health n.e.c.* comprises also only one class 07.6.0 *Health n.e.c.* (CS), which is reserved for collective health services such as the administration, operation or support of activities such as the formulation, administration, co-ordination and monitoring of overall health policies, plans, programmes and budgets; preparation and enforcement of legislation and standards for the provision of health services, including the licensing of medical establishments and medical and paramedical personnel; and the production and dissemination of general information, technical documentation and statistics on health. It includes: health affairs and services that cannot be assigned to (07.1), (07.2), (07.3), (07.4) or (07.5). For the compilation of SHA, it might be necessary to split this group between HC.6 *Preventive care* and HC.7 *Governance and health system & financing administration.*

COICOP

As mentioned above, the structure of the COICOP division 06 *Health* follows a breakdown into groups similar to the COFOG for the individual services. While the first group 06.1 *Medical products, appliances and equipment* comprises exactly the same classes as COFOG, 07.1 *Medical products, appliances and equipment*, the following two groups 06.2 *Outpatient services* and 06.3 *Hospital services* differ in their classes. However, countries might apply more detailed classifications of individual expenditures, *e.g.* in the household budget survey, so that the correspondence between SHA and COICOP shown in Table A.1.6 gives only tentative information.

The second COICOP group 06.2 *Outpatient services* includes three classes: 06.2.1 *Medical services* (S), 06.2.2 *Dental services* (S) and 06.2.3 *Paramedical services* (S). The third group 06.3 *Hospital services* comprises only one class 06.3.0 *Hospital services* (S) and no further breakdown in comparison with the COFOG. The services of residential care for elderly persons, institutions for disabled persons and rehabilitation centres providing primarily long-term support are covered under COICOP class 12.4.0 *Social protection* (S). As in the COFOG, no distinction is made between curative and rehabilitative health care.

One special problem related to the COFOG and COICOP is the identification of administrative costs related to public and private insurance financing. In SNA, private health insurance is a part of non-life insurance. The compilation of the output of private insurance, which is relevant for the compilation of administrative costs in SHA, follows the rules set for non-life insurance. The output of the insurance industry is determined in a manner intended to mimic the premium-setting policies of the insurance corporations. The basic method for measuring non-life insurance output is the following: Output equals total premiums earned plus premium supplements less adjusted claims incurred (SNA 2008, 6.185). Further details are provided in Chapter 6 of SNA 2008. In the case of social insurance, the output is determined in the same way as all non-market output as the sum of costs. Administrative records kept by social insurance and private insurance companies usually contain sufficient information to separate transactions on individual consumption and administration. The administration of social and private insurance corresponds roughly to COFOG 07.6 *Health n.e.c.* and COICOP 12.5.3 *Insurance connected with health*.

COPNI

COPNI (Classification of the Purposes of Non-profit Institutions) is used to identify the socio-economic objectives of current transactions, capital outlays and acquisition of financial assets by NPISH. Many of NPISH have a single purpose and therefore can be unambiguously allocated to one of the purposes listed in the classification. Some of them even if broadly defined NPISH – as religious organisation, can perform two types of activities that serve different purposes, for example they can run hospitals and organise religious ceremonies. If it is not possible to identify a separate institutional unit for each purpose, then the NPISH as a whole will have to be assigned to that purpose which predominates in terms of employment or total expenditures. Following SNA 2008, COPNI can normally[15] be assumed to include only individual consumption.

The health division of COPNI is structured similarly to COFOG and comprises six groups: 02.1 *Medical products, appliances and equipment*, 02.2 *Outpatient services*, 02.3 *Hospital services*, 02.4 *Public health services*, 02.5 *R&D Health*, 02.6 *Other health services*. The three classes of the first group 02.1 Medical products follow exactly the structure of COFOG and

Table A.1.6. Correspondence between classification of health care functions (ICHA-HC) and COFOG and COICOP-Households

ICHA-HC	Functions	COFOG	COICOP-Households	Comments
HC.1	**Curative care**			
HC.1.1	Inpatient curative care	07.3 Hospital services	06.3 Hospital services	These COFOG and COICOP groups refer to inpatient services. A further split into curative, rehabilitative and long-term care health is required based on additional information.
		07.3.1General hospital services (IS)	06.3.0 Hospital services (S)	HC.1.1 includes stay overnight of non-rehabilitative services and excludes hospital day-care and home-based hospital treatment.
		07.3.2 Specialised hospital services (IS)	As above	SHA splits further into HP.1.2 Mental health hospitals and HP.1.3 Specialised hospitals (other than mental health hospitals).
		07.3.3 Medical and maternity centre services (IS)	As above	SHA includes stay overnight in maternity clinics under HP.1.3 Specialised hospitals; see also RI.3.1 Maternal and child health; family planning and counselling.
		07.3.4 Nursing and convalescent home services (IS)	As above	Rehabilitation centres providing inpatient health care and rehabilitative therapy to be reported under HC.2 in SHA, long-term care (health) under HC.3.
HC.1.2	Day curative care	As above	As above	HC.1.2 includes *e.g.* elective surgery carried out within one day.
HC.1.3	Outpatient curative care	07.2 Outpatient services	06.2 Outpatient services	These COFOG and COICOP groups include outpatient services in hospitals. HC.1.3 requires the separation of outpatient acute and curative services from rehabilitative, ancillary and preventive services.
HC.1.3.1	General curative outpatient care	07.2.1General medical services (IS)	06.2.1 Medical services (S)	SHA excludes under outpatient curative care HC.4.1 Laboratory services + HC.4.2 Imaging diagnosis directly delivered to consumers.
HC.1.3.2	Dental curative outpatient care	07.2.3 Dental services (IS)	06.2.2 Services of dentists (S)	HC.1.3.2 includes dentures except delivery directly to patients, but excluded in COFOG: to be reported under 07.1.3 and in the COICOP under 06.1.3.
HC.1.3.3	Specialised curative outpatient care	07.2.2 Specialised medical services (IS)	06.2.1 Medical services (S)	SHA excludes under outpatient curative care HC.4.1 Laboratory services + HC.4.2 Imaging diagnosis directly delivered to consumers.
HC.1.4	Home-based curative care	07.2.4 Paramedical services (IS)	06.2.3 Paramedical services (S)	The COFOG includes ambulance services under this item.
HC.2	**Rehabilitative care**			
HC.2.1	Inpatient rehabilitative care	07.3.1 General hospital services (IS)	06.3.0 Hospital services (S)	HC.2.1 depends very much on the organisation of rehabilitation in a country; the cases of inpatient rehabilitation are treated either in specialised departments or hospitals; excludes acute services.
		07.3.2 Specialised hospital services (IS)	As above	See above.
		07.3.3 Medical and maternity centre services (IS)	As above	HC.2.1 inpatient rehabilitative care includes maternity convalescent services; preventive care and delivery needs to be separated, see also RI.3.1 Maternal and child health; family planning and counselling.
		07.3.4 Nursing and convalescent home services (IS)	As above	COFOG 07.3.4 Nursing and convalescent home services should include rather curative and rehabilitative care than long-term support
HC.2.2	Rehabilitative day care	As above	As above	The cases of day care rehabilitation are either to specialised departments or to hospitals within the same day
HC.2.3	Rehabilitative outpatient care	07.2.2 Specialised medical services (IS)	06.2.1 Medical services (S)	Rehabilitative outpatient care is rather included under COFOG 07.2.2 and 07.2.4; HC.2.3 excludes HC.4.1 Laboratory services + HC.4.2 Imaging diagnosis directly delivered to consumers

Table A.1.6. **Correspondence between classification of health care functions (ICHA-HC) and COFOG and COICOP-Households** *(cont.)*

ICHA-HC	Functions	COFOG	COICOP-Households	Comments
HC.2.4	Rehabilitative home-based care	07.2.4 Paramedical services (IS)	06.2.3 Paramedical services (S)	See above
		07.3.4 Nursing and convalescent home services (IS)		COFOG 07.3.4 Nursing and convalescent home services should include rather curative and rehabilitative care than long-term support
HC.3	**Long-term care (health)**			Less intensive treatment than in hospital curative care; the COFOG division 10 Social protection and COICOP division 12.4 Social protection might also include expenditures for long-term care (health),
HC.3.1	Long-term inpatient care (health)	07.3.4 Nursing and convalescent home services (IS)	06.3.0; Hospital services (S)	Excludes rehabilitation centres providing inpatient health care and rehabilitative therapy where the objective is to treat the patient rather than to provide long-term support
HC.3.2	Day cases of long-term care (health)	07.3.2 Specialised hospital services 07.3.4 Nursing and convalescent home services (IS)		HC.3.2 has no corresponding item in COFOG and requires special separation of expenditures for day cases of long-term care
HC.3.3	Outpatient long-term care (health)	07.2.4 Paramedical services (IS)		HC.3.3 refers to regular outpatient visits or to the provision of remote monitoring services.
HC.3.4	Home-based long-term care (health)	07.2.4 Paramedical services (IS)		HC.3.4 can involve specialised health care at home and services in support of informal (family or community) care. IADL services are long-term care (social), see HC.R.1.
		10.1.1 Sickness (IS) 10.1.2 Disability (IS)	12.4.0 Social protection (S)	These COFOG and COICOP items might include assistance with daily tasks, but which is in general rather long-term care (social) than (health). They might include also long-term inpatient and day care.
HC.4	**Ancillary services n.s.f.**			HC.4 requires services that only in the case directly delivered to patients to be considered
HC.4.1	Laboratory services non-specified by function	07.2.4 Paramedical services (IS)	06.2.3 Paramedical services (S)	Outpatient medical services of COFOG and COICOP exclude public health service laboratories (07.4.0); laboratories engaged in determining the causes of disease (07.5.0).
HC.4.2	Imaging services n.s.f.	As above	As above	See above
HC.4.3	Patient transportation n.s.f.	07.2.4 Paramedical services (IS)	06.2.3 Paramedical services (S)	Ambulance services operated by hospitals not included in COFOG and COICOP under paramedical services but in expenditures for hospital services
		07.3 Hospital services	06.3 Hospital services (S)	See above
HC.5	**Medical goods non-specified by function**	07.1 Medical products, appliances and equipment	06.1 Medical products, appliances and equipment	Not included in COFOG products directly dispensed by medical doctors to outpatients.
HC.5.1	Pharmaceuticals and other non durable goods			HC.5.1 includes all pharmaceuticals delivered to outpatients except veterinary products
HC.5.1.1	Prescribed medicines	07.1.1 Pharmaceutical products (IS)	06.1.1 Pharmaceutical products (ND)	HC.5.1.1 includes prescribed medicines provided in response to a prescription issued by a licensed medical practitioner or pharmacist; includes as COFOG and COICOP administration, operation or support of the provision of pharmaceutical products
HC.5.1.2	Over-the-counter drugs (OTC)	As above	As above	HC.5.1.2 excludes products of personal care such as those stated in COICOP 12.1 and notably in 12.1.3 class with articles for personal hygiene: toilet soap, medicinal soap, cleansing oil and milk, shaving soap, shaving cream and foam, toothpaste, etc.; beauty products: sunbathing products, etc; other products: sanitary towels, etc.
HC.5.1.3	Other medical non durable goods	07.1.2 Other medical products (IS)	06.1.2 Other medical products (ND)	HC.5.1.3 is comparable with these items of COFOG and COICOP
HC.5.2	Therapeutic appliances and other medical goods	07.1.3 Therapeutic appliances and equipment (IS)	06.1.3 Therapeutic appliances and equipment (D)	COFOG and COICOP includes here dentures: SHA includes dentures in HC.1.3.2, if not directly provided by laboratories to consumers;

Table A.1.6. **Correspondence between classification of health care functions (ICHA-HC) and COFOG and COICOP-Households** *(cont.)*

ICHA-HC	Functions	COFOG	COICOP-Households	Comments
HC.5.2.1	Glasses and other vision products	As above	As above	SHA excludes sunglasses not fitted with corrective lenses
HC.5.2.2	Orthopaedic appliances and other prosthetics	As above	As above	COFOG and COCOP excludes: hire of therapeutic equipment (included in paramedical services)
HC.5.2.3	Hearing aids	As above	As above	SHA reports audiological diagnosis and treatment by physicians under HC.1.3.3; hearing implants if delivered directly by the physician as benefit In-kind under curative care; audiological training under HC.1.3.9.
HC.5.2.4	All other medical durables including medical technical devices	As above	As above	SHA excludes: protective goggles, belts and supports for sport
HC.6	**Preventive care**			
HC.6.1	Information, education and counselling programmes	07.4 Public health services 07.6 Health *n.e.c.* (CS)	Not available	COFOG 07.4 includes individual preventive services. Collective preventive services are part of 07.6 Health *n.e.c.* as monitoring (infant nutrition, child health), epidemiological data collection, family planning services and so forth. As Governance and health system and financing administration is also included in COFOG 07.6 further separation is needed
HC.6.2	Immunisation programmes	As above	As above	Separation only at the level of administrative data possible
HC.6.3	Early disease detection programmes	As above	As above	HC.6.3 includes also ancillary services as diagnostic services and imaging
HC.6.4	Health condition monitoring programmes	As above	As above	See above
HC 6.5	Epidemiologic surveillance and risk and disease control programme	07.6 Health *n.e.c.* (CS)	Not available	In COFOG 07.6 only collective services included: Excluded individual services; in COICOP no items.
HC 6.6	Preparing for disaster and emergency response programmes	07.6 Health *n.e.c.* (CS)	Not available	As above
HC.7	**Governance and health system & financing administration**			
HC.7.1	Governance and health system administration	07.6.0 Health *n.e.c.* (CS)	Not available	SHA involves in this category the general public service component which is part of the government function health COFOG 07.6. However, also the health part of the overall planning and statistical services (as expressed in COFOG 01.3) might be relevant
HC.7.2	Administration of health financing	07.6.0 Health *n.e.c.* (CS)	Not available	See above
		10.9.0 Social protection *n.e.c.* (CS)		COFOG does not classify all relevant expenditures for administration under 07.6.0; one should therefore also check other relevant items.
HC.9	**Other health care services not elsewhere classified**			
Reporting items:				
HC.RI.1	Total pharmaceutical expenditure (TPE)	Not available	Not available	Not available in COFOG, COICOP.
HC.RI.2	Traditional, Complementary and Alternative Medicines (TCAM)	Not available	Not available	Included in other items mentioned above.
HC.RI.2.1	Inpatient TCAM	Not available	Not available	Included in other items mentioned above.
HC.RI.2.2	Outpatient and home-based TCAM	Not available	Not available	Included in other items mentioned above.
HC.RI.2.3	TCAM goods	Not available	Not available	Included in other items mentioned above

Table A.1.6. **Correspondence between classification of health care functions (ICHA-HC) and COFOG and COICOP-Households** *(cont.)*

ICHA-HC	Functions	COFOG	COICOP-Households	Comments
HC.RI.3	Prevention and public health services	07.4.0 Public health services (IS) 07.6.0 Health *n.e.c.* (CS)	Not available	See HC.6 above; includes both individual and collective services; therefore collective preventive care items to be split from COFOG 07.6.
HC.RI.3.1	Maternal and child health; family planning and counselling	07.4.0 Public health services (IS)	06.2.1 Medical services (S)	See above.
HC.RI.3.2	School health services	07.4.0 Public health services (IS)	Not available	See above.
HC.RI.3.3	Prevention of communicable diseases	07.4.0 Public health services (IS)	Not available	See above.
HC.RI.3.4	Prevention of non-communicable diseases	07.4.0 Public health services (IS)	Not available	See above.
HC.RI.3.5	Occupational health care	07.4.0 Public health services (IS) 07.6.0 Health *n.e.c.* (CS)	Not available	COFOG includes only public provided occupational health care as expenditures for Occupational health institute; see also ONS 2004 SHA-Guidelines.
HC.RI.3.9	All other miscellaneous preventive care services	07.4.0 Public health services (IS) 07.6.0 Health *n.e.c.* (CS)	Not available	See above.
Health care related items:				
HCR.1	Long-term care (social)	10.1.2 Disability IS) 10.2.0 Old age (IS) 10.7.0 Social exclusion *n.e.c.* (IS)		• Only benefits in kind, such as assistance with daily tasks provided to persons temporarily unable to work due to sickness or injury (home help, transport facilities, etc.). • Administration of social protection only to be considered with the relevant share.
HCR.1.1	In-kind long-term social care		See above	See above
HCR.1.2	Long-term social care cash-benefits		See above	See above
HCR.2	Health promotion with multi-sectoral approach			Activities under this item are part of various COFOG functions [COFOG, 04 Economic Affairs (various industries); and 06.3 Water supply which includes Supervision and regulation of water purity].

n.e.c.: not elsewhere classified; n.s.f.: non-specified by function; n.s.k.: not specified by kind.

CS: Collective services; IS: Individual services; ND: non-durable goods; SD: semi-durable goods; D: durable goods; S: services.

Note: Research and development is considered as current consumption only when it relates to improvements in the day to day operation of services. It is defined as investment when it refers to innovations leading to additional income and generation of assets such as patents. This means that current expenditure on research and development has been transferred to an item of factors of provision. Following the SNA, the output of research and development should be capitalised as "intellectual property products" except in cases where it is clear that the activity does not entail any economic benefit to its producer (and hence owner) in which case it is treated as intermediate consumption.

Spending on army field hospitals is not included in COFOG 07.3 but is to be included in the SHA functional classification.

Source: IHAT for SHA 2011.

COICOP. The breakdown of the second group 02.2 *Outpatient services* into classes goes in line with COICOP, which means there is one class 02.2.1 Medical services and not two classes as in COFOG distinguishing between general and specialised medical services. The other four groups of COPNI contain only one class.

The correspondence codes between HC and COPNI are listed in Table A.1.5. As COPNI follows the structure of COFOG and COICOP, Table A.1.6 might also be used to get further information about the correspondence of the items.

CPC/CPA

In order to study transactions in goods and services in detail, the SNA uses the Central Product Classification (CPC). Products are goods and services in the terminology of the SNA. The main purpose of the CPC is to provide a framework for the international comparison of statistics dealing with products. In the construction of CPC, the nature of the product and the industry of origin were taken into account. With regard to health care services and goods various categories of the CPC are relevant. Most health care goods and services fall into the division 93 *Human health and social care services* which comprises five classes 931 *Human health services*, 932 *Residential care services for the elderly and disabled*, 933 *Other social services with accommodation* and 934 *Social services without accommodation for the elderly and disabled* and 935 *Other social services without accommodation*. Table A.1.7 gives an overview on the correspondence between the CPC and SHA 2011. The European Classification of Products by Activity (CPA) is the corresponding European classification to CPC.[16] Further information about CPC is presented in Annex E.

Correspondence between classification of health care functions (ICHA-HC) and ESSPROS

ESSPROS aims to provide a comprehensive and coherent description of social protection interventions[17] performed by both public and private bodies that intend to relieve households and individuals of the burden of a defined set of risks or needs, provided that there is neither a simultaneous reciprocal nor individual arrangement involved. In practice, various bodies, both government-controlled schemes and those not controlled by government, can be included in the countries' list of social protection schemes; the most frequent of these include:[18]

- Social security funds;
- Central, state and local government agencies;
- Insurance companies (in Denmark, the pension funds running labour market pensions can delegate the administration of these pensions to insurance companies);
- Mutual benefit societies;
- Public or private employers that provide benefits to their current and former employees directly;
- Private welfare assistance institutions and charitable organisations (for instance, the Red Cross).

Consequently, all insurance policies taken out on the private initiative of individuals or households solely in their own interest (voluntary insurance) are excluded. For instance, the payment of a capital sum or an annuity to the holder of a savings account or of voluntary health insurance is not considered to be social protection. SHA is broader on this point, because it includes also individual arrangements, including all household out-of-pocket expenditure as well as those of corporations and NPISH.

Social benefits are broken down by ESSPROS function and by type. The *function* of a social benefit refers to the primary purpose for which social protection is provided, irrespective of legislative or institutional provisions. In other words, the functional breakdown of social benefits reflects all interventions of social protection schemes by grouping them according to the eight types of risks, *i.e.* sickness/health care, disability, old age, survivors, family/children, unemployment, housing and social exclusion. The *type of*

Table A.1.7. **Correspondence between classification of health care functions (ICHA-HC) and CPC**

ICHA-HC	Functions	CPC Code	Title of headings	Comments
HC			**HEALTH**	
HC.1	**Curative care**			
HC.1.1	Inpatient curative care	9311	Inpatient services	HC.1.1 includes stay overnight of non-rehabilitative services and excludes hospital day-care and home-based hospital treatment.
HC.1.2	Day curative care	93119	Other services for inpatients	HC.1.1 includes only day cases of non-rehabilitative services within the same day; *e.g.* elective surgical services 93111for inpatients and gynaecological services for inpatients.
HC.1.3	Outpatient curative care	9312	Medical and dental services	The CPC excludes, like the COICOP and COFOG, Laboratory services (93195 Medical laboratory services) + Imaging diagnosis (93196 Diagnostic-imaging services). SHA excludes only diagnostics directly delivered to consumers.
HC.1.3.1	General curative outpatient care	93121	General medical services	HC.1.3.1 requires separation between curative, rehabilitative and preventive services.
HC.1.3.2	Dental curative outpatient care	93123	Dental services	The CPC includes also dental services delivered in hospitals to inpatients under this item. HC.1.3.2 includes dentures except delivery directly to patients.
HC.1.3.3	Specialised curative outpatient care	93122	Specialised medical services	The CPC excludes Laboratory services + Imaging diagnosis directly delivered to consumers (see above).
HC.1.4	Home-based curative care	93121 93122 93192 93199	General medical services, Specialised medical services Nursing services Other human health services *n.e.c.*	Curative services delivered at home are included in the categories of outpatient medical services. The separation of HC.1.4 needs further information.
HC.2	**Rehabilitative care**			
HC.2.1	Inpatient rehabilitative care	9311 93119	Inpatient services Other services for inpatients	HC.2.1 excludes acute services. The cases of inpatient rehabilitation are referred either to specialised departments or to specialised hospitals.
HC.2.2	Rehabilitative day care	93119	Other services for inpatients	The cases of day care rehabilitation refer either to specialised departments or to hospitals within the same day.
HC.2.3	Rehabilitative outpatient care	93121 93122 93193 93199	General medical services Specialised medical services Physiotherapeutic services Other human health services *n.e.c.*	Rehabilitative outpatient care is not an item of CPC and has therefore to be derived from medical and non-medical rehabilitative services accordingly.
HC.2.4	Rehabilitative home-based care	As above	As above	See above.
HC.3	**Long-term care (health)**			SHA includes under long-term care (health) less intensive care than in hospitals.
HC.3.1	Long-term inpatient care (health)	93210 93301 93303	Residential health care services other than by hospitals; Residential care services for children and for adults suffering from mental retardation, mental health illnesses or substance abuse	HC.3.1 includes only long-term inpatient care (health) with stay overnight and excludes day-care and home-based treatment; no separate item in CPC.
HC.3.2	Day cases of long-term care (health)	93210	Residential health care services other than by hospitals	HC.3.2 only includes day cases of long-term care; no separate item in CPC.
HC.3.3	Outpatient long-term care (health)	93192	Nursing services	HC.3.3 includes personal "body help" type. services (*e.g.* help with ADL, while "assistance or home help" type services (*e.g.* help with IADL) should be separately counted separately as long-term care (social); see also HCR.1 below.
HC.3.4	Home-based long-term care (health)	93192 93199	Nursing services Other human health services *n.e.c.*	HC.3.4 includes ADL services at patient's home; long-term social personal care is reported in SHA as HC.R.1. See above.
HC.4	**Ancillary services n.s.f.**			
HC.4.1	Laboratory services n.s.f.	93195	Medical laboratory services	The CPC might include also services delivered to other providers as "intermediate consumption". HC.4.1 includes only services in the case directly delivered to patients.

Table A.1.7. **Correspondence between classification of health care functions (ICHA-HC) and CPC** *(cont.)*

ICHA-HC	Functions	CPC Code	Title of headings	Comments
HC.4.2	Imaging services n.s.f.	93196	Diagnostic imaging services	See above.
HC.4.3	Patient transportation n.s.f.	93194	Ambulance services	The CPC comprises services involving the transport of patients by ambulance, with or without resuscitation equipment or medical personnel; HC.4.3 includes transportation in conventional vehicles by non-specialised providers, such as taxis when authorised and the costs are reimbursed by health insurance.
HC.5	**Medical goods non-specified by function**			The CPC distinguishes different forms of retail trade 621 Non-specialised store retail trade services; 622 Specialised store retail trade services; 623 Mail order or internet retail trade services; 624 Other non-store retail trade services Medical goods are usually distributed by specialised store retail trade services, therefore only this group is listed below.
HC.5.1	Pharmaceuticals and other non- durable goods	62273	Specialised retail trade of pharmaceutical products	The CPC classifies pharmaceutical products from the perspective of production as defined in "352 Pharmaceutical products".
HC.5.1.1	Prescribed medicines	62273	As above	The CPC makes no distinction in prescribed/non-prescribed.
HC.5.1.2	Over-the-counter drugs (OTC)	62273	As above	SHA excludes products of personal care such as those stated in COICOP 12.1 and notably in the 12.1.3 class with articles for personal hygiene: toilet soap, medicinal soap, cleansing oil and milk, shaving soap, shaving cream and foam, toothpaste, etc.; beauty products: sunbathing products, etc; other products: sanitary towels, etc.
HC.5.1.3	Other medical nondurable goods	62274	Specialised retail trade of Medical and orthopaedic goods	The CPC classifies the production of medical non-durable goods, such as clinic thermometers or bandages, under various headings.
HC.5.2	Therapeutic appliances and other medical goods	62274	Specialised retail trade of Medical and orthopaedic goods	SHA classifies denture in HC.1.3.2 if not delivered directly by denturists.
HC.5.2.1	Glasses and other vision products	62522 87154	Specialised retail trade of Photographic, optical and precision equipment Maintenance and repair services of medical, precision and optical instruments	SHA excludes sunglasses not fitted with corrective lenses.
HC.5.2.2	Orthopaedic appliances and other prosthetics	62274	Specialised retail trade of Medical and orthopaedic goods	
HC.5.2.3	Hearing aids	62274 87154	Specialised retail trade of Medical and orthopaedic goods Maintenance and repair services of medical, precision and optical instruments	SHA excludes under HC.5.2.3 audiological diagnosis and treatment by physicians. (HC.1.3.3) and hearing implants (HC.1, curative care) as well as audiological training covered under outpatient rehabilitation (HC.2.3).
HC.5.2.4	All other medical durables including medical technical devices	62733	Mail order or internet retail trade services	Includes specialised telematic equipment for emergency calls from the patient's home and/or for the remote monitoring of medical parameters.
HC.6	**Preventive care**	91122 9312	Public administrative services related to health care Medical and dental services	The CPC does not include a special class for preventive care; collective preventive care partly included under public administrative services, individual preventive care partly included human health services. HC.6 requires more detailed information
HC.6.1	Information, education and counselling programmes	As above	As above	See above.
HC.6.2	Immunisation programmes	As above	As above	See above.
HC.6.3	Early disease detection programmes	As above	As above	See above.
HC.6.4	Health condition monitoring programmes	As above	As above	See above.

Table A.1.7. **Correspondence between classification of health care functions (ICHA-HC) and CPC** *(cont.)*

ICHA-HC	Functions	CPC Code	Title of headings	Comments
HC.6.5	Epidemiologic surveillance and risk and disease control programme	As above	As above	See above.
HC 6.6	Preparing for disaster and emergency response programmes	As above	As above	See above.
HC.7	**Governance and health system & financing administration**			
HC.7.1	Governance and health system administration	91122 91310	Public administrative services related to health care Administrative services related to sickness, maternity or temporary disablement benefit schemes	SHA includes in this category the general public services that are part of the government function through the overall planning and statistical services.
HC.7.2	Administration of health financing	71322 91310	Health insurance services Administrative services related to sickness, maternity or temporary disablement benefit schemes	For compilation, see Chapter 6 of SNA 2008. Administration is only a part of the premiums paid for private insurance (see ONS 2004, SHA-Guidelines, p. 142).
HC.9	**Other health care services not elsewhere classified (*n.e.c*)**			
Reporting items				
HC.RI.1	Total pharmaceutical expenditure (TPE)	352	Pharmaceutical products	The CPC allows the identification of the whole supply/ use of pharmaceuticals in the country, which differs from use by residents.
HC.RI.2	Traditional, Complementary and Alternative Medicines (TCAM)			Included in other items mentioned above.
HC.RI.2.1	Inpatient TCAM			Included in other items mentioned above.
HC.RI.2.2	Outpatient and home-based TCAM			Included in other items mentioned above.
HC.RI.2.3	TCAM goods			Included in other items mentioned above.
HC.RI.3	Prevention and public health services			See HC.6.
HC.RI.3.1	Maternal and child health; family planning and counselling			See HC.6.
HC.RI.3.2	School health services			See HC.6.
HC.RI.3.3	Prevention of communicable diseases			See HC.6.
HC.RI.3.4	Prevention of non-communicable diseases			See HC.6.
HC.RI.3.5	Occupational health care			See HC.6.
HC.RI.3.9	All other miscellaneous preventive care services			See HC.6.
Health care-related items				
HCR.1	Long-term Social Care	9322 9330	Residential care services for the elderly and persons with disabilities; Other social services with accommodation	Only benefits in kind, such as assistance with daily tasks provided to persons temporarily unable to work due to sickness or injury (home help, transport facilities, etc.).
HCR.1.1	In-kind long-term social care			See above.
HCR.1.2	Long-term social care cash-benefits			Cash benefits are not part of CPC.
HCR.2	Prevention with multi-sectoral approach			Private expenses, if any, included in different non-health categories.

n.e.c.: not elsewhere classified; n.s.f.: non-specified by function; n.s.k.: not specified by kind.
Source: IHAT for SHA 2011.

benefit refers to the form in which the protection is provided. These can take many forms; however, in the core ESSPROS system these are limited to benefits in cash, *i.e.* cash payment to protected people, and benefits in kind that include reimbursements of expenditure made by protected people and goods and services directly provided to protected people. A brief description of other ESSPROS functions and their relevance to SHA are presented below in Table A.1.8

Table A.1.8. **Definitions of the functions of social protection (ESSPROS)**

Function	Description	Relevance for SHA
1. Sickness/ Health care	Income maintenance and support in cash in connection with physical or mental illness, excluding disability. Health care intended to maintain, restore or improve the health of the people protected irrespective of the origin of the disorder.	All medical care falls under this function irrespective of the need or risk against which it is provided. For example, specific medical care provided to expectant mothers and disabled persons is included here and not under the Family/children and Disability functions.
2. Disability	Income maintenance and support in cash or kind (except health care) in connection with the inability of physically or mentally disabled people to engage in economic and social activities. All medical care specific to disability is reported under the Sickness/health care function	Long-term care (social): Practical help provided to disabled people to assist them with daily tasks. Home help is included in this category, as well as the payment of an allowance to the person who looks after the disabled person. Furthermore, provision of specific goods and services (other than medical care) and vocational training to further the occupational and social rehabilitation of disabled people are included. These services may be provided in specialised institutions. Medical rehabilitation – such as physiotherapy – is included in the Sickness/health care function.
3. Old age	Income maintenance and support in cash or kind (except health care) in connection with old age.	Long-term care (social) in connection with elderly. This function includes provision of lodging and sometimes board to retired people either in specialised institutions (old people's homes, nursing homes) or staying with families. Assistance in carrying out daily tasks: practical help provided to old people to assist them with daily tasks. Home help is included in this category, as well as the payment of an allowance to the person who looks after an elderly person. Other benefits in kind: miscellaneous goods and services for retired people to enable them to take part in leisure and cultural activities, to travel and/or participate in community life. These include reductions in prices, tariffs and fares for old age pensioners where they are expressly granted for social protection; these other benefits are outside the boundary of SHA.
4. Survivors	Income maintenance and support in cash or kind in connection with the death of a family member.	Not relevant to SHA
5. Family/children	Support in cash or kind (except health care) in connection with the costs of pregnancy, childbirth and adoption, bringing up children and caring for other family members.	Not relevant to SHA
6. Unemployment	Income maintenance and support in cash or kind in connection with unemployment.	Not relevant to SHA
7. Housing	Help towards the cost of housing.	Not relevant to SHA
8. Social exclusion not elsewhere classified	Benefits in cash or kind (except health care) specifically intended to combat social exclusion where they are not covered by one of the other functions.	Social care in relation health care: Rehabilitation of alcohol and drug abusers: treatment of alcohol and drug dependency aimed at reconstructing the social life of the abusers, making them able to live an independent life. The treatment is usually provided in rehabilitation centres or special institutions.

Source: IHAT for SHA 2011.

For the purposes of a mapping exercise between SHA and ESSPROS functions, the benefits in kind recorded under sickness/health care function are of particular relevance. The prevalence of one or other form of benefit in kind depends on the way in which the health care system is organised and how health care goods and services are financed within it. In that respect, the following three main patterns of health care provision can be mentioned:

- Under the indirect system, the social protection scheme provides medical care benefits for protected people by paying all or part of the cost of the medical care supplied by the providers. The patient pays the medical bill, all or part of which is then reimbursed by the social protection scheme. *The benefits therefore take the form of reimbursements*. This pattern of provision is predominant in outpatient medical care and in private hospital care in France and Luxembourg, but can be found elsewhere too, for example in Belgium, and partially in Greece, Cyprus and Switzerland.
- Under the direct system, the institutional unit running the social protection scheme owns, operates and controls the necessary medical facilities and employs the medical, paramedical and administrative staff. In this system *benefits are directly provided to the protected people*. This pattern of provision is typical for inpatient and specialised outpatient medical care in national health services (Denmark, Cyprus Malta, Sweden and United Kingdom) and for some sickness insurance schemes for employees (Spain, Greece);
- In an alternative pattern of provision, *intermediate between the two above* – known as a direct settlement system – the social protection scheme enters into a variety of contracts or agreements with health care providers. The medical care is provided to the beneficiary free or at a co-payment rate by the providing unit (which is not a social protection scheme). The providing unit is then reimbursed by the social protection scheme. This type of benefit is also recorded as directly provided. This mode of provision is typical for primary care practices in most European countries and can be found in the case of hospital care and specialised outpatient medical care in Belgium, Germany, the Netherlands and Austria, but also in other countries (in Bulgaria, the Czech Republic, Estonia, Lithuania, Hungary, Poland, Romania, Slovenia and the Slovak Republic).

The scope of health care goods and service that are covered under the Sickness/health care function includes in particular:

- Services: medical and paramedical services provided by general practitioners, specialists and other health care personnel; laboratory tests and other examinations; dental care; physiotherapy; thermal cures; transport of sick people; preventive treatment such as vaccinations; and accommodation in the case of a stay in hospital or other medical institution. Medical services as defined here cover those services provided within and outside medical institutions.
- Goods: pharmaceutical products; medical prosthesis (optical and acoustical aids; orthopaedic; dental and other prosthesis); and dressings and medical supplies.

Although the mapping between ESSPROS social protection schemes and the HF financing schemes classification is close to a one-to-one relation, divergences appear in the HC classification of functions and the scope of ESSPROS benefits in kind/functions, which differ since the two frameworks have different health care boundaries. With respect to preventive care, the Sickness/Health care function of ESSPROS covers only those preventive measures through which an individual may benefit (for example, a medical check-up).

Contrary to the SHA preventive programmes related to various campaigns that alert the general public to health hazards (for example, smoking, alcohol or drug abuse) are not recorded by ESSPROS. It also does not define a function in the case of occupational accidents and diseases. Statistical data on this type of expenditure are not comparable, as they reflect the definition of an occupational hazard adopted by each country in its own legislation and practice. Furthermore, benefits provided in the event of occupational accidents or diseases may range from sickness cash benefits to health care provision, from rehabilitation benefits to disability pensions. Table A.1.9 gives more detailed information about the correspondence between the functional classification of SHA 2011 and social benefits of ESSPROS, which are broken down by function and by type. It clearly shows that the different approaches used in the two frameworks do not allow for direct mapping between detailed functions of SHA and those of the ESSPROSS aggregated level recorded as social benefits. In order to make such links, it would be necessary to trace background information related to benefits in kind and in cash on the level of each country's national schemes.

Table A.1.9. **Correspondence between classification of health care functions (ICHA-HC) and ESSPROS**

Source: SHA 2011		ESSPROS				Comments
ICHA-HC	Functions	Functions	Code	Description	Type	
HC.1	Curative care	S	1111211/1112211 1111212/1112212	Inpatient health care - Direct provision - Reimbursement	bik	Under these ESSPROS items any type of inpatient medical care (preventive, curative, rehabilitative and LTC) is included; to isolate their value, more detailed information from national schemes is necessary; HC.1.2 Day care hospitalisation is by convention recorded under ESSPROS items for inpatient care; requires additional information at the level of national schemes.
		S	1111222/1112222 1111224/1112224	Outpatient health care - Other direct provision - Other reimbursement	bik	Under these items any type of outpatient medical care (prevention, cure, rehabilitation and LTC) is included, with the exception of expenditure on pharmaceutical products. It includes also medical care provided at home. To isolate the value for HC.1.4 more detailed information from national schemes/ providers is necessary.
HC.2	Rehabilitative care	S	1111211/1112211 1111212/1112212	Inpatient health care - Direct provision - Reimbursement	bik	Under these ESSPROS items any type of inpatient medical care (prevention, cure and rehabilitation) is included. To obtain HC.2.1 requires more detailed information at level of schemes/providers; HC.2.2 Day care hospitalisation is by convention recorded under ESSPROS items for inpatient care.
		S	1111222/1112222 1111224/1112224	Outpatient health care - Other direct provision - Other reimbursement	bik	Under these three items any type of outpatient medical care (prevention, cure and rehabilitation) is included. To obtain HC.2.3 requires more detailed information at level of national schemes/ providers.
		S	As above	As above	bik	HC 2.4 is part of ESSPROS items for outpatient care; To obtain HC.2.4 requires more detailed information at level of schemes/ providers.
		SE	1181202/1182202	Rehabilitation of alcohol and drug abusers	bik	Special item of ESSPROS; separation of rehabilitation requires additional information about type of services at the level of schemes.
HC.3	Long-term care (health)	S	1111211/1112211 1111212/1112212	Inpatient health care - Direct provision - Reimbursement	bik	HC.3 is only partly covered in the sickness/health care function and requires additional information for separation from curative and rehabilitative care.
		D	1121201/1122201	Accommodation	bik	Not directly comparable; in ESSPROS it is likely that more long-term care (social) is included.
		O/A	1131200/ 1132200	Benefits in kind	bik	See above.
		S	1122202/1121202	Home help means-tested non means tested	bik	HC 3.4 is part of ESSPROS items for outpatient care, but might include also expenditures under home care. To obtain HC.3.4 requires more detailed information at level of schemes/providers.

Table A.1.9. **Correspondence between classification of health care functions (ICHA-HC) and ESSPROS** *(cont.)*

Source: SHA 2011		ESSPROS				Comments
ICHA-HC	Functions	Functions	Code	Description	Type	
		D	1122113/1121113	Periodic care allowance	cb	This is a benefit paid to disabled people who need frequent or constant assistance (which might be considered long-term assistance) to help them meet the extra cost of attendance (other than medical care). Therefore the social aspect should be separated. ESSPROS includes care allowances of compulsory long-term care schemes but not voluntary insurance.
		D	1121202/1122202	Assistance in carrying out daily cases	bik	Only relevant in case of connected health services, otherwise social care, see HCR.1.
		OA	1131202/1132202	Assistance in carrying out daily cases	bik	See above HC.3.1 "assistance in carrying out daily task", can also be for inpatient care.
HC.4	Ancillary services (non-specified by function)	S	1111222/1112222 1111224/1112224 1111230/1121204 1112230/1122204	Outpatient health care - Other direct provision - Other reimbursement Other benefits in kind	bik	In ESSPROS laboratory services and diagnostic imaging are not separately recorded. Therefore the categories HC.4.1-HC.4.2 are included under outpatient care (direct provision and other reimbursement). These SHA items require more detailed information from national schemes/providers. Similarly, transport of sick people is a part of medical care (inpatient or outpatient) in ESSPROS, or included under other benefits
HC.5	Medical goods non-specified by function	S	1111221/1112221 1111223/1112223	Outpatient health care: of which: pharmaceutical products - Direct provision - Reimbursement	bik	Under these ESSPROS items pharmaceutical products provided either directly or reimbursed are recorded. However, it is not possible to distinguish between prescribed and OTC medicines.
		S	1111222/1112222 1111224/1112224	Outpatient health care - Other direct provision - Other reimbursement	bik	Therapeutic appliances and other medical goods: The definition of medical care specifies that goods such as medical supplies are considered as goods covered by medical care (and thus might be included under outpatient health care).
HC.6	Preventive care		1111222/1112222	Outpatient health care: Other direct provision non-means-tested and means-tested		Only *individual* preventive care is covered in ESSPROS, usually under outpatient care. Preventive campaigns/collective preventive care are not part of social protection covered by ESSPROS.
HC.7	Governance and health system & financing administration					Administration costs are explicitly recorded only in the core system of ESSPROS by schemes; sometimes schemes providing sickness/health care benefits can also provide other benefits classified under other functions. Administration costs should be split accordingly; administration of private-non-compulsory insurance not included in ESSPROS.
HC.9	Other health care services not elsewhere classified (*n.e.c*))					
Reporting items						
HC.RI.1	Total pharmaceutical expenditure (TPE)					Not available in ESSPROS
HC.RI.2	Traditional, Complementary and Alternative Medicines (TCAM)					Not available in ESSPROS

Table A.1.9. **Correspondence between classification of health care functions (ICHA-HC) and ESSPROS** *(cont.)*

Source: SHA 2011		ESSPROS				Comments
ICHA-HC	Functions	Functions	Code	Description	Type	
HC.RI.3	Prevention and public health services according to SHA 1.0)	S	1111222/1112222 1111224/1112224	Outpatient health care - Other direct provision - Other reimbursement	bik	See HC.6 above; collective preventive care not included in ESSPROS, *e.g.* anti-smoking campaigns, health education campaigns, etc. Individual preventive care, services of genetic counselling related to mother and child health (HC.RI.3.1) or activities that are related to individual screening, immunisation, and vaccination can be included under core system or under other sickness/health care functions, therefore their separation requires detailed information on the level of national schemes. School health services are often in the educational budget of governments and are therefore often not included in ESSPROS Screening, immunisation, vaccination activities: separation requires detailed information from schemes; Function for the event of occupational accidents and diseases is not separately defined in ESSPROS; therefore either covered in the core system or under other sickness/health care or disability depending on the country's special regulations.
		F/C	1151200/1152204	Other benefits in kind	bik	Difficult to separate health issues in ESSPROS from this item; Family planning services are included here but this item also includes holiday and leisure centres, miscellaneous goods – so social not health.
		F/C	1151200/1152204	Other benefits in kind	bik	Difficult to separate health issues in ESSPROS from this item; Family planning services are included here but this item also includes holiday and leisure centres, miscellaneous goods – so social not health.
Health care related items						
HCR.1	Long-term Social Care	D OA	1121201/1122201 1131201/1132201	Accommodation	bik	ESSPROS contains comprehensive information about social care but in a different structure; therefore, analysis at the level of national schemes is necessary. In-kind long-term care is not directly comparable, see above.
		D OA	1121202/1122202 1131202/1132202	Assistance in carrying out daily cases	bik	Should be included, as it refers to help to assist in daily tasks.
		D	1121203/1122203	Rehabilitation	bik	ESSPROS includes items other than medical rehabilitation, *e.g.* vocational rehabilitation

bik = benefits in kind; cb = cash benefits.
n.e.c.: not elsewhere classified; n.s.f.: non-specified by function; n.s.k.: not specified by kind.
D = Disability; F/C = Family/Children; OA = Old age; S = Sickness/Health care; SE = Social exclusion.

Correspondence between the classification of health care providers (ICHA-HP) and ISIC

In SHA, all statistical units are classified in the HP-classification into groups which deliver health care services and goods or which provide insurance or administration. The consumption of services mirrors the delivery of services. Chapter 6 outlines the classification rules for ICHA-HP. Table A.1.10 which shows the correspondence between the ICHA-HP health care provider classification and the economic classification of providers by the ISIC/NACE highlights the differences in the principal activity used in these two classifications.[19]

Most activities of health care providers fall into ISIC division 86 *Human health activities*, which includes only three classes 8610 *Hospital activities*, 8620 *Medical and dental practice activities* and 8690 *Other human health activities*. The NACE split the second group further into 86.21 *General medical practice activities*, 86.22 *Specialist medical practice activities* and 86.23 *Dental practice activities*.

Several issues need to be considered when comparing provider units and financing units with ISIC/NACE. First, the production value of provider units, *e.g.* hospitals (ISIC 8610), does not usually correspond exactly to the provision of health care. Second, the definition of the economic/institutional units, *e.g.* other health care providers (ISIC 8690), does not necessarily correspond with ICHA-HP. Third, the classification of economic agents/ institutional units in the SNA is different.[20] In the SNA, institutional units are created using the main activity principle. This means that based on the activities performed by any economic unit, the most important activity (in terms of output share, production process or the use of inputs or any combination of these criteria) determines the classification of that unit in the ISIC or NACE classification. As a consequence of this main activity principle, economic units with dominant non-health care activities are considered to be outside the health care branch and are consequently not included in the production value of the units classified in ISIC/NACE 86 (human health activities).

Because of the very broad scopes of the three classes of ISIC, further information from national statistics are required in order to be able to classify providers properly in SHA. Many health care providers are self-employed health care professionals: the corresponding international classification of health care professionals is ISCO. As in ambulatory care, a wide variety of informal and less-than-fully-qualified health care providers might exist in many countries. SHA 2011 recommends that these categories should be recorded in accordance with their qualification, following the rules of ISCO 08. Therefore, Table A.1.10 Correspondence between ICHA-HP – ISIC also refers to the relevant ISCO Codes.

Table A.1.10. **Correspondence between classification of health care providers (ICHA-HP) and ISIC**

Provider code *SHA 2011*	Type of provider	ISIC Rev 3	ISIC Rev 4	Categories	Comments
HP.1	**Hospitals**				Comparable definition
HP.1.1	General hospitals	8511	8610	Hospital activities	The ISIC does not distinguish the type of hospital activity: general, mental or other specialised activity.
HP.1.2	Mental health hospitals	8511	8610	Hospital activities	See above.
HP.1.3	Specialised hospitals (other than mental hospitals)	8511	8610	Hospital activities	See above.
HP.2	**Residential long-term care facilities**				The ISIC includes also establishments with dominant social characteristics in Division 87 *Residential care activities.*
HP.2.1	Long-term nursing care facilities	8519/ 8531	8710	Residential nursing care facilities	Comparable definition between the ISIC and SHA.
HP.2.2	Mental health and substance abuse facilities	8519/ 8531	8720	Residential care activities for mental retardation, mental health and substance abuse	Comparable definition between the ISIC and SHA.
HP.2.9	Other residential long-term care facilities		8730/ 8790	• Residential care activities for the elderly and disabled • Other residential care activities	Not directly comparable; ISIC 8730 and 8790 includes residential facilities where medical treatment is not an important element.

Table A.1.10. **Correspondence between classification of health care providers (ICHA-HP) and ISIC** *(cont.)*

Provider code *SHA 2011*	Type of provider	ISIC Rev 3	ISIC Rev 4	Categories	Comments
HP.3	**Providers of ambulatory health care**				
HP.3.1	Medical practices	8512	8620	Medical and dental practice activities	Comparable definition between the ISIC and SHA, but may include also ambulatory health care centres, see HP.3.4.
HP.3.1.1	Offices of general medical practitioners	8512	8620	Medical and dental practice activities	See ISCO 08: 2211 Generalist medical practitioners.
HP.3.1.2	Offices of mental medical specialists	8512	8620	Medical and dental practice activities	See ISCO-08: 2212 Specialist medical practitioners.
HP.3.1.3	Offices of medical specialists (other than mental medical specialists)	8512	8620	Medical and dental practice activities	See ISCO-08: 2212 Specialist medical practitioners.
HP.3.2	Dental practices	8512	8620	Medical and dental practice activities	See ISCO-08: 2261 Dentists.
HP.3.3	Other health care practitioners	8519	8690	Other human health activities	This ISIC item compromises all activities for human health not performed by hospitals, medical doctors or dentists. See ISCO 08: 2221 Nursing professionals, 2222 Professional midwife, 3230 Traditional and complementary medicine associate professionals, 3255 Physiotherapy technicians and assistants, 3259 Health associate professionals *n.e.c.*
HP.3.4	Ambulatory health care centres				
HP.3.4.1	Family planning centres	8519	8620	Medical and dental practice activities	ISIC item comprises family planning centres providing medical treatment on outpatient basis, such as sterilisation and termination of pregnancy, without accommodation; *e.g.* fertility clinics.
HP.3.4.2	Ambulatory mental health and substance abuse centres	8519	8620 8690	Medical and dental practice activities Other human health activities	Outpatient detoxification centres, drug addiction centres, mental health centres etc., without medical doctors providing services.
HP.3.4.3	Free-standing ambulatory surgery centres	8519	8620 8690	Medical and dental practice activities Other human health activities	Medical Centres primarily engaged in providing surgical and not conservative services.
HP.3.4.4	Dialysis care centres	8519	8620 8690	Medical and dental practice activities Other human health activities	If not included in hospitals, *e.g.* centres of nephrologists with dialysis units.
HP.3.4.9	All other ambulatory multi-speciality centres	8519/ 8531	8620 8690	Medical and dental practice activities Other human health activities	Multi-speciality outpatient polyclinics.
HP.3.5	Providers of home health care services	8519/ 8531	8690/ 8810	Other human health activities Social work activities without accommodation for the elderly and disabled	See ISCO 08: 0322 Nursing and midwifery associate professionals; 5322 Home-based personal care workers.
HP.4	**Providers of ancillary services**				
HP.4.1	Providers of patient transportation and emergency rescue		8690	Other human health activities	The ISIC item includes ambulance transport of patients by any mode of transport including airplanes. These services are often provided during a medical emergency: not included is transportation by taxis; see ISCO 08: *e.g.* 3258 Ambulance workers.

Table A.1.10. Correspondence between classification of health care providers (ICHA-HP) and ISIC *(cont.)*

Provider code *SHA 2011*	Type of provider	ISIC Rev 3	ISIC Rev 4	Categories	Comments
HP.4.2	Medical and diagnostic laboratories	8519	8690	Other human health activities	The ISIC includes X-ray laboratories and other diagnostic imaging centres as well as blood analysis laboratories. Medical and diagnostic laboratory activities for inpatients are included under ISIC 8610 hospital services.
HP.4.9	Other providers of ancillary services	8519	8690	Other human health activities	HP.4.9 comprises other providers of ancillary services not explicitly listed above
HP.5	**Retailers and other providers of medical goods**				
HP.5.1	Pharmacies	5231	4772	Retail sale of pharmaceutical and medical goods, cosmetic and toilet articles in specialised stores	The ISIC also includes retail sale of medical and orthopaedic goods, perfumery and cosmetic articles. See ISCO 08: 2262 Pharmacists, 3213 Pharmaceutical technicians and assistants.
HP.5.2	Retail sellers and other suppliers of durable medical goods and appliances	5239	4773	Other retail sale of new goods in specialised stores	ISIC 4773 also includes *e.g.* retail sale of watches, clocks and jewellery, etc. See also ISIC 3313: Repair of electronic and optical equipment included.
HP.5.9	All other miscellaneous sale and other suppliers of pharmaceuticals and medical goods	5231/ 5239	4772/ 4773	See above	See above.
HP.6	**Providers of preventive care**	7512	8412	Regulation of the activities of providing health care, education, cultural services and other social services, excluding social security	ISIC division 84 includes activities of a governmental nature that are normally carried out by the public administration, including the enactment and judicial interpretation of laws and their pursuant regulation; the administration of programmes based on them; legislative activities; taxation.
HP.7	**Providers of health care system administration and financing**				
HP.7.1	Government health administration	7512	8412	Regulation of the activities of providing health care, education, cultural services and other social services, excluding social security	The ISIC also includes other public programs, *e.g.* education, culture, sport, recreation, environment, housing and social services.
HP.7.2	Social health insurance agencies	7530	8430	Compulsory social security activities	Social security, workers compensation, unemployment insurance and similar social welfare programs.
HP.7.3	Private health insurance administration agencies	6603	6512	Non-life insurance	The ISIC also includes *e.g.* travel insurance, property insurance, motor, marine, aviation and transport insurance, pecuniary loss and liability insurance.
HP.7.9	Other administration				
HP.8	**Other secondary health care providers**				
HP.8.1	Households as providers of home health care	9700	9820	Undifferentiated service-producing activities of private households for own use	Only to be considered in the case of paid services (*e.g.* through cash allowances for LTC)

Table A.1.10. **Correspondence between classification of health care providers (ICHA-HP) and ISIC** *(cont.)*

Provider code *SHA 2011*	Type of provider	ISIC Rev 3	ISIC Rev 4	Categories	Comments
HP.8.2	All other industries as secondary provider of health care				This class of SHA might include a wide set of industries with health care as a secondary industry
HP.8.9	Rest of the economy				This class of SHA comprises social care providers and establishments that promote health with a multi-sectoral approach but do not provide health care services.
		8519/ 8531	8730 8790 8810/ 8890	Residential care activities for the elderly and disabled Social work activities without accommodation	Long-term social care providers.
			7120	Technical testing and analysis	Testing activities in the field of food hygiene; testing and measuring environmental indicators: air and water pollution etc; periodic road-safety testing of motor vehicles.
HP.9	**Rest of the world**				

Correspondence between the Classification of Financing Schemes (ICHA-HF) and institutional sectors of the SNA

As mentioned above, the structure of health care financing is shown in SNA from an institutional perspective by the breakdown of final consumption based on the three institutional sectors: households, NPISH and government.[21] In SHA 2011, the ICHA-HF Classification of Financing Schemes provides a classification for health care expenditures from the financing side. ICHA-HF is following a concept of schemes that differs from the institutional sectors of SNA. In SHA, the following criteria have been selected for the classification of schemes: a) the legal basis of the financing scheme, b) the mode of participation, c) the basis for benefit entitlement, d) the benefits (covered package; coverage of services), e) the method of raising funds, and f) the mechanism and extent of the pooling and re-allocation of funds. Further details are given in Chapters 7 and 8.

Users and compilers should be aware of the connection between schemes and institutional sectors. Each statistical unit of SHA, or economic agent, can be aggregated into institutional groups, in SNA institutional sectors (see Table A.1.9). One should note:

- Consumers may in certain circumstances be at the same time providers of home health care;
- Financing schemes (or the financing agents managing them) are providers of administration.

As the classification of statistical units of health care providers includes all provider units and financing units in the universe of health accounts, this allows creating a mutually exclusive classification of economic units. Also, all statistical units of SHA can be classified by industries (ISIC/NACE, see Table A.1.10 herein).

There are three criteria used in SNA to classify institutional units – asset and liabilities, activities and transactions – which must together form an institutional unit. The corporate enterprise is a typical example. It has assets and liabilities, engages in production and sells to other enterprises. In contrast to SNA, in SHA, ownership and control do not play a prominent role in the classification of health care providers and financing schemes. The link to the institutional sectors of SNA can therefore provide useful additional information, *e.g.* the involvement of NPISH. A good example is the Classification of Financing Schemes by their corresponding institutional structure, the financing agents (FA), and the further classification into the SNA institutional sectors (see Table D.1.11 and Annex D).

As mentioned above, SNA exhibits the structure of financing in the breakdown of final consumption expenditures by the three institutional sectors: General government (S.13), Households (S.14) and NPISH (S.15). The financing by non-financial corporations (S.11) and financial corporations (S.12) via reimbursements of household expenditures are integrated into households (S.14) in SNA (see Table A.1.11). SHA provides a more complete picture of "who spends" by disentangling the health care expenditures into out-of-pocket insurance and reimbursements by private insurance (*e.g.* Preferred Provider Organisations (PPOs) with private insurance[22] or voluntary private insurance). In the case where government controls the rates of contributions and benefits of insurance schemes, or if it routinely makes up any shortfall in scheme funds, the scheme would be classified under the general government sector (S.13) in SNA. For example, the statutory health insurance funds of France and Germany belong to the institutional sector S.13 General Government, which corresponds with FA.1 General Government in SHA.[23] The same holds for Medicare in the United States. In contrast, Private and Non-Profit Health Plans operating in the United States, which are classified as voluntary insurance HF.2.1 in SHA, belong to the institutional sector S.12 Financial corporations in SNA. This item corresponds with FA.2 Insurance corporations in SHA 2011. The same holds for Compulsory Sickness Funds in Switzerland because their premium rates vary and are not income based, members can change funds, and government does not own the funds. The complexity of financing arrangements in health makes the allocation of financing schemes sometimes not easy particular if a scheme is engaged in different activities as health care provision and health care financing and related to different financing agents.

Table A.1.11. **Correspondance between classification of financing schemes (ICHA-HF) and institutional sectors of SNA (examples)**

	Institutional sectors of SNA				
	Non-financial corporations (S.11) FA.3	Financial corporations (S.12) FA.2	Consumption in SNA		
			Households (S.14) FA.5	NPISH (S.15 FA.4)	General government (S.13)FA.1
Financing schemes of SHA 2011					
Governmental schemes (HF.1.1)					Government health administration (HF.1.1)
Compulsory contributory schemes (HF.1.2, HF.1.3)		Medical savings accounts (HF.1.3)			Social health insurance (HF.1.2)
Private insurance (HF.1.2.2 and HF.2.1)		Compulsory private insurance (HF.1.2.2) Voluntary private insurance (HF.2.1)			
NPISH financing schemes (HF.2.2) Enterprise financing schemes (HF.2.3)	Preferred provider organisations with private insurance (HF.2.3.2)	NPISH financing schemes (HF.2.2)			
Households (HF.3)			Household out-of-pocket payment (HF.3)		

Source: IHAT for SHA 2011.

It is not just financing schemes that can be presented using the analytical capacity of the institutional sector classification of SNA, but also health care providers (see Table A.1.12). In many countries a large share of primary providers are part of the institutional sector "Non-financial corporations" (S.11). The grouping of providers into institutional sectors is a precondition of sector accounts, which are outlined in Annex B. Each provider can relate only to one institutional unit in SNA. Chapter 4 of SNA 2008 provides a detailed guide to sectoring institutional units. For example, hospitals, whether public or private, are usually classified under Non-financial corporations (S.11) in the SNA, because most services are provided on market rules. Units supplying health services on a non-market basis remain an integral part of the local government unit to which they belong (S:13). As already mentioned, institutional sectors aim to support the analysis of economic behaviour as provision, consumption, financing, income redistribution or capital accumulation. They are also used to study the public and private mix of the economy. For example, the output measurement of the UK National Accounts distinguishes four private sectors (private non-financial corporations, private financial corporations, households, NPISH) and three public sectors (public corporations, central government and local government). Therefore, for a national analysis of the health economy, one might further subsector the institutional sectors.

Table A.1.12. **Correspondence between classification of health care providers (ICHA-HP) and institutional sectors of SNA (examples)**

Health care providers of SHA 2011	Institutional sectors of SNA				
	Non-financial corporations (S.11)	Financial corporations (S.12)	Households (S.14)	NPISHs (S.15)	General government (S.13)
Primary providers (HP.1-HP.6)	Offices of doctors (HP.3.1), pharmacies (HP.5.1). private hospitals (HP.2); Laboratories (HP.4.2)			Non-profit general hospitals (HP.1.1), ambulances (HP.4.1) etc.	Public university hospitals (HP.1) Public health institute (HP.6)
Health care system administration and financing (HP.7)		Private health insurance administration (HP.7.3) Non-profit insurance plans (HP.7.3, HP.7.9)			Government-funded health administration (HP.7.1) Social health insurance administration (HP.7.2)
Households (HP.8.1)			Households as home health care providers (HP.8.1)		
Other secondary health care providers (HP.8.2)			All other industries as secondary providers of health care (HP.8.2)		
Rest of the economy (HP.8.9)				Social care providers (HP.8.9)	

Source: IHAT for SHA 2011.

Notes

1. SNA 93 includes four classifications of expenditure according to purpose (formerly called functional classifications).
2. The reason for the different approaches of SHA and SNA is that SHA is interested in showing the total outlays on health care spent by insurance, while SNA compiles productive output, which is defined by the following formula to calculate output: Actual premiums earned plus premium

supplements minus adjusted claims incurred, where adjusted claims are estimated from past experience in order to eliminate volatile variations in claims (SNA 2008, 17.27).

3. "The whole of individual consumption of general government is treated as social transfers in kind in the redistribution of income in kind account and in the use of adjusted disposable income account."(SNA 2008, 9.95).
4. SNA paragraph 2.104: "Actual final consumption of households covers goods and services which are effectively available for individual consumption by households, regardless of whether the ultimate bearer of the expense is government, NPISHs or households themselves. Actual final consumption of government and NPISHs is equal to consumption expenditure less social transfers in kind, or, in other words, collective consumption."
5. See SNA 2008, 9.16.
6. In SNA, actual collective consumption (P.42) equals final collective consumption (P.32) in SNA by definition which means "who consumes" equals "who spends" for collective services. In SHA, the concepts "who consumes" and "who spends" might lead to different figures. Take, for example, administrative costs for the treatment of foreigners in domestic hospitals, which should be subtracted in SHA, because the dominant perspective of SHA is the consumption by residents.
7. For the detailed list of all categories of transactions covered by the COFOG, see UN (2000), Table 2.1.
8. When the consumption of fixed capital is additionally deducted, the result is net value added.
9. The individual consumption expenditure of NPISH is usually integrated into the final consumption expenditure of households.
10. In SNA, no final consumption is recorded for corporations, because corporations are not considered to be final users of goods and services, except for capital products (see SNA 2008, A4.16).
11. "A special case of benefits payable in kind is that of reimbursements, when the household initially makes a cash outlay but the government reimburses some or all of the expense. For example, when a payment is made by an employee or other member of a resident household for health or education benefits and these are subsequently reimbursed by government, they are not shown as a social insurance benefit and thus as part of compensation of employees but as part of the expenditure by government on health services provided to individual household members. The expenditure by government on individual services is part of government final consumption expenditure and not part of household final consumption expenditure nor of compensation of employees" (SNA 2008, 8.104).
12. By definition, the other two institutional sectors of the SNA – non-financial corporations and financial corporations – cannot consume.
13. Individual consumption expenditures are those that are made for the benefit of individual persons or households. All consumption expenditures by households are defined as individual; COICOP Divisions 01 through 12 identify the purposes for which these expenditures are made; All consumption expenditures of NPISH are also treated, by convention, as being for the benefit of individual households; COICOP Division 13 identifies the purposes for which the expenditures of NPISH are made; but, only some of the consumption expenditures of general government are defined as individual (COICOP Division 14).
14. The corresponding codes for the COICOP (NIPSH) are 13.2.1, 13.2.2, 13.2.3; for the COICOP (government) 14.2.1, 14.2.2, 14.2.3.
15. "It is possible for NPISH to produce collective services. For example a privately funded non-profit institution may undertake medical research and make its results freely available. However, unless such activities are evident and quantifiable, the assumption can be made that the expenditure of NPISH is on individual goods and services only" (SNA 2008, 9.107).
16. The classification of production activities used in SNA, which is ISIC (in Europe NACE), is closely related to the CPC, or CPA and so one might try to link the items of HCxHP to CPC/CPA. Norway and Portugal have tried to build up correspondence tables between CPC/CPA and HPxHC. In Norway, for example, the classification of products consists of a six-digit code. One can tell by the product number the type of service, the producer of the service, and to some extent the financing source. The CPA product classification combined with data on purpose, also from the national accounts, is the basis for the mapping from Norwegian National Accounts to SHA. For each and every specific combination of product by purpose there is a link to a specific HC, HF and HP. This code list is established as an integral part of the technical framework of the system of Norwegian National Accounts, and the mapping is carried out within this framework. For details see Brændvag (2008).

17. The interventions cover the financing of the benefits and related administrative costs, as well as the actual provision of benefits.

18. See the ESSPROS Manual, Eurostat (2008).

19. The NACE is the European Classification of Economic Activities; it is derived from the ISIC, in the sense that it is more detailed than the ISIC. The ISIC and NACE have exactly the same items at the highest levels, while the NACE is more detailed at lower levels.

20. Several national studies have tried to match the activity classifications used by SNA and SHA. A comparison between the activities of the NAICS and the US NHEA can be found in Hartman *et al.* (2010), Table 4.

21. By definition, corporations do not consume.

22. A PPO is a medical plan where coverage is provided to subscribers through a network of selected health care providers, although in some cases subscribers may go outside the network and pay a larger share of the cost (see CMS, 2010).

23. Following the Eurostat Manual on Government Deficit and Debt, the institutional subsector "social security funds (S.1314)" includes all central, state and local institutional units whose principal activity is to provide social benefits and which fulfil each of the following two criteria: 1) by law or by regulation certain groups of the population are obliged to participate in the scheme or to pay contributions; 2) general government is responsible for the management of the institution in respect of the settlement or approval of the contributions and benefits independently from its role as supervisory body or employer.

ANNEX B

The Relationship between SHA and SNA

Introduction

This annex illustrates the relationship between the System of Health Accounts (SHA) and the System of National Accounts (SNA). Readers who are to some extent familiar with either health accounts or national accounts, but not both, will find a description of how health expenditure and financing data reported in the SHA cross-classified tables relate to the main macroeconomic variables in the SNA. In other words, the point is to develop a common language between the two disciplines, which should be of value both theoretically and practically.

From a theoretical viewpoint, this annex shows how, in principle, SHA data can be reorganised and displayed in a form very similar to the form used by the SNA (*i.e.* supply and use tables and the sequence of integrated economic accounts). This kind of representation would allow users of SHA data to relate the categories included in the SHA to the macroeconomic variables included in SNA (*e.g.* the relationship between current expenditure on health and health consumption of households).

At the same time, this section has a practical value in that it could be useful to health accountants who need to retrieve data from their national accounts (for example, if basic information included in SNA represent the sole source to compile SHA tables, or if a comparison with related national accounting aggregates is required). Moreover, it provides basic guidelines for the compilation of a full set of additional SNA-type accounts, which can supplement the information included in the SHA cross-classified tables. The choice of whether national authorities compile the SHA cross-classified tables only or, additionally, the corresponding SNA-type tables, will depend on the priorities set at a national level. It is not intended that the assembly of the additional set of SNA-type tables should be an integral and essential part of the data compilation under the revised SHA methodology. Those interested in enhancing the analytical power of SHA can use this annex as guidance for studying and reporting health expenditure from a different perspective.

A dual representation of the health system

The statistical information included in SHA can be presented by means of two groups of tables, also called accounts: the typical SHA cross-classified tables, and a set of tables similar to those proposed by the System of National Accounts (SNA). It is worth noting that the elementary information forming the basis of the two representations is the same, that is, the flows and stocks identified by SHA boundaries.[1]

When delimiting the health system, SHA 2011 identifies two sets of boundaries (see Chapter 4): the first, known as the "core accounting framework", refers essentially to the value of health care products (goods and services) consumed by the population; the second, labelled the "extended accounting framework", gives a fuller economic picture of the health system. The information included in the "extended framework" can in turn be clustered in two groups: the first includes health specific information (such as health expenditure by disease, age or gender, or by health products) is classified by means of SHA-specific classifications and is generally presented via various cross-classified tables set out in this Manual. The second group includes information which, by its nature, is not necessarily specific to the health system (*e.g.* inputs used in the production of hospital services, such as water and electricity) and can be organised and presented using a set of T-accounts.[2]

As shown in Figure B.1.1, the two information sets partially overlap and identify three subsets of statistical information: a first set of information which is typical of the health system and which can be displayed by using SHA tables only (area A in Figure B.1.1), for example, expenditure on health broken down by beneficiaries' characteristics or expressed in terms of health-specific purchasing power parity standards (PPP). A second set consists of macroeconomic information referring to the consumption of health products and its financing, which can be represented using either SNA-type tables or SHA-specific tables. Finally, there is a third set of economic information (the components of the demand side of the health system other than consumption and the supply-side components) which can be represented using SNA tables only. Examples of the first and third sets were given above (health expenditure by provider and disease on the one hand and the production account on the other); while an example of the overlapping set could be information concerning the consumption of medicines.

In principle, the information recorded in SHA on health expenditure and its financing is also included in SNA, as the latter covers all the economic activities (and financial transactions) that take place in a country.[3] The two systems, however, report the information differently: SHA, for example, employs its own specific classifications (*i.e.* the ICHA classification of providers, of financing schemes (derived from agents) and health functions,) to break down the health expenditure at a high level of detail. In addition, SHA highlights the origin and destination of the economic (and financial) flows through the use of cross-classified tables. SNA, on the other hand, is composed of two main sets of tables: the supply and use (SUT) framework (including the symmetric input-output table and the accounts by industry) and the sequence of integrated economic accounts (IEA) for the institutional sectors. The supply and use (SUT) framework describes in detail the production process (*i.e.* cost structure, output, income generated and employment) plus the imports and the use of goods and services (*i.e.* intermediate and final consumption, exports and capital formation), while the sequence of integrated economic accounts (IEA) provides information on how income is generated, distributed and used as final consumption or saving as well as the process of the accumulation of financial and non-financial assets.

Although the approach proposed here uses the SNA structure of accounts (*i.e.* the supply and use tables and the sequence of integrated economic accounts), it retains SHA concepts, including definitions of variables and classifications. For example, all accounts based on the SNA sequence of integrated economic accounts are developed with reference to the health providers (see Chapter 6) and to the health financing agents (see Annex D)

Figure B.1.1. **SHA 2011 information set**

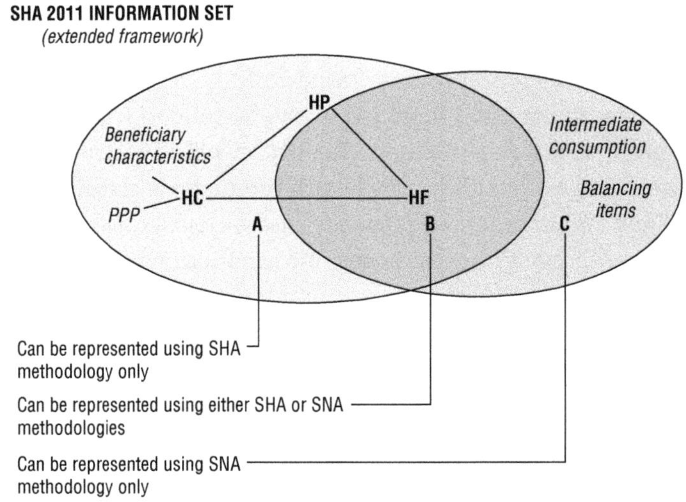

Source: IHAT for SHA 2011.

rather than to the institutional sectors in SNA. Also, the health care goods and services identified by SHA boundaries are classified using the SHA functional classification (see Chapter 5) instead of the CPC, COICOP or COFOG (for a correspondence between the different classifications see Annex A).

Figure B.1.2 below outlines the links between the two representations. The unbroken lines show the links across SHA tables, while dashes show the correspondence between

Figure B.1.2. **Links between the System of National Accounts (SNA) and the System of Health Accounts (SHA)**

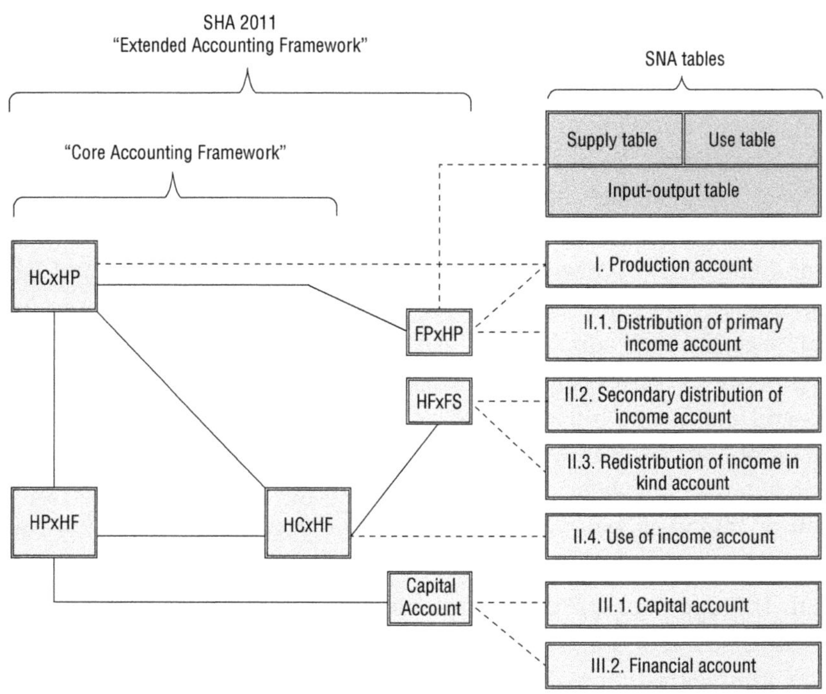

Source: IHAT for SHA 2011.

SHA aggregates and their counterpart included in the supply and use tables or in the relevant account in the sequence of integrated economic accounts (IEA). In short, the following links can be established:

- Current health expenditure reported in SHA is the sum of health care goods and services for final consumption of resident units (see Chapter 3). When broken down by providers (as in SHA table HCxHP), it also represents the value of that part of the output of the health providers which is consumed by households, Non-profit institutions serving households (NPISH) and General Government are valued at market prices. SHA calls "provision" the value of the health providers' output used as final consumption. The same information would be recorded in SNA in the supply and use tables and in the production account, which is the account showing output as a resource and intermediate consumption as use. The value of goods and services consumed as intermediate consumption by the health providers is also recorded in SHA in the HCxFP tables, which makes use of a specific Factors of provision classification.
- The compensation of employees of the health providers is also reported in the HPxFP table. Compensation of employees corresponds to the "compensation of employees" reported in the distribution of primary income account in SNA.
- In SHA 2011, the HFxFS table reports the revenues of the financing schemes (see Chapter 8), that is, the funds which have been transferred to the financing agents from the bodies collecting and pooling the funds. Revenues might be collected by different bodies (*e.g.* central/local government, social security agency, commercial insurance fund, employer fund, health care provider, etc.) using a variety of contribution mechanisms (*e.g.* direct taxes, indirect taxes, payroll tax revenues, often called "social health insurance contributions", voluntary prepayment, usually for voluntary health insurance). In SNA, each health contribution mechanism is included in different items of the classification of economic flows (called the classification of transactions) and recorded in a different stage of the sequence of accounts. Consider, for instance, taxes on cigarettes used in some countries to fund health care programmes. In the SNA, these would be included under the category of taxes on products and would be reported in the "Distribution of primary income accounts", which is the account showing how much of the value added is generated by labour in the form of the compensation of employees and how much of the value of output is payable to the government in the form of taxes (less subsidies) on products. In the same way, the "social health insurance contributions" would be included in the broader category of "social contributions" and reported in the "Secondary distribution of income accounts", which reflects the redistribution of (primary) income through monetary transfers (income and property taxes, social contributions, social benefits other than social benefits in kind, other current transfers). SHA, instead, focuses only on the last step, that is, only the resources of the financing schemes (that pay the health providers) are recorded in the HFxFS table, while SNA reports all the transactions, some in the "Distribution of primary income accounts" and the remainder in the "Secondary distribution of income accounts". The latter accounts also record all the transfers made between the different actors (*e.g.* the transfer of funds from the central government to local governments), which in the health financing literature is referred to as "pooling", and which is not recorded in SHA (see Chapter 8 and Annex D).

- The purchase of health products from health care providers made either by the entities pooling the funds (third-party payers) or by households as out-of-pocket expenditure is recorded in SHA in the table HPxHF. In SNA, these expenditures are recorded in the "use of disposable income account".
- Finally, the SNA Capital account records the value of the non-financial assets that are acquired, or disposed of. The information on the acquisitions less disposals can be combined with the saving and the capital transfers to calculate the change in net worth. A similar account is developed in SHA (see Chapter 11). The SHA version of the capital accounts, however, is extended to also include the relevant changes in financial assets. These would be recorded in SNA in the financial accounts.

To conclude, all aggregates included in SHA to account for the health activities of production, collection of funds, pooling of funds, purchase of health goods and services and accumulation are in principle also recorded in SNA. Therefore, a set of empty SNA-type tables could be populated by using the information collected in the SHA extended accounting framework.

Differences between SHA and SNA

Although SHA adopts definitions and concepts derived from SNA, there exist a few important differences that ought to be borne in mind whenever comparing the two systems. Of particular note are the extension of the production boundaries in the SHA, the inclusion of some ancillary services in final consumption, the treatment of goods purchased and resold by retailers, and the capitalisation of research and development.

SHA extends the SNA production boundaries by including, under certain conditions, a part of the household production of health services for own final use. The extension of the production boundaries is limited to those health services whose costs are partially or completely covered by dependency allowances. Therefore, if households receive transfers in cash to cover a sizeable share of the costs of services to persons with severe functional mobility or cognitive handicaps, the transfers are treated as quasi-salary in SHA and a corresponding "production value" is then calculated and included in current health expenditure.

Secondly, the final consumption of health services in the SHA also includes the services of "occupational health" (*e.g.* surveillance of employee health and therapeutic care on or off business premises, see Chapter 5), which are considered as an ancillary activity in the central framework of the SNA and treated as intermediate consumption.

Thirdly, SHA considers the goods purchased and resold by retailers as their intermediate consumption, whereas SNA excludes them, as only minimal processing such as grading, cleaning, packaging, etc. are performed. Two consequences derive from the different approaches: 1) producers of health goods are excluded from the provider classification, and 2) retailers' output is measured in SHA by the sum of the total value of the goods they purchase for resale plus the trade margins realised, while in SNA only the latter component is considered.

Lastly, research and development is considered as a non-financial asset in the SNA (and therefore included in the capital accounts) whereas SHA 2011 has excluded the creation of R&D assets on practical grounds.

Box B.1.1. **Final consumption expenditure and actual final consumption of households**

Final consumption consists of expenditure on final goods and services (goods and services that are not used for the purpose of production). Final goods or services are acquired for the direct satisfaction of human needs, whether individual or collective. Three different sectors can acquire consumption products:

- *Household* acquire goods and services (for individual consumption), which are then used to satisfy the needs and wants of members of that household.
- *Government* spends to benefit specific individuals (*e.g.* health care, education, food aid, etc.). Besides expenditure for individual benefit, the government also spends for collective purposes, such as public administration, defence, security, general health improvement, etc., which benefit the society as a whole but not specific individuals.
- The final consumption expenditure of *non-profit institutions serving households* (NPISH) is by convention classified as individual consumption only.

Therefore, to satisfy their needs, households actually benefit from some goods and services paid for by themselves or by other institutions (government and NPISH). The products acquired by the government sector or by NPISH are transferred to households as social transfers in kind. The table below shows final consumption expenditure by institutional sectors (that actually spent) and by purposes (individual or collective consumption).

Final consumption expenditure and actual final consumption of households

Purpose	Sector			
	Households	Government	NPISH	Total acquisitions
Individual	X	X (=Social transfers in kind)	X (=Social transfers in kind)	Households' actual individual final consumption
Collective		X		Government's actual collective final cons.
Total	Household final cons. Expenditure	Government final cons. expenditure	NPISH final cons. expenditure	Actual final cons. = Total final cons. exp.

Source: IHAT for SHA 2011.

Thus, the overall expenditure for individual consumption that actually benefits households equals the sum of:

- Final consumption expenditure of households;
- Social transfers in kind from the government;
- Social transfers in kind from NPISH.

The sum of the three components is the "*Households actual individual final consumption*". This concept was introduced in SNA93 with the objective of better comparing final consumption of households across space and time in the country and internationally, while taking into account government social policies and NPISH activities.

Box B.1.1. **Final consumption expenditure and actual final consumption of households** *(cont.)*

Social transfers in kind

Social transfers in kind include:

- *Individual final expenditure of the government sector (less sales)*. This includes the output of individual goods and services which are produced by the government sector and distributed free to individuals, such as education, health, social security and welfare, sports and recreation, culture, provision of housing, collection of household refuse and operation of transport. It excludes general administration and regulatory and research expenditures in each category.
- *Social benefits in kind,* which include:
  - *Reimbursements* from government's social security funds to households on specified goods and services bought by households on the market;
  - *Other social security benefits in kind except reimbursement.* This includes goods and services that are not produced by the government sector but are bought and distributed free or almost free to households under the social security funds (any payment by household must be deducted);
  - *Social assistance benefits in kind.* This includes goods and services similar to other social security benefits, but not under social security schemes.

Health supply and use tables

This section looks more closely at the example of supply and use tables for health care. Any health care good or service available within an economy must have been produced domestically or have been imported. At the same time, any health good or health service entering an economy must be used for intermediate consumption, final consumption, capital formation (including changes in inventories) or exports (Figure B.1.3). These two statements can be combined to give the following accounting identity:

Equation 1. Goods and services accounting identity

Supply		Use
Output + Imports	=	Intermediate consumption + Final consumption + Capital formation + Exports

By subtracting the item "Intermediate consumption" from both sides of the previous identity we obtain the so-called "goods and services account", which is one of the most basic, if not the most basic, identity in the SNA.[267,268] This kind of identity can be compiled for any health good or service. A complete set of health care product (goods and services) identities can be arranged in a matrix, in which each row represents a health product and each column the supply and use.

Health supply table (H-ST)

Taking only the left-hand side of the identity, it is possible to isolate a smaller matrix, with the health care products in the rows while the columns show whether the products

Figure B.1.3. **Health supply and use tables (H-SUT)**

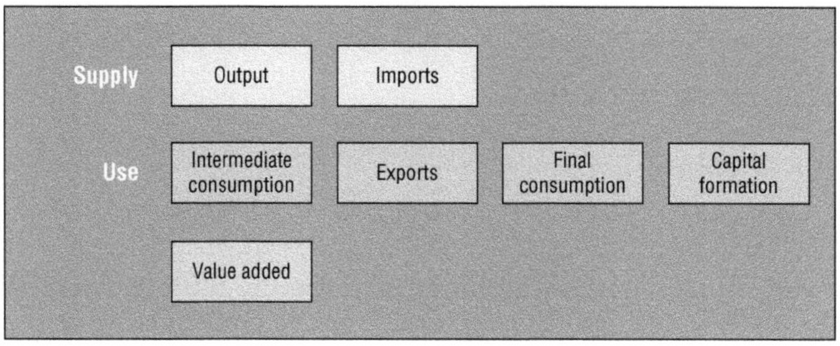

Source: IHAT for SHA 2011.

are the output of a domestic producer or have been imported. As such a matrix would be difficult to handle due to its large number of rows, it is convenient to group the health care products. Products may be classified either according to the health functional classification (see Chapter 5) or a classification of health care products (see Annex E).

For analytical purposes, however, it could also be of interest to identify the different domestic producers of health goods and services. This could be done by introducing separate columns for each group of providers and using the classification of health providers (see Chapter 6). However, a provider can also produce health-related output and non-health products. These health-related and non-health products can also be recorded in separated rows. In this way all the information on the output of each provider can be kept, which might then facilitate a consistency check. For the same reason it would also be helpful to record taxes (less subsidies) on each product.

An example of a complete matrix could thus have the following form:

The health supply table (Table B.1.1) shows, along each row, the health product (classified according to the functional classification) produced both by domestic providers

Table B.1.1. **Health supply table (H-ST)**

		Providers of health goods and services			Taxes less subsidies on products	Total output	Imports (*f.o.b.*)	Total resources
		HP_1		HP_j HP_9				
		(1)	…	(9)	(10)	(11)=(1)+..+(9)+(10)	(12)	(13)=(11)+(12)
Health goods and services (*)	**HC_1 : HC_i : HC_9**	$A_{i,j}$			$(T\text{-}S)_i$	$THO_i = \Sigma_j A_{i,j} + (T\text{-}S)_i$	I_i	$TR_i = THO_i + I_i$
Health output		$B_j = \Sigma_i A_{i,j}$			$\Sigma_i (T\text{-}S)_i$	$\Sigma_i \Sigma_j Ai_{,j} + (T\text{-}S)_i$	$\Sigma_i I$	$\Sigma_i TR_i$
Health-related output	**HCR.1 . HCR_k**	$C_{k,j}$						
Total health-related output		$D_j = \Sigma_k C_{k,j}$						
Non-health output		E_j						
Total output		$F_j = B_j + D_j + E_j$						

*: The health products correspond to the health functions.
Source: IHAT for SHA 2011.

and imported.[8] The sum of the two components (production and imports) represents the value of the health resources that are available.

Description of the elements of the H-ST

- Columns of the H-ST

Health providers

In the health supply table H-ST, matrix A shows the different categories of health products produced by each health care provider. The total health output by each provider of health products is shown in vector B. Each element Bj of the vector B would represent the total health output of each provider included in the HP classification.

The value of the secondary production of the health care providers (health-related output and non-health output) should be recorded in the matrix C and the vector E, respectively. When a provider produces health–related products as a secondary activity, these products are recorded under matrix C, by the type of health-related product. The vector D corresponds to the total of health-related output that is produced on a secondary basis by each provider. Take, for instance, a long-term nursing care facility that is linked to a facility providing social care: the fees for the latter activity should be recorded under column HP.2.1 (Long-term nursing care facility) in row HCR.1 (for example, if it corresponds to long-term social care) in cell $C_{1,2.1}$ in matrix C, and if this is the only amount of health-related output that is produced, then the respective amount should also be recorded in vector D as a total of health-related-output that is provided additionally by the health care provider. Elements Dj of vector D represent the total value of the health-related output of each provider.

As health care providers may also provide non-health output on a secondary basis, this could be recorded under vector E. For instance, many providers sell non-health products, such as renting space for small shops, charging visitors for parking spaces or serving meals to visitors (other than meals provided to inpatients and personnel).

Finally, the vector F shows the total output of Health providers, which is likely to be composed mainly of health goods and services, but which could also include health-related and non-health products. The elements Fj of vector F would be the sum of the corresponding elements Bj+Dj+Ej Non-health providers which produce health services on a secondary basis.

Some producers of health-related products could also produce, as secondary production, health products. For instance, home help providers produce mainly health-related output in social care, but could provide nursing care services as well as other non-health services. The health-related output could be recorded in matrices C; the sales of nursing services could be recorded in A; while any non-health output could be recorded under vector E. The total output should be the sum of the three types of output and should be recorded in vector F.

Finally, there are non-health producers that manage their own occupational health schemes in a private way by producing their own health output for their employees and their families. Sometimes these productive units create separate establishments for the provision of health goods and services, and therefore these establishments can be considered as health providers, because their output is mainly health. In other cases these non-health producers provide health products without creating a separate establishment, that is, output that is produced on a secondary basis or, as is more often the case, as an ancillary activity. Moreover, many non-health producers provide occupational medical services to their own employees as an ancillary service. According to SHA, these ancillary services must be considered as separate output. This is a conceptual difference between national accounts and SHA. The ancillary services would be recorded as output of non-health producers in matrix A. The total health output of these non-health producers would be recorded under vector B.

Taxes less subsidies on products

The supply table would also record the taxes less subsidies on products that are imposed on health care products. For instance, in some countries there are some taxes, such as value added tax (VAT), that are imposed on pharmaceuticals and other medical goods durables and non-durables and therapeutic appliances. In other countries there may also be health services on which taxes on products are imposed.

The sum of the value of the health goods (valued at basic prices) plus taxes less subsidies equals the value of the health output at purchasers' prices. Column I corresponds to the imports of health goods and services. The total resources available to be used in the health system are shown in column TR.

- Rows of the H-ST

Data for each health and health-related product category that is produced is shown in rows. The value of Health goods and services is broken down by providers and is measured at basic prices, in matrix A. The value is also expressed at purchasers' prices by adding taxes less subsidies. Each element of the column Total output represents the value of health products produced in the economic territory. By adding the imports by product, we get the total resources by health products/functions that are available to be used by the resident units.

Health use table (H-UT)

In a way similar to the supply table, in the H-UT information included in the right-hand side of Equation [1] can be arranged in a matrix that gives a full picture on the use of the output produced by the health providers. The matrix would take the form of a rectangular matrix, where the rows represent all health products available in an economy, valued at purchasers' prices, and the columns indicate the various types of uses.

Although the production of health goods and services is likely to be mainly for final domestic use, a minor part of the total production of the health care system could be exported or consist of intermediate products acquired by other health providers. The value of the output of the health providers can therefore differ from the value of final consumption on health. Consider, for example, a physician in private practice who may also work part-time for a hospital. In that case, a part of his/her output is acquired by another health provider as intermediate consumption. If the health providers' output were wrongly assumed to equal final consumption, a double-counting issue would arise. The reason would be that the sum of the output of the hospital plus the output of the physician would double-count the value of the service that the hospital has purchased from the physician.

The same consideration can apply to imported health products. Imports can be employed either as final consumption or also as intermediate consumption. Using the same example as above, if the physician working part time for a domestic hospital were resident abroad, the purchase of his/her service would be an imported service used as intermediate consumption.

In addition, the beneficiary of the health services provided by resident providers may be either a resident or a non-resident unit. For example, the service provided by a domestic hospital to a foreign tourist should be considered as an exported service.

Therefore, health care goods and services available in any given economy may in principle be used as intermediate and final consumption, or exported.

At the same time, health providers might be acquiring health-related or non-health products as input for their production process. For instance, consider the use of chemicals in ancillary diagnosis services, such as imaging or clinical laboratory.

However, health products are most likely employed as final consumption. The perspective of final consumption is the actual consumption of the households, regardless of the fact that part of the expenditures are financed by health insurance schemes and the collective consumption of services and administration funds.

Description of the elements of the H-UT

- Columns of the H-UT

The health providers use inputs of a different nature to produce their output. These could include heath products produced by other providers, health-related products or non-health products.

The health products employed as intermediate consumption by other health providers should be recorded in matrix HIC. Examples could include the case of a hospital using an external laboratory to perform blood tests. Also, health providers may subcontract with self-employed health professionals who work as own-account workers. These could be doctors, nurses and other health professionals who are not employees of the provider. The subcontracting of these workers should be recorded as the intermediate consumption of the provider to whom these self-employed render their services.

The health providers also consume health-related and non-health products. Those inputs should be recorded in the matrices HRIC and NHIC, respectively. An example of health-related products used as intermediate consumption would be a self-employed clinical social worker who renders their services to a hospital (family planning, individual and group therapy in Mental health and substance abuse), whereas non-health products would include water, electricity, etc.

Final uses includes three broad categories: final consumption, gross capital formation and exports.

The final consumption of health goods and services describes all the health goods and services that are used for the final use of households individually and collectively. Individual final consumption (vector IFC) includes all the health care products/functions that are supplied to the households for final use, such as services of curative care, rehabilitative care, long-term care, ancillary services and pharmaceuticals, among others. All the healthcare services are part of personal health expenditure, regardless of who finances these healthcare services. The column represented in the vector IFC shows total individual final consumption by product or health care service.

Table B.1.2. **Health use table (H-UT)**

		Intermediate consumption				Final uses			
		Providers of health goods and services			Total intermediate consumption	Final consumption of health goods and services		Gross capital formation	Exports
		HP_1	HP_i	HP_9		Individual cons.	Collective cons.		
		(1)	...	(9)	(10)	(11)	(12	(13	(14
Health goods and services (*)	HC_1		$HIC_{i,j}$		$\Sigma_j HIC_{i,j}$	IFC_i	$CCAF_i$	$HGCF_i$	X_i
	:								
	HC_i								
	:								
	HC_9								
	Totals		$\Sigma_i HIC_{i,j}$		$\Sigma_i \Sigma_j HIC_{i,j}$	$\Sigma_i IFC_i$	$\Sigma_i CCAF_i$	$\Sigma_i HGCF$	$\Sigma_i X$
Other products	**Health-related products**		$HRIC_j$		$\Sigma_j HRIC_j$			Software produced by hospitals for other hospitals	
	Non-health products		$NHIC_j$		$\Sigma_j NHIC_j$			Other assets produced by health care providers	
Totals			TIC_j		TIC				
Gross value added (Health)			GVA_j		GVA				
Net value added (Health)			NVA_j		NVA_j				
Compensations of employees			$D1_j$		D1				
Other taxes less subsidies on production			$(D29\text{-}D39)_j$		(D29-D39)				
Gross operating surplus /Gross mixed income			$(GOS/GMI)_j$		$(GOS/GMI)_j$				
Net operating surplus/Net mixed income			$(NOS/NMI)_j$		$(NOS/NMI)_j$				
Consumption of fixed capital			CCF_j		CCF				
Gross fixed capital formation			$GFCF_j$		GFCF				
Health labour input, of which: **- Employees** **- Self-employed**			L_j		L				

*: The health products classified according to the health functions classification.
Source: IHAT for SHA 2011.

The collection and administration of funds that are final consumption correspond to the health products/functions of prevention and health services and health administration and health insurance. It includes the administrative cost not only of public health insurance but also of private health insurance. The respective amounts should be recorded in vector CCAF.

The vector gross capital formation (HGCF) records all the assets produced by health providers and also acquired as gross capital formation. In practice, intellectual properties are considered in this column, plus "Changes in inventories" (*e.g.* pharmaceuticals and other medical non-durables and therapeutic appliances and other medical durables).

The column "Exports (X)" shows the amounts of health products that are provided to non-resident units.

- Rows of the H-UT

As previously mentioned, this table shows the health products (resources) that are available to be used as intermediate consumption by other providers, and as final consumption, individually and collectively by households, or exported. For the medical goods dispensed to outpatients, it shows how much is available to be used as intermediate consumption, final consumption, held in stocks or exported.

The first section "Health goods and services" is shown by type of product/function, with an extension for other products that are used to provide some medical services, and shows the way these products are used in the health system. The section "Non-health products" that is represented as one row only provides an indication of the other inputs that are used to produce, by provider, health and health-related services. For instance, the inpatient services as part of curative care, by Hospital A, is mainly used as individual final consumption. However, if Hospital B subcontracts Hospital A to provide these kinds of services to patients, then the provision of these services is considered as the intermediate consumption of Hospital B. The output of these services (shown in the health supply table) provided by Hospital A to Hospital B is already included in the output provided by Hospital B, and therefore is allocated as being used by households as Individual Final Consumption.

The output of collective health care services (prevention and public health services and health administration and health insurance) are totally allocated in the respective product code to final consumption as the collective consumption and administration of funds (vector CCAF). In the proposed H-UT, the cost of private health insurance is considered as a final consumption of administration funds, together with collective consumption of general government.

The health goods and services that are provided to non-residents are recorded by type of health-service in vector X, as exports. For instance, services provided by hospitals to non-residents are recorded in this vector by type of service rendered. Moreover, the exports of pharmaceuticals and other medical goods are recorded under vector X in the respective product. In fact, the medical goods may be used by other providers as intermediate consumption, are allocated to final consumption of households when dispensed to outpatients, and may be exported or held in stocks (Column GCF).

The row "Gross value added, by provider", results from the difference between the total output, by provider, and the Intermediate consumption, by provider.

The row "Other taxes less subsidies on production" includes eventual "Other taxes on production" (equal to D29 in SNA93) and "Other subsidies on production" (equal to D39 in the SNA) that are paid/received by providers of health goods and services.

The operating surplus corresponds to the income obtained by the producers from the use of their own production facilities. It is the balancing item of the generation account, and it can be estimated separately or as a balancing item. "Gross operating surplus" is one of the components of "Gross value added" in the income approach.

The self-employed and the own-account workers obtain income that cannot be split between their profit and what should be considered as remuneration for their work. This income is called "mixed income".

"Gross capital formation" includes the investment carried out by health providers in health assets (tangible and intangible). Gross capital formation comprises: gross fixed capital formation; changes in inventories; and acquisitions less disposals of valuables.

It is worth noting the difference between the aggregate "Gross capital formation" reported in the vector HGCF and the vector GFCF. The former refers to the capital goods produced by the health providers. The latter records the capital goods acquired by the providers.

The row "Consumption of fixed capital" measures the decrease of the value of fixed assets as a consequence of their use in the process of production. It enables the change from "Gross balancing items" to "Net balancing items". It is also a component of non-market output, for it is considered as a cost of production. In this case it reflects only health providers.

Health labour measures employment in health, which can be divided into health employees and the self-employed. It can be measured in persons, posts or full-time equivalent/hours worked. The income received by employees for their participation in the production process is recorded under "Compensation of employees". The income paid to the self-employed is "mixed income". A person can be working as an employee as well as self-employed. Under such circumstances, usually the former is the main activity.

The shaded areas in Table B.1.2 show the information set identified by the SHA boundaries, which can be represented through the SHA cross-classified tables as well as through the health use table (*i.e.* current expenditure on health + capital formation). The first area (top right-hand side) includes the final consumption of health products classified through the functional classification. The second reports the gross capital formation broken down by providers.

The sequence of Health Integrated Economic Accounts (H-IEA)

The health supply and use tables, together with the health input-output table, provide detailed analyses of the process of production and the use of health goods and services. The information reported in the supply and use tables can be further elaborated to show, on the one hand, how the income derived from the production of health goods and services is divided between the factors of production (labour and capital) and used for the acquisition of capital goods by health providers. It can then show, on the other hand, how the income available to households is increased by the provision of health goods and services and how the resources needed for the provision of health products are collected, pooled, transferred and finally used.

Consider, for example, the consumption of health services. As with any other products, the consumption of health services is the result of a choice between spending the available resources or saving them for future use. These two possible uses of the available money, that is, consumption (called "final consumption expenditure" in the national accountants' jargon) and saving, are recorded in the sequence of integrated accounts in a table called "use of disposable income account".

Using the same example, we might wonder who has purchased that particular service. Was it the household itself using its own resources, or was it the government (or social security or an NPISH)? If it was the government that purchased the health service, it would obviously not be the government itself that actually consumed the health service. Rather, households would actually benefit from the service. As a consequence, the value of goods and services consumed by households (the "final consumption expenditure" included in the "use of disposable income account") could be adjusted by adding the value of those goods and services which, although paid by the government, were actually consumed by the households. Therefore, National Accounts employ a different table to report the "actual consumption", as opposed to the "final consumption expenditure". This table is entitled

Box B.1.2. **T-Account**

A T-Account is a standard accounting tool whose name comes from its distinctive shape, like the capital letter T.

Account name	
Uses	Resources

The account title is reported above the top portion of the T. The left side of the base of the T includes the *uses* (*i.e.* the amount spent), while the right side shows the *resources* (*i.e.* the amount received). The vertical part of the T accounts shows the transactions, each of which identifies a row where entries can be reported, either under uses or under resources.

The difference between the total resources recorded on one side of the account and the total uses recorded on the other side gives the *balancing item*. Balancing items are economic constructs of considerable interest and analytical significance. Examples of balancing items in National Accounts include value added, disposable income and saving. Balancing items can be expressed gross or net, the difference being the consumption of fixed capital.

T-accounts can be built for any statistical unit (*i.e.* households and providers) or groups of statistical units. In order to simplify the reading and the comparison of different groups of units, T-Accounts can be presented in a more compact form. Using just one table, it is possible to present in adjacent columns on the left-hand side the uses of each single T-Account. The same occurs for the resources grouped in a set of columns on the right-hand side.

Account name			
Uses		Resources	
Households	Providers	Providers	Households

It is worth noting that each transaction implies that the amount spent by a unit corresponds to the amount received by another unit. This gives rise to a pair of matching entries within the accounts, the first recorded as use for the unit making the payment, the other as resource for the unit receiving the payment. This bookkeeping principle is traditionally called *double-entry*.

A further step is the "consolidation" of the accounts. A *consolidated T-account* is simply an aggregation of single T-Accounts.

Account name	
Uses	Resources
All Units	All Units

"Use of adjusted disposable income account". In an accounting logic, where consistency is a stringent requisite, if the amount spent is adjusted, then the resources available also need to be adjusted, in that to spend more you need more. Therefore the concept of "disposable income" also needs to be modified to take into account the value of goods and services transferred to the households. Therefore the algebraic sum of disposable income and the transfers (called social transfers in kind) results in "Adjusted disposable income", which is reported in the "Redistribution of income in kind account". The "Adjusted disposable income" exceeds the "Disposable income" of those economic units, like households, receiving the transfers, whereas the contrary applies to the units offering the goods and services (*e.g.* the government).

Besides the purchase of health care goods and services on behalf of households, the health system is characterised by a number of other transfers and, more generally, by other kind of transactions.[9] For example, consider transfers of funds between central and local government, or between central government and the National Health Service; another example could be the payment of contributions to the National Health Insurance or the payment of premiums to private health insurance companies, or the transfer of funds from abroad for health-specific projects (*e.g.* AIDS programmes). All the transactions related to the health system can be grouped according to the economic activities that they refer to, such as production of health goods and services, and the generation, distribution, redistribution and use of income. In National accounts each transaction is recorded in a specific account.

Each account shows the resources available to the institutional units and the uses made of these resources. The difference between the total resources recorded on one side of any account and the total uses recorded on the other side of the same account gives a balancing item (*e.g.* value added, disposable income and saving), which encapsulates the net result of the activities covered by the account in question. The balancing item from one account is carried forward as the first item in the following account. Consider for example the "adjusted disposable income", which is the balancing item of the "Redistribution of income in kind account" and, at the same time, the starting point for the construction of the "Use of adjusted disposable income account". The balancing items are therefore the chain element which allows the different tables showing the economic activities (production, the generation, distribution, redistribution and use of income) to be connected and thereby make the set of accounts an articulated whole. For this reason, the set of economic accounts are called "integrated economic accounts".

Integrated economic accounts (IEA) provide a flexible and powerful tool to record in a systematic way all the transactions taking place between the economic units included in the health boundaries. They are a powerful tool as they allow all transactions to be recorded, and most of all this provides a methodology to record all the transactions in a systematic way. This tool is flexible because, although presented in the SNA to provide a synthesis of a country's whole economy, it can be adapted to a specific sector and to specific analytical needs. The following example shows how the elements of the sequence of integrated economic accounts can be re-aggregated to meet specific SHA needs.

- *The accounts of the health system*

When referring to a country's whole economy, the SNA sequence of integrated economic accounts (IEA) provides information on how the entire national income is

Box B.1.3. **Interpreting expenditure by financing schemes as an aggregation of transactions**

Chapter 7 presents the concept of the financing scheme as a category for international comparisons of health expenditure. In this section we show how the concept of the financing scheme would fit in the sequence of accounts.

Consider a household subscribing to a mandatory health insurance policy with a private insurance company: the value of the premium is recorded as a use under the household accounts and as a resource under the insurance company accounts. If the same household also subscribes with the same insurance company a complementary voluntary insurance, a new transaction is recorded in both accounts (again under uses for the households and resources for the insurance company). However, as the two transactions differ in nature (one being voluntary and the other mandatory), the payment of the two premiums can be registered using two different headings (payment of premium for voluntary insurance vs. payment of premium for mandatory insurance). The same distinction could be applied to the claims, in that claims paid by the insurance company in force of a voluntary insurance policy are distinguished from those made because a mandatory insurance was subscribed (see figure below).

Voluntary and mandatory insurance

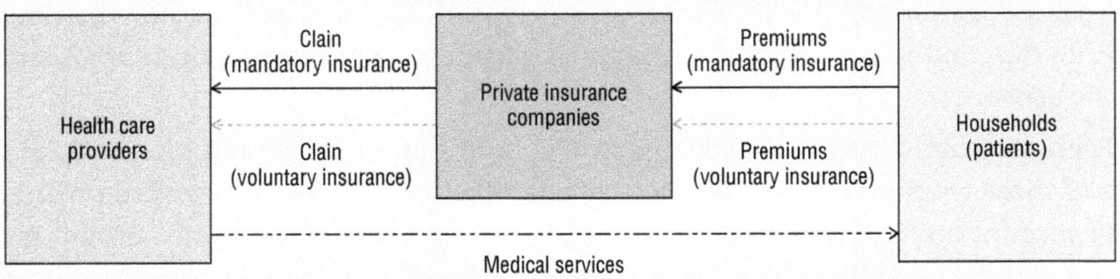

Source: IHAT for SHA 2011.

If for international comparison, it is deemed more convenient to separate voluntary premiums and claims from mandatory ones and then aggregate them into the categories of the financing schemes classification, this can be done by aggregating the transactions that take place between the financing agents, the providers and the units providing the resources to the financing schemes. All those transactions are in principle reported in the integrated sequence of economic accounts (IEA).

generated, distributed and used as final consumption or saving. This is done by reporting in different accounts all the transactions that take place both between resident units and between these units and non-resident units. A similar set of accounts can be developed for a specific sector of the economy, like the health sector. As in the case for the supply and use table, the basic idea in SHA is to consider a set of empty tables, similar to those used in SNA, and populate them with the information available either in the core or in the extended SHA accounting frameworks.

The two main differences between the SNA and SHA sequence of integrated economic accounts are first, the way resident units are grouped and second, the classification used for transactions. In SNA, units are grouped into five institutional sectors, while the non-resident units form the rest of the world; in SHA, resident units engaging in health transactions are classified according to the Provider (if they provide health goods and services), the financing agents (if they collect, pool and use resources) or as households, with the rest of the world being included in both the provider and financing agents classifications. The classification of transactions used in a health-IEA would differ slightly from the corresponding SNA classification so as to show the required level of disaggregation, which is usually more detailed.

- *Behind the delivery of health products: the production and generation of income accounts*

Health care products (goods and services) consumed by resident households are recorded in the SHA core accounting framework as Current health expenditure. In doing this, SHA privileges a demand-side approach, in that the purchase of health products is considered together with its financing. However, a supply-side approach is also possible, in that health products consumed by the resident households can be regarded as delivered by resident health providers or as imported. Whenever a supply approach is adopted, the structure of production costs becomes of interest. Hence, an account showing at once the value of the output of the health providers together with the set of costs can be derived from the SNA sequence of accounts by combining the production and generation of income accounts (see Table B.1.3 below).

The health providers can, however, also deliver health services to non-resident households (*i.e.* tourists) or to other health providers, which then employ those services as inputs into their production process. Services delivered to non-resident households and to non-resident providers are regarded as "exports", while the services acquired by other resident health providers constitute the intermediate consumption of those provisions. Both exports and intermediate consumption are excluded from the SHA core accounting framework and considered only in the SHA extended framework (see Chapter 3 and 4). Health providers can also produce health-related services or even non-health services. Health-related and non-health services are also excluded from the core framework. So, if the Current health expenditure broken down by providers corresponds to the output of the same health provider, the contrary is not necessarily true. The right-hand side of the production and generation of income account reports all health provider outputs, possibly broken down into health goods and services, delivered to either resident or non-resident units, and the health-related products and non-health products.

The left-hand side of the account (uses side) records the purchase of all goods and services acquired by the health providers for the production of their output. As shown in Chapter 9, the inputs can be broken down into health care goods and services (*e.g.* pharmaceuticals delivered to inpatients or specific tests performed by other providers), non-health care goods and services (*e.g.* electricity, water, disposable equipment) or health-related products. The sum of all the products used by the providers to perform their activities is called "intermediate consumption" in national accounts terminology.

The difference between output and intermediate consumption is the value added, which is the balancing item of the production account. Value added represents the contribution of the factors of production (*e.g.* labour and capital) to increasing the value of goods and services bought as inputs to the production process. Hence, the value added corresponds to the incomes received by the owners of these factors. Value added can be presented gross or net of the consumption of fixed capital. The concepts of intermediate consumption and value added are part of the SHA extended framework, but not of the core framework.

The sum of the value added of all health providers results in the value added of the health system as a whole. The value added of the health system can be used as an important indicator to assess the relative importance of the health system compared with the rest of the economy.[10]

Box B.1.4. **Intermediate consumption**

Intermediate consumption represents the value of the basic materials, components and semi-manufactured goods going into the product, as well as the value of the electricity, the cost of rents, IT services, insurance, legal and accounting services, etc., used in the production of a good or a service. In short, intermediate consumption consists of everything needed to produce other goods and services intended for sale, other than the labour of the workforce and the services provided by plant and machinery, offices and factory buildings. Just as output is not equal to sales, intermediate consumption is not equal to the purchases of goods and services intended to be intermediately consumed. This is because certain intermediate goods used in the production during the period may have been bought and stocked in a previous period. Similarly, some purchases during the period may be consumed after the period has ended, having been stocked in the meantime. In the end, intermediate consumption is equal to the purchases during the period minus the change (positive or negative) in the value of the inventories of goods and services for intermediate consumption. Firms often refer to these inventories as "materials inventories". Like output, intermediate consumption is a flow, corresponding to what has been consumed during a period (a year or a quarter). This leads to the exclusion from the definition of intermediate consumption of the goods used for production but not entirely consumed during the period, such as machinery or software. These capital goods are classified as "gross fixed capital formation" (GFCF).

Source: Lequiller and Blades (2007).

The value added that has been created in the production process is distributed between the factors of production (*i.e.* labour – as compensation of employees, and capital – as gross operating surplus) and taxes on production. The information on the remuneration of the health work-force reported in the table HPxFP corresponds to the information included in this account.

The compensation of employees includes employees' contributions and income tax withheld at source. Similarly, although employees do not in practice receive the employers' social contributions (which, like the employees' contributions, are paid directly to social insurance plans, tax authorities, etc.), the national accounts treat them as if employees did receive them, in such a way as to show the total cost of the labour factor to employers. The contributions included comprise both those actually paid by the employers and so-called imputed contributions. In addition, the account records taxes less subsidies on production under the uses side. These taxes on production are made up of taxes on wages or capital paid by the health providers. The balancing item is operating surplus or mixed income for self-employed providers. The gross operating surplus of a non-market health producer is equal to consumption of Fixed Capital only, as the net operating surplus is by definition nil.

Table B.1.3. **Production and generation of income account of health providers**

	Uses	Resources	
Y	Intermediate consumption	Output at basic prices	X
	FP.3 Materials and services used	*Health goods and services*	
	FP.3.1 Health care services	*Delivered to residents*	
	FP.3.2 Health care goods	*Delivered to non-residents*	
	FP.3.2.1Pharmaceuticals		
	FP.3.2.2 Other health care goods	*Health-related products*	
	FP.3.3 Non-health care services	*Non-health products*	
X-Y	Gross value added at basic prices		
	Gross value added at purchasers' prices		
K	Consumption of fixed capital		
(X-Y)-K	Net value added		
	RC.2. Compensation of employees and operating surplus/mixed income		
w	*D1 Compensations of employees*		
	D11 Wages and salaries		
T	*(D29-D39) Other taxes less other subsidies on production*		
(X-Y)-W-T	B2 Gross operating surplus/mixed income		
(X-Y)-W-T-K	B2N Net operating surplus		

Source: IHAT for SHA 2011.

By using the health supply and use table it is possible to derive the production and generation of income account for each category of the health provider classification and for the health system as a whole. The production and generation of income accounts represent the link between the SHA HPxHF or HCxHP tables and SNA.

Where does the money come from? And where does the money go to?

The previous sections covered information related to the provision of health care and the related transactions. Besides the provision of health care, SHA also addresses two basic questions: 1) where does the money spent on health go? and 2) where does the money come from? To answer these questions, two different perspectives are available:

- The first perspective aims at a breakdown of expenditure on health into the complex range of third-party payment arrangements plus direct payments by households or other direct funders of, *e.g.*, government-provided health care.
- The second perspective considers the ultimate burden of financing borne by sources of funding. In this kind of analysis, the sources of financing of the intermediary sources of funding (social security funds; private social and other private insurance; NPISH) are traced back to their origin. Additional transfers – such as inter-governmental transfers, tax deductions, subsidies to providers, and financing by the rest of the world – are included to complete the picture.

To record health care financing, SHA has developed a specific set of classifications (*i.e.* the HP classification of providers, the HF Classification of Financing Schemes, the FS Classification of the Revenues of Financing Schemes and the FA Classification of Financing Agents) plus a set of specific tables (*e.g.* HPxHF, HFxFS, HFxFA). The remainder of this annex shows how the information recorded in SHA via a set of cross-classified tables can also be displayed using a section of the SNA sequence of accounts. If the primary interest is the financing of current health expenditure, the redistribution of income accounts and the use of income accounts are the most relevant accounts, whereas the capital account and the financing accounts can be employed to report the capital formation of health care providers and its financing.

- *Redistribution of income accounts*

Health systems are financed differently (*e.g.* through taxes or contributions) depending on the organisational set-up in each country. Moreover, within the same country, each health financing unit can raise its revenues in different ways (see Chapters 7 and 8): for example, general government can collect taxes or social contributions paid by households or other economic actors, or it can receive transfers from abroad; private insurance companies typically use premiums. All these financing mechanisms can be classified using the classification of transactions and reported in the secondary distribution of income accounts. This account is the first of the two accounts which in the SNA form the set called the "Redistribution of income accounts". The second is the "Redistribution of income in kind account".

The secondary distribution of income account

The secondary distribution of income account can be compiled for every group of financing units of the health system. Each transaction will be recorded either as a resource (revenue) if the subject is receiving the funds, or as a use if the subject is making the payment. For example, social contributions paid by households to the government will be recorded as uses (expenditures) in the household secondary distribution of income account and as resources in the government account. More generally, the Secondary distribution of income account shows how the balance of primary incomes of a health financing unit is transformed into its disposable income by the receipt and payment of current transfers,[11] excluding social transfers in kind (*i.e.* current taxes on income and wealth, social benefits, and other current transfers as both resources and uses, since what is a resource for one sector is a use for another). The balancing item is "Disposable income". Disposable income is the amount available for consumption-expenditure and/or saving (investment and capital transfers).

The main transactions included in the Secondary distribution of income account are (Table B.1.4):

- *Taxes on income*, which comprises taxes on incomes, profits and capital gains. They are assessed on the actual or presumed incomes of individuals, households, NPISH or corporations;[12]
- *Social contributions for health benefits* paid by employers to social security funds, insurance enterprises administering social insurance to secure social benefits for their employees;[13]
- *Social benefits other than social transfers in kind,* which includes all health care social benefits that are either in cash or are not provided by social security funds.

Redistribution of income in kind account

Health goods and services provided to individual households by government units (including social security funds) and NPISH, whether purchased on the market or produced as non-market output by government units or NPISH, are called "transfers in kind".[14] They may be financed out of taxation, other government income or social security contributions,

Table B.1.4. **Secondary distribution and use of income accounts**

Account	Transactions	Health care providers HP1. + HP-6		Health administration and system of financing HP-7		Others HP-8		Rest of the world HP-9		Total	
		U	R	U	R	U	R	U	R	U	R
Secondary distribution of income	D.3.1 Subsidies										
	D.5 Current tax on icome, wealth, etc.										
	D.5.1 Tax deduction (private households)										
	D.6.1 Social contributions										
	D.6.1.1 Actual social contributions										
	D.6.1.1.1 Employers' actual social contributions										
	D.6.1.1.1.1 Compulsory										
	D.6.1.1.1.2 Voluntary										
	D.6.1.1.2 Employees' actual social contributions										
	D.6.1.1.2.1 Compulsory										
	D.6.1.1.2.2 Voluntary										
	D.6.1.1.3 Actual social contributions by self- and non-employed persons										
	D.6.1.1.3.1 Compulsory										
	D.6.1.1.3.2 Voluntary										
	D.6.2 Social benefits other than social transfers in kind										
	D.7 Other current transfers										
	B.6 Disposable income										
Reditribution of income in kind	D.6.3 Social transfer in kind										
	D.6.3.1 Social benefits in kind										
	D.6.3.1.1 Social security benefits, reimbursements										
	D.6.3.1.2 Other social security benefits in kind										
	D.6.3.1.3 Social assistance benefits in kind										
	D.6.3.2 Transfers of individual non-market goods and services										
	B.7 Adjusted disposable income										
Use of (adjusted) disposable income	P.3 Final consumption expenditure										
	P.3.1 Individual consulption expenditure										
	P.3.2 Collective consumption expenditure										
	B.8 Saving										
	P.4 Actual final consumption										
	P.4.1 Actual indicidual consumption										
	P.4.2 Actual collective consumption										

Source: IHAT for SHA 2011.

or out of donations and property income in the case of NPISH. The Redistribution of income in kind account takes the balancing item of the Secondary distribution of income account, disposable income, and adjusts this for the value of social transfers in kind to reach a new balancing item, called adjusted disposable income. Adjusted disposable income will be higher than disposable income for the household sector, and lower for the government and the NPISH (SNA 2006, 8.140). The Redistribution of income account records social benefits in kind, which includes both benefits for which the households do not incur the expense and benefits for which the households make the initial outlay and are later reimbursed. The account also records the transfer of individual non-market goods and services, such as education and health, not included in social benefits in kind. Both types of transactions are included under the heading Social transfers in kind.

This account is relevant only for the household sector, which is the recipient of the social benefits in kind, and the government sector and the non-profit institutions serving households (NPISH), which are both "serving" the households.

The purposes of this account are 1) to give a clearer picture of the role of government and NPISH, 2) to deliver a more complete measure of household income, 3) to give a more complete picture of the redistribution process between sectors, and 4) to facilitate international comparisons and comparisons over time when economic and social arrangements differ or change.

- *Use of the disposable income account*

This account shows how disposable income is used either for the purpose of consumption expenditure or for saving. The account records disposable income as a resource and consumption expenditure as a use. The balancing item is saving.

Consumption expenditure covers the amount used on goods and services for final consumption. Excluded here is consumption of goods and services used in a production process (intermediate consumption is recorded in the production account).

Only the households, the government and the non-profit institutions serving households have final consumption expenditure.

Final consumption expenditure consists of the expenditure, including imputed expenditure, incurred by general government on individual and collective goods and services, and incurred by households and NPISH on individual goods and services.

An adjustment for the change in the net equity of households on pension funds is done by imputation. Pension funds are considered to be assets of households, not of the institutional units that manage them (the financial sector). The households pay contributions to and receive benefits (when retired) from the financial sector. Any difference between the contributions paid and the benefits received should be considered part of household's saving, since the household is the owner of the assets. To accomplish this, an adjustment item is introduced. The adjustment is a resource (positive or negative) for the household sector and a use for the financial sector.

- *Use of the adjusted disposable income account*

The purpose of this account is to measure the sector's actual final consumption. Actual final consumption for households covers goods and services that are effectively available for individual consumption by households, regardless of whether the ultimate bearer of the expense is the household itself, the government or NPISH. Consequently, actual final consumption for the government refers only to collective consumption, while NPISH by definition have no actual final consumption, since all their consumption is individual by nature, and transferred to the households.

- *Capital account*

Non-financial assets like hospital buildings, ambulances, scan machines and so on are an important component in the production of health services. The value of the assets acquired or disposed of by health providers is recorded in the capital account (see Chapter 11). This account records also how the acquisition of the assets is financed (*e.g.* through own funds – saving – or capital transfers from resident or non-resident units) and finally reports the change in net worth due to saving and capital transfers. The transactions may take place either with other institutional units, both resident and non-resident, or could be internal transactions in which units retain products that they have produced themselves for use as capital formation (*e.g.* software produced in a hospital).

Saving plus capital transfers constitute the total of capital revenues, which finances what in the SNA is called changes in net worth due to saving and capital transfers. The difference between the latter and the level of non-financial investments defines the capacity of the sector to lend to (+) or its need to borrow from (-) other sectors. The detail on financial instruments used in lending or borrowing is presented in the financial accounts.

- *Financial accounts*

The financial account records all transactions in financial assets and liabilities – financial instruments – *i.e.* all borrowing and lending. The account shows net acquisitions of financial assets on the left-hand side and net incurrence of liabilities on the right. The balancing item of this account is net lending/net borrowing, the same balancing item as in the capital account.

Setting priorities

SHA compilers might wonder whether it would be possible to set priorities for which accounts in the sequence of integrated economic accounts should be compiled first. To address this issue, it is worth noting that:

- This depends very much on the policy relevance assigned to the data in each country at any point in time. For example, there may be cases where the efficiency of the financing system is considered a priority. In such a case, the secondary distribution of income and the redistribution of income in kind accounts would be paramount. It could be the case that the containment of costs is the main issue, so that the information included in the production accounts could become the primary objective. Also, the availability of equipment and infrastructure of the health system could be considered as the main issue: in this situation the capital account together with the estimation of capital stock (not included yet in this annex) would be considered as a priority.
- The great majority of the information included in the sequence of IEA is the same information as included in the cross-classified tables (the main difference being the level of detail). As a consequence, the issue of setting priorities in the sequence of IEA is strictly linked to the priority assigned to the compilation of SHA cross-classified tables. As an example, consider the remuneration reported in the HPxFP table: if this table is

compiled, then the same information can be displayed in the generation of income account, but if the compilation of the HPxFP is not a priority for a given country because the analysis of the remuneration of the health personnel is not an issue, then the same also applies to the compilation of the generation of income account.

- One of the advantages of compiling the IEA is the possibility of calculating the balancing items, which are taken forward into the following account. So, unless a certain balancing item is estimated directly, it would not be possible to isolate one account from the rest of the sequence. As an example, consider the capital account. The entry balancing item is "saving", which is taken forward from the use of disposable income account. If a direct estimation of saving were made, then it would be possible to compile the capital account without compiling the previous accounts.
- Finally, the accounts could also be compiled without taking into consideration the entry balancing items. In that case, they would only include the information on transactions, which would correspond to the information included in the cross-classified tables. However, compiling the accounts in this way might still have some advantages, in that it would be possible to display the information at a higher level of disaggregation as compared to the cross-classified tables. This could also be of great use for the compilers, as the consistency of information coming from different sources could then be checked, which would enhance the quality of the data.

Note on the practicality of implementing the supply and use tables and the sequence of IEA

As for any other statistical manual, the main concern for users is whether the approach proposed is feasible, and whether is it worth the time, costs and effort of implementing it. Obviously, a sound assessment depends on the specific features of the national statistical system (*i.e.* to what extent different statistical bodies – the Ministry of Health and the National Statistics Office to mention just two – co-operate and exchange information; the quality of the survey, the availability and reliability of administrative data sources, etc). However, it is worth repeating that the greater part of the information required for the compilation of the supply and use tables and the IEA sequence is the same information used in the compilation of SHA cross-classified tables. This is essentially due to the specific characteristics of the health system, notably the high share of non-market production, and therefore the lack of economically significant prices and in the case of non-market providers the output of the health providers is indirectly estimated using the sum of production costs. As a result, all the information required to compile the supply tables and the production accounts should be available, at least for the non-market production, when SHA cross-classified tables are compiled. The sole set of information that is not required for the compilation of SHA cross-classified tables is the "intermediate consumption" of the market providers. Similarly, demand-side aggregates (consumption, gross capital formation, exports) need to be estimated to compile SHA cross-classified tables: first, the final consumption expenditure, but also exports need to be estimated, as the SHA boundaries require their exclusion. Similar considerations apply to the compilation of the secondary distribution of income, as the information corresponds to the HFxFS table.

Advantages and disadvantages of the SHA- and SNA- type representations

The SNA-type representations of the health system supplement those of SHA cross-classified tables rather than being in competition. Each has its own advantages as well as disadvantages:

- The main advantage of the system of SHA cross-classified tables is to show the origin and destination of the flows (*i.e.* "from whom to whom"). In addition, the matrix approach imposes consistency on the use of different data sources and helps to identify information gaps and needs. The principal disadvantage, however, is that the cross-classified tables are limited in that the transactions are not explicitly reported, and the surplus/deficit and net lending/borrowing of health actors are not accommodated.
- The SNA-type accounts could provide instead a richer set of information that has the potential to increase the analytical power of the SHA. The main benefits are:
- The SNA sequence of accounts provides information on the nature of the economic flows (*i.e.* transactions) that are not explicitly reported in SHA cross-classified tables. SNA-type accounts show whether funds have been collected using taxes (local or central, direct or indirect), contributions (paid by employers or employees), donations, or transfers from the rest of the world; or whether they are redistributed among actors that purchase health products; or whether the purchase is for own final use or as third-party payments. Also, the SNA sequence of accounts provides estimates of the surpluses or deficits (net lending or net borrowing) of the actors in the health system (balancing items, which are currently not included in SHA cross-classified tables). The analysis of surpluses or deficits is required to address the issue of the financial sustainability of the health system. A drawback of the sequence of accounts is that it is not possible to identify the origin and the destination of the transactions ("from whom to whom"). However, this might be overcome by employing a sufficiently detailed classification of transactions.
- SNA-type accounts and tables also allow the analysis of the supply side of the health system. The analysis of the production structure of the health providers (through the supply tables and the production and generation of income accounts) includes the share of intermediate consumption, the integration of the health system into the rest of the economy and its financial and non-financial dependence on the rest of the world. The cross-classified tables of current health expenditures and capital formation focus only on the demand side of the health system.

It is worth noting that, although the compilation of the tables derived from the SNA could enhance the analytical power of the SHA, its compilation should be considered as an advanced stage in the different stages of SHA implementation.

Notes

1. See Chapter 4 for the definition of SHA boundaries. Please note that the boundaries of health in the SNA (COFOG or ISIC) are not considered here. Therefore, the total value of the corresponding aggregates (*i.e.* current health expenditure) is in principle the same.
2. See Box B.1.2 for a definition of the T-Accounts.
3. An important difference is the way trade and transport margins for pharmaceutical goods are treated in SHA. See Annex A.

4. Because the uses of products are usually valued at purchasers' prices, but production at basic prices, it is necessary to add trade and transport margins, and taxes on products less subsidies on products to the left-hand (or supply) side of the identity so both sides are expressed in purchasers' prices. Therefore a more precise accounting identity is given by:

5. Output (at basic prices) + Imports + Non-deductible VAT + Other taxes on products – Subsidies on products + Trade margins + Transport margins= Uses.

6. Also, imports and exports require special consideration due to the cif/fob valuation.

7. See SNA 2008, 14.11.

8. Health products are valued either in basic prices or c.i.f. The total supply of each product in purchasers' prices is obtained by adding in trade and transport margins, and taxes less subsidies on products. C.i.f./f.o.b. adjustment is for obtaining total imports in f.o.b.

9. Most economic actions are undertaken by mutual agreement between economic units. They are either an exchange of economic value or a voluntary transfer by one unit to another of a certain amount of economic value without a counterpart. These actions undertaken by mutual agreement between two institutional units are called transactions in the SNA.

10. In the SNA, §6.37 "In the System, the intermediate inputs are recorded and valued at the time they enter the production process, while outputs are recorded and valued as they emerge from the process. Intermediate inputs are normally valued at purchasers' prices and outputs at basic prices, or alternatively at producers' prices if basic prices are not available. The increase between the value of the intermediate inputs and the value of the outputs is the gross value added against which must be charged the consumption of fixed capital, taxes on production (less subsidies) and compensation of employees. The positive or negative balance remaining is the net operating surplus or mixed income. The definition, measurement and valuation of outputs and inputs is, therefore, fundamental to the System and is described in detail in the following sections."

11. A transfer is a transaction in which one institutional unit provides a good, service or asset to another unit without receiving from the latter any good, service or asset in return as a direct counterpart. Transfers are separated into current transfers and capital transfers. Capital transfers are unrequited transfers where either the party making the transfer realises the funds involved by disposing of an asset (other than cash or inventories) or by relinquishing a financial claim (other than accounts receivable), or the party receiving the transfer is obliged to acquire an asset (other than cash), or both conditions are met. Capital transfers are often large and irregular, but neither of these are necessary conditions for a transfer to be considered a capital rather than a current transfer. Other transfers are described as current. A current transfer is a transaction in which one institutional unit provides a good or service to another unit without receiving from the latter any good or service directly in return as a counterpart, and does not oblige one or both parties to acquire, or dispose of, an asset.

12. Normally, there are no income taxes "earmarked" for health. Government policy regarding income taxed on individual households can, however, indirectly influence household decisions on health care financing, *e.g.* where tax deductions are granted to private households on private health insurance or on the direct out-of-pocket payment of health care services. For health policy analysis, however, this is an important piece of information.

13. The SNA makes a distinction between Employers' actual social contributions (D.6111); Employees' actual social contributions (D.6112); and Social contributions by self- and non-employed persons (D.6113). Although it is administratively more efficient for employers to pay the contributions on behalf of their employees, this must not be allowed to obscure the underlying economic reality. The payment made by the employer to the social security fund, insurance enterprise or autonomous pension fund is not a current transfer by the employer. The transfer takes place between the employee and the social security fund, insurance enterprise or autonomous pension fund out of remuneration provided by the employer. It is customary to describe the employers' social contributions as being re-routed in the accounts via the employees' primary and secondary distribution of income accounts. A further breakdown of social contributions for health benefits into compulsory contributions and voluntary contributions would be a useful tool.

14. The SNA states: "In principle, social transfers in kind may be paid to non-residents. One simple example is emergency medical care provided to a foreign tourist by a hospital within general government. However, just as non-resident households may benefit from social transfers in kind from the national government, so resident households may benefit from social transfers in kind paid by the government of another economy. In general these flows to non-residents will be small relative to the total level of social transfers in kind and, unless there is strong evidence to the contrary, by convention it may be assumed that the flows to non-residents are balanced by flows from governments (and NPISH) of other economies. Subject to this convention, it is therefore the case that total disposable income for the total economy is exactly equal to total adjusted disposable income" (SNA08 8.141). This is a difference between the SNA and SHA, as in the latter the two flows should be recorded: the exports to be subtracted from domestic production, and the imports included in consumption.

ANNEX C

Health and Health Associate Professionals and ISCO-08

International Standard Classification of Occupations (ISCO)[1]

The sub-major groups of ISCO-08 that are relevant to SHA 2011 are 22 (Health professionals) and 32 (Health associate professionals).

22 Health professionals

Health professionals conduct research, improve or develop concepts, theories and operational methods, and apply scientific knowledge relating to medicine, nursing, dentistry, pharmacy and the promotion of health.

Tasks performed by workers in this sub-major group usually include: conducting research and obtaining scientific knowledge through the study of human disorders and illnesses and ways of treating them; advising on or applying preventive and curative measures, or promoting health; and preparing scientific papers and reports. Supervision of other workers may be included.

Occupations in this sub-major group are classified into the following minor groups:[2]

221 Medical doctors

222 Nursing and midwifery professionals

223 Traditional and complementary medicine professionals

224 Paramedical practitioners

226 Other health professionals

32 Health associate professionals

Health associate professionals perform technical and practical tasks to support the diagnosis and treatment of illness, disease, injuries and impairments in humans, and to support the implementation of health care, treatment and referral plans usually established by medical, nursing and other health professionals.

Tasks performed by workers in the sub-major group usually include: testing and operating medical imaging equipment and administering radiation therapy; performing clinical tests on specimens of bodily fluids and tissues; preparing medications and other pharmaceutical compounds under the guidance of pharmacists; designing, fitting, servicing and repairing medical and dental devices and appliances; providing nursing and personal care and midwifery support services; and using herbal and other therapies based on theories, beliefs and experiences originating in specific cultures.

Occupations in this sub-major group are classified into the following minor groups:[3]

321 Medical and pharmaceutical technicians

322 Nursing and midwifery associate professionals

323 Traditional and complementary medicine associate professionals

325 Other health associate professionals

Table C.1.1. **ISCO-08 structure for health professionals and health associate professionals**

Code	Description
22	**Health professionals**
221	Medical doctors
2211	Generalist medical practitioners
2212	Specialist medical practitioners
222	Nursing and midwifery professionals
2221	Nursing professionals
2222	Midwifery professionals
223	Traditional and complementary medicine professionals
2230	Traditional and complementary medicine professionals
224	Paramedical practitioners
2240	Paramedical practitioners
226	Other health professionals
2261	Dentists
2262	Pharmacists
2263	Environmental and occupational health and hygiene professionals
2264	Physiotherapists
2265	Dieticians and nutritionists
2266	Audiologists and speech therapists
2267	Optometrists and ophthalmic opticians
2269	Health professionals not elsewhere classified
32	**Health associate professionals**
321	Medical and pharmaceutical technicians
3211	Medical imaging and therapeutic equipment technicians
3212	Medical and pathology laboratory technicians
3213	Pharmaceutical technicians and assistants
3214	Medical and dental prosthetic technicians
322	Nursing and midwifery associate professionals
3221	Nursing associate professionals
3222	Midwifery associate professionals
323	Traditional and complementary medicine associate professionals
3230	Traditional and complementary medicine associate professionals
325	Other health associate professionals
3251	Dental assistants and therapists
3252	Medical records and health information technicians
3253	Community health workers
3254	Dispensing opticians
3255	Physiotherapy technicians and assistants
3256	Medical assistants
3257	Environmental and occupational health inspectors and associates
3258	Ambulance workers
3259	Health associate professionals not elsewhere classified

Source: ILO (2008).

Notes

1. See ILO (2008) for a detailed structure of ISCO-08.
2. The minor group for Veterinarians (225) has been excluded as it is not relevant for SHA 2011.
3. The minor group for Veterinary technicians and assistants (324) has been excluded as it is not relevant for SHA 2011.

ANNEX D

Financing of Health Systems – Supplementary Tools

Classification of Financing Agents (ICHA-FA)

This annex complements Chapter 7 "Classification of financing schemes" with the Classification of Financing Agents. Chapter 7 discusses, among other things, the concept of institutional units of the health system and financing agents as elements of the accounting framework for health financing. Chapter 7 also presents the relationship between financing schemes and financing agents.

Definition of financing agents

A financing agent is an institutional unit involved in the management of one or more financing scheme. It may collect revenues, pay for (purchase) services under the given health financing scheme(s), and be involved in the management and regulation of health financing.

A financing agent may manage the payment for health services and goods in different ways:

- Finance the services produced in its own institutions (*e.g.*, a local government may own and finance a hospital);
- Purchase services from providers owned by other entities (*e.g.*, social insurance funds purchase services from hospitals owned by local governments);
- Reimburse the cost of services to the patients who first pay the bill directly to the providers.

Main categories of the Classification of Financing Agents

- *FA.1 General government*

This item comprises all institutional units of central, state, regional or local government, and social insurance funds.[1] Included are non-market non-profit institutions that are controlled and mainly financed by government units.

Note: FA.1 does not include public corporations, even when all the equity of such corporations is owned by governments units. It also does not include quasi-corporations that are owned and controlled by government units (see SNA 2008, Chapter 4).

Table D.1.1. **Classification of financing agents**

Code	Description
FA.1.	**General government**
FA.1.1	Central government
FA.1.1.1	Ministry of Health
FA.1.1.2	Other ministries and public units (belonging to central government)
FA.1.1.3	National Health Service Agency
FA.1.1.4	National Health Insurance Agency
FA.1.2	State/Regional/Local government
FA.1.3	Social security agency
FA.1.3.1	Social Health Insurance Agency
FA.1.3.2	Other social security agency
FA.1.9	All other general government units
FA.2	**Insurance corporations**
FA.2.1	Commercial insurance companies
FA.2.2	Mutual and other non-profit insurance organisations
FA.3	**Corporations (other than insurance corporations)**
FA.3.1	Health management and provider corporations
FA.3.2	Corporations (other than providers of health services)
FA.4	**Non-profit institutions serving households (NPISH)**
FA.5	**Households**
FA.6	**Rest of the world**
FA.6.1	International organisations
FA.6.2	Foreign governments
FA.6.3	Other foreign entities

Source: IHAT for SHA 2011.

FA.1.1 Central government

This item comprises all institutional units making up the central government. These entities would not necessarily be just the health ministry, but any central government entity involved in the financing of the health sector. Included are centralised, national level agencies strongly controlled by the central government, such as the National Health Service Agency and National Health Insurance Agency.

Note:

- A central government unit generally acts as financing agent for a governmental scheme (HF.1.1).
- Governmental schemes (HF.1.1) are generally managed by government units. However, NPISH or corporations may also act as financing agents for such schemes. For example, the Ministry of Health may design and set a separate budget for a cancer screening programme, but contract out the financial management to an NPISH or a management company, which then will contract providers to make the screening examinations.

FA.1.1.3 National Health Service Agency

In several countries, universal access to basic health services is ensured by a central government funded and managed programme: the National Health Service Agency (NHSA) is a centralised government agency managing the National Health Service (part of HF1.1.1), usually under the supervision of the Ministry of Health. The NHSA is usually also responsible for provision of the health services, but the NHSA may also purchase services from private providers. The NHSA has a separate legal identity, a separate budget and a certain level of autonomy and discretion over the allocation of its expenditure. As it is controlled by the central government, it is considered part of the central government sub-sector.

FA.1.1.4 National Health Insurance Agency

Social health insurance schemes (HF.1.2.1) may involve different ways of pooling the financial resources. A country may have a centralised national insurance fund, or a decentralised structure of funds. In the case of a decentralised system, pooling may be based on a territorial or professional principle or funds may compete with each other.

The National Health Insurance Agency is a centralised government agency for managing social health insurance schemes (HF.1.2.1). It has a separate legal identity, a separate budget and a certain level of autonomy and discretion over the allocation of its expenditure. As it is controlled by the central government, it is considered part of the central government sub-sector.

Note: Social health insurance (HF.1.2.1) is a financing scheme characterised by a great variety of institutional arrangements in different countries. Social health insurance can be managed by different financing agents: a centralised national agency (FA.1.1.4.), social insurance funds (FA.1.3) or insurance corporations (FA.2). In some countries, social health insurance may be managed by both government agencies and commercial insurance companies at the same time (for example, in the Slovak Republic).

FA.1.2 State/Regional/Local government

This item comprises all institutional units making up local government. The terms "state" and "provincial" may be used for "regional" in different countries. In small countries, individual state/provincial governments may not exist.

Regional/local governments may act for different financing schemes:

- Regional/local governments may have the primary responsibility for providing access to health care and thus establish their health financing scheme for this purpose. In this case, regional/local governments act as the financing agent for regional/local governmental schemes HF.1.1.2.
- Regional/local governments may also manage central governmental schemes (HF.1.1.1).

FA.1.3 Social security agency

Social insurance funds are economic units with a specific legal status whose purpose is to operate social insurance schemes (HF.1.2.1). They have a non-profit status. They have substantial autonomy in their operations, *e.g.* engaging in financial transactions, and they hold their own assets and liabilities. They are classified as part of the general government sector, as their operation is controlled by the government. Social insurance funds may operate one or more types of social insurance (pension, health, accident, long-term care, etc.).

Note: Recent reforms have brought considerable changes: in some countries, for-profit insurance companies may also be allowed to participate in the operation of a social insurance scheme. Thus, both sickness funds and private insurance companies may take part in the operation of a social health insurance scheme.

FA.1.3.1 Social health insurance agency

Social health insurance agencies[2] are legal entities with the obligation, defined by law, to ensure access to a defined health service package. Social health insurance funds have a non-profit status and are based on the principle of self-governance through representatives of the insured and the employers. Traditionally, social health insurance funds directly collect contributions from their members, and have the right to determine what contribution rate is necessary to cover expenditure. (Reforms over the last two or three decades have changed the characteristics of revenue collection in several countries.)

FA.1.3.2 Other social security agencies

Other social security agencies may also be involved in operating social health insurance or voluntary insurance schemes. For example, in Germany accident funds cover curative and rehabilitative care services for work-related accidents and diseases; retirement funds are responsible for some rehabilitative measures; and long-term care funds manage the long-term care insurance.

FA.1.9 All other public units

This item includes non-market non-profit institutions that are controlled and mainly financed by government units.

- *FA.2 Insurance corporations*

Insurance corporations may act as financing agent for different types of insurance. Traditionally, insurance corporations offer voluntary health insurance (HF.2.1). However, due to recent reforms, in several countries insurance corporations take part in operating compulsory health insurance (HF.1.2.1 or HF.1.2.2). In these countries, an insurance corporation may act as financing agent both for compulsory insurance and voluntary insurance at the same time.

- *FA.3 Corporations (other than insurance corporations)*

Based on the SNA, the category of corporations is used in a wider sense: this sector comprises all corporations or quasi-corporations whose principal activity is the production of market goods or services. Included are all resident government-owned and non-profit institutions that are market producers of goods or non-financial services. Included are non-profit health maintenance organisations and health management corporations managing insurance schemes.

In several countries, there exist a variety of health sector-specific corporations other than traditional health service providers, such as *health management corporations*. These may act as financing agents for several types of financing schemes.

Corporations (including health management corporations) may act as financing agents for:

- Enterprises health financing schemes (H.F.2.3);
- Employer-based insurance (HF.2.1.1.1) and other voluntary health insurance schemes;
- Governmental schemes (HF.1.1); and
- RoW financing schemes (HF.4).

- *FA.4 Non-profit institutions serving households (NPISH)*

Non-profit institutions serving households (NPISH) are a special type of non-profit organisation. NPISH consist of non-profit institutions that provide financial assistance, goods or services to households free or at prices that are not economically significant. Their operation is not controlled by the government.

NPISH may act as financing agent for different financing schemes:

- Non-profit institutions financing schemes (HF.2.2);
- Governmental schemes (HF.1.1);
- RoW financing schemes (HF.4).

Included are charities, relief or aid agencies that are created for philanthropic purposes and not to serve the interests of the members of the association controlling the NPISH. These NPISH provide goods or services on a non-market basis to households in need. The resources of such NPISH are provided mainly by donations in cash or in kind from the general public, corporations or governments. They may also be provided by transfers from foreign entities, including similar kinds of NPISH that are resident in other countries (see SNA 2008, 4.169).

Religious institutions are treated as NPISH, even when mainly financed by government units if this majority financing is not seen as empowering control by the government.

Note: Experience has shown that there is ambiguity in distinguishing between the different types of non-profit organisations (market producers, units of government and NPISH), and also between the different roles that NPISH may play. Therefore, when producing NHAs, it is important to make a qualitative analysis to distinguish between these different roles and statuses of non-profit organisations.

Non-profit institutions may have specific health programmes (with separate funds and management of the funds) and carry out the programmes themselves (as providers of care) or finance health care providers that do so. In this case, the financing scheme is: Non-profit institutions financing scheme, with NPISH playing the role of financing agents. The funds may be provided by households, government, foreign entities or foundations, so that they themselves do not manage the health programmes – they only provide resources for them.

Non-profit institutions that provide assistance to households to buy certain health services (for example, abroad) are considered financing agents, even when the households first pay the bill directly for the services to the providers and are then reimbursed by the NPISH.

- *FA.5 Households*

A household is defined by the SNA as a group of persons who share the same living accommodation, who pool some, or all, of their income and wealth, and who consume certain types of goods and services collectively, mainly housing and food.

Under SHA 2011, households are categorised as the financing agent for households' out-of-pocket payments.

- *FA.6 Rest of the world*

This item comprises institutional units that are resident abroad:

- International and supranational agencies;
- Foreign governments;
- Financial intermediaries (insurance, NGOs, charities and foundations).

RoW institutional units may act as financing agents for RoW-funded schemes (HF.4).

Sectoral accounts

The HFxFS table provides aggregate information about revenue collection in the whole health care sector. There may be a need for more in-depth information about the collection and use of resources concerning major financing schemes that is separate from the HFxFS table. Sectoral accounts can provide important information from the perspective of a given financing scheme or institutional units/sectors that cannot be directly gained from any of the SHA tables; for example, the operating balance (surplus or deficit) of the financing schemes.

In the following, three types of sectoral accounts are presented:

- Sectoral accounts of *revenues and expenses of financing schemes* (except households[3]). The approach of these accounts is similar to the way the Government Finance Statistics Manual (GFSM) accounts for government revenues and expenses. For example, Table D.1.2 presents the account of revenues and expenses of governmental health financing schemes (HF.1.1).
- Sectoral accounts of *health-specific revenues and expenses of institutional units/sectors of the economy*. For example, Table D.1.4 presents the account of total health-specific revenues and expenses of government (including expenses made by government as providers of financial resources).
- The sectoral account of private *households' health-specific transfers and net financing of health care out of own resources*. This shows the overall role of households in health care financing from a macroeconomic perspective. This account is taken from SHA Manual 1.0, which applies an approach similar to the way the SNA accounts for transactions. Such a sectoral account can be produced for all the institutional sectors (as presented in SHA 1.0).

Guidelines available separately from this Manual will be developed for the preparation of sectoral accounts.

The classification of expenses

Based on the GFSM, two approaches can be applied in classifying expenses: an economic or a functional classification of expenses. Sectoral accounts can be useful in both ways.

Table D.1.2 provides an illustration for the accounts of revenues and expenses of financial schemes, using the category of governmental health financing schemes as an example.

Table D.1.2 shows revenue collection and allocation of financial resources under governmental health financing schemes (HF.1.1). The shaded cells in the table are those categories of expenses that cannot occur in this case. Expenses show both expenses on services and goods provided by government units (E1, E2 and E3) and services and goods purchased from providers outside the government sector (E5, E7). This table excludes those expenses that relate to the role of government as a financing source (FS) for other financing schemes (such as expenditure on grants).

Note: In Table D.1.2 "Expense on social benefits" is a narrower category than health services and goods financed by government. Health services and goods produced by a government unit (*e.g.*, hospitals managed by local governments) are not classified as social benefits. The expenses of producing such services are part of compensation of employees, use of goods and services and consumption of fixed capital.

Table D.1.2. **Revenues and expenses of governmental health financing schemes (HF.1.1)**

Expenses		Revenues	
E1	Compensation of employees	**FS.1**	**Transfers from government domestic revenue**
E.1.1	Wages and salaries	FS.1.1	Internal transfers and grants
		FS.2	**Transfers distributed by government from foreign origin**
E.1.2	Social contribution	**FS.6**	**Other domestic revenues *n.e.c.***
E2	Use of goods and services	FS.6.1	Other revenues from households *n.e.c.*
E3	Consumption of fixed capital	FS.6.2	Other revenues from corporations *n.e.c.*
E4	Interest	FS.6.3	Other revenues from NPISH *n.e.c.*
E5	Subsidies	**FS.7**	**Direct foreign transfers**
E6	Grants	**FS.7.1**	**Direct foreign financial transfers**
E7	Social benefits	FS.7.1.1	Direct bilateral financial transfers
E8	Other expense	FS.7.1.2	Direct multilateral financial transfers
		FS.7.1.3	Other direct foreign financial transfers
		FS.7.2	**Direct foreign aid in kind**
		FS.7.2.1	Direct foreign aid in goods
		FS.7.2.1.1	Direct bilateral aid in goods
		FS.7.2.1.2	Direct multilateral aid in goods
		FS.7.2.1.3	Other direct foreign aid in goods
		FS.7.2.2	Direct foreign aid in kind: services (including technical assistance – TA)
		FS.7.3	Other direct foreign transfers (*n.e.c.*)
Net/gross operating balance			

*: For the definition of the categories of expenses, see: Government Finance Statistics Manual, *www.imf.org/external/pubs/ft/gfs/manual/pdf/all.pdf*.
Source: IHAT for SHA 2011.

Revenue less expenses equals the *net operating balance,* which is an important summary measure of the sustainability of the given financing scheme. (The gross operating balance equals revenue minus expenses other than consumption of fixed capital.)

Table D.1.3 shows the account of governmental financing schemes with a functional classification of health expenditure (ICHA-HC).[4]

Sectoral accounts of health-specific revenues and expenses of institutional units

This type of account includes all health-specific revenues and expenses of the main types of institutional units of the health system, regardless of whether these relate to their role as financing agent or as provider of financial resources. Table D.1.4 serves as an example, presenting total health-specific revenues and expenses of the government.

The sectoral account of total health-specific revenues and expenses of the government (Table D.1.4) concerns all components of government involvement in health care financing, including their roles as financing agent and provider of financial resources. For example, under its role as a provider of financial resources, government may provide

Table D.1.3. **Revenues and expenses of governmental health financing schemes (HF.1.1)**

Expenses		Revenues	
HC.1	Curative care	**FS.1**	**Transfers from government domestic revenue**
HC.2	Rehabilitative care	FS.1.1	Internal transfers and grants
HC.3	Long-term care (health)	**FS.2**	**Transfers distributed by government from foreign origin**
HC.4	Ancillary services non-specified by function	**FS.6**	**Other domestic revenues *n.e.c.***
HC.5	Medical goods non-specified by function	FS.6.1	Other revenues from households *n.e.c.*
HC.6	Preventive care	FS.6.2	Other revenues from corporations *n.e.c.*
HC.7	Governance and health system & financing administration	FS.6.3	Other revenues from NPISH *n.e.c.*
HC.9	Other health care services not elsewhere classified (*n.e.c.*)	**FS.7**	**Direct foreign transfers**
		FS.7.1	**Direct foreign financial transfers**
		FS.7.1.1	Direct bilateral financial transfers
		FS.7.1.2	Direct multilateral financial transfers
		FS.7.1.3	Other direct foreign financial transfers
		FS.7.2	**Direct foreign aid in kind**
		FS.7.2.1	Direct foreign aid in goods
		FS.7.2.1.1	Direct bilateral aid in goods
		FS.7.2.1.2	Direct multilateral aid in goods
		FS.7.2.1.3	Other direct foreign aid in goods
		FS.7.2.2	Direct foreign aid in kind: services (including TA)
		FS.7.3	Other direct foreign transfers (*n.e.c.*)
Net/gross operating balance			

Source: IHAT for SHA 2011.

grants to an NPISH which acts as a financing scheme, *e.g.* to pay social contributions on behalf of children or elderly persons to compulsory social insurance schemes and so on.

The sectoral account of government (as an institutional sector) includes social insurance contributions among the revenues and social security benefits among the expenses, as social insurance schemes can be managed by a government unit. Sectoral accounts also provide a tool for analysing the role of foreign revenues in financing health care.

The accounting of private households health-specific transactions and net financing out of own resources

The purpose of the account of private households' health-specific transactions and net financing of health care out of own resources is to provide a comprehensive macroeconomic view of the households' role in health care financing. This account tracks back the transfers to the level of households' primary income and therefore treats households differently than does the ICHA-FS classification (HFxFS matrix). See Table D.1.5.

The account of private households consists of two parts: the first part shows the transfers that households make and receive *relating to health care financing*. (It does not show households' resources and revenues gained/used for purposes other than health care.) The second part shows the amount of Actual final consumption and how much of Actual final consumption is ultimately financed by households, including not only direct payments, but payments through third-party payers (for which funds originally stem from households' primary income).

Table D.1.4. **Total health-related revenues and expenses of government**

	Expenses		Revenues
E1	Compensation of employees	**FS.1**	**Transfers from government domestic revenue**
E.1.1	Wages and salaries	FS.1.1	Internal transfers and grants
E.1.2	Social contribution	**FS.3**	**Social insurance contributions**
E2	Use of goods and services	FS.3.1	Social insurance contributions from employees
E3	Consumption of fixed capital	FS.3.3	Social insurance contributions from employers
E4	Interest	FS.3.3	Social insurance contributions from self-employed
E5	Subsidies	FS.3.4	Other social insurance contributions
E6	Grants		
E7	Social benefits	**FS.6**	**Other domestic revenues *n.e.c.***
	Social security benefits	FS.6.1	Other revenues from households *n.e.c.*
	Social assistance benefits	FS.6.2	Other revenues from corporations *n.e.c.*
	Employer social benefits	FS.6.3	Other revenues from NPISH *n.e.c.*
E8	Other expenses	**FS.7**	**Direct foreign transfers**
		FS.7.1	**Direct foreign financial transfers**
		FS.7.1.1	Direct bilateral financial transfers
		FS.7.1.2	Direct multilateral financial transfers
		FS.7.1.3	Other direct foreign financial transfers
		FS.7.2	**Direct foreign aid in kind**
		FS.7.2.1	Direct foreign aid in goods
		FS.7.2.1.1	Direct bilateral aid in goods
		FS.7.2.1.2	Direct multilateral aid in goods
		FS.7.2.1.3	Other direct foreign aid in goods
		FS.7.2.2	Direct foreign aid in kind: services (including TA)
		FS.7.3	Other direct foreign transfers (*n.e.c.*)
Net/gross operating balance			

*: For the definition of the categories of expenses, see: Government Finance Statistics Manual, *www.imf.org/external/pubs/ft/gfs/manual/pdf/all.pdf*.
Source: IHAT for SHA 2011.

The account of private households' health-specific transfers provides the following information:

- The "uses" side shows all the transfers that households make relating to health care financing. The source of these payments is households' incomes that, however, are not explicitly shown in this account.
- The "resources" side shows all the health-specific transfers and benefits that households receive, including benefits in-kind.
- The "Net balance of health specific transfers" shows the difference between transfers made and received. This is the amount by which households' health-specific transfers received from other actors of the economy (mostly benefits in-kind and in-cash) exceed the health-related transfers that households made.[5]
- This part of the account, however, does not show explicitly the out-of-pocket payments that households make for health services (as they are not transfers). This amount can be calculated from the second part of the account.

The second part of the account shows, tracing back to primary incomes, ultimately, to what extent households' own resources cover the actual individual consumption of health services.

- "Actual final consumption" shows the total resources devoted to health care financing, except gross capital formation. Actual individual consumption refers to services consumed by individuals (regardless of who pays for it), and Actual collective consumption refers to those services that are a public good, in an economic sense (that is consumption by one individual does not exclude others from consumption of the same services). Examples are anti-smoking advertisements and health care administration.

- "Net financing of health care out of own resources" shows the total amount households devoted to health care from their primary income: this is partly channelled through third-party payers (health-specific transfers) and out-of-pocket payments paid directly to providers. This latter amount (OOPs) can be calculated as the difference between "Net financing of health care out of own resources" and the sum of the transfers made by households; or as the difference between actual individual consumption and transfers received by households. (In the example, OOP amounts to 375.)

Table D.1.5. **Account of households' health-specific transfers and net financing out of own resources**

	Uses			Resources	
D.51	Tax deduction (per household)	–22	**D.62**	Social benefits other than social transfers in kind	97
			D.621	Social security benefits in cash	8
D.61	Social contributions	651	D.622	Private funded social benefits	75
D.611	Actual social contributions	639	D.623	Unfunded employee social benefits	9
D.6111	Employers' actual social contributions	322	D.624	Social assistance benefits in cash	5
D.6112	Employees' actual social contributions	241			
D.6113	Social contributions by self- and non-employed persons	76	**D.63**	Social transfers in kind	749
D.612	Imputed social contributions	12	D.631	Social benefits in kind	720
			D.6311	Social security benefits, reimbursements	313
D.7	Other current transfers	59	D.6312	Other social security benefits in kind	372
D.71	Net insurance premiums	51	D.6313	Social assistance benefits in kind	35
D.75	Miscellaneous current transfers	8	D.632	Transfers of individual non-market goods and services (charity from NPISH)	29
			D.7	Other current transfers	109
			D.72	Net insurance claims	50
			D.75	Miscellaneous current transfers	59
B.1	*Net balance of health specific transfers*	267			
			B.1	*Net balance of health-specific transfers*	267
P.4	Actual final consumption	1330			
P.41	Actual individual consumption	1330			
P.42	Actual collective consumption				
B.2	*Net financing of health care out of own resources*	-1063			

Source: SHA Manual, 1.0, p. 82.

The accounts presented in the main text and Tables in this annex describe health care financing from three different perspectives:

- Focusing on financing schemes (direct or third-party payers). For example, in the case of households as a financing scheme (HF.3), only out-of-pocket payments are accounted;

- Focusing on financing sources. For example, in the case of households as a provider of financial resources, social and voluntary insurance contributions paid by households, etc., are also accounted for (besides out-of-pocket payments);
- Focusing on, based on the SNA, the net balance of own resources devoted by institutional sectors of the economy to health care financing. As already mentioned, in the case of households, all social contributions (including employers' social contributions) are reported as uses (expenses of) households.

An in-depth analysis of households could be made from the comparison of these three approaches.

Main problems of the health financing classification (ICHA-HF) in SHA 1.0

Over time, a number of problems both from health policy and health accounting perspectives have emerged with the ICHA-HF classification in SHA 1.0. The classification for health care financing under SHA 1.0 is shown below in Table D.1.6.

Table D.1.6. **ICHA-HF classification of health care financing in SHA 1.0**

ICHA-HF code (SHA 1.0)	ICHA-HF category
HF.1	**General government**
HF.1.1	General government excluding social security funds
F.1.1.1	Central government
HF.1.1.2	State/provincial government
HF.1.1.3	Local/municipal government
HF.1.2	Social security funds
HF.2	**Private sector**
HF.2.1	Private social insurance
HF.2.2	Private insurance enterprises (other than social insurance)
HF.2.3	Private household out-of-pocket expenditure
HF.2.3.1	Out-of-pocket excluding cost-sharing
HF.2.3.2	Cost-sharing: Central government
HF.2.3.3	Cost-sharing: State/provincial government
HF.2.3.4	Cost-sharing: Local/municipal government
HF.2.3.5	Cost-sharing: Social security funds
HF.2.3.6	Cost-sharing: Private social insurance
HF.2.3.7	Cost-sharing: Other private insurance
HF.2.3.9	All other cost-sharing
HF.2.4	Non-profit institutions serving households (other than social insurance)
HF.2.5	Corporations (other than health insurance)
HF.3	Rest of the world

Source: IHAT for SHA 2011.

The categories of ICHA-HF in SHA 1.0 do not adequately reflect the complex and changing systems of health financing

In both the OECD area and in middle- and lower-income countries outside the OECD, insurance and financing schemes are heterogeneous and have evolved significantly as a result of recent reforms and policy initiatives (Gottret and Schieber, 2006; OECD, 2004). A few examples are listed below, illustrating that the categories of ICHA-HF in SHA 1.0 do not enable the complex and changing systems of health financing to be reflected adequately:

- In the Netherlands prior to 2006, non-profit sickness funds operated the social insurance scheme; and they were accounted under HF.1.2. Social security funds. Following the 2006 reform, the same purpose, that is, to provide access to care for the whole population, is performed by compulsory health insurance that is managed by private insurance enterprises. If the definitions of ICHA-HF were strictly applied, this expenditure should be accounted under HF.2.2 Private insurance enterprises. However, health spending would not be comparable with the previous Dutch system, nor that of other OECD countries. In fact, Netherlands reported expenditure by compulsory insurance funds under HF.1 General government. Strictly speaking, this is not appropriate. Furthermore, the same insurance companies also offer voluntary health insurance, which is accounted for under HF.2.2. If the SHA 1.0 definitions of ICHA-HF were strictly applied, payment under both mandatory cover and voluntary health insurance should be counted under HF.2.2.

- In the Slovak Republic, the compulsory social insurance scheme is managed by a state-owned insurance agency and also by private insurance enterprises. Thus the same role is played by institutional units belonging to the general government and institutional units belonging to private insurance enterprises. Strictly speaking, according to the ICHA-HF in SHA 1.0, spending by the state-owned insurance agency should be reported under HF.1.2 and spending by the other insurers under HF.2.2 Private insurance enterprises. This obviously would not be appropriate.
- The spending by the U.S. Medicare programme is reported under HF.1 General government. However, beneficiaries are allowed to obtain Medicare coverage through certain private health insurers if they want, or they can remain in the traditional Medicare programme. These private health insurers (primarily managed care plans) act for the government. According to the SHA 1.0 ICHA-HF, in a strict sense, expenditure by private insurers should be classified as HF.2.2 Private insurance enterprises.
- In Switzerland, basic health insurance is mandatory for the entire resident population. Mandatory health insurance is provided by private funds, but their activity is heavily regulated (OECD, 2006b). Several insurers that offer mandatory health insurance also sell voluntary health insurance, which is not subject to stringent regulation. Mandatory health insurance in Switzerland is at present reported under HF.1.2 Social security funds (as part of General government). If Switzerland classified mandatory health insurance according to the ICHA-HF classification and criteria in SHA 1.0, both mandatory and voluntary insurance should appear under "private insurance" (HF.2.1 or HF.2.2) as part of private sector financing (HF.2). While it is not correct to report the Swiss mandatory system under "social security", it would not be satisfactory to place it with voluntary health insurance under the category private health insurance.
- In some middle- and lower-income countries, there are specific arrangements for health care financing, such as community insurance and medical savings accounts, which would require new categories, as their decisive characteristics are not reflected by any of the categories of ICHA-HF in SHA 1.0.

In fact, in most of the above-mentioned cases, countries apply a practical approach that best reflects the nature of the financing arrangements: as if the ICHA-HF categories were defined as financing schemes. (In a strict sense, this means that some of the data – according to SHA 1.0 – are "misclassified" by countries.)

Ambiguity regarding the current definitions of the ICHA-HF categories

There is a great deal of ambiguity regarding the definitions of the ICHA-HF categories: SHA 1.0 did not make a clear distinction between financing schemes and institutional units (organisations) that manage financing schemes.

The definitions provided in SHA 1.0 for several categories can be interpreted in two different ways: as schemes or as institutional units (which, however, may manage more than one different scheme). For example:

- HF.1 General government: "This item comprises *all institutional units* of central, state or local governments and social security funds on all levels of government."
- HF.1.2 Social security funds: "Social security funds are social insurance *schemes covering the community as a whole,* or large sections of the community, and that are imposed and controlled by government units."
- HF.2 Private sector: "This sector comprises all resident institutional units which do not belong to the government sector."
- HF.2.2 Private insurance enterprises (other than social insurance): "This sector comprises all private *insurance enterprises* other than social insurance. Note: this sector comprises both *for-profit and non-for-profit insurance schemes* other than social insurance."

HF.2.3 "Private households' out-of-pocket expenditure" obviously is not a category for an institutional sector. (Households as an institutional sector also pay social insurance contributions and voluntary insurance fees.)

One source of this ambiguity between schemes and institutional units is that the definitions for most of the categories of ICHA-HF in SHA 1.0 were taken from SNA 93 (definitions for the institutional sectors) without adequate interpretation for the health care sector. Furthermore, health systems have undergone considerable changes since SNA 93 was prepared that the SNA obviously cannot reflect.

In fact, in the cases of a few countries (*e.g.*, Netherlands, Slovak Republic, Switzerland, etc.), a decision already had to be made about whether to apply a financing scheme or an institutional approach. In all cases, countries applied a financing scheme approach, as that more accurately reflected the characteristics of their financing systems. (In a strict sense, however, there is a discrepancy between the ICHA-HF definitions under SHA 1.0 and the new schemes. This is one of the key reasons for the revision of the ICHA-HF.)

What information is expected from SHA 2011?

To answer this question, our starting point is SHA 1.0. It emphasises:

"The set of core tables in the System of Health Accounts (SHA) addresses three basic questions:

- Where does the money come from (source of funding)?
- Where does the money go to (provider of health services and goods)?
- What kind of (functionally defined) services are performed and what types of goods are purchased?

Consequently, SHA is organised around a tri-axial system for the recording of health expenditure, by means of a newly proposed International Classification for Health Accounts (ICHA), defining:

- Health care by function (ICHA-HC);

- Health care service provider industries (ICHA-HP);
- Sources of funding health care (ICHA-HF)."

In fact, the HCxHF and HCxHP tables reflect the answer to the first question from the perspective of the providers. It would be more precise to say: Where does the money come from that is *received by the providers*.

During the implementation of SHA, the ambiguity regarding the "where does the money come from" question resulted in changes in the name of the ICHA-HF classification. The JHAQ 2006 used two terms: financing agent/financing schemes, reflecting the lack of agreement.

The SHA 2011 Revision consultation process thoroughly discussed whether ICHA-HF should be defined as a Classification of Financing Schemes or as Classification of Financing Agents (institutional units).

Concerning the interpretation of "where", two approaches can be applied:

- *From a health policy perspective*, the "where" should refer to the main "building blocks" of the health financing system of a country: government programmes, compulsory insurance, voluntary insurance, out-of-pocket payment, etc. From a health policy perspective, the tri-axial system (HCxHF and HPxHF tables) should provide information focusing on *how the resources of the main financing schemes are allocated among services/providers.*
- *From a statistical/micro-economic perspective*, the "where" refers to the economic units executing the payments. If the ICHA-HF were defined as a classification for financing agents (institutional units), the HCxHF and HPxHF tables would provide information concerning the economic units executing the payments to the providers, *regardless of the financing schemes they manage.*

To highlight the differences between the two perspectives, take the following example. In a given country, private insurance companies manage both compulsory and voluntary insurance:

- The key health policy focus is on the difference between the spending by the compulsory insurance scheme and by the voluntary insurance scheme (regardless of which economic units execute the payment under the compulsory insurance scheme);
- The micro-economic focus is on the operation of private insurance companies. However, even in this case the data that includes payments under both compulsory insurance and voluntary insurance are not very meaningful. Information would be needed about financing schemes and institutional units together.

Conclusion for the interpretation of the ICHA-HF classification

The essential information needs for health policy analysis is what puts the health financing schemes at the centre of the accounting framework for health financing under SHA 2011. Therefore, ICHA-HF is interpreted as a Classification for Financing Schemes.

This does not mean, however, that the institutional settings of the allocation of resources and revenue-raising are not important. The proposal for a Classification of Financing Agents (ICHA-FA) and the relevant tables (Expenditure by functions, financing schemes and financing agents and expenditure by providers, financing schemes and financing agents) address this issue.

Notes

1. In SNA the relevant terminology is: social security funds. In the literature on health financing generally the expression "social insurance fund" or "sickness fund" is used.
2. In some countries, social insurance funds are called sickness funds. In many European countries, when compulsory social health insurance for industrial workers was introduced in the late 19th or early 20th century, its operation was built on the organisational structure of the voluntary self-help and self-regulatory funds established by the industrial workers to alleviate the risk of poverty due to sickness and death. The period since the 1960s has witnessed the increasing involvement of state regulations and a considerable concentration of the number of funds. For example, in Germany there were more than 2000 sickness funds in the early 1960s but only about 300 in the early 2000s (Busse and Riesberg, 2004).
3. Under ICHA-HF, only households' out-of-pocket expenditures are accounted under households (HF.2.2.). Producing a sectoral account for households' direct purchase of health services and goods would not provide additional information to the HFxFS table.
4. The table shows only the first-digit level categories of ICHA-HC.
5. Technically, the two sides of the T-account should be equal. Therefore a positive net balance (on the "uses" side) means that the transfers received exceeds the transfers made. A negative net balance means that the transfers made exceed the transfers received of the given actors.

ANNEX E

Classifying Health Care Products

Introduction

The health system provides health care goods and services to the population in the form of health care products. Health products are repeatedly referred to throughout the SHA 2011 Manual and, as such, a standardised concept of what a health product is should be established as a basis for any analysis of the production and consumption processes. This annex discusses the development of a classification of health care products based on their composition and characteristics. The categories presented are not intended as a definitive classification at this stage. The annex also includes an initial overview of the potential uses of such a classification and a brief reference to products as mentioned in the main chapters.

In SHA 2011, the functional classification aims at grouping together health care products according to their purpose, with the purpose categories relating to the natural history of disease (see Chapter 5). The content of the functional classes, which is the various health care goods and services, is further categorised by the Mode of Provision (MoP). A product classification may thus enable a deeper analysis of the consumption of health care products according to the type of MoP and the purpose.

The boundary of the health accounts is set according to the functions of health care. The basic feature of a functional approach concerns final consumption expenditure, which refers to the health goods and services purchased by households, NPISH and government for a health purpose (see Chapter 4 for a description of the boundary setting).

The health care provider (HP) classification in SHA 2011 is organised around the health care functions, so that its equivalence with regard to the underlying health care products is to be expected, at least implicitly: that is, the health care consumed has also been provided (see Chapter 6). There is, however, no one-to-one relationship of the provider to the type of product; usually providers generate a mix of products. A product classification may allow a definition of the profile of the health care mix by provider. It may also support an easier identification of provision outside of the health care boundary. For example, health care technology can be used for non-health care purposes, as is the case in some cosmetic procedures, as well as for the provision of non-health goods and services in pharmacies.

The product classification may be used to identify the quantity[1] of health care goods and services produced and consumed in a country and to see how much is spent on specific items. This may enable an examination of whether a country is achieving better performance indicators because of differences in the quantities consumed/provided or due to price changes. In order to monitor changes in consumption/provision over time, one strategy frequently used is to monitor price dynamics for a health care basket selected on a country-by-country basis. Several international initiatives have targeted comparable price monitoring through purchasing power parities for a selected basket of inputs and products. The development of a health care product classification could assist in the construction of health specific PPPs[2] (see Chapter 13 for a description of price and volume analysis).

Uses of a product classification[3]

As with any classification, standardisation enables international comparability as well as comparison over time. The definition of health care products and their characteristics can help reduce any ambiguity with regard to decisions about classifications.

A primary use of a product classification should therefore be to facilitate the boundary-setting in each health system and to select what should be considered as health care expenditure. The international use of an explicit listing of health care products should improve the comparability of expenditure on health. To achieve this clarity, the expectation is not that a Health Accounting table using the product classification as an axis can be generated, but only that the scope of the accounts can be selected in a standardised way.

The development of a standard classification of products would also help make the content of each of the various functional classes more explicit. Many products may be labelled in a generic way, but it is only the use of the purpose of the consumption that allows them to be integrated into a specific function. For example, the same transportation service may be linked to education or leisure, but only in some specific conditions classified as health care. The health care products target health needs, but they do not have a one-to-one relationship in most cases: different products can target the same need, or one product can target multiple needs. The same health care contact can be considered preventive or curative based on its purpose. It is clear that the classification of health care products and functions are related. In fact, the value of functions is established as equivalent to the value of the groups of products consumed with a specific health purpose. To this end, one expected use of the product classification is to elaborate the content of the HC classes and not necessarily to generate a table of products cross-classified by HC. An explicit listing of products can contribute to identifying the primary product characteristics of health care providers and thus can support decision-making when classifying the health care providers.

Measurement of the consumed quantities of products appears to be a basic though not yet fully standardised process in most of the world's countries. The reporting services among a country's provider institutions may be improved if there is agreement on a selection of products to monitor, so that the identification of the most important ones is comparable. Some products have already been used in an extensive way as indicators of health system practices, such as the number of caesarean sections.

Information on products may be used as an input into more complex analyses, such as productivity and effectiveness. For this purpose, the classification can be adjusted to select the relevant products in the appropriate level of aggregation so that the measurement is made on a comparative basis. The level of product aggregation should be explicit and adjusted for the purpose of the measurement. That is, products may be expressed as individual goods or services, or as a composite or a bundle (see definitions and specific uses below).

The level of aggregation of products to be used is very much dependent on the analysis to be performed. The specific uses of the product classification can be linked to the analysis of specific types of provider and by type of product, such as hospitals and hospital services or nursing homes and LTC services. However, a more detailed level can be required for an analysis by beneficiary, in which case a treatment or type of disease or patient is the level to consider. Each of these uses may lead to different levels of aggregation of products, as appropriate.

A classification of products can be used in the data collection of price statistics. A consumer price index measures the prices paid at the retail sale level. The collection of such prices involves a detailed specification of each representative product. As regular price surveys are expensive, only a selection of products is priced. In some cases, products are grouped at a higher level of aggregation to reduce the cost of the data collection. One example of this is inpatient care, which contains a bundle of products, including those related to diagnosis and treatment as well as nursing and food provision during the stay. An average amount would be generated instead of capturing the amount for each product contained. On the other hand, a larger level of detail could be required for specific areas of interest, in which case the product level needs to be more detailed. Selected health care products are part of the Consumer Price Index (CPI), which is measured on a recurrent basis in many countries.[4]

In summary, a classification can contribute to the framework for international comparison of health care products and should promote the harmonisation of the various types of statistics that deal with goods and services and should strengthen the role of national health accounts as an instrument for co-ordination so as to provide the basis for preparing production and consumption statistics on health care.

Definition of a health care product

A health care product is the result of the interaction of capital, labour and entrepreneurship in the production process which has the primary purpose of improving, maintaining or preventing the deterioration of the health status of persons or mitigating the consequences of ill-health.

Products can consist of both goods and services. Goods are physical objects over which ownership rights can be established and whose ownership can be transferred from one institutional unit to another by engaging in transactions on markets. Goods are in demand either because they may satisfy the needs or wants of households or the community or because they can be used to produce other goods or services. The production and exchange of goods are quite separate activities. The separation of the production of a good from its subsequent sale or resale is an economically significant characteristic of a good (not a characteristic of services). Goods can be stored.

Services are products over which ownership rights cannot be established, although they typically generate changes in the conditions of the consuming units, including health benefits for the receiving individuals. They cannot be traded separately from their production, and they are the result of the activities of producers at the demand of consumers. By the time their production is completed, the services must have been provided to the consumers. Goods may have a very constant set of characteristics depending on the way they are produced, whereas services are heterogeneous outputs as they are linked to the situation when they were provided/consumed. SNA 2008 (paragraphs 6.10-6.22) provides a further discussion of products as goods and services.

- *Products for final and intermediate consumption*

Products can be used for final consumption and intermediate consumption. The focus in the classification of health care products is on products used for final consumption. Products for the intermediate consumption of providers are included in this classification only when these products relate to health care as defined in the functional classification, such as laboratory diagnosis and imaging, medicine provision and patient transport whenever these are provided for final consumption. Other intermediate consumption products, such as electricity, paper and food, are not presented in the classification.

To correctly define the product(s) of a service industry, it is essential to specify exactly what the producer agrees to sell and what the customer agrees to buy. That is, a determination must be made of what is implicitly or explicitly "contracted for" when a transaction takes place. The final service products may include one or more of the following broad types:

- *Simple service:* a standard service whose real output can often be measured in physical units or counts, *e.g.*, a vaccination.
- *Composite service:* a product that embodies several distinct services that are produced together (by virtue of regulations, production process, safety or hygiene requirements, or industry practice). The customer is not free to pick and choose among the several services in the composite – the consumer buys all or none, *e.g.*, a conventional outpatient visit includes diagnosis services as well as a therapeutic plan by a health worker.
- *Service bundle:* a product containing a collection of services negotiated between the service provider and the customer whose composition may vary by customer, *e.g.* a hospital admittance can contain some nursing, medical and "hotel" services and goods. When products reach the level of disease treatments, they implicitly deal with a bundle or a composite service set.

Product identification is easier at a level of detail that accords with prevailing marketing practices and record-keeping practices in the industry. Composite and bundled products are usually integrated in a cost centre and/or in a billing system. A progressive agreement on recording and reporting practices may be advantageous for both health comparisons and the use of health accounts.

- *Criteria used in the construction of the classification*

The product classification is designed to categorise health goods and services that have common characteristics. The classes proposed are a first attempt to cover all the health goods and services, notably in alignment with the purpose (functions) and the provider classifications (by type of services provided), and linked to the mode of provision. This classification is also linkable to the nationally and internationally used product classifications,[5] which could facilitate the use of national accounts data for health accounts.

In order to generate the various categories, differences in technology have been taken into account to delineate the various products. Products defined according to technology can help health care providers to assess the optimality of the methods being used and of health care quality.

The integrated system of statistical classifications includes a classification of products. The health care product classification is based upon CPC Ver. 2 and CPA Rev. 2, adjusted to cover the scope of SHA.[6] Both the CPC and the CPA classify products based on the physical properties of the product, their intrinsic nature as well as the principle of industrial origin. The link between the CPA and the harmonised commodity description and coding system (HS) is less strict than the link between the CPC and the HS, since the CPA gives a high priority to industrial origin. Industrial origin may be very useful for production statistics, but it is not so relevant for other types of statistics, such as those by purpose. For health care products, these criteria can be translated as follows:

- The physical properties of the goods (these cannot be applied to services) relate to their health care purpose and their durability, meaning the medical goods can be non-durable, such as consumables like pharmaceuticals and other medical inputs as well as durable goods, such as medical tools and equipment and prostheses and orthoses whose usability is more than a year.
- The intrinsic nature applies both for goods and services, which in principle must also have a primary purpose of health and must deal with health technology to various extents, and thus has a character of being general or specialised, *e.g.* surgery, a minor procedure, a consultation, a community visit or counselling, for which the human resources and equipment involved can be radically different.
- The industrial origin should be in agreement with the providers as specified in the provider classification.[7] Whether a surgery is in an outpatient unit, a day care centre or a hospital may imply different levels of technology and complexity.

The basic criteria set out in the internationally-used product classifications are supplemented by a specific set of criteria that is necessary for the delineation of health care products:

- The classes at the more aggregated level deal with one of the bundles by purpose that is listed in the functional classification, and can include the simplest aggregation, such as the name of a medicine or medical good, or the specific intervention performed, such as a vaccination (see Box E.1.1 below);
- For the various functional classes split by MoP, the classification of products follows that split;
- When a greater detail in the level of aggregation is required, the proposal is to split by technology levels and differentiate them as general or specialised;
- Specialised services can be further detailed by type of specialty, such as an otolaryngologist consultation/admittance or a gynaecologist consultation/admittance-stay;
- The content of the composite product or contact can then be used to label the product, *e.g.* an ophthalmologist sight test examination, or a cardiologist consultation with an electro-cardiograph diagnosis.

The content of the contact can be a combination of any of the following activities:

- Establish a diagnosis;
- Formulate a prescription and therapeutic plan;
- Complement the process by imaging, laboratory and functional tests for diagnosis and clinical evolution assessment;

- Complement the therapeutic plan to include pharmaceuticals and other medical goods, as well as procedures, such as surgery;
- Monitor and assess the clinical evolution.

Products that are excluded from the health care boundary but are relevant for analytical purposes can also be included in the classification as memorandum items.

- *Adaptations and changes to the basic classifications*

The classification as presented in this chapter is based on both the CPC and the CPA,[8] including the health classes and those components external to the human health branch used to cover the scope of SHA 2011. The starting point is the health functions, which also underlie the provider categories in the classification to set the area of health and the purpose they serve. They also include the products non-specified by functions (contained as retail trade and laboratory services as well as ancillary services such as the transportation of patients) and governance products and some products related to the secondary production of providers. The secondary production of providers could include in-house education programmes for specialisation in the medical and nursing professions. Another example could be services that prepare a hospital's dietetic meals delivered *e.g.* to a nursing home. Many groups and classes are expanded with additional digit groups to create a more complete overview of the products of health care.

A classification of products

The classification of products at its most detailed level contains up to six digits. While for some uses of the classification this might not be detailed enough (*e.g.* for a specific price survey on a selected section of products), for other uses the level of detail may be too large.

An example of the level of detail in the classification is presented in Box E.1.1, where the retail trade in pharmaceuticals and medical non-durables is provided for the issue of "other articles for medical purposes". For general purpose statistics, the detail could be too high, but for a specific survey on wound dressings the level of detail might need to be expanded greatly.

Box E.1.1. **An example of the possible level of detail in wound dressings and other medical non-durables**

07.1	Retail trade services of pharmaceutical goods and medical non-durables
07.1.3	Other articles for medical purposes
07.1.3.1	wound dressing (excl bandages)
07.1.3.1.1	Classic wound dressings
07.1.3.1.1.1	dry wound dressings
07.1.3.1.1.2	Moisture-keeping wound dressings
07.1.3.1.2	bioactive dressings & skin substitutes
07.1.3.2	other medical non-durables
07.1.3.2.1	adhesive and non-adhesive bandages
07.1.3.2.2	hypodermic syringes, first-aid kits,and ice bags (disposables)
07.1.3.2.3	medical hosiery items such as elastic stockings and knee supports
07.1.3.2.4	pregnancy tests
07.1.3.2.5	condoms and other mechanical contraceptive devices

In the health care branch, many products are delivered as composite services or as bundles of services. The distinction is important in understanding the classes proposed below. A composite service is a combination of activities that cannot be separated, *i.e.* they are inseparable. One cannot exist without the other. A bundle of services is a combination of services that depends on the specific intervention needed. Each package of services is customised to the health need and the resource availability, and thus may involve different product bundles, different combinations of the components in the same product aggregate. A bundle can be a combination of composite services and simple services.

Overview of health care products

01 *Hospital services* (CPC/CPA 9311, 86.1)

This category includes bundles of services for:

- Short- or long-term hospital services for patients admitted for a minimum of 24 hours, *i.e.* medical, diagnostic and treatment services, of general hospitals (*e.g.* community and regional hospitals, hospitals of non-profit organisations, university hospitals, military-base and prison hospitals) and specialised hospitals (*e.g.* mental health and substance abuse hospitals, hospitals for infectious diseases, maternity hospitals, specialised sanatoriums).

The services are directed to inpatients and are carried out under the direct supervision of medical doctors (ISCO groups 2212 Specialist medical professionals as well as group 2230 Traditional and complementary medical professionals) and contain:

- Medical, rehabilitative, nursing day care services;
- Emergency room, operating room, etc., services;
- Laboratory, imaging and all other ancillary services.

This also includes pharmaceutical services and laboratory and technical services delivered to inpatients as part of the bundle of services.

This category excludes:

- Services delivered by hospital outpatient wards (03.2, 03.3), services delivered to day care patients (02), and laboratory, imaging, transport and other ancillary services for outpatients (04.5).

• *01.1 Hospital surgical services* (CPC/CPA 93111, 86.10.11)

This subcategory includes:

- Surgical services delivered under the direction of medical doctors (ISCO group 2212 Specialist medical professionals as well as group 2230 Traditional and complementary medical professionals) to inpatients, principally aimed at curing and restoring the health of a patient. Surgical services involve the use of operative manual and instrumental techniques on a patient to investigate and/or treat a pathological condition such as a disease or injury or to help improve bodily function. It also includes pharmaceutical services, nursing services and laboratory and technical services delivered to inpatients as part of the bundle.

Rehabilitative and preventive services are included only if these are part of the bundle of services supplied.

This subcategory excludes day care surgical services (02.1); small surgery services provided in general and specialised practice (03.1 and 03.2); dental surgery in hospitals

(03.3). This type of service also excludes surgery related to the field of gynaecology and obstetrics (01.2).

• *01.2 Hospital gynaecological and obstetrical services (CPC/CPA 93112, 86.10.12)*

This subcategory includes:

- Gynaecological and obstetrical services delivered under the direction of medical doctors (ISCO group 2212 Specialist medical professionals as well as group 2230 Traditional and complementary medical professionals) to inpatients, aimed at the health of a patient. It also includes pharmaceutical services, nursing services and laboratory and technical services delivered to inpatients as part of the bundle.

This subcategory also includes family planning services, including medical treatment such as sterilisation or the termination of pregnancy, with accommodation. Also included are preventive services provided as part of the bundle.

This category excludes gynaecological and obstetrical services delivered in day care (02.2), by independent specialists to outpatients (03.2.2.3) and by independent midwives (not being part of the bundle) (04.1).

• *01.3 Hospital rehabilitation services (CPA 86.10.13)*

This subcategory includes:

- Rehabilitation services delivered under the direction of medical doctors (ISCO group 2212 Specialist medical professionals as well as group 2230 Traditional and complementary medical professionals) to inpatients, aimed at restoring and/or maintaining the health of a patient. Rehabilitation is a process intended to enable people with functional limitations to reach and maintain optimal physical, sensory, intellectual, psychological and/or social function. It also includes pharmaceutical services, nursing services and laboratory and technical services delivered to inpatients as part of the bundle.

Preventive activities provided as part of the bundle are included.

Rehabilitation products include:

- Physical, psychological, speech, and occupational therapy and support services.

This category excludes rehabilitation services provided in day care (02.3), in general practice (03.1) and in other human health services (04), such as physiotherapy services for outpatients.

• *01.4 Hospital psychiatric services (CPC/CPA 93113, 86.10.14)*

This subcategory includes:

- Psychiatric services delivered under the direction of medical doctors (ISCO group 2212 Specialist medical professionals as well as group 2230 Traditional and complementary medical professionals) to inpatients, aimed at curing or maintaining the mental health of a patient. It also includes pharmaceutical services, nursing services and laboratory and technical services delivered to inpatients. Included is also the preventive services provided as part of the service bundle.

This category excludes mental health services delivered in day care settings (02.4) and specialist practices services (03.2.3)

- *01.5 Intensive care services*

Intensive care includes extensive medical and continuous care and treatment provided for an acutely ill patient, in a specially designated section (intensive care unit) of a hospital. It includes nursing, ancillary, laboratory, imaging, prevention and all other services provided as part of the bundle.

- *01.9 Other hospital services (CPC/CPA 93119, 86.10.15, 86.10.19)*

This subcategory includes:

- Other hospital services delivered under the direction of medical doctors (ISCO group 2212 Specialist medical professionals as well as group 2230 Traditional and complementary medical professionals) to inpatients, aimed at curing, restoring and/or maintaining the health of a patient, not mentioned separately above. It also includes other hospital services (radiotherapy, chemotherapy, dialysis services, etc.) delivered to inpatients as part of the bundle of services.

This subcategory excludes specialist medical practice services to inpatients (03.2, and specialised dental services (03.3.1) that are not part of the bundle. Day care services (02) are also excluded. Also excluded are ambulance services (04.4) and medical laboratory services for outpatients (04.5) that are not part of the bundle.

01.9.1 Radiotherapy services

Radiotherapy is the treatment of disease by means of ionising radiation; tissue may be exposed to a beam of radiation, or a radioactive element may be contained in devices (*e.g.*, needles or wire) and inserted directly into tissue (interstitial radiotherapy), or it may be introduced into a natural body cavity (intracavitary radiotherapy).

This category includes these services only if they can be separately identified.

01.9.2 Chemotherapy services

Chemotherapy is the treatment of disease using chemical agents or drugs that are selectively toxic to the causative agent of the disease, such as a virus, bacterium or other microorganism.

This category includes these services only if they can be separately identified.

01.9.3 Dialysis service

A procedure for removing metabolic waste products or toxic substances from the bloodstream by dialysis (either Haemodialysis, Peritoneal dialysis, Haemofiltration, Haemodiafiltration or Intestinal dialysis).

This category includes these services only if they can be separately identified.

01.9.9 Other hospital services n.e.c.

All services delivered in a hospital environment relating to admitted patients including those by medical doctors (ISCO groups 2212 Specialist medical professionals as well as group 2230 Traditional and complementary medical professionals) or under the supervision of medical doctors not elsewhere classified are to be included here.

02 Day care services

This category includes:

- Short-term "hospital" services for admitted patients for less than 24 hours (day care), *i.e.* medical, diagnostic and treatment services. The delivery of day care services is not limited to hospitals, but can also be delivered in ambulatory premises or self-standing centres.

This also includes pharmaceutical services, nursing services and laboratory and technical services delivered to day care patients as part of the bundle of services.

The services are directed to day care patients and are carried out under the direct supervision of medical doctors (ISCO groups 2212 Specialist medical professionals as well as group 2230 Traditional and complementary medical professionals) and contain:

- Medical, rehabilitative, nursing day care services;
- Emergency room, operating room, etc., services;
- Laboratory, imaging and all other ancillary services.

This category excludes services delivered by hospital to inpatients (01) and outpatients (03, 04), laboratory services for outpatients (04.5).

- *02.1 Day care surgical services*

This subcategory includes:

- Surgical services delivered under the direction of medical doctors (ISCO groups 2212 Specialist medical professionals as well as group 2230 Traditional and complementary medical professionals) to day care patients, aimed at curing or restoring the health of a patient. It also includes pharmaceutical services, nursing services and laboratory and technical services delivered to day care patients, when these are part of the bundle.

Rehabilitative and preventive services are included only if these are part of the bundle of services supplied.

This type of service also excludes surgery related to the field of gynaecology and obstetrics (02.2) and dental surgery in hospitals (03.3).

- *02.2 Day care gynaecological and obstetrical services*

This subcategory includes:

- Gynaecological and obstetrical services delivered under the direction of medical doctors (ISCO group 2212 Specialist medical professionals as well as group 2230 Traditional and complementary medical professionals) to day care patients, aimed at the health of a patient. It also includes pharmaceutical services, nursing services and laboratory and technical services that are delivered to day care patients as part of the bundle.

This subcategory also includes family planning services, including medical treatment such as sterilisation or the termination of pregnancy, without accommodation (with admission but a stay of less than 24 hours).

Also included are preventive services provided as part of the bundle.

- *02.3 Day care rehabilitation services*

This subcategory includes:

- Rehabilitation services delivered under the direction of medical doctors (ISCO group 2212 Specialist medical professionals as well as group 2230 Traditional and complementary medical professionals) to day care patients, aimed at restoring and/or maintaining the health of a patient.

Rehabilitation products include:

- Physical, psychological, speech, and occupational therapy and support services as part of the bundle.

It also includes pharmaceutical services, nursing services and laboratory and technical services delivered to day care patients as part of the bundle.

Preventive activities provided as part of the bundle are included.

- *02.4 Day care psychiatric services*

This subcategory includes:

- Psychiatric services delivered under the direction of medical doctors (ISCO groups 2212 Specialist medical professionals as well as group 2230 Traditional and complementary medical professionals) to day care patients, aimed at curing the health of a patient. It also includes pharmaceutical services, nursing services and laboratory and technical services delivered to day care patients as part of the bundle.

Included is also the preventive services provided as part of the service bundle.

- *02.5 Other day care services*

This subcategory includes:

- Other day care services (radiotherapy, chemotherapy, dialysis services, etc.) delivered to day care patients as part of the bundle.

This subcategory excludes laboratory testing/checking and inspection services for all types of materials and products, except medical, ambulance services (04.4), medical laboratory services (04.5).

02.5.1 Day care radiotherapy services

This subcategory includes radiotherapy services provided in day care.

This category includes these services only if they can be separately identified.

02.5.2 Day care chemotherapy services

This subcategory includes chemotherapy services provided in day care.

This category includes these services only if they can be separately identified.

02.5.3 Day care dialysis services

This subcategory includes dialysis services provided in day care (either Haemodialysis, Peritoneal dialysis, Haemofiltration, Haemodiafiltration or Intestinal dialysis).

This category includes these services only if they can be separately identified.

02.5.9 Other day care services n.e.c.

All services delivered in a day care environment relating to patients, including those by medical doctors (ISCO groups 2212 Specialist medical professionals as well as group 2230 Traditional and complementary medical professionals) or under the supervision of medical doctors not elsewhere classified, are to be included here, as long as these services are provided as part of the bundle.

03 Medical and dental practice services (CPC/CPA 9312, 86.2)

The medical services subcategory includes:

- General and specialised medical services consisting in the diagnosis and treatment by medical doctors (ISCO groups 2211 Generalist medical professionals, 2212 Specialist medical professionals as well as group 2230 Traditional and complementary medical professionals) of physical and/or mental diseases or health needs, such as:
  - ❖ Consultations, visits, house calls, telephone services for aiding a patient and establishing a diagnosis;
  - ❖ A prescription and therapeutic plan;
  - ❖ Diagnostic tests and clinical evolution assessment;
  - ❖ Prescription of pharmaceuticals and other medical goods, as well as medical procedures, such as surgery;
  - ❖ Monitoring and assessing the clinical evolution, etc.

Included are preventive services that are part of the composite package provided, meaning these services cannot be separated from the other services delivered at the same time.

Excluded are check-ups in the case that these can be separately identified, when they are not part of the composite package (see 08.4).

The dental services subcategory includes:

- Diagnosis and treatment services of diseases affecting the patient's teeth or mouth or aberrations in the cavity of the mouth, and services aimed at the prevention of dental diseases, including orthodontic services and jaw surgery services. Services aimed at prevention are included only if these services cannot be separately identified in the accounts and are provided as part of the composite package.

The dental services can be delivered in health clinics, such as those attached to schools, firms, homes for the aged, etc., as well as in own consulting rooms.

They cover services in the field of general dentistry, such as routine dental examinations, preventive dental care, treatment of caries, etc., as well as services in the specialised dental area.

When the medical or dental service has as part of the composite the delivery of medical goods, they are included. Whenever the consumption of goods and ancillary services linked to these subcategories is made as an outpatient final consumption, they are excluded. The consumption of pharmaceuticals and therapeutic appliances is an essential component of the health care process, but the retail distribution records are distinct from the health services records. This means that these goods and services are in that case not a part of the composite package.

- 03.1 *General medical practice services (outpatient) (CPC/CPA 93121, 86.21)*

The medical services subcategory includes:

- General medical services that consist of the diagnosis and treatment by medical doctors (ISCO groups 2211 Generalist medical professionals, as well as group 2230 Traditional and complementary medical professionals) of physical and/or mental diseases and health needs, such as:
  - ❖ Consultations, visits, house calls, telephone services for aiding a patient and establishing a diagnosis;
  - ❖ A prescription and therapeutic plan;
  - ❖ Diagnostic tests and clinical evolution assessment;
  - ❖ Prescription of pharmaceuticals and other medical goods, as well as medical procedures, such as surgery;
  - ❖ Monitoring and assessing the clinical evolution, etc.

These services are not limited to specified or particular conditions, diseases or anatomical regions. They can be provided in general practitioners' practices and also delivered by outpatient clinics, at home, in firms, schools etc., or by phone, Internet or other means.

Included are preventive services that are part of the composite package provided, meaning these services cannot be separated from the other services delivered at the same time.

Excluded are check-ups whenever these can be separately identified, *i.e.* they are not part of the composite package (part of 08.4).

The composite package can contain any of the following activities, but any of these can also be delivered as a simple product.

03.1.1 Diagnosis

The act or process of identifying or determining the nature and cause of a condition, disease or injury through evaluating the patient's history, considering signs, symptoms and/or the results of various diagnostic procedures, such as examination and laboratory and imaging data.

03.1.2 Providing medication/prescription of medication/renewal of prescription

This class involves ordering the use of a medicine or other treatment. Preventive activities provided as part of the composite package are included.

03.1.3 Physical medicine/rehabilitation services/physiotherapeutic services

The treatment and diagnosis of a condition, disease or injury by essentially physical means, including manipulation, massage and exercise, often with mechanical devices, and the application of heat, cold, electricity, radiation and water. Rehabilitation products include:

- Physical, psychological, speech, and occupational therapy and support services as part of the composite.

Prevention is included only if it is part of the composite package and cannot be separately identified.

03.1.4 Minor surgery services

Restricted to the management of conditions, diseases or injuries by operative procedures not involving anaesthesia or respiratory assistance.

03.1.5 Evaluation and analysis of medical images and tests

This subcategory includes:

- The analysis and interpretation of medical images (X-rays, electrocardiograms, endoscopies and the like) and all other laboratory test results by medical generalists.

Preventive activities provided as part of the composite package are included. Separately identifiable preventive services are classified in 08.4.

03.1.9 All other general medical practice services (outpatient)

This subcategory includes all services not mentioned above and it excludes inpatient hospital services (01); day care services (02); services of medical laboratories (04.5).

• *03.2 Specialist medical practice services (CPC/CPA 93122, 86.22)*

This category includes:

- Specialist medical practice services that can be provided in specialised practitioners' practices and also delivered by outpatient clinics, at home, in firms, schools, etc., or by phone, Internet or other means. There are four basic medical specialised fields separately mentioned: internal medicine, gynaecology and obstetrics, surgery and paediatrics. Specialised services often involve a further breakdown of each of those fields, as surgery (such as neurosurgery), internal medicine (such as allergology), paediatrics (such as paediatric allergology), and gynaecology and obstetrics (such as reproductive medicine, genetics), etc.
  - ❖ Specialised medical services consisting in diagnosis and treatment by medical doctors (ISCO groups 2212 Specialist medical professionals as well as group 2230 Traditional and complementary medical professionals) of physical and/or mental diseases and health needs, such as:
  - ❖ Consultations, visits, house calls, telephone services for aiding a patient and establishing a diagnosis;
  - ❖ A prescription and therapeutic plan;
  - ❖ Diagnostic tests and clinical evolution assessment;
  - ❖ Prescription of pharmaceuticals and other medical goods, as well as medical procedures, such as surgery;
  - ❖ Monitoring and assessing the clinical evolution, etc.

This subcategory includes:

- Specialised medical services provided to inpatients in case these services can be separately identified and are not part of the composite package of services delivered.

The analysis and interpretation of medical images (X-rays, electrocardiograms, endoscopies and the like) and all other laboratory test results by medical specialists as part of the composite package.

Included are the preventive services as part of the composite package provided, meaning that these services cannot be separated from the other services delivered at the same time.

This subcategory excludes inpatient hospital services (01); day care services (02); services of medical laboratories (04.5).

Excluded are check-ups in case these can be separately identified, *i.e.* they are not part of the composite package (part of 08.4).

Excluded are the services of specialised medical practice as part of a bundle of inpatient or day case services.

03.2.1 *Internal medicine*

This is the branch of medicine that deals with the diagnosis and (nonsurgical, non-gynaecologic, or paediatric) treatment of diseases of the internal organs.

The composite package can contain any of the below-mentioned activities, but any of these can also be delivered as a simple product.

Excluded are the services of internal medicine practice as part of a bundle of inpatient or day case services.

03.2.1.1 *Diagnosis*

The act or process of identifying or determining the nature and cause of a condition, disease or injury in internal medicine practice through the evaluation of a patient's history, considering signs, symptoms and/or the results of various diagnostic procedures, such as examination and laboratory and imaging data.

03.2.1.2 *Providing medication/prescription of medication/renewal of prescription*

Ordering the use of a medicine or other treatment in internal medicine practice. Preventive activities provided as part of the composite package are included.

03.2.1.3 *Physical medicine/rehabilitation services/physiotherapeutic services*

The treatment and diagnosis of a condition, disease or injury in internal medicine practice by essentially physical means, including manipulation, massage and exercise, often with mechanical devices, and the application of heat, cold, electricity, radiation and water.

Rehabilitation products include:

- Physical, psychological, speech and occupational therapy and support services as part of the composite.

Prevention is included only if it is part of the composite package and cannot be separately identified.

03.2.1.4 *Minor surgery services*

Restricted to management of conditions, diseases or injuries in internal medicine practice by operative procedures not involving anaesthesia or respiratory assistance.

03.2.1.5 Evaluation and analysis of medical images and tests

Analysis and interpretation of medical images (X-rays, electrocardiograms, endoscopies and the like) and all other laboratory test results by medical specialists in internal medicine practice.

03.2.1.9 All other internal medicine services

This subcategory includes all services not mentioned above and excludes:

- Inpatient hospital services (0.1), day care services (0.2), services of medical laboratories (04.5).

03.2.2 Surgery (excluding surgery in gynaecology and obstetrics), excluding minor surgery in other fields (outpatient)

Surgical services involve the use of operative manual and instrumental techniques on a patient to investigate and/or treat a pathological condition such as a disease or injury to help improve bodily function.

Surgical services involve:

- Elective surgery: to correct a non-life-threatening condition, which is carried out at the patient's request, subject to the availability of the surgeon and the surgical facility;
- Emergency surgery: must be done quickly to save life, limb, or functional capacity;
- Exploratory surgery: performed to aid or confirm a diagnosis;
- Therapeutic surgery: treats a previously diagnosed condition.

All types of surgery with a primary health purpose are to be included.

- Minimally invasive surgery involves smaller outer incision(s) to insert miniaturised instruments within a body cavity or structure, as in laparoscopic surgery or angioplasty,
- Open surgical procedures require a large incision to access the area of interest.
- Laser surgery involves the use of a laser to cut tissue.
- Microsurgery involves using an operating microscope so that the surgeon can see small structures.
- Robotic surgery makes use of remote control of the instrumentation operated under the direction of the surgeon.

Excluded are the services of specialised surgical practice as part of a bundle of inpatient or day case services.

03.2.2.1 Diagnosis

The act or process of identifying or determining the nature and cause of a condition, disease or injury in surgical medicine practice through the evaluation of a patient's history, considering signs, symptoms and/or the results of various diagnostic procedures, such as examination and laboratory and imaging data.

03.2.2.2 Providing medication/prescription of medication/renewal of prescription

Ordering the use of a medicine or other treatment in surgical medicine practice. Preventive activities provided as part of the composite package are included.

03.2.2.3 Evaluation and analysis of medical images and tests

Analysis and interpretation of medical images (X-rays, electrocardiograms, endoscopies and the like) and all other laboratory test results by medical specialists in surgical medicine practice.

03.2.2.9 All other surgical specialist services

This subcategory includes all services not mentioned above and excludes:

- Inpatient hospital services (0.1), day care services (0.2), services of medical laboratories (04.5).

03.2.3 Gynaecology and obstetrics

This is the specialty dealing with the care of women, including the health of the female reproductive system (uterus, vagina and ovaries) and of their children during pregnancy, childbirth and postnatal. Midwifery is the non-surgical equivalent.

The composite package can contain any of the below-mentioned activities, but any of these can also be delivered as a simple product.

Excluded are the services of specialised gynaecological and obstetric practice as part of a bundle of inpatient or day case services.

03.2.3.1 Diagnosis

The act or process of identifying or determining the nature and cause of a condition, disease or injury in gynaecological and obstetric medicine practice through the evaluation of a patient's history, considering signs, symptoms and/or the results of various diagnostic procedures, such as examination and laboratory and imaging data.

03.2.3.2 Providing medication/prescription of medication/renewal of prescription

Ordering the use of a medicine or other treatment in gynaecological and obstetric medicine practice. Preventive activities provided as part of the composite package are included.

03.2.3.3 Physical medicine/rehabilitation services/physiotherapeutic services

The treatment and diagnosis of a condition, disease or injury in gynaecological and obstetric medicine practice by essentially physical means, including manipulation, massage and exercise, often with mechanical devices, and the application of heat, cold, electricity, radiation and water.

Rehabilitation products include:

- Physical, psychological, speech, and occupational therapy and support services as part of the composite.

Prevention is included only if it is part of the composite package and cannot be separately identified.

03.2.3.4 Surgery services related to gynaecology and obstetrics

Surgical services involve the use of operative manual and instrumental techniques on gynaecology and obstetric patients to investigate and/or treat a condition, disease or injury to help improve bodily function.

03.2.3.5 Evaluation and analysis of medical images and tests

Analysis and interpretation of medical images (X-rays, electrocardiograms, endoscopies and the like) and all other laboratory test results by medical specialists in gynaecological and obstetric medicine practice.

03.2.3.9 All other gynaecological and obstetrical services (outpatient)

This subcategory includes all services not mentioned above and excludes:

- Inpatient hospital services, day care services, services of medical laboratories (04.5).

03.2.4 Paediatrics

This specialty is concerned with the treatment of conditions, diseases and injuries in infants and children.

The composite package can contain any of the below-mentioned activities, but any of these can also be delivered as a simple product.

Excluded are the services of specialised paediatric practice as part of a bundle of inpatient or day case services.

03.2.4.1 Diagnosis

The act or process of identifying or determining the nature and cause of a condition, disease or injury in paediatric medicine practice through the evaluation of a patient's history, considering signs, symptoms and/or the results of various diagnostic procedures, such as examination and laboratory and imaging data.

03.2.4.2 Providing medication/prescription of medication/renewal of prescription

Ordering the use of a medicine or other treatment in paediatric medicine practice. Preventive activities provided as part of the composite package are included.

03.2.4.3 Physical medicine/rehabilitation services/physiotherapeutic services

The treatment and diagnosis of a condition, disease or injury in paediatric medicine practice by essentially physical means, including manipulation, massage and exercise, often with mechanical devices, and the application of heat, cold, electricity, radiation and water.

Rehabilitation products include:

- Physical, psychological, speech, and occupational therapy and support services as part of the composite.

Prevention is included only if it is part of the composite package and cannot be separately identified.

03.2.4.4 Minor surgery services

Restricted to the management of conditions, diseases or injuries in paediatric medicine practice by operative procedures not involving anaesthesia or respiratory assistance.

03.2.4.5 Evaluation and analysis of tests

Analysis and interpretation of medical images (X-rays, electrocardiograms, endoscopies and the like) and all other laboratory test results by medical specialists, in paediatric medicine practice.

03.2.4.9 All other paediatric services

This subcategory includes all services not mentioned above and excludes:

- Other hospital services (0.1), other day care services (0.2), services of medical laboratories (04.5).

03.2.5 All other specialisations

This subcategory includes all services not mentioned above.

The composite package can contain any of the below-mentioned activities, but any of these can also be delivered as a simple product.

Excluded are the services of all other specialised medical practices as part of a bundle of inpatient or day case services.

03.2.5.1 Diagnosis

The act or process of identifying or determining the nature and cause of a condition, disease or injury in all other specialised medicine practice through the evaluation of a patient's history, considering signs, symptoms and/or the results of various diagnostic procedures, such as examination and laboratory and imaging data.

03.2.5.2 Providing medication/prescription of medication/renewal of prescription

Ordering the use of a medicine or other treatment in all other specialised medicine practice. Preventive activities provided as part of the composite package are included.

03.2.5.3 Physical medicine/rehabilitation services/physiotherapeutic services

The treatment and diagnosis of a condition, disease or injury in all other specialised medicine practice by essentially physical means, including manipulation, massage and exercise, often with mechanical devices, and the application of heat, cold, electricity, radiation and water.

Rehabilitation products include:

- Physical, psychological, speech, and occupational therapy and support services as part of the composite.

Prevention is included only if it is part of the composite package and cannot be separately identified.

03.2.5.4 Minor surgery services

Restricted to management of conditions, diseases or injuries in all other specialised medicine practice by operative procedures not involving anaesthesia or respiratory assistance.

03.2.5.5 Evaluation and analysis of medical images and tests

Analysis and interpretation of medical images (X-rays, electrocardiograms, endoscopies and the like) and all other laboratory test results by medical specialists in all other specialised medicine practice.

03.2.5.9 All other services by other medical specialisms

This subcategory includes all services not mentioned above and excludes:

- Other hospital services (0.1), other day care services (0.2), services of medical laboratories (04.5).

- *03.3 Dental practice services (CPC/CPA 93123, 86.23)*

The dental services subcategory includes:

- Diagnosis and treatment services of diseases affecting the patient's teeth or mouth or aberrations in the cavity of the mouth, and services aimed at the dental diseases and dental health needs, including orthodontic services and jaw surgery services.

The dental services can be delivered in health clinics, such as those attached to schools, firms, homes for the aged, etc., as well as in own consulting rooms.

Dental services consist in diagnosis and treatment by the dentist (generalists and specialists), such as:

- Consultations, visits, house calls, telephone services for aiding a patient and establishing a diagnosis;
- A prescription and therapeutic plan;
- Diagnostic tests and clinical evolution assessment;
- Prescription of pharmaceuticals and other medical goods, as well as medical procedures, such as surgery;
- Monitoring and assessing the clinical evolution, etc.

They cover services in the field of general dentistry, such as routine dental examinations, treatment of caries, etc., as well as services in the specialised dental area.

Included are preventive services included as part of the composite package provided, meaning these services cannot be separated from the other services delivered at the same time.

Excluded are the services of dental practice as part of a bundle of inpatient or day case services.

03.3.1 Orthodontic services (CPA 86.23.11)

This subcategory includes:

- Orthodontic services, *e.g.*, treatment of protruding teeth, crossbite, overbite, etc., including dental surgery; services in the field of oral surgery; other specialised dental services, *e.g.*, in the field of periodontics, paedodontics, endodontics and reconstruction.

This subcategory includes:

- Preventive services included as part of the composite package provided, meaning these services cannot be separated from the other services delivered at the same time.

Excluded are the services of orthodontic dental practice as part of a bundle of inpatient or day case services.

03.3.9 Other dental practice services (CPA 86.23.19)

This subcategory includes:

- Diagnosis and treatment services of diseases affecting the patient or aberrations in the cavity of the mouth, and services aimed at dental diseases.

These dental services can be delivered in health clinics, such as those attached to schools, firms, homes for the aged, etc., as well as in own consulting rooms.

This subcategory includes:

- Specialised dental services including dental surgery provided to inpatients in case these services can be separately identified and are not part of the bundle of services delivered.

They cover services in the field of general dentistry, such as routine dental examinations, treatment of caries, etc. Preventive dental care is included only when part of the composite package provided, meaning these services cannot be separated from the other services delivered at the same time.

***04 Other medical services* (CPC/CPA 9319, 86.9)**

This subcategory includes:

- Services provided by authorised persons, other than medical doctors in the fields of Midwives' services, Nursing services, Physiotherapeutic services, Ambulance services and Medical laboratory services delivered as part of the composite package.

This subcategory excludes all the services delivered to inpatients and day cases as part of the package of services, *i.e.* the service bundle consumed.

- *04.1 Midwives' services* (CPC/CPA 93191, 86.90.11)

This subcategory includes:

- Services provided by authorised persons, other than medical doctors:
  - ❖ Supervision and delivery services during pregnancy and childbirth; supervision of the mother after birth; family planning services involving medical treatment.

This subcategory includes the midwifery services delivered to inpatients and day care cases, which are not part of the bundle of inpatient services.

This subcategory excludes day cases if these are part of a bundle delivered by a medical specialist. However, in case the midwife conducts a delivery in a hospital setting on her own authority, these services are included in this subcategory.

- *04.2 Nursing services* (CPC/CPA 93192,86.90.12)

This subcategory includes:

- Services provided by authorised persons other than medical doctors:
  - ❖ Services in the field of nursing care (without admission), advice and prevention for patients at home, the provision of maternity care, children's hygiene, etc.

This subcategory excludes residential nursing care facility services (05). This subcategory also excludes all services delivered in an inpatient or day case setting delivered as part of the bundles of services mentioned in inpatient and day cases.

- *04.3 Physiotherapeutic services (CPC/CPA 93193, 86.90.13)*

This subcategory includes:

- Services provided by authorised persons, other than medical doctors:
  - Services in the field of physiotherapy, ergotherapy, etc.

Excluded are the services provided to inpatients and day case as part of the bundles of services.

- *04.4 Patient transport services, among others Ambulance services (CPC/CPA 93194, 86.90.14)*

This subcategory includes:

- Transportation of patients to the health care premises or a required inter-facility transfer to complement a bundle of services, *e.g.* emergency transportation to health facilities and transportation between health facilities to complement imaging diagnosis or rehabilitative treatment. The transportation can be delivered in a specially-equipped surface vehicle or in a designated air or water ambulance (with or without resuscitation equipment or medical personnel) to and from facilities for the purpose of receiving medical and surgical care.

This also includes transportation in conventional vehicles, such as a taxi, when there is either a transaction involved or an overhead *e.g.* in the case of inter-hospital diagnosis imaging procedures.

Excluded are the transportation services provided to inpatients and day cases as part of the bundle of services.

- *04.5 Medical laboratory services (CPC/CPA 93195, 86.90.15)*

This entry comprises a variety of tests of clinical specimens in order to get information about the health of a patient. Laboratory tests are an integral part of the workup of any patient, and constitute a guide for diagnosis and treatment choice. This class involves all prescribed tests that are not part of a bundle of services (inpatient and day case) or of a composite service for outpatient. Laboratory diagnosis includes the areas of Anatomic Pathology (histopathology, cytopathology); Clinical Microbiology (bacteriology, virology, parasitology, immunology and mycology); Clinical Biochemistry (enzymology, toxicology and endocrinology); Haematology (coagulation and blood bank); Cytology (semen and organ banks); and Genetics (cytogenetics).

Also included are clinical tests that are directed to specific organs and require additional technology to measure the activity, which are linked to most medical specialties: cardiovascular: *e.g.* electrocardiographic diagnosis; allergy: *e.g.* allergy test, food sensitivity tests; audiology, etc. Other diagnostic services include tests such as electrocardiographic diagnosis and effort assessment.

Excluded are all laboratory services provided as part of the bundle of services delivered during an inpatient stray or day case treatment as well as laboratory services that are part of the composite service for outpatients.

Also excluded are the interpretation and evaluation of the laboratory testing results (0.1, 0.2 and 0.3).

04.5.1 Sensitivity tests

A sensitivity test is a procedure that determines how responsive the subject is to certain outside stimuli. Each test is performed differently and may help both the subject and those administering the test better understand certain behaviour patterns or symptoms and how to treat them.

04.5.2 Microbiological/immunological tests

Laboratory techniques involving the use of microorganisms and the interaction of antigens with specific antibodies.

04.5.3 Blood, urine and faeces tests

Laboratory diagnosis through the physical, chemical and microscopic examination of blood, urine and faeces samples.

04.5.4 Histological/exfoliative cytology

Study of changes caused by disease within cells.

04.5.5 Other laboratory tests NEC

This subcategory includes all laboratory tests not mentioned above.

04.5.6 Physical function tests

The physical function examination consists of exercises designed to measure particular aspects of musculoskeletal strength and flexibility in a standardised manner

04.5.7 Diagnostic endoscopy

Examination of the interior of a canal or hollow organ by means of an endoscope to reach a diagnosis. The endoscope usually has a fibre optic camera, which allows a greatly magnified image to be projected onto a video screen, to be viewed by the operator. Many endoscopes also allow the operator to retrieve a small sample (biopsy) of the area being examined, in order to more closely view the tissue under a microscope.

04.5.9 Other medical laboratory services n.e.c.

This subcategory includes all medical laboratory services not elsewhere classified.

- *04.6 Diagnostic imaging services without interpretation (CPC/CPA 93196, 86.90.17)*

This subcategory includes:

- A variety of services applying imaging technology like X-rays and radiation to diagnose and monitor patients. Includes an array of imaging technologies to diagnose and treat diseases, such as plain X-rays, bone; Soft tissue imaging, contrast X-rays or photo-imaging, diagnostic ultrasound, computed tomography (CT), Computer Assisted Tomography, Nuclear medicine, Nuclear magnetic imaging; Nuclear scanning, Positron Emission Tomography (PET), Magnetic resonance imaging (MRI) and other miscellaneous diagnostic imaging (arteriography using contrast material, angiocardiography, phlebography, thermography, bone mineral density studies).

Excluded are all imaging services provided as part of the bundle of services delivered during an inpatient stay or day case treatment as well as imaging services that are part of the composite service for outpatients.

Also excluded are the interpretation and evaluation of the imaging service results (0.1, 0.2 and 0.3).

04.6.1 Diagnostic radiology/imaging (CPC/CPA revised: 86. 90.17)

Specialised study through the application of imaging technology such as X-rays to diagnose and monitor conditions, disease or injuries.

- *04.7 Blood, sperm and transplant organ bank services (CPC/CPA 93197, 86.90.16)*

This subcategory includes:

- Services provided by blood, semen, embryo, tissue and transplant organ banks, including storing and cataloguing available specimens, matching donated specimens and potential recipients, etc.

In the majority of cases, these services are not directly delivered to patients as final consumption but are used in the process of some medical procedure and as such are part of intermediate consumption.

- *04.9 Other medical services n.e.c. (CPC/CPA 93199, 86.90.19)*

This subcategory includes:

- Other paramedical human health services *n.e.c.*, such as occupational therapy (ISCO 2263 occupational health professionals), speech therapy (ISCO 2266 Audiologists and speech therapists) and services of TCAM (traditional, complementary and alternative medicine), such as acupuncture, aroma therapy, homeopathy, nutrition therapy, services of traditional birth attendants, traditional healers (see description of ISCO group 2230 Traditional and complementary medicine professionals).

These services are provided by authorised persons other than medical doctors.

This subcategory excludes services such as physiotherapy and ergotherapy (04.3). Also excluded are these services whenever they are part of the bundle of services delivered to inpatients and day cases as well as the services part of the composite services delivered to outpatients.

05 Residential care services (CPC/CPA 932, 87)

This category includes:

- Services provided in nursing homes, homes for the elderly and disabled, services provided for mental retardation, mental health and substance abuse and other residential care services, with respect to the medical, nursing, ancillary and ADL components.

In principle, only the activities related to nursing, ancillary and ADL are to be recorded as part of the health care package.

Excluded are Nursing services (04.2) provided by independent qualified nurses.

- 05.1 *Residential nursing care services* (CPC/CPA 9321, 87.1)

This subcategory includes:

- Combined accommodation and medical, nursing, ancillary and ADL services provided without the supervision of a medical doctor located on the premises, *e.g.* nursing homes, homes for the elderly with nursing care, convalescent homes and rest homes with nursing care.

In principle, only the activities related to nursing, ancillary and ADL are to be recorded as part of the health care package.

Excluded are nursing services (04.2) provided by independent qualified nurses.

- 05.9 *Other residential care services* (CPC/CPA 9330, 87.90)

This category includes:

- Other social work services with accommodation, halfway group homes for persons with social or personal problems; other social rehabilitation services, in so far as medical, nursing, ancillary and ADL services are separable parts of the packages.

In principle only activities related to nursing, ancillary and ADL are to be recorded as part of the health care package.

Excluded are nursing services (04.2) provided by independent qualified nurses.

06 *Nursing care services without accommodation* (CPC/CPA 934, 88)

This category includes:

- All nursing, ancillary and ADL services provided by authorised and unauthorised persons delivered to children and adults with a large dependency for activities of daily living and instrumental activities of daily living (IADL). Included are services provided by volunteers (for their remunerated services).

In principle only activities related to nursing, ancillary and ADL are to be recorded as part of the health care package.

Excluded are nursing services (04.2) provided by independent qualified nurses.

- 06.1 *Nursing care services without accommodation for the elderly and disabled* (CPA 88.1)

All nursing, ancillary and ADL services provided by authorised and unauthorised persons delivered to elderly and disabled with a large dependency for activities of daily living and instrumental activities of daily living (IADL), but without the supervision of a medical doctor located on the premises during a part of the day. Included are nursing care services delivered at the patient's home.

In principle only activities related to nursing, ancillary and ADL are to be recorded as part of the health care package.

Excluded are nursing services (04.2) provided by independent qualified nurses.

- 06.9 *Other nursing care services without accommodation* (CPC/CPA 935, 88.9)

This subcategory includes all services not mentioned above.

07 Retail trade services in medical products (CPC/CPA Division 62, 47)

This item comprises medical goods dispensed to outpatients and the services connected with dispensing, such as retail trade, fitting, maintaining and renting of medical goods and appliances. Included are the services of public pharmacies, opticians, sanitary shops and other specialised or non-specialised retail traders, including mail ordering and teleshopping.

This group covers medicaments, prostheses, medical appliances and equipment and other health-related products provided to individuals, either with or without a prescription, usually from dispensing chemists, pharmacists or medical equipment suppliers, and intended for consumption or use by a single individual or household outside a health facility or institution.

Included is the information and education service provided as part of the (simple) product delivery.

- *07.1 Retail trade services of pharmaceutical goods and medical non-durables (CPC/ CPA 62273, 47.00.74)*

This item comprises pharmaceuticals such as medicinal preparations, branded and generic medicines, drugs, patent medicines, serums and vaccines, vitamins and minerals and oral contraceptives. This item also comprises a wide range of medical non-durables such as bandages, elastic stockings, incontinence articles, condoms and other mechanical contraceptive devices.

Included is the information and education service provided as part of the (simple) product delivery.

07.1.1 Medicaments, for therapeutic or prophylactic uses

Medicaments are any chemical substance intended for use in the medical diagnosis, cure, treatment or prevention of disease. The level of detail in the category of medicaments for therapeutic and prophylactic use corresponds to the distinctions used in the Anatomical Therapeutic Classification.

07.1.1.1 Medicaments aimed at alimentary tract and metabolism

07.1.1.2 Medicaments aimed at blood and blood-forming organs

07.1.1.3 Medicaments aimed at cardiovascular system

07.1.1.4 Dermatologicals

07.1.1.5 Medicaments aimed at genito-urinary system and sex hormones

07.1.1.6 Systemic hormonal preparations, excluding sex hormones and insulins

07.1.1.7 Anti-infectives for systemic use

07.1.1.8 Antineoplastic and immunomodulating agents

07.1.1.9 Medicaments aimed at musculo-skeletal system

07.1.1.10 Medicaments aimed at nervous system

07.1.1.11 Antiparasitic products, insecticides and repellents

07.1.1.12 Medicaments aimed at respiratory system

07.1.1.13 Medicaments aimed at sensory organs

07.1.1.14 Various other medicaments

07.1.2 Other pharmaceutical products

07.1.2.1 Serums and vaccines

07.1.2.2 Vitamins and minerals

07.1.2.3 Cod liver oil and halibut liver oil

07.1.2.4 Oral contraceptives

07.1.2.9 All other pharmaceutical products

07.1.3 Other articles for medical purposes

07.1.3.1 Wound dressing (excluding bandages)

07.1.3.1.1 Classic wound dressings

07.1.3.1.1.1 Dry wound dressings

07.1.3.1.1.2 Moisture-keeping wound dressings

07.1.3.1.2 Bioactive dressings & skin substitutes

07.1.3.2 Other medical non-durables

07.1.3.2.1 Adhesive and non-adhesive bandages

07.1.3.2.2 Hypodermic syringes, first-aid kits and ice bags (disposables)

07.1.3.2.3 Medical hosiery items such as elastic stockings and knee supports

07.1.3.2.4 Pregnancy tests

07.1.3.2.5 Condoms and other mechanical contraceptive devices

07.1.9 All other retail trade services of pharmaceutical goods and medical non-durables

- *07.2 Retail trade services of medical durables and orthopaedic products (CPC/CPA 62274, 7.00.75)*

This item comprises a wide range of medical durable goods such as hearing aids and other medical devices.

Included is the information and education service provided as part of the (simple) product delivery.

07.2.1 Medical durables for household use (such as clinical thermometers, hot-water bottles and (re-usable) ice bags

07.2.2 Hearing aids

07.2.3 Artificial limbs and other prosthetic devices

07.2.4 Orthopaedic braces and supports, surgical belts, trusses and supports, neck braces

07.2.5 Orthopaedic footwear

07.2.6 Wheelchairs and invalid carriages, crutches, electronic and other devices for monitoring blood pressure, etc.

Included in this item are also items such as walking canes (such as for the blind), wigs, etc.

07.2.7 Repair of such articles

07.2.9 All other retail trade services of medical durables and orthopaedic products and their repair

- *07.3 Retail trade services of optical goods and services of opticians*

This item comprises a wide range of medical durable goods such as glasses, rims, lenses, fluids and the fitting and related services to the sales of these items.

Included is the information and education service provided as part of the (simple) product delivery.

07.3.1 Spectacles, corrective eyeglasses and contact lenses and analogous articles for correction, protection, or of another type; lens fluids; frames for spectacles, eyeglasses and analogous articles; binoculars, monoculars.

07.3.2 Repair of such articles

- *07.4 Mail order or internet retail trade services in medical goods (CPC 623)*

- *07.9 All other retail trade services in medical products and their repair*

08 *Preventive services*

Prevention is any service that reduces the burden of mortality or morbidity from disease. This takes place at primary, secondary and tertiary prevention levels.

- Primary prevention anticipates the emergence and lessens the severity of diseases. Most population-based health promotion activities are primary preventive measures, *e.g.* vaccination.

- Secondary prevention activities are aimed at early disease detection, thereby increasing opportunities for less costly and invasive interventions to prevent progression of the disease and emergence of symptoms, *e.g.* screening for TB, diabetes, breast cancer, etc.
- Tertiary prevention reduces the negative impact of an already-established disease by restoring function and reducing disease-related complications.

In SHA, prevention is limited to primary and secondary prevention, that is to say, it involves specific benefits aimed at avoiding contact with disease-producing risk factors to reduce the onset of a disease and to detect diseases early.

Although most primary and secondary prevention services are offered as part of health care while delivering curative and rehabilitative services, in some cases they have a set of specific resources, as in the case of vaccination campaigns and screening campaigns, for which health services can be delivered outside the health care premises. These services are also provided by special teams or individual health professionals not connected with a hospital, clinic or practitioner, but in public health laboratories, by researchers, by toxicological experts and community health workers, among others.

Any preventive services provided as part of a bundle for inpatients and day cases as well as part of a composite service delivered to outpatients are not part of these (sub) categories.

- *08.1 Information and counselling programmes*

Information, education and communication (IEC) combines strategies, approaches and methods to enable individuals, families, groups, organisations and communities to play active roles in achieving, protecting and sustaining their own health. Embodied in IEC is the process of learning that empowers people to make decisions, modify behaviours and change social conditions, including better knowledge, beliefs, attitudes, use and interaction with the health system.

This includes products in the various formats:

- Printed documents, internet and other electronic formats;
- Media;
- Personal interaction.

Mass media content can cover movie, radio, theatre and TV advertisements and programmes, and flyers, posters, documents of all sizes, mass media publicity, interpersonal interaction and special dissemination activities at all levels of detail.

The content aims to inform individuals about specific health problems, their conditioning factors and particular risks. This can be related to risk-avoidance strategies, self-protection, medication adherence, self-management guidelines of diseases, pre-operative education, or discharge plans, self-applied tests to monitor health conditions, orienting individuals on how to stay well if the results are negative, and orienting and referring them for follow-up, if positive.

- *08.2 Immunisation programmes*

These aim to prevent the development of a disease, before or after exposure, through the use of pharmaceutical products, such as vaccines.

This involves consumption both as a control programme and upon individual demand. For accounting purposes, it is recommended that this class be further disaggregated as:

- Immunisation through mass vaccination campaign (intra- or extramural);
- Immunisation requested by individuals.

Vaccination can be related to a predefined package related to specific population groups (children, pregnant women, individuals at imminent risk, etc.).

Most frequent vaccines:

- Diphtheria, measles, mumps, pertussis (whooping cough), rubella, tetanus, varicella (chicken pox), polio;
- Hepatitis, herpes zoster, HPV, influenza, meningococcal infections, pneumococcal infections, rabies and yellow fever.

- *08.3 Early disease detection programmes*

This item concerns the active search for a disease early in its course, before symptoms appear, within the risk groups. These are directed to specific diseases, such as breast cancer, cervical cancer, colon rectal cancer, diabetes, HIV/AIDS, malaria, tuberculosis, prostate cancer and so on.

This involves consumption both as a control programme and upon individual demand. For accounting purposes, it is recommended that this class be further disaggregated as:

- Early disease detection campaign (intra- or extramural);
- Early disease detection requested at the consumer's initiative.

These can involve one or more of the following services (not being part of a bundle of services delivered to inpatients or day cases or part of a composite service delivered to outpatients):

- Medical examinations;
- Laboratory and imaging diagnostic;
- Endoscopic and other procedures.

- *08.4 Healthy condition monitoring programmes*

This item concerns the active monitoring of healthy conditions, not focused on specific diseases. These can target, for example, specific conditions such as pregnancy (antenatal and postnatal care), age groups such as children (*e.g.* child growth and development) or ageing groups and specific health domains, such as general health check-ups.

- General check-ups;
- Essential preventive interventions for healthy groups, *e.g.* distribution of contraceptive methods, including emergency contraception, anaemia prevention and control in maternal and child conditions: iron and folic acid supplementation;
- Monitoring growth and development, *e.g.* progress of pregnancy and assessment of maternal and foetal well-being, including nutritional status; monitoring child growth; post-abortion care and family planning;
- Support for routine care and follow-up visits;
- Recognition of problems, illness and timely care-seeking, *e.g.* for the elderly.

Includes early detection and management of common conditions of ageing groups; early identification and management of newborn problems, for pregnancy complications (*e.g.*, anaemia, hypertensive disorders, bleeding, mal-presentations, multiple pregnancy).

- *08.5 Epidemiologic surveillance and risk and disease control programme*

This class involves the technical effort to manage knowledge and resources with a preventive and control focus. It can be developed through global, regional or national protocol-based programmes.

This includes:

- Programme control documents and related planning, monitoring and evaluation of interventions;
- Information systems for epidemiology and health and management to track cases, records and health system responses;
- Operational programme interventions, for improvement of the programme: supervision, hands-on training and operational research;
- Reports and systems for surveillance and analysis of communicable and non-communicable diseases, injuries and exposure to environmental agents harmful to health;
- Records to measure selected health conditions and diseases of community significance, such as tuberculosis.

- *08.6 Disaster and emergency response programmes of health systems*

Includes the preparation for an appropriate response in case of humanitarian emergencies whether of human or natural origin. The aim is to protect health and to reduce mortality and morbidity due to health hazards through, notably, field epidemiology and training to follow technical standards.

This involves:

- Documents with instructions and guidance;
- Training and exercises to set strategies;
- Generating and handling information during emergency periods to identify the nature of the emergency and the health effects as well as the magnitude and location of health damages;
- Strategies for the enlargement of resources on a very short-term basis;
- Preparation and adjustment strategies on operations and the referral of patients, such as reorganising triage and coverage based on the nature of the emergency.

This class can be adjusted to country-specific needs, as the health risks can differ in different areas. However, in all cases health rules and a health infrastructure should be prepared to cope with emergency health care needs.

09 Governance, management and health system administration (CPC/CPA Division 91, 84)

The focus of these services is on the health system rather than directly on health care. They are considered to be collective, as they may not be allocated to specific individuals but benefit all users. They direct and support the functioning of the health system. These services are expected to maintain and increase the effectiveness and efficiency of the health system and may enhance its equity.

This category includes:

- The formulation and administration of government policy;
- The setting and enforcement of standards;
- The regulation, licensing or supervision of producers;
- The management of funds collection;
- The administration, monitoring and evaluation of these resources.

Excluded are: the administrative costs of the health providers and the health goods and services they provide. Also excluded are the opportunity costs of paperwork for consumers and the associated general revenue tax collection.

- *09.1 Governance and administrative health (excluding those for mandatory schemes) care services (CPC/CPA 911, 84.1)*

Governance and health system administration together form a single class. One class is proposed at the second-digit level due to its relatively low share of spending and the low feasibility of it being separated.

Governance has been defined as "the careful and responsible management of the population's well-being", and comprises three broad tasks: providing vision and direction, collecting and using intelligence and exerting influence through regulation and other means. It includes planning, policy formulation and information intelligence for the entire health system, such as:

- Monitoring of health needs and health care interventions;
- Specific resource monitoring and auditing;
- Research, development and implementation of innovative interventions to set standards;
- Development of policies and planning;
- Health promotion partnerships, social participation and empowerment.

Administration involves a management focus on the design of measures to regulate, to generate incentives and to control organisations and resources in the system, such as general and specialised medical establishments, including dental services, hospitals and clinics, nursing and convalescent home services as well as independent practices. This includes directive and operational roles as well as the resources involved in such operations.

- Strategic management of health systems and services to improve the population's health;
- Regulation to protect public health, including accreditation and quality assurance;
- Human resources development and planning.

- *09.2 Administrative services regarding mandatory schemes (CPC/CPA 913, 84.3)*

Health administration and health insurance activities concern mandatory schemes that are executed by private insurers and central and local authorities and social security institutions. Included are the planning, management, regulation and collection of funds and the handling of claims by the delivery system.

This class involves a subcomponent specific to health financing. It includes management of fund collection and the administration, monitoring and evaluation of mandatory schemes. Among these are the specific services linked to:

- Resource mobilisation: Member identification of the schemes, their enrolment, billing and collection of contributions, as well as managing exemptions.
- Pooling: Risk equalisation is one important service;
- Purchasing function: Selecting, negotiating with health providers and purchasing and contracting;
- Claim processing system, gate-keeping, payments to providers and patient reimbursement.

09.2.1 Administration of governmental schemes and compulsory health insurance

09.2.1.1 Administration of governmental schemes

This subcategory includes:

- Administrative and operational services related to compulsory governmental health delivery schemes, involving the provision of benefits due to sickness, childbirth or temporary disablement.

09.2.1.2 Administration of compulsory health insurance schemes

This subcategory includes:

- Administrative and operational services related to compulsory health insurance schemes, involving the provision of benefits due to sickness, childbirth or temporary disablement.

10 Health insurance, except mandatory schemes (CPA 65)

- *10.1. Health insurance services* (CPC/CPA 7132, 65.12.1)

The administration of private health insurance essentially involves the health insurance service and the service charge[9] for this. This covers expenditure on sales, the enrolment and policy service, claim adjudication, actuarial functions, legal support services, investment functions, corporate overheads and risk charges.

Excluded are: the administrative costs of the health providers and the health goods and services they provide. Also excluded are the opportunity costs of paperwork for consumers and the associated general revenue tax collection.

11 Health and social care goods and services produced by households for own use

This item contains all services generated within the household for own final use, which are reimbursed or the subject of transfers. It usually refers to care provided on a long-term basis through relatives and friends.

All services that are not associated with a transaction lie outside the boundary, but they can be accounted for, when relevant, as a memorandum item.

Memorandum items

MP.1 Room or unit accommodation services for visitors (CPA 55.10.10)

This subcategory includes:

- Accommodation services consisting of rooms or units with daily housekeeping and other services, for persons away from their place of residence, in, for example, hospitals or other health care-type institutions offering accommodation, provided on a daily basis for relatives and others related to patients.

MP.2 Food and drink served to visitors

This subcategory includes:

- Food and drink preparation and supply services to visitors in hospitals and related health care-type institutions.

These services provide meals and drinks, usually at reduced prices, to groups of clearly defined persons who are usually linked to health care-admitted patients.

MP.3 Transportation of persons accompanying patients

This subclass includes the expenditure related to persons who need to accompany a patient seeking health care services.

MP.4 Health and social care goods and services produced by households for own use, not associated with transactions.

This item contains all services generated within the household for own final use, which are not reimbursed nor the subject of transfers. It usually refers to care provided on an acute or long-term basis through relatives and friends.

Notes

1. For an explanation of the differences between quantity and volume see Chapter 13.
2. Although in some OECD/EU countries health-specific PPPs are constructed based on a DRG system, it should be noted that DRGs are usually valid only for inpatient care settings. In outpatient settings more use is made of bundles of products in the construction of internationally comparable data on the quantities provided (and consumed) in the health branch. The PPP strategy for middle- and low- income countries is also related to bundles of products. These goods and services are usually linked to the CPC/CPA. See Chapter 13.
3. The classification of products in the national statistical system is used for various purposes: a) products provide the basis for preparing statistics on the production, distributive trade, consumption, foreign trade and transport of such products, of which a section pertains to health; b) product data is used in the construction of the supply and use tables: health products are an important means for the construction of both economy-wide supply and use tables as well as health-specific supply and use tables. The comparison of products contributes to learning from best practices and links performance with institutional and health policy-related factors, and helps identify potential gains by improving performance.
4. Agreement on the basket and the ideal level of detail faces operational challenges in the various countries, depending on the statistical system and resources available for price surveys. In WHO, some of the recommendations involve *e.g.* 30 widely used medicines and their prices in the various sectors (public, private, and private not-for-profit), innovator brands, the most sold and lowest-priced generics as well as a parallel measurement of the reference international prices, see WHO (2011a).

5. Here the reference to linkages to CPC: Central Product Classification and CPA: Classification of Products by Activities is made, though health system statistics really rely on some modified version of SNA reference classifications, for purposes, industries and products. All of these in the health-related area have been used in SHA and all of them have been slightly modified for analytical purposes. The main characteristic of these classifications is that inpatient and outpatient services and medical good provision are seen from the various perspectives: the industry producing them, the purpose of consumption as well as the object of consumption. See Annex A for a detailed view of the interaction of SHA with the various reference classifications.

6. The integrated system of statistical classifications has a close connection with the harmonised commodity description and coding system, which makes it possible to compare statistics produced in different statistical domains. The CPA is the European counterpart of the CPC, although the components of the CPA are in a different structural order. The CPC structures products based on the physical properties and intrinsic nature of the products as well as on the principle of industrial origin; the CPA has the same criteria but gives first priority to industrial origin. Both the CPC and the CPA cover the entire economy, including the health care branch: in the CPC by section 93 Human health and social care services; in the CPA by section Q Human health and social work services. Although the two global classifications contain sections covering health care, this does not mean that the boundaries are identical to what is used in SHA. On the one hand, the CPC and CPA contain in these sections products that are not part of health care as defined in SHA (such as the majority of the social services). On the other hand, SHA covers areas that are treated elsewhere in the CPC and CPA (such as the delivery of medical goods and government services related to health care).

7. This means that all providers of health care are taken into consideration, not only the providers whose main activity is health care (as in the ISIC and NACE).

8. The basis for the classification of health care products is the CPC and CPA. A few additional sources of products are used to create more detail in specific classes. For general medical practice services, the classification of the International Classification of Primary Care (ICPC, 2005) is used. Government preventive programme services are supplemented by various services mentioned in the Essential Public Health publication of WHO (WHO, 2002). There are various sources for details on the retail trade services of pharmaceutical goods. First, some details of pharmaceutical production are added in the retail sales structure. The details are found in the Harmonised system (headings and subheadings of HS 2007). Some examples are the sale of vitamins, provitamins and antibiotics, vaccines and serums and oral contraceptives. For medicaments for therapeutic or prophylactic use, additions are found in the Anatomic Therapeutic Classification (ATC; WHO, 2011b) classification. Details for wound dressings and other medical non-durables can be found on various internet sites on wound repair and related products (see *e.g.* Derm Net NZ, 2011; MedScape, 2011). Also, some details for the heading of medical and orthopaedic goods are found in the Harmonised System. Details in the CPC and CPA that are not relevant for the classification of health products are not included.

9. SNA 2008 defines the value of an insurance service or insurance output in paragraph 6.185.

ANNEX F

Medical Classifications

Table F.1.1. International Classification of Primary Care (ICPC-2)

ICPC-2 – English

International Classification of Primary Care – 2 nd Edition

Wonca International Classification Committee (WICC)

Wonca

Process codes

-30 Medical Exam/ Eval-Complete
-31 Medical Examination/Health Evaluation-Partial/Pre-op check
-32 Sensitivity Test
-33 Microbiological/Immunological Test
-34 Blood Test
-35 Urine Test
-36 Faeces Test
-37 Histological/Exfoliative Cytology
-38 Other Laboratory Test NEC
-39 Physical Function Test
-40 Diagnostic Endoscopy
-41 Diagnostic Radiology/Imaging
-42 Electrical Tracings
-43 Other Diagnostic Procedures
-44 Preventive Imunisations/Medications
-45 Observe/Educate/Advice/Diet
-46 Consult with Primary Care Provider
-47 Consultation with Specialist
-48 Clarification/Discuss Patient's RFE
-49 Other Preventive Procedures
-50 Medicat-Script/ Reqst/Renew/Inject
-51 Incise/Drain/Flush/Aspirate
-52 Excise/Remove/Biopsy/Destruction/ Debride
-53 Instrument/Catheter/Intubate/Dilate
-54 Repair/Fixate-Suture/Cast/Prosthetic
-55 Local Injection/Infiltration
-56 Dress/Press/Compress/Tamponade
-57 Physical Medicine/Rehabilitation
-58 Therapeutic Counselling/Listening
-59 Other Therapeutic Procedure NEC
-60 Results Tests/Procedures
-61 Results Exam/Test/Record
-62 Administrative Procedure
-63 Follow-up Encounter Unspecified
-64 Encounter Initiated by Provider
-65 Encounter Initiated third person
-66 Refer to Other Provider (EXCL. M.D.)
-67 Referral to Physician/Specialist/ Clinic/Hospital
-68 Other Referrals NEC
-69 Other Reason for Encounter NEC

General and Unspecified — A

A01 Pain general/multiple sites
A02 Chills
A03 Fever
A04 Weakness/tiredness general
A05 Feeling ill
A06 Fainting/syncope
A07 Coma
A08 Swelling
A09 Sweating problem
A10 Bleeding/haemorrhage NOS
A11 Chest pain NOS
A13 Concern/fear medical treatment
A16 Irritable infant
A18 Concern about appearance
A20 Euthanasia request/discussion
A21 Risk factor for malignancy
A23 Risk factor NOS
A25 Fear of death/dying
A26 Fear of cancer NOS
A27 Fear of other disease NOS
A28 Limited function/disability NOS
A29 General symptom/complaint other
A70 Tuberculosis
A71 Measles
A72 Chickenpox
A73 Malaria
A74 Rubella
A75 Infectious mononucleosis
A76 Viral exanthem other
A77 Viral disease other/NOS
A78 Infectious disease other/NOS
A79 Malignancy NOS
A80 Trauma/injury NOS
A81 Multiple trauma/injuries
A82 Secondary effect of trauma
A84 Poisoning by medical agent
A85 Adverse effect medical agent
A86 Toxic effect non-medicinal substance
A87 Complication of medical treatment
A88 Adverse effect physical factor
A89 Effect prosthetic device
A90 Congenital anomaly OS/multiple
A91 Abnormal result investigation NOS
A92 Allergy/allergic reaction NOS
A93 Premature newborn
A94 Perinatal morbidity other
A95 Perinatal mortality
A96 Death
A97 No disease
A98 Health maintenance/prevention
A99 General disease NOS

Blood, Blood Forming Organs and Immune Mechanism — B

B02 Lymph gland(s) enlarged/painful
B04 Blood symptom/complaint
B25 Fear of aids/HIV
B26 Fear cancer blood/lymph
B27 Fear blood/lymph disease other
B28 Limited function/disability
B29 Sympt/ complt lymph/immune other
B70 Lymphadenitis acute
B71 Lymphadenitis non-specific
B72 Hodgkin's disease/lymphoma
B73 Leukaemia
B74 Malignant neoplasm blood other
B75 Benign/unspecified neoplasm blood
B76 Ruptured spleen traumatic
B77 Injury blood/lymph/spleen other
B78 Hereditary haemolytic anaemia
B79 Congen.anom. blood/lymph other
B80 Iron deficiency anaemia
B81 Anaemia, Vitamin B12/folate def.
B82 Anaemia other/unspecified
B83 Purpura/coagulation defect
B84 Unexplained abnormal white cells
B87 Splenomegaly
B90 HIV-infection/aids
B99 Blood/lymph/spleen disease other

PROCESS CODES
SYMPTOMS/COMPLAINTS
INFECTIONS
NEOPLASMS
INJURIES
CONGENITAL ANOMALIES
OTHER DIAGNOSES

Digestive — D

D01 Abdominal pain/cramps general
D02 Abdominal pain epigastric
D03 Heartburn
D04 Rectal/anal pain
D05 Perianal itching
D06 Abdominal pain localized other
D07 Dyspepsia/indigestion
D08 Flatulence/gas/belching
D09 Nausea
D10 Vomiting
D11 Diarrhoea
D12 Constipation
D13 Jaundice
D14 Haematemesis/vomiting blood
D15 Melaena
D16 Rectal bleeding
D17 Incontinence of bowel
D18 Change faeces/bowel movements
D19 Teeth/gum symptom/complaint
D20 Mouth/tongue/lip symptom/ complt.
D21 Swallowing problem
D23 Hepatomegaly
D24 Abdominal mass NOS
D25 Abdominal distension
D26 Fear of cancer of digestive system
D27 Fear of digestive disease other
D28 Limited function/disability (d)
D29 Digestive symptom/complaint other
D70 Gastrointestinal infection
D71 Mumps
D72 Viral hepatitis
D73 Gastroenteritis presumed infection
D74 Malignant neoplasm stomach
D75 Malignant neoplasm colon/rectum
D76 Malignant neoplasm pancreas
D77 Malig. neoplasm digest other/NOS
D78 Neoplasm digest benign/uncertain
D79 Foreign body digestive system
D80 Injury digestive system other
D81 Congen. anomaly digestive system
D82 Teeth/gum disease
D83 Mouth/tongue/lip disease
D84 Oesophagus disease
D85 Duodenal ulcer
D86 Peptic ulcer other
D87 Stomach function disorder
D88 Appendicitis
D89 Inguinal hernia
D90 Hiatus hernia
D91 Abdominal hernia other
D92 Diverticular disease
D93 Irritable bowel syndrome
D94 Chronic enteritis/ulcerative colitis
D95 Anal fissure/ perianal abscess
D96 Worms/other parasites
D97 Liver disease NOS
D98 Cholecystitis/ cholelithiasis
D99 Disease digestive system, other

Eye — F

F01 Eye pain
F02 Red eye
F03 Eye discharge
F04 Visual floaters/spots
F05 Visual disturbance other
F13 Eye sensation abnormal
F14 Eye movements abnormal
F15 Eye appearance abnormal
F16 Eyelid symptom/complaint
F17 Glasses symptom/complaint
F18 Contact lens symptom/complaint
F27 Fear of eye disease
F28 Limited function/disability (f)
F29 Eye symptom/complaint other
F70 Conjunctivitis infectious
F71 Conjunctivitis allergic
F72 Blepharitis/ stye/ chalazion
F73 Eye infection/inflammation other
F74 Neoplasm of eye/ adnexa
F75 Contusion/haemorrhage eye
F76 Foreign body in eye
F79 Injury eye other
F80 Blocked lacrimal duct of infant
F81 Congenital anomaly eye other
F82 Detached retina
F83 Retinopathy
F84 Macular degeneration
F85 Corneal ulcer
F86 Trachoma
F91 Refractive error
F92 Cataract
F93 Glaucoma
F94 Blindness
F95 Strabismus
F99 Eye/ adnexa disease, other

Ear — H

H01 Ear pain/earache
H02 Hearing complaint
H03 Tinnitus, ringing/buzzing ear
H04 Ear discharge
H05 Bleeding ear
H13 Plugged feeling ear
H15 Concern with appearance of ears
H27 Fear of ear disease
H28 Limited function/disability ear
H29 Ear symptom/complaint other
H70 Otitis externa
H71 Acute otitis media/ myringitis
H72 Serous otitis media
H73 Eustachian salpingitis
H74 Chronic otitis media
H75 Neoplasm of ear
H76 Foreign body in ear
H77 Perforation ear drum
H78 Superficial injury of ear
H79 Ear injury other
H80 Congenital anomaly of ear
H81 Excessive ear wax
H82 Vertiginous syndrome
H83 Otosclerosis
H84 Presbyacusis
H85 Acoustic trauma
H86 Deafness
H99 Ear/mastoid disease, other

Cardiovascular — K

K01 Heart pain
K02 Pressure/tightness of heart
K03 Cardiovascular pain NOS
K04 Palpitations/awareness of heart
K05 Irregular heartbeat other
K06 Prominent veins
K07 Swollen ankles/oedema
K22 Risk factor cardiovascular disease
K24 Fear of heart disease
K25 Fear of hypertension
K27 Fear cardiovascular disease other
K28 Limited function/disability (k)
K29 Cardiovascular sympt./complt. other
K70 Infection of circulatory system
K71 Rheumatic fever/heart disease
K72 Neoplasm cardiovascular
K73 Congenital anomaly cardiovascular
K74 Ischaemic heart disease w. angina
K75 Acute myocardial infarction
K76 Ischaemic heart disease w/o angina
K77 Heart failure
K78 Atrial fibrillation/flutter
K79 Paroxysmal tachycardia
K80 Cardiac arrhythmia NOS
K81 Heart/arterial murmur NOS
K82 Pulmonary heart disease
K83 Heart valve disease NOS
K84 Heart disease other
K85 Elevated blood pressure
K86 Hypertension uncomplicated
K87 Hypertension complicated
K88 Postural hypotension
K89 Transient cerebral ischaemia
K90 Stroke/cerebrovascular accident
K91 Cerebrovascular disease
K92 Atherosclerosis/ PVD
K93 Pulmonary embolism
K94 Phlebitis/ thrombophlebitis
K95 Varicose veins of leg
K96 Haemorrhoids
K99 Cardiovascular disease other

Musculoskeletal — L

L01 Neck symptom/complain
L02 Back symptom/complaint
L03 Low back symptom/complaint
L04 Chest symptom/complaint
L05 Flank/axilla symptom/complaint
L07 Jaw symptom/complaint
L08 Shoulder symptom/complaint
L09 Arm symptom/complaint
L10 Elbow symptom/complaint
L11 Wrist symptom/complaint
L12 Hand/finger symptom/complaint
L13 Hip symptom/complaint
L14 Leg/thigh symptom/complaint
L15 Knee symptom/complaint
L16 Ankle symptom/complaint
L17 Foot/toe symptom/complaint
L18 Muscle pain
L19 Muscle symptom/complaint NOS
L20 Joint symptom/complaint NOS
L26 Fear of cancer musculoskeletal
L27 Fear musculoskeletal disease other
L28 Limited function/disability (l)
L29 Sympt/ complt. Musculoskeletal other
L70 Infections musculoskeletal system
L71 Malignant neoplasm musculoskeletal
L72 Fracture: radius/ulna
L73 Fracture: tibia/fibula
L74 Fracture: hand/foot bone
L75 Fracture: femur
L76 Fracture: other
L77 Sprain/strain of ankle
L78 Sprain/strain of knee
L79 Sprain/strain of joint NOS
L80 Dislocation/subluxation
L81 Injury musculoskeletal NOS
L82 Congenital anomaly musculoskeletal
L83 Neck syndrome
L84 Back syndrome w/o radiating pain
L85 Acquired deformity of spine
L86 Back syndrome with radiating pain
L87 Bursitis/ tendinitis/synovitis NOS
L88 Rheumatoid/ seropositive arthritis
L89 Osteoarthrosis of hip
L90 Osteoarthrosis of knee
L91 Osteoarthrosis other
L92 Shoulder syndrome
L93 Tennis elbow
L94 Osteochondrosis
L95 Osteoporosis
L96 Acute internal damage knee
L97 Neoplasm benign/ unspec musculo.
L98 Acquired deformity of limb
L99 Musculoskeletal disease, other

Neurological — N

N01 Headache
N03 Pain face
N04 Restless legs
N05 Tingling fingers/feet/toes
N06 Sensation disturbance other
N07 Convulsion/seizure
N08 Abnormal involuntary movements
N16 Disturbance of smell/taste
N17 Vertigo/dizziness
N18 Paralysis/weakness
N19 Speech disorder
N26 Fear cancer neurological system
N27 Fear of neurological disease other
N28 Limited function/disability (n)
N29 Neurological symptom/ complt. other
N70 Poliomyelitis
N71 Meningitis/encephalitis
N72 Tetanus
N73 Neurological infection other
N74 Malignant neoplasm nervous system
N75 Benign neoplasm nervous system
N76 Neoplasm nervous system unspec.
N79 Concussion
N80 Head injury other
N81 Injury nervous system other
N85 Congenital anomaly neurological
N86 Multiple sclerosis
N87 Parkinsonism
N88 Epilepsy
N89 Migraine
N90 Cluster headache
N91 Facial paralysis/bell's palsy
N92 Trigeminal neuralgia
N93 Carpal tunnel syndrome
N94 Peripheral neuritis/neuropathy
N95 Tension headache
N99 Neurological disease, other

Table F.1.1. **International Classification of Primary Care (ICPC-2)** *(cont.)*

Psychological P

Code	Description
P01	Feeling anxious/nervous/tense
P02	Acute stress reaction
P03	Feeling depressed
P04	Feeling/behaving irritable/angry
P05	Senility, feeling/behaving old
P06	Sleep disturbance
P07	Sexual desire reduced
P08	Sexual fulfilment reduced
P09	Sexual preference concern
P10	Stammering/stuttering/tic
P11	Eating problem in child
P12	Bedwetting/enuresis
P13	Encopresis/bowel training problem
P15	Chronic alcohol abuse
P16	Acute alcohol abuse
P17	Tobacco abuse
P18	Medication abuse
P19	Drug abuse
P20	Memory disturbance
P22	Child behaviour symptom/complaint
P23	Adolescent behav. Symptom/ complt.
P24	Specific learning problem
P25	Phase of life problem adult
P27	Fear of mental disorder
P28	Limited function/disability (p)
P29	Psychological symptom/ complt other
P70	Dementia
P71	Organic psychosis other
P72	Schizophrenia
P73	Affective psychosis
P74	Anxiety disorder/anxiety state
P75	Somatization disorder
P76	Depressive disorder
P77	Suicide/suicide attempt
P78	Neuraesthenia/ surmenage
P79	Phobia/compulsive disorder
P80	Personality disorder
P81	Hyperkinetic disorder
P82	Post-traumatic stress disorder
P85	Mental retardation
P86	Anorexia nervosa/bulimia
P98	Psychosis NOS/other
P99	Psychological disorders, other

Respiratory R

Code	Description
R01	Pain respiratory system
R02	Shortness of breath/dyspnoea
R03	Wheezing
R04	Breathing problem, other
R05	Cough
R06	Nose bleed/epistaxis
R07	Sneezing/nasal congestion
R08	Nose symptom/complaint other
R09	Sinus symptom/complaint
R21	Throat symptom/complaint
R23	Voice symptom/complaint
R24	Haemoptysis
R25	Sputum/phlegm abnormal
R26	Fear of cancer respiratory system
R27	Fear of respiratory disease, other
R28	Limited function/disability (r)
R29	Respiratory symptom/complaint oth.
R71	Whooping cough
R72	Strep throat
R73	Boil/abscess nose
R74	Upper respiratory infection acute
R75	Sinusitis acute/chronic
R76	Tonsillitis acute
R77	Laryngitis/tracheitis acute
R78	Acute bronchitis/ bronchiolitis
R79	Chronic bronchitis
R80	Influenza
R81	Pneumonia
R82	Pleurisy/pleural effusion
R83	Respiratory infection other
R84	Malignant neoplasm bronchus/lung
R85	Malinant neoplasm respiratory, other
R86	Benign neoplasm respiratory
R87	Foreign body nose/larynx/ bronch
R88	Injury respiratory other
R89	Congenital anomaly respiratory
R90	Hypertrophy tonsils/adenoids
R92	Neoplasm respiratory unspecified
R95	Chronic obstructive pulmonary dis
R96	Asthma
R97	Allergic rhinitis
R98	Hyperventilation syndrome
R99	Respiratory disease other

PROCESS CODES

SYMPTOMS/COMPLAINTS

INFECTIONS

NEOPLASMS

INJURIES

CONGENITAL ANOMALIES

OTHER DIAGNOSES

Skin S

Code	Description
S01	Pain/tenderness of skin
S02	Pruritus
S03	Warts
S04	Lump/swelling localized
S05	Lumps/swellings generalized
S06	Rash localized
S07	Rash generalized
S08	Skin colour change
S09	Infected finger/toe
S10	Boil/carbuncle
S11	Skin infection post-traumatic
S12	Insect bite/sting
S13	Animal/human bite
S14	Burn/scald
S15	Foreign body in skin
S16	Bruise/contusion
S17	Abrasion/scratch/blister
S18	Laceration/cut
S19	Skin injury other
S20	Corn/callosity
S21	Skin texture symptom/complaint
S22	Nail symptom/complaint
S23	Hair loss/baldness
S24	Hair/scalp symptom/complaint
S26	Fear of cancer of skin
S27	Fear of skin disease other
S28	Limited function/disability (s)
S29	Skin symptom/complaint other
S70	Herpes zoster
S71	Herpes simplex
S72	Scabies/other acariasis
S73	Pediculosis/skin infestation other
S74	Dermatophytosis
S75	Moniliasis/candidiasis skin
S76	Skin infection other
S77	Malignant neoplasm of skin
S78	Lipoma
S79	Neoplasm skin benign/unspecified
S80	Solar keratosis/sunburn
S81	Haemangioma/ lymphangioma
S82	Naevus/mole
S83	Congenital skin anomaly other
S84	Impetigo
S85	Pilonidal cyst/fistula
S86	Dermatitis seborrhoeic
S87	Dermatitis/ atopic eczema
S88	Dermatitis contact/allergic
S89	Diaper rash
S90	Pityriasis rosea
S91	Psoriasis
S92	Sweat gland disease
S93	Sebaceous cyst
S94	Ingrowing nail
S95	Molluscum contagiosum
S96	Acne
S97	Chronic ulcer skin
S98	Urticaria
S99	Skin disease, other

Endocrine/Metabolic and Nutritional T

Code	Description
T01	Excessive thirst
T02	Excessive appetite
T03	Loss of appetite
T04	Feeding problem of infant/child
T05	Feeding problem of adult
T07	Weight gain
T08	Weight loss
T10	Growth delay
T11	Dehydration
T26	Fear of cancer of endocrine system
T27	Fear endocrine/metabolic dis other
T28	Limited function/disability (t)
T29	Endocrine/met./ sympt/ complt other
T70	Endocrine infection
T71	Malignant neoplasm thyroid
T72	Benign neoplasm thyroid
T73	Neoplasm endocrine oth/unspecified
T78	Thyroglossal duct/cyst
T80	Congenital anom endocrine/ metab.
T81	Goitre
T82	Obesity
T83	Overweight
T85	Hyperthyroidism/thyrotoxicosis
T86	Hypothyroidism/myxoedema
T87	Hypoglycaemia
T89	Diabetes insulin dependent
T90	Diabetes non-insulin dependent
T91	Vitamin/nutritional deficiency
T92	Gout
T93	Lipid disorder
T99	Endocrine/ metab/ nutrit. dis. other

Urological U

Code	Description
U01	Dysuria/painful urination
U02	Urinary frequency/urgency
U04	Incontinence urine
U05	Urination problems other
U06	Haematuria
U07	Urine symptom/complaint other
U08	Urinary retention
U13	Bladder symptom/complaint other
U14	Kidney symptom/complaint
U26	Fear of cancer of urinary system
U27	Fear of urinary disease other
U28	Limited function/disability urinary
U29	Urinary symptom/complaint other
U70	Pyelonephritis/pyelitis
U71	Cystitis/urinary infection other
U72	Urethritis
U75	Malignant neoplasm of kidney
U76	Malignant neoplasm of bladder
U77	Malignant neoplasm urinary other
U78	Benign neoplasm urinary tract
U79	Neoplasm urinary tract NOS
U80	Injury urinary tract
U85	Congenital anomaly urinary tract
U88	Glomerulonephritis/nephrosis
U90	Orthostatic albumin./proteinuria
U95	Urinary calculus
U98	Abnormal urine test NOS
U99	Urinary disease, other

Pregnancy, Childbearing, Family Planning W

Code	Description
W01	Question of pregnancy
W02	Fear of pregnancy
W03	Antepartum bleeding
W05	Pregnancy vomiting/nausea
W10	Contraception postcoital
W11	Contraception oral
W12	Contraception intrauterine
W13	Sterilization
W14	Contraception other
W15	Infertility/ subfertility
W17	Post-partum bleeding
W18	Post-partum symptom/complaint oth.
W19	Breast/lactation symptom/complaint
W21	Concern body image in pregnancy
W27	Fear complications of pregnancy
W28	Limited function/disability (w)
W29	Pregnancy symptom/complaint other
W70	Puerperal infection/sepsis
W71	Infection complicating pregnancy
W72	Malignant neoplasm relate to preg.
W73	Benign/ unspec. neoplasm/pregnancy
W75	Injury complicating pregnancy
W76	Congenital anomaly complicate preg.
W78	Pregnancy
W79	Unwanted pregnancy
W80	Ectopic pregnancy
W81	Toxaemia of pregnancy
W82	Abortion spontaneous
W83	Abortion induced
W84	Pregnancy high risk
W85	Gestational diabetes
W90	Uncomplicate labour/delivery live
W91	Uncomplicate labour/delivery still
W92	Complicate labour/ delivery livebirth
W93	Complicate labour/delivery stillbirth
W94	Puerperal mastitis
W95	Breast disorder in pregnancy other
W96	Complications of puerperium other
W99	Disorder pregnancy/delivery, other

Female Genital X

Code	Description
X01	Genital pain female
X02	Menstrual pain
X03	Intermenstrual pain
X04	Painful intercourse female
X05	Menstruation absent/scanty
X06	Menstruation excessive
X07	Menstruation irregular/frequent
X08	Intermenstrual bleeding
X09	Premenstrual symptom/complaint
X10	Postponement of menstruation
X11	Menopausal symptom/complaint
X12	Postmenopausal bleeding
X13	Postcoital bleeding
X14	Vaginal discharge
X15	Vaginal symptom/complaint other
X16	Vulval symptom/complaint
X17	Pelvis symptom/complaint female
X18	Breast pain female
X19	Breast lump/mass female
X20	Nipple symptom/complaint female
X21	Breast symptom/ complt. female other
X22	Concern breast appearance female
X23	Fear sexually transmitted disease (f)
X24	Fear of sexual dysfunction female
X25	Fear of genital cancer female
X26	Fear of breast cancer female
X27	Fear genital/breast disease other (f)
X28	Limited function/disability (x)
X29	Genital symptom/ complt female oth.
X70	Syphilis female
X71	Gonorrhoea female
X72	Genital candidiasis female
X73	Genital trichomoniasis female
X74	Pelvic inflammatory disease
X75	Malignant neoplasm cervix
X76	Malignant neoplasm breast female
X77	Malignant neoplasm genital other (f)
X78	Fibromyoma uterus
X79	Benign neoplasm breast female
X80	Benign neoplasm female genital
X81	Genital neoplasm oth/ unspecied (f)
X82	Injury genital female
X83	Congenital anomaly genital female
X84	Vaginitis/vulvitis NOS
X85	Cervical disease NOS
X86	Abnormal cervix smear
X87	Uterovaginal prolapse
X88	Fibrocystic disease breast
X89	Premenstrual tension syndrome
X90	Genital herpes female
X91	Condylomata acuminata female
X92	Chlamydia infection genital (f)
X99	Genital disease female, other

Male Genital Y

Code	Description
Y01	Pain in penis
Y02	Pain in testis/scrotum
Y03	Urethral discharge
Y04	Penis symptom/complaint other
Y05	Scrotum/testis sympt/ complt. other
Y06	Prostate symptom/complaint
Y07	Impotence NOS
Y08	Sexual function sympt./ complt.(m)
Y10	Infertility/ subfertility male
Y13	Sterilization male
Y14	Family planning male other
Y16	Breast symptom/complaint male
Y24	Fear of sexual dysfunction male
Y25	Fear sexually transmitted dis. male
Y26	Fear of genital cancer male
Y27	Fear of genital disease male other
Y28	Limited function/disability (y)
Y29	Genital sympt./ complt.male other
Y70	Syphilis male
Y71	Gonorrhoea male
Y72	Genital herpes male
Y73	Prostatitis/seminal vesiculitis
Y74	Orchitis/ epididymitis
Y75	Balanitis
Y76	Condylomata acuminata male
Y77	Malignant neoplasm prostate
Y78	Malign neoplasm male genital other
Y79	Benign/ unspec. neoplasm gen. (m)
Y80	Injury male genital
Y81	Phimosis/redundant prepuce
Y82	Hypospadias
Y83	Undescended testicle
Y84	Congenital geni anomaly (m) other
Y85	Benign prostatic hypertrophy
Y86	Hydrocoele
Y99	Genital disease male, other

Social Problems Z

Code	Description
Z01	Poverty/financial problem
Z02	Food/water problem
Z03	Housing/neighbourhood problem
Z04	Social cultural problem
Z05	Work problem
Z06	Unemployment problem
Z07	Education problem
Z08	Social welfare problem
Z09	Legal problem
Z10	Health care system problem
Z11	Compliance/being ill problem
Z12	Relationship problem with partner
Z13	Partner's behaviour problem
Z14	Partner illness problem
Z15	Loss/death of partner problem
Z16	Relationship problem with child
Z18	Illness problem with child
Z19	Loss/death of child problem
Z20	Relationship prob. parent/family
Z21	Behaviour problem parent/family
Z22	Illness problem parent/family
Z23	Loss/death parent/family member
Z24	Relationship problem friend
Z25	Assault/harmful event problem
Z27	Fear of a social problem
Z28	Limited function/disability (z)
Z29	Social problem NOS

Abbreviations

Anom	anomaly
behav.	behaviour
bronch.	bronchus
complicat.	complication
congen.	congenital
dis.	disease
eval.	evaluation
exam.	examination
gen.	genital
malig.	malignant
metab.	metabolic
musculo.	musculoskeletal
NEC	not elsewhere classified
NOS	not otherwise specified
nutrit.	nutrition
oth	other
preg.	pregnancy
prob.	problem
RFE	reason for encounter
sympt.	symptom
unspec.	unspecified
w	with
w/o	without

Source: WICE (2011).

Table F.1.2. **Anatomical Therapeutic Chemical (ATC)**

The main groups of the ATC classification system

A	Alimentary tract and metablism
B	Blood and blood forming organs
C	Cardiovascular system
D	Dermatologicals
G	Genito urinary system and sex hormones
H	Systemic hormonal preparations, excl. sex hormones and insulins
J	Anti-infectives for systemic use
L	Antineoplastic and immunomodulating agents
M	Musculo-skeletal sustem
N	Nervous system
P	Antiparasitic products, insecticides and repellents
R	Respiratory system
S	Sensory organs
V	Various

Source : *www.who.int.*

Table F.1.3. **International Shortlist for Hospital Morbidity Tabulation (ISHMT)**

ICD chapter	Group	Code	Heading	ICD-10 code	ICD-9 code
I		**0100**	**Certain infectious and parasitic diseases**	**A00-B99**	**001-033, 0341-0992, 0995-134, 1360, 1362-139, +042-044 or 2795, 2796 for HIV (varies according to country)**
I	**1**	**0101**	Intestinal infectious diseases except diarrhoea	A00-A08	001-008
I	**2**	**0102**	Diarrhoea and gastroenteritis of presumed infectious origin	A09	009
I	**3**	**0103**	Tuberculosis	A15-A19, B90	010-018, 137
I	**4**	**0104**	Septicaemia	A40-A41	038
I	**5**	**0105**	Human immunodeficiency virus [HIV] disease	B20-B24	042-044 or 2795, 2796 (varies according to country)
I	**6**	**0106**	Other infectious and parasitic diseases	remainder of A00-B99	remainder of 001-139, except 0340, 0993, 0994, 135, 1361
II		**0200**	**Neoplasms**	**C00-D48**	**140-239**
II	**7**	**0201**	Malignant neoplasm of colon, rectum and anus	C18-C21	153, 154
II	**8**	**0202**	Malignant neoplasms of trachea, bronchus and lung	C33-C34	162
II	**9**	**0203**	Malignant neoplasms of skin	C43-C44	172, 173
II	**10**	**0204**	Malignant neoplasm of breast	C50	174, 175
II	**11**	**0205**	Malignant neoplasm of uterus	C53-C55	179, 180, 182
II	**12**	**0206**	Malignant neoplasm of ovary	C56	1830
II	**13**	**0207**	Malignant neoplasm of prostate	C61	185
II	**14**	**0208**	Malignant neoplasm of bladder	C67	188
II	**15**	**0209**	Other malignant neoplasms	remainder of C00-C97	remainder of 140-208
II	**16**	**0210**	Carcinoma in situ	D00-D09	230-234
II	**17**	**0211**	Benign neoplasm of colon, rectum and anus	D12	2113, 2114
II	**18**	**0212**	Leiomyoma of uterus	D25	218
II	**19**	**0213**	Other benign neoplasms and neoplasms of uncertain or unknown behaviour	remainder of D00-D48	remainder of 210-239
III		**0300**	**Diseases of the blood and blood-forming organs and certain disorders involving the immune mechanism**	**D50-D89**	**135, 2790-2793, 2798. 2799*, 280-288*, 2890*, 2894-2899***
III	**20**	**0301**	Anaemias	D50-D64	280-285

Table F.1.3. **International Shortlist for Hospital Morbidity Tabulation (ISHMT)** *(cont.)*

ICD chapter	Group	Code	Heading	ICD-10 code	ICD-9 code
III	**21**	**0302**	Other diseases of the blood and blood-forming organs and certain disorders involving the immune mechanism	D65-D89	135, 2790-2793, 2798, 2799*, 286-288*, 2890*, 2894-2899*
IV		**0400**	**Endocrine, nutritional and metabolic diseases**	**E00-E90**	**240-278**
IV	**22**	**0401**	Diabetes mellitus	E10-E14	250
IV	**23**	**0402**	Other endocrine, nutritional and metabolic diseases	remainder of E00-E90	remainder of 240-278
V		**0500**	**Mental and behavioural disorders**	**F00-F99**	**290-319**
V	**24**	**0501**	Dementia	F00-F03	2900-2902, 2904-2909, 2941
V	**25**	**0502**	Mental and behavioural disorders due to alcohol	F10	291, 303, 3050
V	**26**	**0503**	Mental and behavioural disorders due to use of other psychoactive substance.	F11-F19	292, 2940, 304, 3051-3059
V	**27**	**0504**	Schizophrenia, schizotypal and delusional disorders	F20-F29	295, 2970-2973, 2978-2979, 2983-2989
V	**28**	**0505**	Mood [affective] disorders	F30-F39	296, 2980, 3004, 3011, 311
V	**29**	**0506**	Other mental and behavioural disorders	remainder of F00-F99	remainder of 290-319
VI		**0600**	**Diseases of the nervous system**	**G00-G99**	**320-359, 435**
VI	**30**	**0601**	Alzheimer's disease	G30	3310
VI	**31**	**0602**	Multiple sclerosis	G35	340
VI	**32**	**0603**	Epilepsy	G40-G41	345
VI	**33**	**0604**	Transient cerebral ischaemic attacks and related syndromes	G45	435
VI	**34**	**0605**	Other diseases of the nervous system	remainder of G00-G99	remainder of 320-359
VII		**0700**	**Diseases of the eye and adnexa**	**H00-H59**	**360-379**
VII	**35**	**0701**	Cataract	H25-H26, H28	366
VII	**36**	**0702**	Other diseases of the eye and adnexa	remainder of H00-H59	remainder of 360-379
VIII	**37**	**0800**	**Diseases of the ear and mastoid process**	**H60-H95**	**380-389**
IX		**0900**	**Diseases of the circulatory system**	**I00-I99**	**2891-2893*, 390-459 except 435, 446 and 4590***
IX	**38**	**0901**	Hypertensive diseases	I10-I15	401-405
IX	**39**	**0902**	Angina pectoris	I20	413; ICD-9-CM: 4111*, 413*
IX	**40**	**0903**	Acute myocardial infarction	I21-I22	410
IX	**41**	**0904**	Other ischaemic heart disease	I23-I25	411-412, 414; ICD-9-CM: 4110*, 4118*, 412*, 414*
IX	**42**	**0905**	Pulmonary heart disease & diseases of pulmonary circulation	I26-I28	415-417
IX	**43**	**0906**	Conduction disorders and cardiac arrhythmias	I44-I49	426, 427
IX	**44**	**0907**	Heart failure	I50	428
IX	**45**	**0908**	Cerebrovascular diseases	I60-I69	430-434, 436-438
IX	**46**	**0909**	Atherosclerosis	I70	440
IX	**47**	**0910**	Varicose veins of lower extremities	I83	454
IX	**48**	**0911**	Other diseases of the circulatory system	remainder of I00-I99	2891-2893*, remainder of 390-459 except 435, 446 and 4590*
X		**1000**	**Diseases of the respiratory system**	**J00-J99**	**0340, 460-519**
X	**49**	**1001**	Acute upper respiratory infections and influenza	J00-J11	0340, 460-465, 487; ICD-9-CM: 0340*, 460-465, 487, 488*
X	**50**	**1002**	Pneumonia	J12-J18	480-486
X	**51**	**1003**	Other acute lower respiratory infections	J20-J22	466 (acute lower respiratory infections other than acute bronchitis, acute bronchiolitis and pneumonia were not separated in ICD-9, no J22 equivalent)

Table F.1.3. **International Shortlist for Hospital Morbidity Tabulation (ISHMT)** *(cont.)*

ICD chapter	Group	Code	Heading	ICD-10 code	ICD-9 code
X	**52**	**1004**	Chronic diseases of tonsils and adenoids	J35	474
X	**53**	**1005**	Other diseases of upper respiratory tract	J30-J34, J36-J39	470-473, 475-478
X	**54**	**1006**	Chronic obstructive pulmonary disease and bronchiectasis	J40-J44, J47	490-492, 494, 496; ICD-9-CM: 490-492, 4932*, 494, 496
X	**55**	**1007**	Asthma	J45-J46	493; ICD-9-CM: 4930*, 4931*, 4938*, 4939*
X	**56**	**1008**	Other diseases of the respiratory system	J60-J99	remainder of 460-519
XI		**1100**	**Diseases of the digestive system**	**K00-K93**	**520-579**
XI	**57**	**1101**	Disorders of teeth and supporting structures	K00-K08	520-525
XI	**58**	**1102**	Other diseases of oral cavity, salivary glands and jaws	K09-K14	526-529
XI	**59**	**1103**	Diseases of oesophagus	K20-K23	530
XI	**60**	**1104**	Peptic ulcer	K25-K28	531-534
XI	**61**	**1105**	Dyspepsia and other diseases of stomach and duodenum	K29-K31	535-537
XI	**62**	**1106**	Diseases of appendix	K35-K38	540-543
XI	**63**	**1107**	Inguinal hernia	K40	550
XI	**64**	**1108**	Other abdominal hernia	K41-K46	551-553
XI	**65**	**1109**	Crohn's disease and ulcerative colitis	K50-K51	555, 556
XI	**66**	**1110**	Other non-infective gastroenteritis and colitis	K52	558
XI	**67**	**1111**	Paralytic ileus and intestinal obstruction without hernia	K56	560
XI	**68**	**1112**	Diverticular disease of intestine	K57	562
XI	**69**	**1113**	Diseases of anus and rectum	K60-K62	565, 566, 5690-5694
XI	**70**	**1114**	Other diseases of intestine	K55, K58-K59, K63	557, 564, 5695, 5698, 5699
XI	**71**	**1115**	Alcoholic liver disease	K70	5710-5713
XI	**72**	**1116**	Other diseases of liver	K71-K77	570, 5714-573
XI	**73**	**1117**	Cholelithiasis	K80	574
XI	**74**	**1118**	Other diseases of gall bladder and biliary tract	K81-K83	575, 576
XI	**75**	**1119**	Diseases of pancreas	K85-K87	577
XI	**76**	**1120**	Other diseases of the digestive system	remainder of K00-K93	remainder of 520-579
XII		**1200**	**Diseases of the skin and subcutaneous tissue**	**L00-L99**	**680-709**
XII	**77**	**1201**	Infections of the skin and subcutaneous tissue	L00-L08	680-686
XII	**78**	**1202**	Dermatitis, eczema and papulosquamous disorders	L20-L45	690-693, 6943, 696-6983, 6988, 6989
XII	**79**	**1203**	Other diseases of the skin and subcutaneous tissue	remainder of L00-L99	remainder of 680-709
XIII		**1300**	**Diseases of the musculoskeletal system and connective tissue**	**M00-M99**	**0993, 1361, 2794, 446, 710-739**
XIII	**80**	**1301**	Coxarthrosis [arthrosis of hip]	M16	Not a concept in ICD-9 at four-digit level. Can only be defined by using the optional fifth digit 5 to 715, *i.e.* 715.15, 715.25, 715.35 and 715.95
XIII	**81**	**1302**	Gonarthrosis [arthrosis of knee]	M17	Not a concept in ICD-9 at four-digit level. Can only be defined by using the optional fifth digit 6 to 715, *i.e.* 715.16, 715.26, 715.36 and 715.96
XIII	**82**	**1303**	Internal derangement of knee	M23	717
XIII	**83**	**1304**	Other arthropathies	M00-M15, M18-M22, M24-M25	0993, 711-716, 718, 719, 7271*, 7284*
XIII	**84**	**1305**	Systemic connective tissue disorders	M30-M36	1361, 2794, 446, 710, 725, 7285

Table F.1.3. **International Shortlist for Hospital Morbidity Tabulation (ISHMT)** *(cont.)*

ICD chapter	Group	Code	Heading	ICD-10 code	ICD-9 code
XIII	**85**	**1306**	Deforming dorsopathies and spondylopathies	M40-M49	720, 721, 7230, 7235*, 7240, 737
XIII	**86**	**1307**	Intervertebral disc disorders	M50-M51	7220-7227*, 7229*
XIII	**87**	**1308**	Dorsalgia	M54	7231, 7234, 7236, 7241-7243, 7245
XIII	**88**	**1309**	Soft tissue disorders	M60-M79	726*, 7270*, 7272-7279*, 7280-7283, 7286-7289, 729
XIII	**89**	**1310**	Other disorders of the musculoskeletal system and connective tissue	M53, M80-M99	remainder of 710-739
XIV		**1400**	**Diseases of the genitourinary system**	**N00-N99**	**0994, 580-5996, 5998-629, 7880**
XIV	**90**	**1401**	Glomerular and renal tubulo-interstitial diseases	N00-N16	580-5834, 5838, 5839, 5900-5902, 5908, 5909, 591, 5933-5935, 5937, 5996
XIV	**91**	**1402**	Renal failure	N17-N19	5836, 5837, 584-586
XIV	**92**	**1403**	Urolithiasis	N20-N23	592, 594, 7880
XIV	**93**	**1404**	Other diseases of the urinary system	N25-N39	0994, 587-589, 5903, 5930-5932, 5936, 5938, 5939, 595- 597, 5980, 5981, 5988, 5989, 5990-5995, 5998, 5999, 6256
XIV	**94**	**1405**	Hyperplasia of prostate	N40	600
XIV	**95**	**1406**	Other diseases of male genital organs	N41-N51	601-608
XIV	**96**	**1407**	Disorders of breast	N60-N64	610, 611
XIV	**97**	**1408**	Inflammatory diseases of female pelvic organs	N70-N77	614-616
XIV	**98**	**1409**	Menstrual, menopausal and other female genital conditions	N91-N95	6250-6255, 6258-627
XIV	**99**	**1410**	Other disorders of the genitourinary system	remainder of N00-N99	remainder of 580-629 except 5997*
XV		**1500**	**Pregnancy, childbirth and the puerperium**	**O00-O99**	**630-676 (no exactly equivalent ICD-9 codes for the three phases); ICD-9-CM: 630-677* (no exactly equivalent ICD-9 codes for the three phases)**
XV	**100**	**1501**	Medical abortion	O04	635
XV	**101**	**1502**	Other pregnancy with abortive outcome	O00-O03, O05-O08	630-634, 636-639
XV	**102**	**1503**	Complications of pregnancy predominantly in the antenatal period	O10-O48	640-646, 651-659
XV	**103**	**1504**	Complications of pregnancy predominantly during labour and delivery	O60-O75	660-668, 6690-6694, 6698, 6699
XV	**104**	**1505**	Single spontaneous delivery	O80	650
XV	**105**	**1506**	Other delivery	O81-O84	6695, 6696, 6697
XV	**106**	**1507**	Complications predominantly related to the puerperium	O85-O92	670-676
XV	**107**	**1508**	Other obstetric conditions	O94*, O95-O99	647, 648; ICD-9-CM: 647*, 648*, 677*
XVI		**1600**	**Certain conditions originating in the perinatal period**	**P00-P96**	**760-779**
XVI	**108**	**1601**	Disorders related to short gestation and low birth weight	P07	765
XVI	**109**	**1602**	Other conditions originating in the perinatal period	remainder of P00-P96	remainder of 760-779
XVII	**110**	**1700**	**Congenital malformations, deformations and chromosomal abnormalities**	**Q00-Q99**	**740-759**

Table F.1.3. **International Shortlist for Hospital Morbidity Tabulation (ISHMT)** *(cont.)*

ICD chapter	Group	Code	Heading	ICD-10 code	ICD-9 code
XVIII		**1800**	**Symptoms, signs and abnormal clinical and laboratory findings, not elsewhere classified**	**R00-R99**	**780-799 except 7880, but including 4590* and 5997**
XVIII	**111**	**1801**	Pain in throat and chest	R07	7841, 7865
XVIII	**112**	**1802**	Abdominal and pelvic pain	R10	7890
XVIII	**113**	**1803**	Unknown and unspecified causes of morbidity (incl. those without a diagnosis)	R69	7999
XVIII	**114**	**1804**	Other symptoms, signs and abnormal clinical and laboratory findings	remainder of R00-R99	remainder of 780-799 except 7880, but including 4590* and 5997
XIX		**1900**	**Injury, poisoning and certain other consequences of external causes**	**S00-T98**	**800-999**
XIX	**115**	**1901**	Intracranial injury	S06	8001-8004, 8006-8009, 8011-8014, 8016-8019, 8031-8034, 8036-8039, 8041-8044, 8046-8049, 850-854 (Definition includes relevant ICD-9-CM codes.)
XIX	**116**	**1902**	Other injuries to the head	S00-S05, S07-S09	8000, 8005, 8010, 8015, 802, 8030, 8035, 8040, 8045, 830, 870-873, 900, 910, 918, 920, 921, 925, 950*, 951* (Definition includes relevant ICD-9-CM codes.)
XIX	**117**	**1903**	Fracture of forearm	S52	813
XIX	**118**	**1904**	Fracture of femur	S72	820, 821
XIX	**119**	**1905**	Fracture of lower leg, including ankle	S82	823, 824
XIX	**120**	**1906**	Other injuries	S10-S51, S53-S71, S73-S81, S83-T14, T79	805-812, 814-819, 822, 825-829, 831-848, 860-869, 874-897, 901-904, 911-917, 919, 922-924, 926-929*, 952-959*
XIX	**121**	**1907**	Burns and corrosions	T20-T32	940-949
XIX	**122**	**1908**	Poisonings by drugs, medicaments and biological substances and toxic effects of substances chiefly non-medicinal as to source	T36-T65	960-989
XIX	**123**	**1909**	Complications of surgical and medical care, not elsewhere classified	T80-T88	996-999
XIX	**124**	**1910**	Sequelae of injuries, of poisoning and of other consequences of external causes	T90-T98	905-909
XIX	**125**	**1911**	Other and unspecified effects of external causes	remainder of S00-T98	930-939*, 990-995
XXI		**2100**	**Factors influencing health status and contact with health services**	**Z00-Z99**	**V01-V82**
XXI	**126**	**2101**	Medical observation and evaluation for suspected diseases and conditions	Z03	V710-V712*, V717-V719*
XXI	**127**	**2102**	Contraceptive management	Z30	V25
XXI	**128**	**2103**	Live-born infants according to place of birth ("healthy newborn babies")	Z38	V30-V39
XXI	**129**	**2104**	Other medical care (including radiotherapy and chemotherapy sessions)	Z51	V071, V58
XXI	**130**	**2105**	Other factors influencing health status and contact with health services	remainder of Z00-Z99	remainder of V01-V82
		0000	**All causes**	**A00-Z99 (excluding V, W, X and Y codes)**	**001-V82 (excluding E800-E999)**

Source: WHO (2005d).

Table F.1.4. **Global Burden of Disease (GBD)**

Code	GBD cause name	ICD-9 code	ICD-10 code
U000	**All causes**		
U001	**I. Communicable, maternal, perinatal, and nutritional conditions**[a]	001-139, 243, 260- 269, *279.5,* 280-281, 285.9, 320-323, 381-382,460-465, 466, 480-487, 614-616, 630-676, 760-779	A00-B99, G00-G04, N70-N73, J00-J06, J10-J18, J20-J22, H65-H66, O00-O99, P00-P96, E00-E02, E40-E46, E50, D50-D53, D64.9, E51-64
U002	**A. Infectious and parasitic diseases**	001-139, *279.5,* 320-323, 614-616, 771.3	A00-B99, G00, G03-G04, N70-N73
U003	1. **Tuberculosis**	010-018, 137	A15-A19, B90
U004	2. **Sexually transmitted diseases excluding HIV/AIDS**	090-099, 614-616	A50-A64, N70-N73
U005	a. Syphilis	090-097	A50-A53
U006	b. Chlamydia	—	A55-A56
U007	c. Gonorrhea	098	A54
U008	d. Other sexually transmitted diseases	099, 614-616	A57-A64, N70-N73
U009	3. **HIV/AIDS**	279.5 (3042-044)	B20-B24
U010	4. **Diarrheal diseases**	001, 002, 004, 006-009	A00, A01, A03, A04, A06-A09
U011	5. **Childhood-cluster diseases**	032, 033, 037, 045, 055, 138, 771.3	A33-A37, A80, B05, B91
U012	a. Pertussis	033	A37
U013	b. Poliomyelitis	045, 138	A80, B91
U014	c. Diphtheria	032	A36
U015	d. Measles	055	B05
U016	e. Tetanus	037, 771.3	A33-A35
U017	6. **Meningitis**	036, 320-322	A39, G00, G03
U018	7. **Hepatitis B**	070.2-070.9	B16-B19 (minus B17.1, B18.2)
U019	**Hepatitis C**	—	B17.1, B18.2
U020	8. **Malaria**	084	B50-B54
U021	9. **Tropical-cluster diseases**	085, 086, 120, 125.0, 125.1, 125.3	B55-B57, B65, B73, B74.0-B74.2
U022	a. Trypanosomiasis	086.3, 086.4, 086.5,	B56
U023	b. Chagas' disease	086.0, 086.1, 086.2, 086.9	B57
U024	c. Schistosomiasis	120	B65
U025	d. Leishmaniasis	085	B55
U026	e. Lymphatic filariasis	125.0, 125.1	B74.0-B74.2
U027	f. Onchocerciasis	125.3	B73
U028	10. **Leprosy**	030	A30
U029	11. **Dengue**	061	A90-A91
U030	12. **Japanese encephalitis**	062.0	A83.0
U031	13. **Trachoma**	076	A71
U032	14. **Intestinal nematode infections**	126-129	B76-B81
U033	a. Ascariasis	127.0	B77
U034	b. Trichuriasis	127.3	B79
U035	c. Hookworm disease (Ancylostomiasis and necatoriasis)	126	B76
U036	Other intestinal infections	127.1, 127.2, 127.4-127.9, 128, 129	B78, B80, B81
U037	Other infectious diseases	003, 005, 020-027, 031, 034, 035, 038-041, 046-049, 050-054, 056-057, 060, 062.1-066, 070.0-070.1, 071-075, 077-079, 080-083, 087-088, 100-104, 110-118, 121-124, 125.2, 125.4, 125.5, 125.6, 125.7, 125.9, 130-136, 139, 323	A02, A05, A20-A28, A31, A32, A38, A40-A49, A65-A70, A74-A79, A81, A82, A83.1-A83.9, A84-A89, A92-A99, B00-B04, B06-B15, B25-B49, B58-B60, B64, B66-B72, B74.3-B74.9, B75, B82-B89, B92-B99, G04
U038	**B. Respiratory infections**	460-466, 480-487, 381-382	J00-J06, J10-J18, J20-J22, H65-H66
U039	1. Lower respiratory infections	466, 480-487	J10-J18, J20-J22
U040	2. Upper respiratory infections	460-465	J00-J06
U041	3. Otitis media	381-382	H65-H66
U042	**C. Maternal conditions**	630-676	O00-O99
U043	1. Maternal hemorrhage	640, 641, 666	O44-O46, O67, O72
U044	2. Maternal sepsis	670	O85-O86
U045	3. Hypertensive disorders of pregnancy	642	O10-O16

Table F.1.4. **Global Burden of Disease (GBD)** *(cont.)*

Code	GBD cause name	ICD-9 code	ICD-10 code
U046	4. Obstructed labor	660	O64-O66
U047	5. Abortion	630-639	O00-O07
U048	Other maternal conditions	643-659, 661-665, 667-669, 671-676	O20-O43, O47-O63, O68-O71, O73-O75, O87-O99
U049	**D. Conditions arising during the perinatal period**	760-779 (minus 771.3)	P00-P96
U050	1. Low birthweight	764-765	P05-P07
U051	2. Birth asphyxia and birth trauma	767-770	P03, P10-P15, P20-P29
U052	Other perinatal conditions	760-763, 766, 771 (minus 771.3), 772-779	P00-P02, P04, P08, P35-P96
U053	**E. Nutritional deficiencies**	243, 260-269, 280-281, 285.9	E00-E02, E40-E46, E50, D50-D53, D64.9, E51-E64
U054	1. Protein-energy malnutrition	260-263	E40-E46
U055	2. Iodine deficiency	243	E00-E02
U056	3. Vitamin A deficiency	264	E50
U057	4. Iron-deficiency anemia	280, 285.9	D50, D64.9
U058	Other nutritional disorders	265-269, 281	D51-D53, E51-E64
U059	**II. Noncommunicable diseases**[a]	140-242, 244-259, 270-279 (minus 279.5), 282-285 (minus 285.9), 286-319, 324-380, 383-459, 470-478, 490-611, 617-629, 680-759	C00-C97, D00-D48, D55-D64 (minus D 64.9) D65-D89, E03-E07, E10-E16, E20-E34, E65-E88, F01-F99, G06-G98, H00-H61, H68-H93, I00-I99, J30-J98, K00-K92, N00-N64, N75-N98, L00-L98, M00-M99, Q00-Q99
U060	**A. Malignant neoplasms**	140-208	C00-C97
U061	1. Mouth and oropharynx cancers [b]	140-149	C00-C14
U062	2. Esophageal cancer [b]	150	C15
U063	3. Stomach cancer [b]	151	C16
U064	4. Colon and rectal cancers [b]	153-154	C18-C21
U065	5. Liver cancer	155	C22
U066	6. Pancreas cancer	157	C25
U067	7. Trachea, bronchus and lung cancers	162	C33-C34
U068	8. Melanoma and other skin cancers [b]	172-173	C43-C44
U069	9. Breast cancer [b]	174-175	C50
U070	10. Cervix uteri cancer [b]	180	C53
U071	11. Corpus uteri cancer [b]	179, 182	C54-C55
U072	12. Ovarian cancer	183	C56
U073	13. Prostate cancer [b]	185	C61
U074	14. Bladder cancer [b]	188	C67
U075	15. Lymphomas and multiple myeloma [b]	200-203	C81-C90, C96
U076	16. Leukemia [b]	204-208	C91-C95
U077	Other malignant neoplasms [b]	152, 156, 158-161, 163-171, 181, 184, 186-187, 189-199	C17, C23, C24, C26-C32, C37-C41, C45-C49, C51, C52, C57-C60, C62-C66, C68-C80, C97
U078	**B. Other neoplasms**	210-239	D00-D48
U079	**C. Diabetes mellitus**	250	E10-E14
U080	**D. Endocrine disorders**	240-242, 244-246, 251-259, 270-279 (minus 274, 279.5), 282-285 (minus 285.9), 286-289	D55-D64 (minus D64.9), D65-D89, E03-E07, E15-E16, E20-E34, E65-E88
U081	**E. Neuropsychiatric conditions**	290-319, 324-359	F01-F99, G06-G98
U082	1. Unipolar depressive disorders	296.1, 311	F32-F33
U083	2. Bipolar affective disorder	296 (minus 296.1)	F30-F31
U084	3. Schizophrenia	295	F20-F29
U085	4. Epilepsy	345	G40-G41
U086	5. Alcohol use disorders	291, 303, 305.0	F10
U087	6. Alzheimer's disease and other dementias	290, 330, 331	F01, F03, G30-G31
U088	7. Parkinson's disease	332	G20-G21

Table F.1.4. **Global Burden of Disease (GBD)** *(cont.)*

Code	GBD cause name	ICD-9 code	ICD-10 code
U089	8. Multiple sclerosis	340	G35
U090	9. Drug use disorders	304, 305.2-305.9	F11-F16, F18-F19
U091	10. Post-traumatic stress disorder	308-309	F43.1
U092	11. Obsessive-compulsive disorder	300.3	F42
U093	12. Panic disorder	300.2	F40.0, F41.0
U094	13. Insomnia (primary)	307.4	F51
U095	14. Migraine	346	G43
U096	15. Mental retardation, lead-caused	317-319	F70-F79
U097	Other neuropsychiatric disorders	292-294, 297-300.1, 300.4-302, 305.1, 306-307 (minus 307.4), 310, 312-316, 324-326, 333-337, 341-344, 347-349, 350-359	F04-F09, F17, F34-F39, F401-F409, F411-F419, F43 (minus F43.1), F44-F50, F52-F69, F80-F99, G06-G12, G23-G25, G36, G37, G44-G98
U098	**F. Sense organ diseases**	360-380, 383-389	H00-H61, H68-H93
U099	1. Glaucoma	365	H40
U100	2. Cataracts	366	H25-H26
U101	3. Vision disorders, age-related	367.4	H524
U102	4. Hearing loss, adult onset	389	H90-H91
U103	Other sense organ disorders	360-364, 367-380 (minus 367.4), 383-388	H00-H21, H27-H35, H43-H61 (minus H524), H68-H83, H92-H93
U104	**G. Cardiovascular diseases**	390-459	I00-I99
U105	1. Rheumatic heart disease	390-398	I01-I09
U106	2. Hypertensive heart disease	401-405	I10-I13
U107	3. Ischemic heart disease [c]	410-414	I20-I25
U108	4. Cerebrovascular disease	430-438	I60-I69
U109	5. Inflammatory heart diseases	420, 421, 422, 425	I30-I33, I38, I40, I42
U110	Other cardiovascular diseases [c]	415-417, 423-424, 426-429, 440-448, 451-459	I00, I26-I28, I34-I37, I44-I51, I70-I99
U111	**H. Respiratory diseases**	470-478, 490-519	J30-J98
U112	1. Chronic obstructive pulmonary disease	490-492, 495-496	J40-J44
U113	2. Asthma	493	J45-J46
U114	Other respiratory diseases	470-478, 494, 500-508, 510-519	J30-J39, J47-J98
U115	**I. Digestive diseases**	530-579	K20- *K92*
U116	1. Peptic ulcer disease	531-533	K25-K27
U117	2. Cirrhosis of the liver	571	K70, K74
U118	3. Appendicitis	540-543	K35-K37
U119	Other digestive diseases	530, 534-537, 550-553, 555-558, 560-570, 572-579	K20-K22, K28-K31, K38, K40-K66, K71-K73, K75-K92
U120	**J. Genitourinary diseases**	580-611, 617-629	N00-N64, N75-N98
U121	1. Nephritis and nephrosis	580-589	N00-N19
U122	2. Benign prostatic hypertrophy	600	N40
U123	Other genitourinary system diseases	590-599, 601-611, 617-629	N20-N39, N41-N64, N75-N98
U124	**K. Skin diseases**	680-709	L00-L98
U125	**L. Musculoskeletal diseases**	710-739, 274	M00-M99
U126	1. Rheumatoid arthritis	714	M05-M06
U127	2. Osteoarthritis	715	M15-M19
U128	3. Gout	274	M10
U129	4. Low back pain	720-724 (minus 721.1, 722.0, 722.4)	M45-M48, M54 (minus M54.2)
U130	Other musculoskeletal disorders	710-713, 716-719, 721.1, 722.0, 722.4, 723, 725-739	M00-M02, M08, M11-M13, M20-M43, M50-M53, M54.2, M55-M99
U131	**M. Congenital anomalies**	740-759	Q00-Q99
U132	1. Abdominal wall defect	756.7	Q79.2-Q79.5
U133	2. Anencephaly	740.0	Q00
U134	3. Anorectal atresia	751.2	Q42
U135	4. Cleft lip	749.1	Q36
U136	5. Cleft palate	749.0	Q35, Q37

Table F.1.4. **Global Burden of Disease (GBD)** *(cont.)*

Code	GBD cause name	ICD-9 code	ICD-10 code
U137	6. Esophageal atresia	750.3	Q39.0-Q39.1
U138	7. Renal agenesis	753.0	Q60
U139	8. Down syndrome	758.0	Q90
U140	9. Congenital heart anomalies	745-747	Q20-Q28
U141	10. Spina bifida	741	Q05
U142	Other congenital anomalies	740.1, 740.2, 742-744, 748, 749.2, 750.0, 750.1, 750.2, 750.4-751.1, 751.3-751.9, 752, 753.1-753.9, 754, 755, 756.0-756.6, 756.8, 756.9, 757, 758.1-758.9, 759	Q01-Q04, Q06-Q18, Q30-Q34, Q38, Q392-Q399, Q40-Q41, Q43-Q56, Q61-Q78, Q790, Q791, Q796, Q798, Q799, Q80-Q89, Q91-Q99
U143	**N. Oral conditions**	520-529	K00-K14
U144	1. Dental caries	521.0	K02
U145	2. Periodontal disease	523	K05
U146	3. Edentulism	—	—
U147	Other oral diseases	520, 521.1-521.9, 522, 524-529	K00, K01, K03, K04, K06-K14
U148	**III. Injuries**	E800-999	V01-Y89
U149	**A. Unintentional injuries**[d]	E800-949	V01-X59, Y40-Y86, Y88, Y89
U150	1. Road traffic accidents	E810-819, E826-829, E929.0	e
U151	2. Poisonings	E850-869	X40-X49
U152	3. Falls	E880-888	W00-W19
U153	4. Fires	E890-899	X00-X09
U154	5. Drownings	E910	W65-W74
U155	6. Other unintentional injuries	E800-E807, E820-E848, E870-E879, E900-E909, E911-E949	Rest of V, W20-W64, W75-W99, X10-X39, X50-X59, Y40-Y86, Y88, Y89
U156	**B. Intentional injuries**[d]	E950-978, 990-999	X60-Y09, Y35-Y36, Y870, Y871
U157	1. Self-inflicted injuries	E950-959	X60-X84, Y870
U158	2. Violence	E960-969	X85-Y09, Y871
U159	3. War	E990-999	Y36
U160	Other intentional injuries	E970-E978	Y35

a) Deaths coded to "Symptoms, signs and ill-defined conditions" (780-799 in ICD-9 and R00-R99 in ICD-10) are distributed proportionately to all causes within Group I and Group II.

b) Cancer deaths coded to ICD categories for malignant neoplasms of other and unspecified sites including those whose point of origin cannot be determined, and secondary and unspecified neoplasms (ICD-10 C76, C80, C97 or ICD-9 195, 199) were redistributed pro rata across the footnoted malignant neoplasm categories within each age-sex group, so that the category "Other malignant neoplasms" includes only malignant neoplasms of other specified sites.

c) Ischemic heart disease deaths may be miscoded to a number of so-called cardiovascular "garbage" codes. These include heart failure, ventricular dysrhythmias, generalised atherosclerosis, and ill-defined descriptions and complications of heart disease. Proportions of deaths coded to these causes were redistributed to ischemic heart disease as described by Lozano *et al.* (2001). Relevant ICD-9 codes are 427.1, 427.4, 427.5, 428, 429.0, 429.1, 429.2, 429.9, 440.9; relevant ICD-10 codes are I47.2, I49.0, I46, I50, I51.4, I51.5, I51.6, I51.9, I70.9.

d) Injury deaths where the intent is not determined (E980-989 of ICD-9 and Y10-Y34, Y872 in ICD-10) are distributed proportionately to all causes below the group level for injuries.

e) For countries with three-digit ICD-10 data, use: V01-V04, V06, V09-V80, V87, V89, V99. For countries with four-digit ICD-10 data, use: V01.1-V01.9, V02.1-V02.9, V03.1-V03.9, V04.1-V04.9, V06.1-V06.9, V09.2, V09.3, V10.4-V10.9, V11.4-V11.9, V12.3-V12.9, V13.3-V13.9, V14.3-V14.9, V15.4-V15.9, V16.4-V16.9, V17.4-V17.9, V18.4-V18.9, V19.4-V19.6, V20.3-V20.9, V21.3-V21.9, V22.3-V22.9, V23.3-V23.9, V24.3-V24.9, V25.3-V25.9, V26.3-V26.9, V27.3-V27.9, V28.3-V28.9, V29.4-V29.9, V30.4.V30.9, V31.4-V31.9, V32.4-V32.9, V33.4-V33.9, V34.4-V34.9, V35.4-V35.9, V36.4-V36.9, V37.4-V37.9, V38.4-V38.9, V39.4-V39.9, V40.4-V40.9, V41.4-V41.9, V42.4-V42.9, V43.4-V43.9, V44.4-V44.9, V45.4-V45.9, V46.4-V46.9, V47.4-V47.9, V48.4-V48.9, V49.4-V49.9, V50.4-V50.9, V51.4-V51.9, V52.4-V52.9, V53.4-V53.9, V54.4-V54.9, V55.4-V55.9, V56.4-V56.9, V57.4-V57.9, V58.4-V58.9, V59.4-V59.9, V60.4-V60.9, V61.4-V61.9, V62.4-V62.9, V63.4-V63.9, V64.4-V64.9, V65.4-V65.9, V66.4-V66.9, V67.4-V67.9, V68.4-V68.9, V69.4-V69.9, V70.4-V70.9, V71.4-V71.9, V72.4-V72.9, V73.4-V73.9, V74.4-V74.9, V75.4-V75.9, V76.4-V76.9, V77.4-V77.9, V78.4-V78.9, V79.4-V79.9, V80.3-V80.5, V81.1, V82.1, V83.0-V83.3, V84.0-V84.3, V85.0-V85.3, V86.0-V86.3, V87.0-V87.8, V89.2, V89.9, V99, Y850.

Source: Global Burden of Disease 2008, forthcoming.

ANNEX G

International Standards and Classifications of Trade and Tourism

International trade in services by mode of supply

Trade statistics play an important information role in analysing the strengths and weaknesses of economies and in assessing the impacts of different policies and identifying opportunities offered by partners' markets. The World Trade Organisation, recognising the increasing role of the service sector, concluded the General Agreement of Trade in Services (GATS) in 1995, bringing services more into the spotlight of considerations about international trade. In addition to the general obligations that apply across all service sectors of all WTO Members, countries can choose which service sector and mode they wish to open up to trade. GATS has been an important driving force for the development of statistics on the international supply of services,[1] and has influenced the establishment of a classification of four different modes of trade in services. The supply of health care services can take place in all four of these GATS modes, although not all are relevant to the measurement of trade under the System of Health Accounts.

To date, WTO Members have only made relatively limited commitments in health services (Mattoo *et al.*, 2007). However, services are an important part of ongoing multilateral trade negotiations, and further liberalisation is expected in the future.

The following paragraphs describe the GATS four modes of supply, with particular reference to health services. GATS also sets out a classification that identifies relevant sectors and sub-sectors for the purposes of trade negotiating purposes, rather than for statistical purposes. The classification known as GNS/W/120 comprises 12 major categories, including "Health-related and social services".

Mode 1: Cross-border supply

Mode 1 "Cross-border supply" takes place when a service is supplied "from the territory of one Member into the territory of any other Member". This is comparable to trade in goods where the product is delivered across borders and the consumer and the supplier remain in their respective territories.

In the domain of health services, Mode 1 can take different forms: tele-health services[2] are the most prominent method, such as a physician providing a medical diagnosis to a patient via email, internet or telephone. A variety of services includes tele-diagnosis, tele-pathology, tele-radiology and tele-psychiatry and can cover preventive and curative care. The service can be delivered in real time (for example, through video conferences) or by store-and-forward, which means that the analysis is done at a different moment in time. For example, hospitals in the United States may send X-ray images electronically to India, where they are analysed by radiologists (Pollack, 2003). Another area relevant to SHA is the provision of health insurance by non-resident entities.

In addition to electronic delivery of health services, this also includes the shipment of laboratory samples, diagnosis and clinical consultations via traditional mail channels.

Mode 2: Consumption abroad

Mode 2 "Consumption abroad" takes place when the service is supplied "in the territory of one Member to the service consumer of any other Member", *i.e.* either the consumer or his property is abroad.

In theory, all health services could be purchased abroad; however, there exist practical constraints, such as the non-portability of health insurance or the capacity of the providing country. To date, the most prominent and most easily identifiable part of trade in health services is when patients travel abroad to receive medical treatment. This phenomenon is often called "medical or health tourism", hinting at a mix of health, well-being and leisure activities. In some instances this may be the objective, and the marketing of services may play upon opportunities to visit and experience a country at the same time as receiving quality care, but more often this concerns travel specifically and often exclusively for health care purposes and thus may more correctly be termed "health (or medical) travel" or "patient mobility". In other cases, tourists or persons on business travel may become sick or suffer an accident and need to seek medical care in the destination country.

The medical treatment of non-resident persons, *i.e.* person travelling abroad to the home country of the provider, can often be categorised into those seeking:

- Specialised or advanced treatment not available in the home country, generally sought by affluent patients from developing countries travelling to hospitals in industrialised countries or in neighbouring developing countries with superior health care standards;
- Or a price or quality advantage over the home country, generally sought by patients from industrialised countries who purchase affordable, high-quality treatment or alternative medicines and treatments in less developed countries.

Mode 3: Commercial presence

Mode 3 "Commercial presence" takes place through "the supply of a service by a service supplier of one Member, through commercial presence in the territory of any other Member". GATS recognises that it is often necessary for service suppliers to establish a commercial presence abroad to ensure closer contact with the consumer at various stages of production, distribution, marketing, sale and delivery as well as after-sales service. Commercial presence in a market abroad covers not only juridical persons in the strict legal sense, but also legal entities that share some of the same characteristics, such as representative offices and branches, *e.g.* medical services provided by a foreign-owned hospital.

The commercial presence of a foreign health care provider through, for example, capital investment, branches or affiliates, falls under mode 3. Commercial presence is mainly represented by the activities of foreign-controlled affiliates' trade. Health care companies in industrialised and some developing countries are increasingly engaging in joint ventures and alliances, resulting in several regional health care networks and chains.

It should be noted that commercial presence is *not* defined as trade under the SHA (or balance of payments) framework.[3] However, it may be of policy interest for some countries to monitor separately the extent of services delivered by foreign health care providers on the territory.

Figure G.1.1. **The four modes of supply for trade in health services as defined by GATS**

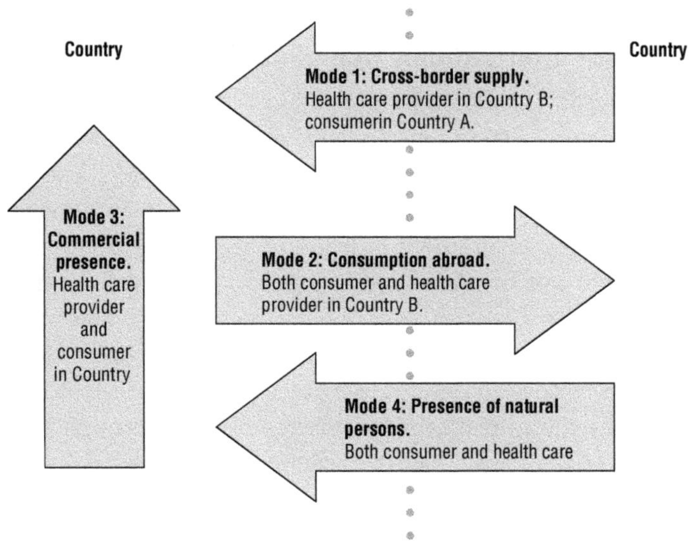

Source: IHAT for SHA 2011.

Mode 4: Temporary presence of natural persons

Mode 4 "Temporary presence of natural persons" takes place when an individual is temporarily present in the territory of an economy other than their own to provide a commercial service. GATS defines Mode 4 as the supply of a service by "a service supplier of one member, through the presence of natural persons of a Member in the territory of any other Member". Mode 4 is generally understood as covering:

- Contractual service suppliers, whether employees are of a foreign service supplier or self-employed;
- Intra-corporate transferees and foreign employees directly recruited by foreign established companies;
- Service sellers who enter the host country to establish contractual relationships for a service contract, or persons responsible for setting up a commercial presence.

It might sometimes be difficult to distinguish between those service providers that fulfil Mode 4 criteria and those that do not. However, it needs to be emphasised that from a public health perspective, it is very important to generate information on both the movement of health professionals under Mode 4 as well as outside Mode 4.

Examples in the health field include the movement of nurses, physicians, paramedics, midwives and other professionals from one country to another to provide health services. Short-term flows have been driven mainly by conscious strategies to promote the export of health services in order to earn foreign exchange and foster co-operation between governments.

Balance of payments and national accounts

The balance of payments is a statistical statement that provides a record of an economy's economic transactions with the rest of the world. In general terms, transactions in goods, services and incomes come under the current account, while a capital and financial account shows the financial resource flows. Services are arranged according to 12 broad standard services components. The 2008 System of National Accounts and the BPM6 have a common conceptual framework.

Manual on Statistics of International Trade in Services (MSITS)

The *Manual on Statistics of International Trade in Services* (UN, 2010) is built not only around the requirements of GATS but also on the key concepts of the System of National Accounts (SNA 2008) and the balance of payments (BPM6). The MSITS provides recommendations for the measurement of international trade in services and therefore provides a clear link to the measurement of trade in services under the System of Health Accounts. The MSITS sets out the Extended Balance of Payments Services Classification (EBOPS 2010), which provides a greater level of detail to the BPM6 classification of services and has correspondence tables with standard product and industry classifications.[4] The coverage of the MSITS goes beyond that required by the System of Health Accounts, in that it allows for the separate identification of services delivered through locally established, but foreign controlled enterprises. Such transactions are covered by Foreign Affiliates Statistics (FATS). Although this information may be of importance to governments and policy makers, this distinction among health care providers is not made in the SHA supplementary trade tables.

Within the EBOPS 2010 classification (Table G.1.1), health services approximating to personal health care[5] are split between two classes, depending on their mode of supply:

- 4.2.1. Health-related travel (corresponding to Mode 2 of GATS);
- 11.2.1. Health services (either Mode 1 or part of Mode 4).

Health-related travel

Of the two categories, the more important for most countries is "health-related travel"; the nature of most health care requires the presence and co-location of patient and healthcare provider, entailing the movement of one or the other. In this case, it is the movement of the patient abroad that is covered under the item "Travel" (EBOPS 4). Any services provided as a result of a non-resident provider moving (temporarily) across the border would be included under the "Health services" category.

The concept of "Travel" as part of services under the MSITS and BPM6 differs from most other traded services in that it does not refer to a specific product. Travel is defined as "goods and services, for own use or to give away, acquired from an economy, by non-residents during visits to that economy". It covers stays of any length, provided there is "no change in residence" (normally taken as less than a year). However, in contrast to tourism statistics (see the next section), this also covers students and patients staying more than a year, as well as the consumption of seasonal, border and other short-term workers. Also important from the SHA perspective is the inclusion of third-party payments, *e.g.* health costs paid or reimbursed by government or insurers and in theory the imputation of social transfers in kind, *e.g.* government consumption expenditure on non-market health services.

Travel is broken down into *Business travel* and *Personal travel*. *Business travel* covers all the goods and services acquired by persons whose primary purpose of travel is business. This includes not only employees and self-employed persons travelling on business, but also cross-border, seasonal and short-term workers. Therefore, all expenditure items, including any health goods and services, would be included under *Business travel*. On the other hand, *Personal travel* covers the goods and services acquired by persons going abroad for any purpose other than business. MSITS 2010 recommends a further breakdown of personal travel into three subcomponents, one of which is *Health-related*. This, in effect, measures the consumption of all goods and services (*i.e.* food, transport, accommodation, etc.) – not just the health services acquired – by persons whose primary purpose for travelling is for health or medical reasons.

However, an alternative breakdown of *Travel* by product is also recommended, which provides a much closer link to the requirements of health accounts. There is a split into subcategories such as local transport and accommodation, as well as a category of other travel-related services, with health services as a suggestion. This kind of breakdown would gather together the consumption of health services by residents abroad, irrespective of the main purpose of travel. Note, however, that the purchase of any medical goods by travellers would not be included in this category.

Health services

Health services forms one part of the EBOPS first-level category "Other personal, cultural or recreational services" and equates to CPC Ver. 2 Group 931 (and class 9321 Residential health-care services other than by hospitals) covering human health services provided by hospitals, doctors, nurses and paramedical and similar personnel, as well as laboratory and similar services, whether rendered remotely (through telemedicine or tele-diagnosis) or on-site. Included are diagnostic-imaging services, pharmaceutical, radiology and rehabilitation services. This equates to the cross-border provision of health services (Mode 1), but also includes the presence of a non-resident health-care provider on the territory (Mode 4). It should be noted that in contrast to health services under travel, health services here can include both services provided provider-to-provider (*i.e.* diagnosis services from a laboratory in one country provided to a laboratory or hospital in another country) in addition to services provided directly to a patient. This important distinction is further discussed under the section intermediate and final use.

Any health services supplied by and to governments should also be included under health services. In practice it may be that some services will not be able to be separately identified and are included under "Government goods and services not included elsewhere (n.i.e)". This can be relevant to health services provided to embassy or military staff posted abroad.

MSITS 2010 also provides suggestions for the complementary grouping of EBOPS 2010 categories, including C.8. *Total health services*. This aggregates the two components:

- *Health services* (product breakdown of *travel, other services*); and
- *Health services* (under other personal, cultural and recreational services).

Reporting of this complementary grouping is a close proxy to what is required under trade in health services under the SHA framework. Some additional items and adjustments related to SHA boundaries would in principle still be required.

Table G.1.1. **Health services under the EBOPS 2010 classification**

Code	Description	
4 Travel	**4.1 Business**	
	Acquisition of goods and services by border and seasonal workers	
	Other	
	4.2 Personal	***4.2.1* Health-related**
		4.2.2 Education-related
		4.2.3 Other
11 Personal, cultural and recreational services	*11.1 Audiovisual and related services*	
	11.2 Other personal, cultural and recreational services	***11.2.1 Health services***
		11.2.2 Education services
		11.2.3 Other
Alternative EBOPS groupings		
8 Health services = health services in travel + health services in personal, cultural and recreational services		

Source: UN (2010).

Other relevant EBOPS categories

To achieve a full mapping to health care according to the boundaries of SHA, reference should also be made to other EBOPS categories, such as business services, other personal services and insurance services. It is clear that the EBOPS classification (and data sources) is not sufficiently detailed to provide much information that is relevant to health spending.

In the case of insurance, accident and health insurance provided to and by non-residents cannot be separately identified from a broader sub category of *Other direct insurance*. In theory, the service charges for resident policyholders with non-resident insurers (and vice versa) should be taken into account in estimating health spending (as a component of HC.7 Governance, and health system & financing administration).

Similarly, despite the increased use of overseas outsourcing in such areas as health system governance, planning and administration (or research and development), this does not warrant any explicit categorisation in *Business services*.

Finally, the boundaries of health expenditure under SHA mean that some areas of personal care related to parts of care services to the elderly and disabled lie outside the boundaries of Health care services under the EBOPS and are included instead under *Other personal, cultural and recreational services n.i.e.*

Tourism statistics and the Tourism Satellite Account (TSA)[6]

Definitions of trade in health goods and services under the SHA framework and the concepts adopted for tourism satellite accounting show many similarities that may be useful in identifying relevant data sources. First and foremost, tourism is primarily a demand-side phenomenon that refers to the activities of visitors and their role in the acquisition of goods and services across many different industries, including health goods and services. Tourism, as defined under tourism statistics, goes beyond what may be traditionally perceived to include persons travelling (under certain conditions explained below) for holiday, leisure and recreation purposes and also includes, among others, business, education, and importantly, health. However, if the purpose of a trip is for employment or to earn an income, then the trip is not considered as a tourist trip, and the individual cannot be considered as a visitor. Therefore, in the case of seasonal and border workers, any expenditure on health would be excluded from the Tourist Satellite Account.

The concepts of economic territory and residence are defined in the same way as in the balance of payments. Tourism statistics make the further distinction between "the country of residence" and citizenship or nationality. Nationality or citizenship is related to the country issuing the passport or identity card; a person may be resident in one country but hold the nationality of another – or indeed hold dual nationality in some cases. This may be an important distinction regarding health services abroad, since much of the cross-border traffic involves nationals returning for treatment to their country of origin, where they still hold nationality. In addition, statistics of travellers collected at borders may often identify only the nationality (as stated in the passport) rather than the country of residence. For the purpose of tourism statistics and indeed for health accounts, persons are classified according to their country of residence.

IRTS 2008 makes a clear distinction between "travel" and "travellers" in the BoP sense, and "tourism" and "visitors" – the latter terms being subsets of the former: such a distinction builds on the concept of "usual environment" (one of the key concepts in tourism statistics). The purpose of introducing such a concept is to exclude from visitors those travellers who commute regularly between their place of usual residence and their place of work or study, or who frequently visit places as part of their regular life routine, for instance, for health care.

In relation to the country of reference, the following three basic forms of tourism can be distinguished:

- Domestic tourism,[7] which comprises the activities of a resident visitor within the country of reference either as part of a domestic tourism trip or part of an outbound tourism trip;
- Inbound tourism, which comprises the activities of a non-resident visitor within the country of reference on an inbound tourism trip;
- Outbound tourism, which comprises the activities of a resident visitor outside the country of reference, either as part of an outbound tourism trip or as part of a domestic tourism trip.

Although visitors are then divided into residents and non-residents for the purposes of domestic and inbound tourism, non-resident visitors are a category distinct from non-residents abroad. For example, border workers living in Belgium and regularly crossing into France would be excluded from visitors, and any expenditure on health goods and services made in France would not be included in the French inbound tourist consumption figures. Some other differences exist between the scope of visitors in tourism statistics and that of non-residents used in SHA, *e.g.* refugees, long-term students and patients (that is, those staying longer than one year) are also excluded from visitors.

The main priority of the TSA is to provide information on internal tourism, *i.e.* to measure the consumption of inbound and domestic visitors in the economy. The consumption of residents abroad is of a lesser priority to TSA compilers, since there is no direct impact in the economy of reference. Therefore, from the SHA point of view, information coming from the TSA on inbound tourism may be most useful in identifying the consumption of health services by non-residents, *i.e.* exports. Visitor flows – in non-monetary terms – can be split between visitors and other travellers with no tourist purpose. The standard classification of a tourism trip according to main purpose includes a category: "health and medical care".

In addition to the traditional measurement of the characteristics and activities of visitors by means of non-monetary data, IRTS 2008 also refers to the measurement of tourism expenditure defined as "the amount paid for the acquisition of consumption goods and services, as well as valuables, for own use or to give away, for and during tourism trips. It includes expenditure by visitors themselves as well as expenses that are paid for or reimbursed by others." The wider measure of tourism consumption is a TSA concept that is more inclusive because it also includes "services associated with vacation accommodation on own account, tourism social transfers in kind and other imputed consumption". For the purposes of health, this distinction can be useful, since it includes, in theory, government consumption expenditure on individual non-market services or products including social services and health that can be considered as benefiting visitors (social transfers in kind).

The Tourism Satellite Account is organised according to products (using the internationally approved classifications of products CPC Ver. 2) – that is, the goods and services consumed by visitors. However, since the product breakdown of tourist expenditure is based primarily on information provided by visitors, the classification for collection of this expenditure is usually based on purpose, in this case the COICOP. Consequently, there is a need to adapt data based on the COICOP – a functional classification – to the CPC – a product classification – which can be linked to products (CPC) and activities (ISIC). Tourism products are classified according first to broad categories: consumption products/non-consumption products. The former category is further divided into tourism characteristic products (characterised by the fact that the tourism expenditure on the product accounts either for a significant share of total tourism expenditure and/or represents a significant share of the supply of the product in the economy) and other consumption products. Tourism characteristic products are then sub-divided into internationally comparable tourism characteristic products, which are a standard list of products defined in terms of CPC Ver. 2, such as accommodation services, food and beverages and transport. The other subcategory refers to country-specific tourism characteristic products, and this is where individual countries can include products that may have particular relevance to their countries, but are limited worldwide. This may be the case for countries where the promotion of health or medical tourism is seen as an important area, and as such the inclusion of specific questions related to health in tourist surveys or the development of specific surveys of health providers can be seen as an important source of information.[8]

It should be noted that a specific category "health and medical care" corresponds closely to the main purpose of the trip, and as such the incidental purchase of health care products and occasional health services may be allocated into non-tourism-related consumption products in the first instance.

Additional tables of the TSA show both how this tourist demand is met by domestic supply and imports as well as the link with non-monetary information.

Notes

1. Although the supply of health services by governmental organisations such as national health services is included in the SHA and SNA views of trade in health services, it should be noted that GATS does not cover these.
2. There are currently a number of alternative terms in use: tele-medicine, e-medicine and e-health.
3. Foreign ownership is not a criterion applied in determining the resident status of health care providers under SHA. Thus, foreign-owned resident health care providers are classified under the appropriate domestic provider category, and the health care goods and services consumed are treated accordingly.
4. The MSITS provides correspondence tables between the EBOPS classification, CPC Ver. 2 and GNS/W/120 (a Services Sectoral Classification drawn up by the GATT Secretariat for trade negotiating purposes rather than statistical classification).
5. Note that medical goods consumed abroad are considered as part of services and reported under the category "Travel" in the MSITS.
6. In order to provide internationally comparable data on the different aspects of tourism, the World Tourism Organisation (UNWTO) has developed a set of basic concepts, definitions and classifications. The International Recommendations for Tourism Statistics 2008 (IRTS 2008) includes an alignment with other economic statistics. The development of a Tourism Satellite Account analyses in detail all the aspects of demand for goods and services associated with tourism. The Tourism Satellite Account: Recommended Methodological Framework 2008 (TSA: RMF 2008) provides the link between tourism statistics and the standard tables of the SNA 2008.
7. It is important to note differences in the use of the word "domestic". In tourism statistics, "domestic" refers to activities of residents *within the country of residence*, whereas in national accounts and SHA, "domestic" refers to activities of residents *irrespective* of where this takes place. In tourism statistics, the latter corresponds to "national tourism".
8. For example, Switzerland specifically includes "Health care" as a tourism-connected product in their Tourism Satellite Account (Swiss Federal Statistical Office, 2008).

OECD PUBLISHING, 2, rue André-Pascal, 75775 PARIS CEDEX 16
(81 2017 00 1 P) ISBN 978-92-64-27097-8 – 2017

www.ingramcontent.com/pod-product-compliance
Ingram Content Group UK Ltd.
Pitfield, Milton Keynes, MK11 3LW, UK
UKHW051456290926
15471UKWH00008B/1229

9 789264 270978